KW-034-681

CO-OPERATION BETWEEN NATIONAL COMPETITION AGENCIES IN THE ENFORCEMENT OF EC COMPETITION LAW

In May 2004, the enforcement of the EC competition rules changed radically. Under Regulation 1/2003, the national competition authorities (NCAs) of all 27 Member States are called upon to actively participate, together with the European Commission, in the enforcement of Articles 81 and 82 EC. In order to ensure the efficient and consistent application of the law, Regulation 1/2003 provides for a number of co-operation mechanisms at the heart of which lies the European Competition Network (ECN). The ECN acts as a common forum for information exchange, coordination and discussion. This book provides an in-depth analysis of the rules governing co-operation within the ECN. It is a valuable source for all working in the field of EC competition law: practitioners, company lawyers, competition authority officials and academics.

The author focuses on horizontal co-operation between the NCAs of different Member States. She starts by looking at the arrangements for case allocation, discusses the rules on information exchange and also deals with the consultation procedure prior to the adoption of final NCA decisions. The existing rules are assessed not only in the light of their purpose, ensuring efficiency and consistency in the application of the law, but also reviewed against the requirements of the EU Charter and the European Convention on Human Rights. Particular attention is devoted to issues arising in the event of parallel procedures by several NCAs. This includes the applicability of the *ne bis in idem* principle and the question of which duties of the NCAs result from the loyalty obligation enshrined in Article 10 EC. Finally, the author explores whether the ECN concept of co-operation and networking could be applied more broadly in the context of European integration.

Co-operation between National Competition Agencies in the Enforcement of EC Competition Law

SILKE BRAMMER

·HART·
PUBLISHING

OXFORD AND PORTLAND, OREGON
2009

Published in North America (US and Canada) by

Hart Publishing
c/o International Specialized Book Services
920 NE 58th Avenue, Suite 300
Portland, OR 97213-3786
USA
Tel: +1 503 287 3093 or toll-free: (1) 800 944 6190
Fax: +1 503 280 8832
Email: orders@isbs.com
Website: www.isbs.com

© Silke Brammer 2009

Silke Brammer has asserted her right under the Copyright, Designs and Patents Act
1988, to be identified as the author of this work.

All rights reserved. No part of this publication may be reproduced, stored in a
retrieval system, or transmitted, in any form or by any mean, without the prior
permission of Hart Publishing, or as expressly permitted by law or under the terms
agreed with the appropriate reprographic rights organisation. Enquiries concerning
reproduction which may not be covered by the above should be addressed to Hart
Publishing at the address below.

Hart Publishing, 16C Worcester Place, Oxford, OX1 2JW
Telephone: +44 (0)1865 517530 Fax: +44 (0)1865 510710
Email: mail@hartpub.co.uk
Website: http//:www.hartpub.co.uk

British Library Cataloguing in Publication Data
Data Available

ISBN: 978-1-84113-931-9

Typeset by Forewords, Oxford
Printed and bound in Great Britain by
TJ International Ltd, Padstow

For Gerd A Brammer
(1930–1973)

Acknowledgements

This book is the result of a research project that I carried out at the *Katholieke Unversiteit Leuven* (KU Leuven). The project was partly funded by the *Fonds Wetenschappelijk Onderzoek—Vlaanderen* (Research Foundation—Flanders). An earlier version of this research work was accepted as a doctoral dissertation by the KU Leuven in April 2008.

I am very grateful to my promoter Professor Dr Wouter Devroe and my co-promoter Professor Dr Jules Stuyck for the trust they put in me, their academic and moral support and the freedom they gave me in composing my work. We had many fruitful discussions and their comments and suggestions were always useful and constructive. Warm thanks are also due to Professor emeritus Walter Van Gerven, who did me the honour of serving on the jury of my doctoral examination and encouraged me to pursue the publication of the dissertation.

This work would not have been possible without the constant encouragement, patience and support of my husband, Hans M Gilliams.

I have aimed to state the law as it stood on 1 February 2009.

Contents

Table of Cases

European Court of Justice and Court of First Instance

Alphabetical

Chronological

France

Germany

Netherlands

Dutch Competition Authority/Nederlandse Mededingingsautoriteit

United Kingdom

United States

Table of Legislation

Czech Republic

European Community

Decisions

Directives

Regulations

Italy

Luxemburg

Netherlands

United States

Table of Conventions and Agreements

Introduction

I N 2004, EUROPEAN competition law underwent the most radical reform since its conception. The changes that this reform involved were so significant that it has been described as a 'legal and cultural revolution'.[1] The centrepiece of the reform, commonly referred to as 'modernisation', is Regulation No 1/2003 on the implementation of Articles 81 and 82 EC,[2] which entered into force on 1 May 2004. Regulation 1/2003 has brought about a fundamental reorganisation of the division of responsibilities between the European Commission, the national competition authorities (NCAs) and the courts of the Member States of the European Union. It is said to entail a decentralisation of the enforcement of EC competition law.

Regulation 1/2003 has in fact established a system of full parallel competences in which the Commission, the NCAs and the courts of the Member States share the responsibility to enforce the EC competition rules. Shared competences and 'decentralised' application of EC competition law through a multitude of enforcers (instead of one central body—the Commission) make it necessary that the numerous enforcement bodies[3] collaborate and coordinate their action in order to avoid conflicts and to ensure the efficient and consistent application of the law. Therefore, Regulation 1/2003 provides for certain co-operation mechanisms. At the heart of these mechanisms lies the creation of a network of public authorities, to act as a common forum for information exchange, coordination and discussion.[4] However, Regulation 1/2003 only establishes a general

---

[1] C-D Ehlermann, 'The Modernization of EC Antitrust Policy: A Legal and Cultural Revolution' (2000) 37 *CML Rev* 537, 537. Wißmann even calls it a 'quantum leap' and Kallaugher/Weitbrecht speak of a 'seismic shift'. T Wißmann, 'Decentralised Enforcement of EC Competition Law and the New Policy on Cartels: The Commission White Paper of 28th April 1999' (2000) 23 *World Competition* 123, 154. J Kallaugher and A Weitbrecht, 'Developments under Articles 81 and 82 EC—The Year 2004 in Review' (2005) 26 *European Competition Law Review* 188, 188. *Contra* A Riley, 'EC Antitrust Modernisation: The Commission Does Very Nicely—Thank You! Part One: Regulation 1 and the Notification Burden' (2003) 24 *European Competition Law Review* 604, 615. According to Riley, the reform looked a lot more radical than it actually was. It must be said, however, that the elimination of the notification/ authorisation requirement, coupled with the duty imposed on NCAs to actually apply Arts 81 and 82 EC, are unprecedented, drastic steps which justify the view that the reform involves a certain amount of radicalism.

[2] Council Regulation (EC) No 1/2003 of 16 December 2002 on the implementation of the rules on competition laid down in Articles 81 and 82 of the Treaty [2003] OJ L1/1.

[3] The term 'enforcement bodies' as employed here refers to both administrative authorities and courts that are involved in the (public or private) enforcement of EC competition law.

[4] Cf recitals 15 and 19 of Regulation 1/2003.

framework for the co-operation process, which needs to be complemented by more detailed rules.

Moreover, the co-operation mechanisms established by Regulation 1/2003 are essentially limited to vertical aspects, ie the relationship between the national enforcement bodies on the one hand and the Commission on the other. Little is said on horizontal co-operation between the NCAs of different Member States, and Regulation 1/2003 remains completely silent as to the question of co-operation between NCAs and courts of foreign Member States.[5]

In summary, the entire horizontal dimension of the modernisation process appears underdeveloped.[6] The rights and duties of the national enforcement bodies of a Member State vis-à-vis the enforcement bodies of other Member States appear to be ill-defined, yet are quintessential for the proper functioning of Regulation 1/2003.

This book focuses on these horizontal aspects of the decentralisation of EC competition law enforcement. It analyses and evaluates the arrangements for horizontal co-operation foreseen by Regulation 1/2003 in the light of their purpose, namely to ensure efficiency and consistency.

Chapter 1 describes the history of the reform, focusing on the drawbacks of the old regime that ultimately led to the adoption of Regulation 1/2003. It also provides an overview of the new enforcement system established by Regulation 1/2003 by briefly discussing the respective roles of all players involved, ie the Commission, NCAs and national courts. Chapter 2 contains a general description of the network of public authorities created by Regulation 1/2003 and those provisions which determine horizontal co-operation between the NCAs, most notably the exchange of confidential information. Chapter 3 examines in more detail the rules on co-operation applicable at the beginning of a procedure, in particular the principles governing the allocation of cases and their implementation in practice. It also discusses certain drawbacks of these rules. Chapter 4 analyses the provisions regarding information exchange and administrative

---

[5] Similarly, the question of a possible co-operation between national courts of different Member States is not at all addressed by Regulation 1/2003. However, as this book is focusing on co-operation between the NCAs, it will not, in principle, treat horizontal issues involving national courts.

[6] Riley describes the co-operation measures contained in Regulation 1/2003 as marginal compared to the centralising and supervisory elements of that regulation. A Riley, 'EC Antitrust Modernisation: The Commission Does Very Nicely—Thank You! Part Two: Between the Idea and the Reality: Decentralisation under Regulation 1'(2003) 24 *European Competition Law Review* 657, 664. It is true that both aspects are present in the reform. Whether this justifies the view that the co-operation mechanisms are only marginal is, however, doubtful. After all, the supervisory powers provided for the Commission are primarily meant to ensure consistency and coherence of enforcement and, on this basis, are ancillary to the decentralisation efforts. Moreover, Regulation 1/2003 does set the stage for intense horizontal co-operation, albeit on a purely voluntary basis. Yet it remains a fact that the mechanisms for vertical co-operation and coordination are much more strongly developed.

assistance in the course of an investigation. Special attention is devoted to problems resulting from divergent national procedural rules and the need to guarantee the fairness of proceedings and the protection of confidential information. Chapter 5 deals with information rights and duties before the termination of a case. Chapter 6 discusses particular issues arising in case of multiple (parallel) proceedings regarding the same infringement. The main focus of the analysis are the fundamental principle of *ne bis in idem* and the obligation of loyalty imposed on Member States by Article 10 EC. In Chapter 7, the main conclusions of the previous chapters are recapitulated and the co-operation mechanisms critically assessed. There is less literature regarding co-operation in international administrative law. If the network of public authorities proves to operate successfully in the field of EC competition law enforcement, it may serve as a model for other areas of European (administrative) co-operation. Therefore, the epilogue seeks to give an answer to the question of whether the network concept as created by Regulation 1/2003 and supplementing (legislative) acts could be applied more broadly in the context of European integration.

It is not the purpose of this book to provide a thorough comparative analysis of the procedural rules of all 27 Member States. Divergencies between the national laws are highlighted by way of example only in order to demonstrate issues arising in the context of horizontal co-operation between the competition authorities of different Member States.

1

Overview of the Decentralised Enforcement of EC Competition Law

I. BACKGROUND TO THE REFORM—HISTORY OF THE REFORM PROCESS, PRINCIPAL OBJECTIVES AND MAIN CRITICISM OF THE REFORM PROPOSAL

T HE COMMISSION'S APPROACH to the modernisation of EC competition law embraced several steps. It had a substantive and a procedural element.[1] First, the Commission adopted a more economic approach towards the evaluation of restrictive agreements and practices[2] under Article 81 EC. Instead of focusing on the wording and content of agreements, it decided to put a stronger emphasis on market structure and market power.[3] Secondly, a reform of the procedural rules implementing Articles 81 and 82 EC[4] was undertaken. Thirdly, one could

---

[1] R Wesseling, 'The Draft-regulation Modernising the Competition Rules: the Commission is Married to One Idea' (2001) 26 *EL Rev* 357, 361. Cf also M Van Der Woude, 'National Courts and the Draft Regulation on the Application of Articles 81 and 82 EC' in J Stuyck and H Gilliams (eds), *Modernisation of European Competition Law. The Commission's Proposal for a New Regulation Implementing Articles 81 and 82 EC* (Antwerp, Intersentia, 2002), 41, 41.

[2] The words 'agreements and practices' are used in this document to embrace all forms of agreements between undertakings, decisions by associations of undertakings and concerted practices within the meaning of Art 81 EC.

[3] This was reflected inter alia in the adoption of a new block exemption for vertical restraints (Commission Regulation (EC) No 2790/1999 of 22 December 1999 on the application of Article 81(3) of the Treaty to categories of vertical agreements and concerted practices, [1999] OJ L336/21). Reg 2790/1999 no longer lists clauses that vertical agreements have to contain in order to benefit from the exemption, but rather exempts vertical agreements in general provided that they do not contain hard-core restrictions and certain market share thresholds are not exceeded. The block exemptions for horizontal co-operation were equally revised by Commission Regs No 2658/2000 of 29 November 2000 on the application of Article 81(3) of the Treaty to categories of specialisation agreements ([2000] OJ L304/3) and No 2659/2000 of 29 November on the application of Article 81(3) of the Treaty to categories of research and development agreements ([2000] OJ L304/7), as well as the Commission's guidelines on the applicability of Article 81 of the Treaty to horizontal co-operation agreements ([2001] OJ C3/2). Similarly, the Commission has started a revision of its policy under Art 82 EC with a view to basing also the application of Art 82 EC on sound economic assessment which takes into account the reality on the market.

also consider the 2004 review of the 1989 Merger Regulation[5] as part of the modernisation package, although this step is not directly linked with the other two elements of the reform.[6] Regulation 1/2003 thus forms one of the cornerstones of a more comprehensive reform of EC competition law. It replaced Council Regulation No 17 of 6 February 1962, First Regulation implementing Articles 85 and 86 (now Articles 81 and 82) of the Treaty,[7] which had remained in force essentially unchanged for more than 40 years.

A. The Previous Enforcement System—Overview, Justification, Drawbacks

In order to place the reform into context and understand the fundamental changes resulting from the modernisation, it is useful to briefly recall the main structure of the EC cartel provisions, ie Article 81 EC, and the previous enforcement system.[8]

1. Regulation 17

Article 81(1)[9] prohibits agreements between undertakings and concerted practices that restrict competition and may affect trade between Member States. Agreements/practices that fulfil the four conditions set out in Article 81(3) are eligible for exemption. These conditions essentially ensure that the agreement has sufficient redeeming virtues outweighing the negative

---

[4] Unless otherwise stated, I use the numbering as laid down by Art 12 of the Treaty of Amsterdam ([1997] OJ C340/1) throughout the entire document.

[5] Council Regulation (EEC) No 4064/89 of 21 December 1989 on the control of concentrations between undertakings, [1989] OJ L395/1. The review was prompted by the legal obligation imposed by the 1989 Merger Regulation itself to re-examine certain of its provisions (see Arts 1(4) and 9(10) of that Reg). However, the Commission took the opportunity to examine the operation of the 1989 Merger Regulation as a whole and, on 11 December 2001, published the Green Paper on the Review of Council Regulation (EEC) No 4064/89. The process eventually lead to the adoption of a revised set of merger control rules contained in Council Regulation (EC) No 139/2004 of 20 January 2004 on the control of concentrations between undertakings (the EC Merger Regulation), [2004] OJ L24/1, which also entered into force on 1 May 2004 ('2004 Merger Regulation' or 'EC Merger Regulation').

[6] Finally, the Commission also undertook to revise certain aspects of the Community's rules on state aid. Thus, 'modernisation' in fact involves a general overhaul of all areas of Community competition law, although the primary attention seems to have been (and arguably still is) on the reform (of the enforcement) of Arts 81 and 82 EC. See H Vedder, 'Spontaneous Harmonisation of National (Competition) Laws in the Wake of the Modernisation of EC Competition Law' (2004) 1 *The Competition Law Review* 5, 7.

[7] [1962] OJ 13/204 (Special Edition 1959–1962, 87).

[8] Art 82 EC, which prohibits the abuse of a dominant position, will not be discussed in detail here since the enforcement of this provision has not been changed significantly by Reg 1/2003.

[9] Articles without addition are those of the EC Treaty.

effects of the restriction so that on balance it can be considered pro-competitive. [10]

Article 83 EC grants the Council of the European Union the power to adopt regulations 'to give effect to the principles set out in Articles 81 and 82' and, in particular, 'to lay down detailed rules for the application of Article 81(3)'.[11] On the basis of this provision (formerly Article 87), the Council adopted Regulation 17, which established a system of prior notification and authorisation and the Commission's monopoly to apply Article 81(3).

The Member States, ie NCAs and national courts, could apply Articles 81(1) and 82 EC as long as the Commission had not initiated any procedure.[12] However, the Commission had the sole power to grant exemptions pursuant to Article 81(3) in the form of either individual decisions or so-called block exemption regulations which cover groups of agreements.[13] In order to benefit from an individual exemption, agreements had to be notified to the Commission.[14] Without any notification no exemption could be granted, and the agreement was null and void pursuant to Article 81(2).

The choice made by the Council to set up a centralised authorisation system by giving the Commission exclusive competence to apply Article 81(3) is understandable if one considers the historical background and the environment in which EC competition law was initially implemented.

Regulation 17 was adopted in 1962, ie at a time when there were only six Member States, two of which—Italy and Luxemburg—had no competition laws at all. The competition rules of the four other Member States were not homogeneous. Only the French and German competition laws were based on a prohibition principle (*Verbotsprinzip*)[15] similar to the EC

---

[10] The four requirements are: (i) the agreement must improve the production or distribution of goods or promote technical or economic progress; (ii) consumers can benefit from the results; (iii) restrictions are kept to a minimum; and (iv) competition is not eliminated completely.

[11] Art 83(1) and (2)(b) EC.

[12] Art 9(3) of Reg 17.

[13] Art 9(1) of Reg 17. It is noteworthy that, until Reg 17 entered into force, the Member States were responsible for granting exemptions in application of Art 81(3). This followed from Art 88 (now Art 84) EC: C-D Ehlermann, 'The Modernization of EC Antitrust Policy: A Legal and Cultural Revolution' (2000) 37 *CML Rev* 537, 539; D Goyder, *EC Competition Law* (Oxford, Oxford University Press, 4th edn, 2003), 438. See also T Wißmann, 'Decentralised Enforcement of EC Competition Law and the New Policy on Cartels: The Commission White Paper of 28th April 1999' (2000) 23 *World Competition* 123, 133, who mentions that the German competition authority, the Federal Cartel Office (*Bundeskartellamt*) in fact took three exemption decisions between 1958 and 1962, ie before the enactment of Reg 17.

[14] Art 4(1) of Reg 17.

[15] As concerns Germany, this applied only to horizontal agreements. Vertical restrictions were subject to abuse control (*Missbrauchskontrolle*) except for resale price maintenance which was per se prohibited. Nonetheless, in 1958, Germany was the only Member State having a national competition law which remotely resembled that of then EEC. A Weitbrecht, 'From Freiburg to Chicago and Beyond—the First 50 Years of European Competition Law' (2008) 14 *European Competition Law Review* 81, 82.

rules, while Belgium and the Netherlands operated a system of abuse control.[16] Moreover, the founding Member States lacked the administrative structures necessary for an efficient (decentralised) enforcement of the EC competition rules, not to mention the absence of a common 'competition culture'.[17]

It must also be considered that abuse control was the prevailing cartel policy in Continental Europe (including Germany) until World War II. At that time cartels were even used as instruments of governmental policies, and the protection of the national market was considered a prerogative of the nation state.[18] Against this background, the introduction of a general prohibition on restrictive agreements and practices in all Member States in 1958 seems nothing less than revolutionary.[19]

Finally, it should be noted that in 1962 the national markets of the Member States were not integrated to such an extent as they are now and that the concept of an 'internal market' did not even exist.[20] Competition policy was viewed as a device for overcoming the partitioning of the common market,[21] and Article 81 has indeed been interpreted and applied by both the Commission and the European Court of Justice (ECJ) so as to promote economic integration,[22] one of the goals of the EC Treaty.

Establishing a rather centralised system of prior authorisation therefore appeared mandatory to ensure the uniform interpretation and the efficient and coherent implementation of the EC cartel provisions.

---

[16] White Paper, para 18.

[17] Ehlermann, above n 13, 540. In the early 1960s, only Germany and France had an independent authority (respectively the *Bundeskartellamt* and the *Conseil de la concurrence*) entrusted with the enforcement of (national) competition law. However, Germany was probably the only Member State with an effective authority having at its disposal both a set of substantive rules and sufficient resources to enforce them. Goyder, above n 13, 447.

[18] D Edward, 'Competition and the Law—Where Are We Going?' (2001) 51 *Wirtschaft und Wettbewerb* 1185, 1185.

[19] E-J Mestmäcker, 'The EC Commission's Modernization of Competition Policy: a Challenge to the Community's Constitutional Order' (2000) 1 *European Business Organization Law Review* 401, 406–7. W Wils, *The Optimal Enforcement of EC Antitrust Law. Essays in Law and Economics* (The Hague, Kluwer Law International, 2001), 102.

[20] The term 'internal market' was introduced in 1986 with the Single European Act ([1987] OJ L169/1), by which Art 8a (now Art 14) was added to the EC Treaty.

[21] See eg Joined Cases 56 and 58/64 *Consten and Grundig v Commission* [1966] ECR 299, 343 (English special edition), where it was held that maintaining artificially separate national markets within the EC for products of a well-known brand amounted to a distortion of competition within the meaning of Art 85 (now Art 81).

[22] R Burnley, 'Interstate Trade Revisited—The Jurisdictional Criterion for Articles 81 and 82 E.C.' (2002) 23 *European Competition Law Review* 217, 222; C-D Ehlermann, 'The Contribution of EC Competition Policy to the Single Market' (1992) 29 *CML Rev* 257, 261.

2. *Major Deficiencies of the Centralised System under Regulation 17*

It soon became obvious that the enforcement system under Regulation 17 had a number of important drawbacks.[23]

The Commission interpreted the notion 'restriction of competition' rather broadly. The mere presence of a clause that technically restricted the parties' freedom of action was sufficient reason to consider the agreement as restrictive within the meaning of Article 81(1).[24] The application of Article 81(1) also depends on whether an agreement 'may affect trade between Member States'. The ECJ gave a broad meaning to this requirement which should determine the Commission's scope of jurisdiction.[25] It held that the inter-state trade criterion is fulfilled if the agreement in question is capable of having 'an influence, direct or indirect, actual or potential, on the pattern of trade between Member States'.[26] Due to these interpretations by the Commission and the ECJ, Article 81(1) had a very extensive scope. Combined with the Commission's monopoly over Article 81(3), this meant that almost all agreements of any commercial relevance, including essentially benign agreements, had to be notified to the Commission in order to escape invalidity under Article 81(2).[27]

It is thus not surprising that, by 1 February 1963, the Commission had

---

[23] For a concise description of the deficiencies, the so-called 'system failure', see J Venit, Working Paper VI in s 8 ('Future Competition Law'), in C-D Ehlermann and L Laudati (eds), *European Competition Law Annual 1997. Objectives of Competition Policy* (Oxford, Hart Publishing, 1998), 567.

[24] I Forrester and J MacLennan, 'EC Competition Law 1999–2000' (2001) 20 *Yearbook of European Law* 365, 365.

[25] See *Consten and Grundig*, above n 21, 341, where the ECJ ruled that the effect on inter-state trade criterion 'defines . . . the boundary between the areas respectively covered by Community law and national law'. According to Wesseling, however, the broad interpretation of this criterion by the ECJ rendered it useless as a tool to demarcate the Commission's jurisdiction. Wesseling, above n 1, 365. A similar proposition is made by P Marsden, 'Inducing Member State Enforcement of European Competition Law: A Competition Policy Approach to "Antitrust Federalism"' (1997) 18 *European Competition Law Review* 234, 237. This view is probably too radical.

[26] The test was first stated in Case 54/65 *Société Technique Minière v Maschinenbau Ulm* [1966] ECR 235, 249 (English special edition) and subsequently became settled case law. For a more recent judgment, see eg Joined Cases C–215/96 and C–216/96 *Carlo Bagnasco and others v Banca Popolare di Novara, Cassa di Risparmio di Genova* ('*Italian Banks*') [1999] ECR I–135, para 47. Riley points out, however, that the scope of the interstate trade criterion has been narrowed down by that judgment, even though on its face the ECJ applied the same test. A Riley, 'EC Antitrust Modernisation: The Commission Does Very Nicely—Thank You! Part Two: Between the Idea and the Reality: Decentralisation under Regulation 1' (2003) 24 *European Competition Law Review* 657, 664. On the recently reduced scope of Art 81 see also Wesseling, above n 1, 366–7 and J Venit, 'The Decentralised Application of Article 81: Italian Banks, Cohabitation, Private Enforcement and Other Issues Raised by the White Paper' in C-D Ehlermann and I Atanasiu (eds), *European Competition Law Annual 2000. The Modernisation of EC Antitrust Policy* (Oxford, Hart Publishing, 2001), 457, 466 ff. See also below n 113.

[27] See Wesseling, above n 1, 365.

been swamped with roughly 34,500 notifications.[28] Since adopting a formal exemption decision was not a simple administrative act but a 'major piece of rule-making'[29], the Commission only granted very few formal exemptions each year, rarely more than three or four.[30] In order to cope with the caseload, the Commission developed the practice to issue so-called comfort letters. These were informal statements, signed by a director or other senior official of the Competition Directorate-General (DG Competition, formerly known as DG IV), informing the parties that the Commission was closing the file and did not intend to take any further action.[31] Even though comfort letters could carry great weight due to their persuasive authority, they did not formally bind national authorities and courts and therefore did not provide any legal certainty as to the lawfulness and validity of the notified agreement.[32] Nonetheless, formal exemption decisions remained very rare. In almost 40 years of EC competition law enforcement under Regulation 17, only about 225 individual exemption decisions have been taken.[33] In its White Paper on the modernisation of the rules implementing Articles 85 and 86 of the EC Treaty[34] ('White Paper'), the Commission states that more than 90% of notifications were closed informally.[35]

[28] Goyder, above n 13, 41. In 1967, the number of cases had reached 37,450. White Paper, para 25.

[29] I Forrester, 'The Modernisation of EC Antitrust Policy: Compatibility, Efficiency and Legal Security' in Ehlermann and Atanasiu, above n 26, 75, 76. The adoption of a formal (exemption) decision under Reg 17 by the Commission, ie the College of Commissioners, is a cumbersome procedure involving extensive publication, consultation and translation requirements. Cf also the commentary by V Emmerich, 'Zur Mär von der Arbeitsüberlastung der Kommission' (2001) 51 *Wirtschaft und Wettbewerb* 3: 'Nicht jede Entscheidung zu Art 81 EGV muss einem Lehrbuch des Wettbewersbrechst gleichen.'

[30] V Korah, *An Introductory Guide to EC Competition Law and Practice* (Oxford, Hart Publishing, 7th edn, 2000), 209. See also n 33.

[31] C Kerse, *EC Antitrust Procedure* (London, Sweet & Maxwell, 3rd edn, 1994), para 6.54.

[32] See L Ritter and D Braun, *EC Competition Law, A Practitioner's Guide* (The Hague, Kluwer Law International, 3rd edn, 2004), 91. For this reason they were criticised as creating discomfort rather then comfort on the side of the parties. T Wißmann, 'Decentralised Enforcement of the EC Competition Law and the New Policy on Cartels: the Commission White Paper of 28th April 1999' (2000) 23 *World Competition* 123, 130; F Montag, 'The Case for a Reform of Reg 17/62: Problems and Possible Solutions from a Practitioner's Point of View' in B Hawk (ed), *1998 Proceedings of the Fordham Corporate Law Institute* (New York, Juris Publishing, 1999), 157, 164. Cf also S Kingston, 'A "New Division of Responsibilities" in the Proposed Regulation to Modernise the Rules Implementing Articles 81 and 82 E.C.? A Warning Call' (2001) 22 *European Competition Law Review* 340, 342. In order to 'upgrade' their status, the Commission developed the practice to indicate in the comfort letter whether it favoured a 'negative clearance' or rather an exemption. See C-D Ehlermann, 'The European Administration and the Public Administration of Member States with Regard to Competition Law' (1995) 16 *European Competition Law Review* 454, 457. However, the non-binding legal character remained.

[33] This number refers to the period 1962–2000. Forrester and MacLennan, above n 24, 366. According to Ehlermann, the Commission took on average not more than five formal exemption decisions per year during the 1990s. Ehlermann, above n 13, 541.

[34] Commission Programme No 99/027of 28 April 1999 [1999] OJ C132/1.

[35] White Paper, para 34. The number of comfort letters issued each year amounted to 150–200.

The introduction of comfort letters allowed the Commission to speed up the processing of notifications considerably and 'close' more cases within a relatively short time frame.[36] And there were other measures to reduce the caseload. Following the judgment of the ECJ in *Völk v Vervaeke*,[37] the Commission introduced the concept of 'appreciable' effects by which cases with negligible effects on trade and competition were excluded from the scope of Article 81(1). The concept was set out in a notice of the Commission on agreements of minor importance ('*de minimis* Notice').[38] Furthermore, between 1983 and 1996, the Commission adopted a series of block exemption regulations.[39] Finally, the Commission developed the policy to reject the investigation of cases that did not reveal a sufficient 'Community interest'.[40]

However, the situation still proved unsatisfactory. In spite of the above measures, the Commission could not properly cope with the large number of notifications which it had received and continued to receive each year. At the end of 1994, the statistics still showed a backlog of 1,052 cases.[41] Moreover, parties often had to wait years before finally obtaining a (formal or informal) decision of the Commission.[42]

---

[36] Between 1988 and 1994, the backlog of unfinished cases could be reduced from 3,451 to 1,052. See XXVth Report on Competition Policy 1995, 346.

[37] In this judgment, the ECJ held that 'an agreement falls outside the prohibition in Article 85 when it has only an insignificant effect on the markets'. Case 5/69 *Völk v Vervaecke* [1969] ECR 295, para 5/7.

[38] The first *de minimis* Notice was published in 1970 ([1970] OJ C64/1), ie shortly after the ECJ's judgment in *Völk*. The notice was updated several times. For the latest version see [2001] OJ C368/13. This version now only covers the appreciability element with regard to the restriction on competition, while the question of whether the effects on trade are appreciable are laid down in a separate notice. See below Chapter 1.II.B.1.b(2) and n 291.

[39] In 1999, block exemptions were available for five different categories of agreements, namely exclusive distribution, exclusive purchasing, motor vehicle distribution, franchising and technology transfer.

[40] This practice was upheld by the Court of First Instance (CFI). See Case T–24/90 *Automec v Commission* (*Automec II*) [1992] ECR II–2223, para 85 *et seq*. It allowed the Commission to set enforcement priorities and 'refer' complainants to the national competition authorities or courts arguing that the matter did not warrant an intervention by the Commission but could effectively be handled at national level, in particular in cases where the effects, albeit not being *de minimis*, were essentially limited to the territory of a single Member State. Cf paras 87–96 of the judgment in *Automec II*.

[41] See the XXVth Report on Competition Policy 1995, 346 (table 2.1). This number even increased slightly the following year, then remained essentially unchanged for a while. There were roughly 1,200 cases pending from 1995 to 1998. At the end of 1999, the number of unfinished cases had dropped to 1,013. In 2000 there were still 935 open matters, and 841 were reported for 2001. See the XXVIIIth Report on Competition Policy 1998, 403 (table 2.1) and the XXXIst Report on Competition Policy 2001, 412 (table 2.1). Admittedly, the number of new notifications which the Commission received each year may have been manageable. However, there was still the backlog of old cases, many of which were difficult. Moreover, 'unorthodox' methods of reducing the huge backlog from more than 34,000 to roughly 1,000 (comfort letters, block exemptions, appreciability requirement, etc) seemed to have been exhausted. It is therefore doubtful that the remaining backlog could have been removed by a single major effort. Ehlermann, above n 13, 546–7.

[42] A notorious example for the extremely lengthy procedures is Case IV/31.400 *Ford Agricultural* [1993] OJ L20/1, which the Commission took almost 30 years (from 1964 to 1992)

While that situation had been accepted in the first decades of Regulation 17, the general attitude started to change in the 1980s, and in the 1990s the Commission was increasingly criticised[43] inter alia for the backlog of cases, the length of procedures, and the lack of transparency and motivation of comfort letters.[44]

In a further attempt to reduce its workload, the Commission issued two notices which aimed at stimulating the (decentralised) enforcement of the EC competition rules by national courts and competition agencies of the Member States. In 1993, the Commission published the Notice on co-operation between national courts and the Commission in applying Articles 85 and 86 of the EC Treaty ('1993 Co-operation Notice')[45] and in 1997 the Notice on co-operation between national competition authorities and the Commission in handling cases falling within the scope of Articles 85 and 86 of the EC Treaty ('1997 Co-operation Notice').[46] By offering co-operation and support to national courts and authorities, the Commission had hoped to share the burden of enforcement with the Member States. However, the mechanisms set out in these notices had little success, and the Commission's efforts to involve the Member States' authorities and courts in the enforcement of EC competition law largely failed.[47]

The continuing incapacity of the Commission to fulfil the tasks entrusted to it by Regulation 17 effectively and on time increased the pressure to improve the enforcement process. At the end of the 1990s, it was common ground that a reform of the existing implementation rules was imperative.[48] In view of the rapidly progressing enlargement of the

---

to decide. See I Forrester, C Norall and J MacLennan, 'Competition Law' (Annual Survey) (1998) 18 *Yearbook of European Law* 511, 512. This example is certainly not representative. Generally, the Commission reached a formal decision after 2–3 years. K Holmes, 'The EC White Paper on Modernisation' (2000) 23 *World Competition* 51, 53.

[43] Eg D Wolf and R Fink,'Mit der Verordnung Nr 17 ins nächste Jahrtausend?' (1994) 44 *Wirtschaft und Wettbewerb* 289. More conciliatory is C-D Ehlermann, 'Ist die Verordnung Nr 17 noch zeitgemäss?' (1993) 43 *Wirtschaft und Wettbewerb* 997.

[44] Cf Ehlermann, above n 13, 541.

[45] [1993] OJ C39/6.

[46] [1997] OJ C313/3.

[47] See M Paulweber, 'The End of a Success Story? The European Commission's White Paper on the Modernisation of European Competition Law' (2000) 23 *World Competition* 3, 15; Riley, above n 26, 661 and 665; A Schaub, 'The Reform of Regulation 17/62: The Issues of Compatibility, Effective Enforcement and Legal Certainty' in Ehlermann and Atanasiu, above n 26, 241, 249.

[48] For instance, at a workshop organised by the EUI/RSC in 1997, all participants, including high-level (Commission) officials, renowned scholars and practitioners specialising in competition law, agreed that the competition policy under Art 81 had to be adapted. Interestingly enough, there also seems to have been a basic consensus among those participants that the problems could be remedied just by reducing the scope of Art 81(1), namely by narrowing the concept of 'restriction of competition' (a suggestion that was firmly rejected by the Commission; see paras 56–7 of the White Paper). See the Introduction in Ehlermann and Laudati, above n 23, vii–xviii, xiii–xiv. See also Paulweber, *ibid*, 12: 'As of today, nobody really

European Union, the need for (structural) changes of the system seemed even more urgent. It was likely that the problems which the Commission was facing would be exacerbated by the accession of new Member States.[49] Given their recent transition from state-directed to free market economies, the candidate countries presented a potentially high number of competition issues.[50] As a matter of principle, a 'modernisation' of the enforcement procedures was therefore welcomed.

B. The Reform

1. Main Objectives of the Reform

Regulation 1/2003 was adopted on 16 December 2002 after a wide-ranging debate among the Commission, the Member States and other interested parties, such as industry, competition lawyers and European Economic Area (EEA) States.[51] The Commission had already published the White Paper in April 1999, in order to launch the discussion on a possible reform of Regulation 17.

In the White Paper, the Commission set out the main objectives of such a reform:

1. to refocus the Commission's activities on combating the most serious violations of EC competition law;
2. to decentralise the enforcement of EC competition law; and
3. to simplify procedures in order to ease the administrative burden on undertakings.[52]

It then put forward five options (i–v) available for reforming the system. Four of these options concerned the improvement of the existing notification and exemption system by: (i) changing the interpretation of Article 81(1) in order to reduce the scope of the provision; (ii) sharing the power to grant exemptions pursuant to Article 81(3) with the NCAs; (iii) broad-

---

denies the need for a reform.' Wißmann, above n 32, 137, therefore calls the White Paper a 'declaration of capitulation by the Commission'.

[49] See A Schaub and R Dohms, 'Das Weißbuch der Europäischen Kommission über die Modernisierung der Vorschriften zur Anwendung der Artikel 81 und 82 EG-Vertrag. Die Reform der Verordnung Nr. 17' (1999) 49 *Wirtschaft und Wettbewerb* 1055, 1056; J Temple Lang, 'Decentralised Application of Community Competition Law' (1999) 22 *World Competition* 3, 4; R Whish, 'Recent Developments in Community Competition Law 1998/99' (2000) 25 *EL Rev* 219, 244.

[50] Holmes, above n 42, 54.

[51] See the Commission's summary of observations (Competition DG Document of 29 February 2000) at http://europa.eu.int/comm/competition/antitrust/others/wp_on_modern isation/summary_observations.html ('Summary of Observations').

[52] White Paper, paras 43–51.

ening the scope of Article 4(2) of Regulation 17 to waive the prior notification requirement for certain agreements; and (iv) simplifying the procedures for the adoption of formal exemption decisions.[53] (v) The fifth option considered by the Commission consisted in replacing the notification system by a directly applicable exception system (*Legalausnahme/exception légale*).[54] It is based upon two key elements: the abolition of the notification requirement and the elimination of the Commission's monopoly to apply Article 81(3).

It is understandable that the Commission opted for the fifth alternative and presented this option as the (only) adequate reform proposal ('the Proposal').[55] Abolishing the notification procedure seems, at first sight, the most effective way to decrease the caseload as all measures previously introduced in this respect (*de minimis* rule, block exemptions etc) still did not sufficiently lower the number of new cases. Indeed, the aim of significantly reducing its workload appears to be the major motivation of the Commission's Proposal, permeating the entire White Paper,[56] though clearly it is not an end in itself.

The Commission felt that processing notifications was not the best way of using its limited resources, as that approach diverted it 'from its true mission'.[57] Since notified agreements or practices hardly ever raise any competition issues, the handling of notifications did not, according to the Commission, sufficiently contribute to the protection of competition in the EU.[58] The Commission therefore wanted to free up resources in order to be able to retarget its work on the detection and prosecution of the most harmful antitrust infringements so that it could ultimately ensure a more effective protection of competition.[59]

Against this background, the decentralisation of EC competition law enforcement, allegedly the second objective of the reform, appears to be a tool rather than a goal in itself:[60] it helps the Commission to reduce its workload by shifting the burden of enforcement partly to the Member States. Similarly, the third objective put forward by the Commission, ie the reduction of bureaucracy (for companies), seems to be more of a welcome

---

[53] *Ibid*, paras 55–68.
[54] *Ibid*, paras 69 *et seq.*
[55] Cf paras 74 and 75 of the White Paper.
[56] Cf Kingston, above n 32, 345–6.
[57] White Paper, para 43.
[58] *Ibid*, para 77.
[59] *Ibid*, paras 42 and 72.
[60] Ehlermann, above n 13, 560. Cf also E Mohr Mersing, 'The Modernisation of EC Competition Law—The Need for a Common Competition Culture' in B Hawk (ed), *1999 Proceedings of the Fordham Corporate Law Institute* (New York, Juris Publishing, 2000), 259, 264, who believes that the main driving force behind the reform is the Commission's wish to transform the enforcement system 'in such a way that it can be administered with the Commission's present resources'.

by-product of the elimination of the notification procedure than a true objective of the reform.[61]

2. Development of the Reform Process

The Commission contended that the White Paper merely set out its preliminary views. It was supposed to serve as a point of departure for a comprehensive discussion of the various alternatives for a reform.[62] However, the way in which the White Paper was drafted suggests that the Commission had already made up its mind about the direction which the reform should take when it published the White Paper.[63] This impression is confirmed by the further development of the reform process.

Following the publication of the White Paper, the Commission received approximately 120 submissions from the Member States and EU institutions, as well as from a variety of other interested parties, including European Free Trade Association (EFTA) countries, associations of undertakings, law firms and the competition authorities of some of the candidate countries. Scholars and other competition experts also contributed to the discussion of the reform proposals.

The comments submitted to the Commission were not entirely favourable and some even rejected the Proposal. For instance, two Member States and several retail companies were opposed to abolishing the notification system. Some Member States also expressed doubts as to the compatibility of the proposed system with the EC Treaty.[64] Discussions at conferences and legal publications revealed that academics also viewed the Proposal with scepticism, if not opposition.[65] Important contributions were also made by national institutions such as the German Monopoly Commission (Monopolkommission).[66]

However, in spite of the severe criticism[67] which the White Paper encountered and the important issues raised during the consultation

---

[61] *Ibid.*

[62] In para 140 of the White Paper, the Commission namely invited interested parties to submit 'observations on any aspect of the reform proposed *and* on the *options* outlined in this document' (emphasis added).

[63] Holmes, above n 42, 51.

[64] Sections 3 and 4 of the Commission's summary of observations (Competition DG Document of 29 February 2000) at europa.eu.int/comm/competition/antitrust/others/wp_on_modernisation/summary_observations.html.

[65] See eg Paulweber, above n 47, 48, who states that the White Paper 'does not provide a convincing concept'. Wißmann, above n 32, 154, finds that the Commission, by abolishing the notification requirement, 'overshoots the mark'.

[66] Monopolkommission, *Kartellpolitische Wende in der Europäischen Union. Zum Weißbuch der Kommission vom 28. April 1999* (1999), 28. Sondergutachten.

[67] See eg Wesseling, above n 1,378: '. . . the remedy the Commission proposes to (ill-identified) problems may be worse than the disease'.

process[68], the Commission did not reconsider its approach or reopen the (public) debate. Instead, it simply moved on to the next step by presenting a proposal for a Council Regulation implementing Articles 81 and 82 EC[69] ('Draft Regulation') on 28 September 2000.[70] The Draft Regulation was in fact based on the Proposal which the Commission had seemingly viewed as the preferred option at the time it drafted the White Paper.[71] Article 1 of the Draft Regulation established the system of direct applicability of Article 81(3) in that it provided that agreements or concerted practices falling within the scope of Article 81(1) 'which do not satisfy the conditions of Article 81(3) . . . shall be prohibited, no prior decision to that effect being required'. In other words, where the conditions of Article 81(3) are met, without any prior decision, the agreement or practice would not be prohibited. The Commission thus presented a formal proposal to abolish the notification requirement and remove its monopoly to apply Article 81(3). There was no further discussion of alternative reform steps.[72]

The debate that followed concentrated instead on the details of the system of direct applicability as proposed in the Draft Regulation. Interested parties discussed in particular the various mechanisms which the Commission suggested in order to ensure coherent and uniform application of the rules and legal certainty in a system in which the enforcement of EC competition law lies in the hands of a multitude of agencies and courts, and for which constitutive exemptions are no longer available.[73]

---

[68] Major concerns were raised in relation to the effectiveness of competition law enforcement with the argument that the prohibition of Art 81(1) would de facto be 'reduced' to a system of abuse control (*Mißbrauchskontrolle*). Moreover, the question was raised how legal certainty and consistency could be ensured if the notification/authorisation system was abolished.

[69] Proposal for a Council Regulation on the implementation of the rules on competition laid down in Articles 81 and 82 of the Treaty and amending Regulations (EEC) No 1017/68, (EEC) No 2988/74, (EEC) No 4056/86 and (EEC) No 3975/87, [2000] OJ C365 E/284.

[70] Cf Holmes, above n 42, 52. It is suspected, however, that between February 2000 (publication of the Summary of Comments) and September 2000 (publication of the Draft Regulation), secret discussions took place between the Commission and the Member States on the basis of strictly confidential so-called 'non-papers'. Wesseling, above n 1, 358. Cf also Holmes, above n 42, 52.

[71] While the discussion of the other four options always included a critical assessment of the associated risks and disadvantages or simply the conclusion the solution would not be wholly satisfactory (see paras 57, 62, 65 and 68 of the White Paper), the introduction of the directly applicable exception system was presented only in positive terms (see paras 69–73 of the White Paper).

[72] Against this background, it is not surprising that Wesseling proclaims: 'Clearly, the Commission *is* married to one idea' (Wesseling, above n 1, 378). Basedow less provokingly describes it as 'the political resolve of the Commission to have its way'. Basedow, 'Who will Protect Competition in Europe? From Central Enforcement to Authority Networks and Private Litigation' in T Einhorn (ed), 'Liber Amicorum Ernst-Joachim Mestmäcker' (2001) 2 *European Business Organization Law Review* 443, 446.

[73] There was also considerable debate about the envisaged exclusivity clause (Art 3 of the Draft Regulation) which provided that in all cases where there is an effect on interstate trade, EC competition law should apply to the exclusion of national competition laws. See eg Mestmäcker, above n 19, 426–35; A Pappalardo, 'Modernisation of EC Competition Law: Some Doubts and Questions on the Forthcoming Reform' in B Hawk (ed), *2000 Proceedings of the Fordham*

The process eventually led to the enactment of Regulation 1/2003, which was adopted by the Council on 16 December 2003 and became applicable on 1 May 2004.[74]

C. Résumé of Criticism

This book centres upon specific aspects of the decentralisation process rather than providing an overall assessment of the whole of Regulation 1/2003. However, in order to evaluate the implications of the reform and keep a critical eye on the new rules, it is useful to briefly summarise the major points of criticism.

The critique essentially focuses on five issues, notably: (i) the compatibility of the new system with the EC Treaty; (ii) the problem of effective control; (iii) the question of efficiency; (iv) the lack of legal certainty; and (v) the risk of incoherence and inconsistency.[75]

1. Compatibility

In the White Paper, the Commission states that the wording of Article 81(3) is the result of a compromise between those favouring an authorisation system and those favouring a directly applicable exception system, and contends that the EC Treaty negotiators deliberately left it to the Community legislator to choose between these two systems.[76] On this

---

Corporate Law Institute (New York, Juris Publishing, 2001), 365, 367–8. However, this proposal was not accepted by the Council. Instead, the principle of concurrent applicability has been maintained. In accordance with Art 3 of Reg 1/2003, national competition law and EC competition law can be applied in parallel in the same case.

[74] Art 45 of Reg 1/2003. The regulation also became immediately and fully applicable in the Central and Eastern European states which joined the EU since 2004. In this respect, neither the accession treaty nor Reg 1/2003 provide for a transition period for those new Member States. See K Cseres, 'The Interface between EC Competition Law and the Competition Laws of the New Member States: Implementation or Innovation?' in D Obradovic and N Lavranos (eds), *Interface between EU Law and National Law* (Groningen, Europa Law Publishing, 2007), 203, 210 and 211.

[75] Some critical comments concerned the strengthening of the Commission's powers of investigation. In contrast to the former rules, Reg 1/2003 authorises the Commission to search private homes of directors, managers and staff members, to seal offices and records, to interrogate company representatives and staff during inspections and record the answers, and to interview any person that might possess useful information (Arts 19–21 of Reg 1/2003). Criticism concerned in particular the right to carry out on-the-spot interrogations. See eg M Siragusa, 'A Critical Review of the White Paper on the Reform of the EC Competition Law Enforcement Rules' in B Hawk (ed), *1999 Proceedings of the Fordham Corporate Law Institute* (New York, Juris Publishing, 2000), 273, 295–301. However, since the Commission's investigatory powers are not related to the issue of decentralisation, this problem will not be further discussed here.

[76] Para 12 of the White Paper. *Contra* A Deringer, 'Stellungnahme zum Weißbuch der Europäischen Kommission über die Modernisierung der Vorschriften zur Anwendung der Art. 85 und 86 EG-Vertrag (Art. 81 und 82 EG)' (2000) 11 *Europäische Zeitschrift für*

basis, the Council would be free to transform the notification/authorisation system into a regime of directly applicable exception. However, some authors believe that the elimination of the notification and authorisation procedure would require an amendment of the EC Treaty. Their opinion is based mainly on textual considerations (Article 81(3) states that paragraph 1 may be *declared* inapplicable)[77] and the ECJ's doctrine of direct effect, according to which only Treaty provisions that establish clearly defined and unconditional rights or obligations can produce direct effects.[78]

It is curious to note that doubts concerning the compatibility of the new system with the EC Treaty appear to be largely confined to commentators

---

Wirtschaftsrecht 5, 5–6, who states: 'Ausdrücklich ausgebrochen ist der Meinungsstreit [regarding the two systems]erst bei der Beratung der späteren Verordnung Nr 17 . . .' Deringer further argues that the Commission's view is not reflected in the wording of Art 81(3). Interestingly, the Commission does not quote any evidence for its contention. Forrester has conducted some 'legal archaeology' browsing through the Council's archives. His conclusions do not exactly confirm the Commission's position. According to Forrester, the drafters of the EC Treaty did not contemplate the competition rules in the way that we examine them today, their debate was not as focussed and scientific as it is conducted nowadays: '. . . they certainly looked at every possible variant, procedurally speaking . . . What they produced was an *amalgam* [emphasis added] of several countries' preferences.' Forrester, above n 29, 93–4. Since many different procedural models were discussed, Appeldoorn concludes that there is no historical obstacle to switching to a directly applicable exception system. J Appeldoorn, 'Are the Proposed Changes Compatible with Article 81(3) E.C.?' (2001) 22 *European Competition Law Review* 400, 401. See also G Marenco, 'Le régime de l'exception légale et sa compatibilité avec le Traité' in (2001) 37 *Cahiers de Droit Européen* 135, 142, who agrees with the Commission's interpretation of the *travaux préparatoires*.

77 Therefore, the EC Treaty is said to presuppose the interposition of a constitutive administrative act before Art 81(3) can be invoked. Deringer, *ibid*, 6; W Möschel, 'Systemwechsel im Europäischen Wettbewerbsrecht?' (2000) 55 *Juristenzeitung* 61, 62; Paulweber, above n 47, 31; *contra* Forrester, above n 29, 95–6; Ehlermann, above n 13, 556. Ehlermann admits, however, that the wording of Art 81(3) seems to suggest a positive action being taken by someone other than a judge; *ibid*, 555. Similarly, in the *Bosch* case, Advocate General Lagrange recognised that the constitutive decision theory accorded best with the wording of Art 81(1), while a system depending on a legal exception (*exception légale*) would have required a different text (opinion of Advocate General Lagrange in Case 13/61 *de Geus v Bosch and van Rijn* [1962] ECR 45, 67 (English special edition)). Lagrange has described the issue perfectly well. In my view, the language of Art 81(3) can hardly be reconciled with a directly applicable exception system. The wording clearly suggests that there must be a 'declaration', ie some form of public intervention in the form of an administrative act which states ('declares') that the requirements of para 3 are fulfilled and the exemption/exception thus is applicable in the case at hand.

78 This is settled case law. See Case 26/62 *van Gend & Loos* [1963] ECR 1, 13 (English special edition). According to the critics, Art 81(3) does not fulfil these conditions as it provides for a wide margin of discretion. Moreover, Art 81(1) and (3) form a unity and must be applied as a whole. Since Art 81(3) is not susceptible to having direct effects, the directly applicable exception system would also deprive Art 81(1) of its direct effect. Consequently, such a system would be contrary to the EC Treaty. Mestmäcker, above n 19, 420; Möschel, above n 77, 62. Paulweber, above n 47, 32. Cf also D Wolf, 'Comment on the White Paper on the Reform of EC Competition Law' in B Hawk (ed), *1999 Proceedings of the Fordham Corporate Law Institute* (New York, Juris Publishing, 2000), 307, 311 and Wißmann, above n 32, 140. These arguments are less convincing. There are more provisions in the EC Treaty which allow for some discretion and still are considered to have a direct effect, such as Art 82, Art 86 or certain provisions in the field of social policy (see the judgment of the ECJ in Case 149/77 *Defrenne* [1978] ECR 1365 regarding Art 141 (ex Art 119) EC).

in Germany and the Netherlands.[79] Moreover, it seems that this debate is purely academic as, to date, the ECJ has not been called upon to review the legality of Regulation 1/2003.[80]

2. Effectiveness

Eliminating the notification/authorisation system also means that there is only *ex post* control of restrictive agreements and practices. Preventive control mechanisms allowing the Commission or NCAs to screen and, where necessary, prohibit anti-competitive agreements or practices in advance, ie before they are put into effect, no longer exist.

Some authors have criticised this, saying that, as a consequence, restrictive agreements that do not satisfy the conditions of Article 81(3) would in fact be tolerated and could be implemented until they are detected and prohibited. The damage that is thereby caused for competition could not be remedied. The risk of illegal agreements being effectively operated for years before a prohibitive decision is issued would be even greater with regard to horizontal agreements, where, in contrast to vertical restrictions, the parties usually have homogeneous interests, and the negative effects are less visible for third parties and therefore more difficult to detect.[81] These writers therefore contend that the new scheme

---

[79] See Ehlermann, above n 13, 554, n 61. Cf also A Komninos, ch 16: 'Modernisation and Decentralisation: Retrospective and Prospective' in G Amato and C-D Ehlermann (eds), *EC Competition Law. A Critical Assessment* (Oxford, Hart Publishing, 2007), 629, 647, who describes Germany as 'the centre of most negative reactions'. In addition to Deringer, Mestmäcker, Möschel, Wißmann and Wolf (see above nn 32, 76, 77 and 78), the German Government and the German Monopoly Commission (Monopolkommission) disputed the compatibility of a directly applicable exception system with the EC Treaty (see Monopolkommission, 28. Sondergutachten, above n 66, paras 14–17). Serious doubts as to the compatibility were also expressed by F Montag, 'The System of Legal Exception' (2001) 37 *Cahiers de Droit Européen* 145, 149. More recently, S Heutz, 'Legalausnahme und Gruppenfreistellungsverordnungen im System der VO (EG) Nr 1/2003' (2004) 54 *Wirtschaft und Wettbewerb* 1255, 1262, argued, on the basis of wording, history and teleological interpretation of Art 81 EC, that the provision requires an authorisation system. It appears that, outside Germany, these views are only shared by M Mok, 'Naar 'modernisering' van het Europees kartelbeleid. Witboek Europese Commissie mei 1999' (1999) 47 *Sociaal-Economische Wetgeving* 314, 319; F Vogelaar, *Marktwerking moet! Enkele kanttekeningen bij een zich snel ontwikkelend dogma* (Amsterdam, Vossiuspers AUP, 2000), 13; Pappalardo, above n 73, 366.

[80] Member States can no longer challenge Reg 1/2003 before the ECJ, as proceedings against the validity of a Commission act must be instituted within 2 months after its publication in the OJ (Art 230 EC). However, the validity of Reg 1/2003 could still be challenged indirectly, eg in the course of a private litigation in which the compatibility of an agreement with EC competition law is disputed and the question of the direct applicability of Art 81(3) EC arises. In such a case, the national court seized with the matter could ask the ECJ, pursuant to Art 234 EC, for a preliminary ruling on the legality of Art 1 of Reg 1/2003. One would expect that sooner or later an undertaking will raise this issue and the question will be submitted to the ECJ. See Vogelaar, *ibid*, 14, who observes: '. . . zal men bijna kunnen wachten op het moment dat aan het Hof de vraag van rechtsgeldigheid van de nieuwe procedureverordening wordt voorgelegd . . .'.

[81] M Paulweber and R Kögel, 'Das europäische Wettbewerbsrecht am Scheideweg' in (1999) 44 *Die Aktiengesellschaft* 500, 511.

would reduce the control mechanism, at least de facto, to a system of abuse control (*Mißbrauchskontrolle*).[82]

However, other commentators have pointed to the fact that the new system deprives undertakings of the privilege to exclude the risk of fines simply by notifying their agreements to the Commission. This could increase the effectiveness of the prohibition laid down in Article 81(1).[83] Moreover, also in the notification/exemption system, violations could go on undisturbed for quite some time, because undertakings were free to implement their agreements once they had been notified and Regulation 17 did not impose a time limit on the Commission within which it had to decide.[84]

Some observers have further suggested that, in a directly applicable exception system, companies against which proceedings are initiated could always claim to have acted bona fide assuming their agreements or practices were covered by Article 81(3). It would therefore become more difficult for the authorities to actually impose fines on undertakings.[85] On the other hand, it seems that, also in the past, the Commission has never imposed fines in cases where the companies involved had serious and honest grounds to believe that their agreement would be eligible for exemption.[86]

3. Efficiency

A number of authors have expressed doubts as to whether the new system will indeed allow a more efficient enforcement of Articles 81 and 82 EC. The Commission has made it clear that it plans to change its role from a purely reactive to a really proactive stance. It wants to concentrate on investigating the most serious infringements by increasing the number of own-initiative procedures.[87] In view of its scarce resources, the Commission asserted that the only way to achieve this was to abolish the notification/authorisation system thereby freeing resources that were otherwise locked up by the processing of notifications.

---

[82] Paulweber and Kögel, *ibid*, 504; Wißmann, above n 32, 140; Wolf, above n 78, 308; F Rittner, 'Zurück zum Missbrauchsprinzip im EG-Kartellrecht?' (1999) 52 *Der Betrieb* 1485, 1485; Mestmäcker, above n 19, 410–12.

[83] R Bechtold, 'Modernisierung des EG-Wettbewerbsrechts: Der Verordnungsentwurf der Kommission zur Umsetzung des Weissbuchs' (2000) 55 *Betriebs-Berater* 2425, 2427.

[84] Wils, above n 19, 126.

[85] Cf Paulweber and Kögel, above n 81, 511. Mestmäcker, above n 19, 410. Wißmann, above n 32, 149. *Contra* A Bartosch, 'Von der Freistellung zur Legalausnahme—was geschieht mit der Rechtssicherheit?' (2000) 50 *Wirtschaft und Wettbewerb* 462, 469, who maintains the contrary, namely that, in the new system, it is more difficult for companies to escape fines by proving that they were in good faith, even though the failure to notify can no longer be used against them.

[86] Bechtold, above n 83, 2427. Cf also Schaub, above n 47, 253, who quotes Case IV/36.888 *1998 Football World Cup* [2000] OJ L5/55, paras 123–5, where the Commission imposed only a symbolic fine of €1,000 in view of the lack of clarity of the law.

[87] White Paper, para 45.

However, it is feared that the new functions which the Commission has to perform in a directly applicable exception system in order to ensure the consistent application of the competition rules throughout the EU could compromise this goal. These are in particular consultation, coordination, monitoring and intervention tasks with regard to cartel investigations and court proceedings at national level.[88] Additional work may result from companies lobbying for a positive decision,[89] the only sort of Commission 'blessing' for restrictive agreements that is available in the new system, or requesting informal guidance.[90] It has been feared that these new tasks could easily absorb all those resources that the Commission wanted to free up by abolishing the notification procedure.[91] It must be noted, however, that the misgivings about an enormous 'demand' for positive decisions or guidance letters do not seem to have materialised. In the first 10 months of application of Regulation 1/2003, ie in the period between 1 May 2004 and 28 February 2005, the Commission did not issue a single Article 10 decision or guidance letter.[92]

[88] The Commission may be requested to provide assistance to national judges pursuant to Art 15(1) of Reg 1/2003; it has to monitor proceedings before national courts in order to decide whether an own-initiative intervention pursuant to Art 15(3) of Reg 1/2003 (*amicus curiae* provision) is recommended; eventually it may have to intervene as *amicus curiae* in national proceedings; and, above all, it has to play a central role in the network of competition authorities by monitoring the investigations carried out at national level and reviewing draft decisions of NCAs (Art 11(3) and (4) of Reg 1/2003).

[89] Pursuant to Art 10 of Reg 1/2003, the Commission may, in exceptional cases, find by way of decision that Art 81 EC is not applicable to a particular agreement or practice. Such decisions are adopted solely in the public interest on the Commission's own initiative. In other words, an undertaking cannot formally apply for a positive decision. See below, section II.A.1.a(2).

[90] See the Commission notice on informal guidance relating to novel questions concerning Arts 81 and 82 of the EC Treaty that arise in individual cases (guidance letters), [2004] OJ C101/78 ('Notice on Guidance Letters'). (In earlier documents and publications this type of informal guidance was also called 'reasoned opinion'.) According to Böge, this is what it will all boil down to in practice anyway, namely the discussion of 'critical proposals in informal talks with the undertakings concerned'. U Böge, 'The Discussion on the Modernisation of EC Antitrust Policy. An Update on the Bundeskartellamt's Point of View' in Ehlermann and Atanasiu, above n 26, 67, 72. Wolf, above n 78, 310, anticipates that the Commission will be 'swamped' with informal requests. See also Paulweber, above n 47, 38; Vogelaar, above n 79, 15, predicting 'een drukke praktijk van "business reviews"' for the Commission.

[91] See Möschel, above n 77, 65; Wesseling, above n 1, 377; Mestmäcker, above n 19, 443; K Lenaerts, 'Modernisation of the Application and Enforcement of European Competition Law—An Introductory Overview' in Stuyck and Gilliams, above n 1, 11, 35 and 40; F Jenny, 'On the Modernisation of EC Antitrust Policy' in Ehlermann and Atanasiu, above n 26, 361, 367. According to A Fuchs, 'Kontrollierte Dezentralisierung der europäischen Wettbewerbsaufsicht' (2005) 40 *Europarecht* (Beiheft 2), 77, 85, there is even a risk that the Commission might again be overburdened. The Commission seemed to ignore that it would acquire many new responsibilities when it proclaimed: 'Freed from the burden of having to process notifications, the Commission for its part could concentrate on taking action against the most serious infringement.' White Paper, para 72.

[92] E Paulis and E De Smijter, 'Enhanced Enforcement of the EC Competition Rules since 1 May 2004 by the Commission and the NCAs', paper for the conference 'Antitrust Reform in Europe: A Year in Practice', organised jointly by the International Bar Association (IBA) and the European Commission, Brussels, 9–11 March 2005, 15. F Montag and S Cameron, 'Effective enforcement: the practitioner's view of recent experiences under Reg 1/2003', paper for the

4. Legal Certainty

Another issue raised in legal doctrine is the question of whether the new enforcement system can guarantee an adequate level of legal certainty. The notification procedure undoubtedly provided a high level of legal certainty, at least to the extent that companies actually obtained a formal exemption.[93] Being directly applicable Community measures, formal (exemption) decisions of the Commission had to be given full legal force and effect (*effet utile*) in all Member States.[94] They were binding for national courts and could be invoked against anyone (ie contracting parties and third parties) who challenged the validity of the agreement in question.[95] Moreover, pursuant to Article 15(5)(a) of Regulation 17, undertakings achieved immunity from fines by notifying their agreements to the Commission.

In the directly applicable exception system, formal exemptions of a constitutive nature at the request of an undertaking (ie after notification) are no longer available.[96] Undertakings themselves have to assess the legality of an agreement or practice without the possibility of obtaining

---

conference 'Antitrust Reform in Europe: A Year in Practice', organised jointly by the International Bar Association (IBA) and the European Commission, Brussels, 9–11 March 2005, 5. It must be noted, though, that there are numerous strict requirements which must be fulfilled before a company can successfully request a guidance letter. In many cases, these conditions are probably not met or undertakings are simply discouraged from resorting to this instrument. On the dissuading effect of the long list of cumulative conditions for the issuance of guidance letters which make it difficult for firms to qualify for such guidance see Montag and Cameron, *ibid*, 5–6. Moreover, applicants have to disclose in detail all relevant facts of the potentially unlawful agreement or conduct, and the guidance letters will also be published on the Commission's website, but do not bind NCAs or courts. Arhold therefore concludes that, given this combination of absolute transparency with no legal certainty, guidance letters are unlikely to have much success. C Arhold, 'Die Reform der europäischen Wettbewerbsaufsicht aus praktischer Sicht' (2005) 40 *Europarecht* (Beiheft 2), 119, 125. This assumption seems to be confirmed in practice. Also at the time of writing, ie more than four years after Reg 1/2003 came into force, the Commission still has not issued a single guidance letter under the relevant procedure. G Bruzzone and M Boccaccio, 'Taking Care of Modernisation after the Start-up: A View from a Member Sate' (2008) 31 *World Competition* 89, 101.

[93] As concerns comfort letters, see above n 31. In view of the fact that the vast majority of cases were decided by comfort letters, Gilliams states that the legal certainty obtained from the notification system in many cases was rather illusory. H Gilliams, 'Modernisation: From Policy to Practice' (2003) 28 *EL Rev* 451, 470. Forrester, above n 29, 103, even calls it a 'fiction' that most notifications led to a formal decision providing legal certainty.

[94] See the judgment of the ECJ in Case 106/77 *Amministrazione delle Finanze v Simmenthal* [1978] ECR 629, paras 21–2. See further K Lenaerts and P Van Nuffel, *Constitutional Law of the European Union* (London, Sweet & Maxwell, 2nd edn, 2005), paras 17-008–17-010.

[95] Cf Ritter and Braun, above n 32, 132. Some authors even consider constitutive formal exemption decisions to have effect *erga omnes*. Schaub, above n 47, 251 and 254; E Paulis, 'Coherent Application of EC Competition Law in a System of Parallel Competences' in Ehlermann and Atanasiu, above n 26, 399, 409. This seems, however, not to be entirely in line with Art 249 (ex Art 189), which provides that a decision shall be binding 'upon those to whom it is addressed'.

[96] Positive decisions (see below, section II.A.1.a(2)) only have declaratory character and cannot be obtained on demand by companies.

confirmation of their views from the Commission. The reduction in legal certainty is probably less dramatic than has often been pretended since most applications resulted in comfort letters.[97] Moreover, in the notification system parties themselves also had to make an assessment of their agreement in order to determine the likelihood of an exemption before filing a notification.[98] The block exemption regulations which continue to apply, as well as notices and guidelines issued by the Commission, help undertakings to understand and correctly apply the law. However, concerns for legal certainty are not triggered by those agreements that benefit from a block exemption or by those that contain hard-core restrictions that are plainly illegal. The issue here is the legal uncertainty pertaining to the large number of grey area cases (for instance, agreements between parties with significant market shares) for which a (formal or informal) Commission blessing is no longer available.[99] On this basis, the new enforcement system under Regulation 1/2003 has reduced legal certainty.[100]

In contrast, the Commission claims that, after 40 years of implementation, the conditions for applying Article 81(1) and (3) have been sufficiently clarified by its own decision-making practice and the case law of the European courts at Luxemburg, and are known to undertakings.[101] However, the interpretation of Article 81 EC has recently undergone significant changes. The Commission itself has radically changed its approach

---

[97] See Gilliams, above n 93, 470. J Venit, 'Brave New World: The Modernization and Decentralization of Enforcement under Articles 81 and 82 of the EC Treaty' (2003) 40 *CML Rev* 545, 554–5. On the other hand, it has been pointed out that, in practice, even comfort letters provided some relative assurance since they were hardly ever ignored or 'overruled' by national courts or authorities. W Deselaers and S Obst, 'Weissbuch zum Europäischen Kartellrecht—Rechtssicherheit ade?' (2000) *Europaisches Wirtschafts- und Steuerrecht* 41, 43.

[98] If the assessment lead to the conclusion that the agreement was not exemptible, parties would not notify it generally. Venit, above n 97, 555. K Pijetlovic, 'Reform of Antitrust Enforcement: Criticism of the New System is Highly Exaggerated' (2004) 25 *European Competition Law Review* 356, 365. See also Wils, above n 19, 113, who notes that, in practice, only a limited number of agreements were notified.

[99] Gilliams, above n 93, 459, calls them the 'tough' cases that will involve much debate about market definition, potential market entry, alleged efficiencies, possible foreclosure effects and so forth. See also Deselaers and Obst, above n 97, 44. Venit, above n 97, 555, additionally points to the fact that in these less clear-cut cases the parties can no longer obtain immunity from fines by lodging a notification.

[100] A Bartosch, 'Von der Freistellung zur Legalausnahme: Der Vorschlag der EG-Kommission für eine "neue Verordnung Nr. 17"' (2001) 12 *Europäische Zeitschrift für Wirtschaftsrecht* 101, 105. Cf also Möschel, above n 77, 64; Wolf, above n 78, 309; and H Bourgeois (below n 106).

[101] Cf para 78 of the White Paper. *Accord* Schaub and Dohms, above n 49, 1069; Wils, above n 19, 122, who contends that, after four decades of implementation, the novel character of Art 81 EC, which certainly was revolutionary in 1957, would no longer justify an ex *ante* control system. *Contra* Paulweber, above n 47, 38, who predicts a multitude of informal inquiries by undertakings. It should be noted here that the bulk of the Commission's so-called decision practice on Art 81(3) has not been publicised because it is 'hidden' in comfort letters. Holmes, above n 42, 64.

towards a more economic analysis.[102] This may entail some departures from previous case law. Therefore, it is quite uncertain whether those earlier decisions and judgments still have full precedent value. In fact, they may even provide incorrect guidance.[103]

Moreover, it is doubtful whether one can expect an undertaking to properly strike a balance between the pro- and anti-competitive effects of its own agreements.[104] Seemingly, the Commission believes it can trust the cat to keep the cream. However, the self-assessment by companies in matters where there is an inherent conflict between the self-interest of the undertaking concerned (to maximise profits) and the public interest (to preserve effective competition) may turn out to be a poor way of regulating business conduct.[105]

In any event, undertakings are forced, to a far greater extent, to take recourse to (external) legal advice. They require a more detailed and in-depth analysis, ideally from more than one law firm. The assessment of the four conditions of Article 81(3), more particularly the proof of economic efficiencies and their passing on to consumers, which must moreover be substantiated by hard and convincing numbers, may often require a full-blown market analysis.[106] This certainly calls for the involvement of economic experts.[107] In other words, the cost of legal and

---

[102] This aspect is also underlined by Deselaers and Obst, above n 97, 44. On the new analytical framework for the application of Art 81 and the Commission's 'break with the past', see further G Van Gerven, 'The Application of Article 81 in the New Europe' in B Hawk (ed), *2003 Proceedings of the Fordham Corporate Law Institute* (New York, Juris Publishing, 2004), 415, in particular 421–3. According to Fuchs, above n 91, 92, the Commission' new approach even results in a 'creeping alignment' of the concept of restriction of competition under Art 81 EC with the 'rule of reason' doctrine applied in the US. See also the interpretation of the interstate trade criterion by the ECJ in the *Italian Banks* case (above n 26 and below n 113).

[103] Gilliams, above n 93, 458. Cf S Bishop, 'Modernisation of the Rules Implementing Articles 81 and 82' in Ehlermann and Atanasiu, above n 26, 55, 59–61, and also Wesseling, above n 1, 362, who finds that, due to inconsistencies between the Commission decisions and judgments of the Luxemburg courts, the reliability of the case law and decision practice was already doubtful before the Commission changed its approach. Against this background, it is a little surprise that, during the first months of application of Reg 1/2003, there were only a few requests for guidance letters (which did not fulfil the criteria set out in the Notice on Guidance Letters) and no positive decisions by the Commission. See further above n 92.

[104] In particular, the grey area cases will require the (self-)assessment of highly complex issues. Even within a single authority, the same agreement or practice is sometimes viewed and evaluated differently, eg by two case handlers dealing successively with the same matter. See Deselaers and Obst, above n 97, 44. It is therefore hard to imagine that the undertakings concerned can adequately evaluate such issues themselves.

[105] Cf Möschel, above n 77, 63: 'Ein potentieller Sünder ist aufgerufen, sich selbst freizusprechen.' J Basedow, 'La renationalisation du droit communautaire de la concurrence' (2001–2002) 11/12 *Revue des Affaires Européennes* 92, 95. Also sceptical is Mestmäcker, above n 19, 411.

[106] H Bourgeois, 'The Impact of Modernisation on Companies and their Counsels' in D Geradin (ed), *Modernisation and Enlargement: Two Major Challenges for EC Competition Law* (Antwerp, Intersentia, 2004), 257, 263–5. Bourgeois even contends that anticipating the likely outcome of a public policy decision, a qualification which was at least appropriate for exemption decisions of the old type, may after all require 'a fair amount of crystal ball gazing'. *Idem*, 264.

[107] Holmes, above n 42, 64.

economic advice will in most cases be substantial. This, in turn, raises the question of whether the new system is in fact more favourable for undertakings in terms of procedure and (associated) costs.[108] Whilst the undertakings have been freed from the burden and expense of having to prepare lengthy notifications, the overall cost of ensuring compliance with Article 81 is unlikely to have decreased; rather, the contrary is true.[109]

Another loss of legal certainty arises in relation to proceedings at national level. The risk of double jeopardy, ie parallel NCA investigations or court actions in several Member States concerning the same agreements or practice, and the possibility of inconsistent results of such parallel proceedings obviously entails a considerable degree of uncertainty.[110]

5. Coherence and Consistency

One of the major challenges of the reform is to maintain coherence in the application of EC competition law throughout the EU and avoid conflicting decisions of different enforcement bodies.[111] This is also acknowledged by the Commission.[112]

Since Article 81 EC only applies where there is an effect on interstate trade, it is highly unlikely that agreements or practices which have no cross-border elements at all will fall within the ambit of this provision. As a consequence, in the majority of cases, more than one Member State can legitimately claim to have jurisdiction because there exists a material link with its territory in that the agreement affects competitors or consumers on the domestic market.[113] Parallel NCA investigations regarding the same agreement/practice or network of agreements are therefore likely,[114] even though Regulation 1/2003 provides for some limited mechanisms to avoid duplication of procedures.

---

[108] This is, however, what the Commission seems to suggest when it argues that undertakings should be freed from administrative constraints (ie the notification requirement) that generate major costs. White Paper, para 50.

[109] See Gilliams, above n 93, 472.

[110] Holmes, above n 42, 61–2 and 67–8.

[111] Cf L Idot, 'A French Point of View on the Radical Decentralisation of the Implementation of Article 81(1) and (3)' in Ehlermann and Atanasiu, above n 26, 335, 336. As Idot points out, the issue of coherence is typical for any decentralised application of the law.

[112] White Paper, para 101.

[113] Cf J Venit, above n 26, 461 and 469. Venit points to the judgment of the ECJ in the *Italian Banks* case (above n 26) which is said to exclude the application of Article 81 to so-called domestic agreements, ie agreements that primarily affect consumers in a single Member State only.; *idem*, 468. Venit even concludes that, as a result of this judgment, the White Paper may turn into 'an invitation for the Member States to apply Art 81 to agreements or practices that primarily affect competitors or consumers *in other Member States*'; *ibid*, 474.

[114] Cf Venit, above n 26, 470, who thinks that agreements with cross-border effects will attract 'the competing attentions of other Member State authorities'. Cooke even speaks of 'inter-agency rivalry': J Cooke, 'Commission White Paper on Decentralisation of Competition Rules. The Threat to Consistency' in Ehlermann and Atanasiu, above n 26, 551, 552.

On the other hand, not all of the 27 NCAs in the EU have the same legal traditions and experience, the same level of expertise and staffing, the same degree of independence, the same national sensitivities. They do not apply the same procedural rules and probably do not follow the same policy considerations.[115] One can therefore easily imagine that these 27 authorities may have quite different views both on procedural questions and substantive issues. Disagreements may also arise concerning the general enforcement practice, ie the (political) question of which infringements and/or sectors deserve priority.[116] However, there are no clear rules, let alone binding principles, for the relationship between NCAs.[117] Co-operation and consultation at the horizontal level as provided by Regulation 1/2003 take place on a voluntary basis only. Neither the Advisory Committee on Restrictive Practices and Monopolies ('Advisory Committee') nor the Commission have any decisional power regarding the allocation or referral of cases or the resolution of other conflicts between NCAs.[118] Moreover, NCA decisions formally have no legal effects outside the territory of the NCA which adopted them.[119] It thus appears that there is considerable scope for divergent NCA decisions.[120]

[115] Cf Cooke, *ibid*, 553; Riley, above n 26, 658–61; Forrester, above n 29, 105–6. For instance, the economic and legal heritage of the 12 new Member States (which joined the EU since 2004) as former communist countries may play a role. The domestic markets of these Member States are (still) characterised by certain distinct features, notably the transition economy and the small size of their markets, which may require different responses in terms of competition policy and enforcement measures. See Cseres, above n 74, 205–6 and 218–19.

[116] Gilliams, above n 93, 466. In this context, it is interesting to note that several of the 12 new Member States have enacted competition legislation with a broader scope, covering not only the classical competition rules but also other fields of market law such as unfair commercial practices, which then also come under the responsibility of the NCA. Cseres, above n 74, 225. The situation is similar in Italy and France. This combination of the functions of antitrust law enforcement and (traditional) consumer protection in a single authority may not only influence the outcome of a particular case, but may already guide the NCA when deciding whether (or not) to pursue certain matters. As Cseres notes: 'Considerations in one policy area can provide useful guidelines in the other policy area . . .'

[117] See below, section II.B.3 and also Chapters 4 and 6.

[118] Cf J Bourgeois and C Humpe, 'The Commission's Draft "New Regulation 17"' (2002) 23 *European Competition Law Review* 43, 47, who notice that the Draft Regulation is 'remarkably silent' on the issue of case allocation. U Immenga, 'Coherence: A Sacrifice of Decentralization?' in Ehlermann and Atanasiu, above n 26, 353, 355.

[119] K Ritter in U Immenga and E-J Mestmäcker (eds), *Wettbewerbsrecht, Band 1. EG/Teil 2. Kommentar zum Europäischen Kartellrecht* (Munich, CH Beck, 4th edn, 2007), Art 5 VO 1/2003, para 7; D Dalheimer in D Dalheimer, C Feddersen and G Miersch, *EU-Kartellverfahrensverordnung. Kommentar zur VO 1/2003* (Munich, CH Beck, 2005), Art 5 no 24.

[120] Evidently the risk of inconsistencies has not only a horizontal, but also a vertical dimension. Cooke, above n 114, 553. However, as regards the (vertical) relationship between the Commission, on the one hand, and the NCAs or national courts, on the other hand, the potential for conflicting decisions is much smaller, mainly for three reasons. First, the Commission has an evocation right allowing it to relieve an NCA at any time of its competence (Art 11(6) of Reg 1/2003). Secondly, national courts and NCAs are under an explicit duty to avoid decisions that would run counter to a (contemplated) Commission decision (Art 16 of Reg 1/2003). Thirdly, the Commission has the right to intervene in national court proceedings using the new instrument of *amicus curiae* submissions. Similar provisions do not exist with regard to the horizontal relations between NCAs and/or national courts of different Member States.

Similarly, multiple private litigation regarding the same agreement or network of agreements before national courts of different Member States can lead to inconsistent outcomes. Regulation 1/2003 does not provide for any coordination or consultation mechanisms regarding national courts. The scope of application of Article 27 of Council Regulation (EC) No 44/2001[121] is too limited to prevent conflicting decisions.[122]

Double jeopardy caused by multiple litigation in different Member States or parallel investigations by several NCAs therefore poses a real threat to consistency and coherence. Admittedly, these issues could have arisen under Regulation 17. However, the problem has become much more urging since NCAs are now obliged to effectively apply Articles 81 and 82 EC. Moreover, both NCAs and national courts can apply Article 81 EC in full, which means, at the same time, that there will generally be no reason to put their own procedure on hold in order to await an EU-wide binding Commission decision. Against this background, the horizontal aspects, ie the need for coordinating preventive and corrective measures with regard to investigations and decisions of national enforcement bodies, seem to have been neglected in the White Paper and subsequently in Regulation 1/2003.[123] Several writers therefore doubt that it will be possible to maintain the same level of coherence and consistency that existed under Regulation 17.[124]

---

[121] Council Regulation (EC) No 44/2001 of 22 December 2000 on jurisdiction and the recognition and enforcement of judgments in civil and commercial matters, [2001] OJ L12/1. This regulation replaces the former Brussels Convention.

[122] Bourgeois and Humpe, above n 118, 46–7; Van Der Woude, above n 1, 47. Art 27 of Reg 44/2001 obliges national courts to decline jurisdiction if the court of another Member State has been seized of the same matter (principle of *lis pendens*). It applies only to the extent that the cause of action and the parties are identical. However, where a company practices, for instance, a pan-European distribution system, it may well be faced with private litigation in several Member States regarding the same subject matter (ie the 'standard' distribution agreement), while the parties are different. It is also quite doubtful that in such a case the actions could be considered as 'related' within the meaning of Art 28 of Reg 44/2001, which would allow one court to stay proceedings if a another court is dealing with a related matter. D Edward, 'The Modernization of EC Antitrust Policy. Issues for Courts and Judges' in Ehlermann and Atanasiu, above n 26, 565, 570.

[123] Cf Immenga, above n 118, 357 and 359; B Hawk and N Denaeijer, 'The Development of Articles 81 and 82: Legal Certainty' in Ehlermann and Atanasiu, above n 26, 129, 143.

[124] Cf Immenga, above n 118, 358, stating that 'it hardly seems possible to have both uniform application and the direct applicability of Art 81(3)'. Cooke, above n 114, 552, finds that 'the White Paper is at its weakest when it seeks to suggest how this risk (to the uniform and consistent application) might be minimised'. Gilliams, above n 93, 473, expects a significant number of erroneous assessments and inconsistent decisions at least during an initial period. *Contra* Pijetlovic, above n 98, 369, and Wils, above n 19, 146–7, who does not see any need for mechanisms to reduce the incidence of conflicting decisions since, in his view, disagreements about the interpretation of the law would be normal and excessive divergencies would not be sustained long. Wils even suggests that the Commission should not use the provisions available in Reg 1/2003 to minimise the number of conflicting decisions as this would detract it from other work.

6. *Alternative Solutions*

It seems that the Commission, early in the reform process, had set its mind on the abolition of the notification/authorisation system.[125] It therefore appears to be one of the main shortcomings of the reform process that the Commission did not seriously consider any of the other options outlined in the White Paper as a viable solution.[126] In particular, it seems that the Commission failed to examine the possibility of combining several of the alternatives, thereby restricting itself unnecessarily to an all-or-nothing approach.[127] Arguably, such a combination might have presented an effective way of improving the enforcement system as it existed at that time.[128]

This is all the more true since certain reform measures were already underway when the Commission published the White Paper in April 1999. These measures included the reform on vertical restraints, which could be expected to decrease the number of new notifications significantly.[129] Moreover, at the beginning of the 1990s, the Commission managed to reduce the backlog of cases substantially (from roughly 3,000 to about 1,000 pending cases).[130] There are also reasons to believe that the alleged workload problem was less dramatic than the Commission claimed. While the number of agreements notified each year still varied between 236 and 368 at the beginning of the 1990s,[131] there were only 206 notifications in 1996 and roughly 220 notifications in 1997 and 1998. In 1999, the number dropped to only 162,[132] prompting Ehlermann to concede that the

---

[125] See above n 71.

[126] See Vogelaar, above n 79, 15.

[127] Wißmann, above n 32, 150.

[128] Cf Ehlermann, above n 13, 544; Venit, above n 26, 473; Wißmann, above n 32, 151. On the insufficient discussion of alternative solutions in general, see R Wesseling, 'The Commission White Paper on Modernisation of E.C. Antitrust Law: Unspoken Consequences and Incomplete Treatment of Alternative Options' (1999) 20 *European Competition Law Review* 420.

[129] See Pappalardo, above n 73, 366; Wißmann, above n 32, 153; Wolf, above n 78, 309. Following the publication of the Green Paper on vertical restraints in EC competition policy (COM(96) 721 final) in January 1997, the Commission was planning to replace the rules for exclusive purchasing, exclusive selling and franchising by a single block exemption regulation with a much broader scope. It would cover all types of vertical agreements. The relevant proposals led to the adoption of Reg 2790/1999 (see above n 9). Moreover, in November 1998, the Commission had published a proposal to amend Art 4 of Reg 17 ([1998] OJ C365/30) so as to enable the Commission to exempt vertical agreements with retroactive effect thereby dispensing them from the requirement of prior notification. The proposal was adopted shortly after the publication of the White Paper, ie in June 1999 ([1999] OJ L148/5).

[130] Ehlermann, above n 13, 546.

[131] 1991 to 1995. See the XXVth Report on Competition Policy 1995, 346 (table 2.2). The peak of 368 notifications in 1995 may have been caused by the accession of Austria, Finland and Sweden to the EU. Siragusa, above n 75, 280, n 26. (NB: Later reports on competition policy state only 360 notifications for 1995; see eg XXVIIth Report on Competition Policy 1997, 396 (table 2.2)).

[132] See statistics in the XXXIst Report on Competition Policy 2001, 81. In 2000 and 2001 there were only 101 and 94 notifications respectively. This recent drop in notifications may have

annual average of notifications 'looks quite manageable'.[133] Other writers have suggested that the backlog existing at the end of the 1990s (approximately 1,000 cases pending)[134] could easily be removed by one big effort.[135]

Furthermore, the Commission seems to have misjudged the relevance of the notification process. According to the Commission, the notification system no longer ensured an effective protection of competition because notifications hardly ever revealed serious competition issues, and prohibition decisions[136] resulting from a notification were extremely rare.[137] However, this argument is not compelling. In fact, the question is not how many of the notified agreements are prohibited, but rather how many prohibitions are avoided because parties either do not include in their agreements restrictions that are not eligible for exemption or modify their agreements in the course of the notification procedure in order to meet the concerns of the competition authority.[138] On this basis, the pre-screening of restrictive agreements in a notification/authorisation system can be a valuable and quite effective way of protecting competition.[139] The

---

been due partly to the availability of a broader block exemption and the possibility of retroactive individual exemptions for vertical restraints (see above n 129) and partly to the reform plans outlined in the White Paper which signalled that the Commission was not likely to issue any more individual exemption decisions.

[133] Ehlermann, above n 13, 544. A Riley, 'EC Antitrust Modernisation: The Commission Does Very Nicely—Thank You! Part One: Regulation 1 and the Notification Burden' (2003) 24 *European Competition Law Review* 604, states that '200 or so cases a year is truly minimal'. Cf also Lenaerts, above n 91, 14, n 37, who believes that the caseload to be expected in an enlarged EU has been 'clearly exaggerate(d)' by the Commission. In his commentary (see above n 29), Emmerich even calls the alleged administrative overload a tale invented by the Commission: 'Das Massenproblem ist im wesentlichen eine Erfindung der Kommission . . .'

[134] See above n 41.

[135] W Möschel, 'Guest Editorial: Change of Policy in European Competition Law?' (2000) 37 *CML Rev* 495, 495. Emmerich, above n 29.

[136] The term 'prohibition decision' (or 'negative decision') is used here to capture decisions requiring that an infringement be brought to an end (see Reg 1/2003, Art 7(1), 1st sentence).

[137] To support this argument, the Commission quotes the fact that, in more than 35 years of application of Reg 17, only nine prohibition decisions have been taken following a notification without an (additional) complaint having been lodged. White Paper, para 77 note 53. *Accord* Wils, above n 19, 129.

[138] See PM Roth and V Rose (eds), *Bellamy & Child. European Community Law of Competition* (Oxford, Oxford University Press, 6th edn, 2008), para 3.005.

[139] Möschel, above n 77, 63–4; I Forrester, 'Modernisation of EC Competition Law' in B Hawk (ed), *1999 Proceedings of the Fordham Corporate Law Institute* (New York, Juris Publishing, 2000), 181, 195, agrees to the extent that the system is functioning well. See also Paulweber and Kögel, above n 81, 513. Paulweber and Kögel further point out that notifications are also an important source of information for the competition authority allowing it to accumulate market and sector specific know-how (*ibid*, 511). This has also been acknowledged by the Commission in Green Paper on Vertical Restraints, para 188. On this issue see also H Sauter, 'Die Globalisierung der Wettbewerbsbehörden durch die Erweiterung der Europäischen Union' in A Fuchs, H-P Schwintowski and D Zimmer (eds), *Wirtschafts- und Privatrecht im Spannungsfeld von Privatautonomie, Wettbewerb und Regulierung. Festschrift für Ulrich Immenga zum 70. Geburtstag* (Munich, CH Beck, 2004), 351, 358–9, who believes that the abolition of the notification system is particularly unfortunate with regard to the 10 new Eastern

Commission may therefore have been too quick to conclude that the notification system had become irrelevant or even useless[140] and should be abolished altogether.[141]

On the other hand, it is undoubtedly one of the major advantages of the directly applicable exception system that it puts an end to the artificial procedural division between the implementation of Article 81(1) and the application Article 81(3), which ran counter to the unitary character of Article 81.[142] In fact, it has often been stated that the possibility of so-called dilatory notifications, ie notifications lodged for the (sole) purpose of bringing court proceedings to halt, were a major obstacle to a more extensive and more frequent application of the EC competition rules by national courts.[143]

II. THE NEW SHARING OF COMPETENCES UNDER REGULATION 1/2003—A BRIEF OVERVIEW

In the White Paper,[144] the Commission describes the (new) tasks to be assumed by itself, the NCAs and the national courts of the Member States in a directly applicable exception system under the heading 'new division of responsibilities'. However, the term 'division' does not seem appropriate since there is no clear dividing line between cases falling within the jurisdiction of the Commission and cases falling within the jurisdiction of the Member States' authorities.

Whenever a restrictive agreement or practice affects trade between Member States, the Commission as well as the Member States are theoretically competent to apply Article 81. Neither the White Paper nor Regulation 1/2003 contains any criteria for attributing that responsibility

and Central European Member States whose competition authorities are still in the phase of building up important know-how and experience and where a real competion culture still has to grow.

[140] Cf Forrester, *ibid*, 194, quoting A Schaub, former Director General at DG Competition.

[141] Moreover, in my view, the legal exception system cannot be reconciled with the wording of Art 81(3) EC and therefore would have required a Treaty amendment. See above n 77.

[142] In the *Bosch* case (n 77, 52), the ECJ held that Art 81(1) and 81(3) form an 'indivisible whole'. However, due to the Commission's monopoly, under Reg 17, over Art 81(3) exemptions, national courts and NCAs could only apply Art 81(1) but not Art 81(3) in the past, and thus had to abort their examination after the 1st para. D Smeets, 'Nouveau règlement européen en matière d'ententes et nouveau rôle du Conseil de la concurrence' (2004) 71 *DAOR* 21, 23, called this situation schizophrenic. On the procedural difficulties resulting from this unfortunate partitioning see Bundeskartellamt, *Praxis und Perspektiven der dezentralen Anwendung des EG-Wettbewerbsrechts, Diskussionspapier für die Sitzung des Arbeitskreises Kartellrecht am 8. und 9. Oktober 1998*, 13. See also para 49 of the White Paper.

[143] White Paper, para 100. The term 'dilatory notification' was used by the Commission in para 55 of the 1997 Cooperation Notice (abve n 46).

[144] Paras 83–100.

either to the Commission or the NCAs, or for distributing cases among the NCAs. Article 11 of Regulation 1/2003 only provides that the Commission and the NCAs shall apply the EC competition rules 'in close cooperation'.

Consequently, for as long as the Commission has not initiated any proceedings,[145] both the Member States and the Commission have concurrent jurisdiction over one and the same Article 81 case.[146] Regulation 1/2003 does not establish a system of mutually exclusive spheres of responsibility. Therefore, it appears more accurate to speak of the 'sharing' of competences or authority.[147]

A. The Commission's Role

Under Regulation 17, the Commission had the exclusive power to declare Article 81(1) inapplicable by granting an exemption pursuant to Article 81(3). It thus performed the function of a central antitrust authority in the EU. As stated above, under Regulation 1/2003, the Commission shares the competence to apply Article 81(1) *and* (3) with the NCAs and the courts of the Member States. However, the Commission maintains a key role with regard to both the enforcement of the competition rules and the orientation of the competition policy.[148]

---

[145] If the Commission initiates proceedings, the NCAs are relieved of their competence pursuant to Art 11(6) of Reg 1/2003 (right of evocation). As concerns national courts, they shall stay proceedings pursuant to Art 16(1) of Reg 1/2003 if the Commission is dealing with the matter.

[146] See Paulis, above n 95, 403, describes this as 'a system of full parallel competencies'.

[147] Cf J Bourgeois, 'Decentralized Enforcement of EC Competition Rules by National Competition Authorities. Some Remarks on Consistency, Coherence and Forum Shopping' in Ehlermann and Atanasiu, above n 26, 323, 331.

[148] Which corresponds to the role and discretion afforded to it by the *Automec II* case law (n 40) and also reflected in the *de minimis* Notice (above n 38). The changes (compared to Reg 17) regarding the Commission's powers are only discussed here to the extent that they are relevant to co-operation between the competition authorities of the EU. For the sake of completeness, it is simply mentioned here that Reg 1/2003, in addition to the new supervision, coordination and co-operation mechanisms, also entailed a number of changes as regards the Commission's investigatory and sanctioning powers. These include, inter alia, the right to interrogate persons (Art 19 of Reg 1/2003), ask for any kind of explanation relating to the subject matter of an inspection (Art 20(2)(e) of Reg 1/2003), search private homes of company directors and staff members (Art 21 of Reg 1/2003), and seal business premises (Art 20(2)(d) of Reg 1/2003). Finally, the rules on procedural fines were amended to allow the Commission to impose fines of up to 1% of the aggregate annual turnover where a company supplies incorrect, incomplete or misleading information and periodic penalty payments of up to 5% of the average daily turnover per day where a company needs to be compelled to comply with a Commission decision. See also above n 75.

1. Enforcement

The Commission's role is not reduced to that of a guardian of the Treaty. The Commission maintains the power to enforce itself the EC rules on competition.[149] In addition to the right to adopt prohibition decisions, Regulation 1/2003 confers a number of 'new' decisional powers[150] on the Commission. Some of these additional powers had already been acknowledged by the ECJ, even though they were not explicitly laid down in Regulation 17. Furthermore, while the Member States have concurrent jurisdiction, the Commission retains control over the outcome of proceedings conducted by NCAs due to certain supervisory and interventionary powers. In addition, the possibilities of the Commission for assisting national courts are extended. Finally, the Commission's policy with regard to the handling of complaints is set out in more detail.

a. Decisional Powers

The Commission's principal decisional powers are laid down in Articles 7–10 of Regulation 1/2003. It can essentially take three different types of decisions, notably prohibition (or infringement) decisions, positive decisions and decisions accepting commitments.

(1) Prohibition Decisions—Article 7 of Regulation 1/2003. Pursuant to Article 7(1) of Regulation 1/2003, the Commission can prohibit agreements or practices that restrict competition and do not satisfy the conditions of Article 81(3). The Commission may also find that an infringement has been committed in the past; it can make such a finding without imposing a fine.[151] Moreover, the provision now expressly grants the Commission the power to impose (behavioural or structural) remedies[152] on the undertakings concerned if this is necessary to bring the infringement effectively

---

[149] See Paulis, above n 95, 405.

[150] Riley, above n 133, 607, distinguishes between three categories of Commission powers: decisional, investigatory and penal powers. Investigatory and penal powers are not discussed here. In my view, however, a fourth category should be added—namely, all those supervisory and interventionary powers that are conferred upon the Commission to ensure the consistent and uniform application of the EC competition rules throughout the EU.

[151] Reg 1/2003, Art 7(1), 4th sentence. This right had already been confirmed by the ECJ before Reg 1/2003 was adopted with regard to cases where there is a real danger of repetition. See Case 7/82 GVL [1983] ECR 483, paras 16–28.

[152] At p 14 of the explanatory memorandum of 27 September 2000 which preceded the publication of the Draft Regulation on the Commission's website (COM(2000) 582 final; not published in the OJ) ('Explanatory Memorandum'), the Commission states explicitly that structural remedies may include the divestiture of (parts of) a business. However, the power to break up an entire company is an extremely strong weapon and must only be used under strict conditions, such as the principle of proportionality. See A Jones and B Sufrin, *EC Competition Law* (Oxford, Oxford University Press, 3rd edn, 2008), 1206.

to an end.[153] In addition, Article 8 of Regulation 1/2003 explicitly entitles the Commission to order interim measures in cases which pose the risk of serious and irreparable damage to competition.[154]

Since the Commission's major goal is to concentrate its forces on the detection, investigation and punishment of the most serious infringements of competition law, the number of prohibition decisions that it will adopt may be expected to increase substantially. Prohibition decisions may set out important precedents.[155] Since they state that an infringement of the EC competition rules has occurred, they can be combined with a decision pursuant to Article 23(2)(a) of Regulation 1/2003 imposing a fine on the undertaking(s) having violated Article 81 or 82 EC.

(2)   Positive Decisions—Article 10 of Regulation 1/2003. Since Article 81(3) is directly applicable without any further act being required, the Commission no longer issues exemption decisions. However, the Commission felt that, where a transaction raises novel or unresolved questions, it might be expedient to clarify the law in order to provide the economic operators as well as the other decision makers with guidance regarding the Commission's approach. This may be the case, for instance, if a new type of agreement is concluded that has not yet been settled in the existing case law or administrative practice.[156] Therefore, Article 10 of Regulation 1/2003 provides for a completely new power of individual decision. It entitles the Commission to issue positive decisions, ie decisions finding that Article 81 is not applicable to a particular agreement or practice, either because it falls outside the scope of Article 81(1) EC or because it is covered by the legal exception of Article 81(3) EC.

It is important to note that positive decisions will be adopted only on the Commission's own initiative and exclusively on grounds of public interest. Formally, there is no possibility for undertakings to request that a positive decision be issued in favour of a particular agreement or practice. As a consequence, the adoption of a positive decisions is not actionable under Article 232 EC (action for failure to act).[157] Clearly, positive decisions are supposed to serve not so much the interest of individual operators in obtaining legal certainty, but primarily the general interest of

---

[153] Reg 1/2003, Art 7(1), 2nd sentence. This power had also been recognised by the ECJ prior to the adoption of Reg 1/2003. Joined Cases C–241/91 P and C–242/91 P *Magill* [1995] ECR I–743, para 91. See also Joined Cases 6 and 7/73 *Commercial Solvents* [1974] ECR 223, para 45.

[154] This right had equally been acknowledged by the ECJ prior to the enactment of Reg 1/2003. See Case 792/79R *Camera Care* [1980] ECR 119, para 18. The case law will remain relevant with regard to the application of Art 8 of Reg 1/2003. Jones and Sufrin, above n 152, 1209.

[155] White Paper, para 87.

[156] Recital 14 of Reg 1/2003.

[157] See Paulis, above n 95, 424.

the EC.[158] In this sense, they fulfil a policy-making role[159] rather than a legal function in settling a specific case. It is therefore within the sole discretion of the Commission—which must, of course, take due account of the public interest—whether or not it issues a positive decision. Accordingly, the Commission has made it quite clear that it will adopt positive decisions only in exceptional cases and that it will not allow this instrument to function as a backdoor notification procedure.[160] It is a fundamental principle of the enforcement system established by Regulation 1/2003 that all forms of voluntary notification be excluded.[161] Against this background, it is not surprising that, at the time of writing, ie more than four years after Regulation 1/2003 entered into force, not a single Article 10 decision had been adopted by the Commission.[162]

In contrast to exemption decisions under Regulation 17, positive decisions are, according to the Commission, of a purely declaratory nature.[163] It is not clear what message the Commission intends to convey with this statement. Since positive decisions are formal acts of the Commission adopted by the College of Commissioners, they are decisions within the meaning of Article 249 EC and thus have binding legal force.[164] As a consequence, they must be considered to have precedence. NCAs and national courts could not disregard them.[165] They are, however, different from constitutive decisions in that they declare lawful an agreement or practice the legality of which results in fact directly from the law without it

---

[158] A Schaub, 'Modernisation of EC Competition Law: Reform of Regulation no 17' in B Hawk (ed), *1999 Proceedings of the Fordham Corporate Law Institute* (New York, Juris Publishing, 2000), 143, 150. However, the purpose of the positive decision may also be to ensure consistency throughout the common market, eg in cases where the lawfulness of the same (type of) agreement under Art 81 EC has been evaluated differently by several NCAs. Dalheimer, in Dalheimer *et al*, above n 119, Art 10 no 4. In such a situation, a positive decision would seem to serve the public interest (consistency) as much as the individual interest in obtaining legal certainty (through consistency).

[159] D Gerber and Cassinis, 'The "Modernisation" of European Community Competition Law: Achieving Consistency in Enforcement—Part I' (2006) 27 *European Competition Law Review* 10, 16.

[160] Recital 14 of Reg 1/2003. See also Riley, above n 133, 608 and the Explanatory Memorandum, 19.

[161] See Schaub, above n 47, 251 and L Idot, 'Le nouveau système communautaire de mise en oeuvre des articles 81 et 82 CE (Règlement 1/2003 et projets de textes d'application)' (2003) 39 *Cahiers de Droit Européen* 283, 367, para 211. See also Explanatory Memorandum, 19 (with regard to informal guidance in form of reasoned opinions). Ehlermann, above n 13, 568, anticipated, however, that, in practice, positive decisions would be taken at the request of undertakings submitting their agreements for approval.

[162] See Bruzzone and Boccaccio, above n 92, 101.

[163] This is explicitly stated in recital 14 of Reg 1/2003. In para 89 of the White Paper, the Commission had already announced that positive decisions would have the same legal effect as negative clearance decisions had under Reg 17.

[164] Explanatory Memorandum, 19: 'Non-infringement decisions will have the effects of Community acts.' See also Ehlermann, above n 13, 567.

[165] Dalheimer, in Dalheimer *et al*, above n 119, Art 10 no 14; C Kerse and N Khan, *EC Antitrust Procedure* (London, Sweet & Maxwell, 5th edn, 2005), para 2-067. See also Ehlermann, above n 13, 567.

being necessary for the Commission to intervene. The reason is that, due to the direct applicability of Article 81(3) EC, a formal act of the Commission is no longer required for an agreement to benefit from the exemption. In other words, a positive decision only restates the law. Accordingly, if the relevant facts and circumstances (on which the Commission's positive decision is based) change, the agreement or practice becomes automatically illegal in direct application of Article 81. No intervention by the Commission is needed. This is a further difference to the former exemption decisions which the Commission formally had to repeal if it wanted to withdraw the benefit of the exemption from the undertaking concerned.[166] In this respect, ie its validity over time, positive decisions are thus more akin to negative clearances than to (individual) exemptions under the old system.[167]

(3) Commitment Decisions—Article 9 of Regulation 1/2003. Another entirely new power is laid down in Article 9(1) of Regulation 1/2003, which enables the Commission to make commitments binding on undertakings.

In the course of an infringement procedure, commitments can be either offered by the companies themselves or proposed by the Commission. In both cases, the purpose is to overcome objections raised by the Commission and prevent a prohibition decision from being issued against the companies.[168] Under Regulation 17, the Commission could not terminate infringement proceedings by accepting legally binding commitments from the companies concerned;[169] it could only make an exemption decision subject to conditions and obligations. However, since the latter option for shaping restrictive agreements is no longer available in the directly applicable exception system, it was even more important to fill the gap regarding commitments. Pursuant to Article 9(1) of Regulation 1/2003, the Commission now has the power to render such commitments binding upon the companies by way of a decision. This new instrument provides the Commission with possibilities of 'fine tuning' similar to those that existed in the context of notification procedures.[170] Since the Commission is

---

[166] Dalheimer, in Dalheimer *et al*, above n 119, Art 10 no 13; Kerse and Khan, above n 165, para 2-067.

[167] Cf Kerse and Khan, above n 165, para 2-065, who describes positive decisions as something more than the old negative clearances, but something less than an exemptions. (NB: Negative clearances granted under Reg 17 automatically ceased to have effect if the facts changed on which they were based. Goyder, above n 13, 33.)

[168] Schaub and Dohms, above n 49, 1062.

[169] The possibility of terminating infringements, pursuant to Art 3(3) of Reg 17, by the instrument of non-binding recommendations was rarely used. In practice, the Commission usually entered into an informal settlement with the companies concerned and closed the file. Riley, above n 133, 607. Kerse, above n 31, 6.53 *et seq.*

[170] Schaub, above n 158, 151. The new instrument of commitment decisions is comparable to the possibility of the Commission, in merger control proceedings, accepting commitments

obliged to publish a summary of the case and the commitments offered at least one month before adopting its decision (Article 27(4) of Regulation 1/2003), interested third parties are able to make comments and influence the final drafting of the commitments.[171] Moreover, compliance with the binding commitments is effectively ensured through the threat of sanctions for non-observance.[172] This new instrument thus removes one of the major deficits of the practice of informal settlements[173] which the Commission had developed under Regulation 17.[174]

Commitment decisions may be adopted for a specified period.[175] They are based on a preliminary assessment of the case[176] and therefore do not establish whether or not there really has been or still is an infringement. Commitment decisions rather conclude that there are no longer grounds for action by the Commission.[177] The Commission may reopen the

offered by the undertakings with a view to modifying the originally notified concentration so as to render it compatible with the common market. See Arts 6(2) and 8(2) of the EC Merger Regulation.

[171] Montag and Cameron, above n 92, 10.

[172] The new power under Art 9 is coupled with the possibility of the Commission being able to impose fines or periodic penalty payments on the companies concerned in order to enforce compliance or punish non-compliance with the commitments (Arts 23(2) (c) and 24(1) (c) of Reg 1/2003). These sanctions can be applied for the mere disobedience with the formal Commission decision which made the commitment binding, ie without the need for the Commission to actually prove an infringement of Art 81 or 82 EC. M Busse and A Leopold, 'Entscheidungen über Verpflichtungszusagen nach Art. 9 VO (EG) Nr. 1/2003' (2005) 55 *Wirtschaft und Wettbewerb* 146, 152; C Cook, 'Commitment Decisions: The Law and Practice under Article 9' (2006) 29 *World Competition* 209, 221.

[173] Under the Commission's new terminology, the term 'settlement' now has a different meaning. See below n 180 and accompanying text.

[174] See W Wils, 'Settlements of EU Antitrust Investigations: Commitment Decisions under Article 9 of Regulation No 1/2003' (2006) 29 *World Competition* 345, 347. The other deficit was the lack of transparency. This defect has also been remedied. The Commission not only announces envisaged commitment decisions by way of a short notice (summary of the case and main content of the proposed commitments) so that interested third parties can submit comments; the actual Art 9 decisions are also published in the Official Journal (see Art 30 of Reg 1/2003). Beyond these legal obligations, the Commission has even developed the practice of releasing the full (non-confidential) text of the draft commitments in original language on its website. Cook, above n 172, 216.

[175] Busse and Leopold, above n 172, 148.

[176] See Art 2(1) of the Implementing Regulation, from which it follows that the preliminary assessment in principle is an act distinct from the statement of objections. Cook, above n 172, 215–16, believes that it has a largely symbolic function and therefore rather constitutes a formality.

[177] See recital 13 of Reg 1/2003. The relevant passage reads: 'Commitment decisions should find that there are no longer grounds for action by the Commission without concluding whether or not there has been or still is an infringement.' In one of the first articles on this new type of decision, Temple Lang argues, however, that the Commission should make 'the firmest statement it can about the unlikelihood' of an infringement after full implementation of the commitment in order to increase the value of and incentive for commitment decisions. Where possible, it should thus certify that there will be no illegal behaviour outside the scope of the commitment, but within the scope of the statement of objections. J Temple Lang, 'Commitment Decisions under Reg 1/2003: Legal Aspects of a New Kind of Competition Decision' (2003) 24 *European Competition Law Review* 347, 348–9.

proceedings only in certain circumstances specified by Article 9(2) of Regulation 1/2003. This rule applies, for instance, where the companies act contrary to their commitments.

The Commission will use this new instrument only in cases where it does not intend to impose a fine.[178] For this reason, commitments made binding by virtue of a Commission decision under Article 9 of Regulation 1/2003 must be distinguished from the settlement proceedings. The latter are a new kind of instrument which the Commission recently introduced without, however, amending Regulation 1/2003.[179] In contrast to commitments, settlements are possible in cases where the Commission initially envisages the adoption of a formal decision pursuant to Articles 7 and 23 of Regulation 1/2003, ie a prohibition and fining decision.[180]

Article 9 of Regulation 1/2003 has the potential to become an effective, swift and transparent instrument of competition law enforcement. The new tool allows the Commission and the undertakings concerned to avoid a time-consuming and costly infringement procedure the outcome of which is uncertain.[181] Almost five years after Regulation 1/2003 entered into force, the Commission seems to have adopted a total of 11 commitment decisions.[182] Experience with this novel instrument is thus still limited.[183]

---

[178] Recital 13 of Reg 1/2003.

[179] The legislative package regarding settlements comprises Commission Regulation (EC) No 622/2008 of 30 June 2008 amending Regulation (EC) No 773/2004, as regards the conduct of settlement procedures in cartel cases, and the Commission notice on the conduct of settlement procedures in view of the adoption of Decisions pursuant to Article 7 and Article 23 of Council Regulation (EC) No 1/2003 in cartel cases ('Settlement Notice') ([2008] OJ L171/3 and C167/1).

[180] The option for a settlement essentially aims at simplifying and expediting the Commission procedure in cartel cases. It centres on the idea that the Commission can issue a much shorter, 'settled' (but non-negotiated) statement of objections and also skip the procedural step of an oral hearing where the parties, by way of written settlement submissions, acknowledge their involvement in the cartel and their liability under Art 81 EC (Art 10a(2) and (3) of the amended Implementing Regulation and paras 23–8 of the Settlement Notice). In return, the parties will normally be rewarded for their contribution to procedural savings by receiving a certain reduction in the fine (paras 31–3 of the Settlement Notice). On this new instrument, including a comparison of settlements and commitments and their respective contributions to optimal antitrust enforcement, see W Wils, 'The Use of Settlements in Public Antitrust Enforcement: Objectives and Principles' (2008) 31 *World Competition* 335.

[181] Paulis and De Smijter, above n 92, 11–12.

[182] At the time of finalising this manuscript (January 2009), the Commission had adopted Art 9 decisions in the following cases: *German Football League (Bundesliga)* (Case COMP/37.214; decision of 19 January 2005), *Coca-Cola* (Case COMP/39.116; decision of 22 June 2005), *De Beers* (Case COMP/38.381; decision of 22 February 2006), *FA Premier League* (Case COMP/38.173; decision of 22 March 2006), *Repsol* (Case COMP/38.348 decision of 12 April 2006), *Cannes Extension Agreement* (Case COMP/38.681; decision of 4 October 2006), *DaimlerChrysler* (COMP/39.140; decision of 14 September 2007), *Fiat* (COMP/39.141; decision of 14 September 2007); *Toyota* (COMP/39.142; decision of 14 September 2007); *General Motors (Opel)* (COMP/39.143; decision of 14 September 2007) and *Distrigaz* (Case COMP/37.966; decisions of 11 October 2007).

[183] See Cook, above n 172, 214. However, the CFI already had to deal with an Art 9 decision (see Case T–170/06 *Alrosa*, judgment of 11 July 2007 [2007] ECR II–2601). The case concerns an action for annulment of the commitment decision in *De Beers* (see above n 182) filed by the company Alrosa. De Beer, which occupies the number one position on the world market for the

It must also be acknowledged that the Article 9 process is still surrounded by numerous important uncertainties which may ultimately compromise its attractiveness for undertakings and thus question the usefulness of this new instrument.[184] One of the major unanswered questions is whether NCAs retain the competence to investigate and prosecute the same practices as those which form the subject of a commitment decision.[185] It follows from recital 13 of Regulation 1/2003 that commitment decisions include neither a finding that the past conduct was in breach of the EC competition rules nor a finding that future conduct consistent with the commitments will not infringe these rules.[186] Moreover, recital 13 states that 'Commitment decisions are without prejudice to the powers of competition authorities and courts of the Member States to make such a finding and decide upon the case'.[187] On this basis, further action by NCAs or national courts regarding the same practice as that addressed by the commitment decision is not precluded.[188] Companies thus

production and sale of rough diamonds, used to purchase large quantities of the diamonds produced by Alrosa, the number two on that market. By virtue of the contested decision, as of 2009, any trading relations between the two suppliers regarding rough diamonds would have been completely and permanently prohibited. The CFI annulled the decision mainly for violation of the proportionality principle. In the present context, it is interesting to note that the CFI draws a parallel between commitment decisions and prohibition decisions (Art 7 of Reg 1/2003) considering that both essentially have the same objective, which is to put an end to a (potential) infringement (see paras 87 and 95 of the judgment in *Alrosa*). The only distinctive feature, according to the CFI, is that in the case of an Art 9 decision the Commission is relieved from pursuing the entire regulatory procedure and, while being required to establish the reality of its competition concerns, does not have to adduce evidence to actually prove the infringement (see paras 100 and 125 of the judgment in *Alrosa*). The consideration of the CFI concerning the identity of the purpose of both types of decisions is not in line with recital 13 of Reg 1/2003. It is submitted that, if the court wanted to hold that also commitment decisions must definitely bring to an end the reputed infringement, it should have ruled on the compatibility of Art 9 *juncto* recital 13 of Reg 1/2003 with Arts 81 and 82 EC and the objectives of the EC Treaty.

[184] See M Sousa Ferro, 'Committing to Commitment Decisions—Unanswered Questions on Article 9 Decisions' (2005) 26 *European Competition Law Review* 451, 457. See also Jones and Sufrin, above n 152, 1207.

[185] See Sousa Ferro, *ibid*, 455–7; Cook, above n 172, 224–7. Another open issue is whether the company which is the addressee of a commitment decision can challenge that decision by bringing an action for annulment. *Pro* Wils, above n 174, 363; *contra* Cook, above n 172, 222. It is also uncertain whether companies that plan to or have already offered commitments with a view to obtaining an Art 9 decision have a right of access to the Commission's file. See Wils, above n 174, 353–5 and Cook, above n 172, 220.

[186] See above *n* 177. O Armengol and Á. Pascual, 'Some Reflections on Article 9 Commitment Decisions in the Light of the Coca-Cola Case' (2006) 27 *European Competition Law Review* 124, 129 call this the 'neutrality of Art. 9 decisions as to the substance of the case'.

[187] Similarly, recital 22 of Reg 1/2003 explicitly provides that commitment decisions of the Commission 'do not affect the power of the courts and the competition authorities of the Member States to apply Articles 81 and 82 of the Treaty'.

[188] On the contrary, as Cook, above n 172, 226, puts it, recitals 13 and 22 of Reg 1/2003 'seem expressly to contemplate the possibility of such action'. Against the binding force of Art 9 decisions, see also Fuchs, above n 91, 106, and D Gerber and P Cassinis, 'The "Modernisation" of European Community Competition Law: Achieving Consistency in Enforcement—Part II' (2006) 27 *European Competition Law Review* 51, 51, note 3, who note that the conflict rule of

have no assurance that they will not be prosecuted by one or more NCAs or exposed to private damages claims.[189]

Nonetheless, it can be attractive for undertakings to settle an infringement procedure under Article 9 of Regulation 1/2003. Apart from the obvious advantage that the company will not have to pay a fine[190] and can dispute civil liability as the decision does not involve the admission of an infringement,[191] there are also considerable cost savings, in terms of both management time and legal fees, resulting from the shorter procedure. Moreover, commitment decisions may avoid negative publicity and reputational damage as they do not carry the blame of illegal conduct on the part of the company concerned, given that there is no finding of a past infringement.[192] Also from the authority's perspective, Article 9 decisions have significant advantages even if, as has been argued, commitments do not necessarily put an end to the alleged infringement in that they are based on a preliminary assessment and may thus omit relevant aspects of the case which only an in-depth inquiry would bring to light.[193] The Commission notably benefits from a cost-efficient and quick resolution of the case since it does not have to engage in a full and lengthy procedure, but can skip some of the procedural steps that would be required in the event of an infringement decision.[194] In addition, there is normally little prospect of an

Art 16(2) of Reg 1/2003, which prohibits NCAs from taking decisions that would run counter to a Commission decision, does not apply to commitment decisions.

[189] However, NCAs or private claimants would still have to prove the existence of an infringement. In this respect, Art 9 decisions cannot be construed so as to imply a presumption of illegality of the relevant practice prior to or failing compliance with the commitment nor its lawfulness after the commitment is implemented. See Armengol and Pascual, above n 186, 125–6 and Sousa Ferro, above n 184, 453–4. Such interpretation would run counter to the content of the commitment decision, which only states that there are no longer grounds for action, and would discourage companies from offering commitments. See Cook, above n 172, 223 and 225. On the other hand, the Commission may only issue commitment decisions where it initially intended to adopt an infringement decision (see the terms of Art 9 of Reg 1/2003). It must thus have had serious doubts regarding the lawfulness of the undertaking's past conduct. Obviously, this an element which NCAs and national courts may take into account. Wils, above n 174, 361. Conversely, where undertakings are faced with a national inquiry regarding their conduct post-decision, compliance with the commitment may be a persuasive argument against any further action by the NCA. Armengol and Pascual, above n 186, 126–7.

[190] Although commitments under Art 9 of Reg 1/2003 are not offered in exchange for a reduction or non-imposition of a fine (recital 13 provides that this instrument is not appropriate where the Commission intends to impose a fine), this can be seen as an advantage because a full investigation may lead the Commission to change its mind on this point.

[191] Indeed, private parties claiming antitrust damages would have to start from scratch to prove the existence of an infringement. Bruzzone and Boccaccio, above n 92, 99.

[192] See Cook, above n 172, 211–12; Armengol and Pascual, above n 186, 127.

[193] Armengol and Pascual, above n 186, 125–6. These authors in fact argue that the objective of Art 9 decisions is not to bring the infringement to an end but, rather, to remove the case from the Commission's list of priorities. In this way, commitment decisions would be fully in line with the *Automec II* case law. See also Wils, above n 174, 357–8.

[194] Wils, above n 174, 350; Cook, above n 172, 212. For instance, statement of objection and hearing are dispensable. Wils, above n 174, 353. Also frequently controversial issues such as the definition of the relevant market(s) can largely be left aside. Cook, above n 172, 211.

appeal against Article 9 decisions by their addressees as they have offered, negotiated and accepted the commitments.[195]

In practice, commitment decisions may thus prove a useful tool for both Commission and undertakings to swiftly terminate infringement procedures, even though the precise objective and exact legal effect of such decisions vis-à-vis third parties remains dubious.[196]

b. Supervisory and Interventionary Powers

In the system of decentralised enforcement established by Regulation 1/2003, the Commission has a special responsibility for ensuring the consistent application of the EC competition rules.[197] Therefore, in addition to traditional decisional powers, the Commission has been granted certain limited supervisory and interventionary powers vis-à-vis the NCAs. Further, the Commission has the possibility of monitoring, to some extent, proceedings before the national courts of the Member States and to 'intervene' in such proceedings.

(1) Supervision of NCAs. The Commission is empowered to review the measures adopted by the NCAs in application of the EC rules on competition. When acting under Article 81 or Article 82 EC, the NCAs have to inform the Commission of the initiation of proceedings and before their termination. The information has to be given in writing and must, in principle, be provided prior to the first formal investigative measure or the adoption of a prohibition or commitment decision.[198] The information duties imposed on the NCAs thus enable the Commission to closely

---

[195] Cf Wils, above n 174, 363. Cook, above n 172, 222–3, even argues that addressees are not entitled to appeal commitment decisions as this would undermine 'a potentially useful mechanism. . . to the detriment of all concerned'. See, however, the successful appeal of a competitor and trading partner against the commitments decision binding De Beer in the *Alrosa* case (above n 183).

[196] See Temple Lang, above n 177, 348–9. One may indeed wonder what purpose such decisions actually serve. If the Commission does not (have to) take a definitive position on the existence of an infringement in the past nor its effective removal for the future, the question arises of which legitimate concerns of the Commission the commitments are supposed to address and whether they can actually remedy those concerns. What it seems to boil down to is that the Commission makes undertakings offer potential remedies for potential violations in return for the potential avoidance of a potentially burdensome and costly infringement procedure which would, however, potentially not result in the imposition of fines. In any event, it follows from the wording of Art 9, in conjunction with recital 13 of Reg 1/2003, that such decisions must be very carefully drafted so as to strike a balance between expressing a preliminary view (and thus avoiding the impression that the past conduct is definitely considered illegal) and firmly setting out the Commission's concerns and reasons why, in view of the commitments offered, there is no further need for action on the part of the Commission (without affirming, however, that compliance with the commitments makes the relevant conduct compatible with EC competition law). See Cook, above n 172, 219.

[197] Explanatory Memorandum, 19.

[198] Art 11(3) and (4) of Reg 1/2003. The Commission must also be informed in advance if an NCA plans to withdraw the benefit of a block exemption.

monitor infringement proceedings conducted at the national level. In particular, the Commission is able to review drafts of the decisions that the NCAs intend to issue in order to bring an infringement to an end.

In the White Paper, the Commission explains that the information to be provided by NCAs pursuant to Article 11(3) and (4) of Regulation 1/2003 'together with any correspondence that might take place with the national authorities' should allow the Commission to ensure consistency and coherence in the enforcement of the EC competition rules. Special mechanisms allowing the Commission to impose solutions in case of a conflict regarding the application of the law would not be required.[199]

These explanations seem to imply that the Commission will inform the NCAs of its view in a particular matter and expect the NCAs to comply with it.[200] Since the Commission preserves the right to relieve the NCAs of their competence (Article 11(6) of Regulation 1/2003), there will presumably be sufficient pressure on the NCAs to adhere to the Commission's view.[201] In other words, the Commission will try to influence the outcome of NCA proceedings where this is necessary to avoid divergent decisions and preserve consistency throughout the EU. Therefore, the supervisory powers have a preventive character.

(2) Intervention in NCA Proceedings. The Commission can also adopt measures which are of a more corrective nature. It can intervene in national infringement proceedings as it has retained the power to take a case out of the jurisdiction of an NCA. Pursuant to Article 11(6) of Regulation 1/2003, the Commission can, at any time, relieve the NCAs of their competence to apply Articles 81 and 82 EC in a particular case by initiating itself proceedings regarding the same matter (the so-called right of evocation).[202]

---

[199] Para 105 of the White Paper.

[200] In practice, consultation usually takes place in an informal way, mostly by telephone. In some cases, the observations and comments submitted orally are summarised in a follow-up letter from DG Competition. K Dekeyser and M Jaspers, 'A New Era of ECN Co-operation' (2007) 30 *World Competition* 3, 9.

[201] Jones and Sufrin (1st edn, 2001), above n 152, 1027. Similarly, F Jenny describes the situation in this way: '. . . NCAs are invited to handle Articles 81 and 82 cases. . . in strict accordance with the Commission's view of these cases and under the constant threat of losing them cases if they diverge from the Commission's view.' F Jenny, 'Does the Effectiveness of the EU Network of Competition Authorities Depend on a Certain Degree of Homogeneity of its Membership (with respect to status, structure, powers, responsibilities, etc)?' in C-D Ehlermann and I Atanasiu (eds), *European Competition Law Annual 2002: Constructing the EU Network of Competition Authorities* (Oxford, Hart Publishing, 2003), 203, 205. Cf also the allegory used by K Stockmann to describe the relationship between the BKartA and the competent Federal Minister, quoted below Chapter 2, n 11. In contrast, Commission officials tend to emphasise the informal character of such contacts and the openness of the dialogue. They contend that the consultation process under Art 11 (4) of Reg 1/2003 is akin to the kind of exchange of views that colleagues within the same authority would engage in. See Dekeyser and Jaspers, *ibid*, 9.

[202] See Ehlermann, above n 13, 578. R Smits, 'The European Competition Network: Selected Aspects' (2005) 32 *Legal Issues of Economic Integration* 175, 180 note 26, describes this situation more metaphorically as 'hijacking' of a case. Art 9(3) of Reg 17 contained an equivalent provision.

As a consequence, the Commission would itself take the appropriate decision, while the NCAs lose the power to rule on the relevant case.[203] The Commission's measure could be a prohibition decision (possibly imposing fines) or a commitment decision, or, where there are no sufficient grounds for action, the Commission could simply close the file.[204]

Despite the fact that the Commission considers the right of evocation to be of crucial importance,[205] Regulation 1/2003 does not set out the circumstances under which it may be exercised. In the notice on co-operation within the Network of Competition Authorities[206] ('Network Notice'), the Commission has established a number of rules which it intends to respect when taking a case out of the competence of the NCAs. However, there is no doubt that the initiation of proceedings[207] by the Commission can occur at any stage of the investigation of the case, be it a Commission or a national investigation.[208] When the Draft Regulation was published, it even seemed that the Commission would be allowed to take this drastic step without giving any warning or explanation to the NCA which is already investigating the matter.[209] However, the final version of Article 11(6) of Regulation 1/2003 requires the Commission to consult with the NCA before removing a case on which the NCA is already acting from its juris-

---

[203] The Commission's action has a preclusive effect only as far as the same matter is concerned, ie there must be identity of the agreement or conduct, the undertakings and the geographic and product markets. Gerber and Cassinis, above n 188, 17. Thus, where the Commission decision does not cover a specific national market, the NCA of the relevant Member State would not be precluded to prosecute and penalise the infringement with regard to the 'omitted' territory. See Gerber and Cassinis, above n 188, 53 note 13.

[204] Provided that it concerns an *ex officio* investigation. In this case, proceedings are normally terminated informally. Schaub, above n 47, 251–2. In a case involving a complaint, the rules regarding the handling of complaints by the Commission (see Arts 5–9 of Commission Reg No 773/2004 relating to the conduct of proceedings by the Commission pursuant to Arts 81 and 82 of the EC Treaty; [2004] OJ L123/18) would probably have to be followed, which means that the Commission may have to adopt a formal decision rejecting the complaint. Theoretically, the Commission could also adopt a positive decision if it considers that there is no infringement. It is unlikely, however, that the Commission would take over a case where an NCA wants to take a negative decision while the Commission finds that there is no violation of Art 81 or 82 EC. See the White Paper, para 102, subpara (3). In such a situation, the Commission apparently wants to leave it to the undertakings concerned, whose agreement or practice has incorrectly been considered unlawful, to take legal action in order to have the national decision rectified.

[205] Explanatory Memorandum, 21. On the other hand, it must be noted that in the first four years of application of Reg 1/2003, ie until mid-2008, the Commission had not exercised this right in an Art 11(4) situation even once. Dekeyser and Jaspers, above n 200, 9; Bruzzone and Boccaccio, above n 92, 107.

[206] [2004] OJ C101/43.

[207] According to the case law of the ECJ, the initiation of proceedings by the Commission is a formal act by which the Commission indicates its intention to adopt a decision under ch III of Reg 1/2003. The simple confirmation by the Commission that it has received a complaint does not qualify as a formal act within this meaning. See the judgment of the ECJ in Case 48/72 *Brasserie de Haecht* [1973] ECR 77, paras 16 and 17. See also para 52 of the Network Notice.

[208] Cf para 52 of the Network Notice.

[209] See Pappalardo, above n 73, 368.

diction, but it does not contain any further obligations.[210] In the Network Notice, the Commission commits itself to explaining the reasons for the application of Article 11(6) of Regulation 1/2003 in writing to the NCA concerned as well as to the other Network members.[211]

Where the Commission considers initiating proceedings in a case pending before one or more NCAs, an NCA (or the Commission) can request that the matter be discussed in the Advisory Committee pursuant to Article 14(7) of Regulation 1/2003.[212] The Commission will therefore announce its intention to apply Article 11(6) in due time so that a meeting of the Advisory Committee can take place before the Commission actually exercises the right.[213] According to paragraph 62 of the Network Notice, the Advisory Committee may issue an (albeit) informal statement on the matter.

The Network Notice lists five specific scenarios which may trigger the Commission's intervention after a case has been allocated to one or several NCAs. These are:

1. the possibility of conflicting decisions by several NCAs in the same case;
2. the possibility of an NCA decision obviously conflicting with consolidated case law;
3. the need to develop EC competition policy (eg where similar issues arise in several Member States) or to ensure effective enforcement;
4. an NCA is unduly drawing out proceedings in a particular case;
5. the NCA(s) concerned do not object.

Beyond the situations listed above, the Commission will in principle not apply Article 11(6) of Regulation 1/2003 after a case has been 'allocated' to an NCA. It can be expected that the Commission will only use this mechanism exceptionally and as a last resort, ie in the extreme case of a

---

[210] For general criticism of the lack of precise rules regarding the operation of Art 11(6) of Reg 1/2003, see Monopolkommission, *Folgenprobleme der europäischen Kartellverfahrensreform*, 32. Sondergutachten (2001), paras 47–8; C Mavroidis and D Neven, 'The White Paper: A Whiter Shade of Pale. Of Interest and Interests' in Ehlermann and Atanasiu, above n 26, 207, 219–20, and the Summary of Observations at s 6.4. Cf also Kingston, above n 32, 344; Immenga, above n 118, 358; and Bourgeois, above n 147, 328, who suggests to make the right of evocation at least subject to strict time limits. A Kist and L Tierno Centella, 'Coherence and Efficiency in the Decentralised Enforcement of EC Competition Rules. Reflections on the White Paper on Modernisation' in Ehlermann and Atanasiu, above n 26, 369, 381, ask that the right be used sparingly. Temple Lang, above n 49, 14, also pleads for a careful exercise of this right.

[211] Para 55 of the Network Notice.

[212] Art 14(7) of Reg 1/2003 provides that cases which are dealt with by an NCA shall be included on the agenda of the Advisory Committee at the request of an NCA or on the Commission's initiative.

[213] Para 56 of the Network Notice.

substantial disagreement that could not be resolved by intensive consultation and discussion.[214]

Strictly speaking, the right of evocation is the only formal way of intervention in proceedings that are still pending before an NCA. However, where an NCA has adopted a 'positive decision', which cannot be appealed anymore, the Commission still considers that it can 'always intervene to prohibit the agreement'.[215] This approach raises a number of questions.

Since (positive) decisions of the NCAs cannot be revoked by the Commission, it is unclear what legal effect and practical implications such a subsequent prohibition would have for the agreement and the parties in question.[216] The Commission states that its intervention would always be subject to the principle of *res iudicata*. It would thus not affect any decision made between the parties to the dispute.[217] It is also likely that the term 'positive decision' as employed in paragraph 102 (2) of the White Paper does not actually refer to a decision of inapplicability within the meaning of Article 10 of Regulation 1/2003 but, rather, to a decision whereby an NCA rejects a complaint or closes a file, finding that there are no grounds for action on its part.[218] The function of such 'non-action' decisions is to terminate a procedure rather than to define EC competition policy.[219] The Commission takes the view that a non-action decision only binds the NCA

---

[214] See Schaub, above n 158, 156; Holmes, above n 42, 72, who refers to the evocation right as the 'nuclear' option. Van der Woude, on the other hand, emphasises the corrective nature of the measure by calling it the 'headmaster's ruler'. M Van Der Woude, 'The Modernization Paradox: Controlled Decentralization', paper for the IBC's 10th Annual Advanced Competition Law Conference, Brussels, 6 and 7 November 2003, 15.

[215] White Paper, para 102, subpara (2). It is curious to note that the Commission normally tends not to intervene where an NCA has issued a prohibition decision with which the Commission does not agree, but rather leaves it to the parties concerned to challenge that decision (see para 102 subpara (3) of the White Paper). The simple reason may be that the Commission is more worried about 'wrong authorisations' of anti-competitive agreements than about 'wrong prohibitions' of benign ones. Jones and Sufrin, above n 152, 1026. Such a kind of 'overapplication' of the EC competition rules does not really affect the public interest. A Komninos, 'Effect of Commission Decisions on Private Antitrust Litigation: Setting the Story Straight' (2007) 44 *CML Rev* 1387, 1420–1. See also above n 204.

[216] Cf Cooke, above n 114, 558, with regard to a similar question that arises where the Commission prohibits an agreements that has been upheld as valid by a national judgment which is no longer open to appeal.

[217] See para 102 subpara (2) of the White Paper. Where a court has delivered a 'positive' judgment, the parties to the dispute would have to respect that judgment, but third parties (eg another distributor of the same producer whose exclusive distribution system has incorrectly been held lawful) could still challenge the system. Similarly, where an NCA has issued a 'positive' (unappealable) decision, that same NCA could no longer prohibit the agreement or practice at issue or impose a fine. However, the practical value of the Commission's respect regarding the *res iudicata* remains doubtful. Cf Komninos, above n 215, 1412, on the parallel issue, in the context of Art 16 of Reg 1/2003, of Commission decisions 'overturning' national court judgments.

[218] See Paulis, above n 95, 425 and Ehlermann, above n 13, 578, n 158. The adoption, by NCAs, of decisions finding that there are no grounds for action is provided for by Reg 1/2003, Art 5, 3rd sentence.

[219] Schaub, above n 47, 252.

that adopted it and therefore does not preclude other competition author-
ities from acting in respect of the same agreement.[220] On this basis, the
Commission could subsequently prohibit the agreement for the future in
order to prevent the parties from implementing or further honouring it.
This negative Commission decision would supersede the earlier 'positive'
NCA decision. The parties would therefore be obliged to respect the later
Commission decision.

(3) Co-operation with National Courts of the Member States. In order to
ensure uniformity and consistency also with regard to the application of EC
competition law by national courts, Regulation 1/2003 aims at further
intensifying co-operation between the Commission and national judges.
Therefore, Article 15(1) and (2) of Regulation 1/2003 sets out three
principal ways in which the Commission can effectively support national
courts by playing an active role in the national court proceedings.[221]
Further details of these co-operation mechanisms are set out in the notice
on the co-operation between the Commission and the courts of the EU
Member States in the application of Articles 81 and 82 EC[222] ('National
Courts Notice').[223]

Pursuant to Article 15(1) of Regulation 1/2003, the Commission can
first of all provide to national courts information that is in its possession or
secondly render its opinion on issues concerning the application of the EC
competition rules. Such non-binding opinions can concern questions of law
or fact.[224] This is important to note, as the Commission is no longer
restricted to supply purely factual information. It can thus assist national
courts in dealing with factual as well as economic and legal issues.[225] On
this basis, the existing co-operation mechanism is further developed into a
kind of preliminary legal advice procedure.[226] However, the Commission
will not hear the parties before drafting an opinion, nor will it consider the

---

[220] Explanatory Memorandum, 16. See also A Schaub, 'Continued Focus on Reform: Recent Developments in EC Competition Policy' in B Hawk (ed), *2001 Proceedings of the Fordham Corporate Law Institute* (New York, Juris Publishing, 2002), 31, 42.

[221] At p 9 of the Explanatory Memorandum, the Commission points to the fact that co-operating with national courts is an existing obligation incumbent on the Commission by virtue of Art 10 EC.

[222] [2004] OJ C101/54.

[223] For a critical review of these new instruments see W Devroe, 'De Europese Commissie en nationale mededingingsautoriteiten als amicus curiae. Huidig en komend recht' in P Van Orshoven and M Storme (eds), *Amice curiae, quo vadis?* (Antwerpen, Kluwer, 2002), 211, paras 17 *et seq*, in particular paras 21–9.

[224] Paulis, above n 95, 406. The Commission cannot provide binding answers to legal questions as this is the prerogative of the ECJ.

[225] See para 27 of the National Courts Notice.

[226] See M Van Der Woude, 'De herziening van het Europese mededingingsrecht en de gevolgen daarvan voor de nationale rechter' (2002) 50 *Sociaal-Economische Wetgeving* 176, 181, who calls it 'een alternatief voor een prejudiciële procedure' (an alternative for a preliminary ruling).

merits of the case. Its opinion will be limited strictly to the economic or legal clarification asked for by the national judge.[227] It is for the national courts to decide whether they want to avail themselves of this instrument. The Commission cannot impose this type of assistance on national courts. Co-operation under Article 15(1) of Regulation 1/2003 is possible only at the request of the national judge.

The third type of assistance, by contrast, can be provided on the Commission's own initiative without approval of the national court concerned. Pursuant to the third sentence of Article 15(3) of Regulation 1/2003, the Commission can intervene in national court proceedings by submitting written observations if the coherent application of Article 81 or 82 EC so requires.[228] This provision grants the Commission a novel power. It is based on the premise that the Commission will present its view as *amicus curiae*, not as protagonist for the individual interests of one of the parties to the national dispute. Accordingly, the observations will be confined to an economic and legal analysis of the relevant facts.[229] The power will be exercised solely in the public interest to avoid divergent or conflicting decisions.[230]

The procedural details of the Commission's intervention are not laid down in Regulation 1/2003. In particular, Regulation 1/2003 fails to specify what formal role and standing the Commission has in the national proceedings.[231] It is therefore unclear whether the Commission, when acting as *amicus curiae*, must be considered an intervening party *sensu stricto*, an expert witness or a sort of advocate general, or whether it will have a legal status of its own.[232] Consequently, these details are determined by the applicable national rules on civil procedure and may vary considerably from one Member State to another.[233]

---

[227] Paras 29 and 30 of the National Courts Notice.

[228] With the permission of the national judge, it may also make oral observations (see Reg 1/2003, Art 15(3), 4th sentence).

[229] Para 32 of the National Courts Notice.

[230] In para 19 of the National Courts Notice, the Commission states that its assistance to national courts is part of its duty to defend the public interest. Therefore, the Commission is committed to remain neutral and objective, and has no intention to serve the private interests of the parties involved. See also Wils, above n 19, 156.

[231] Recital 21 of Reg 1/2003 only states that such observations are submitted 'within the framework of national procedural rules and practices'.

[232] The legal qualification of the Commission's role will determine the procedural rights and duties associated with the intervention as *amicus curiae* (eg right of appeal, access to file, need to advance proof, possibility of cross-examination). See Cooke, above n 114, 557, who observes that the regulation itself should precisely state the role and standing of the Commission because only then will the national judge know exactly how to treat information and documents presented by the Commission as well as the arguments that it advances.

[233] The classification of the Commission's assistance, in terms of civil procedure, eg as 'evidence' or 'expert evidence', may have profound procedural consequences. Edward, above n 122, 566.

Both mechanisms, the provision of information or opinions and the intervention as *amicus curiae*, have been qualified as preventive measures,[234] the purpose of which is to help national judges to solve competition issues and minimise the risk of inconsistent judgments. Certainly, the *amicus curiae* provision aims at the avoidance of conflicts rather than their resolution. It is, however, obvious that it also has an interventionary aspect to it in that the provision empowers the Commission to interfere in matters pending before a national court without authorisation of the judge concerned.[235]

The *amicus curiae* instrument is coupled with another important provision, an information requirement which is intended to allow the Commission to monitor national court proceedings that involve the application of EC competition law. Pursuant to Article 15(2) of Regulation 1/2003, Member States must inform the Commission about any written judgment of a national court applying Article 81 or 82 EC by forwarding it a copy of the decision. This procedure should keep the Commission sufficiently well informed and enable it to uncover rulings which contain an erroneous application of Article 81 or 82 EC and may therefore require the Commission's intervention.[236] However, since the information on national cases involving competition matters is not automatically provided when the cases are pending before a national court, but only after the national court has handed down a judgment, the Commission will normally be able to intervene only at the stage of appeal proceedings.[237]

Finally, as in the case of a 'positive decision' of an NCA, the Commission also reserves to itself the prerogative to prohibit an agreement which a national court has held to be lawful and valid where the judgment cannot

---

[234] Paulis, above n 95, 413.

[235] An authorisation is only required to the extent that the Commission wants to make oral observations (see above n 228). The power of the Commission to 'intervene' *ex officio* which is coupled with the right of evocation, is one of the reasons why, according to Devroe, above n 223, paras 28–9, this instrument does not deserve the denomination '*amicus curiae*' as it has too little in common with traditional concepts of the role of an *amicus curiae* as they can be found both at national and supranational level.

[236] It may, however, be doubted that the Commission will have sufficient resources to effectively follow up such information on all national judgments applying Art 81 or 82 EC. Cf Cooke, above n 114, 556. Non-confidential versions of the national judgments notified to the Commission—in the original language—are uploaded into a special database (National Court Cases Database) that is made available to the public at DG Comp's website (see www.ec.europa.eu/comm/competition/antitrust/national_courts/index_en. html).

[237] See Lenaerts, above n 91, 35. An earlier intervention is only possible where the Commission is informed about the case by one of the parties to the proceedings who wants to 'provoke' the Commission's interference. See Van Der Woude, above n 226, 182, who notes that judges should be aware of the fact that the Commission's intervention might be the result of an initiative of one of the parties who tries to make the Commission dance to his/her tune. It is also conceivable that a simple information request from a national judge could trigger an intervention as *amicus curiae*, ie a response by the Commission that goes beyond the request of the judge.

be appealed anymore.[238] Such a prohibition decision of the Commission would of course be subject to the principle of *res iudicata* applying to the dispute between the parties themselves which cannot be altered by the subsequent Commission decision.

The approach is based on the understanding that the Commission cannot be bound by the decisions of national courts given in application of Article 81(1) EC.[239] However, it is unclear what legal effects and practical implications the subsequent prohibition would have. Since the legality of the agreement has been definitively confirmed by the national court, it would seem that the parties are perfectly entitled to perform their contract. It is therefore doubtful to whom the prohibition should apply and which third parties could benefit from it. In any event, the prerogative that the Commission wants to reserve to itself could lead to legally inappropriate or practically undesirable situations.[240] It may be expected that such prohibitions overturning a national court ruling that is no longer open to appeal will regularly be challenged before the CFI.

c. Handling of Complaints

The Commission's major goal is to combat the most serious violations of Articles 81 and 82 EC. This requires an intensified *ex post* control which is considered an indispensable corollary to the removal of the notification procedure.[241] To a large extent, the *ex post* control will be performed on the basis of own-initiative procedures. However, the Commission has repeatedly emphasised that complaints will play an even more important role in the new system as they are a very valuable means of detecting infringements.[242] Another important objective of the reform therefore is to clarify and streamline the Commission's approach for responding to complaints.

---

[238] White Paper, para 102(2). The Commission uses again the terminology 'positive' judgment (see above, section II.A.1.b(2).

[239] This principle has been confirmed by the ECJ in Case C–344/98 *Masterfoods* [2000] ECR I–11369, para 48.

[240] See Cooke, above n 114, 559. If, for example, the litigation before the national judge involves only one of the parties to the agreement in question (the other party in the dispute being a natural person or a third-party undertaking), could the other contracting party, following the Commission's prohibition decision, refuse to fulfil its contractual obligations in view of the invalidity of the agreement pursuant to Art 81(2)? Cf also Bourgeois, above n 147, 329, who wonders 'why the undertakings' legal certainty should be sacrificed on the altar of competition correctness', just because the Commission failed to intervene at an earlier stage of the co-operation and consultation process. An excellent analysis of the possible legal and practical consequences of a subsequent negative Commission decision on a 'positive' national court ruling is provided by Komninos, above n 215, 1411–20.

[241] White Paper, para 108.

[242] White Paper, paras 117 and 118. See also the Explanatory Memorandum, 7. According to the White Paper, para 44, formal complaints accounted for 29% of the new cases in the 10-year period from 1988 to 1998.

In the first place, the Commission seeks to encourage and facilitate the lodging of complaints. This includes providing guidance to potential complainants with respect to the choice of the appropriate forum (ie Commission, NCA or national court) and introducing time limits for the handling of complaints.[243] The relevant rules are laid down in chapter IV of Regulation No 773/2004, relating to the conduct of proceedings by the Commission pursuant to Articles 81 and 82 of the EC Treaty[244] ('Implementing Regulation'). In addition, the Commission has published a notice on the handling of complaints by the Commission under Articles 81 and 82 of the EC Treaty ('Notice on Complaints').[245]

As concerns the dismissive powers conferred upon the Commission with regard to complaints, it is important to note that the Commission retains the right, in accordance with the case law of the Court of First Instance (CFI), to set priorities in its enforcement activities and, consequently, to reject complaints for lack of Community interest.[246] As a natural consequence, Article 13 of Regulation 1/2003 stipulates that the Commission may reject a complaint merely on the ground that an NCA is already dealing with the case.

This does not mean, however, that the Commission can only reject a complaint where another NCA is effectively pursuing the matter. Indeed, recital 18 of Regulation 1/2003 specifically states that the Commission may reject a complaint for lack of Community interest 'even if no other competition authority has indicated its intention of dealing with the case'. In other words, there appears to be no duty to act for the Commission. At least, such duty is not laid down in Regulation 1/2003.[247] At the same time,

---

[243] White Paper, paras 119 and 120. The possibility of the Commission adopting interim measures (Art 8 of Reg 1/2003) could also be mentioned in this context. See para 122 of the White Paper. Interestingly, the four-month time limit for the handling of complaints (see paras 120 and 121 of the White Paper) has not been fixed by a legislative act. It is only mentioned as an 'indicative time frame' in a Commission notice (see below n 245).

[244] See above n 204.

[245] [2004] OJ C101/65. The Notice on Complaints sets out, in particular, the requirements that a formal complaint must fulfil (paras 29–40) the main principles of assessment (paras 41–52) and the procedure to be followed by the Commission (paras 53–82). As concerns the time limit mentioned above, the notice states that: 'The Commission will in principle endeavour to inform complainants of the action that it proposes to take on a complaint within an indicative time frame of four months from the reception of the complaint. Thus . . . the Commission will in principle inform the complainant within four months whether or not it intends to investigate his case further' (para 61 of the Notice on Complaints). More importantly, perhaps, the Notice on Complaints gives indications as to the choice of the appropriate forum. In pt II (paras 7–25) of the Notice, the Commission namely illustrates the different possibilities of bringing a lawsuit before a national court or lodging a complaint with a competition authority and also explains the criteria for the work sharing between Commission and NCAs.

[246] See in particular Case T–24/90 *Automec II* (n 40), para 85.

[247] See, however, Bourgeois, above n 147, 326, who, referring to the judgment of the CFI in *Automec II* (above n 40), contends that arguably such a duty already exists. His argument is, however, difficult to reconstruct. *Automec II* concerned precisely the opposite, notably the Commission's right not to act on a complaint. Moreover, in that case, the Commission had

the Commission has no formal means of compelling an NCA to investigate a particular matter, ie there is no mechanism for the resolution of negative conflicts of jurisdiction.[248] However, non-action may pose a serious risk to the consistency and coherence of EC competition law enforcement.[249]

2. Competition Policy

The Commission is regarded as the guardian of the Treaty (in competition matters) and guarantor of the Community interest.[250] Pursuant to Article 85 EC, the Commission has therefore been entrusted with the task of ensuring that the principles laid down by Articles 81 and 82 EC are applied. In other words, the Commission is responsible for the implementation and orientation of the EU competition policy.[251] This important task of defining the EU's competition policy has not been decentralised by Regulation 1/2003.[252] Also under Regulation 1/2003, the central, guiding role remains with the Commission who retains control over the EU competition policy.[253]

The EU competition policy therefore continues to be reflected in individual Commission decisions which generally have a strong precedent value beyond the specific case that is decided.[254] These individual decisions now include prohibitions as well as positive decisions and, to a lesser extent, commitment decisions.[255] In particular, positive decisions are an important instrument for clarifying or determining the Commission's

referred the complainant to the national courts, a path that would still be available even if no NCA intends to pursue the matter.

[248] The only way for the Commission to counteract a lack of enforcement by an NCA is to enforce the law itself. Cf Paulis, above n 95, 412. Only in the exceptional case that there appears to be a general policy of not applying EC competition law, ie where an NCA systematically disregards the EC competition rules, the Commission could institute proceedings against the Member State in question pursuant to Art 226 (ex Art 169). See Van Der Woude, above n 226, 181.

[249] Cf Bourgeois, above n 147, 326, who observes that complainants 'risk being smashed between the Charybdis of the "no Community interest" of the Commission and the Scylla of the NCAs' indifference'.

[250] This follows inter alia from Art 211 (ex Art 155). See also the judgment of the CFI of 11 December 2003 in Case T–66/99 *Minoan Lines* [2003] ECR II–5515, para 52.

[251] Case C–234/89 *Delimitis* [1991] ECR I–935, para 44. According to Schaub, however, the Commission does not have a policy monopoly; in the new system the NCAs will be involved in the elaboration of the competition policy. Schaub, above n 220, 44.

[252] Only the enforcement of EU competition law is decentralised. Kist and Tierno Centella, above n 210, 380.

[253] Jones and Sufrin, above n 152, 119 and 1279; White Paper, para 14. See also Weitbrecht, above n 15, 87, who even argues that the reform as a whole has the opposite effect to decentralisation precisely because the Commission effectively guides and supervises the NCAs.

[254] Paulis, above n 95, 406.

[255] Commitment decisions are less suitable for defining the competition policy to the extent that they do not establish whether or not there has been an infringement. See above, section II.A.1.a(3).

policy in competition matters[256] since they are only adopted on grounds of public interest, ie not at the request of an individual market operator.[257]

However, individual decisions are only one of the Commission's tools for establishing its competition policy. In a directly applicable exception system, the legislative framework is considered to be of primary importance.[258] Therefore, the Commission retains the power to adopt block exemption regulations in accordance with Article 1 of Council Regulation No 19/65/EEC of 2 March 1965 on the application of Article 85(3) [now Article 81(3)] of the Treaty to certain categories of agreements and concerted practices.[259] Since the exception of Article 81(3) is directly applicable, there is strictly speaking no longer any need to 'exempt' certain categories of agreements or practices en bloc by means of a general regulation. Agreements or practices which fulfil the conditions of Article 81(3) automatically benefit from the legal exception.[260] However, the Commission takes the view that block exemption regulations are an essential tool for ensuring consistency and uniformity and providing legal certainty to undertakings.[261] In practice, they thus offer useful help for the companies which now have to self-assess their agreements.

In addition, the Commission intends to provide informal guidance regarding the interpretation and application of Articles 81 and 82 EC to undertakings and other decision makers. For this reason, the Commission has announced that it will draw up further notices and guidelines to explain its policy, set out its approach in certain matters and clarify particular concepts of the EC competition rules.[262] The Commission even

---

[256] See Schaub, above n 47, 250–1. Positive decisions will be adopted in particular to clarify the law with regard to new types of agreements or practices which raise novel questions of law. Explanatory Memorandum, 19. L Idot, 'Le futur « règlement d'application des articles 81 et 82 CE »: chronique d'une révolution annoncée' (2001) 177 *Recueil Dalloz*, 1370, 1374. See however above n 162 and accompanying text.

[257] See above, section II.A.1.a(2).

[258] White Paper, para 84.

[259] [1965] OJ 36/533 (special edition 1965–66, 35); amended by Council Regulation (EC) No 1215/1999 of 10 June 1999, [1999] OJ 148/1.

[260] For this reason, a number of commentators consider block exemption regulations as alien to the directly applicable exception system. See Pappalardo, above n 73, 366; Bechtold, above n 83, 2426–7; Wißmann, above n 32, 142; Deringer, above n 76, 7; Holmes, above n 42, 57 note 6. *Contra* Lenaerts, above n 91, 17. See also K Schmidt, 'Umdenken im Kartellverfahrensrecht!' (2003) *Betriebsberater* 1237, 1241, who even takes the position that block exemption regulations would be of a constitutive nature.

[261] Cf paras 71, 78, 84 and 85 of the White Paper and 10 of the Explanatory Memorandum. According to the Commission, block exemption regulations help to simplify the applicable rules for most undertakings; para 71 of the White Paper.

[262] White Paper, para 86. In addition to the Notice on Complaints (see above n 251), the Notice on Guidance Letters (see above n 96), the Network Notice (see above n 212) and the National Courts Notice (see above n 228), the Commission has published three other informal documents relating to the interpretation of Arts 81 and 82 EC. These are guidelines on the effect on trade concept contained in Arts 81 and 82 of the Treaty ([2004] OJ C101/81), guidelines on the application of Art 81(3) of the Treaty ([2004] OJ C101/97) and a guidance on the Commission's enforcement priorities in applying Article 82 EC to abusive exclusionary conduct by dominant undertakings (COM(2008) of 3 December 2008).

considers that notices and guidelines become part of the binding rules that NCAs are obliged to apply once the approach set out therein has been confirmed by individual decisions provided that these decisions are upheld by the ECJ.[263]

3. The Commission's Role in the Network of Competition Authorities

Article 11(1) of Regulation 1/2003 provides that the Commission and NCAs 'shall apply the Community competition rules in *close co-operation*'.[264] To this end, the NCAs and the Commission together have created a network of public authorities called 'European Competition Network'[265] (ECN or 'the Network'). The purpose of the Network is to provide an infrastructure for the co-operation of European competition authorities in Articles 81 and 82 cases and to facilitate mutual information, consultation and, where necessary, coordination of enforcement measures.[266] Co-operation within the Network shall be based on the principles of mutual respect and trust.[267]

However, in view of the significant supervisory and interventionary powers vis-à-vis NCAs, in particular the right of evocation and its special responsibility for defining the EU competition policy, the Commission can be expected to occupy a pre-eminent position among the members of the ECN. Moreover, the modalities for the co-operation within the Network are determined and revised by the Commission.[268] Co-operation within the meaning of Article 11 of Regulation 1/2003 does not seem to be based on

---

[263] White Paper, para 86.

[264] Emphasis added. In fact, according to Paulis, above n 95, 406, the 'Commission monopoly will be replaced by co-operation'.

[265] The name, as well as further modalities of the operation of the Network, are laid down in the Network Notice.

[266] From early on, it had been planned that the Network would be supported by an intranet which should allow the instant and simultaneous flow of information between all EU competition authorities. See Paulis, above n 95, 407 and Schaub, above n 220, 39 note 23. Even though such electronic means of communication was apparently even mentioned in an earlier (unpublished) draft of the Network Notice, the final version of the Network Notice does not indicate the precise methods of communication. See A Burnside and H Crossley, 'Co-operative Mechanisms within the EU: A Blueprint for Future Co-operation at the International Level' (2004) 10 *International Trade Law & Regulation* 25, 27. However, Commission officials have confirmed that an electronic case management system was at place and working effectively at the date when Reg 1/2003 entered into force.

[267] Ehlermann, above n 13, 578; Kingston, above n 32, 344; Schaub, above n 220, 43, and Paulis, above n 95, 411–12, who emphasises that the Commission should not systematically play the role of policeman or controller. See also the joint statement of the Council and the Commission on the functioning of the network of competition authorities of 10 December 2002 (Council of the European Union, document no 15435/02 ADD 1; 'Joint Statement') which states at para 7: 'Co-operation between the NCAs and with the Commission takes place on the basis of equality, respect and solidarity.'

[268] Recital 15 of Reg 1/2003. The Network Notice, however, was drafted in close co-operation with the Member States.

the principle of equal powers.[269] The Commission clearly has a central, leading role in the Network and thereby ranks de facto above the NCAs[270], even though there is no formal hierarchy by which NCAs are subordinated to the Commission.[271] It is therefore submitted that the Commission is more than just a *primus inter pares*.[272]

B. The Competences of the National Competition Authorities

The introduction of the directly applicable exception system lies undoubtedly at the heart of the reform. However, it is not only due to the suppression of the Commission's exclusive right to apply Article 81(3) EC that the role of NCAs in the enforcement of EC competition law has changed significantly. The obligation imposed on NCAs by Article 3(1) of Regulation 1/2003 to apply Articles 81 and 82 EC in all cases where they apply national competition law and trade between Member States may be affected has probably had a far larger impact on the position of the NCAs compared to the situation prior to 1 May 2004. In addition, the possibilities for NCAs to co-operate with each other and to assist national courts have been strengthened and formalised.

1. Rights and Duties of NCAs under Regulation 1/2003

a. The Right to Apply Article 81(3)

Article 1(2) of Regulation 1/2003 provides that agreements, decisions or practices which are caught by Article 81(1) EC and which satisfy the condi-

---

[269] Another illustration of this inequality is the fact that NCAs are obliged to inform the Commission at the outset and before the termination of their proceedings, while the provision of such information to other NCAs is not mandatory. Information exchange at the horizontal level takes place on a purely voluntary basis. Accordingly there is no formal right of NCAs to be informed simultaneously with the Commission. Not surprisingly, U Böge, former President of the Bundeskartellamt, considers the core function of Art 11 of Reg 1/2003 to be that of a control instrument of the Commission vis-à-vis the NCAs. In his view, the extensive powers accorded to the Commission counteract the aim of creating a network based on genuine partnership. U Böge, 'The Commission's Position within the Network: The Perspective of the NCAs' in Ehlermann and Atanasiu, above n 201, 247, 248 and 251.

[270] Schaub, above n 47, 255. Kingston, above n 32, 344, takes the view that the 'true Community blueprint is still a "hierarchical" institutional architecture with the Commission at superior level'. In the same vein, Devroe, above n 223, para 22, notes that 'deze autoriteiten [NCAs] de Commissie niet als gelijken maar als ondergeschikten zullen benaderen' and further (at para 30) 'dat de nationale mededingingsautoriteiten opgaan in een hecht en hiërarchisch gestructureerd netwerk'.

[271] M Wezenbeek-Geuke, 'Het voorstel voor een verordening van de Raad betreffende de uitvoering van de mededingingsregels van de artikelen 81 en 82 van het verdrag' [2001] *Nederlands tijdschrift voor Europees recht* 17, 26.

[272] Ehlermann, above n 13, 569 note 125. *Contra* Van Der Woude, above n 214, 14, who maintains that the Commission just is a *primus inter pares*.

tions of Article 81(3) EC are not prohibited, 'no prior decision to that effect being required'. In other words, the legality and validity of a restrictive agreement or practice no longer depends on a notification and subsequent (Commission) decision stating that the agreement or practice fulfils the criteria of Article 81(3) EC. As a consequence, NCAs can also apply Article 81 EC as a whole. They can decide themselves whether or not an agreement or practice that restricts competition meets the requirements of Article 81(3) EC and thus whether it is compatible with the EC Treaty or illegal.

The removal of the notification and authorisation requirement has particular relevance for the competences of the NCAs. It not only confers more rights on the NCAs, but also shifts part of the responsibility for the enforcement of the EC competition rules to the NCAs. As of 1 May 2004, the Commission shares with the authorities of the Member States not only the competence (and hence responsibility) to apply Article 81(1) EC,[273] but also the competence and hence responsibility to apply Article 81(3) EC. Under Regulation 17, NCAs could well apply Article 81(1) EC and, to this extent, the former system could be said to have included some limited form of decentralisation. However, where an issue of Article 81(3) EC arose, an NCA could not decide the case itself, but usually had to stay proceedings and await the Commission decision on the granting (or denial) of an exemption, for which the Commission had the monopoly.[274] Under Regulation 1/2003, such a suspension is no longer necessary since the NCAs can apply Article 81 in full.

b. The Obligation to Apply Articles 81 and 82 EC and the Effect-on-trade Concept

In view of their increased responsibility for the enforcement of EC competition law, it seems vital that all NCAs are actually given the power, as a matter of national law, to apply Articles 81 and 82 EC.[275] Moreover, decentralisation will be successful only if the NCAs effectively use this power.

---

[273] Cf the judgment of the ECJ in *Delimitis* (above n 251), para 45 (with regard to the sharing of competences between the Commission and national courts).

[274] Unless it was crystal clear that the agreement or practice at issue either could benefit from an existing block exemption or, on the contrary, could under no circumstances meet the conditions for an individual exemption.

[275] At the time of the White Paper (1999), only seven Member States (out of 15) had empowered their NCAs to apply EC competition law. These were France, Germany, Greece, Italy, the Netherlands, Portugal and Spain. In Belgium, the legal situation was unclear. In Austria, Denmark, Finland, Ireland, Luxemburg, Sweden and the UK, the NCAs were not entitled, as a matter of national law, to apply Arts 81 and 82 EC. See White Paper, para 94.

(1) Mandatory Application of EC Competition Law. It is therefore no surprise that Regulation 1/2003 makes the application by NCAs of Articles 81 and 82 EC mandatory. Article 3(1) of Regulation 1/2003 provides that, where NCAs

> apply national competition law to agreements, decisions by associations of under-takings or concerted practices within the meaning of Article 81(1) of the Treaty which may affect trade between Member States within the meaning of that provi-sion, they shall also apply Article 81 of the Treaty to such agreements, decisions or concerted practices.[276]

This means that NCAs are under a legal obligation to apply EC compe-tition law in all cases where they apply national competition law to agreements, decisions or practices within the meaning of Article 81(1) provided that there may be an effect on intra-Community trade. It further means that Member States are indirectly required to empower their respective competition authorities to apply Articles 81 and 82 EC.[277] With the entering into force of Regulation 1/2003, all Member States, including the 12 new Member States of Central and Eastern Europe, have given their NCAs the requisite powers.

The competence of the NCAs to apply Articles 81 and 82 EC is obviously subject to the Commission's right of evocation described above.[278] The possibility to be deprived at any moment of their right to apply Article 81 or 82 EC may create some insecurity on the side of the NCAs.[279] Moreover, the question arises of what consequences the removal of an Article 81 or 82 case from an NCA's jurisdiction will have for the applicability of national competition law. Since the NCAs can no longer comply with their obligation to apply both national and EC competition law when the Commission has opened a procedure, it has been argued that the NCAs consequently may also not apply their national competition law to the same set of facts as those which form the subject of the Commission procedure.[280] This would mean that in all cases handled by the

---

[276] Reg 1/2003, Art 3(1), 1st sentence. An equivalent obligation exists with regard to Art 82 EC. See Reg 1/2003, Art 3(1), 2nd sentence.

[277] Read in combination with Art 35(1) of Reg 1/2003, this includes an obligation for the Member States to provide their NCAs with a minimum of resources that are necessary to enable them to effectively enforce the EC competition rules. Cf W Wils, 'The Reform of Competition Law Enforcement—Will it Work?', Community Report for the FIDE XXI Congress, Dublin, 2–5 June 2004, in D Cahill (ed), *The Modernisation of EU Competition Law Enforcement in the EU—FIDE 2004 National Reports* (Cambridge, Cambridge University Press, 2004) (available at SSRN: http://ssrn.com/abstract=1319249), 661, para 141.

[278] See above, section II.A.1.b(2).

[279] Böge, above n 269, 251, believes that Art 11(6) of Reg 1/2003 will create not only uncertainty, but also mistrust at the level of the NCAs. He points to the fact that, due to the Member States' obligation to apply Arts 81 and 82 EC, the number of cases potentially affected by the Commission's right of evocation is drastically increased. *Ibid.*

[280] C Gauer, D Dalheimer, L Kjolbye and E De Smijter, 'Regulation 1/2003: A Modernised Application of EC Competition Rules' (2003) (Spring) *Competition Policy Newsletter* 3, 6; W

Commission the parallel application of national competition law is entirely excluded and companies are fully protected against multiple proceedings at both the EU and the national level. This would evidently constitute an important advantage for undertakings. It would effectively create a real one-stop shop—similar to that existing under the Merger Regulation—for cartel cases handled by the Commission.

On the other hand, the obligation enshrined in Article 3(1) of Regulation 1/2003 shall guarantee that EC competition law is effectively enforced not only by the Commission, but also by the Member States.[281] It shall prevent NCAs from having recourse only to the domestic competition rules merely because they are more familiar with their national law and seek to avoid the trouble of applying rules with which they feel less acquainted and which seem more complex to them. However, an effective enforcement of Articles 81 and 82 EC does not require that NCAs be precluded altogether from applying their national competition rules where the application of the EC competition rules to the relevant facts is ensured by the Commission. The doctrine of supremacy of Community law and the specific conflict rules laid down in Article 3(2) of Regulation 1/2003 prevent the NCAs in any event from taking decisions which would contradict the Commission's decision. It would thus go not only beyond the purpose of Article 3(1) of Regulation 1/2003, but also beyond what is necessary to ensure effective enforcement of EC competition law if one construed that provision so as to prohibit NCAs from applying their national competition law altogether because they have been relieved by the Commission of their competence to apply Articles 81 and 82 EC.[282]

One may of course wonder about the usefulness of an NCA applying national competition law in parallel in a case which is already handled by the Commission under Article 81 or 82 EC since the national procedure may in any event not lead to a different outcome than the Commission procedure.[283] However, this argument would in general militate against the parallel application of EC and national competition law by one and the same (national) authority and would thus cast doubt on the concept of Article 3(1) of Regulation 1/2003 as a whole. The right of Member States to apply their national competition law must not be curtailed more than is absolutely necessary to guarantee an effective enforcement of EC compe-

---

Wils, 'The Principle of "Ne Bis in Idem" in EC Antitrust Enforcement: A Legal and Economic Analysis' (2003) 26 *World Competition* 131, 144 note 44; S Blake and D Schnichels, 'Leniency Following Modernisation: Safeguarding Europe's Leniency Programmes' (2004) 25 *European Competition Law Review* 765, 766 and 768. This also seems to be the position of E Rehbinder, 'Zum Verhältnis zwischen nationalem und EG-Kartellrecht nach der VO Nr 1/2003' in Fuchs et al, above n 139, 303, 308.

[281] See recital 8 of Reg 1/2003.

[282] Such an interpretation could also be regarded as incompatible with the principles of subsidiarity and proportionality. Cf Monopolkommission, above n 210, para 22.

[283] Idot, above n 161, 331 para 102.

tition law. If the principles set out in Articles 3(1) and 11(6) of Regulation 1/2003 are interpreted as broadly as suggested by some authors, these provisions might not be covered by the competence conferred upon the Council by Article 87 EC.

It is therefore submitted that NCAs are entitled to apply national competition law in cases which are investigated and sanctioned by the Commission under Articles 81 and 82 EC provided they respect the principle of supremacy of EC law and the special conflict rule of Article 3(2) of Regulation 1/2003.[284]

(2) The Effect-on-trade Criterion—Double Dilemma and Parallel Application. Another major uncertainty surrounding the enforcement of EC competition law by NCAs is the question of whether or not the agreement/practice at issue is actually capable of affecting inter-state trade in the EU. As of 1 May 2004, this question must be examined in each competition case, since the NCA's duty to apply Article 81 or 82 EC depends on this effect-on-trade criterion. Where there are no effects on inter-state trade, the case falls outside the scope of Articles 81 and 82 EC and, consequently, the NCA's decision must be based exclusively on national competition law. On the other hand, where the agreement or practice is likely to effect trade between Member States, the NCA must (also) apply Article 81 or 82 EC. In the latter case, however, the NCA is free to either apply EC competition law solely or base its decision on both EC and national competition law. Regulation 1/2003 does not establish a system of mutually exclusive scopes of application for national and EC competition rules. Both sets of law may be applied in parallel (principle of concurrent application).[285] Nonetheless, the requirement of effects on intra-Community trade is a crucial element. It is a jurisdictional criterion which defines the scope of application of Community competition law[286] and thus ultimately determines to what extent NCAs can still rely exclusively and autonomously on their national competition law regimes in accordance with Article 3(1) of Regulation 1/2003.

Since the effect-on-trade concept has been given a rather vague meaning

---

[284] Such parallel application of national and Community competition law may, however, raise concerns of double jeopardy. See below Chapter 6, n 279.

[285] In contrast, the Commission had initially proposed that the application of EC and national competition law would be based on a system of mutual exclusivity. See Art 3 of the Draft Regulation, which stipulated: 'Where an agreement, a decision by an association . . . may affect trade between Member States, Community competition law shall apply to the exclusion of national competition laws' (emphasis added). The Commission wanted to make sure that agreements and practices affecting inter-state trade would be scrutinised under a single set of rules, thereby removing the costs and risks attached to a parallel application of EC and national law. Explanatory Memorandum, 15. However, the Council did not endorse this proposal of the Commission.

[286] See para 12 of the Guidelines on the effect on trade concept contained in Arts 81 and 82 of the Treaty (see above n 262; 'EOT Guidelines').

in the past by interpreting it extremely broadly, the Commission has published the EOT Guidelines with the aim of clarifying this concept.[287] In view of the jurisdictional aspects involved, this is an important step. In the EOT Guidelines, the Commission sets out the principles developed by the ECJ and the CFI in relation to the interpretation of the concept. It also attempts to indicate when agreements are in general unlikely to *appreciably* affect intra-Community trade.[288] The ECJ introduced the requirement of appreciable effects as long ago as 1969 in *Völk v Vervaeke*, albeit without using the term 'appreciable',[289] by ruling that an agreement would not be caught by the prohibition of Article 81 EC when its effects on the markets are insignificant.[290] In the Commission's view, the appreciability criterion incorporates a quantitative element limiting the EC law jurisdiction. Accordingly, the Commission seeks to define this criterion by setting cumulative market share and turnover thresholds below which an agreement would in principle not be capable of affecting trade between Member States to an appreciable extent.[291] On the other hand, agreements which do not remain within the limits of the thresholds are not automatically regarded as capable of appreciably affecting inter-state trade. Rather, where the thresholds are exceeded, a case-by-case analysis is required.[292]

The EOT Guidelines must be distinguished from the *de minimis* rule. The market share thresholds laid down in the *de minimis* Notice are aimed at defining an economic parameter below which an agreement or practice is, in general, unlikely to appreciably restrict competition within the meaning of Article 81 EC. Where, by contrast, the thresholds of the EOT Guidelines are respected, the agreement or practice is considered to have only a marginal (inappreciable) impact on intra-Community trade, and for

---

[287] On the broad interpretation of this criterion, see above, section I.A.2.

[288] Paras 50 *et seq* of the EOT Guidelines. The criterion of not appreciable affecting intra-Community trade is also referred to as the NAAT-rule (see paras 3 and 45 of the EOT Guidelines).

[289] Roth and Rose, above n 138, para 2.078. Apparently, the term 'appreciable' (in French: 'sensible') was first used incidentally by the ECJ in *Technique Minière* (seeabove n 26) and then systematically employed by the Commission in its *de minimis* Notice of 1970 (above n 38). It was later endorsed by the ECJ in *Béguelin*, where the ECJ held that 'in order to come within the prohibition imposed by Art 85, the agreement must affect trade between Member States and the free play of competition to an *appreciable* extent' (emphasis added). Case 22/71 *Béguelin Import v SAGL Import Export* [1971] ECR 949, para 16.

[290] Para 5/7 of the judgment (n 37). Roth and Rose, above n 138, para 2.078, observed that this principle was already foreshadowed in *Technique Minière* where the ECJ referred inter alia to the quantity of the products covered by the agreement at issue and the position and importance of the parties on the relevant market when considering the effects of the agreement under Art 81 EC (see p 250 of the judgment, above n 26). In that judgment, the ECJ uses in fact the term 'appreciable' in relation to the effects on competition that the agreement must have in order to be caught by the prohibition of Art 81 (p 249 of the judgment).

[291] Paras 44 and 52 of the EOT Guidelines. The relevant thresholds are a 5% market share of the relevant market in the Community and an aggregate annual turnover of €40 million of the undertakings concerned in the relevant products.

[292] Para 51 of the EOT Guidelines.

this reason would fall outside the scope of Articles 81 and 82 EC. Both criteria are not necessarily interlinked.[293]

It would be overly critical to deny that the EOT Guidelines provide some guidance as to when the effect-on-trade criterion is fulfilled. But it would also be too optimistic to claim that they grant NCAs (and national courts) a safe harbour where EC competition does not have to be applied. There remain uncertainties. Where an NCA erroneously considers that trade between Member States is affected and consequently bases its decision solely on EC competition law, the decision will be vitiated. Conversely, the legality of a decision based exclusively on national competition law will be affected where the NCA errs in concluding that intra-Community trade is not affected.

This leaves NCAs with two main problems. They may be relieved at any moment (during an investigation) from their competence to apply Article 81 or 82 EC. Where they decide to (dis)apply the EC rules on competition, their decisions may be vitiated due to a wrongful assessment of the effect-on-trade criterion. This double dilemma might make NCAs very much inclined to base any investigation and subsequent decision systematically on both domestic and EC competition law. On this basis, the effect-on-trade criterion may turn out to be of little relevance in practice.[294]

In order to help overcome possible difficulties, the Commission has committed itself to assisting NCAs with the enforcement of EC competition law. In accordance with the principles laid down by the ECJ in *Delimitis*,[295] Article 11(5) of Regulation 1/2003 provides that NCAs 'may consult the Commission on any case involving the application of Community law'. The right of NCAs to seek information from the Commission on the status of an individual procedure as well as economic and legal information in cases where the application of EC competition law raises particular difficulties was already contained in the 1997 Co-operation Notice.[296] It is, however, doubtful whether there is still much room for this type of general support, given the numerous notices and guidelines that have since been adopted by

---

[293] See para 16 of the EOT Guidelines and, by way of example, the *Dutch Banks* case ([1989] OJ L253/1), in which the Commission granted negative clearance for certain agreements between several Dutch banks and certain other Dutch financial organisations finding that the agreements, while appreciably restricting competition within the common market (because of the banks' large combined market share), did not have any appreciable effect on trade between Member States (see paras 54–9 of the Commission decision). The appeal against that decision was held to be inadmissible since the negative clearance did not adversely affect the parties' interests and the legal assessment, which contained the statement on the restrictive character of certain clauses that was disputed by the applicants, could not be challenged separately (judgment of the CFI in Case T–138/89 *Nederlandse Bankiersvereniging and others v Commission* [1992] ECR II–2181).

[294] Cf Van Der Woude, above n 214, 5–6.

[295] Above n 257.

[296] See para 52 of the 1997 Co-operation Notice.

the Commission and are designed to clarify the law. After all, it cannot be the Commission's task to solve cases that are handled by NCAs in a national procedure.

It should also be mentioned that in those Member States which have a dual institutional structure, meaning that two separate bodies are in charge of inquisition and decision-taking, the latter body often has a judicial or quasi-judicial character and might thus qualify as a 'court' within the meaning of Article 234 EC.[297] In such a case, the NCA taking the (final) decision can request a preliminary ruling of the ECJ on issues concerning the interpretation of Articles 81 and 82 EC and secondary legislation of the Commission.[298]

c. The Duty to Avoid Conflicting Decisions

The obligation to apply EC competition law entails a number of secondary obligations intended to avoid divergences between the implementation of Articles 81 and 82 EC by NCAs on the one hand and the Commission on the other, as well as conflicts between the application of EC and national competition rules to the same case. Regulation 1/2003 contains two major conflict rules.

First, Article 16(2) of Regulation 1/2003 provides that NCAs cannot take decisions running counter to a decision adopted by the Commission. This rule should ensure the uniform application of EC competition law throughout the Union in order to preserve the proper functioning of the single market and the EU's legal order. It requires all NCAs to make every effort to avoid taking decisions that would contradict an existing Commission decision. The scope of the obligation depends on the facts on which the Commission decision is based. To the extent that the material facts examined at national level are the same, the NCA cannot deviate from the operative part of the Commission decision.[299] It would seem, however, that Article 16(2) of Regulation 1/2003 does apply where the NCA decision relates to a different geographical area than the Commission decision.[300] In other words, in that situation, the NCA could not adopt a divergent (legal) assessment of the agreement or conduct at issue (eg certain

[297] See, eg the Stockholm District Court, which is the competent body in Sweden to impose fines for the infringement of Arts 81 and 82 EC; the Vienna Court of Appeal (Oberlandesgericht Wien) which has similar competences in Austria; and the Raad voor de Mededinging, the Belgian competition council which, under Belgian law, is qualified as an administrative court (*administratief rechtscollege*) (see Art 2 §1 Wet tot oprichting van een Raad voor de mededinging of 10 June 2006). On the (dual) institutional structure see below Chapter 2 IA

[298] See below, section II.C.3.c.

[299] See Explanatory Memorandum, 24. The reason why the obligation is limited to instances where the relevant facts are identical is that Commission decisions do not set general precedents. Van Der Woude, above n 226, 180.

[300] Gerber and Cassinis, above n 188, 53 note 13.

cartel activities) in respect of the national territory unless the factual circumstances with regard to the domestic market are also materially different.[301]

Secondly, the first sentence of Article 3(2) of Regulation 1/2003 lays down the more general rule that national competition law cannot be more severe than Article 81 EC.[302] It states that the application of national competition law may not lead to the prohibition of agreements or practices which are likely to affect trade between Member States but which are compatible with Article 81 EC because they either do not restrict competition within the meaning of that provision or satisfy the conditions of Article 81(3) EC. The provision mainly aims at ensuring coherence in cases where EC and national competition law are applied simultaneously. It does not apply, though, where NCAs prohibit or penalise unilateral conduct, ie in Article 82 EC cases.[303] The conflict rule would not have been necessary in a system of mutual exclusivity, as originally proposed by the Commission in Article 3 of the Draft Regulation.

One may wonder whether it was really necessary to enshrine this rule in Regulation 1/2003. It would seem to follow already from the principle of supremacy of EC law[304] that national competition law cannot prohibit what EC competition law allows, at least to the extent that the legality of the agreement or practice is based on (the direct application of) Article 81(3) EC.[305] Otherwise, the uniform application of EC competition law would be frustrated and the attainment of the objectives of the EC Treaty would be impeded.[306] Indeed, the ECJ ruled in *Walt Wilhelm* that conflicts between national rules and EC rules on competition 'must be resolved by

[301] If Art 16(2) of Reg 1/2003, like Art 11(6) of Reg 1/2003, were to apply only to identical matters (ie same agreement/conduct, same parties, same product and geographic markets), the provision would almost be deprived of any purpose, as in this case (the Commission has decided the identical case or contemplates a decision on it) NCAs are anyway relieved of their competence to act pursuant to Art 11(6) of Reg 1/2003 and thus no risk of conflicting decisions exists.

[302] NB: where the alleged infringement concerns unilateral conduct that comes within the ambit of Art 82 EC, stricter national rules may be applied. This is expressly laid down in the Reg 1/2003, Art 3(2), 2nd sentence. The considerations in this paragraph thus only apply where a (potential) conflict between national law and Art 81 EC is at issue.

[303] Reg 1/2003, Art 3(2), 2nd sentence.

[304] The principle was established by the ECJ in Case 6/64 *Costa v ENEL* [1964] ECR 585, 593–4 (English special edition).

[305] This is the view taken by Advocate General Tesauro in *VW and VAG Leasing*, where he states that 'since the agreements are liable to affect trade between Member States and therefore fall in principle within the prohibition set out in Article 85(1), the exemption granted to them cannot but prevent the national authorities from ignoring the positive assessment put on them by the Community authorities'. Case C–266/93 *Bundeskartellamt v Volkswagen and VAG Leasing* [1995] ECR I–3477, para 51 of the opinion of the Advocate General.

[306] It would clearly jeopardise the system of free, undistorted competition (Art 3(g) EC) if a company having a pan-European business and benefiting from an Art 81(3) exemption is precluded from pursuing its activities in a certain Member State due to the application of more stringent domestic competition rules in that country.

applying the principle that Community law takes precedence'. The ECJ further stated that the parallel application of EC and domestic law is subject to the condition 'that the application of national law may not prejudice the full and uniform application of Community law'.[307] Despite these seemingly clear statements, some commentators have argued that *Walt Wilhelm* does not provide a conclusive answer to the question of whether an agreement or practice permitted at EC level can be prohibited under national competition law.[308] Others have taken the position that, in any event, an exemption precludes Member States from condemning the same agreement or practice on the basis of a stricter national regime.[309] Due to the explicit conflict rule in Article 3(2) of Regulation 1/2003, this dispute is now obsolete.

On the other hand, considering the ECJ's judgment in *Walt Wilhelm* and the supremacy doctrine, there seems to have been general agreement, in the past, that a prohibition under EC competition law will prevail over any authorisation granted on the basis of less rigorous national provisions.[310] In other words, national competition law cannot be more lenient than EC competition law. Curiously enough, Regulation 1/2003 does not restate this basic rule, which is a clear expression of the principle of supremacy of EC

---

[307] Case 14/68 *Walt Wilhelm v Bundeskartellamt* [1969] ECR 1, paras 6 and 9.

[308] Eg Roth and Rose, above n 138 (5th edn), 10-078; R Whish, *Competition Law* (London, LexisNexis, 5th edn, 2003), 76; Jones and Sufrin, above n 152, 1282. Cf Venit, above n 97, 557–8. See also the opinion of Advocate General F Jacobs in *Bronner*: 'The limits placed by Community law on the divergent application of national law in cases falling within the scope of Arts 85 and 86 remain unclear'. Case C–7/97 *Oscar Bronner v Mediaprint* [1998] ECR I–7791, para 22 of the opinion.

[309] Goyder, above n 13, 444, with regard to both individual and block exemptions. This also seems to have been the Commission's view; see Roth and Rose, above n 138 (5th edn), 10-078, with reference to the Commission's observations in the *Perfumes* cases where it was submitted: 'Where . . . the national court is led to conclude that the agreement is conclusively valid from a Community point of view . . . (it) must be prevented from applying its national law in so far as it is more rigorous' (p 2369 of the judgment, below n 315). Ritter and Braun, above n 32, 91, equally support this position when they state that national authorities and courts are legally bound by block exemption regulations in the same way as by individual exemptions and prevented from applying stricter national law. A more differentiated approach is advocated by Temple Lang, who sees good reasons to distinguish between individual and group exemptions and also suggests that, even in the case of group exemption regulations, the question of whether they really preclude, with regard to every single clause in a given contract, the application of stricter national rules must be carefully considered on a case-by-case basis. See J Temple Lang, 'European Community Constitutional Law and the Enforcement of Community Antitrust Law' in B Hawk (ed), *1993 Proceedings of the Fordham Corporate Law Institute* (New York, Juris Publishing, 1994), 525, 553–66, in particular 560–1.

[310] Whish above n 308 (3rd edn), 37; Roth and Rose, above n 138 (5th edn), 10-075; Ritter and Braun, above n 32 (2nd edn), 71. Goyder, above n 13, 442. This conclusion was based inter alia on the judgment of the ECJ in Case 66/86 *Ahmed Saeed Flugreisen and others v Zentrale zur Bekämpfung unlauteren Wettbewerbs* [1989] ECR 803, para 49, where the court held that the approval, by national regulatory authorities, of tariff agreements in the air transport sector which were contrary to Art 81 was incompatible with the EC Treaty, notably Art 10 (ex Art 5) thereof.

law.[311] For the sake of clarity, it would have been desirable to have had this rule also codified in Regulation 1/2003.[312]

Nonetheless, one can conclude that the conflict rules in Regulation 1/2003 fully confirm the supremacy of EC competition law over national competition law, in line with the case law of the ECJ and, in particular, in the spirit of the judgment in *Walt Wilhelm*, where the ECJ held:

> It would be contrary to the nature of such a system [of law] to allow Member States to introduce or to retain measures capable of prejudicing the practical effectiveness of the Treaty. The binding force of the Treaty and of measures taken in application of it must not differ from one state to another as a result of internal measures, lest the functioning of the Community system should be impeded and the achievement of the aims of the Treaty placed in peril.[313]

Only where the agreement or practice is not prohibited by EC competition law because it falls outside the scope of Article 81 or 82 EC may the question be answered differently. Arguably, in such a case, there is no conflict between the two sets of rules.[314] In view of the non-applicability of EC competition law, the agreement or practice is not accorded an explicit validity at EC level that could override national law. Articles 81 and 82 EC simply do not cover the situation, and thus cannot preclude the application of more restrictive national provisions.[315] Accordingly, the conflict rule of Article 3(2) of Regulation 1/2003 is limited to conduct having an effect on trade between Member States. In the absence of such an effect, the case is outside the ambit of Community competition law[316] and stricter national law may be applied.

d. *Types of NCA Decisions—Old and New Instruments*

When NCAs apply EC competition law, they do so according to their own procedural rules. Equally, the sanctions that can be imposed by NCAs for an infringement of Article 81 or 82 EC are determined by the national laws of the Member States. Regulation 1/2003 harmonises neither the relevant procedures nor the applicable penalties.

---

[311] Apparently, the codification of this principle was considered unnecessary. Dalheimer, in Dalheimer *et al*, above n 119, Art 3 no 19.

[312] Cf Van Der Woude, above n 214, 3 and Rehbinder, above n 280, 309. *Contra* Wils, above n 277, para 153 note 229, who finds it 'so obvious an application of the general principle of primacy of Community law' that there was no need to restate it in Reg 1/2003.

[313] Para 6 of the judgment (n 307).

[314] Ritter and Braun, above n 32 (2nd edn), 71–2.

[315] This was confirmed by the ECJ in the *Perfumes* cases. See Joined Cases 253/78 and 1–3/79 *Procureur de la République v Giry and Guerlain* [1980] ECR 2327, para 18.

[316] See Dalheimer, in Dalheimer *et al*, above n 119, Art 3 no 12, who points out that Art 3(2) of Reg 1/2003 clearly distinguishes between the criterion of capability to affect intra-Community trade which delineates the scope of application of Art 81 and the existence of a restriction of competition.

However, in order to guarantee a minimum level of equivalence and effectiveness of the enforcement measures taken at national level, Article 5 of Regulation 1/2003 lists the types of decisions that NCAs may adopt when applying EC competition law. These are: (i) decisions requiring that an infringement be brought to an end (prohibitions); (ii) decisions ordering interim measures; (iii) decisions accepting commitments; and (iv) decisions imposing fines or periodic penalty payments. The purpose of this provision appears to be twofold. On the one hand, it ensures that NCAs are given the necessary powers to effectively enforce the EC competition rules.[317] On the other hand, Article 5 of Regulation 1/2003 limits the variety of national decisions.

(1) Negative Decisions and Non-action Decisions. The types of decisions that NCAs may take are essentially equivalent to those that the Commission can adopt in application of Articles 81 and 82 EC, including interim measures and commitment decisions.[318] There is, however, one exception. Article 5 of Regulation 1/2003 seems to preclude NCAs from taking positive decisions (findings of inapplicability) within the meaning of Article 10 of Regulation 1/2003.

As concerns the non-application of EC competition law, Article 5 of Regulation 1/2003 only provides that NCAs 'may likewise decide that there are no grounds for action on their part'. This last sentence of Article 5 of Regulation 1/2003 was included to take account of those Member States where NCAs, on the basis of the relevant national law, cannot close a file informally but have to adopt a formal decision at the end of every procedure. In order to enable NCAs in such Member States to properly terminate proceedings or reject complaints in cases where they do not find an infringement, the possibility of 'non-action' decisions (*non-lieu*) was added.[319] These would be akin to negative clearances in the former system, where companies could apply for an individual exemption or, alternatively, request the Commission to certify that the notified agreement or practice fell outside the scope of Article 81.[320]

---

[317] Art 5 of Reg 1/2003 could even be interpreted as having direct effect and empowering the NCAs to apply the measures enumerated therein. See Smits, above n 202, 176 note 5, and 184. This would imply that, in the absence of further implementing rules at the national level, NCAs could rely directly on that provision to adopt a certain type of decision listed in that article (eg a commitment decision).

[318] For the sake of completeness, it should be mentioned that NCAs like the Commission are entitled to withdraw the benefits of a block exemption in individual cases. Pursuant to Art 29(2) of Reg 1/2003, however, the withdrawal right of an NCA is limited to situations where the territory of its Member State or a part thereof constitutes a distinct geographic market. A similar power of NCAs already existed with regard to the block exemption for vertical restraints (see Art 7 of Reg 2790/1999).

[319] Schaub, above n 47, 252. Schaub also explains that the Commission, for its part, would not adopt a non-action decision in order to bring an end to an *ex officio* procedure which has not revealed any infringement, but would rather close the file informally.

[320] See Goyder, above n 13, 33.

However, the different wording, as compared to Article 10 of Regulation 1/2003, suggests that such decisions are not decisions of inapplicability within the meaning of Article 10 of Regulation 1/2003.[321] Rather, the decision simply pronounces that the NCA will no longer pursue the matter.[322] This interpretation would be in line with the fact that the option of sharing the Commission's exemption monopoly with NCAs was rejected.[323] Against this background, it seems logical that it should be the Commission's prerogative to adopt positive decisions.[324] Moreover, the Commission wants to ensure, by all means, that the instrument of positive decisions is not turned into a backdoor notification/exemption procedure.[325] The risk of such an abuse of positive decisions can be best minimised if the Commission fully controls the application and devel-

---

[321] Cf Kerse and Khan, above n 165, para 5-004, who also note that the wording of Art 5 of Reg 1/2003 must be contrasted with that of Art 10 of the Reg, but still maintains that the list provided in Art 5 is not exhaustive. *Accord* J Stuyck, 'Hoofdstuk II Restrictieve mededingings-praktijken' in J Stuyck, W Devroe and P Wytinck (eds), *De nieuwe Belgische Mededingingswet 2006* (Mechelen, Kluwer, 2007), 21, 26.

[322] Schaub, above n 47, 252: 'The function of these decisions would be to bring an end to the procedure rather than to define Community competition policy.' See also Paulis, above n 95, 411 (no decision of compatibility). Both authors also point out that such decisions only bind the NCA adopting the decision.

[323] See Wils, above n 19, 139.

[324] Cf L Idot, 'A Necessary Step Towards Common Procedural Standards of Implementation for Articles 81 & 82 EC without the Network' in Ehlermann and Atanasiu, above n 201, 211, 219; Ehlermann, above n 13, 569; Wils, above n 277, para 49. Cf also Art 52 no 2 of the Belgian Competition Act of 2006 (consolidated version; see below Chapter 2, n 45), which provides that the Belgian competition authority can adopt decisions stating that a certain agreement or practice does not constitute an unlawful restriction of competition (*déclaration d'inexistence*) only to the extent that the agreement or practice in question does not affect inter-state trade. In contrast, pursuant to Art 51 of that act, the Belgian competition authority can also decide that there are no grounds for action (*geen aanleiding om op te treden*). This latter power is not restricted to cases which have no effect on intra-Community trade. These provisions evidently built on the presumption that the national authority has the competence to adopt positive decisions merely with regard to the application of national competition law, but not with regard to the application of Community competition law. See also the explanatory memorandum (*Verslag aan de Koning*) to Art 4 of the Royal Decree of 25 April 2004 amending the Belgian Competition Act of 1999 (n 610): 'Nochtans voorziet artikel 10 van de Verordening, voor zaken waarin een mogelijke beïnvloeding van handel tussen de lid-Staten van de Europese Gemeenschap aanwezig is, dat de exclusieve bevoegdheid om vast te stellen dat er geen sprake is van een restrictieve mededingingspraktijk voorbehouden is aan de Europese Commissie.' This is also the position of the Austrian appellate cartel court (*Kartellobergericht*); see J Barbist, 'Das österreichische Kartellobergericht und die VO Nr 1/2003' (2005) 55 *Wirtschaft und Wettbewerb* 756, 758–9. See further P Nihoul, 'Le projet de loi belge sur la protection de la concurrence économique' (2006) 1 *TBM-RCB* 4, para 17. *Contra* Stuyck, above n 321, 25–6, who argues that the list of possible decisions in Art 5 of Reg 1/2003 is not exhaustive since an exclusivity (of the power to take positive decisions) in favour of the Commission would have to be explicitly stated in the law. That provision could therefore not preclude NCAs from adopting positive decisions. See also above n 321.

[325] See Schaub, above n 47, 252, emphasising that non-action decisions of NCAs would only be adopted to terminate an *ex officio* procedure and not at the request of undertakings. However, Reg 1/2003 does not explicitly state this. Theoretically, companies could thus approach an NCA with a view to inducing it to issue a non-action decision.

opment of this particular instrument by precluding NCAs altogether from taking any form of positive decision.[326]

Yet there remains some uncertainty. First, it is true that Regulation 1/2003, in particular its Article 5, does not explicitly preclude NCAs from adopting positive decisions. Secondly, the explanations given by the Commission in relation to Article 5 of the Draft Regulation could be understood to leave open the possibility for NCAs to also adopt positive decisions. The Commission in particular stated:

> If the competition authority of a Member State finds that behaviour, acting on a complaint or on its own initiative *does not infringe Article 81 as a whole or Article 82*, it can close the proceedings or reject the complaint by decision finding that there are no grounds for action.[327]

These words seem to imply that the decisions that NCAs may adopt in accordance with the last sentence of Article 5 of Regulation 1/2003 are in fact non-infringement decisions, ie decisions whereby the NCA confirms that the investigated agreement or conduct does not infringe the EC competition rules. There can be only two reasons why Articles 81 and 82 EC are not violated: either the requirements for application of Article 81(1) or 82 EC are not met or the conditions of Article 81(3) are satisfied. These are exactly the situations covered by Article 10 of Regulation 1/2003. It means, however, that on substance a non-action decision pursuant to Article 5 of Regulation 1/2003 could hardly be distinguished from a positive or non-infringement decision pursuant to Article 10 of Regulation 1/2003. In view of the (implicit or explicit) motivation, they are virtually the same.[328] The fact that, pursuant to Article 5 of Regulation 1/2003, NCAs shall (only) state that 'there are no grounds for action'[329] would appear to be nothing but a camouflage of the real nature of NCA decisions adopted in accordance with that provision.

This is all the more so where proceedings are terminated by formal decision. If a formal decision is to be adopted, it would follow from general principles of law that such a decision must be sufficiently reasoned. It is

---

[326] Cf Ehlermann, above n 13, 568, who points to the fact that the introduction of individual positive decisions will in practice come relatively close to establishing a system of voluntary notifications.

[327] Emphasis added. Explanatory Memorandum, 16.

[328] Cf Kerse and Khan, above n 165, para 5-004, who submit 'that NCAs may take decisions *the substantive effect* of which is to find that, in the wording of Art 10, "the conditions of Art 81(1) of the Treaty are not fulfilled, or. . . the conditions of Art 81(3) are satisfied"' (emphasis added). *Contra* Van Der Woude, above n 214, 7, who maintains that NCAs only decide on the expediency of their action when they take decisions within the meaning the last sentence of Art 5 of Reg 1/2003. Cf also Schaub, above n 220, 42 note 31, who submits that the difference between Art 10 decisions and non-action decisions lies in the operative part. Indeed, it is only the operative part of a decision which produces legal effects. See the judgment of the CFI in *Dutch Banks* (n 293), para 31.

[329] Instead of confirming that the agreement or conduct at issue does not infringe Art 81 or 82 EC.

settled case law of the ECJ that the statement of reasons required by Article 253 EC must disclose in a clear and unequivocal fashion the reasoning followed by the institution which adopted the measure in question in such a way as to enable the persons concerned to ascertain the reasons for the measure and the competent Community court to verify its lawfulness.[330] These general principles derived from the rule of law and the requirements of sound administration also apply *mutatis mutandis* to measures which are taken by national authorities in the context of Community law and are subject to review by national courts of the Member States. It is doubtful that the simple declaration by the NCA that there are no grounds for action on its part would suffice as reasoning. If, however, a more extensive and detailed statement of reasons were required, non-action decisions of NCAs would be hardly any different from positive decisions taken by the Commission.[331] They could be differentiated on the basis of purely formalistic criteria, but not as regards their real content and meaning. Due to the statement of reasons, non-action decisions, it is submitted, may therefore de facto provide persuasive authority if the same infringement is subsequently investigated by another competition authority even though they formally do not bind other NCAs or the Commission.

(2) Commitment Decisions. Article 5 expressly empowers NCAs to adopt commitment decisions. For most, if not all, Member States this means the introduction of an entirely new kind of competition decision. The innovative power may pose difficulties in Member States where, in contrast to the system at EU level, the prosecutorial and adjudicative functions are

---

[330] See, eg judgment of the ECJ of 22 June 2004 in Case C–42/01 *Portugal v Commission* [2004] ECR I–6079, para 66.

[331] Cf Kerse and Khan, above n 165, who also note in this context that an NCA rejecting a complaint may have to explain itself. Cf further J Schwarze and A Weitbrecht, *Grundzüge des europäischen Kartellverfahrensrechts* (Baden-Baden, Nomos, 1st edn, 2004), 165, para 17. Schwarze and Weitbrecht in fact state that the non-infringement considerations are not contained in the operative part of the decision and therefore do not bind courts. However, they also point to the fact that such considerations forming part of the motivation would bind the authority itself which issued the decision. Apparently, § 32c of the German Competition Act (*Gesetz gegen Wettbewerbsbeschränkungen*, GWB), which was introduced by the seventh amendment act of 1 July 2005 (7. GWB-Novelle) to implement Reg 1/2003, tries to avoid this dilemma by providing that a non-action decision shall in fact simply state that the competition authority will not use its powers (to order the termination of an infringement or adopt interim measures) unless it is presented with new facts or evidence. Furthermore, the provision emphasises that such a decision does not grant an exemption from the prohibitions contained in Arts 81 and 82 EC. Sentences 2 and 3 of § 32c GWB read: 'Die Entscheidung hat zum Inhalt, dass die Kartellbehörde vorbehaltlich neuer Erkenntnisse von ihren Befugnissen nach den §§ 32 und 32a keinen Gebrauch machen wird. Sie hat keine Freistellung von einem Verbot im Sinne des Satzes 1 zum Inhalt.' It is, however, equally doubtful that the mere statement of the NCA not to use its powers unless new facts or evidence become known constitutes a sufficient motivation of a formal administrative act closing infringement proceedings. Cf also Van Der Woude, above n 214, 8, who takes the view that NCAs can express themselves, in a non-binding way, on the positive application of Art 81(3). It can be concluded that the legal character and implications of non-action decisions remain doubtful.

divided and the latter function is vested in a court or administrative tribunal.[332] Indeed, it may not be attractive for companies to negotiate commitments with the body investigating and/or prosecuting the infringement to the extent that this body cannot provide any guarantee that the body finally adjudicating the case will effectively accept them. On the other hand, there might be fundamental objections against the idea that the body which has been entrusted with the adjudicative function and, by definition, is required to remain impartial and independent[333] could negotiate the outcome of the proceedings. However, the new power has been introduced by Article 5 of Regulation 1/2003 and, pursuant to Article 35(1) of Regulation 1/2003, the provision must be complied with.

It is thus up to the Member States concerned to find appropriate arrangements in order to ensure that commitment decisions can be adopted at the national level. There seem to be different ways to do this. It is, for instance, conceivable that the prosecutorial body may formally accept commitment of the undertakings in exchange for a commitment, on its part, not to bring a claim before the adjudicative body. Belgium, which operates a dual enforcement system,[334] has opted for a different solution. The law provides that the body investigating the case can be requested to suggest such a commitment decision by making a proposal to this effect in its report for the adjudicative body. In practice, however, commitments seem to be actually negotiated with the adjudicative body, formally an administrative tribunal (*administratief rechtscollege*).[335] Surprisingly, this does not appear to raise any major concerns in terms of independence and impartiality of the relevant tribunal. The need to find workable solutions seems to prevail over the abstract legal principles.

(3) Suspension of Proceedings. Another important instrument foreseen by Article 13(1) of Regulation 1/2003 is the right for NCAs to suspend proceedings or reject a complaint, without considering the merits of the case, for the sole reason that another NCA is dealing with it. This provision is particularly relevant with regard to multiple complaints lodged simultaneously or successively with several competition authorities as it provides the NCAs with a simple mechanism to avoid parallel proceedings. Similarly, pursuant to Article 13(2) of Regulation 1/2003, NCAs may also reject a complaint where the case has already been dealt with by another NCA. It is

---

[332] Idot, above n 201, 219. On the so-called dual enforcement model see below Chapter 2, section I.A.2.

[333] On the principles of impartiality and independence of judges in general, which seem to be universally acknowledged also at the level of national law, see P Rädler, 'Independence and Impartiality of Judges' in D Weissbrodt and R Wolfrum (eds), *The Right to a Fair Trial (Beiträge zum ausländischen öffentlichen Recht und Völkerrecht Band 129)* (Berlin, Springer, 1998), 727.

[334] On the different models for the institutional architecture, see below Chapter 3, section I.A.

[335] See Art 11 §1 of the Belgian Competition Act (consolidated version; see below Chapter 2, n 45).

irrelevant, in this respect, whether the other NCA has adopted a negative decision or equally rejected the complaint. Both provisions set aside any national rule to the contrary which might oblige an NCA to assess a case irrespective of the fact that the same infringement is or has already been subject to an investigation in another Member State.[336]

2. The Relation Between National and Community Competition Law

While the parallel application of Community and national competition law is also possible under Regulation 1/2003, the Commission has made an attempt to define more closely the relationship between the two sets of norms. The special conflict rule of Article 3(2) of Regulation 1/2003 is aimed at ensuring an almost total convergence of the implementation of the national and EC competition rules. However, there remain some uncertainties as to the exact scope of the provision.

a. Background

It is common ground that, under the previous system established by Regulation 17, the parallel application of national and Community competition law was possible. As long ago as 1969, the ECJ ruled in *Walt Wilhelm* that the same infringement could be subject to two proceedings, one based on Community competition law and one based on national competition law, provided that such parallel proceedings did not compromise the uniform application of the EC competition rules throughout the Community. In the case of a conflict between the two sets of rules, the principle of supremacy would apply, meaning that Community law would take precedence over national law.[337] The acceptability of dual procedures was derived from the 'special system of the sharing of jurisdiction between the Community and the Member States with regard to cartels' existing at the time.[338] As is evident, that system was essentially based on Regulation 17.

When the Commission presented its proposal for new implementation rules to replace Regulation 17, it obviously intended to create a simple, clear-cut provision on the relationship between national and Community competition law that would exclude any ambiguities and guarantee the full effectiveness of Community law without leaving any room for inconsis-

---

[336] Such a rule exists, for instance, in France, where the Conseil de la concurrence is obliged to examine each and every case provided the complaint is admissible. A complaint can only be declared inadmissible by formal decision which is subject to judicial review. See Idot, above n 201, 216. Similar principles apply in Belgium, where complaints can only be rejected by formal reasoned decision which can be challenged before the adjudicative body, the Raad voor de Mededinging.

[337] Paras 3, 4 and 6 of the judgment in *Walt Wilhelm* (n 307).

[338] Para 11 of the judgment in *Walt Wilhelm* (n 307).

tencies.[339] In the Commission's view, mutual exclusivity of national and Community law would have represented such a clear system. Article 3 of the Draft Regulation accordingly provided that, in competition matters affecting trade between Member States, Articles 81 and 82 EC would apply to the exclusion of national competition law.[340] However, this proposal was vigorously rejected by a number of Member States and therefore not retained in the final version of Regulation 1/2003.[341] It would indeed have marked another drastic change of the EC competition policy, notably the end of the *Walt Wilhelm* doctrine on parallel application.[342]

b. Scope of the Convergence Rule

Instead, Article 3(2) of Regulation 1/2003 allows for the parallel application of national and Community competition law, but at the same time provides for detailed conflict rules based on the principle of supremacy.[343] The possibility of a parallel application of national and Community competition law is said to have one major advantage: it helps to avert the risk of national decisions being flawed where there are uncertainties as to whether or not there is an effect on intra-Community trade since, in such doubtful cases, national measures can be based on both rules, Article 81 (or 82) EC and the relevant provision of domestic law.[344] However, the question is still in which situations the convergence rule precludes the application of more severe national standards.

Three preliminary observations can be made. First, it should be recalled that Article 3(2) of Regulation 1/2003 regulates only the non-prohibition side. The general primacy rule continues to apply to the prohibition side of Articles 81 and 82 EC: agreements and practices that are prohibited by Article 81 or 82 EC cannot be 'approved of' on the basis of more lenient national rules. This fundamental principle, which was in fact uncontested under Regulation 17, remains unaffected by Regulation 1/2003.[345]

---

[339] See p 14 of the Explanatory Memorandum. The relevant provision was to be based on Art 83(2)(e) EC.

[340] Art 3 of the Draft Regulation reads: 'Where an agreement, a decision by an association of undertakings or a concerted practice within the meaning of Art 81 of the Treaty or the abuse of a dominant position within the meaning of Art 82 may affect trade between Member States, Community competition law shall apply to the exclusion of national competition laws.'

[341] E Paulis and C Gauer, 'La réforme des règles d'application des articles 81 et 82 du Traité' (2003) 11 *Journal des tribunaux. Droit Européen* 65, para19; Komninos, above n 79, 656.

[342] Kingston, above n 32, 343.

[343] See above, section II.B.1.c.

[344] See M Lutz, 'Schwerpunkte der 7. GWB-Novelle' (2005) 55 *Wirtschaft und Wettbewerb* 718, 724; R Bechtold, 'Die Entwicklung des deutschen Kartellrechts seit der 7.GWB-Novelle (Juli 2005 bis Oktober 2007)' (2007) 60 *Neue Juristische Wochenschrift* 3761, 3762; Gerber and Cassinis, above n 188, 12.

[345] Gauer et al, above n 280, 6; Idot, above n 161, para 37 (p. 306). See further above section II.B.1.c.

Secondly, irrespective of the vagueness surrounding the effect-on-trade concept, it is also clear that agreements, concerted practices and decisions of associations of undertakings which cannot even potentially affect trade between Member States are entirely outside the scope of Article 81 EC. The convergence rule does not apply to these agreements and practices,[346] which can be prohibited on the basis of national competition law.[347] Where there is no effect on inter-state trade, national competition law can thus be applied on a stand-alone basis. The absence of an actual or potential impact on intra-Community trade can inter alia result from the *de minimis* character of the relevant agreement or practice, ie from the fact that the effects on inter-state trade are not considered appreciable within the meaning of Article 81 EC.[348]

Thirdly, the second sentence of Article 3(2) of Regulation 1/2003 provides for an exception regarding unilateral conduct. It explicitly provides that Member States are not precluded, by Regulation 1/2003, 'from adopting and applying on their territory stricter national laws which prohibit or sanction unilateral conduct' of undertakings. In other words, in

---

[346] This follows from the wording of the 1st sentence of Art 3(2) of Reg 1/2003, which states: 'The application of national competition law may not lead to the prohibition of agreements, decisions by associations of undertakings or concerted practices *which may affect trade between Member States* but which do not restrict competition within the meaning of Art 81(1) of the Treaty, or which fulfil the conditions of Art 81(3) of the Treaty or which are covered by a Regulation for the application of Art 81(3) of the Treaty' (emphasis added). See also para 8 of the EOT Guidelines and S Hossenfelder and M Lutz, 'Die neue Durchführungsverordnung zu den Artikeln 81 und 82 EG-Vertrag' (2003) 53 *Wirtschaft und Wettbewerb* 118, 120. *Contra* Nihoul, above n 324, para 42, on the basis of the *effet utile* doctrine.

[347] In this context, it is interesting to note that the Belgian legislator has gone further than what is actually required by Reg 1/2003. The Belgian Competition Act of 2006 provides that the national counterpart to the prohibition of Art 81(1) EC does not apply to restrictive agreements and practices the effects of which are confined to the Belgian territory, but which would benefit from a block exemption regulation at Community level, if they had an impact on trade between Member States (see 2nd para of Art 5 of the Belgian Competition Act). An equivalent provision exists in Art 13 of the Dutch Competition Act (Mededingingswet, 'Mededingingswet NL'). The latter norm was actually introduced already in 1998, ie even before the publication of the White Paper. These rules can undoubtedly be called progressive. They establish total convergence between national and Community law in that they require the NCA to treat alike purely national competition cases and cases where Community law is applied. The Belgian and Dutch Competition Acts thus guarantee equal treatment of all market operators on their respective territory regardless of the territorial effects of the restrictive agreements or practices which these operators apply. In particular, smaller companies whose business is too limited, in economic terms, to have any (appreciable) cross-border effects also enjoy the protection offered by EC block exemptions. This approach certainly helps to create a truly level playing field in those two countries. In other respects, the Belgian law is, however, not in conformity with Reg 1/2003. Inter alia, it makes the non-application of the national prohibition dependent on the hypothetical applicability of a block exemption also in cases where there is an effect on trade between Member States, but no restriction of competition within the meaning of Art 81 EC. This condition is incompatible with Art 3(2) of Reg 1/2003. Nihoul, above n 324, para 37. See also below in this section, notably the paragraph regarding the 'first scenario'.

[348] These are typically agreements between small or medium-sized undertakings (see para 50 of the EOT Guidelines) and agreements meeting the conditions of the NAAT-rule as defined on p 52 of the EOT Guidelines.

possible Article 82 cases, the question of whether there is an effect (actual or potential) on trade between Member States is less relevant than in Article 81 cases. Whether or not intra-Community trade is affected and thus regardless of whether Article 82 EC effectively applies, national rules may be stricter. NCAs can therefore prohibit unilateral conduct which, under Article 82 EC, is not prohibited, and also impose sanctions for such conduct. The rule was mainly introduced to allow Member States in which, according to the domestic competition rules, non-dominant firms have special duties vis-à-vis companies that are economically dependent on them, to continue to apply these rules.[349] In addition, the exception (that national rules may be more stringent) also covers unilateral conduct by a dominant company which does not constitute an abuse within the meaning of Article 82 EC.[350] Arguably, abusive conduct of non-dominant firms and unilateral conduct of dominant firms that does not fulfil the notion of abuse are outside the scope of Article 82 EC, so that the supremacy rule could not have prevented Member States from applying conflicting (stricter) national norms.[351] In any event, the second sentence of Article 3(2) of Regulation 1/2003 now explicitly acknowledges the Member States' freedom in this respect. Concerning unilateral conduct, there is consequently no strict convergence between national and Community competition law. It must be noted, though, that some convergence in Article 82 matters is indirectly achieved via Article 12(2) of Regulation 1/2003, which has a broader scope than Article 3(2) in that it does not differentiate between multilateral and unilateral conduct and therefore covers both.[352] The provision authorises NCAs to use information exchanged through the Network in evidence also for the purposes of applying national competition rules where these are applied in parallel to Community competition law—provided, however, that the application of the national rules 'does not lead to a different outcome'. Thus, where NCAs rely on evidence obtained through the Network, Article 12(2) ensures there is convergence between national and Community competition rules also with regard to unilateral conduct.

Uncertainties as to the exact scope of the convergence rule therefore only relate to Article 81 cases where there is an (actual or potential) effect on trade between Member States. The question arises whether, for these cases, it makes a difference for what reasons the agreement or practice is permitted (or, rather, not prohibited) under Article 81 EC or whether the

---

[349] An example of such a national rule is § 20(2) GWB (anti-discrimination rule for companies with relative market power vis-à-vis small and medium-sized firms). A similar provision, prohibiting the 'abus de dépendance économique' exists in France (Art L 420–2 of the Code de Commerce). See Stuyck, above n 321, 27.

[350] Dalheimer, in Dalheimer *et al*, above n 119, Art 3 no 16.

[351] See above n 315 and the accompanying text.

[352] Gerber and Cassinis, above n 188, 13.

first sentence of Article 3(2) of Regulation 1/2003 must be understood in the sense that an agreement which, despite its effects on intra-Community trade, is lawful according to the standards of Article 81 EC can under no circumstances be prohibited on the basis of national law. Three scenarios must be distinguished (see Figure 1).

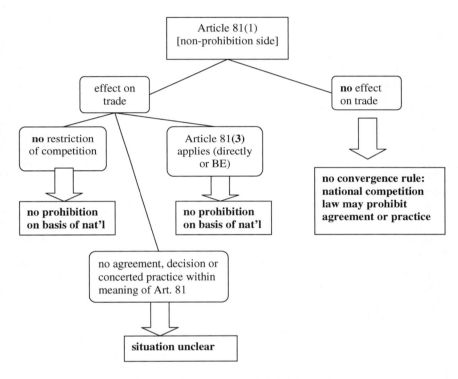

Figure 1: Convergence Rule of Art 3(2)

The first scenario, explicitly described in the first sentence of Article 3(2) of Regulation 1/2003, concerns agreements and practices which do not entail a restriction of competition within the meaning of Article 81(1) EC. These are, for instance, contracts which do not contain any anti-competitive clauses within the meaning of the EC competition rules.[353] But the provision equally covers agreements and practices which do restrict competition, whose anti-competitive effects are, however, considered non-appreciable within the meaning of the relevant jurisprudence of the

---

[353] Eg maximum prices and most-favoured clauses, which were regarded as (illegal) restrictions under German competition law, but not under the EC rules on competition. R Bechtold, *Kartellgesetz (Kommentar)* (Munich, Verlag CH Beck, 3rd edn, 2002), §14 nos 8–10.

Community courts.[354] This generally applies to agreements and practices which qualify as *de minimis* under the Commission notice on agreements of minor importance.[355] Such agreements and practices, according to the Commission, only have negligible effects on competition and thus are not banned by Article 81 EC. Normally, therefore, they may no longer be prohibited on the basis of stricter national competition rules,[356] not even if they affect a significant part of the relevant sales on the domestic territory of a particular Member State.[357]

The second scenario relates to agreements and practices which are restrictive of competition but which benefit from an exception either because they are covered by a block exemption regulation or because they otherwise fulfil the conditions for a legal exception pursuant to Article 81(3). This combination is also formally mentioned in the first sentence of Article 3(2) of Regulation 1/2003. Consequently, these 'exempted' agreements or practices may not be prohibited either on the basis of national competition law.[358] The principle thus seems to emerge that national law may only condemn what is equally condemned under Community competition law.

---

[354] The 'appreciable effects' doctrine is essentially based on the judgment of the ECJ in *Völk v Vervaecke* (above n 37).

[355] H Nyssens, 'Le règlement 1/2003 CE: vers une décentralisation et privatisation du droit de la concurrence' (2003) 109 *Tijdschrift voor Belgisch handelsrecht* 286, 289; Komninos, above n 79, 657 Dalheimer, in Dalheimer *et al*, above n 119, Art 3 no 14. See also E Paulis, 'Latest Commission Thinking and Progress on the Modernisation of Regulation 17' in X, *European Competition Law: A New Role for the Member States/Droit européen de la concurrence: un nouveau rôle pour les Etats membres* (Brussels, Bruylant, 2001), 15, 21. In practice, such a situation is unlikely to arise very often. Most agreements which do not appreciably restrict competition will not have appreciable effects on inter-state trade either and will already fall outside the scope of Art 81 EC for this reason. Rehbinder, above n 280, 310. See, however, para 16 of the EOT Guidelines, where the Commission, quoting the example of a selective distribution agreement based solely on quantitative criteria, argues that non-restrictive agreements also may affect trade between Member States. Cf also J Stuyck, 'L'effet réflexe du droit de la concurrence sur les normes de loyauté de la loi sur les pratiques du commerce (annotation de l'arrêt de la Cour de cassation du 7 janvier 2000 dans l'affaire *Multipharma c Louis Widmer*) 2001- 3 trim' (2001) *Revue critique de jurisprudence belge* 256, para 25, who equally seems to maintain that *de minimis* restrictions can indeed appreciably affect intra-Community trade. Nonetheless, it is submitted that this situation will be limited to very exceptional cases.

[356] Nyssens, *ibid*, 289; Nihoul, above n 324, paras 35–7. See also Stuyck, *ibid*, para 25. The latter author's proposition on the inapplicability of any *règle nationale de concurrence* to *de minimis* restrictions is based on Art 3 Draft Regulation, but is still valid in the present context. While the question arising under the Draft Regulation, in which the Commission had proposed a system of mutual exclusivity, was whether national competition law could be applied at all, the question to be tackled under Art 3(2) of Reg 1/2003 is whether more severe national antitrust rules may be applied. However, the positive answer to both questions depends on the same criterion, namely the absence of an appreciable effect on trade between Member State.

[357] Gilliams, above n 93, 463–4. The definition of the relevant market must of course be the same for the application of national and Community law. *Ibid.*

[358] Hossenfelder and Lutz, above n 346, 120; Nihoul, above n 324, para 44. See also Paulis, above n 355, 21.

Finally, the third scenario concerns the question of how understandings or (parallel) conduct which do not constitute agreements, concerted practices or decisions by an association within the meaning of Article 81(1) are to be treated. Such understandings and conduct may in fact be qualified differently under national law and thus may come within the ambit of a prohibition.[359] Certainly, the notions of 'agreement', 'decision' and 'concerted practice' as used in Article 81 EC are autonomous concepts of Community law. They must be defined and their existence evaluated in accordance with the Community rules.[360] If, however, this evaluation leads to the conclusion that there is no such agreement, concerted practice or decision, can Member States prohibit the relevant understanding or conduct? The wording of Article 3(2) of Regulation 1/2003 suggests that the convergence rule only applies where there is indeed an agreement, decision or concerted practice within the meaning of Article 81(1) and that Member States would thus be free to prohibit types of understandings or conduct which fall entirely outside the scope of that Treaty provision because they do not even qualify as an agreement, decision or concerted practice.[361]

However, when formulated as a general principle, the rule enshrined in the second sentence of Article 3(2) of Regulation 1/2003 seems to imply that Member States may, under no circumstances, condemn an understanding or conduct that is not equally condemned by Article 81(1).[362] On this basis, the convergence rule would indeed also apply where an NCA intends to prohibit an understanding or conduct which is not illegal under Article 81(1) EC simply because it does not reach the level of an agreement or concerted practice within the meaning of Community competition law.

From a Community perspective, the second option is obviously preferable because it effectively guarantees the creation of a level playing field for all undertakings in the EU. It has also been argued that applying different solutions at the national and Community levels would compromise the *effet utile* of Community law.[363] On the other hand, it is

---

[359] An example is price recommendations, which, under German law, used to be prohibited pursuant to § 22 GWB, but which are generally not covered by Art 81(1). See Bechtold, above n 83, 2428. (NB: The relevant German provision has been repealed by the 7. GWB-Novelle.)

[360] Idot, above n 161, para 38 (p 307).

[361] This also seems to be the position of Hossenfelder and Lutz, above n 346, 121; Rehbinder, above n 280, 310; and Idot, above n 161, para 38 (p. 307). Cf also sentences 3 and 4 of recital 8 of Reg 1/2003: 'To that effect it is necessary to provide that the application of national competition laws *to agreements, decisions or concerted practices within the meaning of Art 81(1) of the Treaty* may not lead to the prohibition of *such agreements, decisions and concerted practices* if they are not also prohibited under Community competition law. The notions of agreements, decisions and concerted practices are autonomous concepts of Community competition law covering the coordination of behaviour of undertakings on the market as interpreted by the Community Courts' (emphasis added).

[362] Cf Reg 1/2003, recital 8, sentence 3.

[363] Cf Nihoul, above n 324, para 42.

more difficult to reconcile with the wording of Article 3(2) of Regulation 1/2003. Moreover, the second interpretation would lead to a de facto suppression of national competition law for which there would be hardly any room left. Such a result would probably violate the principle of proportionality in that the de facto exclusion of national law would go beyond what is necessary to give full effect to the principles set out in Articles 81 and 82 EC.[364] It must be concluded that the convergence rule does not apply to understandings and conduct which do not qualify as agreements, concerted practices or decisions within the meaning of Article 81(1). Such understandings and conduct may be prohibited by NCAs on the basis of stricter national competition rules.

3. Co-operation with Other Competition Authorities in the ECN

Co-operation within the Network is mainly governed by Articles 11 and 12 of Regulation 1/2003, which set out rules for the exchange of (confidential) information, including evidence between competition authorities in the EU. The Network Notice supplements these rules. In addition, Article 22(1) of Regulation 1/2003 lays down the principle that the NCA of one Member State may carry out inspections in its own territory on behalf and for the account of the NCA of another Member State.[365]

a. General

There are two stages in the course of an investigation where information exchange between the competition authorities in the EU[366] is particularly

---

[364] Cf L Pace, 'Die Dezentralisierungspolitik im EG-Kartellrecht' (2004) 15 *Europäische Zeitschrift für Wirtschaftsrecht* 301, 304–5, who submits that, even on the basis that Art 3(2) of Reg 1/2003 excludes the application of stricter national rules only with regard to agreements, decisions and practices which fall within the scope of Art 81, the provision is illegal as it is disproportionate.

[365] As regards inspections solicited or ordered by the Commission, Art 22(2) of Reg 1/2003 provides that the NCAs of those Member States in whose territory the inspection is to be conducted shall, at the request of the Commission, undertake such inspection either alone or in collaboration with Commission officials. However, co-operation between the NCAs and the Commission in the course of inspections is not an entirely new element: Reg 17 already contained a similar provision. According to Art 14(5) of Reg 17, NCAs were obliged to assist the Commission, at its request, in carrying out inspections in their respective territory. There is an important difference between the two provisions, in that it appears that the primary responsibility for the conduct of the inspections has been shifted from the Commission to the NCAs. Under Reg 17, the inspections were usually carried out under the sole responsibility of the Commission, whose officials could be assisted by officials of the NCA of the Member States concerned. In contrast, under Reg 1/2003, the NCAs seems to be primarily responsible for conducting the inspections solicited or ordered by the Commission, while the Commission officials only provide assistance to the officials of the acting NCA. Schwarze and Weitbrecht, above n 331, 176, para 20. See also Idot, above n 161, 343, para 135, who is, however, less clear on the question of whether the new provision entails a shift of responsibility.

[366] The term 'competition authorities in the EU' is used to refer collectively to the Commission and the NCAs.

important: the very beginning of the proceedings and before their termination. Since Regulation 1/2003 establishes a system of parallel competences,
information exchange at the beginning of the proceedings, ie prior to the
first formal investigative measure, is primarily required to detect possible or
actual multiple proceedings and identify the authority or authorities that
is/are well placed to solve the competition problem at issue or simply to
reallocate a case to a well-placed authority. In other words, information
exchange at this stage is a pre-condition for an efficient division of the
work avoiding multiple control to the largest extent possible. The key
phrase here is 'case allocation'. The ECN must therefore be informed at an
early stage of the proceedings.

At the end of the investigation, prior to the adoption of a final decision,
the exchange of information on the course of action envisaged by the
NCA(s) is required in order to ensure the consistent application of EC
competition law throughout the Union. On the one hand, NCA decisions
that would run counter to an existing Commission decision must be
prevented. On the other hand, conflicting decisions between several NCAs
investigating the same matter must be avoided.

Accordingly, Article 11(3) and (4) of Regulation 1/2003 centralises the
flow of relevant information to the Commission. It stipulates that, at these
stages of the proceedings, certain information must be provided to the
Commission; the same information may also be given to other NCAs.
Pursuant to Article 12(2) of Regulation 1/2003, the information exchanged
may include confidential information.

Furthermore, competition authorities in the EU will have to liaise and
exchange information where one or several authorities require assistance in
fact-finding measures relating to the investigation of an alleged infringement of Article 81 or 82 EC. Such assistance will be particularly relevant
where a single NCA investigates an infringement involving companies or
affecting competition in several Member States and where therefore the
evidence is (also) located outside the territory of the investigating NCA.
Co-operation between NCAs may also be required where the same
infringement is investigated in parallel by several NCAs. In the latter case,
the coordination of the fact-finding measures of all NCAs acting on the
case and the subsequent exchange of evidence between them will be of
great importance. Articles 22(1) and 12(2) of Regulation 1/2003 lay down
the legal framework for such administrative co-operation and exchange of
evidence.

b. Information at the Beginning of the Procedure (Case Allocation)—Article
11(3) of Regulation 1/2003

A need for case allocation may not only arise where several NCAs are
contacted simultaneously or successively regarding the same alleged

infringement (eg a complaint lodged by an undertaking against several competitors in different Member States). Where the case is only brought to the attention of one NCA, the initial investigation may reveal that the agreement or practice at issue also has substantial effects in the territory of other Member States (eg a cartel that turns out to cover competitors not only in one Member State, but in several). In these cases, positive conflicts of jurisdiction may occur, ie several NCAs and even the Commission may consider themselves well placed and thus competent to investigate the matter.[367]

Consequently, Article 11(3) of Regulation 1/2003 imposes on the NCAs an obligation to inform the Commission of any procedure involving Article 81 or 82 EC before or immediately after the first formal investigative measure.[368] The information must be given in writing. It is foreseen that the information be provided by means of a standard form containing limited details of the case, such as the acting authority, the parties, products and territories concerned, the scope and suspected duration of the alleged infringement and the origin of the case.[369]

In order to detect multiple proceedings as early as possible and to allow for the Network to swiftly determine the competition authority that is 'best' placed to act in such cases, it should, however, be the rule that the above information is not only made available to the Commission, but is also provided directly to the other NCAs. However, pursuant to Article 11(3) of Regulation 1/2003, the provision of such information to other NCAs is not an obligation, but a mere faculty.

This is an example illustrating that the horizontal dimension of the decentralisation of EC competition law enforcement is underdeveloped in Regulation 1/2003. In the Network Notice, the Commission tries to remedy this omission by stating that the information given pursuant to

---

[367] Conversely, where an NCA receives a complaint but does not consider itself well placed to act or where the Commission does not want to pursue a matter for a lack of Community interest, a 'referral' of the case to the NCA which is well placed should be considered in order to avoid a negative conflict of jurisdiction, ie a situation where no competition authority investigates the matter. However, Reg 1/2003 does not provide that competition authorities inform each other when they reject a complaint or simply close an *ex officio* procedure. Apparently, the Commission feared that the information system within the Network would be overloaded with less relevant or even unimportant information if these types of decisions (or informal acts) were to be made available to all NCAs and the Commission. See Paulis, above n 95, 411, who points out that such decisions only bind the acting authority and therefore do not pose a real coherence problem. Nonetheless, in order to avoid enforcement lacunae, the simple closure of cases and rejection of complaints should also be systematically notified to the Network.

[368] The Commission, in turn, has to inform the NCAs of all competition cases where it envisages adopting a prohibition, commitment or positive decision, order interim measures or withdraw the benefits of a block exemption, pursuant to Art 11(2) of Reg 1/2003, by transmitting the most important documents of the case to the NCAs. However, this is not a new duty introduced in the course of the modernisation. An equivalent obligation of the Commission already existed under Art 10(1) of Reg 17.

[369] Para 17 of the Network Notice.

Article 11(3) of Regulation 1/2003 should be provided to both NCAs and the Commission. In practice, information on Article 81 or 82 EC cases pending before NCAs will therefore be made available, on a regular basis, to all members of the ECN. Since Article 12 of Regulation 1/2003 explicitly empowers the Commission and the NCAs to provide one another with confidential information, the fact that certain case details may be covered by the obligation of professional secrecy should not, in principle, hinder the exchange of such information within the Network.

The sharing of this information among all members of the Network will also allow NCAs to make ample use of Article 13(1) of Regulation 1/2003, which gives NCAs the right to suspend the proceedings before them or reject a complaint for the mere reason that another NCA is dealing with the case.[370] This provision evidently aims at avoiding unnecessary multiple proceedings regarding the same subject matter. However, it can only be applied if NCAs are effectively aware of the proceedings pending before their counterparts in other Member States.

c. Consultation Before Final Decision Taking—Article 11(4) of Regulation 1/2003

In order to enable the Commission to ensure a uniform application of the EC rules on competition, NCAs are required by Article 11(4) of Regulation 1/2003 to inform the Commission no later than 30 days before the adoption of certain types of final decisions about the proposed course of action. To this effect, they have to transmit a summary of the case and the contemplated decision or any other document indicating the envisaged course of action.[371]

It must be noted at the outset that the duty to inform the Commission in advance only applies with regard to three types of decisions. These are prohibitions, commitment decisions and decisions withdrawing the benefit of a block exemption, ie decisions that can be reversed only with difficulty, while decisions ordering interim measures, rejecting complaints or terminating *ex officio* procedures are not subject to the mandatory consultation process. With regard to these latter three types of decisions, Article 11(5) of Regulation 1/2003 establishes only a right, not an obligation.[372]

---

[370] Pursuant to Art 13(2) of Reg 1/2003, an NCA may even reject a complaint because another NCA has already dealt with the case irrespective of the outcome of that procedure before the other NCA.

[371] At the Commission's request, the NCA has to transmit further documents which are necessary for the assessment of the case (Reg 1/2003, Art 11(4), 4th sentence).

[372] In para 49 of the Network Notice, however, the Commission suggests that all members of the Network should inform each other at least of the termination of all those proceedings that have previously been communicated to the Network pursuant to Art 11(2) or (3) of Reg 1/2003. This is a logical step. Both the Commission and the NCAs need to know whether another

Since the rejection of a complaint and termination of an own-initiative procedure are said to bind only the NCA that adopted it and therefore do not preclude other NCAs or the Commission from investigating and prohibiting the same agreement or practice, such decisions were apparently considered not to pose a serious risk to the consistent application of the law. Interim measures were not submitted to the information duty since they are based on a preliminary assessment and would consequently not prejudice the outcome of the proceedings.[373] However, the Commission acknowledges in the Network Notice that these types of decisions (interim measures, rejection of complaints, closure of *ex officio* procedures) can also be important from a competition policy point of view and ECN members may therefore have an interest in informing each other about such decisions. The Commission continues to state that:

> NCAs can therefore . . . inform the Commission and thereby inform the network of any other case in which EC competition law is applied.[374]

This wording suggests that the information will ultimately be made available to the entire Network. Informing the Commission of the above types of decisions is not an issue since Article 11(5) of Regulation 1/2003 allows the NCAs to 'consult the Commission on any case involving the application of Community law'. Unlike in the case of prohibitions, commitment decisions and withdrawals of block exemptions, Regulation 1/2003 does not provide any legal basis for NCAs to transmit information concerning those other types of decisions directly to all NCAs. Therefore, such information must be channelled through the Commission pursuant to Article 11(5) of Regulation 1/2003. Apparently, the Commission intends to communicate such information provided by an NCA automatically to all other NCAs.

Prior consultation between the Commission and the acting NCA and, where necessary, intensive discussions can certainly help to avoid conflicting decisions. As *ultima ratio* in exceptional cases, the Commission can always de-seize the acting NCA pursuant to Article 11(6) of Regulation 1/2003 by initiating proceedings and itself adopting a decision. Thus, the Commission can prevent the NCA from taking a decision that would contradict its own decision practice or established case law.

However, coherence and consistency have not only a vertical dimension, but also a horizontal one. Regulation 1/2003 does not exclude parallel investigations by several NCAs relating to the same agreement or practice.

authority is still acting on a particular case since they may be confronted with complaints relating to the same matter or may want to take up the case—possibly suspended previously in accordance with Art 13(1) of Reg 1/2003—if the other NCA is no longer pursuing it.

[373] See A Schaub, 'The Commission's Position within the Network' in Ehlermann and Atanasiu, above n 201, 237, 244; Paulis, above n 95, 411.
[374] Para 48 of the Network Notice.

Such multiple proceedings may result in conflicting NCA decisions. Moreover, there may be variances in the legal approach taken by the NCAs towards the same type of agreement or practice. Such divergencies at national level may provide a real threat to the consistent application of the competition rules and to coherence across the EU. These horizontal aspects of decentralisation seem to have been neglected in Regulation 1/2003. In this respect, the information duty imposed on NCAs prior to the final decision taking vis-à-vis the Commission again contrasts with the mere option, under Article 11(3) of Regulation 1/2003, to inform the other NCAs of the proposed course of action.

In this case, the lack of mandatory rules on horizontal co-operation is not really remedied in the Network Notice. Paragraph 45 of the Network Notice only reiterates what is already stated in the third sentence of Article 11(4) of Regulation 1/2003, ie that the information *may* be shared by the NCA informing the Commission with the other members of the Network. That the Commission has indicated, in paragraph 48 of the Network Notice, it will automatically forward certain voluntary information (ie information regarding rejection of complaints and closure of procedures) to all NCAs may partly resolve the problem in practice, but cannot conceal the fact that Regulation 1/2003 lags behind what would have been required to legally ensure full horizontal co-operation.

d. Administrative Assistance (Co-operation in Fact-finding)

Since Articles 81 and 82 EC only apply to the extent that trade between Member States may be affected, it is likely that a (cartel) investigation under these provisions will concern more than one Member State. Typically, the suspected cartel members will be located in different Members States and/or there will be complainants or affected customers in several Member States. Consequently, the relevant evidence will often be scattered over a number of Member States and may therefore require inspections to be conducted in all those countries. It is, however, the objective of Regulation 1/2003 that cases be dealt with by a single NCA as often as possible.[375] At the same time, an NCA can carry out inspections and make formal requests for information only within the territory of the Member State to which it belongs, and is therefore placed at a serious disadvantage when (part of) the relevant evidence is likely to be found outside its own territory. On this basis, it would hardly be feasible to have the majority of EC competition cases handled by a single NCA.

Therefore, Regulation 1/2003 creates the possibility for NCAs to obtain administrative assistance from other NCAs where inspections or other fact-finding measures have to be conducted outside their own territory.

---

[375] See recital 18 of Reg 1/2003 and para 7 of the Network Notice.

Article 22(1) of Regulation 1/2003 establishes the rule that an NCA may carry out, in its own territory, fact-finding measures on behalf and for the account of the NCAs of other Member States (hereafter 'foreign investigations'). This procedure enables an NCA that investigates a particular case in a way to 'instruct' or 'delegate' tasks to other NCAs and have them conduct inspections and other specific fact-finding measures in their respective territory which the investigating NCA considers necessary. The evidence collected as a result of such foreign investigations may be exchanged, albeit within certain boundaries.[376] The investigating NCA is thus in a position to gather evidence which, because of its limited territorial powers, it would otherwise not have been able to obtain.

The weakness of Article 22(1) of Regulation 1/2003 lies in the fact that it establishes only a right, not a duty.[377] NCAs may conduct inspections in their territory that have been asked for by another NCA, but they are not obliged to comply with such a request.[378] By contrast, where the Commission requires the assistance of an NCA, that authority '*shall* undertake the inspections which the Commission considers to be necessary'.[379] This rule demonstrates the centralising effects of Regulation 1/2003, while the horizontal, decentralising elements again seem to have been marginalised.

Moreover, the exchange of information collected in the course of foreign investigations must be carried out in accordance with Article 12 of Regulation 1/2003. This provision puts certain restrictions on the use in evidence of material exchanged between NCAs. In particular, Article 12(3) of Regulation 1/2003 precludes the receiving NCA from using the evidence to impose sanctions on natural persons where the law of the transmitting NCA neither provides for sanctions of a similar kind nor guarantees the same level of protection of the rights of defence of natural persons as the national rules in the Member State of the receiving NCA. In any event, the receiving NCA may not impose custodial sanctions on the basis of evidence transmitted by another NCA unless the law of the transmitting NCA also provides for the sanction of imprisonment. This provision evidently raises a lot of issues. Whether the sanctions foreseen in the national laws of the Member States are of a 'similar kind' will not always be easy to determine. It will probably be even more difficult to verify whether the national laws

---

[376] Reg 1/2003, Art 22(1), 2nd sentence provides: 'Any exchange and use of the information collected shall be carried out in accordance with Article 12.'

[377] However, see below Chapter 4, nn 5 and 206.

[378] The possibility of an NCA refusing such administrative assistance is of course subject to the duty of loyal co-operation enshrined in Art 10 EC. Y Van Gerven, 'Regulation 1/2003: Inspections ("Dawn Raids") and the Rights of Defence' in C Baudenbacher (ed), *Neueste Entwicklungen im europäischen und internationalen Kartellrecht (Dreizehntes St. Galler Internationales Kartellrechtsforum 2006)* (Basel, Helbing & Lichtenhahn, 2007), 326, 339. See further below Chapter 2, n 159.

[379] Emphasis added. Art 22(2) of Reg 1/2003.

at issue ensure 'the same level of protection of the rights of defence'. Finally, it is not entirely clear whether a lack of the equivalence required by Article 12(3) of Regulation 1/2003 would already restrict the right of the NCA possessing the information to transmit it or only preclude the receiving NCA from using the material in evidence. It is likely that uncertainties regarding the question of whether the requirement of equivalence is fulfilled will in many cases effectively prevent NCAs from exchanging evidence.[380]

In spite of these difficulties regarding the operation of Article 12 of Regulation 1/2003, it is clear that the possibility for an NCA to obtain administrative assistance from other NCAs with regard to fact-finding measures to be conducted outside its territory is a prerequisite for having (cross-border) cases assigned to a single NCA.[381] Article 22(1) of Regulation 1/2003 is therefore a necessary complement to the allocation principles,[382] without which decentralisation would not be feasible.

4. Co-operation Between NCAs and the National Judiciary

Regulation 1/2003 gives NCAs the possibility to co-operate with national courts. In fact, Article 15(3) of Regulation 1/2003 empowers not only the Commission, but also the NCAs, to submit written observations, in national court proceedings, on issues concerning the application of Article 81 or 82 EC. Like the Commission, NCAs can make such submissions on their own initiative, ie without requiring the permission of the national court. With the consent of the judge concerned, NCAs may also present oral observations.[383]

It is not, however, foreseen by Regulation 1/2003 that NCAs can make submissions at the national courts of all Member States. The power of an NCA to intervene in court proceedings is limited to the national courts of

---

[380] Cf Riley, above n 133, 611.

[381] Cf also p 11 of the Explanatory Memorandum, which points out that as a result of market integration evidence and information will increasingly be located in several Member States.

[382] See in particular para 7 of the Network Notice.

[383] The differentiation between written submissions, which may be filed without approval of the national court, and oral observations, which may only be presented with the court's consent, was apparently introduced at a late stage of the drafting of Reg 1/2003 in order to address concerns that the *amicus curiae* provisions would compromise the impartiality and independence of the national judge. See B Ponet, 'Enige beschouwingen over de moderniserings-verordening vanuit het perspectief van de Raad voor de Mededinging' in J Stuyck and Wytinck (eds), *De Belgische Mededingingswet anno 2003* (Mechelen, Kluwer, 2003), 75, 84. The Draft Regulation in fact did not distinguish between written and oral submissions. It is unclear, however, why, in the case of oral observations, potential bias would be avoided by the court's consent to the authority making such observations. Even if this was the case, it would then be unclear why such a consent is not required for written submissions. After all, the observations of the NCA (or the Commission) may prove to be influential regardless of whether they are presented orally or in written form, and whether or not the national court has consented to their presentation. The above concerns are therefore likely to persist.

its own Member State.[384] There is another important difference between the intervention as *amicus curiae* of the Commission and that of an NCA. The Commission is only entitled to submit written observations where the coherent application of Article 81 or 82 EC so requires. By contrast, NCAs may always intervene in national court proceedings regarding the application of EC competition law irrespective of any coherency issue. It should also be noted that the intervention by an NCA is the first alternative stated in Article 15(3) of Regulation 1/2003, while intervention by the Commission is mentioned second only.

These differences seem to indicate that the *amicus curiae* instrument is intended to be first and foremost in the hands of the NCAs.[385] It may represent an attractive tool in particular for those NCAs that wish to take a proactive stance. Besides, the reluctance of national courts to accept 'interference' from the own NCA may be less pronounced than the reluctance to tolerate the intervention of the Commission.

Problems may, however, occur where the competent NCA is a judicial or quasi-judicial body. In this case, the national judge may be less inclined to accept the intervention of the NCA, as it may be perceived as paternalism by a colleague. Moreover, intervention by an NCA might be characterised as an 'abuse' of the instrument of *amicus curiae* submissions where it is seemingly used with a view to influencing proceedings before a court that will eventually decide on the lawfulness of an enforcement decision of that same NCA. Obviously, such intervention in matters where it has a vested interest (*in eigener Sache*) is not the purpose of the *amicus curiae* system. Where the matter concerns an actual review procedure, ie an appeal against the NCA decision, that procedure should be conducted exclusively on the basis of the domestic rules applicable to such review and the NCA involved should remain within the confines of those national procedural rules and not take recourse to Article 15(3) of Regulation 1/2003. Where the case concerns a private law dispute in which the lawfulness of the NCA decision must be assessed incidentally, it may be wise for the relevant NCA to refrain from interfering. It should respect the guidelines of the national legislator in terms of separation of powers or division of competences between different courts.

Pursuant to the second subparagraph of Article 15(3) of Regulation 1/2003, the national court has to provide the NCA, upon the latter's specific request, with any document that the NCA requires for an appropriate assessment of the case and the preparation of a qualitatively

---

[384] See the wording of Art 15(3) of Reg 1/2003 ('to the national courts of *their* Member State' (emphasis added)) and the Explanatory Memorandum, 23.

[385] Edward suggests that, in view of the Commission's limited resources, NCAs should be made primarily responsible for assisting national courts. Edward, above n 122, 568. The wording of Art 15(3) of Reg 1/2003 does not in fact exclude the assumption that the Commission intended to leave the main responsibility for *amicus curiae* interventions to the NCAs.

satisfactory submission. There is, however, a practical difficulty with regard to the possibility for NCAs to make such a specific request. Unlike the Commission, NCAs are not automatically informed of national cases involving an application of Article 81 or 82 EC unless the national law of the Member State provides for an obligation to notify the NCA of all cases involving competition law issues[386] or forward copies of all relevant judgments also to the NCA.[387] As a consequence, NCAs may not even be aware of court proceedings that warrant an intervention as *amicus curiae*. This is another example demonstrating the rudimentary treatment of the horizontal aspects of modernisation by Regulation 1/2003. The imbalance of the information process, as laid down in Regulation 1/2003, increases the burden on the Commission, which would have to monitor national courts largely on its own. Ultimately, interventions by NCAs would then depend on the Commission informing the NCAs of court cases for which it might be appropriate to submit observations.

It is probably also in view of this hurdle that the Commission has stated its intention to co-operate closely with the NCAs in exercising its powers under Article 15 of Regulation 1/2003.[388] Indeed, the Commission seems to develop a practice of 'delegating' the submission of *amicus curiae* briefs to NCAs, thereby allowing them to effectively co-operate with the national courts in their Member State. A first step in this direction has already been made by the Commission. Non-confidential versions of all national judgments which it receives are published—in their original language—on DG Comp's website.[389] This allows all NCAs, including those which are not informed automatically on the basis of national provisions, to monitor the decision practice of the courts in their own Member State, provided, of course, that the NCA has the necessary resources for this exercise. NCAs can thus consider independently whether or not a particular matter warrants their intervention as *amicus curiae*, pursuant to Article 15(3) of Regulation 1/2003, at the appeal level.

C. The Position of the National Courts

One of the stated objectives of the Commission's reform proposal was to

---

[386] In Germany, for example, national courts are required to inform the Bundeskartellamt of all matters involving the application of national or EC competition law (see § 90(1) GWB).

[387] Pursuant to Art 15(2) of Reg 1/2003, national judgments are to be sent only to the Commission. However, where NCAs also obtain copies of all relevant judgments, they can—like the Commission—at least consider intervening at the appeal level. In Belgium, for example, both the Competition Council (Raad voor de Mededinging) and the Competition Service (Dienst voor de Mededinging) receive every judgment of a national court which raises antitrust issues, whether under national or Community competition law. See Art 74 of the Belgian Competition Act (consolidated version; see below Chapter 2, n 45).

[388] Note 18 of the Network Notice.

[389] See above n 236.

have national courts play an enhanced role in the application of EC competition law.

1. The Role of National Courts under Regulation 17

It is settled case law that Articles 81(1) and 82 EC have a direct effect and create rights for the benefit of individuals which the national courts must safeguard.[390] However, due to the Commission's exemption monopoly under Regulation 17, national courts were previously prevented from applying Article 81(3). This meant that they could not themselves grant an exemption and therefore could not reject an unjustified 'Euro-defence'[391] by ruling in favour of the validity of an (restrictive) agreement which had not been exempted by the Commission. In cases where it was doubtful whether the agreement would merit exemption, court proceedings could effectively be blocked for a long time if one of the parties invoked Article 81(3) and applied for an individual exemption. In that event, the national judge had to suspend the proceedings since it had to avoid handing down a judgment which would run counter to a decision envisaged by the Commission.[392] Only in cases where the national court could not reasonably doubt the Commission's contemplated decision (eg because the agreement was manifestly not eligible for individual exemption) could it decide the case without awaiting the outcome of the Commission procedure.[393] Consequently, the role of national courts was curtailed and frustrated to some extent. In fact, the Commission considers that the possibility, under Regulation 17, of being confronted with so-called dilatory notifications was a major obstacle to a more extensive and more frequent application of the EC competition rules by national courts.[394]

2. The Enhanced Role of National Courts in the New System

In a directly applicable exception system, these obstacles no longer exist. Under Regulation 1/2003, the courts of the Member States, like the NCAs, are entitled to apply Article 81(1) and (3). They may thus rule on the

---

[390] Case 127/73 *BRT v SABAM* [1974] ECR 51, para 16.

[391] Euro-defence means that the incompatibility of an agreement with Art 81(1), and hence its voidness pursuant to Art 81(2), is raised as a defence to an action for performance of contractual obligations.

[392] These principles deriving from the duty of sincere co-operation laid down in Art 10 (ex Art 5) EC were first established by the ECJ in *Delimitis* (n 251), paras 47–55, and then further developed in *Masterfoods* (n 239), paras 45 *et seq*. They are now 'codified' in Art 16(1) of Reg 1/2003. See Gerber and Cassinis, above n 188, 51. Komninos, above n 215, 1392, notes that the *Masterfoods* principles have indeed been incorporated verbatim.

[393] Cf para 50 of the *Delimitis* judgment (n 251). See also para 30 of the 1993 Commission notice on co-operation between national courts and the Commission in applying Arts 85 and 86 of the EEC Treaty, [1993] OJ 39/6 ('1993 Co-operation Notice').

[394] White Paper, para 100.

(in)compatibility of a restrictive agreement or practice with the EC Treaty without having to stay proceedings and await a Commission decision. As in the case of national authorities dealing with competition matters, the right of national courts to apply Article 81 as a whole is coupled with the obligation to apply this provision (and Article 82 EC) in all cases where national competition law is applied and trade between Member States may be affected.[395]

Undoubtedly, the new system purports to give national courts a greater role in the application of EC competition law. The Commission believes that enforcement by national courts has certain advantages compared to administrative action by the Commission. As it points out in the White Paper, national courts are close to European citizens.[396] In contrast to the Commission, national courts can rule on claims for payment or performance of contractual obligations and award damages to victims of anti-competitive agreements or practices. Moreover, the successful party can usually obtain recovery of its legal costs. Finally, national courts are often better placed to adopt interim measures than the Commission.[397]

Evidently, the Commission focuses only on one aspect of the involvement of national courts in the enforcement of EC competition law, notably private litigation. That is to say, the White Paper lists three kinds of proceedings in which national courts apply Article 81, all of them civil law actions. These are (i) contractual liability proceedings (ie disputes between the parties to an agreement about the legality/validity of the agreement); (ii) non-contractual liability proceedings (ie claims against the parties of an alleged infringement by third parties); and (iii) applications for injunctions.[398] The Commission's main concern is to increase private enforcement of EC competition law.[399]

However, there are two more categories of proceedings—not mentioned in the White Paper—in which national courts may be called upon to apply Articles 81 and 82 EC. These are administrative proceedings and, in certain Member States, even criminal[400] or quasi-criminal prosecu-

---

[395] Art 3(1) of Reg 1/2003.

[396] Para 99 of the White Paper.

[397] These advantages were already stressed by the Commission in para 16 of the 1993 Cooperation Notice and are highlighted again in para 16 of the Notice on Complaints. See also para 100 of the White Paper.

[398] Para 99 of the White Paper.

[399] See also page 9 of the Explanatory Memorandum: 'As the proposal aims at increasing the level of private enforcement before national courts . . .'.

[400] See Edward, above n 122, 565. In Denmark, Ireland, Malta, the UK, Greece, Estonia and France, the sanctions imposed for competition law breaches are (partly) considered to be of a criminal nature. Four of these Member States (France, Ireland, Estonia and the UK) have enacted legislation pursuant to which the infringement of (EC) competition rules may even be punished by imprisonment. (NB: Specific national legislation on bid rigging/collusive tendering has not been included in this analysis.) See C Gauer, 'Does the Effectiveness of the EU Network of Competition Authorities Require a Certain Degree of Harmonisation of National Procedures and Sanctions?' in Ehlermann and Atanasiu, above n 201, 187, 198. Imprisonment for

tions.[401] In particular, the increased relevance of administrative proceedings, ie proceedings where national courts act as judicial review bodies in appeal cases against NCA decisions, should not be neglected. These proceedings will play an enhanced role in the new system. Many more review decisions involving an assessment of Article 81 or 82 EC can be expected, corresponding to the greater number of NCA decisions applying Article 81 or 82 EC that are likely to result from the decentralisation.[402]

Finally, depending on the national enforcement system in place,[403] national courts may also act as public enforcer, meaning that it is a court rather than an administrative body that adopts infringement decisions pursuant to Article 81 or 82 EC. In that event, the national court(s) will be designated by the Member State concerned as the responsible competition authority in accordance with Article 35(1) of Regulation 1/2003.[404]

In all cases where national courts apply EC competition law (or any other directly effective provision of Community law), they act as Community courts.[405] However, their decisions remain national acts which have effects only *inter partes*.[406] Nonetheless, it can be concluded that Regulation 1/2003 transfers a significant part of the responsibility for the

---

competition law violations is also possible in Romania and the Slovak Republic (see Roth and Rose, above n 138, para 14.171 (p 1494)). Recently, the Dutch legislator considered (and still considers) the option 'to go criminal'. On this 'trend' towards criminalisation of competition law infringements. which is also evident in the Netherlands, see F Vogelaar, 'Interface: EC and Dutch Competition Law—In Which Fields or Areas Would the Netherlands Still Have Autonomous Regulating Powers?' in Obradovic and Lavranos, above n 74, 185, 196–9. As a (preliminary) result of the ongoing debate in the Netherlands, the Dutch Competition Act, as of 1 October 2007, provides for a dual system whereby the NCA can not only penalise undertakings, but also impose fines on individuals who gave instructions or exercised de facto leadership with regard to the illegal activities (Art 56 Mededingingswet NL in conjunction with Art 51 Wetboek van Strafrecht (Dutch Criminal Code)). See M Mok, 'Mededingingswet weer gewijzigd' (2008) 56 *Sociaal-Economische Wetgeving* 226, 230. However, these fines are still qualified as administrative sanctions (F Vogelaar, 'Criminalisering van het mededingingsrecht: trendy of noodzaak?' (2005) 54 *Ars Aequi* 1015, 1016–17).

[401] Under German law, for example, infringements of the competition rules are regulatory offences (*Ordnungswidrigkeiten*) which, in many respects (eg concerning certain rights of the defendants), are assimilated with criminal offences.

[402] See C-D Ehlermann and I Atanasiu, 'The Modernisation of EC Antitrust Law: Consequences for the Future Role and Function of the EC Courts' (2002) 23 *European Competition Law Review* 72, 75.

[403] See below Chapter 2, section I.A.2.

[404] Art 35(1) of Reg 1/2003 provides that the Member States shall designate the competition authority or authorities responsible for the application of Arts 81 and 82 EC. The authorities designated may include courts.

[405] Case T–51/89 *Tetra Pak v Commission* [1990] ECR II–309, para 42. See further J Temple Lang, 'The Duties of National Courts under Community Constitutional Law' (1997) 22 *EL Rev* 3.

[406] Paulis, above n 95, 420. It should be noted, however, that a large part of the competition law issues are likely to arise in commercial disputes falling within the scope of Reg 44/2001 under which national judgments can obtain recognition and be enforced in other Member States.

implementation of Articles 81 and 82 EC to the national courts of the Member States.[407]

3. Assistance Offered to National Courts

In a legal exception system, it is even more expedient to provide sufficient guidance to national judges and create an avenue for dialogue and co-operation between the national courts and the Commission in order to preserve the uniformity of EC competition law. The sheer number of decision-makers (national judges) involved in the application of the EC competition rules provides a realistic threat to consistency.

a. Assistance from the Commission

In order to ensure consistent application by the judiciary, the Commission will assist national courts in the three principal ways outlined above.[408] Pursuant to Article 15(1) of Regulation 1/2003, the national judge may ask the Commission for documents (eg statistical data, market studies) or other information (eg information of a procedural nature) in its possession. The national judge may also seek the Commission's advice in relation to economic, factual or legal matters (opinions). Furthermore, the Commission will submit observations (*amicus curiae* briefs) on its own initiative pursuant to Article 15(3) of Regulation 1/2003.

Article 15 of Regulation 1/2003 is largely based on the 1993 Co-operation Notice which, in turn, essentially follows the principles of sincere (or loyal) co-operation developed by the ECJ in *Delimitis*[409] and *Zwartfeld*.[410] According to this case law, Article 10 (ex Article 5) EC imposes on the European institutions and the Member States mutual duties of loyal co-operation. The duty of sincere co-operation imposed on Community institutions is of particular importance vis-à-vis the judicial authorities of the Member States. It is therefore incumbent upon every Community institution and, above all, the Commission to give active assistance to the judiciary.[411]

The possibility for national courts to request procedural or factual information from the Commission or consult the Commission on points of law was provided in the 1993 Co-operation Notice,[412] which was not a legis-

---

[407] Edward, above n 122, 565.
[408] See above, section II.A.1.b(3).
[409] See in particular paras 50–3 of that judgment (n 251).
[410] Case C–2/88 Imm *Zwartveld and others* [1990] ECR I–3365, paras 17–22.
[411] *Ibid*, paras 18 and 22. O'Keeffe, however, takes the view that the duty of sincere cooperation weighs far more heavily on the national courts than on the Commission. S O'Keeffe, 'First Among Equals: The Commission and the National Courts as Enforcers of EC Competition Law' (2001) 26 *EL Rev* 300, 308.
[412] Paras 37–40.

lative act, but a simple communication of the Commission merely setting out its intentions. Article 15(1) of Regulation 1/2003 has converted these principles into a legally binding instrument.

However, Regulation 1/2003 does not simply codify the informal co-operation mechanisms already provided for by the 1993 Co-operation Notice. The Commission clearly wanted to strengthen the co-operation with national courts and therefore introduced a completely new instrument, the submission of *amicus curiae* briefs. This form of imposed assistance represents a novel and quite far-reaching form of co-operation with national courts in that Article 15 (3) of Regulation 1/2003 empowers the Commission to intervene in national court proceedings entirely on its own initiative, ie without invitation or even permission of the national judge(s) concerned. Only the presentation, by the Commission, of oral observations requires the consent of the national court.

It is obvious that, in view of the fundamental principle of separation of powers, national judges and courts can neither co-operate nor be coordinated *sensu stricto* when applying EC competition law.[413] Co-operation with the judiciary of the Member States therefore is a far more delicate task than co-operation with administrative bodies such as NCAs. On the other hand, the co-operation mechanisms may be extremely useful where there is a risk of conflicting decisions in a matter pending before a national court and the Commission. In such an event, Article 16(1) of Regulation 1/2003 suggests that the national court should stay its proceedings and await the Commission's decision.[414] However, initiating one or the other form of co-operation with the Commission under Article 15 of Regulation 1/2003[415] may provide a viable alternative to such a stay of proceedings. There may thus be a strong incentive for national courts to effectively seek

---

[413] Ehlermann, above n 13, 580–1. See also Devroe, above n 223, para 21.

[414] The provision prohibits national courts from taking decisions that would run counter to an existing Commission decision on the same subject matter and obliges them to avoid giving decisions that would conflict with a contemplated Commission decision. Commission decisions are thus effectively binding upon national courts to the extent that they relate to the same agreement or conduct which is at issue in the court proceedings. (This is *contra* Komninos, above n 215, 1395, who submits that Commission decisions are not positively binding. Rather, Art 16(1) of Reg 1/2003 imposes a negative duty of abstention on national courts. The difference between the two views seems to be a purely acadamic one having little or even no impact at all in practice.) Art 16(1) of Reg 1/2003 will play an important role in the context of private enforcement where private parties seek compensation of their loss sustained as a result of a violation of the Community competition rules after the Commission has adopted an infringement decision (so-called follow-on actions) because it will allow the plaintiffs to rely on the Commission's findings. See W Van Gerven, 'Private Enforcement of EC Competition Rules in the ECJ—Courage v Crehan and the Way Ahead' in J Basedow (ed), *Private Enforcement of EC Competition Law* (Kluwer Law International, 2007), 19, 25; E De Smijter, 'Het Groenboek van de Commissie omtrent schadevorderingen wegens schending van de Europese mededingingsregels' (2007) 2 *TBM-RCB* 3, para 14.

[415] Which would arguably include the possibility of 'inviting' the Commission to submit an *amicus curiae* brief.

the Commission's assistance.[416] In fact, the specific mechanisms laid down in Article 15 of Regulation 1/2003 provide all the opportunities for closer interaction between the Commission/NCAs and the national judiciary, thereby creating a sort of 'expanded network' which embraces all European bodies that apply competition law, including judges.[417] However, it is uncertain how national courts will actually receive these partly unprecedented co-operation instruments.

b. Assistance from NCAs

Regulation 1/2003 does not provide for any rules enabling national courts to address themselves to their NCA in order to obtain advice on factual, procedural or legal questions relating to the application of Article 81 or 82 EC. The question of whether a national judge can obtain, at his or her request, the assistance of the NCA therefore depends on the domestic law of the Member State concerned.[418]

The situation is, however, different with regard to own-initiative interventions by the NCAs. Article 15(3) of Regulation 1/2003 empowers not only the Commission, but also the NCAs, to intervene, on their own initiative, as *amicus curiae* in proceedings before the national court of the same Member State if the application of Article 81 or 82 EC is at issue. This power of the NCAs is not limited to cases which raise a coherency problem.[419]

Regulation 1/2003 does not oblige national courts to inform the NCA of their Member State systematically of all pending cases or at least all judgments involving the application of Article 81 or 82 EC. Therefore, where such a duty is not established by national legislation, NCAs may not be aware of some or all proceedings relating to the application of EC competition law. However, nothing prevents national courts from making such cases known to the NCA informally on a voluntary basis. In this way, a national court might be able to trigger an intervention of the NCA pursuant to Article 15(3) of Regulation 1/2003 in a case where it wishes to obtain the NCA's assistance and the national law does not provide the possibility for the court to turn to the NCA for formal

---

[416] R Nazzini, 'Parallel and Sequential Proceedings in Competition Law: An Essay on the Modes of Interaction between Community and National Law (2005) 16 *European Business Law Review* 245, 268–9.

[417] Gerber and Cassinis, above n 188, 54.

[418] Under French law, for example, national courts can request advice from the Conseil de la concurrence, the French Competition Council. See Art L462–3 of the Code de Commerce. (NB: The French rules on competition have been integrated into Part IV (Livre IV) of the Code de Commerce under the heading 'De la liberté des prix et de la concurrence'.) The possibility of a national court requesting an opinion under Art 15(1) of Reg 1/2003 is limited to opinions of the Commission.

[419] See further above section II.B.4.

advice.[420] To the extent that this option is not exercised, *amicus curiae* interventions by NCAs will depend on the Commission informing the NCAs of court cases for which it might be appropriate to submit observations, unless all Member States introduce rules similar to the information duties contained in the German competition act or the right to obtain advice from the Conseil de la concurrence existing under French law.[421]

c. Preliminary References to the ECJ

The Commission has always stressed that the above mechanisms for co-operation with national courts are without prejudice to the existing possibility for national courts to refer a question to the ECJ for a preliminary ruling pursuant to Article 234 (*ex* Article 177) EC.[422] This formal avenue for co-operation between national courts and the ECJ, which has been in place since the Treaty of Rome, is well known and constitutes the central vein (*levensader*) of the Community legal order.[423] It may play an even greater role in the new system. There will be an increasing number of national procedures for judicial review of decisions taken by NCAs on the basis of Articles 81 and 82 EC. These review cases will of course be pending before national courts. It is likely, however, that national judges, when reviewing such NCA decisions based on Articles 81 and 82 EC, will feel the need to request a preliminary ruling from the ECJ more often than in the past.[424] It can be assumed that Article 234 references will in particular be made with respect to the interpretation of Article 81(3).[425] One may also expect that national courts will more frequently refer questions regarding the interpretation and validity of Commission acts such as regulations (eg block exemptions), decisions, notices and guidelines issued in relation to the implementation of Articles 81 and 82 EC.

On the other hand, the Commission apparently does not consider that the preliminary reference procedure is adequate to ensure consistency.[426] It is true that the ECJ gives authoritative and binding answers to the questions referred to it, while the Commission's opinions and observations

---

[420] Even if the NCA has been informed of the case only in very general terms and therefore requires additional information for the preparation of an appropriate submission, an *amicus curiae* intervention is still possible. Pursuant to Reg 1/2003, Art 15(3), 2nd subpara, the NCA may request that the court provide it with any document necessary for the assessment of the case.

[421] See above nn 386 and 418.

[422] Explanatory Memorandum, 23; White Paper, para 27.

[423] Van Der Woude, above n 226, 176.

[424] Ehlermann and Atanasiu, above n 402, 75–6; see also Explanatory Memorandum, 9, where the Commission anticipates an 'initial increase in Art 234 references' due to the fact that the reform aims at increasing the level of private enforcement.

[425] Ehlermann and Atanasiu, above n 402, 76.

[426] Cf White Paper, para 107; Explanatory Memorandum, 9 and 22; Jones and Sufrin, above n 152 (1st edn), 1029.

provided pursuant to Article 15(1) and (3) of Regulation 1/2003 are not binding on the national courts. However, an Article 234 reference inevitably causes serious delays of at least 18 months.[427] National courts may therefore be reluctant to make an Article 234 reference unless they are obliged to do so because they are courts of last instance.[428] The possibility of seeking the Commission's advice pursuant to Article 15(1) of Regulation 1/2003 may therefore appear as a welcome alternative.[429] The Commission has indeed committed itself to providing the requested opinion within four months from the date it receives the request of the national court.[430] On the other hand, it seems a difficult, if not impossible, mission for the Commission to always remain neutral and objective in its assistance and deliver useful (legal or economic) advice without considering the merits of the case.[431] But approaching the Commission has another important advantage. The ECJ only replies to questions of law, while competition law cases are heavily fact-based. Therefore, the request for a Commission opinion which can relate to procedural, legal and economic matters is a valuable complement to the Article 234 procedure.[432]

In any event, which national bodies involved in the implementation of EC competition law can refer questions to the ECJ under the Article 234 EC procedure still needs to be clarified. Obviously, in terms of procedural economy, it would be best if references from all NCAs were admissible. In this way, problems regarding the applicability and interpretation of the Community's competition rules could be tackled at the earliest possible stage of the proceedings.[433] However, it is unlikely that all NCAs could be

---

[427] Jones and Sufrin, above n 152 (1st edn), 1029. According to Goyder, above n 13, 561, Art 234 references normally took up to 21 months. In 2006, the average duration of proceedings in preliminary reference matters was 19.8 months (see Court of Justice, 2006 Annual Report, 87).

[428] Jones and Sufrin, above n 152 (1st edn), 1029. The Commission also stresses the 'need for flexible and rapid mechanisms'. White Paper, para 104.

[429] Yet, consultation with the Commission can certainly not entirely replace the preliminary ruling procedure in that the authoritative interpretation of Community law is an exclusive competence of the ECJ, whose judgments are binding and thus guarantee a higher degree of consistency and legal certainty. See H Tagaras and M Waelbroeck, 'Les autorités nationales de la concurrence et l'article 234 du Traité. Un étrange arrêt de la Cour de justice' (2005) 41 *Cahiers de Droit Européen* 465, 473; A Leopold and E Reiche, 'Zur Vorlageberechtigung mitgliedstaatlicher Wettbewerbsbehörden nach Art 234 EG' (2005) 16 *Europäische Zeitschrift für Wirtschaftsrecht* 143, 144.

[430] Para 28 of the National Courts Notice. If the national court only requests factual information (documents, information of a procedural nature, statistical data etc), the Commission will endeavour to transmit such information within 1 month from receipt of the request.

[431] See paras 19 and 29 of the National Courts Notice.

[432] Paulis, above n 95, 406. Where the Commission actually provides (pure) legal advice, this obviously again raises problems in terms of separation of powers.

[433] G Anagnostaras, 'Preliminary Problems and Jurisdiction Uncertainties: The Admissibility of Questions Referred by Bodies Performing Quasi-judicial Functions' (2005) 30 *EL Rev* 878, 881; A Komninos, 'Art 234 and National Competition Authorities in the Era of Decentralisation' (2004) 29 *EL Rev* 106, 113. Moreover, these issues would be addressed at a stage where a specialised body (as opposed to an ordinary review court) is dealing with the matter which may

classified as judicial bodies within the meaning of Article 234 EC, which reserves the right to request a preliminary ruling of the ECJ to courts and tribunals of the Member States. In *BRT v SABAM*, the ECJ distinguished between those courts which derive their competence to apply Community competition law from Article 84 EC and thus were to be considered as competition authorities for the purposes of Regulation 17 and those courts which apply these competition rules in civil litigation cases between private parties, ie by virtue of their direct effect.[434] The latter type, it is submitted, are traditional civil courts, which will in principle always qualify as a court or tribunal within the meaning of Article 234 EC.[435] However, the distinction drawn by the ECJ in *BRT v SABAM* does not mean that those national judicial bodies that were considered NCAs for the purposes of Regulation 17 or now Regulation 1/2003 are excluded per se from the preliminary reference procedure.[436] Indeed, the judgment of the ECJ in *Spanish Banks* originated from a reference for a preliminary ruling under Article 234 EC submitted by the Spanish competition tribunal, the Tribunal de Defensa de la Competencia (TDC), which until 2007 was the competent authority in Spain to apply Articles 81 and 82 EC.[437] By contrast, in *Syfait*, the ECJ held that the Greek competition commission (Epitropi Antagonismou) did not qualify as a court or tribunal within the meaning of Article 234 EC.[438] The ECJ generally considers five factors in order to

have a positive impact on the relevance and quality of the questions actually referred to the ECJ. Anagnostaras, *ibid*, 881 and 887.

[434] Paras 14–19 of the judgment (n 390). In that case, the ECJ had to define the notion of national competition authority under the former Reg 17 in order to determine which bodies could be de-seized pursuant to Art 9(3) of that regulation by the Commission instituting proceedings. The exact term applied by Art 9(3) of Reg 17 is 'authorities of the Member States'. The provision corresponds to Art 11(6) of Reg 1/2003. See above, section II.A.1.b(2).

[435] *BRT v SABAM* is still good law, and more recent case law of the ECJ regarding the admissibility of references from NCAs (which will be discussed hereafter) does not invalidate the findings therein. See Tagaras and Waelbroeck, above n 429, 472.

[436] In fact, as Komninos, above n 433, 112, puts it, the terms 'authority' and 'court' as used in Art 35 of Reg 1/2003 have no bearing at all on the notion of 'court or tribunal' employed in Art 234 EC and vice versa.

[437] *See Case C–67/91 Dirección General de Defensa de la Competencia v Asociación Española de Banca Privada and others* ('*Spanish Banks*') [1992] ECR I–4785. Under Spanish law, the TDC used to be the primary body to ensure the enforcement of the domestic and Community competition rules together with the *Servicio Defensa de la Competencia* (SDC). While the latter was in charge of the enquiry phase, the TDC's main function was to rule on the existence (or non-existence) of an illegal restriction of competition. However, in the Spanish legal doctrine, the TDC was not considered part of the judiciary. See E Navarro Contreras, 'Chapter 15. Spain' in M Holmes and L Davey (eds), *A Practical Guide to National Competition Rules across Europe* (The Hague, Kluwer Law International, 2004), 313, 313–14. It is understood that, despite its name, the TDC was not a real court, but simply an independent administrative body. Curiously enough, the ECJ did not declare inadmissible the reference made by the TDC under Art 234 EC. (As of 1 September 2007, following the entry into force of the new Spanish Competition Act (Law Nr 15/2007 of 3 July 2007), TDC and SDC have been replaced by the newly created Comisión Nacional de la Competencia, an independent administrative body which combines the investigative and adjudicative functions of the former two agencies. Internally, however, investigative and adjudicative powers remain separated as the relevant functions are assumed by

determine whether a body qualifies as national court or tribunal and thus can make a reference under Article 234 EC.[439] One of these factors is whether the body is truly independent from the executive so as to constitute a third party distinct from those involved in the disputes before it.[440] The court's conclusion in *Syfait* was based on four considerations, which eventually all came down to denying the Greek competition commission the requisite independence. According to the ECJ, the Epitropi Antagonismou was subject to supervision by the Minister for Development; there were no particular safeguards as concerns the dismissal or removal from office of its members; the competition commission further had (too) close operational links with its secretariat, a fact-finding body which also makes proposals for the decisions to be taken by the commission; and finally it could be relieved of its competence in accordance with Article 11(6) of Regulation 1/2003.[441]

Apart from the fact that this judgment has been sharply criticised on grounds of factual inaccuracies,[442] the ruling does not exclude a priori that an NCA can qualify as a court within the meaning of Article 234 EC provided it has all the necessary characteristics of a court as established by the ECJ's case law, in particular in terms of safeguarding the independence of its members. Admittedly, *Syfait* seems to mark a shift in the case law towards a more stringent application of the independence criterion, which is probably to be welcomed. Instead of merely relying on the domestic classification of the referring body as independent, the ECJ puts emphasis on the existence of national provisions which effectively guarantee this independence, such as specific rules in respect of appointment, tenure of office and removal from office. The decisive factor thus is real functional independence (or operational freedom)

---

two different units within the Comisión, the investigations directorate and the council respectively. See E Navarro Varona and L Moscoso del Prado, 'New Spanish Law for the Defence of Competition' (2007) 28 *European Competition Law Review* 571, 571–2.)

[438] See Case C–53/03 *Syfait and others vs GlaxoSmithKline* [2005] ECR I–4609.

[439] See the judgment of the ECJ in Case C–54/96 *Dorsch Consult v Bundesbaugesellschaft* [1997] ECR I–4961, para 23. For a summary discussion of the relevant factors see Tagaras and Waelbroeck, above n 429, 475 *et seq* and Anagnostaras, above n 433, 883 *et seq*.

[440] See Anagnostaras, above n 433, 882.

[441] Paras 30–6 of the judgment in *Syfait* (n 438).

[442] Tagaras and Waelbroeck, above n 429, 479, contend that the court's assumption in para 30 of the judgment (according to which the Minister of Development can review the lawfulness of the decisions of the Epitropi Antagonismou) is inaccurate in that the Minister has specific powers only in merger control proceedings, but not in antitrust matters. Moreover, these powers do not constitute a legal review procedure, but simply entitle him to approve a merger which has previously been prohibited by the competition commission. Similarly, these authors note that the fact that the President of the competition commission is responsible for the coordination and general policy of the secretariat and can exercise disciplinary powers over its personnel would not make the competition commission dependent on the secretariat, but rather the other way round. Thus it would be inconceivable that the referring body (or its President) would be unduly influenced by the secretariat. *Ibid*, 483–4.

rather than structural autonomy.[443] This does not take away that the judgment in *Syfait* is criticisable on account of another important legal consideration. The ECJ based its findings, inter alia, on the fact that, pursuant to Article 11(6) of Regulation 1/2003, an NCA such as the Epitropi Antagonismou can be relieved of its competence, in which case the proceedings pending before it would not lead to a decision of a judicial nature.[444] However, this argument is not compelling. The ECJ seems to have overlooked the special arrangements contained in Regulation 1/2003 in respect of Member States where the final decision in competition matters is taken by a court or tribunal. Article 35(4) of Regulation 1/2003 namely provides that, if the national procedure involves

> a judicial authority which is separate and different from the prosecuting author-
> ity . . ., the effects of Article 11(6) shall be limited to the authority prosecuting
> the case which shall withdraw its claim before the judicial authority.

It is thus the declaration of the prosecuting body to abandon the matter which will actually lead to the termination of the procedure before the judicial authority. By incorporating this rule, the Community legislature clearly acknowledged the fact that 'real' courts of the Member States might be called upon to decide competition cases as NCAs, ie courts which are fully independent and form part of the state's judiciary. Such courts cannot simply be integrated into a hierarchy of agencies with the Commission as superior body, nor be instructed by the national administration. This is why Regulation 1/2003 had to make special provisions for such dual enforcement systems. While the Epitropi Antagonismou probably still does not qualify as a court, the Kartellgericht in Austria and the Stockholm District Court, both of which perform enforcement functions within the respective national competition system, are, in my view, true courts within the meaning of Article 234 EC.[445] Moreover, the considerations of the ECJ regarding Commission's right of evocation apply to all NCAs. It cannot have been the intention of the ECJ to deprive all competition bodies, including those which are almost undoubtedly courts, of the right to make references under Article 234 EC;[446] otherwise there would have been no need for the ECJ to examine in detail the characteristics of the Epitropi Antagonismou and the question of its independence.[447] Also, the fact that a

---

[444] Anagnostaras, above n 433, 884–6. Elements of this more functional approach (as opposed to applying a purely organisational standard) were already present in the ECJ's ruling in *Dorsch Consult* (see para 35–6 of the judgment; n 439).

[444] Paras 34–6 of the judgment in *Syfait* (n 438).

[445] See Komninos, above n 433, 108–9, who even pleads in favour of allowing preliminary references by all NCAs in order to honour the principle of equality amongst them (*id.*, 114). This argument is also advanced by Leopold and Reiche, above n 429, 144.

[446] See Tagaras and Waelbroeck, above n 429, 490.

[447] Anagnostaras, above n 433, 889.

procedure pending before a court may ultimately not result in a judicial decision is not a circumstance that is unique to competition matters or the associated right of the Commission to relieve NCAs of their competence. Equally, in civil proceedings the claimant can typically withdraw the action, at least under certain conditions. If a theoretical possibility that the procedure will not lead to a judicial decision was really a decisive element disqualifying the court from the procedure under Article 234 EC, preliminary references from all civil courts in the Community would be inadmissible. That would be an absurd result of the *Syfait* judgment.

4. New Duties for National Courts

The duty of sincere co-operation not only obliges the Commission to assist the authorities of the Member States, it also implies that the Member States' authorities support the European institutions with a view to attaining the objectives of the EC Treaty. In particular, Member States have an obligation to co-operate loyally with the Commission to enable it to ensure, pursuant to Article 211 EC, that Community law is applied.[448] Consequently, Regulation 1/2003 imposes certain obligations, mainly information requirements, on national courts which aim at facilitating the fulfilment of the Commission's tasks under that Regulation.

a. Information Duties

Pursuant to Article 15(2) of Regulation 1/2003, Member States shall forward to the Commission a copy of all written judgments of the national courts involving the application of Article 81 or 82 EC.[449] This information duty shall allow the Commission to monitor the application of Articles 81 and 82 EC by national courts and make a preliminary assessment as to whether an intervention as *amicus curiae* may be warranted in the appeal proceedings.[450] In the Explanatory Memorandum, the Commission points out that the amount of bureaucracy involved, in particular on the side of the national courts, is kept to a minimum.[451] Formally, the duty is imposed on the Member States, not on the national courts. In practice, the transmission, by the national courts, should take place automatically and should

---

[448] Case C–69/90 *Commission v Italy* [1991] ECR I–6011, para 15.

[449] The copy must be transmitted without delay after the full written judgment has been notified to the parties. The cases are uploaded in the National Court Cases Database (see above n 242).

[450] See para 37 of the National Courts Notice where it is stated that 'the transmission of national judgements . . . and the resulting information on proceedings before national courts primarily enable the Commission to become aware in a timely fashion of cases for which it might be appropriate to submit observations where one of the parties lodges an appeal'.

[451] Explanatory Memorandum, 23. The transmission of judgments in paper form shall be replaced, to the largest extent possible, by electronic transmission.

ideally be effected through a central national institution (court or authority) that has been assigned the task of sending all relevant judgments to Brussels.

Furthermore, the second subparagraph of Article 15(3) of Regulation 1/2003 obliges national courts to supply further information in individual cases, but only upon specific request of the Commission or NCA. They have to transmit all documents that the authority requires to assess the case for the purpose of preparing its observations. This obligation serves two purposes. First, the information shall enable the Commission or NCA to arrive at a well-founded decision about whether or not it is necessary to intervene as *amicus curiae* in the national (appeal) proceedings in order to preserve the coherent application of the EC competition rules.[452] Secondly, where the competition authority does decide to intervene in the appeal proceedings, the information shall enable the Commission or NCA to prepare a helpful and qualitatively satisfactory submission.[453]

It has been observed by some writers that the information duties imposed on national courts only make sense if the Commission also uses the information effectively.[454] It may be doubted, however, that the Commission will have the time and manpower to monitor systematically the decision practice, with regard to Articles 81 and 82 EC, of hundreds of national courts throughout a union of 27 Member States operating in 23 different languages.[455] It is even less likely that the Commission will have the resources to provide those courts with helpful advice or satisfactory *amicus curiae* briefs.[456]

b. Admission of Observations

While information which the Commission holds and opinions on factual, economic or legal matters are provided, in accordance with Article 15(1) of Regulation 1/2003, only at the (explicit) request of the national judge, written observations are submitted on the Commission's (or NCA's) own initiative. An invitation or permission from the national court is not required. Accordingly, national courts are obliged to tolerate such an *ex officio* intervention and admit written observations that the Commission (or an NCA) wants to present pursuant to Article 15(3) of Regulation 1/2003. This would seem to follow from Article 10 EC and the principle of sincere co-operation that national courts have to observe.

---

[452] As noted above (section II.C.3.b), the NCAs have the power to submit written observations even where coherence does not require an intervention.
[453] Explanatory Memorandum, 23.
[454] See, eg Idot, above n 111, 346.
[455] See Edward, above n 122, 567; Idot, above n 111, 346.
[456] Cf Edward, above n 122, 567.

Regulation 1/2003 does not provide for any procedural framework within which such observations can be introduced in the proceedings. Recital 21 of Regulation 1/2003 only states that (written or oral) observations

> should be submitted within the framework of national procedural rules and practices including those safeguarding the rights of the parties.

The National Courts Notice, which lays down further details of the co-operation with national courts, also gives little guidance in this respect. It essentially rehearses some very general principles of Community law.[457] In other words, it is left to the national legislators of the Member States to establish the relevant procedural framework.

In any event, the lack of specific procedural rules for the submission of *amicus curiae* briefs will not be allowed to prevent the Commission (or NCAs) from using this instrument because Article 15(1) of Regulation 1/2003 is considered to be directly effective. If the national law does not yet provide for a procedural framework for the submission of observations by Commission or NCA, it is for the national judge to determine the most appropriate procedural rules to be applied.[458] Even if there are no appropriate rules,[459] written observations by the Commission or NCA may not be rejected. If necessary, national courts have to admit these observations directly on the basis of Article 15(3) of Regulation 1/2003.[460]

Interestingly, the Commission has not reiterated its commitment from the 1993 Co-operation Notice to ensure that its submissions reach all parties to the proceedings. It is true that this commitment was made in relation to requests that did not come from a national court directly, but came indirectly, ie through a party which had been ordered by the court to provide certain information.[461] Apparently, the Commission will no longer approve of such a procedure. It expects all requests to be made directly by the national court itself and does not wish to be involved in direct contacts

---

[457] Eg the principles of effectiveness and equivalence. See para 35, subparas (b) and (c) of the National Courts Notice.

[458] Para 34 of the National Courts Notice.

[459] See, eg the situation in Italy, where there appears to be no judicial tool that would allow a national court to benefit from the Commission's assistance. M Todino, 'Modernisation from the Perspective of National Competition Authorities: Impact of the Reform on Decentralised Application of EC Competition Law' (2000) 21 *European Competition Law Review* 348, 351.

[460] Cf para 35, subpara (a) of the National Courts Notice, where the Commission stresses that the procedural framework applied 'cannot make the submission of such observations excessively difficult or practically impossible'. These rules are derived from the principle of effectiveness established by the ECJ in Joined Cases 46/87 and 227/88 *Hoechst v Commission* [1989] ECR 2859, para 33. Cf also the judgment of the ECJ in Case 45/76 *Comet* [1976] ECR 2043, paras 15, 16 (with regard to rights conferred by Community legislation on individuals).

[461] Para 42 of the 1993 Notice provided that in such a case the Commission would 'ensure that its answer reaches all the parties to the proceedings'.

with the parties.[462] In addition, the National Courts Notice states, with regard to opinions requested by a national judge, that the Commission will not hear the parties before drafting and submitting such opinion. Rather, the national court 'will have to deal with the Commission's opinion in accordance with the relevant national procedural rules'.[463]

The Commission's new approach shows that the sole responsibility for guaranteeing a fair trial and, in particular, a contradictory debate during the proceedings before a civil court has been shifted to the national judge. This also applies with regard to the intervention as *amicus curiae*. The National Courts Notice simply states that the procedural framework for the submission of observations 'has to be compatible with the general principles of Community law, in particular the fundamental rights of the parties'.[464] It is for the national court to ensure that the adversarial character of the civil procedure is preserved and the rights of defence are protected when the Commission or an NCA submits observations.[465] The national judge or legislator therefore has to decide when and how the Commission's (or NCA's) observations are made available to the parties, and whether and how the parties may respond to such observations.[466]

5. *Review of the Commission's Inspection Decisions*

During an investigation, the Commission is entitled, pursuant to Article 20 of Regulation 1/2003, to inspect the business premises of the companies that are investigated. Moreover, pursuant to Article 21 of Regulation 1/2003, the Commission may search the private homes of directors, managers and other staff members of the companies concerned provided there are reasons to believe that books or other records which may be relevant to prove a serious violation of the EC competition rules are kept at these premises.[467]

---

[462] Where it is nonetheless contacted directly by any of the parties, it will inform the national court thereof, independent of whether these contacts took place before or after the national court's request for co-operation (para 19 of the National Courts Notice).

[463] Para 30 of the National Courts Notice.

[464] Para 35, subpara (a) of the National Courts Notice.

[465] This is also true with regard to information and opinions requested by a court. Here, the national court also has to ensure that all parties are duly informed and the rights of defence are respected (in accordance with the applicable national procedural rules) while at the same time protecting confidential information and business secrets that may be contained in the Commission's reply to the court's request. See paras 25 and 30 of the National Courts Notice.

[466] Further questions arising in this context are, for example, whether an official of the Commission or the NCA can be summoned to explain the written observations submitted by the authority, whether such witness is to be regarded as 'expert' witness, and whether the witness can be subject to cross-examination. Edward, above n 122, 566.

[467] The latter provision has been introduced in the course of the modernisation. Reg 17 did not contain an equivalent provision. Art 21 of Reg 1/2003 is based on the Commission's experience that important documents which are relevant to determine an infringement are

As a matter of principle, undertakings are obliged to submit to inspections of their business premises which are ordered by Commission decision.[468] However, where a company objects to such an inspection, the Commission will require assistance by the police or other enforcement authorities and must therefore usually obtain a search warrant from a national court of the Member State concerned.[469] The inspection of non-business premises, by contrast, is always subject to prior authorisation from the judicial authority of the Member State on whose territory the inspection takes place.[470]

In the context of granting these authorisations, national courts may have to review the Commission's inspection decision. However, in both cases, ie inspection of business and non-business premises, the powers of national courts to review the Commission decision are limited. In particular, national courts may not call into question the lawfulness of the inspection decision, since this is the prerogative of the ECJ. Nor may they question the necessity of the inspection. Consequently, national courts may only control whether the Commission decision is authentic and the coercive measures envisaged are not arbitrary or excessive (proportionality test).[471]

The limited scope of control to be exercised by national courts over the Commission's inspection decisions results from the case law of the ECJ. The relevant principles were essentially established in *Hoechst*, where the ECJ held that a national court cannot substitute its own assessment of the need for the investigation at issue for that of the Commission, since the lawfulness of the Commission's assessment of fact and law is subject only to review by the Community courts. The national court must, however, satisfy itself that the inspection decision is authentic and it can subsequently consider whether the measures of constraint envisaged are arbitrary or excessive.[472]

It is important to note, in this context, that national courts may ask the Commission for detailed explanations,[473] including the grounds for the Commission's suspicion, the seriousness of the alleged infringement, the nature of the involvement of the companies concerned and all other elements that the courts must consider in order to reach a well-founded

---

sometimes withheld from the Commission's agents by moving them to the private homes of employees. The new power shall thus ensure the effectiveness of Commission inspections. See Recital 26 of Reg 1/2003.

[468] Art 20(4) of Reg 1/2003.

[469] The Commission may also seek an authorisation of the national court as a precautionary measure in order to overcome possible opposition on the part of the company to be inspected. See Art 20(6) and (7) of Reg 1/2003.

[470] Reg 1/2003, Art 21(3), 1st sentence.

[471] Arts 20(8) and 21(3) of Reg 1/2003.

[472] Para 35 of the *Hoechst* judgment (n 460).

[473] Reg 1/2003, Arts 20(8), 2nd sentence and 21(3), 3rd sentence.

decision about the proportionality of the coercive measures.[474] Such requests for further explanations can be addressed directly to the Commission or channelled through the NCA of the Member State concerned.

The latter principles were developed by the ECJ in *Roquette Frères*.[475] This judgment concerned a request by the French Cour de Cassation for a preliminary ruling on, inter alia, the interpretation of the ECJ's decision in *Hoechst*. The ECJ was thus asked to determine more precisely what the limited review to be exercised by the national court in accordance with the *Hoechst* judgment involved. The ECJ ruled that, in order to enable the national court to satisfy itself that the coercive measures are not arbitrary or disproportionate, the Commission is required to provide that court with explanations showing, in a properly substantiated manner, that the Commission possesses information and evidence providing reasonable grounds for suspecting an infringement of the competition rules by the undertaking concerned.[476]

By contrast, Regulation 1/2003 also provides that national courts may not demand to be presented with the information in the Commission's file.[477] From the mere reading of the relevant provisions in Regulation 1/2003, the difference between 'explanations' and 'information in the Commission's file' is not entirely clear. Would the Commission not have to disclose information from its file when providing the judge with further explanations, such as the grounds it has for suspecting an infringement of the competition rules and other elements relevant for assessing the proportionality of the measures of constraint?

From the judgment in *Roquette Frères*, one can conclude that Regulation 1/2003 refers to documentary evidence such as written testimonies or complaints when excluding the national judge from being provided with 'information in the Commission's file'. In that judgment, the ECJ distinguished between the explanations that the Commission provided giving 'very precise account of the suspicions harboured by it'[478] and the evidence on which these suspicions were based. With regard to the latter, the ECJ held:

> Although the Commission has not indicated the nature of the evidence on which its suspicions are based, such as a complaint, testimony or documents exchanged between the participants in the suspected cartel, the mere fact that no such indication is given cannot suffice to cast doubt on the existence of reasonable

---

[474] Where the inspection relates to non-business premises, the court has to consider in addition the importance of the evidence sought and the likelihood that the relevant documents are kept at the private homes to be searched. Reg 1/2003, Art 21(3), 2nd sentence.

[475] Case C–94/00 *Roquette Frères* [2002] ECR I–9011.

[476] Para 61 of the judgment in *Roquette Frères* (*ibid*).

[477] Reg 1/2003, Arts 20(8), 3rd sentence and 21(3), 2nd subpara.

[478] Para 69 of the judgment in *Roquette Frères* (above n 475).

grounds for those suspicions where . . . the detailed account of the information held by the Commission concerning the specific subject-matter of the suspected cartel is such as to enable the competent national court to establish a firm basis for its conclusion that the Commission does indeed possess such evidence.[479]

In other words, the Commission is obliged to explain to the national judge why it has concluded that the undertaking concerned is engaged in conduct violating Article 81 or 82 EC, but it does not have to disclose the various pieces of evidence underpinning this conclusion.[480]

It is to be welcomed that the rules developed by the ECJ regarding the role of national courts in the context of Commission inspections and, in particular, the exact scope of the limited judicial review of inspection decisions are now laid down in a legislative act, ie Articles 20(8) and 21(3) of Regulation 1/2003. In fact, the rules are formulated in so much detail in Regulation 1/2003 that even the National Courts Notice hardly adds anything; rather, it confines itself to repeating the principles already spelled out in Articles 20(8) and 21(3) of Regulation 1/2003. The only additional element is the indication that, in view of the duty of loyal co-operation, national courts are required to take their decisions within an appropriate timeframe.[481] A timely decision of the national court may, of course, be of crucial importance with regard to the surprise character and thus the effectiveness of the Commission inspection.

The substantive review of the legality and justification of the Commission's inspection decisions thus remains the exclusive right of the ECJ. This review is the only true recourse that the undertakings and individuals concerned have since the national court, if at all, is seized solely at the request of the Commission when it needs or anticipates the need for a search warrant. However, the review by the ECJ inevitably takes place *ex post factum*, which in many cases may be years after the inspection and therefore does not provide an effective protection against illegal searches. It is therefore doubtful whether the limitation of the judicial review at national level, albeit established by the ECJ and now codified in Regulation 1/2003, is at all consistent with the requirements of Community law. After all, the Commission exercises extensive powers under Articles 20 and 21 of Regulation 1/2003 which allow it to interfere with fundamental rights of the (legal or natural) persons whose property is to be raided.[482]

---

[479] Para 70 of the judgment in *Roquette Frères* (above n 475).

[480] In other words, the national judge does not have any means to verify the truthfulness of the Commission's assertions.

[481] Para 41 of the National Courts Notice.

[482] Very critical on the limited review rights of national courts is G McCurdy, 'The Impact of Modernisation of the EU Competition Law System on the Courts and Private Enforcement of the Competition Laws: A Comparative Perspective' (2004) 25 *European Competition Law Review* 509, 516, who argues that Art 21 of Reg 1/2003 'provides a necessary, but not sufficient restraint on the Commission's unfettered powers.' Cf also para 15 of the judgment in *Hoechst* (n 460),

D. New Tasks for the Advisory Committee

The Advisory Committee, composed of representatives of the Member States, was set up by Regulation 17. Under the heading 'Liaison with the Authorities of the Member States', Article 10 of Regulation 17 contained basic rules for the co-operation between the Commission and the NCAs. It provided, in particular, that the Commission had to inform the NCAs of applications and notifications by transmitting copies of the relevant documents. Furthermore, the Commission had to consult the Advisory Committee before the adoption of an infringement, negative clearance or exemption decision.[483] Such consultation took place at a meeting of the Advisory Committee and the Commission. In practice, these meetings were chaired by a senior official of the Commission, while the Committee members were given the opportunity to make observations, raise questions and express their views orally on a case.[484] The Advisory Committee could also deliver a (written) opinion. A 'report of the outcome of the consultative proceedings' had to be annexed to the draft decision. In practice, the opinion of the Advisory Committee accompanied that report.[485] However, it was not foreseen that the report or the opinion would be published.[486]

It is clear from the above rules that, under the former system, the Advisory Committee operated only for vertical consultation, ie consultation between the Commission and the Member States. Its opinions were neither binding on the Commission[487] nor made public in any way. Unlike the situation under the 1989 Merger Regulation, the undertakings concerned and interested third parties had no access to the opinion. In *Pioneer*, the ECJ even ruled that Regulation 17 clearly precluded the possibility of disclosing the Advisory Committee's opinion to the undertakings concerned since the consultation of the Advisory Committee was intended to be the final stage of the administrative procedure before the Commission and a disclosure of the opinion to the undertakings would mean the re-opening of this procedure.[488] Due to the secrecy surrounding the

where the ECJ held in fact that fundamental rights such as the rights of defence may not be 'irremediably impaired during preliminary inquiry procedures'.

[483] Including decisions regarding the renewal, amendment or revocation of an exemption decision pursuant to Art 81(3). See Art 10(3) of Reg 17.

[484] Kerse, above n 31, para 5.23. For the purpose of that meeting, the Advisory Committee was provided with the draft decision and the most important documents. Roth and Rose, above n 138 (5th edn), para 12-055. See also Art 10(5) of Reg 17.

[485] Kerse, above n 31, para 5.24.

[486] Art 10(6) of Reg 17. In contrast, the opinions delivered by the Advisory Committee on concentrations already under the old merger control regime could be published in certain circumstances. See Art 19(7) of the 1989 Merger Regulation. Under the new EC merger control rules (see Art 19(7) of the 2004 Merger Regulation), the publication of the opinion, together with the decision, is even obligatory.

[487] Roth and Rose, above n 138 (5th edn), para 12-055.

[488] Joined Cases 100–103/80 *SA Musique Diffusion Française and others v Commission* [1983] ECR 1825, paras 34–5. Nevertheless, in some cases the Committee's opinions were made

Committee's opinions, they could de facto be disregarded easily by the Commission.[489]

Under Regulation 1/2003, the role of the Advisory Committee has been reinforced considerably. As under the old regime, the Commission has to consult the Advisory Committee before adopting an infringement decision or a decision imposing fines.[490] The Advisory Committee must also be consulted where the Commission plans to issue a positive or a commitment decision, withdraw the benefits of a block exemption or order interim measures.[491] In addition, however, Regulation 1/2003 explicitly states that the Advisory Committee may discuss individual cases handled by an NCA as well as general issues of competition law.[492] Discussions on particular cases can be requested by any Member State and by the Commission itself. The Commission puts individual cases dealt with by an NCA on the agenda after having informed that NCA.

As a consequence, the Advisory Committee can now function as a full-scale forum for the discussion of important general matters as well as for individual cases, including both cases dealt with by the Commission and cases handled at the national level.[493] Since national competition cases involving Article 81 or 82 EC may be discussed, the Advisory Committee no longer operates only for vertical consultation, but has also become a forum for the horizontal coordination of policy and enforcement of EC competition law.[494] It is important to note, however, that the Advisory Committee may not deliver opinions with regard to cases dealt with by an NCA.[495]

As concerns vertical consultation with the Commission, there are also

available to the ECJ, albeit without being shown to the applicants—a practice which can hardly be approved of in the light of the requirements of a fair trial. On this problematic approach of the ECJ see Kerse and Khan, above n 165, para 5-048.

[489] Cf Böge, above n 269, 253. Since the consultation process under Art 10 of Reg 17 was confidential and the opinions delivered by the Advisory Committee were secret, one can only speculate about the question of whether the Commission always gave due regard to the opinion expressed by the Advisory Committee or sometimes ignored it. It is presumed, however, that the Commission has only adopted a decision against the vote of the Advisory Committee on rare occasions. Usually, Commissioners seem to have attached great weight to the opinions of the Advisory Committee and tried to obtain a favourable vote of at least the majority of its members. Goyder, above n 13, 39 and 439.

[490] Consultation can take place either at a meeting or by written procedure. See Art 14(3) and (4) of Reg 1/2003. The latter (written) procedure is new, and was not foreseen by Reg 17 (see Art 10(5)).

[491] Art 14(1) of Reg 1/2003. Under Reg 17, there was no express obligation to consult the Advisory Committee in relation to interim measures, but in practice the Commission did consult the Committee also in these cases. Kerse, above n 31, para 5.22.

[492] Art 14(7) of Reg 1/2003.

[493] See Todino, above n 459, 352.

[494] Paulis, above n 95, 407.

[495] Art 14(7), subpara 3. Nonetheless, it is the Commission's view that discussions in the Advisory Committee will help safeguard the consistent application of the EC competition rules. See Recital 19 of Reg 1/2003. *Accord* Todino, above n 459, 352.

some important changes which strengthen the position of the Advisory Committee: the Commission is under an obligation to take 'the utmost account' of the opinion and inform the Advisory Committee of the manner in which its opinion has been taken into account.[496] The latter obligation, in particular, should prevent the Commission from 'overlooking' the Advisory Committee's opinion. The Commission will be forced to genuinely consider and analyse the opinion, since it has to explain its approach to the Advisory Committee. Moreover, in addition to simply appending the opinion to the Commission's draft decision, the Advisory Committee may also recommend the publication of its opinion.[497] These provisions were clearly modelled after Article 19(6) and (7) of the 1989 Merger Regulation, since they impose the same standards as those which used to apply in relation to opinions delivered by the Advisory Committee on concentrations.[498]

Finally, the composition of the Advisory Committee has been adapted to the needs of a full-scale discussion forum. In principle, the Advisory Committee consists of representatives of the NCAs.[499] Article 14(2) of Regulation 1/2003 provides, however, that, for meetings where issues other than individual cases[500] are being discussed, Member States may appoint an additional representative competent in competition matters who does not necessarily have to belong to the NCA.[501] This allows Member States to have a sort of 'permanent representative' for meetings concerning general issues of EC competition law, while discussions on individual cases will normally take place at the level of case handlers.[502]

It is not entirely clear what the exact relationship between the Advisory Committee and the ECN will be. While the Advisory Committee is expressly provided for by Article 14 of Regulation 1/2003, the ECN has no formal legal basis in Regulation 1/2003.[503] The 'network of public authorities' is only mentioned in some recitals of Regulation 1/2003.[504] Formally,

---

[496] Art 14(5) of Reg 1/2003.

[497] Art 14(6) of Reg 1/2003.

[498] The current merger control regime, which entered into force on the same day as Reg 1/2003, already goes two steps further: not only has the publication of the opinion of the Advisory Committee on concentrations become mandatory; the Commission is also obliged to communicate the opinion, together with its own decision, to the parties. See Art 19(7) of the 2004 Merger Regulation.

[499] This constitutes a change in relation to the rules applicable under Reg 17. Art 10(4) of Reg 17 only provided that the Advisory Committee had to be composed of 'officials competent in the matter of restrictive practices and monopolies' without requiring that such officials came from the NCAs. (Each Member State had the right to appoint one member.) In practice, of course, Member States often nominated officials of the NCA.

[500] In note 23 of the Network Notice, the Commission describes these matters as 'horizontal issues such as block-exemption regulations and guidelines'.

[501] Note 23 of the Network Notice.

[502] Cf Paulis, above n 95, 407.

[503] See Van Der Woude, above n 214, 9.

[504] See recitals 15, 16, 17, 18 and 32 of Reg 1/2003.

the Advisory Committee does not include the Commission as it consists of representatives of the Member States, even though the Commission usually chairs the meetings of the Advisory Committee.[505] The ECN, by contrast, is formed by the NCAs and the Commission together.

The modalities of the operation of the ECN are laid down in the Network Notice, which states that the ECN

> provides a framework for the co-operation of European competition authorities in cases where Articles 81 and 82 EC of the Treaty are applied.[506]

The Network Notice also contains a section on the role of the Advisory Committee in the new system.[507] It describes the Advisory Committee as 'the forum where experts from the various competition authorities discuss individual cases and general issues of Community competition law'.[508] Moreover, pursuant to Article 14(3) of Regulation 1/2003, the meetings of the Advisory Committee are convened and chaired by the Commission. Usually, the Commission will send the competent Director of DG Competition, though other Commission officials (eg the case handler or a member of the Commission's Legal Service) may be present as well.[509] In other words, the Commission is an ordinary member of the ECN and it convenes and chairs the meetings of the Advisory Committee (without being a member thereof). Thus, in terms of participation of Commission and Member State representatives, both bodies appear to be identical. On this basis, one could understand the ECN to be a more general and essentially virtual platform for co-operation and consultation between the competition authorities in the EU, which operates predominantly by electronic means (in particular, through a common intranet which links all NCAs and the Commission (hereafter 'the Intranet')), while the Advisory Committee comes into play when members of the Network meet in person.[510] In that event, the ECN performs its functions through the Advisory Committee, which assumes the task of the ECN to provide a (real) forum for discussion and co-operation.[511]

---

[505] See Art 14(2) and (3) of Reg 1/2003.

[506] Para 1 of the Network Notice.

[507] Paras 58–68 of the Network Notice.

[508] Para 58 of the Network Notice.

[509] This was already the case under Reg 17: Art 10(5) of Reg 17 provided that consultation of the Advisory Committee should take place at a joint meeting to be convened by the Commission. In practice, the Commission also presided the joint meeting and was often represented by more than one official. Cf Kerse, above n 31, para 5.23. This practice is unlikely to change.

[510] Schaub, above n 220, 39. It must be noted, however, that where its consultation by the Commission is mandatory, the Advisory Committee may formulate its observations by way of a written procedure provided that no Member State requests a meeting. See Art 14(4) of Reg 1/2003.

[511] It can even serve as a forum for the discussion of case allocation. Para 62 of the Network Notice. Obviously, these functions are carried out in addition to its traditional role as advisory body in matters where it has to be consulted by the Commission. In the latter case, in particular with regard to the delivery of opinions on certain draft decisions of the Commission, the

In my view, however, the exact relation between these two fora, the ECN and the Advisory Committee, should be further clarified in order to allow the participants to channel information correctly and prevent officials from engaging in discussions from which they should be excluded.[512]

III. SUMMARY

In this first chapter, I have briefly recapitulated the history of the reform process, including the most important criticism voiced during that process. I have also briefly outlined the most important powers and duties of both the Commission and the NCAs in order to place into context the issues and considerations which will be presented in the subsequent chapters.

The replacement of Regulation 17 by Regulation 1/2003 is part of a larger reform process which encompasses three pillars: a more economic approach towards the evaluation of competition issues; the revision of the 1989 Merger Regulation; and, finally, an overhaul of the Community's antitrust enforcement rules, notably Regulation 17.

The reform of Regulation 17, in turn, has three major goals. First, it aims to extend the Commission's investigatory powers, in particular by introducing the right to search non-business premises, to seal rooms and to interview any person who might possess relevant information. Secondly, it aims to eliminate the notification/exemption requirement by making Article 81(3) directly applicable, ie by creating a legal exception system (*exception légale*). Thirdly, it seeks to involve NCAs to a far larger extent in the enforcement of the EC competition rules by conferring more rights and responsibilities upon them.

The second and third goals, which can in fact be summarised by the term 'decentralisation', suggest, however, that the Commission was essentially driven by one objective, ie to reduce its own workload in order to be able to pursue a more proactive competition policy and devote its scarce resources to the detection and punishment of the most serious antitrust violations. On this basis, and contrary to what the Commission maintained in the White Paper, decentralisation is not an end in itself, but rather an instrument to attain the said goal.

Advisory Committee will not include Commission officials (although a Commission official may be present to chair the meeting) and, formally, it will thus be solely for the Member States' representatives to determine the content of such opinion. Cf Kerse, above n 31, para 5.23.

[512] For instance, Member State representatives should only discuss general issues; members of national competition tribunals which fulfil functions of (or similar to) a judge should probably not participate in the discussion of the individual cases they deal with. Again, these considerations are based on the principle of separation of powers in the broadest sense.

Be that as it may, under Regulation 1/2003, NCAs are fully responsible, next to the Commission, for applying Article 81 EC in its entirety as well as Article 82 EC (principle of concurrent jurisdiction). The 'centre of gravity' of EC competition law enforcement is thus (slowly) moving from the European towards the national level.[513] At the same time, the Commission and NCAs are to apply Articles 81 and 82 EC in close co-operation. This co-operation takes place through the ECN. Despite the accrued competences of the NCAs, the Commission certainly retains a central and prominent role in the Network.

In order to guarantee the effectiveness and efficiency of the system, the Network members have been empowered to assist each other in fact-finding and to exchange any kind of relevant information and documents, including confidential items. In view of the need to ensure coherence and consistency, these rights are complemented by certain information duties of the NCAs vis-à-vis the Commission, as well as the faculty to provide the same information to other NCAs. This book will focus primarily on the latter aspect, ie the exchange of information between the NCAs, also called horizontal co-operation (in contrast to the vertical relation between the Commission and NCAs). Since NCAs do not apply a uniform procedure but instead operate in accordance with the domestic procedural rules of their respective Member State, which moreover display large discrepancies, the possibility of a 'free movement' of information created by Regulation 1/2003 raises a number of questions. Possible limits of the information exchange, protection of confidential information, rights of defence and problems of parallel (national) procedures, including the issues of case allocation and double jeopardy, are among the most pressing topics.

---

[513] The expression has been borrowed from D Geradin and N Petit, 'Droit de la concurrence et recours en annulation à l'ère post-modernisation', GCLC Working Paper 06/05, available at www.coleurop.be/content/gclc/documents/GCLC%20WP%2006-05.pdf, 9 (accessed January 2009): 'La réforme. . . a entraîné un glissement du centre de gravité de la mise en œuvre des articles 81 et 82 vers l'échelon national.'

2

Creating a Framework for Co-operation between Competition Authorities in the EU

ARTICLE 11(1) OF Regulation 1/2003 obliges the Commission and the NCAs to apply the EC rules on competition 'in close co-operation'. To this end, they formed the ECN, which provides the framework for co-operation in all cases where Articles 81 and 82 EC are applied. In view of the information duties imposed by Articles 11 of Regulation 1/2003, the Network serves primarily as a platform for information exchange and consultation. Pursuant to Article 14 of Regulation 1/2003, it can also be used as a forum for the discussion of individual cases and general issues of competition law and policy (so-called horizontal issues). The Network thus plays a central role in the decentralised implementation process.

I. WHAT IS THE NETWORK?

The ECN consists of 'public authorities', notably the Commission and the NCAs of the Member States.[1] The first point to note in this context is that the ECN, as defined in Regulation 1/2003 and the Network Notice, does not represent an all-inclusive model in the sense that only competition law officials can participate, while other (private) actors who are regularly involved in the application and interpretation of competition law (eg lawyers, the business community, academics) are automatically excluded from the Network. However, Regulation 1/2003 at least mentions the Network in several of its recitals, thereby recognising its existence and creating some sort of formal framework for its operation, albeit without providing a legal basis *sensu stricto*.[2]

This distinguishes the Network from the (Association of) European Competition Authorities (ECA), a purely informal discussion forum which was founded in 2001 and comprises the competition authorities of the EEA

---

[1] Recital 15 of Reg 1/2003 and recital 1 of the Network Notice.
[2] See above Chapter 1, nn 503 and 504.

countries,[3] as well as the Commission and the EFTA Surveillance Authority. The ECA's main purpose is to enhance co-operation among competition authorities in Europe. Similar to the ECN, the ECA seeks to improve co-operation between its members by organising meetings, setting up working groups and exchanging non-confidential information, expertise and staff. However, the ECA is an entirely informal association which is not supported by any legal framework, such as Regulation 1/2003, providing formal mechanisms for co-operation between the ECA members. It may well be regarded as a kind of predecessor of the ECN.[4] However, having a broader range of members in that it comprises EU and third country competition authorities, the ECA has not become redundant. Another reason for the continuing existence of the ECA alongside the ECN is the fact that, in contrast to the ECN, the ECA is not controlled by the Commission. Moreover, it offers the possibility to intensify co-operation in multi-jurisdictional merger cases, an area where the ECA has been quite active through, inter alia, the adoption of a procedures guide, while the mandate of the ECN is formally limited to questions regarding the enforcement of Articles 81 and 82 EC and thus does not cover merger control.[5] The ECA still exists, and should henceforth be distinguished carefully from the ECN.[6]

The second point is that neither Regulation 1/2003 nor the Network Notice specifies the national public bodies that are members of the Network. Since there exists a variety of competition law institutions in the Member States, including different types of public bodies (administrative agencies, quasi-judicial bodies, courts of law), the question arises which exact body or bodies of each Member State can and should participate in the Network, and whether certain bodies should preferably be excluded.

A. Institutional Architecture of Competition Law in the Member States

In order to understand the composition of the Network and the way it operates, it is useful to recall briefly the most common institutional arrangements for competition law enforcement in the EU.[7] Even though

---

[3] Ie the EU Member States plus Norway, Iceland and Liechtenstein.

[4] L Idot, 'Le nouveau système communautaire de mise en oeuvre des articles 81 et 82 CE (Règlement 1/2003 et projets de textes d'application)' (2003) 39 *Cahiers de Droit Européen* 283, 313, para 58.

[5] A Burnside and H Crossley, 'Co-operative Mechanisms within the EU: A Blueprint for Future Co-operation at the International Level' (2004) 10 *International Trade Law & Regulation* 25, 25–6.

[6] This also means that the communication systems (intranet etc) of the two networks must be kept apart as co-operation within both networks follows different rules in particular with regard to the exchange of confidential data.

[7] The purpose of this section is not to make a thorough and exhaustive comparative study of the institutional models applied in all 27 Member States, but to highlight, by way of examples,

there is a large variety of institutional designs, the enforcement systems can essentially be classified according to two basic models: the monist, unitary or integrated agency model; and the dual or bifurcated model.[8]

The national systems that will be discussed hereafter have been chosen in such a way that there are several examples for each of the two principal models. At the same time, the countries selected allow the existence of many combinations and variations within each category to be demonstrated.[9] Moreover, the countries used to illustrate the diversity of the existing arrangements comprise some of the larger Member States (France, Germany, Italy and the UK), but also some of the smaller ones (Belgium, the Netherlands and Austria). Finally, the Czech Republic and Sweden have been included in the list of selected countries in order to take account not only of some of the more recently acceded Member States,[10] but also of the North and East European enlargements. The models of these nine countries are summarised below.

1. The Integrated Agency Model

Where the integrated agency or 'monist' model is applied, a single authority performs the functions of investigating, prosecuting and adjudicating competition law infringements. Such integrated authorities can have different degrees of independence, depending on whether they have their own budget and can take their own personnel decisions or whether they are subject to the supervision of a ministry which ultimately determines expenditures, human resources and policy priorities and, in some instances, may even give instructions. Examples of an integrated agency are the NCAs of Germany, the Netherlands, the UK, Italy and the Czech Republic. They are briefly presented below.

---

the major differences between the most common enforcement systems which may have an impact on the functioning of the ECN. Interestingly, L Idot, 'A Necessary Step Towards Common Procedural Standards of Implementation for Articles 81 & 82 EC without the Network' in C-D Ehlermann and I Atanasiu (eds), *European Competition Law Annual 2002: Constructing the EU Network of Competition Authorities* (Oxford, Hart Publishing, 2003), 211, 211, finds the absence of any debate about the complex issue of diversity of the NCAs in the running up to the modernisation proposal quite astonishing.

[8] Trebilcock and Iacobucci identify three basic models by distinguishing between the bifurcated *agency* model and the bifurcated *judicial* model. In the latter model, a court performs the adjudicative function, while the first model presupposes the existence of a separate, specialised adjudicative agency. M Trebilcock and E Iacobucci, 'Designing Competition Law Institutions' (2002) 25 *World Competition* 361, 361–2. They concede however that the bifurcated agency model is in fact a compromise between the integrated agency model and the bifurcated judicial model. *Ibid*, 380.

[9] Cf Trebilcock and Iacobucci, *ibid*, 362, who point out that there are a virtually infinite number of potential arrangements. Despite the many possible variants and combinations, the two basic models provide useful points of reference.

[10] Obviously, Austria, which joined the EC in the same year as Sweden (1995), could also be named in this category.

The German competition authority, the Bundeskartellamt (BKartA) is an independent federal agency, which belongs to the area of responsibility of the Federal Minister of Economic Affairs and Technology.[11] It was established on the basis of the GWB, which entered into force on 1 January 1958[12] and is thus one of the oldest competition authorities in Europe. The BKartA is organised into 10 decision-making divisions (*Beschluß-abteilungen*), each of which is responsible for certain industry sectors. These divisions investigate, prosecute and adjudicate competition law infringements. They are entitled to prohibit illegal agreements and practices, and impose (administrative) fines (*Bußgelder*). The President of the BKartA can neither instruct the divisions with regard to individual cases nor decide on a case himself.[13]

In the Netherlands, competition law enforcement lies in the hands of the Nederlandse mededingingsautoriteit (NMa), which is among the youngest competition authorities in the EU. It was only set up in 1998, and originally operated under the responsibility of the Minister of Economic Affairs. In 2005, the NMa was transformed into an independent administrative agency.[14] It has several management departments and five operational

---

[11] § 51(1) GWB. The right of the Minister to issue general directives (*Allgemeine Weisungen*), which have to be published in the official gazette, is exercised at rare occasions only. R Bechtold, *Kartellgesetz (Kommentar), 3. Auflage* (Munich, Verlag CH Beck, 2002), § 52 no 1. Whether the Minister has the power to give instructions in a specific case (*Einzelweisungen*) is still unclear. In any event, even though the respective Ministers regularly claim the right to instruct the BKartA also in individual cases, they have until today not done so in a single case. The BKartA is therefore generally recognised as an independent authority. K Stockmann, 'Zur Stellung der deutschen Kartellbehörden' in A Fuchs, H-P Schwintowski and D Zimmer (eds), *Wirtschafts- und Privatrecht im Spannungsfeld von Privatautonomie, Wettbewerb und Regulierung. Festschrift für Ulrich Immenga zum 70. Geburtstag* (Munich, CH Beck, 2004), 389, 394. Stockmann himself, however, has some critical comments on the general opinion. He suggests that the mere possibility of an intervention by a Federal Minister would already impair the independence of an institution and explains this view with some smug words: 'Bekanntlich erzielte früher die Vorführung der Folterinstrumente häufig schon die gewünschte Wirkung, so dass deren Einsatz gar nicht erst erforderlich wurde.' *Ibid*, 395–6.

[12] Ie on the same day when the Treaty of Rome, which was signed on 25 March 1957, and thus Arts 85 and 86 EEC [now Arts 81 and 82 EC], came into force. It is sometimes believed that German competition law functioned as a model for the Community competition rules. However, given that the German provisions are as 'young' as those of the EC Treaty and that the ECSC Treaty, which was signed in Paris in 1951, already contained antitrust provisions (Arts 65), the GWB cannot really be credited for the fact that competition rules were also included in the EC Treaty. On this question and the influence of North American economic conceptions of free trade and competition on the development and design of the German and Community antitrust rules, see G Marenco, 'The Birth of Modern Competition Law in Europe' in A von Bogdandy (ed), *European Integration and International Co-ordination: Studies in Transnational Economic Law in Honour of Claus-Dieter Ehlermann* (The Hague, Kluwer Law International, 2001), 279.

[13] Bechtold, above n 11, § 52 no 3.

[14] See Arts 2(1) and 4 Mededingingswet NL Initially, the Minister was entitled to give directions both in general matters and individual cases (see former Art 4, in particular para 4, of the Dutch Competition Act). As of 1 April 2004, the Minister of Economic Affairs only remains responsible for defining the competition policy and can therefore give general instructions, but he can no longer instruct the NMa with regard to individual cases (see Arts 5a–5c Mededingingswet NL). In any event, the law in itself does not always reflect exactly the real level

departments, including a directorate for the control of anti-competitive agreements and practices and abuses of dominant positions (*directie Concurrentietoezicht*).[15] All decision-making powers are, however, conferred upon a board of directors (*Raad van Bestuur*), which has three members and heads the NMa. This means that the NMa officials of the aforementioned department (the case handlers) only investigate and prosecute alleged violations of the competition rules and make proposals for a decision.[16] Final decisions, including the imposition of fines, must be taken collectively by the board of directors, which decides by unanimous resolution.[17] In other words, investigative and adjudicative functions in the Netherlands are effectively performed by different units (albeit within the same agency), which are separated by a so-called 'Chinese wall'.[18]

In contrast to the German and the former Dutch approach, Italy has created a fully independent competition agency, the Autorità Garante della Concorrenza e del Mercato ('Autorità Garante'), established in 1990, which

of independence of an institution. C Gauer, 'Does the Effectiveness of the EU Network of Competition Authorities Require a Certain Degree of Harmonisation of National Procedures and Sanctions?' in Ehlermann and Atanasiu, above n 7, 192. Even though under German law, there is, in theory, the possibility of interference at a political level, the BKartA can be characterised as independent authority since interference by the Minister of Economic Affairs hardly ever occurs in practice (see also above n 11). The same applies to the Belgian competition authorities. Similarly, the NMa was an independent agency also at the time when the Dutch Minister of Economic Affairs could still give instructions in individual cases as this right was in fact never used.

[15] The latter, in turn, is divided into four units ('*clusters*') each of which is responsible for a number of specific industry sectors.

[16] See A Knijpenga, 'Chapter 12. The Netherlands' in M Holmes and L Davey (eds), *A Practical Guide to National Competition Rules across Europe* (The Hague, Kluwer Law International, 2004), 237, 238–9. In fact, they handle the case until the issue of the statement of objections, at which point the case file is handed over to the legal service of the NMa (which has not been involved in the investigation and) which is responsible for giving the suspected firms the opportunity to make their views known on the SO. P Kalbfleisch, 'Criminal Competition Law Sanctions in the Netherlands' in K Cseres, M Schinkel and F Vogelaar, *Criminalization of Competition Law Enforcement* (Cheltenham, Elgar, 2006), 312, 314.

[17] See Art 14(2)(a) of the Decree on the Internal Organisation of the NMa (Besluit organisatie, mandaat, volmacht en machtiging NMa 2005). See also B Van Reeken and S Noë, 'Competition Law in the Netherlands', in F Vogelaar, J Stuyck, B Van Reeken (eds), *Competition Law in the EU, Its Member States and Switzerland, Volume I* (The Hague, Kluwer Law International, 2000), 417, 428, 460 and 474 for the situation prior to the 2005 amendments. (NB: In 2005, the internal administrative structure of the NMa was transformed from a system with a single head (Director-General) to a collegiate system with a Board of Directors.) The final decisions of the Board of Directors are in practice prepared and drafted by the NMa's legal service. Kalbfleisch, *ibid*, 314.

[18] Kalbfleisch, *ibid*, 314. The internal separation of the functions is laid down in Art 54a Mededingingswet NL. In practice, the (integrated) Dutch system therefore has certain similarities with the bifurcated model. The inverse situation seems to have emerged in Canada whose enforcement system is formally based on the bifurcated model. However, in practice, the role of the adjudicative body, the Competition Tribunal, has largely been marginalised (at least with regard to merger control) as over 99% of all mergers notified to the Competition Bureau are in fact settled without involvement of the Tribunal (for instance, through modification or undertakings). Thus the Competition Bureau has become a de facto integrated competition agency. Trebilcock and Iacobucci, above n 8, 374.

also formally has full autonomy in that it is not subject to any oversight by the Italian government or parliament[19] and administers its own budget.[20] The Autorità Garante is a collegiate body, consisting of a president and four members, who are chosen among prominent jurists, economists and business executives.[21] The Autorità Garante is organised into various departments, including an investigative directorate-general which is responsible for the handling of competition matters. It is sub-divided into several directorates organised by industrial sectors. These directorates carry out the investigations, while decisions determining the existence of an infringement and/or imposing fines are taken by the panel, ie the president and the other members of the Autorità Garante, deciding by majority vote.[22]

The principal role in enforcing the competition rules in the UK has been assigned to the Office of Fair Trading (OFT), created by the Enterprise Act 2002, which abolished the office of Director General of Fair Trading and transferred his functions to the OFT.[23] In contrast to its predecessor, the OFT is a corporate entity.[24] It has a board, consisting of a chairman and at least four other members, which is responsible for the strategic direction of the OFT. The board therefore takes enforcement action only in cases of strategic importance; decisions in other cases are delegated to the staff.[25] The OFT has the power to conduct investigations and adopt (interim and) final decisions, including decisions imposing financial penalties. Under the Enterprise Act 2002, the infringement of certain important provisions of UK competition law constitutes a criminal offence punishable by imprisonment of up to five years. However, the OFT may not impose such custodial penalties. Criminal cartel offences are in practice prosecuted by the Serious Fraud Office and adjudicated by criminal courts.[26]

[19] See A Frignani, 'Competition Law in Italy', in Vogelaar *et al*, above n 17, 361, 374.

[20] Section 10(7) of Law No 287/90, the Italian Competition and Fair Trading Act (*Norme per la tutela della concorrenza e del mercato*).

[21] Section 10(2) of Law No 287/90.

[22] Frignani, above n 19, 374 and 414. In view of the separation of the investigative and the adjudicative functions and the fact that final decisions are taken by a collegiate body comparable to an adjudicative agency (see n 8 regarding the bifurcated agency model), the Italian system shows as least as many similarities with the bifurcated model than the enforcement system prevailing in the Netherlands.

[23] Additional functions are assigned to the Secretary of State, the Lord Chancellor, the Serious Fraud Office and the Competition Commission. However, their involvement in individual cases is either rare (Secretary of State) or limited to specific procedures (Competition Commission: mergers, general market investigations, regulated sectors; Serious Fraud Office: criminal cartel offences). The Lord Chancellor only has regulatory powers. See R Whish, *Competition Law* (London, LexisNexis, 5th edn, 2003), 64–5, 69, 71.

[24] This means that, in contrast to the functions of the Director General of Fair Trading, the functions of the OFT are not carried out in the name of an individual office-holder. Whish, above n 25, 65.

[25] Whish, above n 23, 65.

[26] Whish, above n 23, 69 and 74. See also D Guy, 'The UK's Experience with Criminal Law Sanctions' in Cseres *et al*, above n 16, 248, 251–2. With regard to cartel violations that are criminal offences, the UK thus applies the bifurcated model.

In the Czech Republic, the Office for the Protection of Competition (Úřad pro ochranu hospodářské soutěž, 'Czech Competition Office') performs the functions of investigation, prosecution and adjudication of cartel infringements. The Czech Competition Office is an independent authority headed by a chairman who is appointed for a six-year term and may not be a member of any political party. The Office has several divisions, among which is a competition unit that, in turn, consists of several departments, including a cartel department.[27] It may carry out investigations, determine the existence of an infringement, prohibit the performance of an illegal agreement or practice and impose fines on the undertakings concerned.[28]

2. The Bifurcated Model

In a dual system, the investigative functions are separated from the adjudicative. Mostly, the power to investigate and prosecute, on the one hand, and the power to adjudicate, on the other hand, are vested in two separate bodies, one of which is often a court of law. Sometimes there are even three different bodies involved. This is notably the case where a specialised body, distinct from the investigative agency, is entrusted with the prosecution of infringements, ie that body must bring formal complaints before a court or another adjudicative body, which will then adopt a final decision.[29] Examples for a dual (or even tripartite) structure are the institutional regimes in France, Belgium, Sweden and Austria.

In France, there used to be two principal bodies involved in the enforcement of competition law. The Direction Général de la Concurrence, de la Consommation et de la Répression des Fraudes (DGCCRF), which forms part of the Ministry of Economic Affairs, is entrusted inter alia with the task to ensure observance of the competition rules and, to this end, could investigate anti-competitive agreements and practices on its own initiative.[30] However, it may not issue prohibition decisions or impose

---

[27] In addition, the Czech Competition Office also comprises a state aid department and a public procurement section. See the organigram available at www.compet.cz/en/about-the-office/structure-of-the-office/.

[28] Arts 7(1), 21(5) and 22(2) of the Czech Competition Act (Act No 143/2001).

[29] See, eg the institutional arrangement in the UK with regard to criminal cartel offences which are prosecuted by the Serious Fraud Office. See above n 26 and accompanying text.

[30] D Voillemot, 'Competition law in France', in Vogelaar *et al*, above n 17, 151, 166 and 204. See also Art L450-1 of the Code de Commerce. Only recently, by Law No 2008-776 of 4 August 2008, has the dual structure of the French enforcement system largely been abandoned. With effect from January 2009, a new competition agency—Autorité de la concurrence—has been established which combines the investigative and decision-making functions formerly divided between the Ministry of Economy and the Conseil de la concurrence. Most notably, the Autorité de la concurrence has its own investigation service and is also vested with decision-making powers in the field of merger control. The Ministry of Economy, however, retains certain limited intervention rights with regard to the control of concentrations.

fines. This was the prerogative of the Conseil de la concurrence, an independent administrative body, composed of 17 members who were former judges, experts in competition, economic or consumer matters, or highly regarded individuals with a professional career in certain sectors of the economy.[31] The Conseil de la concurrence could act either on its own initiative or at the request of the Minister of Economic Affairs. Undertakings, industry and trade associations, and professional or consumer organisations could also bring matters before it.[32] The Conseil de la concurrence had the power to order the termination of an infringement and impose administrative (pecuniary) sanctions on the undertakings concerned.[33] In certain cases, the officers of an undertaking engaged in illegal practices may face criminal sanctions, including imprisonment of up to four years.[34] Such criminal sanctions must, however, be imposed by a criminal court. Therefore, the Conseil de la concurrence could transmit the file to the criminal courts if it considers that the infringements qualify as criminal offences under French competition law.[35]

It must be noted, however, that the separation of investigative and adjudicative functions was not always strictly respected in the French system. The adjudicative body, the Conseil de la concurrence, had a group of permanent reporters who were not only in charge of reporting on the cases, but also responsible for investigating them.[36] Also, the DGCCRF sometimes carried out investigations at the request and under the supervision of the Conseil de la concurrence.[37]

Under Swedish competition law, the tasks are essentially divided between the national competition authority, the Konkurrensverket (KKV), and the Stockholm District Court.[38] The KKV is an independent govern-

---

[31] See Arts L461-1 and L462-6 of the Code de Commerce. The Conseil de la concurrence could hear matters in a plenary session (at least 8 members), in chambers (at least 3 members) or in the permanent commission including the President and the three Vice-Presidents of the Conseil. Art L461-3 of the Code de Commerce; Voillemot, above n 30, 164. Since the Conseil de la concurrence was not a judicial body, but a multi-member commission, Trebilcock and Iacobucci (above n 8) would probably classify the former French system as a bifurcated agency model.

[32] Art L462-5 of the Code de Commerce. Where the DGCCRF, after having conducted an investigation, concluded that the competition rules are violated, it proposed to the Minister of Economy to refer the case to the Conseil de la concurrence. Voillemot, above n 30, 164–5.

[33] Voillemot, above n 30, 191–2.

[34] See Art L420-6 of the Code de Commerce. This concerns officers who fraudulently played a personal and determining role in the infringement.

[35] Voillemot, above n 30, 193. Criminal proceedings against individuals can also be initiated by a public prosecutor (*procureur de la République*). As concerns criminal cartel offences, the French system is thus also based on the bifurcated (judicial) model (like the system in the UK).

[36] Code de Commerce, Art L-450-1, 2nd sentence.

[37] Cf Voillemot, above n 30, 164 and 166.

[38] An additional role is assigned to a specialised court also located in Stockholm, the Marknadsdomstolen ('Market Court'). The Market Court can order the termination of an infringement at the request of an undertaking affected by that infringement in cases where the KKV decides not to take any action. Furthermore, the Market Court hears appeals against

mental body with an administrative organisational structure. It is divided into departments, including three competition law departments, each of which is specialised in certain economic sectors.[39] In contrast to the DGCCRF in France, the KKV, which has equally been vested with fact-finding powers[40] and thus performs the investigative functions within the Swedish system, may also issue cease-and-desist orders.[41] However, it has very limited authority to impose fines. The KKV must normally apply to the Stockholm District Court if it wants undertakings to be penalised for breaching the competition rules.[42] Only in uncontested cases where the companies admit their involvement in the infringement and are willing to accept an administrative fine can the KKV itself impose the sanction by a so-called fee order (*avgiftsföreläggande*).[43] As concerns its jurisdiction under the Swedish Competition Act, the Stockholm District Court mainly hears cases regarding the imposition of fines.[44]

The Belgian rules on competition are mainly laid down in the Law of 10 June 2006 on the Protection of Economic Competition (*Wet tot de bescherming van de economische mededinging/Loi sur la protection de la concurrence économique*) (WEM 2006), which replaces the Law of 5 August 1991.[45] The 2006 amendments were predominantly made in order to take account of the changes at European level.[46] One of the original features of the WEM is the dualism between the two principal competition law institutions, notably the Competition Council (Raad voor

judgments of the Stockholm District Court and certain decisions of the KKV. L Widén and S Lindeborg, 'Competition Law in Sweden', in F Vogelaar, J Stuyck, B Van Reeken (eds), *Competition Law in the EU, Its Member States and Switzerland, Volume II* (The Hague, Kluwer Law International, 2002), 395, 406–7 and 437–8.

[39] Widén and Lindeborg, *ibid*, 406. The KKV also applies the rules relating to public procurement.

[40] See s 5 of the Swedish Competition Act (as amended on 1 November 2008).

[41] See s 3 § 1 of the Swedish Competition Act.

[42] See ss 3 § 5 and 6 § 2 of the Swedish Competition Act.

[43] This possibility was only introduced recently with the amendments to the Swedish Competition Act that entered into force on 1 November 2008 (see s 3 §§ 16–19 of the Swedish Competition Act). It gives suspected companies the opportunity to avoid a lengthy and costly trial before the Stockholm District Court. On these recent amendments see H Andersson and E Legnerfält, 'The New Swedish Competition Act' (2008) 29 *European Competition Law Review* 563

[44] And cases regarding the prohibition of concentrations. Widén and Lindeborg, above n 38, 406. Pursuant to s 3 § 26 of the Swedish Competition Act, the Stockholm District Court is also competent to hear private actions for the award of damages.

[45] They are complemented by the Law of 10 June 2006 on the establishment of a competition council (Wet tot oprichting van een Raad voor de mededinging). The articles are quoted according to the numbering of the consolidated version of the WEM of 15 September 2006, which integrates both the aforementioned laws (published in the *Belgisch Staatsblad/Moniteur Belge* of 29 September 2006, 50613 *et seq*).

[46] K Bourgeois, 'De nieuwe Belgische mededingingswet: enkele belangrijke materiële en procedurele wijzingen' (2007) 55 *Sociaal-Economische Wetgeving* 265, 265; J Stuyck, 'Hoofdstuk II. Restrictieve mededingingspraktijken' in J Stuyck, W Devroe and P Wytinck (eds), *De nieuwe Belgische Mededingingswet 2006* (Mechelen, Kluwer, 2007), 21. The first WEM came into force on 1 April 1993. The most recent amendments took effect on 1 October 2006.

de Mededinging/Conseil de la concurrence, 'Raad'), an administrative tribunal, and the Competition Service (Dienst van mededinging/Service de la concurrence, 'Competition Service'), a department within the Ministry of Economic Affairs. In 1999 the WEM was substantially amended, mainly to remedy the unsatisfactory functioning of the institutions created in 1991.[47] Under the WEM 1999, the institutional structure could even have been described as trinomial since the amendments led to the creation of a third body, the Korps Verslaggevers/Corps des rapporteurs ('Reporters Unit'), which was established to reinforce the Competition Service.[48] Under the WEM 2006, the Reporters Unit, however, has been renamed 'Auditors Unit' (Auditoraat/Auditorat) and has been integrated into the Raad.[49] Even though the Auditors Unit has retained its independent function,[50] the tripartite character of the Belgian system now seems less pronounced. On the other hand, the dual character is beyond doubt in that the Auditoraat independently and autonomously determines the order in which individual matters are treated and also defines the general enforcement priorities.[51] The Competition Service, by contrast, is part of the Ministry of Economic Affairs, and as such is hierarchically subordinate to the competent Minister.[52] It is charged with the detection and investigation of potential infringements. However, as a result of the 1999 amendments, the Auditors Unit already leads the investigations and instructs the staff of the Competition Service, which thus acts under the authority of the Auditors Unit.[53]

---

[47] K Platteau, 'Competition Law in Belgium', in Vogelaar *et al*, above n 17, 489, 502 and 497.

[48] B Ponet, 'Enige beschouwingen over de moderniseringsverordening vanuit het perspectief van de Raad voor de Mededinging' in J Stuyck and P Wytinck (eds), *De Belgische Mededingingswet anno 2003* (Mechelen, Kluwer, 2003), 78.

[49] See Art 11 §2 WEM 2006.

[50] The independence of the Auditors Unit has even been reinforced by the WEM 2006. Being part of the Raad, the Auditors Unit, unlike the Competition Service, may not receive any instructions from the executive. D Arts, 'Enkele krachtlijnen van de nieuwe Belgische mededingingswet' (2007) 2 *TBM-RCB* 4, para 12; see also B Stulens, 'Hoofdstuk IV. De nieuwe Belgische Mededingingswet. Enkele bemerkingen bij de institutionele architectuur' in Stuyck *et al*, above n 46, 103, 110–11. For J Steenbergen, 'Hoofdstuk I. Institutionele bepalingen' in Stuyck *et al*, above n 46, 5, 13, by contrast, the organisational transfer of the Auditors Unit to the Raad mainly has symbolic character.

[51] See Stulens, *ibid*, 107–8. Under the WEM 2006, the Auditors Unit has also been empowered to reject complaints, while the former power of the Raad to initiate investigations *ex offcio* has been repealed.

[52] Stulens, above n 50, 111–12, therefore rightly suggests that the presidency of the Director-General of the Competition Service over meetings of the Auditors Unit at which the order of cases and other priorities are determined does not really fit into this system. If the purpose of this provision was not to allow for political interference at the ministerial level, but simply to involve the Competition Service in the decision process, the same result could have been achieved by providing, as a mandatory rule, that the Director-General must always be invited to the relevant meetings of the Auditoraat. For Steenbergen, above n 50, 13, this chairmanship rule is, however, the logical consequence of the fact that it is for the Competition Service to represent Belgium in international committees and meetings (eg ECN).

[53] See Platteau, above n 47, 502 and 545, with regard to the situation under the WEM 1999. The Competition Service together with the Reporters' Unit had broad investigatory powers. It

The Auditors Unit also monitors compliance with the decisions of the Raad. In Belgium, the decision-making power in competition matters is vested in the Raad which, by definition, is an *administratief rechtscollege* (administrative court) now consisting of 12 members.[54] The Raad decides inter alia on the existence of an infringement and the imposition of fines. It acts on the basis of the reports drawn up by the Auditoraat.[55] Certain prerogatives which originally had been attributed to the President of the Raad have now been assigned to the Auditors Unit, which hence may, for instance, reject applications for interim measures and decide on the (non-)confidential nature of information in the case file.[56]

Competition law in Austria is essentially governed by the Cartel Act 2005 (Kartellgesetz 2005, 'KartG 2005'), which replaced the Cartel Act 1988 as of 1 January 2006.[57] Initially, Austria had domestic competition rules, but no national competition agency. Enforcement of the competition rules was in the hands of specialised divisions of the Vienna Court of Appeals (Oberlandesgericht Wien), acting as the central cartel court (Kartellgericht) for the whole of Austria.[58] Only in 2002, following an amendment of the Cartel Act 1988, which, however, still retained the jurisdiction of the Kartellgericht, the Austrian competition authority (Bundeswettbewerbsbehörde; BWB) was established. The BWB is an

could also set enforcement priorities, ie it determined the order in which cases were dealt with. *Ibid.* While the latter function has been transferred to the Auditoraat, the other powers have remained essentially unchanged. For the current situation, ie the investigatory powers of the Auditoraat, see in particular Arts 34 No1, 44, 45, 47 and 48 §1 WEM 2006.

[54] Art 11 §1 WEM 2006. Prior to October 2006, only four members (out of a total of 20) fulfilled their tasks on a full-time basis. See Art 17(4) WEM 1999. This may have been one of the reasons why the Belgian system was in the past often recorded as less efficient than other competition authorities in the EU. Cf I Forrester, 'The Modernisation of EC Antitrust Policy: Compatibility, Efficiency and Legal Security' in C-D Ehlermann and I Atanasiu (eds), *European Competition Law Annual 2000. The Modernisation of EC Antitrust Policy* (Oxford, Hart Publishing, 2001), 30–1. On the difficulties of the Belgian competition authority, in the past, to guarantee an efficient enforcement policy see also Steenbergen, above n 50, 5–6. Under the new rules introduced in 2006, the total number of members of the Raad has been reduced to 12, but the number of full-time magistrates has been increased to six (see Art 12 §1 WEM 2006).

[55] A report contains the details of the investigation, a proposed statement of objections and a proposal for a decision, as well as an indication of confidential documents (Art 45 §4 WEM 2006). It is important to note that Auditors are entitled to commence investigations on their own initiative (Art 44 §1 No 2 and 47 WEM 2006).

[56] Cf Platteau, above n 47, 503–4 for the former rules and Art 45 §2 and §4 WEM 2006 for the current situation.

[57] On this recent reform see J Barbist, 'Austria Goes Europe—Major Reform in the Austrian Competition System' (2005) 26 *European Competition Law Review* 611 and P Lissel, 'Kartellgesetz 2005 und Wettbewerbsgesetznovelle in Österreich' (2006) 52 *Recht der Internationalen Wirtschaft* 128.

[58] A weakness of that system was the fact that the Kartellgericht could, in principle, only act upon the application of a party (even though certain public entities, such as the Chamber of Economic Affairs (Wirtschaftskammer Österreich), could file an application) and was thus precluded from intervening *ex officio* in the public interest. F Höpfel and R Kert, 'Country Analysis—Austria' in G Dannecker and O Jansen (eds), *Competition Law Sanctioning in the European Union* (The Hague, Kluwer Law International, 2004), 305, 309.

independent administrative agency headed by the Director General for Competition, who is not subject to any governmental instructions.[59] The BWB is entrusted with the preservation of effective competition. To this end, it has been vested with wide-ranging investigative powers.[60] It may, however, not order itself the termination of an infringement or impose fines, the adjudicative function (still) being performed by the Kartellgericht. The Kartellgericht can be seized either by the BWB, the Federal Antitrust Attorney (Bundeskartellanwalt) or other interested parties, such as undertakings affected by the alleged breach of the competition rules and certain public entities enumerated in the law.[61]

The Austrian system is a variant of the bifurcated model since, in addition to the BWB and the Kartellgericht, the institutional arrangements provide for a Federal Antitrust Attorney who represents the public interest in antitrust proceedings before the Kartellgericht.[62] Pursuant to § 40 KartG, the Federal Antitrust Attorney is automatically a party to any such proceedings (*Amtspartei*) whether or not he has filed an application. Together with the BWB, he is the only body entitled to request the Kartellgericht to impose a fine in a specific case. The Federal Antitrust Attorney performs his functions independently of the court, but is placed under the authority of the Federal Minister of Justice, by whom he can be instructed.[63] The BWB and the Federal Antitrust Attorney shall co-operate closely and complement each other in the fulfilment of their respective functions.[64]

B. Which National Bodies Can and Should Participate in the Network?

The above examples illustrate that there is a great diversity in the institutional designs for competition matters in the Member States. Not all Member States have adopted the 'Community model', where a single integrated authority (the Commission) performs the functions of investigating, prosecuting and adjudicating infringements of the competition rules. Often there are two, and sometimes even three, bodies involved in

[59] § 1(3) of the Competition Act, the law on the establishment of the BWB (Bundesgesetz über die Einrichtung einer Bundeswettbewerbsbehörde—Wettbewerbsgesetz). The BWB is, however, part of the Federal Ministry of Economic Affairs and Labour. See § 1(1) of the Competition Act. The institutional system has essentially remained unaffected by the 2005 reform. Barbist, above n 57, 613.

[60] The BWB thus can carry out investigations and collect information. However, it cannot issue legally enforceable information requests or search warrants. This is the prerogative of the Kartellgericht. See Barbist, above n 57, 613.

[61] See § 36 KartG 2005. A public entity that may apply to the *Kartellgericht* is, for instance, the Austrian Chamber of Economic Affairs.

[62] The Austrian enforcement system thus has a trinomial structure.

[63] § 75(1) and (2) KartG 2005.

[64] Höpfel and Kert, above n 58, 310.

the enforcement of competition law in a particular Member State. The Commission is aware of the problem. Consequently, Article 35(1) of Regulation 1/2003 leaves it to the Member States to

> designate the competition authority or authorities responsible for the application of Articles 81 and 82 EC in such a way that the provisions of this regulation are effectively complied with.

Thus Regulation 1/2003 fully recognises the institutional and procedural autonomy of the Member States.[65] It only obliges Member States to have a competition authority and grant it the power to apply Articles 81 and 82 EC. However, the institutional structure is entirely within the discretion of the Member States. Theoretically, (all) those national bodies that are empowered to apply Articles 81 and 82 EC as public enforcers could perform the functions attributed to competition authorities/NCAs[66] by Regulation 1/2003, including collaboration within the ECN.[67] In those Member States where more than one body is involved in the public enforcement of EC competition law, the question then arises which body can and should be a member of the Network. It is conceivable, but probably not always desirable, that several national bodies of the same Member State could participate in the Network, if necessary on an alternating basis, depending on the subject matter of the discussion or consultation. The same bodies that are designated as 'competition authorities' should also be represented in the Advisory Committee.[68]

1. Administrative Agencies versus Courts

As demonstrated above, some Member States (eg Sweden, Belgium) follow the bifurcated model, whereby a court, administrative tribunal or quasi-judicial body is involved in the public enforcement[69] of competition law.

---

[65] A Komninos, 'Art 234 and National Competition Authorities in the Era of Decentralisation' (2004) 29 *EL Rev* 106, 109; W Wils, 'The Reform of Competition Law Enforcement—Will it Work?', Community Report for the FIDE XXI Congress, Dublin, 2–5 June 2004, in D Cahill (ed), *The Modernisation of EU Competition Law Enforcement in the EU—FIDE 2004 National Reports* (Cambridge, Cambridge University Press, 2004) (available at SSRN: http://ssrn.com/abstract=1319249), 661, para 180. See also recital 35 of Reg 1/2003.

[66] Curiously enough, the term 'national competition authorities' is not used either in Reg 1/2003 or in the Network Notice. In both documents, the NCAs are referred to as 'the competition authorities of the Member States'. However, the Network Notice uses the abbreviation 'NCAs', which obviously stems from the term 'national competition authorities'.

[67] The only limitation results from the reference, in recital 35 of Reg 1/2003, to 'public enforcers', which excludes authorities that intervene only in disputes between private parties. See M Van Der Woude, 'Exchange of Information within the European Competition Network: Scope and Limits' in Ehlermann and Atanasiu, above n 7, 369, 377.

[68] *Ibid.*

[69] As opposed to 'private enforcement', which describes the application of competition law in the context of private law suits, such as contractual claims or commercial disputes between private parties.

However, the term 'competition authority' as used in Regulation 1/2003 is a Community law concept[70] and, at first sight, might be understood to encompass only administrative agencies such as the Commission.[71] A preliminary issue arising in this context is therefore the question of whether courts and other (quasi-)judicial bodies involved in the application of EC competition law can be regarded as NCAs for the purposes of Regulation 1/2003.

The ECJ has had to deal with the concept of competition authority on several occasions in the context of interpreting Article 9(3) of Regulation 17. Under that provision, 'the authorities of the Member States' remained competent to apply Article 85(1) [now Article 81(1)] for as long as the Commission had not initiated any procedure. Initially, in *Bilger v Jehle*, the ECJ simply held that 'the concept of "authorities of the Member States" includes national courts'.[72] However, following this judgment, there was considerable debate about the question as to what extent the initiation of proceedings by the Commission would bar national courts from applying Article 81(2).[73] Doubts arose in particular since the ECJ had not clarified whether the notion was limited to courts whose primary function is the direct enforcement of the competition rules or whether it would also include ordinary courts that apply Articles 81 and 82 EC only incidentally, ie as a preliminary point in the context of private law suits. In other words, it was unclear whether any national court qualified as 'authority' within the meaning of Article 9(3) of Regulation 17 or whether the provision applied only to particular courts.[74]

The question was eventually decided by the ECJ in 1974 in *BRT v SABAM*.[75] In that case, the ECJ draw a distinction between courts whose competence to apply Articles 81 and 82 EC derives from the direct effect of those provisions and those which apply Articles 81 and 82 EC by virtue of Article 84 EC. The first category consists of those courts before which the prohibitions contained in those Articles are invoked in a dispute governed by private law.[76] The second category includes only courts which are especially entrusted with the task of enforcing domestic competition law (or ensuring the legality of that enforcement by the administrative

[70] Gauer, above n 14, 188.
[71] Cf para 4 of the 1997 Co-operation Notice, where both the Commission and the NCAs are referred to as 'administrative authorities'.
[72] Case 43/69 *Bilger v Jehle* [1970] ECR 127, para 9.
[73] See C Kerse, *EC Antitrust Procedure* (London, Sweet & Maxwell, 3rd edn, 1994), para 10.02.
[74] In 1973, in *Brasserie de Haecht* [1973] ECR 77, a matter that also concerned the interpretation of Art 9(3) of Reg 17, the issue was still left open. See para 16 of the judgment, where the ECJ simply stated that there was no need to re-examine the question of whether the words 'authorities of the Member States' also refer to national courts acting pursuant to Art 85(2) [now Art 81(2)].
[75] Case 127/73 *BRT v SABAM* [1974] ECR 51.
[76] See para 14 and 15 of the judgment in *BRT v SABAM* (*ibid*).

authorities) and also are rendered competent to apply Articles 81 and 82 EC (public enforcement).[77] Observing that Articles 81 and 82 EC create direct rights in respect of individuals which national courts must safeguard, the ECJ held that it would mean depriving individuals of rights which they hold under the Treaty itself if the national courts' jurisdiction to afford that safeguard was denied. The ECJ concluded that the term 'authorities of the Member States' contained in Article 9(3) of Regulation 17 does not cover courts applying Articles 81 and 82 EC by virtue of their direct effect (ie courts of the first category), but refers solely to those national authorities whose competence derives from Article 84 EC (ie courts of the second category).[78]

It follows from the above that those courts of the Member States which have been entrusted to apply (or ensure the proper application of) domestic and EC competition law (by way of public enforcement) may be regarded as competition authorities within the meaning of Regulation 1/2003. The Commission has taken the diversity of the institutional arrangements in the Member States and the above case law into account. Article 35(1) of Regulation 1/2003 explicitly states that the authorities to be designated by the Member States may include courts. Pursuant to Article 35(2) of Regulation 1/2003, Member States which have a dual enforcement system may give different powers and functions to the different (administrative and judicial) bodies involved. In principle, the Member States are therefore free to designate courts, either alone or in addition to any administrative agency empowered to apply Articles 81 and 82 EC, as an NCA within the meaning of Regulation 1/2003.

2. Designation of the Competition Authorities by the Member States

In view of their obligations under Regulation 1/2003, and in particular Article 35(1) thereof, all Member States have now enacted legislation which, depending on the institutional model, empowers one or several national bodies to implement Articles 81 and 82 EC.

---

[77] See para 18 and 19 of the judgment in *BRT v SABAM* (above n 75).

[78] Para 18 to 20 of the judgment in *BRT v SABAM* (above n 75). Another question is whether an NCA which, under national law, is regarded as or assimilated with a court of law or an administrative tribunal can also be considered a court for the purposes of Community law, in particular as regards Art 234 EC. This question had to be tackled by the ECJ in the *Syfait* case, where the ECJ found that the Greek competition commission (Epitropi Antagonismou) could not be considered a court or tribunal for the purposes of Art 234 EC (see further Chapter 1, section II.C.3.c, in particular n 438 and accompanying text). On the other hand, in the Spanish Banks case (Case C–67/91 Dirección General de Defensa de la Competencia v Asociación Española de Banca Privada and others ('*Spanish Banks*') [1992] ECR I–4785), a reference for a preliminary ruling submitted by the former Spanish competition authority, the Tribunal de defensa de la competencia, the ECJ did not decline jurisdiction and thus implicitly recognised that the Spanish competition authority was as court within the meaning of Art 234 EC.

a. Member States with Integrated Authorities

In the Member States where there is a single integrated competition authority, that authority is usually exclusively responsible for the enforcement of Articles 81 and 82 EC and the fulfilment of the duties arising from Regulation 1/2003. In the Netherlands, for instance, the Board of Directors of the NMa has been designated as responsible authority within the meaning of Regulation 1/2003.[79] In Germany, the Bundeskartellamt is authorised to enforce Articles 81 and 82 EC. It also has to ensure co-operation with the Commission and the other NCAs within the ECN.[80] Equally, the Czech Competition Office is empowered to apply Articles 81 and 82 EC. It enjoys all the rights and has to fulfil all the duties arising in connection with the implementation of Regulation 1/2003, including the appointment of a representative in the Advisory Committee.[81] In Italy, responsibility for enforcing the EC rules on competition lies with the Autorità Garante. It also liaises with the Commission and the other NCAs in accordance with the relevant EU provisions and is a member of the Advisory Committee.[82] In the UK, the OFT has authority to enforce Articles 81 and 82 EC; it is also the OFT that maintains the relations with the Commission and the other NCAs, and is a member of the ECN.[83]

Since only one authority is involved in the enforcement of competition law in these Member States, co-operation and consultation with the Commission and other NCAs should not pose any particular problems from an institutional or organisational perspective.

b. Member States with Dual Enforcement Systems

In those Member States where the enforcement tasks are divided between several bodies, it is not always evident which body may participate in the Network and appoint a representative for the Advisory Committee. Moreover, pursuant to Article 11(3) and (4) of Regulation 1/2003, the Commission must be informed of the initiation of proceedings and shall also be provided with a draft of the final decision. Since, under the bifurcated model, the initiation of proceedings and the final decision taking are

---

[79] Art 88 of the Dutch Competition Act.

[80] See §§ 50 and 50a GWB To the extent that a case falls within the jurisdiction of the cartel authority of a *Land* (*Landeskartellbehörde*), that *Landeskartellbehörde* is also competent to apply Arts 81 and 82 EC. However, the co-operation and consultation process is always channelled through the Bundeskartellamt, which is the only point of contact for the Commission and the NCAs of the other Member States and therefore acts as sole representative in the Advisory Committee. See § 50(2) and (3) GWB

[81] See Art 20a of the Czech Competition Act.

[82] s 10(4) of the Italian Competition Act.

[83] Whish, above n 23, 68.

usually in the hands of different institutions, it is particularly important to determine who communicates with the Commission (and possibly the other NCAs) and forwards the relevant documents.

(1) Involvement of Several Bodies. The situation in Sweden is relatively straightforward, since the KKV is responsible for both investigating and prohibiting Article 81 and 82 infringements. This includes the right to carry out inspections at the request of the Commission or other NCAs.[84] It will therefore be for the KKV, who initiates proceedings and takes the final prohibition decisions, to comply with the obligations under Article 11(3) and (4) of Regulation 1/2003.[85] Co-operation with other NCAs concerning fact-finding measures pursuant to Articles 12 and 22 of Regulation 1/2003 will also be the responsibility of the KKV.[86]

In other Member States with a dual system, the situation is more complex. In France, both the DGCCRF and the Conseil de la concurrence were initially empowered to apply Articles 81 and 82 EC within their respective spheres of competence. [87] This dualism is particularly relevant with regard to the (formal) initiation of proceedings under the EC competition rules, of which the Commission has to be notified, since both the DGCCRF and the Conseil de la concurrence could start investigations at their own initiative.

Similarly, in Austria, the BWB is responsible for implementing Articles 81 and 82 EC to the extent that the Kartellgericht is not competent.[88] In other words, the BWB will investigate potential violations of the EC competition rules, while final decisions regarding the termination of the infringement or the imposition of fines will be taken by the Vienna Court of Appeals acting as Kartellgericht. It is also the BWB which is obliged, where applicable, to assist the Commission and collaborate with other NCAs within the framework of the ECN.[89]

---

[84] Section 5 § 14–17 of the Swedish Competition Act. The KKV must apply to the Stockholm District Court only to have fines imposed on the undertakings and, where necessary, to obtain a search warrant (s 3 § 5 and s 5 § 3 of the Swedish Competition Act).

[85] From an EU law perspective, there is no need to involve the Stockholm District Court in any way in the co-operation process with the Commission or other NCAs (except for cases where a search warrant is required). The obligation, imposed by Art 11(4) of Reg 1/2003, to inform the Commission prior to the adoption of a final decision applies only with regard to prohibition decisions, commitment decisions and decisions withdrawing block exemptions, while decisions which merely impose a fine (after the conduct in question has already been prohibited) would not seem to be subject to the information duty. See above Chapter 1, section II.B.3.c.

[86] It should be mentioned, though, that, by ministerial decree of 27 May 2004, Sweden has designated the KKV, the Stockholm District Court and the Market Court as competition authorities within the meaning of Reg 1/2003, each with regard to its specific sphere of responsibilities under the Swedish Competition Act.

[87] See Art L470-6 of the Code de Commerce.

[88] Section 3(1) of the Competition Act 2002 and s 42f of the KartG.

[89] In this context, it can exchange information with those authorities. On these functions, see Lissel, above n 57, 132. On the other hand, all three actors under the Austrian competition rules, ie BWB, Kartellgericht and Bundeskartellanwalt, are regarded as the Austrian

In Belgium, the three national enforcement bodies, ie the Raad, the Competition Service and the Auditors Unit, are considered to form together the 'national Belgian competition authority'—each with regard to its respective sphere of competence—and as such have been designated as a competition authority within the meaning of Article 35 of Regulation 1/2003.[90] Moreover, Article 71 WEM 2006 explicitly empowers all three bodies to forward information to the Commission and other NCAs, and to use in evidence information received from those authorities. However, the obligation imposed on NCAs by Article 11(4) of Regulation 1/2003 to inform the Commission of any envisaged national decision is not specifically addressed. A provision similar to that of Article 71 WEM 2006 had in fact already been enacted by a Royal Decree (*Koninklijk Besluit*) of 25 April 2004 amending the WEM 1999 in order to adapt it to the requirements of Regulation 1/2003.[91] The preamble to this Royal Decree suggests that the obligation is incumbent on the Raad.[92] Finally, Article 34 No 2 WEM 2006 provides that the Competition Service is to represent Belgium in the European and international competition organisations. Obviously, the Belgian legislator had not only the Advisory Committee in mind, but also the ECN and the ICN (International Competition Network). Apart from the facts that the ECN is not an (international) organisation[93] but predominantly an electronic platform and that its members are not formal representatives of the Member States but simple participants or users of a given infrastructure[94], the most striking effect of this provision is that it

competition authority within the meaning of Art 35 of Reg 1/2003. See J Barbist, 'Das österreichische Kartellobergericht und die VO Nr 1/2003' (2005) 55 *Wirtschaft und Wettbewerb* 756, 757.

[90] Art 1 No 4 WEM 2006. The Auditors Unit is not expressly mentioned in this provision. However, having been integrated into the Raad, the Auditors Unit undoubtedly forms part of the competition authority within the meaning of Reg 1/2003. Cf P Nihoul, 'Le projet de loi belge sur la protection de la concurrence économique' (2006) 1 *TBM-RCB* 4, para 14.

[91] See *Belgisch Staatsblad/Moniteur Belge* of 3 May 2004. Art 50 WEM 1999 as amended by Art 5 of that Royal Decree was, however, slightly incomplete in that it excluded the Competition Service from exchanging information with the Commission and did not mention the right to use information obtained from another Network member as evidence in the own proceedings.

[92] See the explanatory memorandum (Verslag aan de Koning) to Art 2 of the Royal Decree (*ibid*): 'Artikel 11, paragraaf 4 van de Verordening [1/2003] bepaalt dat uiterlijk 30 dagen vóór het aannemen van een beslissing . . . Ten einde de Raad voor de Mededinging in de mogelijkheid te stellen om aan deze verplichting te voldoen'. Further, the explanatory memorandum to Art 5 of the same Royal Decree goes on to say: 'doch ook dient de Belgische autoriteit aan te geven in welke zin zij een beslissing zal nemen, taak die behoort tot de bevoegdheidssfeer van de Raad voor de mededinging'. This is also the position of Nihoul, above n 90, para 58. It is, however, uncertain that this approach is compatible with the fundamental guarantee of a fair trial. See below I.B.2.b(2) and Chapter 5 III.B.

[93] K Dekeyser and M Jaspers, 'A New Era of ECN Co-operation' (2007) 30 *World Competition* 3, 4. Neither can the Advisory Committee or the ICN be regarded as international organisations.

[94] Nihoul, above n 90, para 21. Presumably, the term 'international competition organisations' (*internationale mededingingsorganisaties/organisations internationales de concurrence*) in Art 34 No 2 WEM 2006 is used in a broad sense and meant to encompass all kinds of international bodies, not only international organisations *sensu stricto*.

seems to completely exclude the Raad from this important co-operation mechanism.[95]

In each example, two enforcement bodies of the same Member State (in Belgium even three) would seem to have a legitimate interest in participating in the Network (eg in France in order to avoid unnecessary parallel proceedings being conducted in several Member States; in Austria to be able to liaise with the Commission, thereby complying with the different obligations under Article 11(3) and (4) of Regulation 1/2003). It is therefore important that Member States whose enforcement systems are similar to the French or Austrian model clearly define the national body or bodies which shall liaise with the Commission (and possibly other NCAs) and fulfil the information duties established by Article 11(3) and (4) of Regulation 1/2003. Where they opt for designating both national enforcement bodies as NCAs within the meaning of Regulation 1/2003, precise rules are required that indicate when (ie at which point of the national procedure) each body is to liaise with the Commission and which type(s) of documents it shall provide.[96] Moreover, the participation or representation of each body in meetings of the Advisory Committee must be regulated,[97] in particular with regard to meetings where individual cases

[95] Not only does Art 34 No 2 WEM 2006 not mention the Raad; Art 21 WEM provides that, on its own initiative, the Raad can only participate in meetings of the judiciary (*rechterlijke autoriteiten/autorités juridictionelles*). For other meetings at the European or international level, prior authorisation by the competent Minister is required. According to J Steenbergen, 'Naar een nieuwe Belgische Mededingingswet: de institutionele bepalingen' (2006) 54 *Sociaal-Economische Wetgeving* 61, 66, this arrangement is fully in line with the dualism of the Belgian enforcement system and is meant to preclude the Raad from becoming involved in the Commission's enforcement policy. However, it is submitted, the Raad could also make valuable contributions to discussions on general (horizontal) or even policy issues in the ECN, which is above all a platform for an informal dialogue between the national authorities and the Commission, since the Raad takes part in the actual enforcement of the rules and is thus aware of particular problems arising in this respect (cf Steenbergen, above n 50, 14: 'Het zou jammer zijn indien de Raad niet kan deelnemen aan besprekingen die vooral een informerend en vormend karakter hebben . . .'.) Making its presence in the ECN dependent on a ministerial approval is not a practical solution. Much will depend on the individual Minister's policy in this respect (*ibid*). Apart from the question of practicability, it is not quite clear what the legislator means by the term *autorités juridictionelles*. There is an informal platform pooling competition judges in the EU, but no formal body created under the auspices of the EU or the Commission in implementation of Reg 1/2003. The provision thus appears to be largely meaningless. Nihoul, above n 90, 22.

[96] On this basis, the Belgian rules appear, on the one hand, too vague in that they do not specify, for each information or consultation duty imposed by Reg 1/2003, which of the three national bodies is to assume responsibility. On the other hand, the WEM 2006 seems to be too restrictive. Excluding the Raad altogether from participation in the ECN and the Advisory Committee (unless permission has been granted by the responsible Minister) seems to run counter to the objective of these boards, in particular with regard to possible discussions of horizontal matters and policy issues. Under Belgian law, enforcement priorities are essentially determined by the Auditors Unit (which now is part of the Raad). See Steenbergen, *ibid*, 65. In this respect, for instance, coordinating measures with the Commission may be required to ensure effective and efficient enforcement.

[97] See Idot, above n 7, 214. Cf also the Report of the European Parliament on the Draft Regulation (document no A5-0229/2001], 11 (Amendment 9), which suggests that, where there

are discussed and the attendance of the case handler is requested.[98] Otherwise, there is a risk of conflicts between the national bodies concerned and the danger that their views and interests are not properly represented which might ultimately prevent both relevant bodies from playing an influential or meaningful role in the Network and the Advisory Committee.

The complexity of the matter can be illustrated by the situation in Belgium, where all three bodies are members of the ECN. While the Auditoraat has limited access to the common Intranet and can upload on that system information on new matters initiated by it, requests for information exchange and assistance in fact-finding measures from foreign NCAs must always be directed to the Competition Service that is the 'official' permanent representative of the Belgian NCA in the ECN,[99] even though it is the Auditoraat which will ultimately have to satisfy the request.[100] Meetings of the ECN are usually attended by the Competition Service and a member of the Auditoraat and/or the Raad. The latter can be present only if it has obtained the prior approval of the competent Minister. However, where individual matters are discussed or the NCA's position on general policy issues is determined, the Raad will refrain from participating in the debate in view of the principle of impartiality.[101]

(2) Co-operation and Impartiality of the Judiciary. There may, however, be legal or even constitutional problems where a judicial or quasi-judicial body is to liaise with the Commission and would therefore be expected to participate also in the Network (such as the *Kartellgericht* in Austria, the Conseil de la concurrence in France and the Raad in Belgium). The bifurcated model is evidently inspired by the concept of separation of powers and the principle that nobody should be party and judge in the same case.[102] Executive (investigation of infringements) and adjudicative functions are vested in distinct bodies. The choice for this model also implies that the body performing the adjudicative function is independent from the government and impartial with regard to the parties.[103] There are basically

are two competition authorities in a Member State, (only) one should be represented in the Advisory Committee.

[98] See Art 14(2) of Reg 1/2003. Cf also E Paulis, 'Coherent Application of EC Competition Law in a System of Parallel Competences' in Ehlermann and Atanasiu, above n 54, 399–407.

[99] See Art 34 No 2 WEM 2006.

[100] Because inspections and other fact-finding measures are conducted under the direction of the Auditoraat, which instructs the Competition Service. The reply is again channelled through the Competition Service, which has global access to the Intranet.

[101] See the following paragraph, Chapter 2, section I.B.2.b(2).

[102] *Nemo iudex in causa sua.*

[103] See J Steenbergen, 'Decision-making in Competition Cases: The Investigator, the Prosecutor and the Judge' in L Gormley (ed), *Current and Future Perspectives on EC Competition Law—A Tribute to Professor MR Mok* (London, Kluwer Law International, 1997), 101, 103 and 107. See also D Waelbroeck and D Fosselard, 'Should the Decision-making Power in EC Antitrust Procedures be Left to an Independent Judge?—The Impact of the European

two aspects of the co-operation mechanisms under Regulation 1/2003 that seem hardly reconcilable with this concept.

First, NCAs are obliged to communicate an envisaged prohibition or commitment decision to the Commission.[104] In dual enforcement systems where prohibition decisions are issued by a separate body, this duty would have to be fulfilled by the national body adjudicating competition cases. The communication of the draft decision to the Commission may, however, entail discussions about its content and the contemplated outcome of the proceedings. The Commission has clearly stated that it considers the right of evocation only as last resort. Where conflicts arise, the Commission intends to solve them primarily through intensive discussion and consultation with the NCA concerned.[105] This approach implies that the Commission generally expects NCAs to take due account of the views expressed by it in the course of this consultation process.[106]

Secondly, Articles 81 and 82 cases that are dealt with at national level may be put on the agenda of the Advisory Committee.[107] As a consequence, such cases can be discussed at the meetings of the Advisory Committee and NCAs are likely to exchange views on them. This may unduly influence the adjudicative body that has to render the final decision in the case discussed if it is represented at the meeting.[108]

Both situations may compromise the independence and impartiality[109] of the judicial body concerned. This issue even has a human rights dimension to it.[110] In Member States where the adjudicative body is an

Convention on Human Rights on EC Antitrust Procedures' (1994) 14 *Yearbook of European Law* 111, 113, specifically with regard to the Belgian Raad voor de Mededinging.

[104] The rule also applies with regard to decisions withdrawing the benefit of a block exemption.

[105] A Schaub, 'The Reform of Regulation 17/62: The Issues of Compatibility, Effective Enforcement and Legal Certainty' in Ehlermann and Atanasiu, above n 54, 241, 255.

[106] A Jones and B Sufrin, *EC Competition Law* (Oxford, Oxford University Press, 1st edn, 2001), 1027. Jones and Sufrin presume that the possibility of the Commission taking a case out of the jurisdiction of the NCAs increases the pressure on them to adhere to the Commission's opinion.

[107] Art 14(7) of Reg 1/2003.

[108] In my view, the mere presence of the Raad at these meetings entails the risk of undue influence being exercised upon it even if the Raad does not itself participate in the discussions.

[109] Even though both requirements safeguard the objectivity and fairness of proceedings and are often mentioned in the same breath, they describe two different concepts. While impartiality reflects the open-mindedness of the judge, ie the absence of any predisposition or prejudice on his part, independence is a structural and functional guarantee against interference from outside, eg from the executive. P Rädler, 'Independence and Impartiality of Judges' in D Weissbrodt and R Wolfrum (eds), *The Right to a Fair Trial (Beiträge zum ausländischen öffentlichen Recht und Völkerrecht Band 129)* (Berlin, Springer, 1998), 727, 728–9. However, observations of the Commission or views expressed in the Advisory Committee can affect both concepts in that they can unduly influence the judge, ie cause a predisposition of the judge, and, at the same time, constitute an intrusion from an outside body.

[110] On this issue, see W Wils, 'The EU Network of Competition Authorities, The European Convention on Human Rights and the Charter of Fundamental Rights of the EU' in Ehlermann and Atanasiu, above n 7, 433, 457–61.

independent 'tribunal' within the meaning of Article 6 of the European Convention for the Protection of Human Rights and Fundamental Freedoms (ECHR or 'HR Convention'), such as the Stockholm District Court, its participation in the ECN may be incompatible with the requirements of the ECHR. In this respect it is important to note that, in view of the increasing sensitivity of the public to fair administration and justice, the European Court of Human Rights (ECtHR or 'HR Court') attaches considerable importance to outward appearance of independence and impartiality.[111] Therefore, the mere fact that observations submitted by the Commission in the course of the consultation procedure do not formally bind the national tribunal and may thus be disregarded by it do not exclude a violation of Article 6 ECHR simply because the tribunal may be perceived as being predisposed to subscribe to the Commission's opinion.[112]

In view of the principle of separation of powers, it may also raise serious concerns under the constitutional laws of the relevant Member States if the judiciary, be it a national court, administrative tribunal or quasi-judicial body, engages in discussions with the executive branch (ie the Commission) about the outcome of proceedings that are pending before it. Despite the ECJ's ruling in *BRT v SABAM*,[113] it therefore appears advisable for Member States applying the bifurcated model to preclude the adjudicative body from participating in the Network and the Advisory Committee to the extent that the debate concerns individual cases pending before that body if they want to preserve its genuine independence and impartiality, as well as its unbiased public perception.[114] Since the presence of the case handler is normally required when an individual case is discussed in the Advisory Committee, the relevant NCA should in this event be represented by a member of the investigative/prosecuting authority.

The division between investigative/prosecuting and adjudicating functions and the independence of the judiciary also raises the question of how the obligation to inform the Commission of the envisaged decision can

---

[111] 'What is at stake is the confidence which the courts in a democratic society must inspire in the public . . .' See, eg judgments of the ECtHR of 9 June 1998 in the case of *Incal v Turkey* Reports/Recueil 1998-IV, 1547, para 71 and of 26 October 1984 in the case of *De Cubber v Belgium* Publications Series A no 86, para 26. See also judgment of the ECtHR of 30 October 1991 in the case of *Borgers v Belgium* Publications Series A no 214, 21, para 24.

[112] Cf Rädler, above n 109, 729, who points out that the judiciary must inspire confidence in the public that proceedings are really carried out in accordance with the principles of independence and impartiality.

[113] Above n 75.

[114] Cf Wils, above n 110, 461 and 462, who even goes so far as to suggest that independent and impartial tribunals could be excluded from the notion of 'competition authorities of the Member States'. *Contra* the Report of the European Parliament on the Draft Regulation (above n 97), 11, which proposes that, where there are two competition authorities in a Member State, the one responsible for settlement of the case (ie the adjudicative body) should be represented in the Advisory Committee. Adjudicative bodies will of course have to be empowered to apply also Arts 81 and 82 EC to ensure an effective enforcement of the EC competition rules in accordance with Art 35(1) of Reg 1/2003.

be complied with. If the adjudicative body submits its draft decision to the Commission, it risks becoming involved in discussions with the Commission on the proposed measure.[115] A possible solution would be that the Commission contents itself with obtaining the (draft) application of the investigative body or prosecuting authority (eg the Federal Antitrust Attorney in the Austrian institutional system) bringing the action before the adjudicative body or a similar document which forms the basis of the decision of the adjudicative body (eg the report of the Auditors Unit in Belgium).[116] This draft application or report will usually contain a proposal for the action to be taken by the adjudicative body[117] and should therefore allow the Commission to detect possible inconsistencies with the existing case law or its own decision practice before the court or other (quasi-) judicial body is actually seized with the matter. The approach therefore seems to be in line with the requirements of Article 11(4) of Regulation 1/2003, which gives NCAs the option to forward the envisaged decision to the Commission 'or, in the absence thereof, any other document indicating the proposed course of action'. Another possibility would be to consult with the Commission at the stage of the (draft) statement of objections.[118] In both scenarios, discussions and consultation would take place between the applicant before the national adjudicative body (ie the investigative or prosecuting authority) and the Commission. Problems could, however, arise where the adjudicative body does not follow the proposal eventually submitted by the applicant. In that case, the Commission would have to either induce the applicant to appeal the decision or 'overrule' the national decision (of the adjudicative body) by adopting itself a decision.[119]

[115] See text accompanying n 105.

[116] *Contra* Nihoul, above n 90, para 58, who suggests that, in the absence of a specific provision in the WEM 2006 determining which of the Belgian enforcement bodies is to inform the Commission of an envisaged national decision, it is for the Raad, ie the adjudicative body, to submit its proposal to the Commission. In my view, this approach might violate the principle of equality of arms and thus be incompatible with Art 6 ECHR See below Chapter 5, section III.B.

[117] See, eg Art 45 §4 WEM 2006, which provides that the Auditors' report shall contain a proposal for the decision to be taken by the Raad (*voorstel tot beslissing*).

[118] Gauer, above n 14, 190. Under Belgian law, however, both stages—the proposal to the Raad and the statement of objections—seem to occur simultaneously. Art 45 §4 WEM 2006 provides that the Auditoraat submits a report to the Raad which contains the statement of objections and a proposal for the decision to be taken by the Raad. Pursuant to Art 48 §1 WEM 2006, the undertakings concerned are informed at the same time when the Auditoraat submits its report to the Raad. The Auditoraat thus could choose whether to forward the draft statement of objections or the draft proposal for the decision to the Commission. In practice, however, it is the Raad which informs the Commission. See below Chapter 5, n 18.

[119] Albeit the legal effects and practical implications of such a subsequent Commission decision that contravenes the national decision are unclear. See above Chapter 1, section II.A.1.b(2).

C. The ECN in Practice

One of the objectives of creating the ECN is to provide a platform which globally facilitates co-operation at the horizontal level between the NCAs (as well as vertical co-operation with the Commission). Therefore, the internal structure of the Network is such that it is not limited to make possible formal consultations in individual cases pursuant to Articles 11(3) and (4) and 12 of Regulation 1/2003. In addition to this kind of co-operation on an ad hoc basis, the ECN also seeks to encourage a regular exchange of views between NCAs and between the NCAs and the Commission on general issues of competition policy and practice. The purposes are to promote the further development of a common competition culture and enhance mutual trust-building between the Network members.

Indeed, co-operation between the NCAs and the Commission through the ECN started prior to 1 May 2004. At that time already, officials of the present 27 Member States were involved in the process. In the beginning, considerable part of the work in the ECN was devoted to the drafting of the Network Notice, in particular the rules on case allocation, information exchange and leniency applications. The ECN also contributed to the development of certain standard forms that are designed to facilitate information exchange (eg initial case report, information on the termination of a procedure, request for exchange of information).[120]

Moreover, the ECN not only addresses 'internal' issues of co-operation between its members, but also seeks to establish 'external' relations by informing the business community, legal advisers and citizens over its activities. To this end, in April 2006, the ECN launched a one-stop access website,[121] which provides general information on and from the ECN as well as links to the sites of the Network members, in particular to news releases and online annual reports of the NCAs and the Commission. The site also contains links to the most relevant background documents, notably the text of Articles 81 and 82 EC, the provisions of Regulation 1/2003, the Network Notice and the Joint Statement. It further provides a list of the NCAs operating a leniency programme. Information on activities carried out by or within the ECN itself are still relatively limited.[122] Currently, the

---

[120] K Dekeyser and D Dalheimer, 'Co-operation within the European Competition Network—Taking Stock after 10 Months of Case Practice', paper for the conference 'Antitrust Reform in Europe: A Year in Practice', organised jointly by the International Bar Association (IBA) and the European Commission, Brussels, 9–11 March 2005, 18. S Hossenfelder, 'Erste Erfahrungen des Bundeskartellamtes mit dem Behördennetzwerk' in X, *FIW-Schriftenreihe Band 206. Schwerpunkte des Kartellrechts 2004* (Köln, Carl-Heymanns-Verlag, 2006), 1, 3.

[121] See http://ec.europa.eu/competition/ecn/index_en.html.

[122] At present, the only major sources ofinformation on the ECN are the text of the Model Leniency Programme launched by the ECN on 29 September 2006, which is accompanied by explanatory notes, a memorandum on frequently asked questions (MEMO/06/356) and a list of

site thus mainly functions as a central portal combining the links to relevant EU legislation, Commission documents and information from the individual NCAs. It is probably also an attempt to increase transparency of the operation of the Network. However, in view of the scarcity of information available on the ECN's proper activities, this objective has not (yet) been attained.

1. ECN Plenary and Sub-/Working Groups

The highest level of co-operation within the ECN are the meetings of the directors general. This top level forum tends to focus on major policy issues and usually meets on an annual basis.[123] In addition, there is the ECN Plenary whose meetings are composed of 'liaison officers', ie national officials responsible for liaising with the Network in their respective NCA as well as officials of the ECN unit of DG Competition.[124] The ECN Plenary meets at regular intervals to discusses general questions relating to the implementation of Regulation 1/2003, including substantive, mostly horizontal issues. It also functions as forum for the mutual exchange of experience and know-how.[125] If need be, the ECN Plenary reports to the directors general's meeting.

Moreover, the ECN has created a number of working groups and sector-related subgroups.[126] It should be noted, though, that once working groups or subgroups have fulfilled their purpose they are usually dissolve. Therefore, the internal organisation of the Network is not static, but changes with time.[127] By the end of 2007, the ECN had set up, under the umbrella of the Plenary, 16 subgroups for specific industry sectors, including railway, energy, healthcare, media, sports, liberal professions, financial services, motor vehicles and pharmaceuticals. The subgroups hold a limited number of face-to-face meetings each year and otherwise communicate via the common Intranet which links all Network members. They mostly deal with substantive issues of the relevant sector[128] and are

---

NCAs which accept summary leniency applications. (On the Model Leniency Programme, see further below at Chapter 3, section III.C.2.) Further, there are some statistical data on the number of antitrust cases handled by the Network members and the results of a questionnaire on the Member States' national copetition laws.

[123] D Schnichels, 'The Network of Competition Authorities: How Will It Work in Practice?' in D Geradin (ed), *Modernisation and Enlargement: Two Major Challenges for EC Competition Law* (Antwerp, Intersentia, 2004), 99, 120.

[124] In order to facilitate constant and close co-operation with other NCAs, the Bundeskartellamt, for instance, has created an ECN coordination unit. Hossenfelder, above n 120, 8.

[125] Dekeyser and Jaspers, above n 93, 11.

[126] These are groups where case-handlers of different authorities meet to exchange views and experience and discuss particular issues or sectors. Dekeyser and Jaspers, above n 93, 11.

[127] Dekeyser and Dalheimer, above n 120, 17.

[128] *Ibid*, 18. See also Hossenfelder, above n 120, 10.

used to exchange sector-related knowledge and discuss enforcement priorities.[129]

In addition, the ECN has established several working groups to foster the debate on certain horizontal issues. Participants in these working groups are officials of NCAs that volunteered to contribute to these horizontal discussions. There are usually 15–18 NCAs represented in each working group, while the Commission takes part in all working groups. In March 2005 there was one working group on leniency[130] and another dealing with other questions of procedures and sanctions. A third working group that had initially been set up to discuss transitional issues subsequently evolved to cover a variety of topics. All these working groups seek to address problems lying at the interface between uniform EC law and divergent national laws.[131]

Last but not least, there exists a working group on Article 82 issues. This working group was established in particular to exchange views with the Commission on the relevant draft policy documents.[132] The Commission is planning to provide NCAs and national courts with some guidance in relation to the application of Article 82, and to this end is preparing a number of informal communications. The working group on Article 82 issues follows the Commission's work closely. It allows the NCAs to make their views known and actively participate in the design of policy instruments in this field of law.

2. *Exchange of Officials*

Another important aspect of co-operation is the exchange of officials between the competition authorities. The ECN arranges for short secondments (2–3 weeks) of officials of the NCAs to the Commission. Usually, the national officials are assigned to the sector-specific unit which corresponds to their own field of work. At the same time, they get an introduction to Community competition law. It is envisaged that Commission officials will in turn be seconded to the NCAs.

The exchange of officials between NCAs is organised within the framework of the ECA. Consequently, this horizontal exchange embraces not only officials of the Member States, but also officials of the competition

---

[129] E Paulis and E De Smijter, 'Enhanced Enforcement of the EC Competition Rules since 1 May 2004 by the Commission and the NCAs', paper for the conference 'Antitrust Reform in Europe: A Year in Practice', organised jointly by the International Bar Association (IBA) and the European Commission, Brussels, 9–11 March 2005, 5.

[130] This working group developed a model leniency programme as voluntary standard for all ECN members. See Dekeyser and Jaspers, above n 93, 16 and further below Chapter 3, section III.C.2.

[131] Dekeyser and Dalheimer, above n 120, 18.

[132] *Ibid*, 18.

authorities of Norway, Iceland and possibly the EFTA Surveillance Authority.[133]

The exchange of officials is certainly an important feature of the ongoing co-operation process. It can contribute significantly to mutual trust-building. Personal contacts, in particular at the working level, can help to dissipate prejudices and remove (psychological) barriers, making effective co-operation between the authorities much more likely.

II. THE LEGAL FRAMEWORK FOR CO-OPERATION

Businesses becomes increasingly global and accordingly cartels are operated more and more often on an international or even worldwide basis. While cartelists are able to share any kind of information, competition authorities that want to fight international cartels are constrained by numerous rules and often cannot provide each other with evidence and other confidential information.[134] This used to be true also for the competition authorities in the EU; however, Regulation 1/2003 seeks to enhance and facilitate co-operation between them.

There are two main aspects to the notion of co-operation: communication and coordination. First, Regulation 1/2003 aims to improve communication between the competition authorities by providing the legal basis for an extensive exchange of information between all members of the Network. The key provision in this context is Article 12 of Regulation 1/2003, which grants NCAs and the Commission the power to exchange and use in evidence even confidential information. This is an absolute novelty. Moreover, the competition authorities in the EU can exchange views on general issues of EC competition law as well as individual cases. This will mainly be accomplished through the Advisory Committee. Secondly, the system of parallel competences makes it necessary for the competition authorities in the EU to coordinate their action. At the outset of a procedure, coordination will predominantly concern case allocation. Accordingly, Article 11(3) of Regulation 1/2003 obliges NCAs to inform the Commission of new cases involving the application of EC competition law and provides the option to exchange such information equally with other NCAs.[135] During an investigation, coordinating measures may be required in particular to guarantee the effectiveness of (surprise) inspections. Pursuant to Article 22 of Regulation 1/2003, NCAs can therefore

---

[133] On the exchange of officials, see Hossenfelder, above n 120, 10–11.

[134] M Bloom, 'Exchange of Confidential Information among Members of the EU Network of Competition Authorities: Possible Consequences of a Relatively Broad Scope for Exchange of Confidential Information on National Procedural Law and Antitrust Sanctions' in Ehlermann and Atanasiu, above n 7, 389, 390.

[135] The Commission has assumed a similar information obligation vis-à-vis the NCAs under Art 11(2) of Reg 1/2003.

carry out inspections in their territory and collect evidence on behalf and for the account of another NCA. This is another important improvement compared to the situation under Regulation 17. Finally, before the adoption of a final decision, the NCA concerned has to inform the Commission of the intended course of action pursuant to Article 11(4) of Regulation 1/2003. There is again the faculty to make this information equally available to other NCAs. In particular, the latter option may be crucial where coordination of parallel national proceedings is required.

A. The Previous Situation—Information Exchange under Regulation 17

Regulation 17 was not really concerned with the application of EC competition law by the Member States' authorities. It created a centralised system of application with the Commission as primary and central enforcement agency. The NCAs merely had a supporting function, which was to assist the Commission in assuming its pivotal role.[136] The rules on information exchange reflected this centralised structure. Regulation 17 only provided for vertical flows of information, ie the exchange of information between the Commission on the one hand and the NCAs on the other.

Pursuant to Article 10(1) of Regulation 17, the Commission had to keep the Member States informed on infringement and exemption proceedings by forwarding applications and notifications together with copies of the most important documents to them. When the Commission sent a request for information to an undertaking, it had to transmit a copy of that request to the NCA of the Member State where the undertaking was located.[137] The NCAs, in turn, could provide information to the Commission. They had the right to express their views on the procedure in accordance with Article 10(2) of Regulation 17. Moreover, the Commission had to consult the Advisory Committee before taking a final decision.[138] It was also possible for NCAs to conduct investigations on behalf of the Commission.[139] Finally, the Commission could obtain all necessary information from the NCAs (and the Member States' governments).[140] There is no mention of any sort of horizontal co-operation between the NCAs in Regulation 17. All information exchange was strictly limited to the vertical level. According to the judgment of the ECJ in *Spanish Banks*, an NCA was even prohibited, by virtue of Article 20(2) of Regulation 17, from passing

---

[136] Van Der Woude, above n 67, 371.
[137] Art 11(2) of Reg 17.
[138] Art 10(3) of Reg 17.
[139] Art 13(1) of Reg 17.
[140] Art 11(1) of Reg 17.

on to another NCA information that it had received from the Commission.[141]

Article 20(1) of Regulation 17 further restricted the use of information by the Commission and by NCAs in that it stipulated that information acquired during an investigation must be used only for the purpose of that same investigation. The Commission was thus precluded from transferring evidence from one case to another. In other words, procedures and case files had to be kept separate within the Commission.[142] The same rule applied with regard to parallel procedures pending before the Commission and an NCA. NCAs could not use information stemming from the Commission as direct evidence in a domestic procedure, even if that procedure concerned the application of Community competition law.[143] However, the authorities were not required to ignore or forget what they had read. On the basis of the ECJ's judgment in *Dow Benelux*, both the Commission and the NCAs were entitled to use information that they happened to obtain in a particular procedure merely as intelligence to justify the initiation of a new (second) procedure regarding another subject matter.[144]

Within the framework of the 1997 Co-operation Notice, the Commission tried to broaden the scope of the information exchange. The notice was published in an attempt to promote the (decentralised) application of the EC competition rules by the Member States' authorities by providing for some sort of case allocation.[145] The idea of allocating cases between the Commission and the NCAs, including the possibility of referrals, made some sort of co-operation necessary. Accordingly, the Commission was prepared to transmit the relevant documents in its possession to the NCA to which a case would be referred.[146] In return,

---

[141] See para 41 of the judgment (above n 78). The case concerned inter alia the interpretation of Art 20(2) of Reg 17, which enshrines the professional secrecy obligation.

[142] Van Der Woude, above n 67, 374.

[143] Judgment of the ECJ in *Spanish Banks* (above n 78), para 42.

[144] Case 85/87 *Dow Benelux* [1989] ECR 3137, paras 19–20. In *Spanish Banks*, the ECJ elaborated on this issue by explaining that NCAs are not required to undergo 'acute amnesia'. The prohibition to use information outside the legal context in which it was requested (except as circumstantial evidence to justify a new inquiry) would therefore not run counter to the principle of co-operation between the Community institutions and the Member States. See para 39 of the judgment (above n 78).

[145] See Part II of the 1997 Co-operation Notice headed 'Guidelines on case allocation'. The Commission essentially tried to encourage NCAs to handle Art 81 or 82 cases whenever the effects of the relevant anti-competitive agreement or conduct were mainly confined to one Member State and provided that the restriction would appear unlikely, prima facie, to qualify for an exemption. The Commission, in turn, intended to deal with cases involving companies or business activities in more than one Member State or displaying a particular Community interest. See paras 24 and 26 of the 1997 Co-operation Notice.

[146] Para 46 of the 1997 Co-operation Notice. In the light of the above-mentioned case law (above n 144), one might wonder whether the above provision was in conformity with Art 20 of Reg 17. After all, the ECJ had emphasised that national proceedings, even where they relate to the enforcement of Community competition law, are to be distinguished from proceedings

it expected to be systematically informed by the NCAs of any proceedings that the latter would initiate. The Commission also committed itself to making such information available to the other NCAs.[147] This arrangement was the first step towards a horizontal exchange of information.[148]

B. Co-operation under Regulation 1/2003

The provisions of Regulation 1/2003 governing the vertical flow of information are similar to the rules of Regulation 17 with the exception of Article 12(1), which constitutes a novelty as far as confidential information is concerned. In addition, however, Regulation 1/2003 creates the possibility that information and evidence are also exchanged horizontally between the NCAs.

1. Vertical Flow of Information

It is interesting to note that, under Regulation 1/2003, the Commission has fewer information duties than at the time when Regulation 17 applied. Like under Regulation 17, the Commission has to keep NCAs informed about proceedings that it has initiated with a view of adopting interim measures,

conducted by the Commission. See para 32 of the judgment in *Spanish Banks* (above n 78). The referral of a case by the Commission to an NCA would therefore result in a different investigation within the meaning of Art 20(1) of Reg 17, even though the same infringement would be at issue. For this reason, para 47 of the 1997 Co-operation Notice stressed that NCAs were not entitled to use as evidence the information transmitted by the Commission under the notice, but that they could rely on that information to justify the initiation of national proceedings.

[147] Para 49 of the 1997 Co-operation Notice. For instance, the GWB, as applicable prior to the adoption of Reg 1/2003, provided for such a systematic flow of information. Pursuant to the former § 50(3) GWB, the BKartA had to inform the Commission of any proceedings relating to the application of the EC competition rules and even had to give the Commission the opportunity to express its views. Curiously, this provision has not been retained in the amended GWB after the 7. GWB-Novelle. The official explanation is that provisions of Reg 1/2003 which are sufficiently precise to be directly applicable shall not be 'repeated' in the GWB, a view probably based on the judgment of the ECJ in Case 34/73 *Fratelli Variola* [1973] ECR 981, paras 9–11, where the ECJ considered it unlawful to reproduce, in acts of national legislation, the terms of an EC Regulation. The Commission and BKartA thus have to rely directly on Art 11(3) and (4) of Reg 1/2003 as concerns the provision of information on new cases and immanent final decisions from the German cartel authority to the EU authority and other Network members. It would, however, certainly have benefited the clarity of the German law had this information duty of the BKartA been incorporated in the GWB, possibly with some specifications as to what kind of documents (eg decision proposal of case handler or entire draft text of the contemplated decision) have to be forwarded to the Commission, when this should be done and who within the BKartA's internal organisation is responsible for carrying out the duty. Nothing would have prevented the German legislature from underlining in the law that the duty results from Reg 1/2003.

[148] Van Der Woude, above n 67, 373.

prohibition or commitment decisions, positive decisions, or decisions withdrawing the benefit of a block exemption. Pursuant to Article 11(2) of Regulation 1/2003, which mirrors Article 10(1) of Regulation 17, the Commission shall transmit copies of the most important documents it has collected in relation to such proceedings to the NCAs. Further documentation must be provided at the request of the NCAs. However, the Commission is no longer obliged to automatically forward a copy of each information request to the NCA of the Member State in whose territory the addressee of the relevant request is located.[149] The reason that this very specific obligation was repealed may lie in the fact that the Commission generally expects NCAs to be well informed through the Network. Moreover, if desired, NCAs can always request the Commission to forward them existing documents other than those which have already been supplied under Article 11(2) of Regulation 1/2003. Such other documents would seem to include the Commission's requests for information in a certain case.

By contrast, the co-operation obligations of the NCAs have been increased. The possibility of having NCAs conduct inspections on behalf of the Commission has been retained.[150] Moreover, when NCAs act on the basis of the EC competition rules, they are obliged to liaise with the Commission at two decisive moments of the procedure. At the outset of the proceedings, ie prior to the first formal investigative measure, NCAs have to inform the Commission of the matter.[151] The main purpose of this information exchange is to facilitate case allocation.[152] At the end of the proceedings, ie no later than 30 days before the adoption of a final decision, the NCAs have to inform the Commission a second time by providing it with a summary of the case and a copy of the envisaged decision. The Commission may request a copy of any further document relating to the case.[153] The objective of this second information duty is to give the Commission the opportunity to influence the outcome of the proceedings if it considers this necessary to ensure the uniform application and consistent enforcement of the EC competition rules.

2. Horizontal Flow of Information

Under Regulation 1/2003, information can also be widely exchanged between NCAs. The possibility of a broad horizontal exchange of infor-

---

[149] *Ibid*, 377–8. This obligation was contained in Art 11(2) of Reg 17.

[150] Arts 22(2) and 12 of Reg 1/2003.

[151] Art 11(3) of Reg 1/2003.

[152] Explanatory Memorandum, 19–20.

[153] Art 11(4) of Reg 1/2003. There is only a duty to inform the Commission where the foreseen decision is a prohibition decision, a commitment decision or a decision withdrawing the benefits of a block exemption.

mation is a major novelty and a cornerstone of decentralised enforcement. The key provision is Article 12(1) of Regulation 1/2003, which gives NCAs (and the Commission) the right 'to provide one another with and use in evidence any matter of fact or of law, including confidential information'. In principle, the free flow of (confidential) data and evidence within the Network is thus possible. Certain limits are imposed, in particular by the second paragraph of Article 12 and Article 28 of Regulation 1/2003.[154]

In addition, Article 22(1) of Regulation 1/2003 enables an NCA to carry out inspections and other fact-finding measures in its own territory 'on behalf and for the account' of the NCAs of other Member States. The information collected shall be exchanged and used in evidence in accordance with the provisions of Article 12 of Regulation 1/2003. This type of mutual assistance between NCAs is an important complement to the right to exchange information horizontally. In view of the effect-on-trade criterion, EC competition law cases will often relate to companies or business activities in more than one Member State. It is therefore likely that an NCA, when investigating a breach of Article 81 or 82 EC, requires evidence located outside its area of territorial jurisdiction.[155] Where the NCA in the Member State concerned has not itself initiated proceedings with regard to that matter, Article 22(1) Regulation 1/2003 provides the legal basis for it to collect the relevant information 'in the interest of' the foreign investigating NCA. The provision will therefore be of particular relevance in cross-border cases that have been allocated to a single NCA.[156]

The above rules thus permit NCAs to exchange all relevant information, including confidential data and evidence, horizontally. However, at the same time, these rules show that the horizontal dimension is still underdeveloped. Neither provision imposes an obligation on NCAs; they only confer rights. Consequently, an NCA cannot be compelled to pass on information.[157] Nor can it be forced to respond positively to a request of another NCA to collect evidence on the latter's behalf.[158] Assistance in fact-finding measures remains a matter of discretion, and it is certainly conceivable that NCAs will refuse to provide such assistance, for instance, for reasons of insufficient resources, heavy workloads or different

---

[154] These will be discussed below. See the following paragraph in this chapter and further below Chapter 4, section I.B and I.C.

[155] See p 11 of the Explanatory Memorandum, which points out that, as a result of market integration, evidence and information will increasingly be located in several Member States.

[156] See M Widegren, 'Consultation among Members within the Network' in Ehlermann and Atanasiu, above n 7, 419, 424.

[157] Van Der Woude, above n 67, 378.

[158] F Jenny, 'On the Modernisation of EC Antitrust Policy', above n 7, 208. However, where the Commission requests assistance in fact-finding measures, NCAs have no discretion. Pursuant to Art 22(2) of Reg 1/2003, they 'shall undertake the inspections which the Commission considers to be necessary'.

enforcement priorities.[159] Similarly, while informing the Commission of the initiation of proceedings is mandatory, informing other NCAs at the outset of a new procedure is merely a faculty. Equally, the communication of a draft decision to other NCAs is optional. Article 11(4) makes such communication compulsory only vis-à-vis the Commission.[160]

Regulation 1/2003 allows for extensive co-operation both vertically and horizontally. Whether horizontal collaboration and exchange of information will take place at a satisfactory level depends, however, on the commitment and goodwill of the NCAs, since there is no obligation to engage in such horizontal co-operation.[161]

3. Limits

The exchange of information within the Network and the use of such information in evidence are not unrestricted. As a general rule, Article 28(1) of Regulation 1/2003 still confines the use of information collected during a Commission investigation to the purpose for which it was gathered. The provision mirrors the old Article 20(1) of Regulation 17. The slightly different wording does not seem to entail a different meaning of this rule on substance.[162] As concerns investigations conducted solely by the Commission, there can thus be no doubt that the ECJ's judgment in *Dow Benelux* is still applicable. Information may not be used outside the legal context in which it was acquired. The Commission therefore has to

---

[159] Cf Bloom, above n 134, 398, who assumes, however, that NCAs will assist each other so far as this is legally and practically possible having regard to resources, workloads and priorities of each NCA. In practice, problems in this respect do not really seem to arise. See Dekeyser and Dalheimer, above n 120, 11–12, who notice that the practical experience, at least during the first 10 months of Reg 1/2003, has been positive. Authorities are well committed to assisting each other. There were a number of examples of NCAs carrying out inspections or conducting interviews at the request of other NCAs. The authors state that 'no request for assistance has been simply declined'. It is unclear, however, whether this means that no authority refused to assist another or whether those which refused to grant assistance put forward specific reasons why they could not comply with the request. It seems that fact-finding measures on the basis of requests from foreign NCAs are even given priority over own matters of the requested NCA. This has been indicated by some NCA officials in personal conversations which I had during the preparation of the manuscript.

[160] The facultative character of the information exchange between NCAs on new cases is in contradiction to the rule that any NCA is entitled to request that a particular case handled by one of the other NCAs be put on the agenda of the Advisory Committee (Art 14 (6) of Reg 1/2003). Such a right can only be used effectively if not only the Commission, but all members of the Network have knowledge of the cases pending before NCAs. Cf Widegren, above n 156, 423.

[161] Experience in other fields of law (eg tax law) suggests that, in the absence of binding rules, mutual information and close co-operation on a regular or even systematic basis are difficult to achieve.

[162] See the Explanatory Memorandum, 28, which states that the new provision 'takes over' the old Art 20(1) of Reg 17. Pursuant to Art 28(1) of Reg 1/2003, information must 'be used only for the purpose for which it was acquired', while Art 20(1) of Reg 17 stipulated that information had to 'be used only for the purpose of the relevant request or investigation'.

keep proceedings pending before it separate and may not transfer evidence from one file to another.[163]

However, Article 28(1) of Regulation 1/2003 is 'without prejudice' to Article 12 of Regulation 1/2003. The latter can thus derogate from the former rule.[164] And Article 12 does indeed relax the obligation contained in Article 28(1) of Regulation 1/2003 in that it empowers the Commission and NCAs to exchange and use in evidence any kind of information including confidential data. This explicit permission was necessary to remove the obstacles resulting from the judgment of the ECJ in the *Spanish Banks* case.[165] That case concerned the use, by the Spanish Competition Authority, of confidential information which it had received from the Commission within the framework of an Article 81(3) procedure, for the purpose of enforcing domestic competition law.[166] The ECJ held that, when applying national or EC rules on competition, Member States may not use as direct evidence non-public information contained in applications, notifications or replies to requests for information communicated by the Commission in accordance with Regulation 17. Nor may they pass on such information to other NCAs. These conclusions were based, inter alia, on the professional secrecy obligation,[167] the prohibition to use information outside the legal context in which it was acquired[168] and the understanding that proceedings conducted by a national authority, irrespective of whether they concern the implementation of Community or domestic competition rules, are in any event distinct from the proceedings conducted by the Commission under Regulation 17. The collection of evidence by the national authority must conform with the relevant provisions of national law. Therefore, non-public information provided by the Commission could at best be used by NCAs as intelligence to justify the initiation of a national procedure in which the suspected infringement would then have to be proven by means of evidence acquired under national law.[169]

In the absence of an express provision allowing them to do so, the judgment of the ECJ in *Spanish Banks* thus would have precluded NCAs from exchanging confidential information and relying on evidence obtained

[163] Van Der Woude, above n 67, 379–80.

[164] See p 28 of the Explanatory Memorandum, from where it is stated that the provision on professional secrecy is subject to the application of more specific rules, namely Art 12 of Reg 1/2003.

[165] See above nn 78 and 141, and accompanying text.

[166] The Spanish banks involved in that case had been accused of violating certain provisions of the Spanish Competition Act. They claimed that the Spanish Competition Authority had based its investigations under national law on information contained in the notification which the banks had submitted to the Commission with a view to obtaining negative clearance or an exemption under Art 81(3).

[167] Art 20(2) of Reg 17.

[168] Art 20(1) of Reg 17. See also ECJ in *Dow Benelux* (above n 144), paras 17–18.

[169] Paras 29–43 of the judgment (above n 78). See also n 144 and accompanying text.

from the Commission.[170] Ultimately, this case law may have hampered the exchange of any kind of useful information between the competition authorities in the EU. This (potential) obstacle has been removed by the adoption of Article 12(1) of Regulation 1/2003, making it clear that the *Spanish Banks* doctrine shall no longer apply.[171] Moreover, it sets aside any national provision which would prohibit such exchange.[172]

The use in evidence of confidential information that has been exchanged in the Network is, however, subject to certain limitations set out in the second and third paragraphs of Article 12 of Regulation 1/2003. Pursuant to Article 12(2), the information exchanged may only be used for the purpose of applying EC competition law[173] and in respect of the subject matter for which it was collected. The first condition ensures that information exchanged in the Network is not used outside the legal context of Regulation 1/2003—for instance, to enforce national laws on consumer protection[174]—or for purely national competition law proceedings. The second condition, restricting the use of exchanged evidence to the same subject matter, was not contained in the Draft Regulation. It is an important element for the protection of the rights of defence.

On the one hand, Article 12 derogates from Article 28(1) of Regulation 1/2003 in that it allows information to be used outside 'the legal scope of the procedure under which such information has been obtained', thereby overriding the ECJ's ruling in *Spanish Banks*.[175] On the other hand, it takes

---

[170] Cf J Temple Lang, 'Decentralised Application of Community Competition Law' (1999) 22 *World Competition* 3, 6. White Paper, para 96.

[171] Van Der Woude, above n 67, 378.

[172] Para 27 of the Network Notice. Cf also the text of Art 12(1) as proposed in the Draft Regulation: 'Notwithstanding any national provision to the contrary, the Commission and the competition authorities of the Member States may provide one another with and use in evidence any matter of fact or of law, including confidential information.' See also D Reichelt, 'To What Extent Does the Co-operation within the European Competition Network Protect the Rights of Undertakings?' (2005) 42 *CML Rev* 745, 777–9, who raises the question of whether the Council could alter the case law at all, given the fact that the reasoning in *Spanish Banks* was based inter alia on higher-ranking general principles of law, namely the protection of the rights of defence. The main argument in favour of a right of the Council to override the case law is obviously the fact that Arts 12(2) and (3) and 28(1) of Reg 1/2003 include a number of safeguards in that they limit the use of exchanged information considerably. See below Chapter 4, section I.B.

[173] And for the application of national competition law where it is applied in parallel to Community law, provided its application does not lead to a different outcome.

[174] The DGCCRF in France, for instance, is inter alia responsible for guaranteeing the quality of products and the respect of the rules against unfair trade practices for the benefit of consumers. Similarly, in Italy, the Autorità Garante is also in charge of enforcing the rules on unfair commercial practices and misleading advertising. See G Bruzzone and M Boccaccio, 'Taking Care of Modernisation after the Start-up: A View from a Member Sate' (2008) 31 *World Competition* 89, 95.

[175] See in particular para 48 of that judgment (above n 78). The ECJ's ruling—prohibiting the use by NCAs of evidence derived from the Commission—was based inter alia on the understanding that proceedings conducted by a national authority are distinct from Commission proceedings under Reg 17, even if the national proceedings concern the enforcement of Arts 81 and 82 EC.

account of the judgment in *Dow Benelux*, where the ECJ stated that the rights of defence would be seriously endangered if the Commission could rely on evidence against an undertaking which it had obtained during an investigation but which was not related to the purpose or subject matter thereof.[176] The same must apply in relation to the NCAs. The subject matter of an investigation will usually be determined by the decision or order under which it is carried out. This decision or order must indicate the presumed facts which the authority intends to investigate and must specify the alleged infringement.[177] The second condition of Article 12(2) thus ensures that information gathered by one member of the Network can be used by another only for the purpose of prosecuting and establishing the same material infringement.[178]

The third paragraph of Article 12 limits the use of such information as evidence to impose sanctions on natural persons. In particular, it precludes custodial sanctions being imposed on individuals where such sanctions are not foreseen in the Member State in which the evidence was collected. Other personal sanctions[179] may only be applied—on the basis of the information exchanged—if certain additional requirements are fulfilled which are intended to ensure that the rights of defence are adequately protected.[180]

Finally, the obligation of professional secrecy has been retained in Article 28(2) of Regulation 1/2003. The new provision does not add anything to the rule that already existed in Article 20(2) of Regulation 17. Its aim is to complement the safeguards laid down in Article 12(2) of Regulation 1/2003.[181] Article 28(2) of Regulation 1/2003 does, however, take account of the horizontal dimension of the information exchange under the new enforcement regime. It covers not only information obtained from the

---

[176] Para 18 of that judgment (above n 144).

[177] See paras 41 and 42 of the judgment in Joined Cases 46/87 and 227/88 *Hoechst v Commission* [1989] ECR 2859. In that judgment, the ECJ also emphasised that the Commission's obligation, pursuant to Art 14(3) of Reg 17, to specify the subject matter and purpose of the investigation, the applicable penalties and the right to have the decision reviewed by the ECJ constitutes a fundamental guarantee of the rights of defence of the undertakings concerned. It is therefore fair to assume that similar standards apply where the investigation is conducted by an NCA on the basis of national procedural rules.

[178] For instance, where the transmitting authority acquired information in the context of an investigation involving horizontal price fixing agreements between a number of producers, the receiving authority may not use this evidence to establish a breach of Community law on the basis of the existence of restrictive clauses (accidentally discovered and) contained in the distribution agreements between some of these producers and their customers.

[179] These could be pecuniary sanctions, such as fines or disqualification as company director, and similar non- pecuniary penalties.

[180] The requirements are set out in Art 12(3) of Reg 1/2003. They concern the similarity of the sanctions foreseen in the applicable legal orders of the competition authorities between which the information is exchanged and the equivalence of protection of the rights of defence afforded to natural persons in both systems.

[181] Explanatory Memorandum, 28. *Contra* Van Der Woude, above n 67, 381, who considers this rule not a complement, but a restriction.

Commission, but any information 'acquired or exchanged pursuant to this Regulation'. Consequently, information emanating from national investigations and being transmitted by an NCA is protected in the same way as information collected and forwarded by the Commission.

Evidently, Article 12 derogates from the professional secrecy obligation in that it allows confidential information to be passed on, thereby putting aside the ruling of the ECJ in *Spanish Banks*. Therefore, unlike Article 20(2) of Regulation 17, the professional secrecy provision in Regulation 1/2003 prima facie does not seem to concern the inter-agency relations between the competition authorities in the EU. Rather, Article 28(2) of Regulation 1/2003 will predominantly apply where the undertakings concerned or interested third parties (complainants, competitors, and customers) request access to the file. An important issue in this context will be the question of how it can be ensured that information to which confidentiality has been awarded in the Member State from which it originates is not disclosed after it has been passed on in the Network.

The details of the above rules, their interaction and implementation in practice will be discussed later in the book.[182]

III. CONCLUSION

This chapter has shown that there is a large variety of institutional and procedural settings in which NCAs operate. Regulation 1/2003 does not interfere with these arrangements. On the contrary, it recognises the Member States' prerogatives in this respect and, in Article 35, takes into account the different institutional models for competition law enforcement existing at the national level. It is for the Member States to designate the competent authority. In Member States with dual enforcement models, however, it seems indispensable that the national legislator also determines which body is to assume which responsibilities with regard to the obligations that Regulation 1/2003 imposes on NCAs. A general rule whereby each body is called upon to fulfil the functions under Regulation 1/2003 'within its respective sphere of competence' seems to be too vague and might lead to conflicts or lacunae in the co-operation process.

This concerns, in particular, co-operation within the ECN, including certain information and consultation duties of the NCAs for which Regulation 1/2003 sets the legal framework, albeit without mentioning the ECN as such in its articles.[183] Nonetheless, Regulation 1/2003 radically reforms the existing co-operation process. Mutual information, consultation and assistance, not only in a vertical direction (ie between

[182] Chapter 4, in particular section I.C.
[183] The ECN or, rather, 'a network of public authorities' is referred to only once, notably in recital 15 of Reg 1/2003.

Commission and NCAs), but also horizontally (ie between the NCAs), are key elements of the new system. This covers the possibility for all competition authorities in the EU to assist each other in fact-finding and exchange evidentiary material, including confidential information. Despite the fact that horizontal co-operation is largely designed as a mere faculty rather than an obligation, the relevant powers of the NCAs constitute an important novelty in that they supersede the *Spanish Banks* doctrine, which used to form a major obstacle to effective co-operation.

3

Information Exchange at the Outset—The Issue of Case Allocation

A S POINTED OUT already, Regulation 1/2003 is based on the principle of parallel competences (or concurrent jurisdiction). Each competition authority in the EU has the power (and the duty) to apply Articles 81 and 82 EC with regard to restrictive agreements or practices and abusive conduct that affect trade between Member States. This means that at least 28 competition authorities in the EU share the same competence.[1] Case allocation will therefore be one of the central challenges of the new enforcement system and one of the core functions of the Network.[2] Accordingly, the main objective of the information exchange at the beginning of the procedure is to allow the efficient allocation of cases.[3]

I. CASE ALLOCATION

Even though Regulation 1/2003 does not exclude a priori that the same infringement is investigated and penalised in parallel by two or more NCAs, the ultimate goal of case allocation should be to avoid multiple control, duplication of work and inefficient actions to the largest extent

---

[1] Subject to territorial limitations including the effects doctrine (see below n 11).

[2] A Schaub, 'Continued Focus on Reform: Recent Developments in EC Competition Policy' in B Hawk (ed), *2001 Proceedings of the Fordham Corporate Law Institute* (New York, Juris Publishing, 2002), 31, 39, who mentions two principal roles of the Network: namely, case allocation and contribution to the coherent application of the Community competition rules. *Contra* G Tesauro, 'The Relationship between National Competition Authorities and their Respective Governments in the Context of the Modernisation Initiative' in C-D Ehlermann and I Atanasiu (eds), *European Competition Law Annual 2002: Constructing the EU Network of Competition Authorities* (Oxford, Hart Publishing, 2003), 269, 269. Tesauro refers to the fact that, in the past, no cases have ever raised a conflict of jurisdiction. He seems to neglect, however, that the obligation of NCAs to apply Arts 81 and 82 EC will lead to a considerably larger number of EC competition law cases at national level. See M Widegren, 'Consultation among Members within the Network', in Ehlermann and Atanasiu, *ibid*, 419, 419. On this basis, Tesauro's assumption appears somehow simplistic that conflicts of jurisdiction would not arise and case allocation would not be an important task of the Network.

[3] See Explanatory Memorandum, 19–20.

possible.[4] Parallel procedures relating to substantially identical conduct do not only present a burden on undertakings and increase costs considerably, but may also lead to an unnecessary waste of the limited resources of the authorities involved.[5]

A. Lack of Formal Allocation Criteria in Regulation 1/2003

Probably the most efficient way to allocate cases is to attribute, on the basis of precise abstract rules, the competence for each case to a single authority.[6] This would have meant granting each of the competition authorities in the EU exclusive jurisdiction for pre-defined matters. It is evident, however, that a system of exclusive competences is difficult to realise in a field of law, such as EC competition law, where cases typically have important links with several countries.[7] Thus, Regulation 1/2003 does not contain any abstract criteria that would attribute the competence for a given case to a particular competition authority in the EU, ie a single NCA or the Commission. Apparently, it was not even possible to reach a political consensus regarding the division of competences between the national and the supranational level, ie between the NCAs on the one hand and the Commission on the other.[8] Unlike the Merger Regulation, which creates a system of mutually exclusive spheres of application for EC and national (merger control) law, Regulation 1/2003 does not provide for a

---

[4] There seems to be a certain contradiction between recital 18 of Reg 1/2003 ('the objective being that each case should be handled by a single authority') and the compromise expressed in paras 12 and 13 of the Network Notice, which deal with cases where parallel action by two or more NCAs may be appropriate.

[5] Cf A Schaub, 'The Reform of Regulation 17/62: The Issues of Compatibility, Effective Enforcement and Legal Certainty' in C-D Ehlermann and I Atanasiu (eds), *European Competition Law Annual 2000. The Modernisation of EC Antitrust Policy* (Oxford, Hart Publishing, 2001), 241, 255. The question whether, having regard to the *ne bis in idem* principle recognised by all Member States, parallel competition proceedings regarding the same facts and undertakings are at all permissible, will be discussed in Chapter 6.

[6] See J Basedow, 'Who will Protect Competition in Europe? From Central Enforcement to Authority Networks and Private Litigation' in T Einhorn (ed), 'Liber Amicorum Ernst-Joachim Mestmäcker' (2001) 2 *European Business Organization Law Review* 443, 449.

[7] Cf Basedow, *ibid*, 450. In open markets such as the Internal Market of the EU, competition is intrinsically transnational. *Ibid*. Moreover, Arts 81 and 82 EC only apply where trade between Member States is affected. It is therefore hardly conceivable to find purely national cases, ie cases with no relevant cross-border element, in this field of law. This is all the more so since the judgment of the ECJ in Joined Cases C–215/96 and C–216/96 *Carlo Bagnasco and others v Banca Popolare di Novara, Cassa di Risparmio di Genova* ('*Italian Banks*') [1999] ECR I–135, which excludes the application of Art 81 to so-called domestic agreements. See above Chapter 1, n 113.

[8] This is somehow surprising, given that discussions with Member States on the question how the responsibilities could be divided between the Commission and the NCAs started at the beginning of the 1990s. See C-D Ehlermann, 'Implementation of EC Competition Law by National Anti-Trust Authorities' (1996) 17 *European Competition Law Review* 88, 91. See also below n 16.

'Community dimension' type of test which would confer jurisdiction over certain (economically important) cases exclusively on the Commission,[9] nor does it vest any discretionary power with the Commission, the ECN or the Advisory Committee to allocate cases to a particular authority. The principle of concurrent jurisdiction thus applies at both the vertical and the horizontal level.

The only rule on jurisdiction contained in Regulation 1/2003 is the principle, enshrined in Article 11(6), that the NCAs are relieved of their competence if and when the Commission initiates proceedings on the basis of Article 81 or 82 EC. This provision merely excludes the possibility of parallel proceedings at national and Community level. However, there is no equivalent rule with regard to the horizontal level, excluding parallel investigations of the same case by several NCAs. The competence of the NCAs to apply Articles 81 and 82 EC is also not geographically restricted in any way by Regulation 1/2003. In theory, each and every NCA may investigate any agreement or practice which affects trade between Member States no matter where it is concluded or implemented, where the parties are located or where the restrictive effects are felt.[10] Some limitation may result from the relevant national provisions. Most national competition laws have embodied some sort of 'effects doctrine' that preclude the NCA from prosecuting restrictive agreements or practices which do not affect competition in the domestic territory.[11] Such principles of national law will also

---

[9] The EC Merger Regulation applies to concentrations that have a Community dimension. Such concentrations are within the exclusive jurisdiction of the Commission and subject only to the provisions of that regulation to the exclusion of national competition laws. See Art 21(1)–(3) of the 2004 Merger Regulation. The concept of 'Community dimension' is defined in Art 1 of the 2004 Merger Regulation by means of quantitative criteria (turnover thresholds). The NCAs are only competent to scrutinise concentrations without a Community dimension on the basis of national rules on merger control.

[10] Basedow, above n 6, 450. The potential number of competent authorities is thus only limited by the actual number of NCAs empowered to apply EC competition law. But see also below n 11.

[11] See, eg § 130(2) GWB Under Belgian law, the limited territorial competence of the NCA follows from the substantive law. Arts 2 and 3 of the Belgian Competition Act (WEM 2006), which are modelled upon Arts 81 and 82 EC, only apply to the extent that companies restrict or distort competition or abuse a dominant position respectively on the Belgian market. By contrast, as concerns the application, by the Belgian competition authority, of Arts 81 and 82 EC, the WEM 2006 does not seem to contain an equivalent provision limiting the powers of the NCA to infringements which affect the Belgian market. The force of the effects doctrine in antitrust matters has essentially been developed by US courts, which have been called the 'original pioneers' of this approach. See I Van Bael and J-F Bellis, *Competition Law of the European Community* (The Hague, Kluwer Law International, 4th edn, 2005), 152. The leading case, in this respect, is the *Alcoa* case of 1945. There are, however, discussions within the US on the appropriateness of the doctrine to assert jurisdiction in competition matters and the need to accommodate some sort of comity. For a brief overview of the historical development of the effects test in US law, including the influence of comity considerations, see C Sprigman, 'Fix Prices Globally, Get Sued Locally? US Jurisdiction over International Cartels' (2005) 72 *University of Chicago Law Review* 265, 267–81. The doctrine has also triggered some controversy outside the US regarding its compatibility with public international law. The UK, for instance, has traditionally opposed it and instead adopted the implementation doctrine of the

most likely restrict *mutatis mutandis* the competence of NCAs to prosecute and punish infringements of Article 81 or 82 EC. However, the vast majority of Articles 81 and 82 EC cases will have significant cross-border elements[12] and will thus be likely to produce effects in two or more Member State. The effects doctrine will therefore hardly allow a reduction in the number of competent authorities to one and parallel proceedings by several NCAs with regard to the same matter are not excluded by Regulation 1/2003 per se.[13] Ideally, however, each case should be dealt with by a single authority.[14]

Admittedly, Article 13 of Regulation 1/2003 may help to avoid parallel proceedings at national level. According to that provision, the mere fact that an NCA is dealing with a case or has dealt with it in the past are sufficient grounds for other NCAs (and the Commission) to suspend their own proceedings or reject complaints relating to the same agreement or practice. However, Article 13 of Regulation 1/2003 only applies after several NCAs have been seized with the same matter. It does not determine the competent authority prior to their engagement and therefore cannot be considered an allocation rule.

ECJ. See R Whish, *Competition Law* (London, LexisNexis, 5th edn, 2003), 440–1; A Jones and B Sufrin, *EC Competition Law* (Oxford, Oxford University Press, 3rd edn, 2008), 1362–4. Nonetheless, in practice, the vast majority of states seems to regard the effects doctrine as a reasonable criterion to assert jurisdiction. According to Basedow, above n 6, 450, the effects doctrine is even almost universally acknowledged. See also E Fox, 'International Antitrust and the Doha Dome' (2003) 43 *Virginia Journal of International Law* 911, 916. Among the Member States, only the UK does not accept this approach. See H Schröter in H Schröter, T Jakob and W Mederer (eds), *Kommentar zum Europäischen Wettbewerbsrecht* (Baden-Baden, Nomos, 1st edn, 2003), 134 para 86. E-J Mestmäcker and H Schweitzer, *Europäisches Wettbewerbsrecht* (Munich, CH Beck, 2nd edn, 2004), § 6 para 49. Relatively wide acceptance of the effects doctrine is, however, without prejudice to the fact that a number of elements surrounding this doctrine still remain unclear. See D Zimmer, 'Kruman, Empagran und die Folgen: Internationale Wettbewerbspolitik in Zeiten exorbitanter Durchsetzung nationalen Kartellrechts' in A Fuchs, H-P Schwintowski and D Zimmer (eds), *Wirtschafts- und Privatrecht im Spannungsfeld von Privatautonomie, Wettbewerb und Regulierung. Festschrift für Ulrich Immenga zum 70. Geburtstag* (Munich, CH Beck, 2004), 475, 494. To date, the ECJ has never expressly recognised the effects doctrine, but instead prefers to rely on the so-called 'implementation doctrine' which was essentially established in the *Woodpulp I* judgment of 1988 (Joined Cases 89, 104, 114, 116, 117 and 125–129/85 *Ahlström Osakeyhtiö and others v Commission* (*Woodpulp I*) [1988] ECR 5193). See Van Bael and Bellis, *ibid*, 156–7. In practice, however, the differences between both approaches do not appear to be significant, with the exception, probably, of negative behaviour (non-action), which may be covered by the effects doctrine but fall short of the implementation test. Jones and Sufrin, *ibid*, 1377; see also Van Bael and Bellis, *ibid*, 158, Mestmäcker and Schweitzer, *ibid*, §6 para 42. See further below n 42.

[12] The likelihood of an Art 81 or 82 case having cross-border effects is naturally quite high as EC competition law only applies where trade between Member States is affected. See further above n 7.

[13] See Zimmer, above n 11, 490, who notes that it is inherent to the effects doctrine that it leads to jurisdictional conflicts.

[14] Cf recital 18 of Reg 1/2003 and para 7 of the Network Notice.

This inevitably raises the questions of how the work will effectively be divided between the competition authorities in the EU and which criteria and principles will be applied to allocate cases among them.[15]

B. Case Allocation under the Network Notice

The Commission has repeatedly taken the position that the allocation of cases should not be a mechanical process, but that flexible solutions should be found. Moreover, the Commission would not accept legally binding rules by which certain cases would be excluded a priori from the scope of its own jurisdiction.[16] Thus Regulation 1/2003 itself does not contain any criteria for allocating cases. However, the Commission included allocation criteria in an informal, non-binding document, the Network Notice.[17]

---

[15] Schaub, above n 2, 39, points out that the issue is one of dividing the work, not one of attributing competence.

[16] See K Dekeyser and D Dalheimer, 'Co-operation within the European Competition Network—Taking Stock after 10 Months of Case Practice', paper for the conference 'Antitrust Reform in Europe: A Year in Practice', organised jointly by the International Bar Association (IBA) and the European Commission, Brussels, 9–11 March 2005, 6; C Gauer, D Dalheimer, L Kjolbye and E De Smijter, 'Regulation 1/2003: A Modernised Application of EC Competition Rules' (2003) (Spring) Competition Policy Newsletter 3, 7. See also the judgment in Case C–344/98 *Masterfoods* [2000] ECR I–11369, para 48, where the ECJ ruled that, in order to fulfil the role assigned to it, the Commission is entitled to adopt at any time individual decisions under Arts 81 and 82 EC.

[17] Since the instrument of 'notices' falls outside the typology of measures listed in Art 249 EC, they are generally regarded as not legally binding for Member States. G Pampel, 'Rechtsnatur und Rechtswirkungen von Mitteilungen der Kommission im europäischen Wettbewerbsrecht' (2005) 16 *Europäische Zeitschrift für Wirtschaftsrecht* 11, 12. *Contra* M Schweda, 'Die Bindungswirkung von Bekanntmachungen und Leitlinien der Europäischen Kommission' (2004) 54 *Wirtschaft und Wettbewerb* 1133, 1141, who argues that, in view of the loyalty obligation enshrined in Art 10 EC, notices are binding for national authorities and courts. It has, however, been acknowledged that notices and guidelines have a binding effect on the Commission itself, in accordance with the principle of equal treatment which entails a self-imposed limitation on the exercise of the Commission's discretion. See, eg Case T–214/95 *Vlaams Gewest v Commission* [1998] ECR II–717, para 89 (regarding guidelines in the field of state aid) and Case T–224/00 *Archer Daniels v Commission* ('*Lysine*') [2003] ECR II–2597, para 182 (regarding guidelines for the setting of fines in competition matters). This line of arguments is similar to the German doctrine on *Selbstbindung der Verwaltung*. In addition to the principle of equal treatment, one can also rely on the requirement of protecting legitimate expectations in order to justify that at least the Commission itself is bound by the guidelines and notices which it publishes (Pampel, *ibid*, 12 (note 19)). In Joined Cases C–189/02 P etc. *Dansk Rørindustri and others v Commission* (Pre-insulated Pipes) [2005] ECR I–5425, para 211, the court also mentions this second principle (legitimate expectations) to explain the binding effect of published guidelines. At para 223 of that judgment, the ECJ even holds that rules of conduct such as the Commission's Guidelines on the Calculation of Fines are, in principle, covered by the notion of 'law' within the meaning of Art 7(1) ECHR, provision enshrining the principle of *nulla poena sine lege*. Finally, a third general principle, notably the principle of legal certainty can be invoked to justify that the Commission is bound to respect its own guidelines and notices. See H Hofmann, 'Negotiated and Non-negotiated Administrative Rule-making: the Example of EC Competition Policy' (2006) 43 *CML Rev* 153, 162. Hofmann further argues that the denomination of these instruments as 'soft law' (see, eg B Perrin, 'Challenges Facing the EU Network of Competition

These criteria were elaborated in close co-operation with the NCAs.[18] They are considered by their very nature to be purely indicative.[19]

1. General

The rules on case allocation set out in the Network Notice follow two major principles. In accordance with recital 18 of Regulation 1/2003, the objective is that cases should be dealt with by a single authority as often as possible.[20] The allocation rules are further based on the premise that the competition authority that receives a complaint or commences an *ex officio* procedure will usually remain in charge of the case.[21] If reallocation takes place, it should be done swiftly and efficiently so as not to hold up any ongoing investigations.[22]

There are two main conclusions to be drawn from these principles. First, the Network Notice is not so much concerned with the allocation of cases, but rather with their reallocation.[23]As a general rule, it leaves the responsibility to handle a case with the authority that is the first to be seized or to start an investigation. Thus, the issue of case allocation would only arise on rare occasions, notably where the information available at the outset of the proceedings (and shared in the Network) reveals either a blatant misallocation of the case or the existence of multiple parallel proceedings regarding the same infringement. Normally, however, a case will simply

Authorities: Insights from a Comparative Criminal Law Perspective' (2006) 31 *EL Rev* 540, 545) is not entirely justified since, via the three general principles mentioned above, these originally purely internal measures indirectly produce some limited external legal effect, thereby acquiring certain hard law characteristics (*idem*, 164–5). It is doubtful, however, whether this reasoning can be applied to the Network Notice since the notice predominantly aims at organising and regulating the intra-Network relations and thus is principally not meant to have external effects (see para 4 of the Network Notice). On the other hand, at least the case allocation rules could be said to be directed at the undertakings concerned who arguably have a legitimate interest in knowing to which authority's sanctioning system they will be subject.

[18] This co-operation took place via the ECN, which actually started to operate prior to 1 May 2004. At that time, officials from 25 Member States were involved. Dekeyser and Dalheimer, above n 16, 18.

[19] C Gauer, 'Due Process in the Face of Divergent National Procedures and Sanctions', paper for the conference 'Antitrust Reform in Europe: A Year in Practice', organised jointly by the International Bar Association (IBA) and the European Commission, Brussels, 9–11 March 2005, 3. Dekeyser and Dalheimer, above n 16, 6. It is fair to note that all these principles and premises work very much in favour of the Commission, which seems to have almost unlimited discretion in selecting the cases it will treat. Cf also R Nazzini, 'Parallel and Sequential Proceedings in Competition Law: An Essay on the Modes of Interaction between Community and National Law (2005) 16 *European Business Law Review* 245, 251 and A Fuchs, 'Kontrollierte Dezentralisierung der europäischen Wettbewerbsaufsicht' (2005) 40 *Europarecht* (Beiheft 2), 77, 87 (cited also below at n 282).

[20] Para 7 of the Network Notice. It is curious to note that this principle is mentioned not in respect of the (initial) allocation, but with regard to the reallocation of cases.

[21] Para 6 of the Network Notice.

[22] Para 7 of the Network Notice.

[23] White Paper, para 61; Schaub, above n 2, 39–40.

remain with the authority that has informed the Network after taking up the matter. An allocation *sensu stricto* thus does not take place. Secondly, the reallocation of cases will only take place exceptionally, for instance where the complainant obviously did not choose the proper authority, or the facts known about the case change materially in the course of the investigation conducted by the authority that took up the matter first.[24]

2. Allocation Criteria and the Concept of the 'Well Placed Authority'

In a discussion paper published prior to the White Paper, the German competition authority had advanced the proposal to allocate cases according to the 'centre of gravity' test (or national focus).[25] The concept was further discussed and defended by the German Monopolies Commission in a special report of 2001.[26] Interestingly, the CFI had already referred to this concept in *BEMIM*, a judgment of 1995, when considering whether the Commission could reject a complaint on the ground that there was no sufficient Community interest in any further investigation.[27] The CFI held that the Commission was entitled to reject the complaint for lack of Community interest

> solely because it had determined that the *centre of gravity* of the alleged infringements was in France and that the matter had already been brought before the French courts.[28]

Apparently, the expression had been used by the Commission itself in the letter by which it had definitely rejected the complaint in order to describe the fact that the practices criticised by BEMIM had essentially national effects and were therefore not of any particular importance to the functioning of the common market.[29] Nevertheless, the test was rejected by the Commission as being too vague.[30] Instead, in the Explanatory

---

[24] Cf para 19 of the Network Notice.

[25] So-called '*Schwerpunkttheorie*'. Bundeskartellamt, *Praxis und Perspektiven der dezentralen Anwendung des EG-Wettbewerbsrechts*, Diskussionspapier für die Sitzung des Arbeitskreises Kartellrecht am 8. und 9. Oktober 1998, 19–21.

[26] Monopolkommission, *Folgenprobleme der europäischen Kartellverfahrensreform*, 32. Sondergutachten (2001), paras 35–40.

[27] See P-V Bos, 'Towards a Clear Distribution of Competence between EC and National Competition Authorities' (1995) 16 *European Competition Law Review* 410, 414 and B Rodger and A MacCulloch, 'Community Competition Law Enforcement. Deregulation and Re-regulation: the Commission, National Authorities and Private Enforcement' (1998) 4 *Columbia Journal of European Law* 579, 585.

[28] Emphasis added. Judgment of the CFI in Case T–114/92 *BEMIM v Commission* [1995] ECR II–147, para 93.

[29] See the citation of the Commission's letter at para 77 of the judgment in *BEMIM* (*ibid*).

[30] Para 61 of the White Paper. See also A Schaub, 'Modernisation of EC Competition Law: Reform of Regulation no 17' in B Hawk (ed), *1999 Proceedings of the Fordham Corporate Law Institute* (New York, Juris Publishing, 2000), 143, 145.

Memorandum that was attached to the Draft Regulation, the Commission proclaimed that the Network would

> ensure an efficient allocation of cases based on the principle that cases should be dealt with by the best placed authority.[31]

It is curious to note that the concept of the 'best placed' authority was later replaced by the notion of 'well placed'.[32] The term 'well placed' allegedly provides more flexibility in that it does not necessarily point to a single authority but, rather, implies that several authorities can be (equally) suited and eligible to handle a particular matter.[33] In order to determine which authority is well placed to deal with a case, the Network Notice adopts a pragmatic approach. It uses not quantitative, but qualitative criteria. Broadly speaking, the Network Notice follows the principle that geographical proximity to the relevant facts and evidence is decisive. An authority is well placed if it can effectively maintain or restore competition having regard to the seat of the companies involved, the location of the evidence and the area where the effects of the agreement or practice under investigation are mainly felt.[34]

Accordingly, the Network Notice provides that an NCA is well placed to deal with a case where:

(i)   the agreement or conduct at issue has substantial direct (actual or foreseeable) effects in its territory;

(ii)   the NCA is able to effectively bring to an end the entire infringement, ie it has jurisdiction to prohibit the agreement or practice at issue and, where appropriate, impose adequate sanctions; and

(iii) it can gather the relevant evidence either alone or with the assistance of other authorities.[35]

---

[31] P 6 of the Explanatory Memorandum.

[32] See paras 15–19 of the Joint Statement.

[33] See Gauer, above n 19, 3.

[34] The criteria for determining the 'well placed authority' are apparently based on a proposal of the German and Dutch delegations. U Böge, 'The Commission's Position within the Network: The Perspective of the NCAs' in Ehlermann and Atanasiu, above n 2, 247, 249. Obviously, they were drawing largely on elements that had already been discussed in the context of the German proposal to apply the 'centre of gravity' test. These elements are for example the question of whether the authority can effectively investigate the matter and bring the infringement to an end (discussed by the BKartA under the heading '*Ermittlungs- und Durchsetzungsprobleme*') and the issue of cases that show a particular Community interest. See Bundeskartellamt, above n 25, 21–2.

[35] Para 8 of the Network Notice. R Smits, 'The European Competition Network: Selected Aspects' (2005) 32 *Legal Issues of Economic Integration* 175, 179, calls these criteria the 'three E's' (effect, end and evidence).

If all of the above (cumulative) requirements are fulfilled, the respective NCA can be expected to be able to handle the case alone.[36] To the extent that all NCAs effectively abide by these rules,[37] the above criteria, in particular the first criterion, ensure that jurisdiction is asserted only over cases that have an appropriate nexus with the Member State whose NCA is acting.[38]

The requirement of a jurisdictional nexus is an essential aspect of the case allocation rules.[39] In practice, it will help limit the potential number of competent authorities and could thus be seen as a reinforcement or advancement of the effects/implementation doctrine.[40] This approach is also largely in line with the requirements of public international law,[41]

[36] If one compares these criteria with the results of the discussions on the division of responsibilities in the 1990s (see above n 8), it seems that little progress has been made since those days. As long ago as 1994, the Commission had concluded that NCAs could handle a case if three criteria were fulfilled. First, the effects of the case were mainly within a single Member State; secondly, protection at national level would be efficient; and thirdly, the case did not meet the conditions for an exemption. (See XXIVth Report on Competition Policy 1994, point 42.) The third criterion is now of course redundant given the direct applicability of Art 81(3). For the rest, however, the criteria mentioned in the XXIVth Report on Competition Policy 1994 are essentially identical to the requirements set out in the Network Notice, the only distinctive feature being that the criterion of efficient protection at national level has been translated into two more detailed and specific requirements (regarding termination/punishment of the infringement and collection of evidence) in the Network Notice.

[37] In the first case in which the allocation of a case was challenged, the CFI underlined that the criteria laid down in the Network Notice only represent an optional allocation system, a mere possibility of how the work could be divided (*'une simple possibilité de partage des tâches'*). Para 84 of the judgment of 8 March 2007 in Case T–339/04 *France Télécom v Commission* (*Wanadoo*) [2007] ECR II–521. On this judgment see F Rizzuto, 'Parallel Competence and the Power of the EC Commission under Reg 1/2003 According to the Court of First Instance' (2008) 29 *European Competition Law Review* 286.

[38] The other two criteria are more efficiency related. M Van Der Woude, 'The Modernization Paradox: Controlled Decentralization', paper for the IBC's 10th Annual Advanced Competition Law Conference, Brussels, 6 and 7 November 2003, 10.

[39] The Commission describes this nexus as a 'material link'. See para 9 of the Network Notice. The idea that sovereign states should not assert jurisdiction where there is no (sufficient) nexus with their own territory is also promoted by the ICN in the framework of its recommended practices for merger notification procedures. In these recommendations, the ICN suggests that the jurisdictional nexus should be determined by reference to the activities of at least two parties (or of the acquired business) in the local territory. Worldwide revenues or assets alone should not in any event be sufficient to trigger a notification requirement in a particular state. This approach indicates that, from an international law perspective, it would be difficult to justify that Member States claim unlimited jurisdiction over any Art 81 or 82 case (see the ICN's Recommended Practices for Merger Notification Procedures, points IB and IC; available at www.internationalcompetitionnetwork.org/media/larchive0611/mnprecpractices.pdf (accessed February 2009).

[40] See D Arts and K Bourgeois, 'Samenwerking tussen mededingingsautoriteiten en rechtsbescherming: enkele bedenkingen' (2006) 1 *TBM-RCB* 26, para 40. Similarly, Fuchs, above n 19, 96, considers the criteria to be tied in with the effects doctrine. Cf also Schaub, above n 2, 40, who justifies the requirement of a nexus by referring to the objective of the EC competition rules, ie to protect consumer welfare. For this reason, there must be a link between the acting NCA and the consumers affected by the infringement. On the similitude of effects and implementation doctrine see below n 42.

[41] Public international law traditionally regards state jurisdiction as an expression of the sovereignty of states and therefore as being essentially linked to the territory of the state

which have moreover been acknowledged by the Community judicature. In *Gencor/Lonrho*, the CFI namely held that an extraterritorial application of the Community's Merger Regulation

> is justified under public international law when it is foreseeable that a proposed concentration will have an immediate and substantial effect in the Community.[42]

exercising jurisdiction. See A Cassese, *International Law* (Oxford, Oxford University Press, 2nd edn, 2005), 49; A Verdross and B Simma, *Universelles Völkerrecht* (Berlin, Duncker & Humblot, 3rd edn, 1984), § 1022. There is still some uncertainty as to whether the effects doctrine as such is in conformity with the principles of international law. See Whish, above n 11, 429 (*in fine*); Jones and Sufrin, above n 11, 1370. *Pro* conformity Advocate General Darmon at para 57 of his opinion in *Woodpulp I* (above n 11). However, in the present context, where several authorities have concurrent jurisdiction under Reg 1/2003 to enforce Arts 81 and 82 EC, the nexus established by the three cumulative criteria would also seem to satisfy public international law requirements if these are at all applicable in the framework of supranational Community law.

[42] Judgement of the CFI in Case T–102/96 *Gencor v Commission* [1999] ECR II–753, para 90. On the extraterritorial application of EC competition law and the recognition of the effects doctrine, see J Schwarze, 'Die extraterritoriale Anwendbarkeit des EG-Wettbewerbsrechts— Vom Durchführungsprinzip zum Prinzip der qualifizierten Auswirkung' in J Schwarze (ed), *Europäisches Wettbewerbsrecht im Zeichen der Globalisierung* (Baden-Baden, Nomos Verlagsgesellschaft, 2002), 37, 53–4. Note that the ECJ has not (yet) endorsed the effects-based approach. In *Woodpulp I*, the ECJ held that Community competition law was applicable to companies located in non-member countries because the price concertation at issue had been put into effect within the Community. See the judgment of the ECJ in *Woodpulp I*, above n 11, paras 15–18. However, in *Woodpulp I*, the ECJ could have applied the effects doctrine since the concerted practices of the pulp producers regarding prices charged to customers in the Community certainly had effects in the territory of the Member States. Moreover, it is worth noting that the ECJ, when ruling that the decisive factor was the place of implementation, sought to reject the applicants' argument that the Commission had been wrong in founding itself solely on the repercussions within the Community of conduct adopted outside the Member States' territory. The ECJ noted that the applicability of Arts 81 and 82 EC could not depend on the place where the restrictive agreements or practices are formed as the result would obviously be that undertakings could easily evade those prohibitions. See paras 15 and 16 of the judgment in *Woodpulp I*, above n 11. This line of reasoning indicates that the ECJ was in fact considering how the practices adopted by the pulp producers outside the Community had actually manifested themselves within the Community. Such considerations could also be made in the context of the effects doctrine. See Mestmäcker and Schweitzer, above n 11, § 6, para 41. A careful analysis of the *Woodpulp* judgment made by W Van Gerven suggests that the ECJ's approach represents a sort of qualified version of the effects doctrine as the relevant point of contact or nexus with the Community territory used by the court was in reality the 'constituent effect', ie an appreciable effect on the competitive conditions of the Community market. W Van Gerven, 'EC Jurisdiction in Antitrust Matters: The Wood Pulp Judgment' in B Hawk (ed), *1989 Proceedings of the Fordham Corporate Law Institute* (New York, Juris Publishing, 1990), 451, 474–7. Against this background, implementation doctrine and effects doctrine appear almost interchangeable. It therefore seems that the difference between the effects doctrine and the implementation concept would be of little significance in practice. A Burnside and Y Botteman, 'Networking amongst Competition Agencies' (2004) 10 *International Trade Law & Regulation* 1, 6. One exception is negative behaviour (non-action), which is unlikely to fulfil the implementation criterion but could still be covered by the effects doctrine. Jones and Sufrin, above n 11, 1377; Whish, above n 11, 437. See also P Mavroidis and D Neven, 'Some Reflections on the Extraterritoriality in International Economic Law. A Law and Economics Analysis' in X (ed), *Mélanges en hommage à Michel Waelbroeck. Troisième partie. Droit de la concurrence, libre circulation et politiques communes* (Brussels, Bruylant, 1999), 1297, 1306, who consider the relatively recent *Boeing/McDonell Douglas* case (no IV/M877; decision of 31 July 1997), where the Commission asserted jurisdiction over a merger between two US companies, as proof that the EC legal order has effectively incorporated the effects doctrine even in its most aggressive form. See further above n 11.

These principles should apply, *mutatis mutandis*, also with regard to the extraterritorial application of Articles 81 and 82 EC by a Member State authority.

The situation is, however, far more complex where the relevant facts extend beyond the territory of a single country in such a way that the case has material links with several Member States.[43] In such a case, three scenarios are conceivable.

(i) Where two or three Member States are concerned, the action of only one NCA may, in certain cases, be sufficient to bring the entire infringement to an end. This solution should prevail, for instance, where the companies involved are located in one and the same Member State but are also active in one or two other Member States. The NCA of the Member State where the companies are domiciled can effectively issue and enforce a cease-and-desist order against them.[44] To the extent that evidence must be collected in the other Member States concerned, the acting NCA can request the assistance of the NCAs in these other Member States pursuant to Article 22(1) of Regulation 1/2003.

(ii) Where a single NCA cannot effectively bring the infringement to a halt, two or even three NCAs may act in parallel, though one of them should preferably be designated as lead authority.[45] Where several NCAs pursue the same matter in parallel, it is imperative that they are in constant contact and coordinate their actions closely.[46] Such coordination will be particularly crucial with regard to so-called 'dawn-raids' (surprise inspections), where secrecy and timing are essential.[47] It must be emphasised, though, that multiple parallel control is supposed to be the exception rather than the rule, the Network Notice being based on the premise that cases should be handled by a single NCA whenever possible.[48]

(iii) Finally, the suspected infringement may affect competition in more than three Member States. In such situations, the Commission considers itself to be 'particularly well placed' to handle the case.[49]

[43] This would be the case where the companies involved have their seat in different Member States, the evidence is located in several Member States or the relevant agreement/practice has considerable effects in more than one Member State.

[44] See para 11 of the Network Notice.

[45] This scenario would prevail where the companies involved in illegal agreements or practices are located in different Member States. See paras 12 and 13 of the Network Notice.

[46] Schaub, above n 2, 40.

[47] See Dekeyser and Dalheimer, above n 16, 7.

[48] Para 7 of the Network Notice, which mirrors para 16 of the Joint Statement. Schaub, above n 5, 255.

[49] See para 14 of the Network Notice. In the context of reforming the EC merger control rules, the Commission has taken a similar approach. The new rules provide for the possibility of having a merger which has no Community dimension referred to the Commission, at the request

In addition to this 'three-plus' rule, the Commission is also regarded as well placed where a case displays a particular Community interest. This category includes mainly cases which raise novel competition issues and therefore make it necessary for the Commission to set a precedent by opening proceedings itself, as well as cases which involve legal issues that are closely linked to other EC law provisions which, in turn, are exclusively or more effectively applied by the Commission. Cases which require the adoption of a Commission decision in order to ensure effective enforcement also fall in this category.[50] The latter rule is evidently quite vague and would seem a sort of fall-back provision covering all situations that are not yet covered by any of the other alternatives. It may be seen as a necessary complement to Article 11(6) of Regulation 1/2003, which empowers the Commission to take a case out of the jurisdiction of the NCAs at any stage of a national investigation.

3. Initial Allocation Period

If the Network is to work efficiently, case allocation must be a swift process and may not unduly hold up ongoing investigations. In other words, cases should be (re)allocated as quickly as possible.[51]

The Joint Statement mentions an indicative timeframe of up to three months within which case allocation should be completed.[52] In accordance with this statement, the Network Notice provides for an initial allocation period of two months during which any reallocation issues should be settled. After the two-month period, cases will not be reallocated unless the facts known about the case change materially in the course of the investigation, ie in such a way that it becomes obvious that another authority would be better placed to handle the case.[53]

of the parties, where otherwise it would have to be notified to the national authorities of at least three Member States. See Art 4(5) of the 2004 Merger Regulation. However, Fingleton raises the question of why four (or more) NCAs cannot routinely deal with a case. J Fingleton, 'The Distribution and Attribution of Cases Among the Members of the Network: The Perspective of the Commission/NCAs' in Ehlermann and Atanasiu, above n 2, 327, 333. It would probably be very time consuming to coordinate the activities of four or more NCAs as the involvement of so many NCAs would make the situation quite complex. Therefore action by a central authority, the Commission, appears more efficient in such cases. See A Schaub, 'The Commission's Position within the Network' in Ehlermann and Atanasiu, above n 2, 237, 239. Moreover, where an infringement affects more than three Member States, it seems unlikely that all undertakings involved would be located in one and the same Member State. Consequently, the first option outlined above (a single NCA can bring the entire infringement to an end) would rarely be available.

[50] Para 15 of the Network Notice.
[51] Paras 7 and 18 of the Network Notice.
[52] Para 12 of the Joint Statement.
[53] Paras 18 and 19 of the Network Notice. This situation may occur, for instance, where investigations reveal that a cartel, which initially was believed to affect only two Member States, involves companies from more than three Member States. See D Schnichels, 'The Network of

After the initial allocation period, the Commission is, in principle, excluded from de-seizing an NCA that is dealing with a particular case. However, paragraph 54 of the Network Notice lists five scenarios in which the Commission retains the right to take a case out of the jurisdiction of the NCA(s) even after the two-month period has expired. These relate in particular to situations where NCAs envisage decisions which are in conflict with each other or with established case law.[54] The Commission will also de-seize NCAs where there is a need to develop the Community competition policy or to ensure effective enforcement. Again, the latter twocriteria are quite broad and do not seem to effectively restrict the exercise of the Commission's right of evocation after the initial allocation period.

The two-month period starts to run from the date of the first information sent to the Network.[55] The Commission has been careful, however, not to make this a binding time limit. In addition to the fact that a Commission notice is an informal document which in principle does not create legal rights and obligations, the non-binding character of the initial allocation period is also emphasised by the wording of paragraph 18 of the Network Notice ('should be resolved', 'will endeavour'). Moreover, in paragraph 54 of the Network Notice, the initial allocation period is explicitly referred to as '*indicative* time period'.[56] The two-month time limit may therefore be exceeded at the discretion of the Network members.

II. THE EXCHANGE OF THE RELEVANT INFORMATION

The content of the information shared at this early stage, the authorities involved, the timing and the (technical) process of communication are to be understood in the light of the purpose of the information exchange, namely to allow a quick and efficient allocation of cases.

A. Who will be Informed?

Article 11(3) of Regulation 1/2003 formally establishes an obligation for NCAs to report new cases only vis-à-vis the Commission. Informing other NCAs of new cases is a mere faculty. However, an efficient allocation

---

Competition Authorities: How Will It Work in Practice?' in D Geradin (ed), *Modernisation and Enlargement: Two Major Challenges for EC Competition Law* (Antwerp, Intersentia, 2004), 99, 107.

[54] The other two scenarios are: when an NCA is unduly drawing out proceedings and when the NCA concerned does not object. See also above Chapter 1, section II.A.1.b(2).

[55] Para 18 of the Network Notice.

[56] Emphasis added.

process requires that all members of the Network are aware of new cases.[57] Accordingly, paragraph 17 of the Network Notice provides that information on incoming cases 'should therefore be provided to NCAs and the Commission'. In other words, there is a common understanding that information which must be provided to the Commission under Article 11(3) of Regulation 1/2003 will simultaneously be communicated to all other members of the Network. In practice, the information on new cases is disseminated electronically via the common Intranet, which can be accessed by all Network members.[58]

There may be exceptional situations where the information will only be forwarded to a limited number of NCAs. Such an approach may be justified where, for instance, surprise inspections have to be coordinated, which requires a high level of secrecy.[59] The restricted release of the information on new cases seems to be in line with both Regulation 1/2003 and the Network Notice as NCAs have some discretion as to when they actually notify the Network of new cases.[60] Pursuant to Article 11(3) of Regulation 1/2003, the relevant information may be supplied either before or immediately after the commencement of the formal investigation.

B. What Kind of Information will be Exchanged?

1. Essentials Known at the Outset

Cases can start either as an *ex officio* investigation or following a complaint lodged with one or several competition authorities. In the latter case, it is important that the Network is informed of the case early in order to allow detection of multiple complaints concerning the same infringement. The information transmitted on new matters must therefore be such that it is possible for all Network members, with minimum effort, to identify the case, ie to uncover whether a complaint concerning the same facts has also been addressed to them, or whether they have already dealt with the case in the past or are currently dealing with it. In other words, the transmission must contain all details that are necessary to make a first assessment of the

[57] D Reichelt, 'To What Extent Does the Co-operation within the European Competition Network Protect the Rights of Undertakings?' (2005) 42 *CML Rev* 745, 760.

[58] See Schaub, above n 2, 39 (fn 23); E Paulis, 'Coherent Application of EC Competition Law in a System of Parallel Competences' in Ehlermann and Atanasiu, above n 5, 399, 407.

[59] See also below n 90.

[60] See further below in this section II.C. In the context of the allocation process, this discretion may become relevant as the first information sent to the Network triggers the two-month allocation period (see above in this chapter section I.B.3). For instance, if a complaint is lodged simultaneously with several NCAs, the fact that one of them informs the Network much later than the other NCAs may undermine the objective of an efficient allocation process—to address allocation issues as early as possible and allocate cases swiftly within a relatively short time-frame of two months.

case in terms of the type of infringement and the underlying facts, including the parties involved, the relevant products, the territories affected and the origin of the case.

At the same time, the information should be brief, concise and easily accessible.[61] There can be no doubt that a considerably larger amount of information will be exchanged between the competition authorities in the EU as compared to the situation before 1 May 2004.[62] This body of information has to be analysed, processed and stored by each competition authority participating in the Network. In order to avoid overloading the system, it is important to keep the administrative burden on the Network members to a minimum.

Therefore, the information furnished on newly opened matters should be limited to the essential elements of the case.[63] These should include the name and place of business of the parties involved, the products to which the illegal agreement or practice relates, the territory potentially affected by it, the type of infringement suspected and its duration, and, where applicable, the names of the complainants. Finally, the competition authority supplying the information must be identified. To make the information easily accessible, it should be provided in a consistent format. Accordingly, the Network Notice requires that a standard form be made available to the Network members which should be used for transmitting information on new cases.[64] The official form which is currently used, sometimes referred to as the initial case report, adheres to these principles, enabling Network members to provide standardised information on all the information listed above.[65]

Needless to say, the information furnished at the outset of the proceedings may be incomplete or even erroneous. It can only be based on what is known about the case at that time, ie what has been gathered or received. These facts can be described as 'observable characteristics'.[66] However, some (important) characteristics may not be known at the

---

[61] Widegren, above n 2, 422. See also para 10 of the Joint Statement.

[62] At the end of December 2004, ie only eight months after the coming into force of Reg 1/2003, information on almost 300 cases had been uploaded in the system. Even if one takes into account that this number includes a number of old cases which had already been pending before 1 May 2004, it is evident that the Network members will have to deal regularly with huge amounts of incoming information. In January and February 2005 alone, nearly 50 new cases were reported. Dekeyser and Dalheimer, above n 16, 5. By the end of 2005, the total number of cases reported to the ECN had reached the 500 mark. See statistics at http://europa.eu.int/comm/competition/ecn/statistics.html (accessed February 2009).

[63] Cf J Bourgeois, 'Consultations between National Competition Authorities and the European Commission in a Decentralized System of EC Competition Law Enforcement' in Ehlermann and Atanasiu, above n 2, 427, 429.

[64] Para 17 of the Network Notice.

[65] Dekeyser and Dalheimer, above n 16, 5. Information on the standard form is provided in English.

[66] Fingleton, above n 49, 328.

beginning of the procedure, being revealed only in the course of the investigation. In particular, the location of the evidence, which is an important factor in determining whether a particular authority is well placed to deal with it, and the geographical scope of the effects of an infringement are elements which often become apparent only after the first investigative measures have already been carried out.[67]

2. Risk of a Material Change of Facts

If the facts of a case subsequently turn out to differ significantly from the summary distributed at the outset, ie in such a way that the competition authority which is dealing with the case no longer appears to be well placed to handle it, the case would have to be reallocated in accordance with paragraph 19 of the Network Notice.[68] This would not be very efficient if certain investigative measures would then have to be repeated. However, if the objective is to address any (re)allocation issue as soon as the case is pending, the Network must be notified of new cases at an early stage. The risk of a misallocation resulting from the fact that the observable characteristics at this point in time may be incomplete or incorrect cannot be avoided. In practice, however, it appears that cases have to be reallocated only occasionally.[69] The risk would seem greater with regard to cases originating from complaints or leniency applications since the authorities have to rely on information the accuracy of which they cannot usually verify prior to its dissemination. Experience suggests that complainants often do not have precise knowledge of all relevant factors of the reported infringement, such as the exact geographical coverage of a cartel.[70]

The Notice on Complaints provides some guidance to potential complainants. In combination with the Network Notice, which is in parts reproduced in the Notice on Complaints[71], the latter notice should prevent complainants from addressing their complaints to a competition authority that is a priori not well placed to deal with their case. On the other hand, it can reasonably be assumed that complainants may often be unaware of the fact that the suspected infringement equally affects companies or individuals in other Member States, or that parties from several Member

---

[67] Cf Fingleton, above n 49, 330, pointing to the dilemma between the objective of allocating cases as early as possible and the risk that the relevant allocation information may change at a later stage of the proceedings.

[68] See Schnichels, above n 53, 107.

[69] See K Dekeyser and M Jaspers, 'A New Era of ECN Cooperation' (2007) 30 *World Competition* 3, 7.

[70] See C Gauer and M Jaspers, 'Designing a European Solution for a "One-stop Leniency Shop"' (2006) 27 *European Competition Law Review* 685, 688.

[71] See para 21 of the Notice on Complaints.

States are participating in the suspected cartel.[72] On this basis, there is probably a higher risk that the facts known at the outset of proceedings originating from complaints do not convey a full and correct picture of the case.

As concerns own initiative procedures, it is unlikely that an NCA will commence proceedings in a case that has no material link with the territory of its Member State. On the basis of good faith and impartial co-operation between the Network members, the acting NCA in *ex officio* proceedings may therefore be presumed to be well placed. Where the geographical scope of a case turns out to be larger than initially suspected, reallocation problems can be reduced by interpreting paragraph 19 of the Network Notice in a restrictive way. A material change of facts justifying reallocation[73] should only be assumed where the NCA handling the case can no longer be expected to effectively bring to an end the entire infringement, for instance, because of the inclusion in the investigation of parties located outside its territorial jurisdiction whose involvement was unknown at the outset of the proceedings. If, on the other hand, the investigation reveals that consumers are affected in more Member States than initially presumed, this change of facts alone should not be a reason for reallocating the case provided the suspected parties remain the same.

3. National Cases

Another issue connected with initial information on new cases is the question of whether NCAs should also report purely national cases to the Network. This question is of particular relevance if one considers that an NCA may erroneously conclude that a particular agreement or practice does not affect intra-Community trade and consequently deals with the case exclusively under national competition law even though Community competition law would be applicable as well.

However, neither Regulation 1/2003 nor the Network Notice foresees any exchange of information on purely national cases. The obligation established by Article 11(3) of Regulation 1/2003 to inform the Commission and the right to inform other NCAs of new cases only apply to cases involving the application of Article 81 or 82 EC. Therefore, where an NCA incorrectly assumes the absence of an appreciable effect on intra-Community trade, no case information would be forwarded to the Network.

---

[72] Apart from this lack of information, complainants pursue their own interests and will 'present' their case in such a way as to encourage the adoption by the competition authority of the measures that they want to be taken.

[73] Para 19 of Network Notice provides that '[r]e-allocation of a case after the initial allocation period of two months should only occur where the facts known about the case *change materially* during the course of the proceedings' (emphasis added).

On the one hand, this may be regretted as it could lead to enforcement lacunae. On the other hand, members should be careful not to overload the Network with information. The flow of information between the Network members will increase considerably compared to the situation under Regulation 17, where NCAs were neither obliged to inform the Commission of new cases nor entitled to share such information with other NCAs.[74] In the decentralised enforcement system, NCAs have a duty to furnish certain information to the Commission. The larger burden, however, is likely to result from the need to review the information that they continuously receive via the Network.

In this context, it should be noted that case allocation is based on a simple information duty, not a consultation process *sensu stricto*.[75] A response from the Commission or the other Network members is not required or even expected when information on a new case is submitted to the Network. In the absence of any reaction, the notifying NCA may therefore commence or continue its investigation. Consequently, the NCA reporting a new case remains in charge of the matter even if it is not well placed to act, unless another Network member initiates a genuine discussion on the appropriate allocation of the case.[76] In particular, multiple proceedings will only be detected if the Network members are effectively aware of all pending cases. Therefore, Network members must be given a realistic chance to actually review the information on new cases supplied to the Network in order to be able to react where necessary, otherwise the whole exercise of informing the Network of new cases would be devoid of purpose. However, routine information on purely national cases would increase the amount of information shared in the Network to such an extent that it might paralyse the entire allocation system, as it would be practically impossible for the Network members to duly analyse and process the amounts of information supplied to them. It can therefore not be the purpose to feed all domestic cases systematically into the Network even though this would provide Network members with an opportunity to verify whether a given case should (also) be treated under Community law rather than solely under national law.

---

[74] See para 41 of the judgment of the ECJ in Case C–67/91 *Dirección General de Defensa de la Competencia v Asociación Española de Banca Privada and others* ('*Spanish Banks*') [1992] ECR I–4785 with regard to case information stemming from the Commission.

[75] Consultation can be understood as a process whereby information is shared with other authorities in order to get a reaction from them which may lead to further action. See Widegren, above n 2, 419. However, Art 11(3) of Reg 1/2003 imposes a mere information duty. Neither is the NCA notifying a new case obliged to await any approval of the Commission, nor is the Commission at all required to react in any way.

[76] See A Burnside and H Crossley, 'Co-operative Mechanisms within the EU: A Blueprint for Future Co-operation at the International Level' (2004) 10 *International Trade Law & Regulation* 25, 27.

C. When must the Information be Furnished?

Article 11(3) of Regulation 1/2003 provides that new cases must be notified to the Commission '*before* or without delay *after* commencing the *first formal investigative measure*'.[77] Despite the fact that the term 'first formal investigative measure' is not defined in Regulation 1/2003, it is fair to assume that the purpose of that rule is to ensure that the Network is informed as soon as an NCA starts a new matter in order to allow for a quick (re)allocation of the case. At the same time, however, the provision leaves room for some flexibility as it gives NCAs the choice to notify the Network either before or immediately after the first formal inquiry. The question inevitably arises of how far an authority can go in its investigations before it actually has to notify the Commission and should also notify the other NCAs.

It seems that, as a general rule, the Network should be informed prior to any formal investigations, while investigations of which the Network is not informed in advance should be exceptions which must be justified by special circumstances of the case. If NCAs were to choose freely the moment when they notify the Network, the objective of the information system, namely to address any allocation issue as early as possible, which, in turn, is a precondition for an efficient allocation and handling of cases, might be jeopardised. An exception, ie providing the information subsequently, would be justified in particular where an NCA has to act quickly in order to secure evidence.[78]

Another issue concerning when the Network should be informed of new cases is the definition of the term 'first formal investigative measures': there does not seem to be any common understanding of this notion.[79] In paragraph 17 of the Network Notice, the Commission seeks to explain the term by referring to the measures of investigation that it can undertake itself under Regulation 1/2003, namely simple and formal requests for information, interviews of natural or legal persons, and inspections of the premises of undertakings and private homes.[80] In spite of this attempt to

---

[77] Emphasis added.

[78] Cf Fingleton, above n 49, 335, and the proposal for para 17 of the Network Notice as contained in an early EU-restricted draft (quoted by Fingleton, *ibid*, at note 15) which explicitly provided that '. . . there is some flexibility in the system: if the authority wants to carry out surprise inspections on the spot, the other competition authorities can be informed only after the inspection has been carried out.' See also below n 90.

[79] Fingleton, above n 49, 331.

[80] Arguably, a 'warning letter' sent by the Commission to the undertakings subject to an investigation also falls within this category of measures. It is consistent case law that the entire procedure, under Community competition law, in fact comprises two successive stages, notably the investigation phase preceding the statement of objections and the remainder of the administrative procedure following the statement of objections until the adoption of a final decision. See paras 37–8 of the judgment of the ECJ in Case C–105/04 P *FEG and TU v Commission* [2006] ECR I–8725. The beginning of the first stage can be marked by the sending of a warning letter,

clarify the notion of 'first formal investigative measure', it is likely that the term will not be interpreted uniformly by NCAs as they act under their own national procedural laws, which may contain different rules with regard to the (internal and external) handling of cases, including the opening of new matters, the (formal) institution of proceedings and the conduct of investigations.

NCAs therefore appear to have some discretion as to when they actually forward information on new cases to the Network.[81] However, since the objective clearly is to inform the Network as early as possible, the discretion is limited in the sense that informing the Network only after the first formal investigative measure must be justified by imperative reasons, such as the need to protect evidence.[82] Moreover, it also seems clear from a comparison with the Commission's instruments under Articles 18–21 of Regulation 1/2003 (to which paragraph 17 of the Network Notice refers explicitly) that any measure whereby the NCA acts vis-à-vis a (natural or legal) person outside the ECN will trigger the information duty. Doubts may arise with regard to purely internal acts which, depending on the applicable national rules, could be considered a formal opening of a new matter. On the whole, the problems that could result from the lack of a common definition of the term 'first formal investigative measures' thus seem to be limited.[83]

Interestingly, it seems that in practice Network members often contact each other at a very early stage, ie even before the new case has actually been reported to the Network.[84] In some cases, such contacts were apparently triggered by parallel complaints on the same alleged cartel that had been received by several authorities. In another instance, an NCA approached the Commission because it suspected that the infringement at issue concerned several Member States and therefore might warrant measures at Community level. This meant that when the new case was finally notified to the entire Network, the allocation process was not

which the ECJ, in that case, put on a par with a measure of investigation (see para 49 of the judgment in *FEG and TU*).

[81] Widegren, above n 2, 422. There may even be different opinions about what constitutes a new case.

[82] Thus the NMa usually informs the Network of a new case only after it has carried out an on-the-spot investigation. It considers the risk too great that information on an imminent inspection might leak to the parties concerned if the information on the new case is uploaded in the system prior to the actual inspection. This could put at peril the success of the dawnraid.

[83] Nonetheless, it is one example of many which highlights the difficulties that arise from the divergency of national procedures and are thus ultimately provoked by the Commission's refusal to harmonise the procedural rules of the Member States. Others will follow in the course of this book. However, the Commission did not consider it necessary 'to embark on a full-scale harmonisation' (p 12 of the Explanatory Memorandum).

[84] S Hossenfelder, 'Erste Erfahrungen des Bundeskartellamtes mit dem Behördennetzwerk' in X, *FIW-Schriftenreihe Band 206. Schwerpunkte des Kartellrechts 2004* (Köln, Carl-Heymanns-Verlag, 2006),1 , 7.

started but was in fact already terminated.[85] Such a procedure seems to be in contradiction with the purpose of the initial case information in that it risks excluding potentially 'interested' members of the Network from the allocation process. However, this risk should not be overestimated. The very early contacts are also an indication of the close relationships between the Network members and the smooth operation of the co-operation mechanisms. Apparently, it is not necessary to have a new case entered into the common database of the ECN in order to initiate the allocation process. All Network members seem to be alert to the possibility that another Network member could be better placed to handle a particular matter. This appears to be sufficient to prompt early (informal) contacts between them with a view to case (re)allocation. One may thus expect that all agencies that are potentially concerned will be contacted. The procedure also shows that Network members share the common understanding that the (re)allocation of cases should in any event take place at the earliest stage possible. This is in the interest of the parties subject to the investigation.

D. How is the Information Circulated?

In order to make communication swift and information easily accessible, all Network members are linked by the common Intranet.[86] This technical aspect of the communication process is not mentioned in the Network Notice,[87] even though it is an important feature of the co-operation mechanisms. Moreover, there are important issues linked to the question of electronic communication via this Intranet, namely its security, stability and capacity.[88] Since the information exchanged includes (albeit to a limited extent) confidential data, it is essential that only secured lines are used. There should also be the capability to exchange encrypted information.[89] In particular, in situations such as the coordination and conduct of unannounced inspections, where confidentiality and secrecy are of utmost importance in order to preserve the surprise effect and thus guarantee the success of the measure, it is crucial that the Intranet provides absolute protection against accidental disclosure of the information exchanged to outsiders.[90] In practice, these conditions seem to be met. The relevant

---

[85] Dekeyser and Dalheimer, above n 16, 7–9.
[86] Cf Schaub, above n 2, 39.
[87] See Chapter 1, n 266.
[88] See Fingleton, above n 49, 335.
[89] Widegren, above n 2, 426.
[90] Cf Widegren, above n 2, 423, who even suggests that in such cases it may be justified to limit the number of authorities to whom information is released before the inspection takes place. Such an approach would also seem to be in line with the discretion granted to NCAs under Art 11(3) of Reg 1/2003 to inform (all or some) Network members only after the first formal

information on new cases is uploaded in a common electronic case-management system (ECMS),[91] which is secured against unauthorised access. Moreover, even within each competition authority, access rights are limited, notably to case handlers and other authorised personnel of the Network member.[92] Documents can be uploaded in the ECMS in commonly used formats. It is important to note, though, that the ECMS is generally not used for the exchange of documents which contain confidential data.[93]

Another important issue affecting the communication between competition authorities is the question of the language to be used. It is evident that information sharing and consultation cannot function effectively if the information is routinely exchanged in all 23 official languages of the EU: no NCA would be able to cope with so many different foreign languages. Therefore, the practice of the Commission, established under Regulation 17, to forward copies of the most important documents in the original language of the case must be adapted if NCAs are to participate actively in the consultation process.[94]

The ECN appears to have already developed the practice of using English as the common working language. As a general rule, the standard form containing the initial case report is filed in English.[95] Indeed, a single working language is the most reasonable and efficient solution.[96] However, knowledge of English as a foreign language is not equally prevalent in all Member States. As a result, some NCA officials may perceive the use of a single language as a barrier for communication with their colleagues from other Member States, and this, in turn, could negatively affect the functioning of the Network.[97] To counteract this, some effort should be expected from the Member States in terms of providing adequate education

investigative measures. The importance of the surprise effect for cartel investigations was highlighted back in 1983 by a Commission official. See J Joshua, 'The Element of Surprise: EEC Competition Investigations under Art 14(3) of Reg 17' (1983) 8 *EL Rev* 3, 5.

[91] See International Competition Network, Cartels Working Group (Subgroup 1), 'Co-operation between competition agencies in cartel investigations', report to the ICN Annual Conference, Moscow, May 2007 (Luxemburg, Office for Official Publications of the European Communities, 2007), 20.

[92] Each Network member determines autonomously which officials it authorises to access the ECMS. Hossenfelder, above n 84, 3.

[93] Communication of such documents takes place via encrypted e-mail or secure surface mail. Dekeyser and Dalheimer, above n 16, 5. The ECMS was developed by IT experts of DG Competition. These experts are currently preparing an improved version.

[94] See Widegren, above n 2, 425.

[95] In personal (bilateral) contacts between officials of the competition authorities, a language is used which is understood by both. Hossenfelder, above n 84, 4. See also above n 65.

[96] Widegren, above n 2, 425. It is probably also the only workable solution. Cf L Idot, 'Le nouveau système communautaire de mise en oeuvre des articles 81 et 82 CE (Règlement 1/2003 et projets de textes d'application)' (2003) 39 *Cahiers de Droit Européen* 283, 321 (at note 132).

[97] Cf Fingleton, above n 49, 335.

and training for their competition officials.[98] This would also be in their own interests, as the alternative to the 'single working language model', namely the selection of two, three or more (alternative) mandatory working languages, would cause incalculable costs and would put an enormous administrative burden on the NCAs. Moreover, such a selection, which would most likely include the languages of the larger Member States such as France, Germany and Italy, would increase the risk of offending the officials from the smaller Member States.

Finally, at this initial stage of communication, where only basic information on new cases is exchanged, the translation costs incurred by the sending authority should still be limited as the information to be provided mainly consists of (company) names and a couple of key words, such as the identification of the affected products and territories and the type of the suspected infringement.[99]

E. Confidentiality

Article 12(1) of Regulation 1/2003 entitles Commission and NCAs to exchange confidential information. At the same time, Article 28(2) of Regulation 1/2003 obliges the officials and (civil) servants of the Commission, the NCAs and other national authorities not to disclose information acquired or exchanged by them pursuant to Regulation 1/2003 and of the kind covered by the obligation of professional secrecy.

Stemming from the EC Treaty, namely Article 287 (ex Article 214) EC, 'professional secrecy' is a Community concept[100] and must therefore be interpreted uniformly. The CFI has held that, even though Article 287 EC refers specifically to data collected from undertakings[101] and thus primarily

---

[98] Interestingly, the most recent changes to the Belgian Competition Act provide that the members of the investigative body, the Auditors Unit, must have a functional knowledge not only of two of the official languages spoken in Belgium, notably Dutch and French, but also of the English language. This condition was imposed to the detriment of German (which is still the official language in a small part of Eastern Belgium), knowledge of which no longer seems to be required. See Art 14 §2 WEM 1999 and the 4th paragraph of Art 25 of WEM 2006. This pragmatic and even progressive approach of the Belgian legislature to the 'language issue', which in fact only takes due account of the realities of modern competition law enforcement, could certainly serve as example for other Member States. It is regrettable, though, that the same requirement has not been imposed with regard to the members of the adjudicative body, the Raad.

[99] With regard to the exchange of information in the course of proceedings, including the exchange of documentary evidence or even entire case files, specific rules about the distribution of translation costs could be established. It seems reasonable that such rules should be based on the principle that translation costs should be borne by the authority requesting the information.

[100] C Gauer, 'Does the Effectiveness of the EU Network of Competition Authorities Require a Certain Degree of Harmonisation of National Procedures and Sanctions?' in Ehlermann and Atanasiu, above n 2, 187, 197.

[101] Art 287 makes express reference to 'information about undertakings, their business relations or their cost components'.

aims at safeguarding the legitimate interests of undertakings in the protection of their business secrets, information covered by professional secrecy includes both business secrets and other types of confidential data.[102] The provisions on professional secrecy can therefore be regarded as the expression of a more general principle whereby authorities applying Community law may not divulge information on proceedings to outsiders if this could harm the legitimate interests of defendants, complainants or others involved in the procedure.[103] The interests protected by the professional secrecy obligation are thus not limited to private interests, but would include the public interest of the acting competition authority in protecting the success of its investigation.

At the outset of the proceedings, when generally no formal investigative measure has yet been undertaken, the mere fact that an investigation is underway against certain undertakings in a particular sector or branch must not leak to the public in order to avoid jeopardising the success of the investigative measures to follow. Where inspections of the premises of undertakings are planned, the surprise effect is often a key factor in their success.[104] These investigations therefore have a highly confidential character.[105] All competition authorities are expected to be aware of such interest of their fellow agencies when new cases are notified. Having regard to the principles of sincere co-operation[106] and sound administration, information on new cases could thus be regarded as being protected by the duty of professional secrecy.[107]

---

[102] Para 86 of the judgment of the CFI in Case T–353/94 *Postbank v Commission* [1996] ECR II–921.

[103] Cf judgment of the ECJ in Case 145/83 *Adams v Commission* [1985] ECR 3539, para 34.

[104] This is illustrated by Joshua, above n 90, 5, who describes the clandestine and sophisticated way in which some of the most serious cartels operate and which make surprise inspections indispensable: 'There may even be emergency arrangements to shred documents and warn other participants by coded telex messages in the event of an investigation.'

[105] Widegren, above n 2, 423. This aspect was addressed in the draft text of the Network Notice quoted by Fingleton (above n 78), which expressly provided that '[g]iven the extremely sensitive and confidential nature of certain information before the investigation has effectively started', in case of surprise inspections, the Network may be informed only after the inspection has actually been carried out. See also Dekeyser and Dalheimer, above n 16, 7, who point to the need for confidentiality when inspections are to be organised by Network members.

[106] The duty of sincere co-operation is derived from Art 10 (ex Art 5) EC. See, eg Case 230/81 *Luxemburg v European Parliament* [1983] ECR 255 para 37. It applies not only with regard to the vertical relationship between the Community institutions and the Member States, but also at the horizontal level, ie between the Member States. See Case 42/82 *Commission v France (Italian wine)* [1983] ECR 1013, para 36.

[107] Cf paras 12–20 of the Commission Notice on the rules for access to the Commission file in cases pursuant to Articles 81 and 82 of the EC Treaty, Articles 53, 54 and 57 of the EEA Agreement and Council Regulation (EC) No 139/2004 ([2005] OJ C325/7 ('Notice on Access to File'), where the Commission, in the context of defining non-accessible documents, distinguishes between confidential business information and confidential agency information (ie internal documents such as notes, memos or drafts). The latter category, which also includes correspondence with other public authorities (NCAs, other public authorities of the Member States, authorities of third countries, etc.) are equally protected and may therefore not be accessed. Initial case reports can be regarded as constituting such confidential agency

Apart from this, the information exchanged at this early stage will rarely include confidential data, such as business secrets, since it is confined to the essentials of the forthcoming case. The standard form by which the Network is notified of new cases only provides for the identification of the companies involved, the suspected infringement, the territory and products concerned, and the authority dealing with the case. Business data of the companies subject to the investigation or other confidential information are normally not exchanged at this point.

An exception would be the names of complainants, which may be revealed by the authorities when informing each other of the origin of the case.[108] To the extent that the complainants (or other informants) have requested that their identity not be disclosed, this information must also be treated as confidential, ie it must remain internal to the Network. If the NCA sending the information to the Network classifies the complainants' names as confidential, the other competition authorities are prohibited from disclosing the complainants' identity. This follows from the judgment of the ECJ in *Adams*, where it was held that, even though Article 287 EC refers primarily to information gathered from undertakings, it also covers information supplied by natural persons and accompanied by a request for confidentiality in order to protect the informant's anonymity.[109] A strict

information. The 2005 Notice on Access to File replaces the 1997 Commission Notice on Access to File (Commission notice on the internal rules of procedure for processing requests for access to the file in cases pursuant to Articles 85 and 86 of the EC Treaty, Articles 65 and 66 of the ECSC Treaty and Council Regulation (EEC) No 4064/89, [1997] OJ C23/3), which had also contained similar categories. The revision of the 1997 Notice had become necessary because of new legislation adopted in the course of modernisation both with regard to antitrust and merger proceedings. The 2005 Notice on Access to File also takes account of recent case law and modern forms of information support, such as electronic data storage.

[108] Para 17 of the Network Notice provides that the standard form should also indicate the origin of the case.

[109] Para 34 of the judgment of the ECJ in *Adams* (above n 103). See also para 19 of the Commission's 2005 Notice on Access to File, which states that confidential information, which is regarded as non-accessible, includes 'information that would enable the parties to identify complainants or other third parties where those have a justified wish to remain anonymous'. However, the provision seems to be narrower than *Adams* and the corresponding rule under the 1997 Notice on Access to File in that now the Commission apparently intends to protect the identity of complainants and other informants only if their wish to remain anonymous is objectively justified. This approach is inspired by case law of the ECJ and the CFI in competition and merger cases, inter alia, by the judgment in Case C–310/93 P *BPB Industries & British Gypsum v Commission* ([1995] ECR I–865). In that case, the ECJ held that the Commission may legitimately classify as confidential documents submitted by third-party undertakings which collaborated in an investigation and, as a consequence, refuse access to them provided that a disclosure of such documents would risk exposing the supplier of the information to retaliatory measures taken against him by the suspect undertaking (paras 26–7 of the judgment in *BPB Industries*). Neither the ruling in *Adams* nor the 1997 Notice on Access to File contained a comparable condition of justifying the request for anonymity, even though the judgment in *BPB Industries* had already been made when the 1997 Notice was adopted. Admittedly, the interest of informants in not having their identity revealed must always be balanced against the right of the parties to access to the file as precondition for exercising the rights of defence and an entirely unwarranted request could hardly prevail over the parties' defence rights. However, the

reading of Article 287 EC suggests that it covers only members and officials of the Community institutions. However, Article 28(2) of Regulation 1/2003, which implements Article 287 EC,[110] explicitly requires not only Commission officials and servants, but also officials and (civil) servants of the NCAs and other national authorities to respect the obligation of professional secrecy. On this basis, the principles developed by the ECJ in *Adams* also apply to national officials and civil servants when acting under Regulation 1/2003. Therefore, the Commission and the NCAs are equally bound to protect the anonymity of complainants and other informants.[111]

It can be concluded that, even though the notion of 'confidentiality' may not always be interpreted uniformly by NCAs,[112] it is unlikely that there will be divergencies concerning the confidential treatment of information on incoming cases and the identity of complainants where the latter information has been classified explicitly as confidential. In terms of protection of confidentiality, the exchange of information at the outset of proceedings pursuant to Article 11(3) of Regulation 1/2003 thus does not raise any specific problems.

III. DEFICIENCIES OF THE ALLOCATION SYSTEM

It was the intention of the Network members to create allocation rules which are flexible, but at the same time precise enough to make allocation a predictable process.[113] It may be true that in many cases there will be little or no controversy as to which authority is best placed to handle the case.[114] Whether the criteria ensure that 'the vast majority of cases allocate

---

requirement that the informant might come under 'considerable economic or commercial pressure' (para 19 of the 2005 Notice on Access to File) in the form of retaliatory measures or other reprisals if his identity were disclosed is probably too strict a criterion, as lesser fears or less important disadvantages may also justify the wish to remain anonymous. Moreover, the judgment relates to an Art 82 case. It is therefore doubtful that the considerations of the ECJ in *BPB Industries*, which had specific regard to the allegedly dominant position of the suspect company, could even *mutatis mutandis* be transposed to a cartel case where firms do not necessarily enjoy a comparable degree of market power vis-à-vis competitors, suppliers or customers.

[110] See para 26 of the judgment of the ECJ in Case 53/85 *Akzo v Commission (Akzo I)* [1986] ECR 1965 in respect of Art 20(2) of Reg 17, which has essentially the same wording as Art 28(2) of Reg 1/2003.

[111] The standard form for the initial case report apparently provides room for indicating whether an informant has requested that his identity not be disclosed. See Reichelt, above n 57, 769.

[112] Gauer, above n 100, 197. See also S Martinez Lage and H Brokelmann, 'The Possible Consequences of a Relatively Broad Scope for Exchange of Confidential Information on National Procedural Law and Antitrust Sanctions ' in Ehlermann and Atanasiu, above n 2, 405, 409.

[113] Cf para 13 of the Joint Statement and para 20 of the Notice on Complaints. See also Schaub, above n 2, 39.

[114] Widegren, above n 2, 423. Böge, above n 34, 250, even believes that, in the majority of cases, allocation will be unequivocal.

themselves'[115] is, however, far from certain. Uncertainties and disagreements between the Network members about which authority (or authorities) should best deal with a case cannot be excluded. Moreover, the interests of defendants and complainants in the allocation process seem to have been largely neglected.

A. Conflicts of Jurisdiction

The main drawbacks of the allocation system result from the fact that neither Regulation 1/2003 nor the Network Notice contains any mechanisms for the resolution of conflicts. In particular, it does not address the issue of potential (positive or negative) conflicts of jurisdiction. Where the Network members do not agree about the most efficient allocation of a case, neither the Commission nor the ECN or the Advisory Committee can issue binding instructions or refer the case directly to a particular NCA. In addition, the Commission is not under a duty to pull in such a case.

1. Positive Conflicts of Jurisdiction

The lack of binding allocation rules and conflict resolution mechanisms is perhaps most striking with regard to positive conflicts of jurisdiction.

a. No Formal Remedy

If several Member States are affected by an illicit agreement or practice and the NCAs concerned cannot reach an agreement about who should pursue the matter and who should step back, or about who should take the lead in case of a joint investigation, there is no formal procedure—like an application to the Commission or the Advisory Committee—to determine who the case should be assigned to or who should be appointed the leading NCA. On the contrary, paragraph 5 of the Network Notice emphasises the non-binding nature of the allocation principles by stating that each Network member 'retains full discretion in deciding whether or not to investigate a case'. This almost sounds like an invitation to every NCA to pursue a matter whenever it considers itself well placed to act without taking into account the activities of the other NCAs. This approach may result in parallel proceedings in up to three Member States,[116] leading to an unnecessary and costly multiplication of work for both the undertakings and the NCAs concerned.

---

[115] Schaub, above n 2, 39.

[116] If more than three Member States are affected, the Commission may be expected to initiate proceedings itself in accordance with the 'three-plus' rule (para 14 of the Network Notice). In practice, however, this does not always happen.

The only mechanism foreseen in Regulation 1/2003 that could be used to resolve these types of conflict is Article 11(6), which enables the Commission, by initiating proceedings itself, to take a case out of the jurisdiction of the NCAs. However, nothing obliges the Commission to effectively exercise this right of evocation. And the fact that the Commission is only regarded as well placed where more than three Members States are affected suggests that it normally does not want to pull in a case just because that case may otherwise end up in the hands of up to three national authorities. It would also be against the spirit of the decentralised system were the Commission to handle every case affecting two or three Member States because the NCAs concerned disagree on who is best placed. Where there is no particular Community interest (eg because the NCAs involved envisage conflicting decisions), the Commission is therefore unlikely to intervene on the basis of Article 11(6) of Regulation 1/2003, even in the event that a matter concerns more than three Member States.[117] This assumption appears to be confirmed by the actual practice. Apparently, several cases which have had an impact in more than three Member States have nonetheless not been taken up by the Commission. Instead, they have been handled in parallel by all the NCAs concerned.[118] In this context, it is important to note again that the case allocation rules are considered to be purely indicative.[119] Thus, the 'three-plus' rule by no means binds the Commission.

Another possible solution is provided by Article 20(7) of Regulation 1/2003, which enables the Commission to put cases that are dealt with by NCAs on the agenda of the Advisory Committee. This provision is complemented by paragraph 62 of the Network Notice, which stipulates that in important cases the Advisory Committee may serve as a forum for the discussion of case allocation.[120] However, this avenue is again just an option that can be used only if an NCA or the Commission actually requests that the allocation issue be included in the agenda; and, more importantly, the Advisory Committee cannot decide the question. Unlike in those cases where the Advisory Committee has to be consulted by the Commission, it cannot even issue an (albeit non-binding) opinion on the allocation problem discussed. The possibility of adopting a formal opinion

---

[117] Cf Schaub, above n 49, 239 and 243, who admits that there is a need for a referee which can only be the Commission. Schaub also maintains, however, that the Commission will not let itself be turned (by companies) into an appeal body for case allocation. *Idem*, 243. These two positions seem difficult to reconcile.

[118] And this without designating one of them as lead authority (see para 13 of the Network Notice). The efficiency of such an approach remains to be proven.

[119] Gauer and Jaspers, above n 70, 685 and above n 19.

[120] This paragraph particularly aims at situations where an NCA is already dealing with a case and the Commission intends to de-seize it by applying Art 11(6) of Reg 1/2003. However, nothing prevents the Advisory Committee from discussing other allocation issues.

on cases that are dealt with by NCAs has explicitly been excluded in the last sentence of Article 20(7) of Regulation 1/2003.

It follows that multiple proceedings will only be avoided where the Network members choose to do so.[121] This can be done on the basis of Article 13(1) of Regulation 1/2003, which gives NCAs the right to suspend proceedings or reject a complaint for the mere reason that another Network member is dealing with the matter. However, this provision only provides an option, not an obligation.[122] In other words, if there is no sufficient goodwill, mutual trust and deference, positive conflicts of jurisdiction will not be resolved and the allocation system will not work properly.

b. An Academic Problem?

One may wonder whether positive jurisdictional conflicts are merely an academic rather than a realistic problem. On the one hand, many, if not most NCAs, are understaffed and already overloaded with case work. They may not readily consider increasing their workload by opening a new matter if it were not strictly necessary to ensure the coherent enforcement of the EC competition rules. Against this background, it appears unlikely that an NCA would engage in disputes about the question of whether it is well or better placed to investigate a certain case where another NCA has already declared its willingness to pursue the matter.

On the other hand, there are important differences between the NCAs in terms of legal culture and traditions,[123] expertise, experience, staffing[124] and reputation. It would be unrealistic to deny that some NCAs are less respected than others[125] and consequently may have a weak position in the

---

[121] I Forrester, 'Diversity and Consistency: Can They Cohabit?' in Ehlermann and Atanasiu, above n 2, 341, 344.

[122] This is explicitly confirmed in para 22 of the Network Notice.

[123] See Chapter 1, nn 115 and 116.

[124] Resource austerity seems to be a particular problem of the NCAs of the new Member States. However, the issue is not limited to these countries. The Irish and Belgian competition authorities are notorious for their resources problems. See D Geradin and D Henry, 'Competition Law in the New Member States: Where Do We Come From? Where Do We Go?' in Geradin, above n 53, 273, 297.

[125] Cf L Idot, 'A Necessary Step Towards Common Procedural Standards of Implementation for Articles 81 & 82 EC without the Network' in Ehlermann and Atanasiu, above n 2, 211, 213, who suggests that human resources and budgets have an impact on the way NCAs are perceived by companies. This applies a priori also to their perception by colleague authorities. See also Forrester, above n 121, 346. Moreover, the (un)availability of sufficient resources not only influences perception by others, but can effectively have an impact on the productivity and quality of the authority's work. See Geradin and Henry, above n 124, 297–8. Specifically on the Belgian competition authority, whose lack of efficiency in the early years (resulting from inadequate staffing and poor resources) was often an issue of criticism and political controversy, see D Smeets, 'Nouveau règlement européen en matière d'ententes et nouveau rôle du Conseil de la concurrence' (2004) 71 *DAOR* 21, 31–2 (with citations from two interviews of the then responsible Belgian Minister of Economic Affairs).

Network. One must also consider that the requisite skills and expertise for performing the fact-intensive functions in competition matters can, at least in part, only be acquired by extensive field experience.[126] Younger or smaller competition agencies in particular may lack such experience. NCAs from new Member States, Member States in which competition law does not yet have a long tradition or Member States which only recently created an independent competition authority[127] may want to take on cases which promise to have some publicity effects (*öffentlichkeitswirksame Fälle*) in order to gain credibility and make themselves known as competent and well-experienced agencies, or simply to fight a negative reputation.[128] This approach may collide with the need for an efficient case allocation. On this basis, it does not seem to be a purely academic assumption that several NCAs which are affected by an illegal agreement or practice cannot agree about who is (particularly) well placed and should best proceed with the matter.

Moreover, it appears that the majority of cases (about two-thirds) that have been handled by the Commission had their competition and economic

[126] M Trebilcock and E Iacobucci, 'Designing Competition Law Institutions' (2002) 25 *World Competition* 361, 365–6.

[127] It is often with regard to the competition agencies of the 12 newly acceded Member States that concerns are expressed as to their capabilities. However, one should be careful to overestimate the inexperience of these authorities. As has been noted, the competition laws of some of the 12 new Member States are in fact as 'old' (or rather 'young') as those of certain old Member States. T Tóth, 'EU Enlargement and Modernisation of Competition Law: Some National Experiences' in Geradin, above n 53, 367, 367. Moreover, the long forerun to EU membership, in particular the conclusion of the Europe Agreements which preceded accession and obliged the candidate countries to approximate and adapt their national laws to the Community legal order, stimulated and in fact largely determined the adoption and evolution of the competition law regimes in those countries. This process had lasted for about a decade when the candidates became EU members in May 2004. See Tóth, *idem*, 368–71. (NB: The Europe Agreements, which were concluded with eight of the new Member States, and the somewhat older association agreements with Cyprus and Malta, entirely replicated the competition provisions of the EC Treaty. They also contained a general clause whereby approximation of the candidates' existing and future legislation to that of the Community was made a precondition for integration into the EU. See Geradin and Henry, above n 124, 274–6 and, on the accession and adaptation process, 277–91.) It would thus be manifestly wrong to assume a priori that the competition agencies of the new Member States (alone) are less familiar with Community competition law. Nonetheless, there seem to remain certain structural weaknesses in the new Member States. Geradin and Henry, above n 124, 297–301.

[128] Cf Monopolkommission, above n 26, para 42. See also the statement of S Raes, President of the Belgium Raad: 'Eigenlijk wacht ik op een groot symbolisch dossier, waarbij we kunnen tonen dat de Raad voor de Mededinging opnieuw tanden heeft.' The statement was made in an interview conducted by H Brockmans, 'De kruisweg van Belgiës kartelkraker nr 1'. published in *TRENDS*, 21 April 2005, 33, 34. Equally, in an interview conducted by J Clasper and published in (2005) 8 *Global Competition Review* 29, 31, S Raes declared: 'What we need is an important case . . . where we can impose an important fine—preferably to a company in Belgium—and that would be a sign that something is changing.' Cf also M Van Der Woude, 'De herziening van het Europese mededingingsrecht en de gevolgen daarvan voor de nationale rechter' (2002) 50 *Sociaal-Economische Wetgeving* 176, 184: 'Op dit punt [het aanpakken en sanctioneren van mededingingsrechtlijke vergrijpen] moeten de NMa en de Raad van de Mededinging hun sporen nog verdienen.'

impact in more than one Member State.[129] Also, in view of the ECJ's ruling in *Italian Banks*,[130] it is unlikely that there will be many Article 81 or 82 cases in which the anti-competitive effects, the location of the parties and the evidence are confined to one Member State. Therefore, the cumulative allocation criteria outlined above[131] which allow attributing cases to a single NCA will rarely be satisfied. In order to illustrate how the allocation criteria should operate in practice, the Network Notice lists a number of case examples. However, these examples provide little extra clarity as they cover only a very limited number of factual situations. For instance, none of the examples deals with a case involving three Member States.[132] It is, moreover, unclear how the requirement of 'substantial effects' interacts with the other allocation criteria in cases where the illicit agreement or practice originates in the territory of a Member State other than the one in which the effects are felt.[133] Similarly, the outcome of the allocation process also seems uncertain where an illegal agreement or practice has effects in two or three Member States. This inevitably leads to the conclusion that there will be a considerable number of cases in which the allocation process will not have a clear and predictable result, but rather will indicate that several NCAs are (equally) well placed.[134] Therefore, the risk of disagreements over case allocation and positive conflicts of jurisdiction should not be dismissed as purely academic issues.

Finally, it must be noted that, in practice, there is a non-negligible number of cases which are handled by several NCAs in parallel without designation of a lead authority. This phenomenon is not necessarily an expression of a conflict between the NCAs concerned. Rather, the NCAs seem to agree that each of them should take care of the infringement insofar as it affects its own territory. Apparently, they do not even designate a lead authority in these cases. Whether this is compatible with the spirit of the Network Notice and, more particularly, the allocation principles is doubtful.

---

[129] J Bourgeois, 'Decentralized Enforcement of EC Competition Rules by National Competition Authorities. Some Remarks on Consistency, Coherence and Forum Shopping' in Ehlermann and Atanasiu, above n 5, 323, 331, with reference to an (unspecified) Commission staff analysis of 1994.

[130] See above n 7.

[131] Para 8, subparas 1–3 of the Network Notice.

[132] For example, two companies from Member States A and B enter into a market sharing and price fixing agreement with regard to the sale of their products in Member State C or two companies from Member States A agree to share markets and fix prices with regard to the sale of their products in Member States B and C

[133] See Competition Law Forum, 'Co-operation within the European Competition Network', suggestions submitted to the members of the European Competition Network (2004) 15 *European Business Law Review* 263, 266.

[134] See Bourgeois, above n 129, 332; Competition Law Forum, *ibid*, 269.

2. Negative Conflicts of Jurisdiction—Enforcement Lacunae

It is also possible that no authority, ie neither an NCA nor the Commission, wants to take on a particular case. This can happen, for instance, where a complaint is lodged simultaneously or successively with several NCAs, none of which considers itself well placed to handle the case.

a. Lack of Resources and National Bias

Possible reasons for such a negative conflict of jurisdiction are manifold. The notorious 'lack of resources' or 'priorities' problem of many NCAs may be one reason why NCAs would decline jurisdiction and argue that another NCA is better placed to act. Conversely to the situation described above, it may also be the case that NCAs are not really inclined to pursue a matter as it is not *öffentlichkeitswirksam*[135] or simply not interesting enough,[136] or does not, in their view, sufficiently affect consumers in their jurisdiction. In combination with the problem of limited resources, this may lead NCAs to remain inactive on the assumption that another authority will take up the case.[137] An NCA might also decline investigating a specific case where this would imply the enforcement of EC competition law against a 'national champion' or state-owned company, particularly where there is no perception of anti-competitive effects on the domestic market.[138] However, other NCAs cannot handle the case as effectively since they might encounter difficulties when enforcing a cease-and-desist order or a decision imposing fines against the foreign company.[139] Finally,

---

[135] See above n 128.

[136] Cf Fingleton, above n 49, 337, who speaks of the 'boring cases' that might not get taken by any authority.

[137] Obviously, it depends on the applicable national law whether an NCA has full discretion in deciding whether or not to pursue a matter. Under French law, the Conseil de la concurrence is apparently obliged to examine every case which is brought to its attention by complaint, unless the complaint is inadmissible (see further below n 295). In Belgium, complaints must be lodged with the Auditoraat, which can drop the case if the complaint is inadmissible or unfounded. The latter suggests, however, that the Auditoraat has to make at least an initial investigation of the matter before concluding that there are no reasons to act.

[138] The issue of national bias of NCAs has been risen by many authors. See, eg Bourgeois, above n 129, 325; F Jenny, 'Does the Effectiveness of the EU Network of Competition Authorities Depend on a Certain Degree of Homogeneity of its Membership (With Respect to Status, Structure, Powers, Responsibilities etc.)?' in Ehlermann and Atanasiu, above n 2, 203, 208; and even the German Monopolkommission, above n 26, para 38 (*in fine*). Some illustrative examples of national favouritism (inter alia in relation to the Danish companies *Bang & Olufsen* and *Montana*) are provided by Forrester, above n 121, 346–7. It also seems that in some of the new (Central and Eastern European) Member States, political independence of the NCA is still not fully guaranteed. K Cseres, 'The Interface between EC Competition Law and the Competition Laws of the New Member States: Implementation or Innovation?' in D Obradovic and N Lavranos (eds), *Interface between EU Law and National Law* (Groningen, Europa Law Publishing, 2007), 203, 228.

[139] On the question of whether an NCA can address decisions to companies in other Member States, see below Chapter 6, nn 442 and 481.

general policy considerations and enforcement priorities may also have the effect that certain cases are not being investigated by any NCA.

It has been suggested that the Commission should intervene in situations where no NCA intends to act, even in cases which affect only one Member State, in order to compensate for a lack of enforcement.[140] It is, however, settled case law that the Commission is not bound to initiate proceedings and investigate each alleged infringement that is brought to its attention unless the subject matter falls within its exclusive competence. In *Automec II*, the CFI ruled that the Commission is entitled to assign different degrees of priority to cases submitted to it and, being an administrative authority that must act in the public interest, may refer to the Community interest as criterion for determining such priority.[141] It may therefore reject complaints for lack of Community interest without carrying out a prior investigation. Accordingly, recital 18 of Regulation 1/2003 states that nothing

> prevent[s] the Commission from rejecting a complaint for lack of Community interest . . . even if no other competition authority has expressed its intention of dealing with the case.[142]

This rule must apply a fortiori also in cases where no complaint has been directed to the Commission but where the Commission has learned of a suspected infringement through the Network. Consequently, the Commission cannot be compelled to take up an Article 81 or 82 case for the sole reason that no national authority is ready to pursue the matter. It is therefore not very probable that the Commission will (always) intervene in cases which no NCA wants to handle.[143]

One might, of course, argue that it is precisely the risk of an enforcement lacuna which creates the Community interest. It would, however, run counter to the spirit of Regulation 1/2003 and the ultimate purpose of the modernisation, namely to allow the Commission to refocus its activities on combating the most serious infringements, if it were forced to deal with all cases which no NCA wants to investigate. It is therefore for the Commission to assess the Community interest. The risk of an enforcement lacuna may be one element which the Commission has to take into consideration when making this assessment, but not the only one. It must be balanced against other factors, such as the seriousness of the

---

[140] Schaub, above n 49, 239.

[141] Case T–24/90 *Automec v Commission (Automec II)* [1992] ECR II–2223, paras 74–7 and 85.

[142] Cf also para 28 of the Notice on Complaints.

[143] Bourgeois, above n 129, 326, concludes that complainants 'risk being smashed between the Charybdis of the 'no Community interest' and the Scylla of the NCAs' indifference'. Cf also C-D Ehlermann, 'The Modernization of EC Antitrust Policy: A Legal and Cultural Revolution' (2000) 37 *CML Rev* 537, 582, who argues that the Commission cannot assume responsibilities 'simply because the situation at national level is *de jure* or de facto unsatisfactory'.

suspected infringement and the probability of establishing its existence.[144] Whether the Commission will take up a case will ultimately depend on its appraisal of the already available evidence and the Community relevance of the matter.

b. Rejection of Complaints and National Cases

In the context of enforcement lacunae, one should also consider cases which, due to a lack of information of the Network members, are not investigated. Since there is no obligation of NCAs to inform the Commission or other NCAs of matters that are closed informally, many cases may never be brought to the attention of the Network members. This applies in particular to complaints which, in some Member States, can be rejected by a simple letter without need to adopt a formal decision. But even where national law requires the NCA to issue a formal decision, the closure of a file will usually pass unnoticed if it does not fall within the category of decisions of which the Commission must be informed in advance.[145] It is true that paragraph 48 of the Network Notice provides that NCAs 'may' inform the Network of any case in which EC competition law is applied, including decisions rejecting a complaint or closing an *ex officio* procedure; however, feeding such decisions routinely into the Network risks overloading the system and could ultimately paralyse the communication process.

The only foreseeable exception (to the rule that the rejection of complaints and the closing of files are not communicated to the Network) are therefore cases of which the Network members are already aware because the NCAs concerned have notified the Network, in accordance with Article 11(3) of Regulation 1/2003, prior to or immediately after undertaking investigative measures. In these cases, NCAs will exceptionally inform the Network also of the (formal or informal) closure of the procedure.[146]

Furthermore, no information will be communicated on purely national cases not involving an application of Article 81 or 82 EC. However, these information lacunae would also include cases where NCAs erroneously consider that there is no effect on trade between Member States and therefore incorrectly conclude to disapply Community law.[147] The

---

[144] Cf para 86 of the judgment of the CFI in *Automec II* (above n 141). See also para 44 of the Notice on Complaints.

[145] Art 11(4) of Reg 1/2003 imposes an information duty on NCAs only with regard to negative decisions (ie decisions ordering the termination of an infringement), decisions accepting commitments and decisions withdrawing the benefit of a block exemption. See above Chapter 1, section II.B.3.c.

[146] See para 49 of the Network Notice and para 24 of the Joint Statement.

[147] Fingleton, above n 49, 339, even considers that NCAs may be induced to treat cases solely under national law for fear of losing it due to reallocation if they notify the Network in accordance with Reg 1/2003.

erroneous qualification of a case as purely national is of course a threat to the consistent application of Community law. A solution could be to feed such cases into a separate category of the Intranet. This would allow all Network members to consult the list of national cases, if they wish to do so, without necessarily overloading the system. Some NCAs may have the necessary resources to check this category of cases on a more regular basis, while others may consult the list in particular instances. Thus, there would be at least a limited 'control', and some cases that have been wrongly qualified as national but have attracted attention in another Member State could be detected.

c. Conclusion

The conflicts, attitudes and information rules described above may result in important enforcement lacunae. Since the question of which cases are selected by an NCA is intrinsically linked to the problem of (in)sufficient resources, the risk of negative conflicts of jurisdiction may be more important than that of positive conflicts of jurisdiction. However, the issue of negative conflicts is completely ignored by Regulation 1/2003 and the Network Notice. There are no control mechanisms to detect and avoid a lax or biased application or an erroneous disapplication of Community law.[148] It cannot be denied, however, that the non-enforcement of the EC competition rules poses as much a risk to consistency and coherence as multiple (conflicting) actions of NCAs.[149] Adding a separate category of national cases to the Intranet should therefore be considered.

B. Forum Shopping

One of the most frequently expressed concerns in relation to the reform is the allegation that decentralisation coupled with the principle of concurrent jurisdiction would create a problem of forum shopping.[150] On closer analysis, however, it seems that this risk has been largely exaggerated.[151]

---

[148] See Tesauro, above n 2, 272; Idot, above n 125, 216–17.

[149] Bourgeois, above n 129, 325–6.

[150] Eg J Bourgeois and C Humpe, 'The Commission's Draft "New Regulation 17"' (2002) 23 *European Competition Law Review* 43, 47; J Nazerali and D Cowan, 'Modernising the Enforcement of EU Competition Rules—Can the Commission Claim to be Preaching to the Converted?' (1999) 20 *European Competition Law Review* 442, 443; and Ehlermann, above n 143, 570 (with further references at note 129).

[151] One may also wonder whether forum shopping must really be viewed as a negative occurrence, which must by all means be prevented. At least in an initial phase of implementation of the new enforcement rules, forum shopping might indeed be seen as an incentive for Member States to improve their enforcement practice (and possibly even the relevant procedural regime) and to align it with that of other Network members. This could have the positive effect of

Forum shopping describes a phenomenon whereby an applicant, being able to choose freely among various possible (competent) bodies, selects the one he believes to be the most favourable in terms of protecting his interests.[152] As concerns public enforcement[153] of Community competition law, shopping for the 'right' authority can obviously only be a concern where the competition authority does not act on its own initiative but is seized by a third party, ie in cases triggered by a complaint or possibly a leniency application. For an important part of competition matters, notably *ex officio* procedures,[154] forum shopping is thus a priori a non-issue.[155]

A complainant can be expected to opt for the authority which, in view of the available remedies and its enforcement practice, appears to be the most severe or least lenient. Choosing among several authorities in this way presupposes that all of them can effectively offer the complainant adequate redress.[156] In practice, however, this will rarely be the case. There are two reasons why, in reality, the options for complainants will usually be fairly limited. First, each NCA can provide a remedy only insofar as the negative effects for the complainant have occurred in its own territory. It can address orders (eg cease-and-desist orders, orders to resume supplies) only

reducing or even eliminating a complainant's hope for a more stringent or otherwise more favourable decision of a particular competition authority and thus ultimately discourage forum shopping. Cf C Gauer, L Kjolbye, D Dalheimer, E De Smijter, D Schnichels and M Laurila, 'Regulation 1/2003 and the Modernisation Package fully applicable since 1 May 2004' [2004] (Summer) *Competition Policy Newsletter* 1, 3.

152 J-F Bellis and K Van Hove, 'Multiple Enforcement and Forum Shopping After 1 May 2004: Fear for Fear's Sake?' in Geradin, above n 53, 171, 171–2.

153 As opposed to private enforcement of competition law through private law suits brought in the national courts of the Member States. Private enforcement will not be discussed here, as it would go beyond the scope of this book, which concerns the horizontal relation between the public enforcement bodies of the Member States (NCAs). It is worth noting, though, that considerations similar to those set forth below apply with regard to private enforcement. There are a number of important conditions, in particular under the former Brussels Convention (now Reg 44/2001), that effectively limit the number of potential fora for bringing civil law suits (namely place of residence/registration of the opponent and place where the contractual obligations were to be executed or the damage occurred). See A Schaub and R Dohms, 'Das Weißbuch der Europäischen Kommission über die Modernisierung der Vorschriften zur Anwendung der Artikel 81 und 82 EG-Vertrag. Die Reform der Verordnung Nr 17' (1999) 49 *Wirtschaft und Wettbewerb* 1055, 1068–9.

154 As concerns matters handled by the Commission, only 13% of the new cases registered between 1988 and 1998 accounted for own initiative procedures, while 29% resulted from complaints and 58% from notifications (see para 44 of the White Paper). However, with the abolition of the notification/exemption system, the proportion of own initiative procedures can be expected to increase substantially. After all, it is one of the main purposes of the reform that the Commission be more proactive and refocus its activities on the detection and punishment of serious competition infringements (para 45 of the White Paper).

155 See E Paulis, 'Latest Commission Thinking and Progress on the Modernisation of Regulation 17' in X, *European Competition Law: A New Role for the Member States/Droit européen de la concurrence: un nouveau rôle pour les Etats membres* (Brussels, Bruylant, 2001), 15, 23. W Wils, *The Optimal Enforcement of EC Antitrust Law. Essays in Law and Economics* (The Hague, Kluwer Law International, 2001), 148.

156 Bellis and Van Hove, above n 152, 179.

to offenders located on its territory.[157] In many cases, this territorial limitation of the NCAs' powers will already reduce the number of possible fora. Secondly, the complainant's choices may be determined by the location of evidence. It would seem to make little sense for him to lodge the complaint with an authority that cannot gather any of the relevant evidentiary material on its territory.[158]

In addition, the information exchange in the Network makes it possible to detect multiple complaints, including those submitted to an authority which would not, under any circumstances, appear well placed to pursue the matter, or to direct an individual complaint to a well-placed authority (through the instrument of case allocation). In any event, where an authority is objectively not at all well placed to investigate the case, it will simply reject the complaint or attempt to 'refer' the case and discontinue its own proceedings in accordance with Article 13 of Regulation 1/2003, which offers the possibility for NCAs (and the Commission) to suspend a case or reject a complaint merely because another Network member is dealing with the same matter, ie without having to state any further reasons for the dismissal.[159] This approach should function as a strong disincentive for complainants to shop for a competition authority, ie to select the addressee of their complaint according to purely subjective considerations.

In contrast to a complainant, a potential leniency applicant will be tempted to choose the authority which appears to be the most lenient, ie which has the broadest leniency programme, potentially granting immunity to all kinds of cartel participants (ringleaders, instigators, parties who have coerced other participants into the cartel), including more than just 'cartels' in the programme, applying low thresholds in terms of required information and evidence, and offering simple procedures (eg accepting oral applications). However, due to the possibility of reallocation of the case and the absence of an EU-wide leniency programme, the applicant may be well advised to lodge applications also with (all) other authorities which could be well placed to take on the case.[160] Also in case of a leniency application, the allocation of the matter remains within the discretion of the

---

[157] *Ibid.*
[158] Paulis, above n 155, 24. It must be noted, though, that Art 22(1) of Reg 1/2003 makes it possible for NCAs to co-operate also with regard to the collection of evidence. According to that provision, an NCA may carry out inspections and other fact-finding measures on behalf and for the account of another NCA. However, even in view of this possibility of soliciting the assistance of other NCAs, a national authority is unlikely to take on a case where none of the relevant pieces of evidence is located on its own territory.
[159] See Gauer *et al*, above n 151, 4.
[160] See para 38 of the Network Notice. On the difficulty for a potential leniency applicant to identify the right addressee for his application, see P Hetzel, 'Die Vielzahl kartell-rechtlicher Kronzeugenregelungen als Hindernis für die Effektivität der europäischen Kartellbekämpfung' (2005) 40 *Europarecht* 735, 739–43, who contends, however, that the case allocation criteria of the Network Notice provide sufficient guidance for applicants in this respect (*idem*, 747).

Network members.[161] Hence, what is true for complainants also applies with regard to leniency applicants: they can neither predict with certainty nor influence which authority will ultimately handle the case.[162]

Some commentators' preoccupation with forum shopping seems to be a 'fear for fear's sake' rather than a real threat to effective enforcement in a decentralised system.[163]

C. Leniency Applications

The obligation to inform the Commission of new matters also applies with regard to proceedings which have been instituted by an NCA following a leniency application.[164] Pursuant to paragraph 39 of the Network Notice, however, other NCAs are barred from using such information 'as the basis for starting an investigation on their own behalf'. Procedures under the EC competition rules and those under national (competition) law are both excluded. Evidently, the wording of that paragraph does not only prohibit the use of information stemming from a leniency application as direct evidence against the leniency applicant. It also precludes NCAs from using such information as mere intelligence, ie as 'circumstantial evidence',

---

[161] The case file/leniency information can be exchanged and used by other ECN members within the limits set out at paras 39–42 of the Network Notice. See further below section III.C.1.

[162] Gauer and Jaspers, above n 70, 686.

[163] The expression has been borrowed from Bellis and Van Hove, above n 152, 171.

[164] Art 11(3) of Reg 1/2003 does not provide for any exceptions regarding investigations triggered by a leniency application. For a definition of the term 'leniency programme' see note 14 of the Network Notice. Similarly, according to W Wils, 'Leniency in Antitrust Enforcement: Theory and Practice' (2007) 30 *World Competition* 25, 25, leniency in antitrust enforcement describes the granting of (total) immunity from penalties or the reduction in fines by the competent authority in exchange for co-operation volunteered by the leniency applicant/ offender. Co-operation which qualifies for such favourable treatment will usually be of the kind that allows the authority to detect, establish and/or prove an antitrust violation. The current practice of applying leniency in competition matters is said to have been started by the US antitrust authorities in 1978 (*idem*, 34). The Commission published its first Leniency Notice in 1996 (see the Commission notice on the non-imposition or reduction of fines in cartel cases, [1996] OJ C207/4). However, at that time, leniency was not really something new for the Commission. However, by setting out its policy and publishing the relevant criteria in a notice, the Commission made an explicit commitment and increased transparency. W Wils, 'The Commission Notice on the Non-Imposition or Reduction of Fines in Cartel Cases: A Legal and Economic Analysis' (1997) 22 *EL Rev* 125, 127. In order to remedy certain shortcomings of the 1996 Leniency Notice and converge the EU rules with the US leniency programme, the Commission adopted a new Leniency Notice in 2002 (Commission notice on immunity from fines and reduction of fines in cartel cases, [2002] OJ C45/3). The EU leniency policy is regarded as a very successful tool to detect secret hardcore cartel agreements. It has led to a considerable increase in Commission cartel cases and induced a number of Member States to adopt similar leniency systems. See N Levy and R O'Donoghue, 'The EU Leniency Programme Comes of Age' (2004) 27 *World Competition* 75, 76. More recently (December 2006), the 2002 Leniency Notice was replaced by the 2006 Leniency Notice, which was issued with a view to aligning the leniency policies within the framework of the ECN (see below n 208).

which, even under the *Spanish Banks* doctrine,[165] could be relied upon to justify the initiation of a national procedure.[166]

1. Paragraph 39 of the Network Notice and Outside Information

Those NCAs which have committed themselves to respecting this principle will receive the initial case report.[167] As the notice is a non-binding 'soft-law' instrument, NCAs have been requested to formally acknowledge these rules.[168] A declaration stating that the signing NCA will abide by the principles of the Network Notice, in particular those 'relating to the protection of applicants claiming the benefit of a leniency programme', has been signed by the national competition authorities of all 27 Member States.[169] As a consequence, information on new cases will be communicated on a regular basis to all NCAs and will thus circulate freely within the Network.

However, it is uncertain whether paragraph 39 of the Network Notice together with the above declarations can effectively protect leniency applicants against multiple proceedings being initiated by other NCAs after they have learned of the ongoing investigation against a suspected cartel in a particular Member State.[170] The Network Notice explicitly acknowledges that the prohibition to use the information as the basis for an own investigation does not prejudice the right of the NCAs to initiate proceedings 'on the basis of information coming from other sources'. Obviously, other NCAs can always be tipped off by a complainant[171] or another leniency applicant.[172] NCAs may then use such information to start their own cartel

---

[165] See paras 34–43 of the judgment in *Spanish Banks* (above n 74), where the ECJ held that, under Reg 17, Member States were not allowed to use information obtained from the Commission outside the legal context in which the information had been communicated. NCAs were notably prohibited from using information transmitted to them by the Commission on the basis of Art 10 of Reg 17 as direct evidence in a national procedure. However, Member States could take into account such information as 'circumstantial evidence' when considering whether or not to launch a national investigation.

[166] 'Here, NCAs must indeed suffer "acute amnesia"'. C Swaak and M Mollica, 'Leniency Applicants Face to Modernisation of EC Competition Law' (2005) 26 *European Competition Law Review* 507, 513.

[167] Paras 39 and 42 of the Network Notice.

[168] This is necessary (albeit probably not sufficient) because Art 12 of Reg 1/2003 does not provide for any exceptions to the free flow of information in matters involving a leniency application.

[169] In those Member States which have dual enforcement systems, the document has usually been signed by all relevant bodies. The list of authorities having signed the declaration is available at http://ec.europa.eu/competition/antitrust/legislation/list_of_authorities_joint_statement.pdf.

[170] *Contra* Dekeyser and Dalheimer, above n 16, 15, who submit that leniency applicants are adequately protected against the risk of *ex officio* investigations generated by the information exchange in the Network. The following considerations show that their position might not always be correct.

[171] Dekeyser and Jaspers, above n 69, 13.

[172] Gauer and Jaspers, above n 70, 686.

proceedings. Also, NCAs which know of a specific cartel investigation being conducted by a colleague agency will be more alert than otherwise and can be expected to be extremely vigilant. They will monitor the market more closely and probably even target the relevant sector. They might even actively seek alternative sources of information. Moreover, they can put together the pieces of a puzzle more easily, it would seem, and therefore are likely, for instance, to realise more quickly the seriousness of a complaint. In these circumstances, the smallest piece of additional information may be sufficient to trigger an investigation. Companies thus will be exposed to a considerably higher risk that other NCAs will open parallel procedures once information on a leniency application circulates in the Network.[173] This risk and the resulting exposure of leniency applicants is unavoidably connected with the right of ECN members to exchange (leniency) information and the concomitant existence of a patchwork of different leniency programmes across the EU.[174] It can only be excluded by introducing a Community-wide uniform leniency system applicable to all NCA proceedings.[175] The initiative of the ECN to present a model for all national leniency programmes together with the possibility of a short-form application is a first step in this direction.[176]

2. Exposure of Leniency Applicants

The problem is particularly relevant with regard to NCAs which do not have their own leniency programme and therefore could impose sanctions on the leniency applicant.[177] Moreover, NCAs which operate a leniency

---

[173] See Burnside and Crossley, above n 76, 29. The risk of 'spill-over' effects is also noted by C Arhold, 'Die Reform der europäischen Wettbewerbsaufsicht aus praktischer Sicht' (2005) 40 *Europarecht* (Beiheft 2), 119, 131. *Contra* S Blake and D Schnichels, 'Leniency Following Modernisation: Safeguarding Europe's Leniency Programmes' (2004) 25 *European Competition Law Review* 765, 767, and Dekeyser and Dalheimer, above n 16, 15, who argue that communication in the Network does not generate any greater risk of detection for leniency applicants than the normal risk that anyone runs who infringes the law and which existed before 1 May 2004.

[174] This may ultimately jeopardise the attractiveness and effectiveness of existing leniency programmes in the EU. On this issue, particularly the confidentiality concerns, see Hetzel, above n 160, 743–6, who is, however, confident that the Network Notice, together with the declaration signed by the NCAs, provides a sufficient de facto guarantee for potential applicants not to be pursued in the event of an exchange of leniency information.

[175] Obviously, the risk also vanishes where the Commission takes on the matter thereby relieving the NCAs of their competence.

[176] See the following paragraph (section III.C.2).

[177] This risk has in fact been reduced significantly since 1 May 2004. In 2005, there were still eight Member States without leniency system. See K Dekeyser and E De Smijter, 'The Exchange of Evidence within the ECN' (2005) 32 *Legal Issues of Economic Integration* 161, 166 (at note 13). At the time of finalising this text (January 2009), there are only two Member States that do not operate a leniency programme: Malta and Slovenia (see http://ec.europa.eu/competition/ecn/leniency_ programme_nca.pdf). Interestingly, the Belgian legislature, in the course of the most recent amendments to the WEM, has even opted for incorporating the possibility of total amnesty or reduction in fines, including the conditions for such leniency and the procedure to be

programme are not precluded from imposing sanctions on the leniency applicant if the latter has not lodged, or not lodged in time, a leniency application in the relevant Member State, or if their own leniency programme does not provide for full immunity but only allows for a partial reduction in the fine. Indeed, there is no EU-wide system of fully harmonised leniency programmes. Even though the existing leniency programmes have a number of common features, they still differ considerably in terms of both procedure and substance (ie conditions for and extent of 'reward').[178] Procedural differences concern, for instance, the question of whether the request must be made in writing. Some systems require written statements while others accept oral applications, at least for determining the temporal ranking. Substantive divergencies relate, inter alia, to the treatment of instigators and ringleaders. Some national programmes are still modelled upon the EC's first generation leniency programme, the 1996 Leniency Notice of the Commission, which excluded full immunity for ringleaders and instigators. Others follow the Commission's new approach and already apply a coercion test.[179] Some national leniency systems cover vertical restraints, but in most Member States, immunity for vertical restraints is not available. Evidentiary thresholds can also be quite different.[180] In some respects, the divergencies can go as far as requiring

---

applied, in the actual law (see Art 49 WEM 2006). The same applies to Spain, which recently amended its competition law. See E Navarro Varona and L Moscoso del Prado, 'New Spanish Law for the Defence of Competition' (2007) 28 *European Competition Law Review* 571, 576. In most other Member States, leniency programmes are part of the authority's policy without actually being laid down in a formal legislative act. See, eg the leniency rules (*Bonusregelung*) of the BKartA, which has the form of a simple administrative notice (*Bekanntmachung*). A concise overview of the rationale and economics of leniency is provided by Wils (2007), above n 164, 37–52.

[178] See the non-exhaustive list of key differences between leniency programmes in the EU provided by D Schroeder and S Heinz, 'Requests for Leniency in the EU: Experience and Legal Puzzles' in K Cseres, M Schinkel and F Vogelaar, *Criminalization of Competition Law Enforcement* (Cheltenham, Elgar, 2006), 161, 162–6, and the overview given by M Reynolds and D Anderson, 'Immunity and Leniency in EU Cartel Cases' (2006) 27 *European Competition Law Review* 82, 88 and the examples mentioned by A Schwab and C Steinle, 'Pitfalls of the European Competition Network – Why Better Protection of Leniency Applicants and Legal Regulation of Case Allocation is Needed' (2008) 29 *European Competition Law Review* 523, 525–7.

[179] The purpose of these restrictions in the 1996 Leniency Notice was to prevent some perverse effects of the leniency policy whereby companies would be encouraged to actively set up and lead a cartel in the reassuring knowledge that they could always co-operate with the Commission and thus escape fines, should things go wrong. Wils (1997), above n 164, 134. Under the 2002 Leniency Notice, the 'ringleader' and 'instigator' concepts had already been abandoned. Since then, full immunity is only denied to companies that are found to have 'coerced' others to participate in the cartel. See Levy and O'Donoghue, above n 164, 79–80. The German competition authority has meanwhile abandoned the instigator principle, but it has retained, in its new leniency guidelines (*Bonusregelung*) of 2006, the exclusion of full immunity for 'sole ringleaders'. See J Zöttl, 'Though Shallst Co-operate—New Immunity Guidelines in Germany' (2007) 28 *European Competition Law Review* 197, 199.

[180] See Schroeder and Heinz, above n 178, 165.

the applicant to comply with irreconcilable conditions, for instance, with regard to the point in time when the infringement must be terminated.[181]

Matters get even more complex if Member States are involved which provide for criminal sanctions, since not all leniency programmes cover criminal liability.[182] Therefore, the incentives for an undertaking and its employees to apply for leniency may be quite divergent. On the other hand, companies depend on the willingness of their staff to collect the relevant facts and evidence.[183] However, members of staff involved in the infringement will be reluctant to co-operate if they are not shielded from criminal sanctions.[184] Preparing and corroborating a leniency request in such a situation may turn out to be a very difficult exercise, if not impossible.

These divergencies and difficulties may result in a particular applicant failing to achieve amnesty across the EU despite great efforts and the best of intentions.[185] Even the existence of leniency programmes in all relevant jurisdictions and a timely application do not guarantee protection against sanctions.[186] Different substantive standards may prevent an applicant from qualifying for leniency under all applicable systems. Nor is there a one-stop shop for leniency applications. As a consequence, the leniency application

---

[181] Dekeyser and Dalheimer, above n 16, 17. Leniency programmes generally require the applicant to terminate its involvement in the cartel from the time the infringement is disclosed. However, there is a difference in approach. Some Member States and the Commission (generally) insist that the applicant no longer attend meetings at which illegal arrangements are being made or discussed, while other Member States follow the US approach and allow the applicant to continue attending such meetings in order to avoid arousing suspicion among the other cartel members for as long as the dawn raids are still being prepared. See C Prieto and J-C Roda, 'Quelles évolutions pour la clémence dans l'Union européenne?' [2005/3] *Concurrences—RDLC* 12, 14. As regards the Commission's attitude, the recent amendments to the Leniency Notice (see below n 208) provide for some flexibility in this respect. To the extent that the Commission deems this necessary to preserve the integrity of inspections, the leniency applicant can be asked to end its involvement in the alleged cartel activities at a later point in time than the date on which the leniency application is made (see para 12(b) of the 2006 Leniency Notice). See further below n 196 and accompanying text.

[182] In the UK, for instance, individuals can 'only' benefit from so-called 'no action' letters which confirm that he or she will not be prosecuted and there are still difficulties in guaranteeing absolute immunity. D Guy, 'The UK's Experience with Criminal Law Sanctions' in Cseres *et al*, above n 178, 248, 251. This illustrates one of the practical complications for an effective leniency policy that is associated with the criminalisation of competition law infringements. In fact, such criminalisation inevitably leads to procedural complexity in that prosecution and punishment will have to be separated due to general principals of criminal law and applicable human rights standards. In practice, this means that NCAs will not usually have the power to impose the relevant criminal sanctions (see M Frese, 'The Negative Interplay between National Custodial Sanctions and Leniency' in Cseres *et al*, above n 178, 196, 204 and 206), which, in turn, makes it difficult for NCAs to ensure that amnesty will indeed be granted in a particular case.

[183] Schroeder and Heinz, above n 178, 162–3 and 166–7.

[184] Conversely, in a system where there are no sanctions for individuals, these cannot personally gain from reporting an infringement and hence will have little or no incentive to initiate (and support) a corporate leniency application. Frese, above n 182, 199.

[185] See Reynolds and Anderson, above n 178, 88.

[186] Frese, above n 182, 203, who describes this as the 'multiple risk of not qualifying'.

filed with a given competition authority (Commission or NCA) will not be regarded as an application to another authority and therefore does not bind any other competition authorities in the EU.[187] The applicant will not even be granted the same priority if he subsequently lodges further leniency applications with other NCAs. However, timing is of the essence, as complete immunity, if any, is generally granted only to the first whistle-blower. In some Member States, the applicant who is second in line will not even qualify for a reduction in its fine. Thus, the issue of timing may even lead to a total loss of leniency.[188]

Ultimately, the divergencies may seriously undermine the success of leniency programmes. Companies will weigh up the possible benefits and risks of a leniency application in a given situation.[189] The practical diffi-culties associated with multiple applications and the incertitude about the ultimate payoff are likely to prevent them, in many cases, from opting for leniency.[190]

Commission and Member States are aware of the problem. On 29 September 2006, the ECN launched a Model Leniency Programme ('ECN Model') in order to overcome some of the difficulties and inconsistencies described above.[191] The ECN Model sets out the essential conditions for

---

[187] See para 38 of the Network Notice.

[188] If the applicant is second in line, even if only by a matter of hours (which has reportedly happened several times under the US immunity system; see M Jephcott, 'The European Commission's New Leniency Notice—Whistling the Right Tune' (2002) 23 *European Competition Law Review* 378, 382), he is usually (only) disqualified from full amnesty. Leniency applicants are therefore burdened with the need to organise simultaneous multi-jurisdictional filings to a (great) number of authorities, 'a coordinated "race to the regulator"'. C Canenbley and M Rosenthal, 'Co-operation Between Antitrust Authorities In- and Outside the EU: What Does this Mean for Multinational Corporations?—Part 2' (2005) 26 *European Competition Law Review* 178, 186. See also para 38 of the Network Notice, which states: 'It is therefore in the interest of the applicant to apply for leniency to all competition authorities . . . which may be considered well placed to act against the infringement in question'. In the case of a worldwide cartel, the leniency candidate may (also) have to consider lodging applications with authorities outside the EU (eg the competition agencies in Australia, Canada or the US). Realistically, the number of applications to be made within the EU will exceed four only in rare cases, as world- or Europe-wide cartels are likely to be investigated by the Commission under the 'three-plus' rule. Blake and Schnichels, above n 173, 769. However, there may be cases where the actual effects of a cartel a difficult to determine. Moreover, since the case allocation criteria are merely indicative, the leniency applicant can never be sure that the Commission will effectively assume jurisdiction even though the cartel concerns more than three Member States. He may therefore be inclined to apply to the Commission and all NCAs that might possibly have an interest in prosecuting the infringement in order to reduce risks to a minimum. The whole procedure is not only delicate and complicated, but is above all a cumbersome and costly exercise for companies seeking leniency.

[189] Schroeder and Heinz, above n 178, 166.

[190] As Frese, above n 182, 207, points out, a leniency policy will only be successful if four elements are present: severe sanctions, immunity, transparency and certainty. However, given the current 'patchwork' of leniency programmes in the EU, the two latter conditions do not seem to be fulfilled.

[191] The ECN Model is published on the ECN's website together with some Explanatory Notes and a memorandum addressing frequently asked questions (MEMO/06/356); see

rewarding the voluntary co-operation of undertakings as well as the main procedural aspects which the ECN members believe all leniency programmes should have in common.[192] The objective is to make it easier for potential leniency applicants to anticipate the treatment they may receive and to remove contradictory requirements existing in the various systems.[193] Moreover, the ECN Model introduces a standard for a kind of short-form application, ie a uniform summary application system for immunity requests in matters involving more than three Members States. In these cases, where it is likely but yet not certain that the Commission will take on the matter, undertakings will, as a precautionary measure, usually also apply for immunity in the individual Members States concerned. Under the summary application form, this can be done on the basis of very limited information, which will nonetheless allow the applicant to protect his place in the queue.[194]

The ECN Model has been promoted as a response to the call for a one-stop leniency shop[195] and it certainly offers a number of significant advantages. The removal of contradictory requirements in different programmes concerning termination of a cartel activity will be an important improvement.[196] Also, the possibility of summary applications will alleviate the burden on potential applicants in cases with significant cross-border effects in more than three Member States. However, the ECN Model does not provide all the benefits the business world may have hoped for as it does not really present the desired one-stop shop and its scope is

---

http://ec.europa.eu/competition/ecn/documents.html. On the ECN Model, see M Frese, 'Het ECN Clementiemodel onder de loep' (2006) 6 *Actualiteiten Mededingingsrecht* 228.

[192] See Dekeyser and Jaspers, above n 69, 16. The purpose of the ECN Model is thus twofold: harmonisation of (existing) leniency programmes and alleviation of the administrative burden in case of multiple applications. Frese, *ibid*, 228.

[193] For instance, immediate termination of the alleged cartel conduct shall no longer be an absolute condition for leniency. See para 29 of the Explanatory Notes to the ECN Model. The ECN Model also establishes that oral applications must be possible in all systems, at least for particular cases for which this appears justified and proportionate, such as those entailing the risk that discovery will be ordered in the context of civil damages proceedings. See paras 47–8 of the Explanatory Notes to the ECN Model.

[194] The summary application works very much like an indefinite 'marker'. Gauer and Jaspers, above n 70, 689. The NCAs that receive summary applications will not process them in the usual way, ie they will not grant or deny immunity, but merely confirm the applicant's rank. Only if an NCA actually decides to act on the relevant case will the applicant be required to lodge a full and complete application. In that case, the NCA will grant the applicant a certain time period within which more detailed information must be submitted so that the authority can decide on the substance of the application. See pp 3–4 of MEMO/06/356 and further Dekeyser and Jaspers, above n 69, 20–1.

[195] See p 1 of MEMO/06/356.

[196] Some Member States' systems required the applicant to stop all cartel activities immediately at the time of application, while others had opted against the demand of any abrupt termination in order to avoid alerting other cartel members. These discrepancies constitute the only 'true conflict' between existing programmes. Gauer and Jaspers, above n 70, 686 (at note 11). The ECN Model therefore allows for flexible solutions so that termination may be delayed where this appears necessary to preserve the integrity of an envisaged inspection. *Idem*, 691.

fairly narrow. First, the summary application does not relieve undertakings of the burden of preparing multiple applications, albeit in short form, possibly involving different languages[197] and requiring assistance from several legal advisers. The reason for this is that the model chosen by the ECN is based on 'the fundament of the current system', implying that applicants should lodge applications with each and every authority that could pursue a case against them.[198] In other words, the primal policy approach of Commission and Member States, which could be summarised as 'file wherever you feel you need to—it is your risk',[199] has not been given up. A one-stop shop, it is submitted, is something else.[200] The approach also means that one of the most frequent problems for under-takings in the present context, notably the question of knowing which authority/authorities should be approached,[201] has not been tackled. Moreover, the possibility of a summary application is available only in those cases where it is clear (from the outset) that more than three Member State territories are affected and a complete application has been lodged with the Commission. In addition, short-form applications are only possible where full immunity is requested before an investigation has been started.[202] In more general terms, the ECN Model covers only secret horizontal agreements or practices and thus does not provide for any leniency harmonisation concerning vertical restrictions.[203] Moreover, it

---

[197] The Network members have declared themselves flexible in terms of language requirements. It seems that many are willing, as a matter of principle, to accept English language applications. See Dekeyser and Jaspers, above n 69, 21. However, the ECN Model is not a formally binding instrument and, moreover, the commitment has only been made 'to the extent legally permissible'. See para 45 of the Explanatory Notes to the ECN Model.

[198] Gauer and Jaspers, above n 70, 688.

[199] Reynolds and Anderson, above n 178, 87.

[200] In my view, the term 'one-stop shop' cannot be reduced to a 'catch-word that covers a number of different arrangements' (which seems, however, to be the position of a senior Commission official; see the citation by Reynolds and Anderson, above n 178, 89); rather, it must be understood as a concept whereby the leniency application lodged with one particular authority also counts as an application to other authorities. It is submitted that such a one-stop shop would have been feasible. Arguably, there are a number of different ways to achieve this, such as creating a kind of centralised application system and providing for mutual recognition. See Perrin, above n 17, 563. Irrespective of the exact definition of the term, it must also be noted that the one-stop shop principle alone would not remove the key issues currently associated with leniency, most notably the existing substantive divergencies. Schroeder and Heinz, above n 178, 171. See also Schwab and Steinle, above n 178, 531.

[201] See Hetzel, above n 160, 739 *et seq.*

[202] So-called 'Type 1A' applications. The rule thus excludes cases where an application for a simple reduction in the fine is made and applications for immunity lodged after the commencement of an investigation. Dekeyser and Jaspers, above n 69, 20.

[203] According to the Commission, their inclusion in the leniency policy is not desirable because that would risk reintroducing a de facto notification system. See Dekeyser and Jaspers, above n 69, 19. Also, the need to ensure that the negative effects of leniency (eg unequal treatment of offenders and penalty-lowering effects) are counterbalanced by the positive effects (inter alia improved collection of evidence, lower enforcement costs) can explain why leniency is limited to secret horizontal arrangements since these are typically the most difficult to detect. Wils (2007), above n 164, 45. The Commission's position on this point is in stark contrast, for instance, to the

does not address sanctions on natural persons.[204] In other words, there are many situations that are not covered by the ECN Model. The approach entails the approximation of only a minimal number of features of leniency programmes and thus leads to a very fractional 'common system'.

Finally, it must be noted that the success of the ECN's initiative will depend on the willingness of all Member States to endorse the principles enshrined in the ECN Model and the (political) feasibility, at the domestic level, of their intentions.[205] The purpose of the ECN Model is not to create a self-contained programme under which leniency applications can be lodged, but rather to be an instrument to stimulate soft harmonisation by encouraging NCAs, if necessary, to align their (existing) leniency programme with the requirements of the ECN Model.[206] The ECN Model therefore requires implementation by all NCAs and the Commission. Even though NCAs and Commission have committed themselves to using their best efforts in this respect[207] and some have indeed already adapted their national regime,[208] full implementation of the ECN Model by all 27 Member States (and the Commission) will probably require a couple of years. It has already taken the ECN more than two years, since the entry into force of Regulation 1/2003, to launch this initiative. Moreover, not all NCAs actually have the power, in their respective legal system, to amend their own leniency programme[209] and thus can at most only assist the

Belgian approach, where leniency rules also cover vertical restraints. See K Bourgeois, 'De nieuwe Belgische mededingingswet: enkele belangrijke materiële en procedurele wijzingen' (2007) 55 *Sociaal-Economische Wetgeving* 265, 268.

[204] Dekeyser and Jaspers, above n 69, 19.

[205] See Frese, above n 191, 234.

[206] See para 7 of the Explanatory Notes to the ECN Model.

[207] The ECN Model was endorsed unanimously by the heads of all competition authorities in the EU. See Dekeyser and Jaspers, above n 69, 16.

[208] In fact, the BKartA seems to have anticipated these developments. Its new guidelines for leniency and immunity (*Bonusregelung*), published in March 2006, already include a marker system. It allows potential leniency candidates to secure their rank by submitting a short-form application which has to contain only a minimum number of information (such as type and duration of the infringement, affected product and geographical market, names of other cartel participants). The BKartA will then set a deadline (with a maximum of eight weeks) within which the application must be completed. Otherwise, the applicant loses its rank. Specific rules apply where the applicant is involved in a cross-border infringement and equally seeks immunity/leniency with the EC Commission. On this novel marker system, see Zöttl, above n 179, 201–2. In addition, the Commission has aligned its programme with the ECN Model (see the 2006 Leniency Notice, [2006] OJ C298/17; the possibility of a marker is laid down in para 15). For the situation in Belgium, see below n 209.

[209] In Belgium, for instance, the leniency rules have been incorporated in Art 49 WEM 2006. On that provision, see Bourgeois, above n 203, 268–9, who also notes a number of discrepancies between the Belgian and the Commission's leniency system (mostly in terms of scope). Even though the provision of the WEM is formulated in quite general terms and many details of the Belgian model are in fact laid down in a notice issued by the Raad, an amendment of the legal basis could not be brought about by the Belgian competition authority itself, but would require a legislative act of the Belgian parliament. It must be noted, though, that the recently published leniency notice of the Raad (see *Mededeling van de Raad voor de Mededinging betreffende*

national legislator.[210] In addition, there are still two Member States which do not operate a leniency system at all.[211] Finally, it cannot be excluded that, despite the political commitment (by the heads of the competition authorities), some Member States will be reluctant to adopt significant changes and give up certain features of their domestic pro-grammes.[212] There is thus no instant cure in sight.[213] The discrepancies between the different leniency regimes and the inconveniences resulting therefrom will persist for some time to the disadvantage of potential whistleblowers.[214]

Apart from the particular difficulties for companies associated with multiple leniency filings, even in summary form, it would also appear extremely delicate, if not impossible, for an undertaking concerned to prove that an NCA has in fact disregarded paragraph 39 of the Network Notice and opened an investigation without having in its possession, at the time of the opening, further information not originating from the Network.[215] It cannot entirely be ruled out that an NCA will attempt to argue that it had actually obtained information from an anonymous outside source before commencing its own investigation.

volledige of gedeeltelijke vrijstelling van geldboeten in kartelzaken of 22 October 2007—sometimes also referred to as *clementieprogramma*) makes some allowance for the ECN Model. In Austria, the possibility of immunity or a reduction in fines is equally provided for in the law itself (s 11(3) of the Competition Act (Wettbewerbsgesetz) as amended in 2005). Due to the dual structure of the Austrian enforcement regime, the leniency system is quite different from the Commission's leniency program and entails a number of uncertainties. See J Barbist, 'Austria Goes Europe—Major Reform in the Austrian Competition System' (2005) 26 *European Competition Law Review* 611, 614–15. Also in Spain, the principle rules on leniency are laid down by law. See Navarro Varona and Moscoso del Prado, above n 177, 576.

[210] See Dekeyser and Jaspers, above n 69, 17.

[211] These are Malta and Slovenia (see above n 177).

[212] See Reynolds and Anderson, above n 178, 88. Germany and Greece have already announced that they intend to maintain, for the time being, the exclusion of 'sole ringleaders' from immunity under their respective programmes, even though the ECN Model does not provide for any disqualification of ringleaders at all. See Gauer and Jaspers, above n 70, 690. Similarly, despite recent amendments to the Swedish Competition Act (1 November 2008) that were adopted inter alia to align the Swedish law with the EC rules and the ECN Model Leniency Programme, Sweden has not (yet) implemented the ECN's proposal for a 'marker'. See H Andersson and E Legnerfält, The New Swedish Competition Act' (2008) 29 *European Competition Law Review* 563

[213] This is confirmed by the fact that a review of the state of the convergence process is foreseen only for 2008, while the ECN Model was launched in 2006. See Gauer and Jaspers, above n 70, 692.

[214] As Jephcott, above n 188, 384, points out, 'uncertainty in the qualification process will kill an amnesty programme'. Here, the lack of clarity and legal certainty as to whether a cartelist will ultimately be able to benefit from immunity results from the existing patchwork of programmes. Combined with the total absence of a leniency policy in some jurisdictions, this situation may seriously weaken the attractiveness and effectiveness of existing programmes. Wils (2007), above n 164, 59. See also Schwab and Steinle, above n 178, 525 and 531.

[215] In addition to the inherent risks for companies, individuals (eg directors, managers) might also be exposed as prohibition and fining decisions addressed to undertakings are published and national prosecutors (in jurisdictions providing for criminal sanctions) could probably commence *ex officio* investigations. Frese, above n 182, 207.

3. Consequences of an Abuse of Leniency Information

Finally, it is unclear what consequences a 'violation' of paragraph 39 of the Network Notice will entail. It is far from certain that abuse of information stemming from a leniency application by an NCA or the Commission would be considered so serious a flaw as to render the entire procedure illegal and justify the annulment of a negative decision. The fact that all NCAs have signed the above-mentioned document may underscore their willingness to abide by the rules of the Network Notice. However, this declaration does not turn the Network Notice into a formal legislative act of either the Community or each of the Member States.[216] Regulation 1/2003 itself does not limit in any way the exchange and use of information originating from leniency applications or relating to cases that have been triggered by a leniency application. Eventually, the consequences attached to a failure to comply with paragraph 39 of the Network Notice will depend on the applicable (national or EU) law.

Some guidance may be derived from the case law of the ECJ, which has consistently held that not every procedural defect automatically renders the decision illegal and leads to its annulment. The plaintiff must at minimum be able to show the possibility that the outcome might have been different had the irregularity not occurred.[217] This would also apply where the flaw consists of an unlawful disclosure of confidential information.[218] Exceptions are procedural requirements which are considered so essential (such as the authentication of acts) that the mere failure to observe them invalidates the decision without it being necessary to establish that the infringement actually resulted in harm to the applicant.[219] In the light of this case law, it is uncertain whether the opening by the Commission or an NCA of an investigation on the basis of information which was provided to the Network following a leniency application would be considered as the breach of an essential procedural requirement justifying the annulment of the decision which has been adopted at the end of that procedure. Even if the relevant competition authority had not made 'illegal' use of the information available in the Network, in many cases it would nonetheless have

---

[216] The legal effects of the declaration of the NCAs in fact remain unclear. Since they have not been signed by the national governments, they are in any event unlikely to formally bind the Member States. At best, the declarations may produce legal effects in accordance with the principle of legitimate expectations. Smeets, above n 125, 28.

[217] Case T–62/98 *Volkswagen v Commission* [2000] ECR II–2707, para 283. See also Joined Cases C–238, 244, 245, 247, 250–2 and 254/99 P *Limburgse Vinyl Maatschappij and others v Commission ('PVC II')* [2002] ECR I–8375, para 322. See further Art 230 EC, pursuant to which the ECJ reviews the legality of acts of the Commission (and the Council) with regard to, inter alia, an alleged 'infringement of an *essential* procedural requirement' (emphasis added).

[218] K Lenaerts, D Arts and I Maselis, *Procedural Law of the European Union* (London, Sweet & Maxwell, 2006), 7–142.

[219] See Joined Cases C–287/95 P and C–288/95 P *Commission v Solvay* [2000] ECR I–2391, paras 45–6.

initiated proceedings and issued a negative decision because it would be likely to learn of the relevant suspicion sooner or later from other sources.[220] In any event, it would seem difficult for a company to prove that the relevant NCA would not, under any circumstances, have been in the position to commence an investigation on its own behalf and gather sufficient evidence to prove the infringement. On the other hand, using information in clear defiance of the confidentiality obligation assumed by all NCAs might be considered by the ECJ as an inexcusable mischief leading to such a serious defect of the procedure that annulment of the decision would appear to be the only appropriate remedy.

The above considerations show that the principle enshrined in paragraph 39 of the Network Notice is surrounded by many uncertainties, in addition to the fact that its binding force and the legal nature of the written declarations signed by the NCAs are dubious. The risks connected with these uncertainties will have to be borne by the companies concerned. This may, however, undermine the attractiveness of existing leniency programmes and discourage potential applicants from effectively seeking leniency. Therefore, it cannot be excluded that the current situation will ultimately compromise the effectiveness of the leniency policy pursued by the Commission and the majority of the Member States.[221]

D. Unpredictability of Sanctions

Without going into the details of the human rights issues and constitutional law dimension of parallel proceedings by several NCAs[222], it suffices to note here that the predictability or foreseeability of penalties is an element of the principle of legality enshrined in Article 7 ECHR.[223] A provision similar to that of Article 7 ECHR is contained in Article 49(1) of the EU Charter of Fundamental Rights ('EU Charter') which was solemnly proclaimed by the European Parliament (EP), the Council and the Commission in December 2000 at Nice.[224] It is doubtful whether, in the

---

[220] For instance, the fact that certain companies are under investigation may be leaked to the press or the ongoing investigation by the NCA in one Member State may trigger complaints in other Member States.

[221] W Wils, 'The Reform of Competition Law Enforcement—Will it Work?', Community Report for the FIDE XXI Congress, Dublin, 2–5 June 2004, in D Cahill (ed), *The Modernisation of EU Competition Law Enforcement in the EU—FIDE 2004 National Reports* (Cambridge, Cambridge University Press, 2004), 661, para 223.

[222] These issues will be discussed below in Chapter 4, section II.C.1.a. and Chapter 6, section I.

[223] D Waelbroeck, '"Twelve Feet All Dangling Down and Six Necks Exceeding Long." The EU Network of Competition Authorities and the European Convention on Fundamental Rights' in Ehlermann and Atanasiu, above n 2, 465, 468–9.

[224] [2000] OJ C364/1. From a formal perspective, the EU Charter is a legally non-binding document. This does not mean, however, that it cannot have any material effects on Community law. As to the potential impact of the EU Charter on the development of case law of the

absence of clear and binding allocation principles, the new system of concurrent jurisdiction established by Regulation 1/2003 is compatible with these fundamental rights principles.

1. Applicability of the ECHR in Community Law Matters

Since all EU Member States are signatories of the ECHR, they have to observe the rights of individuals guaranteed by the ECHR.[225] While the exact extent to which the Community institutions have to observe the principles enshrined in the ECHR is still uncertain, all 27 Member States, being contracting parties to the ECHR ('Contracting Parties'), are undoubtedly bound by its Articles and the interpretations given by the ECtHR. The hierarchy of norms within the national legal order of each Member State, which might determine which rules prevails in case of a collision of two treaty regimes (eg diverging protection standards under ECHR and Community law), may be left aside here.[226] The principle of supremacy of Community law does not apply in any event in relation to pre-existing obligations of the Member States arising from other international treaties, notably the ECHR.[227] On the contrary, Article 307 EC preserves contractual (rights and) obligations of the Member States resulting from international agreements that have been concluded by them prior to the entry into force of the EC Treaty or the date of accession respectively.

The initial position of the ECJ whereby, in view of the *ratio legis* of that article (protecting the interests of third countries), the precedence of prior international agreements over Community law could generally not be invoked vis-à-vis other Member States provided that no interests of third states, which are parties to the relevant agreement, were at stake has meanwhile been refined. In its judgment of 1993 in *Levy*, the ECJ ruled that Community law could not be afforded primacy if this would compromise the performance by a Member State of its obligations arising under an international agreement concluded prior to the entry into force of the EC Treaty where such performance may still be required by

---

Community courts, see B De Witte, 'The Legal Status of the Charter: Vital Question or Non-Issue?' (2001) 8 *Maastricht Journal of European and Comparative Law* 81, 84. On the possible legal effects of the EU Charter, see Chapter 6, section I.D.1. and further Chapter 4, n 70.

[225] See K Lenaerts and E De Smijter, 'A "Bill of Rights" for the European Union' (2001) 38 *CML Rev* 273, 290.

[226] On this issue, see L Besselink, 'Entrapped by the Maximum Standard: On Fundamental Rights, Pluralism and Subsidiarity in the European Union' (1998) 35 *CML Rev* 629, 642–62.

[227] See J Callewaert, 'Het EVRM en het communautair recht: een Europese globalisering?' (2001) *Nederlands tijdschrift voor Europees recht* 259, 262 and 264.

non-member states.[228] The ECHR entered into force on 4 November 1950, ie before the Treaty of Rome was signed. In fact, all Member States except France had signed and ratified the HR Convention before becoming a contracting party to the EC Treaty.[229] France joined the Convention only in 1974. For all but one Member State, the ECHR standards therefore take priority.[230] At the same time, a considerable number of non-member states are signatories of the HR Convention. On this basis, there can be little doubt that, even in intra-Community relations, Member States cannot derogate from the guarantees of the ECHR without violating their obligations under the HR Convention. Article 307 EC thus ensures that ECHR obligations prevail in any event over Community law.

The obligation to respect the provisions of the HR Convention also applies where Member States enforce Community law. In *Matthews*, the ECtHR has notably held that, while the ECHR does not exclude the transfer of competences to international organisations such as the EU, the responsibility of the signatories to secure the rights of the ECHR continues after such transfer. Even though acts of the EU as such cannot be challenged before the ECtHR, there is no reason why EU Member States, being also signatories of the ECHR, should not be required to observe the rights of the ECHR in respect of EU legislation in the same way as they have to safeguard those rights in respect of purely domestic legislation.[231] Arguably, on the basis of this judgment, Member States are required to respect the guarantees of the ECHR, as interpreted by the ECtHR, when applying Articles 81 and 82 EC in accordance with

---

[228] Case C–158/91 *Jean-Claude Levy* [1993] ECR 4287, paras 12–13 and 19–20. On the issue of applicability of Art 307 EC in the relations between the Member States, see K Lenaerts and E De Smijter, 'The European Union as an Actor under International Law' (1999–2000) 19 *Yearbook of European Law* 95, 115 and 118–19. The question of how far Member States are bound by the ECHR is still relevant to the extent that the protection of fundamental rights guaranteed by the ECJ as part of the general principles of Community law sometimes deviates from the interpretation of such rights given by the ECtHR.

[229] See A Riley, 'The ECHR Implications of the Investigation Provisions of the Draft Competition Regulation' (2002) 51 *ICLQ* 55, 79–80. Note that the 12 new Member States were signatories of the ECHR prior to their accession to the EU.

[230] See Besselink, above n 226, 660–2; I Canor, 'Primus inter pares. Who is the ultimate guardian of fundamental rights in Europe?' (2000) 25 *EL Rev* 3, 11. The priority rule is difficult to apply in practice where the various protocols to the ECHR are concerned because they have often been ratified at different times only by some Member States, but not by others. A Berramdane, 'La Cour européenne des droits de l'homme juge du droit de l'Union européenne' (2006) *Revue du Droit de l'Union Européenne* 243, 250.

[231] See the judgment of 18 February 1999 in the case of *Matthews v UK* Reports/Recueil 1991-I, 251, paras 32–4. The case concerned an application against the 1976 Act concerning the election of the representatives of the European Parliament by direct universal suffrage ([1976] OJ L278/1) which excluded residents of Gibraltar, a dependent territory of the UK, from participating in the elections to the European Parliament. On that judgment, see K Lenaerts, 'Respect for Fundamental Rights as a Constitutional Principle of the European Union' (2000) 6 *Columbia Journal of European Law* 1, 15–17.

Regulation 1/2003. Such (implementing) national acts are subject to review by the ECtHR.[232]

It is true that *Matthews* concerned the compatibility, with the HR Convention, of primary Community law. This factor, ie the distinction made by the ECtHR between primary Community law, which cannot be reviewed by the ECJ, and secondary Community law, which is subject to legal review by the ECJ, has been considered the most important aspect of the *Matthews* case.[233] On this basis, it has been concluded by some authors that the *M & Co* jurisprudence,[234] according to which the ECtHR would refrain from scrutinising secondary Community law given the equivalent protection of human rights ensured in this respect by the Community courts, continues to apply.[235] It is submitted, however, that this differentiation cannot hold. In my view, it would be unacceptable if Member States (that are parties to the HR Convention) were relieved of their duty to respect Convention rights when adopting national measures regardless of whether those measures are entirely autonomous acts or mandatory measures implementing or enforcing Community legislation, inter alia because the Member States, through the Council, participate in the adoption of such legislation and can challenge Community acts that are incompatible with fundamental rights in accordance with Article 230 EC. Some support for this view may be found in the judgment of the ECtHR in *Waite and Kennedy*, where it was held that:

> where States establish international organisations . . . and where they attribute to these organisations certain competences and accord them immunities, there may be implications as to the protection of fundamental rights. It would be incompatible with the purpose and object of the Convention, however, if the Contracting

[232] See Canor, above n 230, 3–4, who argues that the judgment in *Matthews* marks a turning point in the relationship between the ECJ and the ECtHR in that it has brought a de facto vertical dimension into a relationship which, until then, had been characterised by the absence of any hierarchical subordination or superordination of the two relevant legal orders. Community law and Convention law had rather been seen as distinct, but equal legal orders. In *Matthews*, however, the ECtHR took the position that at least primary Community law is subject to its scrutiny.

[233] Lenaerts, above n 231, 15. This differentiation is also emphasised by S Douglas-Scott, 'A Tale of Two Courts: Luxemburg, Strasbourg and the Growing Human Rights Acquis' (2006) 43 *CML Rev* 629, 637. Indeed, in para 33 of the judgment in *Matthews* (above n 231), the ECtHR noted expressly that the contested 1976 Act, being a treaty rather than a 'normal' Community measure, could not be challenged before the ECJ.

[234] Opinion of the HR Commission of 9 February 1990, *M & Co v Germany*, Application no 13258/87, Decisions and Reports vol 64, 138. In that decision, the HR Commission held that 'the transfer of powers to an international organisation is not incompatible with the Convention provided that within that organisation fundamental rights will receive an equivalent protection'. Noting that the legal system of the Communities would not only guarantee fundamental rights but also provide for control of their observance, the HR Commission concluded that the application was incompatible with the provisions of the ECHR *ratione materiae* and declared it inadmissible (145–6).

[235] Lenaerts, above n 231, 16. See also H Schermers, 'Matthews *v* United Kingdom, Judgment of 18 February 1999' (1999) 36 *CML Rev* 673, 679.

States were thereby absolved from their responsibility under the Convention in relation to the field of activity covered by such attribution.[236]

Incidentally or not, that judgment was handed down on the same day as the judgment in *Matthews*. Admittedly, EU and EC are not international organisations in the traditional sense, but rather supranational organisations *sui generis*. Nonetheless, as in the case of a traditional international organisation, it can hardly be accepted that contracting states of the ECHR escape their obligations under the HR Convention altogether simply by becoming Member States of the EU/EC, at least not for as long as the EU itself is not a signatory of the Convention.[237] Accordingly, the opinion of the European Commission of Human Rights ('HR Commission') in *M & Co* has been criticised as a 'disappointing surrender of competence of the Strasbourg Commission'.[238]

Despite such criticism, the equivalence test applied by the HR Commission in *M & Co* has recently been endorsed by the ECtHR in its judgment in *Bosphorus*, albeit in a more elaborated fashion.[239] The ECtHR first recalled that a contracting state is responsible under the HR Convention

> for all acts and omissions of its organs regardless of whether the act or omission in question was a consequence of domestic law or of the necessity to comply with international legal obligations.[240]

It then ruled, however, that a contracting state can be relieved from its liability under the HR Convention for certain national acts where it has transferred sovereign powers in the relevant field to an international organisation and the impugned act was necessary to comply with the strict legal obligations flowing from its membership in that organisation provided that the international organisation, in turn, protects fundamental rights in a manner which can be considered equivalent (meaning 'comparable', not identical) to the protection afforded by the ECHR. The reason is that the 'equivalence of protection' creates a presumption that the contracting state has not departed from the requirements of the ECHR.[241]

This judgment has revived the academic debate on the so-called 'judicial

---

[236] Judgment of the ECtHR of 18 February 1999 in the case of *Waite and Kennedy v Germany*, Reports/Recueil 1999-I, 393, para 67.

[237] See W Peukert, 'The Importance of the European Convention on Human Rights for the European Union' in P Mahoney, F Matscher, H Petzold and L Wildhaber (eds), *Protection des droits de l'homme: la perspective européenne / Protecting Human Rights: The European Perspective. Mélanges à la memoire de / Studies in memory of Rolv Ryssdal* (Köln, Carl Heymanns Verlag, 2000), 1107, 1114.

[238] A similar view is also expressed by D Harris, M O'Boyle and C Warbrick, *Law of the European Convention on Human Rights* (London, Butterworths, 1995), 28.

[239] See the judgment of the ECtHR of 30 June 2005 in the case of *Bosphorus Hava Yollari Turizm v Ireland*, Application no 45036/98, paras 155–7.

[240] Paras 153 of the judgment in *Bosphorus* (*ibid*).

[241] Paras 154–6 of the judgment in *Bosphorus* (above n 239).

dialogue' between the two European courts, the ECJ and ECtHR, and the possible subordination of Community law under the jurisdiction of the ECtHR.[242] It is questionable whether the Community really passes the equivalence test in all respects, particularly if one considers the restrictive approach of the ECJ to *locus standi* of individuals before the Community courts, which seems to lead to a lack of judicial protection[243] and the limited powers of the ECJ in the second and third pillars.[244] On the other hand, it must be noted that the *brevet de conformité*[245] accorded by the ECtHR is not absolute. In fact, the equivalence test has been alleviated in several respects. First, the ECtHR held that the presumption of equivalent protection is not final, but rebuttable.[246] Secondly, the equivalence test does not apply where the state can still exercise some discretion and the impugned act therefore is not merely a result of that state's compliance with a strict international legal obligation. Thus, where Member States have a margin of discretion in the implementation of Community law, they remain fully responsible for their acts under the HR Convention.[247] Thirdly, unlike the HR Commission in *M & Co*, the ECtHR in *Bosphorus* did not declare the application inadmissible. National measures implementing Community law are thus not automatically placed outside the jurisdiction of the ECtHR, not even in cases where there is no room for appreciation and the Member State complies with its obligations under the EC Treaty. On the contrary, the *Bosphorus* ruling suggests that the question of whether or not the presumption applies will be considered on a case-by case basis.

[242] In fact, the *Bosphorus* judgment seems to have triggered a whole wave of legal publications on the interaction between EC/EU law and Convention law and the relation between the Strasbourg and Luxemburg courts. See, eg V Constantinesco, 'C'est comme si ç'étaitait fait? (Observations à propos de l'arrêt de la Cour européene des droits de l'homme [Grande Chambre], Bosphorus Airlines, du 30 juin 2005' (2006) *Cahiers de Droit Européen* 363; J Bröhmer, 'Die Bosphorus-Entscheidung des Europäischen Gerichtshofs für Menschenrechte' (2006) 17 *Europäische Zeitschrift für Wirtschaftsrecht* 71; T Corthaut and F Vanneste, 'Waves between Strasbourg and Luxembourg: The Right of Access to a Court to Contest the Validity of Legislative or Administrative Measures' (2006) 25 *Yearbook of European Law* 475; N Lavranos, 'Das So-Lange-Prinzip im Verhältnis von EGMR und EuGH—Anmerkung zu dem Urteil des EGMR v. 30.06.2005, Rs. 450 36/98' (2006) 41 *Europarecht* 79.

[243] See Corthaut and Vanneste, *ibid*, 509, who criticise in particular the *Plaumann* test applied by the ECJ (*idem*, 492 and 497), but also the lack of procedural safeguards in the second and third pillar (*idem*, 512).

[244] See A Hinarejos Parga, 'Bosphorus *v* Ireland and the protection of fundamental rights in Europe' (2006) 31 *EL Rev* 251, 258.

[245] Constantinesco, above n 242, 364.

[246] Paras 155–6 of the judgment in *Bosphorus* (above n 239). It is rebutted where the protection of HR Convention rights under Community law in a particular case is considered to be 'manifestly deficient'. Obviously, this criterion is quite vague and much will depend on how it will be applied by the ECtHR in future cases. See Douglas-Scott, above n 233, 638–9; Hinarejos Parga, above n 244, 258.

[247] See para 157 of the judgment in *Bosphorus* (above n 239).

The approach taken by the ECtHR in *Bosphorus* is frequently said to be inspired by the *Solange II* doctrine[248] of the German constitutional court (Bundesverfassungsgericht).[249] Yet there is, in my view, a slight difference. It follows from *Bosphorus*, which is now the leading case,[250] that the ECtHR will in principle not refuse to interfere with the Community legal system[251] in that it will exercise its control even where the contested national act is not the result of an autonomous decision of the contracting state but emanates in one way or another from Community law. The ECtHR has not rejected the application as inadmissible, thereby firmly showing that Member States remain subject to jurisdiction in Strasbourg also in respect of measures involving the application of Community law. The ECtHR will thus indirectly assert jurisdiction over Community law, including secondary legislation.[252] On this basis, there is no doubt that Member States are bound to respect the fundamental rights enshrined in the ECHR when they enforce Articles 81 and 82 EC or otherwise implement Regulation 1/2003.

Finally, the ECJ has held that Member States have to observe human rights standards when they implement Community measures.[253] Since human rights are protected in the Community legal order 'only' as an 'integral part of the general principles of law',[254] and since, in this context, the ECJ frequently refers to the ECHR, which is its principal source of

---

[248] In its *Solange II* decision of 1986 (BVerfGE 73, 339), the Bundesverfassungsgericht enunciated that it would not exercise its jurisdiction to review the compatibility of Community legislation with the fundamental rights guaranteed by the German Constitution (jurisdiction which it had still claimed to have in its *Solange I* decision of 1974 (BVerfGE 37, 271)) for as long as (*solange*) the Communities and the ECJ would generally ensure an effective protection of those rights that can be considered essentially equivalent (*im wesentlichen gleichzuachten*) to the standards of the German Constitution.

[249] Douglas-Scott, above n 233, 636; Constantinesco, above n 242, 364; Berramdane, above n 230, 260; Hinarejos Parga, above n 244, 257. In view of these parallel approaches and the 'double jeopardy' resulting from two courts (potentially) claiming to be the final arbiter, above the ECJ, on fundamental rights issues, Justice Hirsch, wonders whether the Luxembourg judges can still sleep well: 'Damit hängen bereits zwei Damoklesschwerter über dem EuGH: das des EGMR und das des Bundesverfassungsgerichts . . . Bei diesem Waffenarsenal muss es schon erstaunen, dass die Richter in Luxemburg noch ruhig schlafen können'. G Hirsch, 'Schutz der Grundrechte im "Bermuda-Dreieck" zwischen Karlsruhe, Straßburg und Luxemburg' (2006) 41 *Europarecht* (Beiheft I), 7, 15.

[250] Douglas-Scott, above n 233, 637.

[251] Hinarejos Parga, above n 244, 257.

[252] Berramdane, above n 230, 260, who submits that this indirect review of Community or EU law carried out by the ECtHR leads to a de facto accession of the EC/EU to the ECHR (*idem*, 261). One could say that the ECtHR has re-established its position as ultimate guardian of Convention rights. See Douglas-Scott, above n 233, 643; Hinarejos Parga, above n 244, 257.

[253] See Case 5/88 *Wachauf v Bundesamt für Ernährung und Forstwirtschaft* [1989] ECR 2609, para 19.

[254] Para 17 of the judgment in *Wachauf* (*ibid*).

inspiration,[255] compliance of national measures with Convention rights is arguably also required from the Community law perspective.[256]

2. Article 7 ECHR, Article 49(1) EU Charter and the Indetermination of Sanctions for Breaches of EC Competition Law

As regards the basic principles of *nullum crimen sine lege* and *nulla poena sine lege*, Article 49(1) of the EU Charter corresponds entirely to Article 7(1) ECHR, and thus has the same scope and meaning as it.[257] According to established case law of the ECtHR, 'an offence must be clearly defined in the law', so that the individual can know in advance

> from the wording of the relevant provision and, if need be, with the assistance of the courts' interpretation of it, what acts and omissions will make him criminally liable.[258]

Similarly, it is settled case law of the ECJ that the requirements of certainty and forseeability apply to Community acts, in particular with regard to rules which may entail important financial consequence,[259] such as Community antitrust law. It is therefore beyond doubt that the rules on the enforcement of Articles 81 and 82 EC, whether at the national or Community level, must be such that the sanctions which can potentially be imposed for an infringement of those Articles are sufficiently clear and predictable.[260]

---

[255] Corthaut and Vanneste, above n 242, 509. The standard phrase applied by ECJ reads: 'Fundamental rights form an integral part of the general principles of law the observance of which the Court ensures. For that purpose, the Court draws inspiration from the constitutional traditions common to the Member States and from the guidelines supplied by international instruments for the protection of human rights on which the Member States have collaborated or to which they are signatories. *The ECHR has special significance in that respect*' (emphasis added). See, eg para 35 of the judgment in Case C–540/03 *European Parliament v Council* [2006] ECR I–5769. At the same time, however, the ECJ seems to reserve the right to adopt its own (possibly diverging) interpretation of HR Convention rights. See also Chapter 4, n 70.

[256] See, eg paras 23–9 of the ECJ's judgment in Case C–94/00 *Roquette Frères* [2002] ECR 9011.

[257] Art 52(3) of the EU Charter explicitly provides that those rights of the EU Charter which correspond to rights of the ECHR must be understood to have the same scope and meaning as under the ECHR. See also P Lemmens, 'The Relation between the Charter of Fundamental Rights of the European Union and the European Convention on Human Rights—Substantive Aspects' (2001) 8 *Maastricht Journal of European and Comparative Law* 49, 66.

[258] See, eg judgment of the ECtHR of 15 November 1996 in the case of *Cantoni v France* Reports/Recueil 1996-V, 1614, para 29.

[259] See, eg judgment of the ECJ in Case C–30/89 *Commission v France* [1990] ECR I–691, para 23.

[260] The obligation of the Member States to fully observe the rights enshrined in the ECHR applies regardless of whether the Member States' authorities act on the basis of purely domestic law or on the basis of national law which has been enacted to implement Community law. See K Lenaerts and M Desomer, 'Het E.V.R.M. en de Europese Unie' in P Lemmens (ed), *Uitdagingen door en voor het E.V.R.M.* (Mechelen, Wolters Kluwer, 2005), 177, 181. See also above nn 232 and 240, and accompanying text.

In the decentralised system established by Regulation 1/2003, the Commission and each NCA apply their own procedural rules and impose the sanctions available in their respective legal system.[261] There are, however, significant differences between the sanctions applicable under the various national regimes and those applicable under the Community law system. The discrepancies relate to the persons who can be punished, the type of sanctions that can be imposed and, in the case of pecuniary sanctions, the possible amount of fines. While some systems only allow for sanctions to be imposed on undertakings (eg Articles 23 and 24 of Regulation 1/2003), others also provide sanctions for individuals.[262] In some Member States, the breach of substantive prohibitions or hard-core infringements can even be punished by imprisonment.[263] Finally, there are remarkable variations in the level of fines available. Generally, the amount is expressed as a percentage of the annual turnover. However, the maximum percentages that can be applied range from 5% in Spain (for 'serious' violations as opposed to 'very serious' violations) to 15% in Greece.[264] In addition, the relevant turnover which serves as the basis for

---

[261] Since Reg 1/2003 does not contain any provisions regarding the relevant national sanctions, Member States may freely determine the type and magnitude of sanctions applicable to violations of the Community competition rules. The only condition imposed by Community law is that the sanctions must be effective, proportionate and deterrent. E Paulis and C Gauer, 'Le règlement n° 1/2003 et le principe du ne bis in idem' 2005/No 1 *Concurrences—RDLC* 32, para 10.

[262] Penalties for individuals are foreseen inter alia in Estonia, France, Greece, Germany, Ireland, UK (since the Enterprise Act 2002), Slovenia, Spain and (since 1 October 2007) the Netherlands (on this recent amendment of the Dutch law see above Chapter 1, n 400). Cf M Bloom, 'Exchange of Confidential Information among Members of the EU Network of Competition Authorities: Possible Consequences of a Relatively Broad Scope for Exchange of Confidential Information on National Procedural Law and Antitrust Sanctions' in Ehlermann and Atanasiu, above n 2, 386 and the more recent table of national enforcement regimes provided by PM Roth and V Rose (eds), *Bellamy & Child. European Community Law of Competition* (Oxford, Oxford University Press, 6th edn, 2008), para 14.171 (pp 1485–96).

[263] In France, for instance, custodial sanctions can be imposed on the officers of a company who have fraudulently played a personal and determining role in the conception or implementation of anti-competitive practices (see Art L420-6 of the *Code de Commerce*). Imprisonment is also possible in Ireland, Estonia, Romania, Slovak Republic and the UK. The latter introduced this sanction just a few years ago (Enterprise Act 2002), while Austria has repealed the possibility of custodial sanctions (except for collusion between tenderers) in 2002. It is interesting to note that, in Ireland, criminal penalties (for undertakings and individuals) are the only form of sanctions available for infringements of Arts 81 and 82 EC, ie the fines imposed on undertakings are also considered to have a criminal law character. See W Wils, 'Is Criminalization of EU Competition Law the Answer?' (2005) 28 *World Competition* 117, 130. In Estonia, all cartel matters are in practice investigated as crimes, and legal persons can be held criminally liable, while other types of antitrust infringements can be punished as a 'misdemeanour', where a regulatory offences procedure is applied rather than the criminal law procedure. See A Proos, 'Competition Policy in Estonia' in Cseres *et al*, above n 178, 307, 307–8. In Denmark and Malta, fines imposed on undertakings are also qualified as criminal charges. See Wils, *idem*, 118 and 130.

[264] In the Netherlands, the legislator recently considered to increase the maximum percentage from 10 to 25%, but this proposal was rejected. M Mok, 'Mededingingswet weer gewijzigd' (2008) 56 *Sociaal-Economische Wetgeving* 226, 230. In most Member States, however, the

the calculation varies. While in many Member States the fine is calculated on the basis of the aggregate worldwide turnover of the group, others include only the turnover of the company (or legal person) directly involved or the turnover in the market affected by the infringement. In some Member States (Cyprus, Portugal), the law does not specify whether the national or global turnover must be taken into consideration.[265] In stark contrast to these rules, which generally make it possible to inflict fines of hundreds of millions of euros on companies, the maximum fine in Slovenia is only €375,000 (for undertakings). In Denmark, on the other hand, there is no legal maximum at all.[266] Lastly, the Commission's guidelines on the calculation of fines[267] are not applicable where NCAs enforce Articles 81 and 82 EC and impose sanctions in accordance with their national provisions on fines.[268]

In view of these divergencies, the allocation of cases has considerable impact on the sanctions that can ultimately be imposed for a particular infringement. However, the allocation itself is not a very predictable process.[269] The qualitative allocation criteria will not always lead to clear and unequivocal results.[270] As mentioned earlier, the examples listed in the

ceiling is the same as at Community level, namely 10% (of worldwide turnover). See Roth and Rose, above n 262, para 14.171 (table) and I Maher, 'Networking Competition Authorities in the European Union: Diversity and Change' in Ehlermann and Atanasiu, above n 2, 223, 232. Even on this seemingly coherent basis for determining the applicable sanction, the outcome in terms of the individual amount of the penalty can be quite different as the NCAs practise a variety of approaches as to the actual calculation of fines. On these different approaches, see J Killick, 'Is it Now Time for a Single Europe-wide Fining Policy? An Analysis of the Fining Policies of the Commission and the Member States', CLaSF Working Papers Series, Working Paper 07, December 2005, 1, 13–15, available at www.clasf.org/publications/workingpapers.htm.

[265] For some overviews (tables) which illustrate the variations in sanctions for breaches of competition law in the Member States, see Roth and Rose, above n 262, para 14.171 (pp 1485–96) and Killick, *ibid*, 22–34.

[266] See Killick, above n 264, 26 and Roth and Rose, above n 262, para 14.171 (pp 1487 and 1494).

[267] Guidelines on the method of setting fines imposed pursuant to Article 23(2)(a) of Regulation 1/2003 ([2006] OJ C210/2), which replaced the first guidelines on fines adopted in 1998 (guidelines on the method of setting fines imposed pursuant to Article 15(2) of Regulation No 17 and Article 65(5) of the ECSC Treaty; [1998] OJ C9/3) ('Guidelines on the Calculation of Fines').

[268] G Dannecker, 'Die Neuregelung der Sanktionierung von Verstössen gegen das EG-Kartellrecht nach der Verordnung (EG) Nr 1/2003 des Rates vom 16. Dezember 2002 zur Durchführung der in den Art. 81 und 82 des Vertrages niedergelegten Wettbewerbsregeln' in Fuchs *et al*, above n 11, 61, 76. But cf J Temple Lang, 'The Core of Constitutional Law of the Community—Article 5 EC' in L Gormley (ed), *Current and Future Perspectives on EC Competition Law—A Tribute to Professor M.R. Mok* (London, Kluwer Law International, 1997), 41, 49. Temple Lang argues that, in view of the principles of uniform application and equal treatment, NCAs should follow the Commission's practice when imposing fines for EC competition law infringements. Schweda, above n 17, 1141 even takes the position that notices in the field of Community competition law are binding on national courts and authorities pursuant to Art 10 EC.

[269] J Schwarze and A Weitbrecht, *Grundzüge des europäischen Kartellverfahrensrechts* (Baden-Baden, Nomos, 1st edn, 2004), 183, para 41. *Contra* Wils, above n 221, para 194.

[270] Cf Monopolkommission, above n 26, para 40.

Network Notice do not really provide any additional guidance on how the allocation criteria will be used in practice. There is another important drawback with regard to the predictability of the allocation process. The examples are based on the premise that all facts determining the allocation of the matter are known, even though this will obviously not always be the case at the outset of the proceedings.[271] In particular, cartels may turn out, at a later stage of the procedure, to involve more companies or to cover more Member States than initially suspected. To what extent such changes of the known facts will lead to reallocation of cases or parallel proceedings is hardly forseeable.

Moreover, the Commission apparently takes the view that in complex cartel matters, covering the territory of several Member States and involving a variety of products or services, a part of the case can be left or 'referred back' to an NCA while the Commission itself deals with the rest of the case.[272] Such a 'partial referral' is considered possible to the extent that the relevant part can be separated from the rest of the case because the geographical reference markets are national, so that the territory of the NCA's Member State forms a distinct geographical market. Repartitioning would also appear possible where the part assigned to the NCA(s) relates to a different product market.[273] This approach seems to be inspired by Article 9 of the 2004 Merger Regulation, which provides that the Commission may refer the whole or part of a case to a Member State's authority for scrutiny under the domestic law of that authority if the concentration affects competition 'in a market within that Member State, which presents all the characteristics of a distinct market'. However, by slicing off pieces of a cartel case which, at least at first sight, is based on a complex, but coherent and indivisible, set of facts, the Commission seems to be introducing the possibility of parallel procedures at both the Community and national level with regard to the same fact situation.[274] In

---

[271] Schwarze and Weitbrecht, above n 269, 183, para 40.

[272] Such a 'sharing' of a case between the Commission and an NCA has taken place on at least two occasions in the past. See Reynolds and Anderson, above n 178, 87 (at note 26). See also Schroeder and Heinz, above n 178, 167.

[273] Cf para 51 of the Network Notice, which deals with the application of Art 11(6) of Reg 1/2003: 'This means that once the Commission has opened proceedings, NCAs cannot act under the same legal basis against the same agreement(s) or practice(s) by the same undertaking(s) on the *same relevant geographical* and *product market*' (emphasis added). This implies that NCAs can well act on the basis of Art 81 or 82 EC with regard to the same agreement and against the same undertakings where the national investigation concerns another product market and/or another geographical market. See also Hossenfelder, above n 84, 7–8: 'In bestimmten Fallkonstellationen kann es vorkommen, dass Kommission und Bundeskartellamt sich die Verfahren aufteilen.' This practice is confirmed by B Lasserre (President of the French competition authority), 'Le Conseil de la concurrence dans le réseau communautaire' 2005/No 3 *Concurrences—RDLC* 42, 46: 'la Commission peut n'instruire que partiellement une affaire et une ou plusieurs autorités nationales instruiront un pan, une partie du dossier détachable de ce cas'.

[274] It is already doubtful whether such cartel cases can be subdivided into separate violations at all. It follows from the case law of the CFI and the ECJ that a series of acts should be considered

other words, even if the Commission has opened a procedure, NCAs might still enter the arena and claim a piece of the cake for themselves.[275] Matters are further complicated by the possibility of criminal proceedings against individuals. In fact, it is argued that Article 11(6) of Regulation 1/2003 does not preclude NCAs from imposing fines on individuals involved in the same infringement as that covered by the Commission's proceedings. Either such proceedings are considered to be possible after the Commission has closed its procedure[276] or they are regarded to fall entirely outside the ambit of Regulation 1/2003.[277] This approach would effectively open the door for genuine parallel proceedings, ie proceedings at the EU and national level regarding the same infringement based on the same set of facts, except that the Commission procedure is directed against legal persons while the national procedure concerns natural persons. In my view, however, such parallel action not only contradicts Article 11(6) of Regulation 1/2003,[278] but also increases the uncertainty for companies and

---

to constitute a single continuous infringement (SCI) under certain conditions (eg where the undertakings act in the pursuit of a single economic aim or the various factual elements form part of an overall common plan) since, in these circumstances, '[i]t would thus be artificial to split up such continuous conduct, characterized by a single purpose, by treating it as consisting of a number of separate infringements'. Case T–1/89 *Rhône-Poulenc v Commission* (*Polypropylene*) [1991] ECR II–867, para 126. See also Case T–334/94 *Sarrío v Commission* (*Cartonboard*) [1998] ECR II–1439, paras 168–9. Similarly, Advocate General Ruiz-Jarabo Colomer notes in his opinion in Case C–150/05 *van Straaten v Netherlands* [2006] ECR I–9327, para 82: 'Het strafbare feit kan langere tijd duren dan wel uiteenvallen in afzonderlijke feiten, maar voor de bestraffing toch één feit blijven.' On recent developments regarding the concept of SCI, in particular the introduction of a complementarity test by the CFI, see M Frese and F ten Have, 'The Legal Characterization of Several Infringements under Article 81 EC: In Search of an Objective Framework of Assessment' (2008) 35 *Legal Issues of Economic Integration* 375 and K Seifert, 'The Single Complex and Continuous Infringement—"Effet" Utilitarism ?' (2008) 29 *European Competition Law Review* 546.

[275] See also Gauer, above n 19, 6.

[276] *Ibid.*

[277] This appears to be the view of the OFT with regard to the criminal cartel offence introduced by the Enterprise Act 2002. See R Nazzini, 'Criminalisation of Cartels and Concurrent Proceedings' (2003) 24 *European Competition Law Review* 483, 485 and 488. See also W Wils, 'Self-incrimination in EC Antitrust Enforcement: A Legal and Economic Analysis' (2003) 26 *World Competition* 567, 572–3 note 27. The OFT's opinion is apparently inspired by the official position of the UK government regarding the distinction between the first and third pillar. The UK government takes the view that, within the ambit of the first pillar, the Community cannot legislate in criminal law matters. According to the UK, the Community's powers in criminal law matters are confined to the tasks covered by the third pillar. Against this background, it becomes obvious why it is argued in the UK that domestic proceedings to impose criminal sanctions in relation to a competition law infringement 'do not involve the application of Art 81 or 82' (see Roth and Rose, above n 262, para 14.015) and therefore are outside the scope of Reg 1/2003. In this way, such proceedings would not imply that the Community might regulate criminal law issues (that are associated with EC competition law enforcement) in the first pillar. In view of the judgment of the ECJ in Case C–176/03 (see Chapter 6, n 21), the UK's position seems difficult to sustain.

[278] As concerns the criminal cartel offence under UK law, it is submitted that it does not fall outside the scope of Reg 1/2003. Pursuant to recital 8 of Reg 1/2003, the regulation does not apply to national criminal laws imposing sanctions on individuals 'except to the extent that such sanctions are the means whereby competition rules applying to undertakings are enforced'. It is

individuals as to which competition authority or authorities will be responsible for scrutinising the facts of a given 'case' and, as a consequence, to what sanctioning regime(s) they will ultimately be subject.

Finally, the question of which authority will effectively handle a case may also depend on a number of ancillary factors, the exact impact on the allocation process of which is even more difficult to predict. For instance, general policy considerations and enforcement priorities of the NCAs concerned and the Commission may play a role.[279] The available resources or resource constraints of certain NCAs might also be relevant.[280] In this context, it must be emphasised again that the case allocation rules are not binding but only provide indications,[281] thus ensuring a high degree of flexibility. This flexibility seems to be largely in the interest of the authorities, which can ultimately 'cherry-pick' the cases that, according to them, deserve their attention.[282] Indeed, it is reported that the Commission has already declined to take on cases pursuant to the 'three-plus' rule, which, as a consequence, are now handled in parallel by more than three NCAs.[283] Parallel action by several NCAs may, however, result in double punishment.

submitted that, with respect to the UK criminal cartel offence, the latter condition is fulfilled, ie the criminal cartel offence is a means of enforcing the (national and) EC competition rules. First, the criminal cartel offence was introduced by the Enterprise Act 2002 in order to ensure compliance with competition law (Whish, above n 11, 389). Secondly, the criminal cartel offence, while being regarded as distinct from Art 81 EC and being prosecuted in a separate procedure, is not independent of the (administrative) cartel offence committed by undertakings. The cartel offence is framed around the concept of dishonesty (Guy, above n 182, 250). However, the relevant norm also implicitly replicates the main elements of the cartel violation under Art 81 EC in that it applies where individuals (dishonestly) agree that certain undertakings will engage in hard-core cartel activities, such as horizontal price-fixing, market sharing, output limitations (see Whish, above n 11, 390). The criminal cartel offence thus intrinsically presupposes the existence of an infringement of Art 81 EC (or the analogous national competition provision) (*contra* presumably Nazzini, above n 277, 484 and 486, who contends that a breach of Art 81 EC 'is not an ingredient of the cartel offence' as it is 'defined autonomously' without any (explicit) reference to Art 81 EC). The two offences are therefore interlinked, both in legal and factual terms (the latter aspect is also conceded by Nazzini, *ibid*, 484). In my view, the argument that the criminal cartel offence under UK law is outside the ambit of Reg 1/2003 is hardly convincing. It is clearly part of the competition enforcement regime in the UK designed to increase deterrence and thus enhance compliance with Arts 81 and 82 EC.

[279] See also Chapter 1, nn 115 and 116.

[280] Cf Schaub, above n 2, 39; Fingleton, above n 49, 336–7; Schnichels, above n 53, 108. Both Schaub and Schnichels are in favour of taking into account the NCAs' resources in order to ensure effective enforcement. It must be feared, however, that such an approach might lead to an asymmetric involvement of NCAs as some of them are notorious for their resources problems.

[281] Gauer and Jaspers, above n 70, 685; above n 19.

[282] See Fuchs, above n 19, 87, who suspects that the entire decentralisation process has been inspired by the wish of the Commission to be able to concentrate its enforcement efforts on those cases which it considers 'really important, interesting and beautiful' ('die ihrer Meinung nach wirklich wichtigen, interessanten, schönen Fälle'). In view of the principle that 'each network member retains full discretion in deciding whether or not to investigate a case' (para 5 of the Network Notice), one could nourish this suspicion also with regard to NCAs. See also below n 299.

[283] See Schroeder and Heinz, above n 178, 167.

This potential accumulation of sanctions not only adds to the unpredict-ability of the punishment, but also raises the question of whether undertakings are protected against such practice by the *ne bis in idem* principle.[284]

Apart from the above, the sharing of information on new cases also leads to a higher exposure of undertakings. The fact that an NCA suspects a cartel to exist in a certain market may induce other NCAs to examine the same product market in their home jurisdiction.[285] This effect of one national investigation triggering proceedings in other Member States further increases the risk that a particular case will eventually be handled by a different authority or more authorities than initially expected. Finally, the almost unrestricted possibility of the Commission's intervening pursuant to Article 11(6) of Regulation 1/2003 is another factor which escalates uncertainty.

It follows from the foregoing that the outcome of the case allocation process, which, in turn, determines the applicable sanctions, can hardly be predicted in advance.[286] Admittedly, the case law of the ECtHR suggests that Article 7 ECHR is not violated to the extent that the possibility of a criminal punishment 'could reasonably be foreseen'.[287] The theoretical possibility of incurring criminal liability, in certain Member States, for the violation of Article 81 or 82 EC may of course be foreseeable. On the other hand, Article 23(2) of Regulation 1/2003, which entitles the Commission to impose fines of up to 10% of an undertakings' annual global turnover without providing itself further criteria for determining the actual size of the sentence, has been criticised as being far too vague and giving too much leeway to the Commission.[288] As it does not set an absolute maximum limit for the fine, it would de facto allow the Commission to apply sanctions between a thousand euros and several tens of billions of euros, whereby the latter amount would depend on the group turnover of the company

---

[284] This issue will be discussed below at Chapter 6, section I.

[285] Bourgeois, above n 63, 428; Fingleton, above n 49, 337. This also applies with regard to cases that are opened following a leniency application. See Arhold, above n 173, 131.

[286] Cf Gauer and Jaspers, above n 70, 686.

[287] See the judgment of the ECtHR of 22 November 1995 in the case of *CR v United Kingdom* Publications Series A no 335-C, para 34.

[288] See, eg U Soltész, C Steinle and H Bielesz, 'Rekordgeldbußen versus Bestimmheitsgebot' (2003) 14 *Europäische Zeitschrift für Wirtschaftsrecht* 202, 204 ('nahezu uferloser Bussgeldrahmen') and 209 ('schier grenzenloser Spielraum der Kommission'). Their criticism relates to Art 15(2) of Reg 17, the predecessor of Art 23(2) of Reg 1/2003. However, the relevant terms of the former provision, namely that the Commission can impose fines of up to 10% of the total turnover in the preceding business year, have been retained in the latter norm. Only the lower margin of a minimum fine of €1000 has been given up. See also Schwarze and Weitbrecht, above n 269, 150, para 20, who doubt that the provision is compatible with the principle of *nullum crimen sine lege*. It would be for the legislator, not for the Commission (by way of non-binding guidelines), to clarify the relevant criteria for the calculation of fines.

concerned.[289] Such a kind of 'moving' range of penalties (*wandernder Strafrahmen*), it has been argued, is incompatible with the principles of legal certainty and foreseeability of sanctions.[290]

The resulting difficulties for potential offenders to reasonably foresee the penalty they might incur are escalated by the fact that, under Regulation 1/2003, the sanctioning system to be applied *in casu* is determined by means of a relatively unpredictable process of case allocation, combined with the fact that the different (potentially applicable) systems vary considerably. It is doubtful that this is still in line with the requirements of Article 7 ECHR.[291] It must be noted, in this respect, that the

[289] Soltész *et al*, *ibid*, 207. The illustrative example given by the authors is the oil company ExxonMobil, which had a worldwide group turnover of approximately €220 billion in 2001, which would lead to a maximum fine of €22 billion. The authors point out that this amount corresponds to the gross national product of Luxemburg. *Idem*, 203.

[290] Soltész *et al*, above n 288, 208 and 210. *Contra* CFI in Case T–279/02 *Degussa v Commission* [2006] ECR II–897, paras 66–88, where it was held that Art 15(2) of Reg 17 (the predecessor norm of Art 23(2) of Reg 1/2003) is not incompatible with Art 7 ECHR, in particular because the case law of the ECtHR would not require, according to the CFI, that the consequences of a violation be foreseeable with absolute certainty (para 71). In addition, the Commission's discretion would not be unlimited since the applicable provision sets an absolute ceiling for the fine, which is, moreover, determined on the basis of objective criteria (para 74), and the guidelines combined with general principles of law (equal treatment, legitimate expectations) would further narrow the Commission's margin of appreciation (para 82). On this basis, 'kann ein verständiger Wirtschaftsteilnehmer . . . in hinreichend genauer Weise die Methode und die Größenordnung der Geldbußen vorhersehen' (para 83 of the judgment in *Degussa*). It seems, however, that absolute certitude about the sanction (which is admittedly not required) and lack of any binding critera for the determination of the fine (except for the theoretical upper limit) mark the two extreme points of a large spectrum. In my view, this spectrum offers other solutions which would strike a fairer balance between the extremities and (better) fit the requirements of predictability and foreseeability under Art 7 ECHR.

[291] See Waelbroeck, above n 223, 469; Schwab and Steinle, above n 178, 528. Cf also J Schwarze, 'Rechtsstaatliche Grenzen der gesetzlichen und richterlichen Qualifikation von Verwaltungssanktionen im europäischen Gemeinschaftsrecht' (2003) 14 *Europäische Zeitschrift für Wirtschaftsrecht* 261, 268. Schwarze already doubts that the sanctioning system established by Reg 1/2003 as such is compatible with the principle of *nullum crimen sine lege* in that it only fixes the possible maximum amount of the fine without determining the relevant criteria for the actual calculation of the fine (on this question see above n 198 and accompanying text). Such doubts are all the more justified if it is unclear to potential offenders whether this system or one (or more) of the 27 diverging national regimes will be applied. The uncertainties are particularly drastic in relation to the possible liability of individuals such as company directors, managers or other members of staff who do not know, for as long as the competent NCA and therewith the applicable national procedure has not actually been determined, whether they can be punished at all for infringements of competition law 'committed' by the company they work for. (See, however, the UK's position with regard to the permissibility of parallel criminal proceedings, above n 277.) Moreover, even in those countries where individuals can be charged, the conditions vary considerably. In France, for instance, officers of a company are only subject to criminal sanctions if they have fraudulently played a personal and determining role (see above n 263). In contrast, in Germany, the quasi-criminal liability of the individual formally is the rule, while sanctions on the relevant company can be imposed only derivatively to the extent that the violation of the staff member who effectively acted can, in legal terms, be imputed to the company because the individual had some sort of proxy (see R Bechtold, *Kartellgesetz (Kommentar)*, 3. *Auflage* (Munich, Verlag CH Beck, 2002), §81 no 40). In fact, the well-known *Walt Wilhelm* case (Case 14/68 *Walt Wilhelm v Bundeskartellamt* [1969] ECR 1) owes its name to a former company director of Bayer AG who had been charged and fined by the BKartA in

criteria for case allocation are not contained in Regulation 1/2003 and thus are not defined by law.[292] Moreover, there are a number of unknown, non-transparent elements which might influence the allocation process, such as the availability of resources and enforcement priorities of the NCAs concerned, not to mention the fact that no authority can ultimately be compelled to prosecute a case where it does fulfil the allocation criteria of the Network Notice or to suspend a case where it does not fulfil them.[293] Thus, the question of which (national) system of penalties actually applies is not determined by the law itself, but ultimately depends on a number of uncertain and unclear factors. One would overstretch the meaning of 'forseeability' and 'defined by law' if one accepted that the mere existence, in some Member States, of domestic laws criminalising EC competition law infringements is sufficient to satisfy the conditions of Article 7 ECHR, even though the risk of being held criminally liable is nothing more than an abstract possibility as it is highly uncertain whether the relevant national provisions would be applied at all in a specific case.

E. Lack of Transparency and Judicial Control

Another major problem raised by the issue of case allocation and the heterogeneity of national competition laws is the protection of the rights of defence and the safeguards for complainants. Since the question of which competition authority will deal with a case determines the procedural rules to be applied, the sanctions available and the language to be used, case allocation is of great importance for defendants.[294] Similarly, case

connection with the dyestuffs cartel and subsequently appealed that decision (arguing lack of competence of the BKartA because the same matter had simultaneously been the subject of a Commission investigation). On the unpredictability of sanctions, see also Killick, above n 264, 16–17, who submits that the system needs to be reformed (albeit his submission is based not on the requirements of Art 7 ECHR, but rather on the principle of equality before the law).

292 The Court of Human Rights held, however, that Art 7 ECHR 'also embodies, more generally, the principle that only the law can define a crime and prescribe a penalty . . .'.; judgment of 25 May 1993 in the case of *Kokkinakis v Greece* Publications Series A no 260-A, para 52.

293 See para 5 of the Network Notice: 'At the same time each network member retains full discretion in deciding whether or not to investigate a case.'

294 The language of the procedure is an issue whose importance for the companies seems to have been underestimated. In any event, the language issue associated with the question of case allocation is largely neglected by commentators or at least hardly ever discussed. It is, however, evident that procedures before NCAs will usually have to be conducted in the official language of the relevant Member State. Therefore, the (re)allocation of a case to an NCA might deprive the parties of the right to express themselves in a particular language which, in turn, may have a significant impact on the choice of counsel or even make necessary the appointment of a new legal adviser. On the other hand, linguistic protection of private parties is an important principle of the Community legal order (albeit apparently not in the rank of a general principle of Community law) which has also been acknowledged by the Community courts. See K Lenaerts and J Vanhamme, 'Procedural Rights of Private Parties in the Community Administrative

allocation has a significant impact on the position of complainants, as the extent to which they will be involved in the proceedings (eg access to the file, possibility to submit observations) and whether they are entitled to a formal decision if their complaint is rejected will depend on the applicable national law.[295] Yet it is unclear to what extent the undertakings subject to an investigation and complainants have a say in the allocation process,[296] and it is unlikely that the allocation process, as currently designed, will result in a challengeable decision.

1. Case Allocation and the Position of Defendants and Complainants

If case allocation takes place—as foreseen by Article 11(3) of Regulation 1/2003 and paragraph 16 of the Network Notice—at a very early stage, namely before the first formal investigative measures, the companies concerned may not even be aware of the ongoing investigation. In such a case, it would be impossible for them to comment on the question of allocation. Where case allocation is discussed at a later stage, defendants and complainants are still unlikely to be heard.

a. Internal Character of Allocation Discussions

The (re)allocation of cases will normally take place through informal consultation within the Network. However, even when there is agreement between the members of the Network that a particular NCA or several NCAs shall handle a specific case, this common understanding will not result in a formal decision. Neither the Commission nor the ECN, or, indeed, the Advisory Committee, has the power to assign or transfer a case to a particular competition authority.[297] A competition authority can only volunteer to take up a matter where the Commission and/or other NCAs have declined their intention to pursue the case. Obviously, a particular

Process' (1997) 34 *CML Rev* 531, 553–4. Since the PVC I case, it is well known that the ECJ attaches particular importance to the observation of the Community's language rules. In that case, the ECJ annulled a Commission decision inter alia because the text of the decision had not been available in all binding languages at the moment when the College of Commissioners adopted it, and thus it had not been properly authenticated. See Case C–137/92 P *Commission v BASF and others* ('*PVC I*') [1994] ECR I–2555, paras 58–9 and 74–6.

[295] Under Community law, a complainant has a right to obtain a decision if the Commission chooses not to pursue the matter. See Art 7(2) of the Implementing Regulation and para 35 of the Network Notice. In France, the Conseil de la concurrence is not only obliged to adopt a formal decision. It must also examine every case which is brought to its attention by complaint, unless the complaint is inadmissible. Idot, above n 125, 216. By contrast, under German law, a complaint can be rejected by simple letter. On the divergent rules regarding the rights of complainants, see also Gauer, above n 19, 4.

[296] See Jenny, above n 138, 209.

[297] The only thing that the Commission can do is initiate itself proceedings thereby automatically depriving the NCAs of their competence to apply Art 81 or 82 EC to the same case.

NCA or the Commission can be invited by the other Network members to initiate proceedings. However, Regulation 1/2003 does not provide any formal means for obliging an NCA or the Commission to prosecute a specific infringement. Similarly, no competition authority can be compelled not to proceed with a case unless it is relieved of its competence by the Commission.[298] Paragraph 5 of the Network Notice explicitly states that each Network member 'retains full discretion in deciding whether or not to investigate a case'.[299] Consequently, there will be no formal allocation or referral decisions.[300]

In most cases, communication will be effected electronically through the ECN's Intranet or via telephone. Only in exceptional situations will the question of case allocation be discussed by the Advisory Committee. However, there is no (formal) role for the undertakings concerned or third parties such as complainants in the (informal) procedure leading to the (re)allocation of a case. The Advisory Committee may not issue opinions on cases dealt with at the national level. Therefore, the discussions regarding case allocation remain in any event entirely internal to the Network[301] as the whole consultation process under Article 11 of Regulation 1/2003 is meant to be a purely internal matter of the ECN.[302] Accordingly, paragraph 4 of the Network Notice states:

> Consultations and exchanges within the network are matters between public enforcers and do not alter any rights or obligations arising from Community or national law for companies. Each competition authority remains fully responsible for ensuring due process in the cases it deals with.

This approach is also reflected by Article 27(2) of Regulation 1/2003, which specifically excludes correspondence between the members of the Network and documents drawn up pursuant to Article 11 of Regulation 1/2003 from the right of access to the file. Due to this lack of transparency, defendants are simply not in a position to submit comments on the issue of case allocation when it arises.[303]

---

[298] Art 13 of Reg 1/2003 only facilitates the closure of a procedure in that it entitles NCAs and the Commission to suspend proceedings or reject complaints simply on the ground that another competition authority is dealing with the case.

[299] The optional character of the allocation rules is also highlighted by the CFI in para 84 of its judgment in *Wanadoo* (above n 37).

[300] As Gauer puts it, reallocation is actually 'the result of all individual decisions of the Network members to act or not to act on a case'. Gauer, above n 19, 3. See also Arts and Bourgeois, above n 40, paras 18–19, who consequently do not describe case allocation through the Network as 'beslissing', but instead use the term 'doorverwijzingsakkoord'.

[301] See Schaub, above n 2, 42. The discussions will only become known to the extent that they are later reflected in the statement of objections and/or the final decision of the competition authority to which the case has effectively been assigned.

[302] E Paulis and C Gauer, 'La réforme des règles d'application des articles 81 et 82 du Traité' (2003) 11 *Journal des tribunaux. Droit Européen* 65, para73.

[303] Pursuant to para 34 of the Network Notice the undertakings concerned and the complainants must be informed if a case is reallocated. However, this is a mere *ex post*

It is therefore highly unlikely that the allocation process will be open to any exchange of views between the competition authorities and the companies concerned. Neither will there be an allocation decision or any other type of official (published) document after the case has been assigned that would set out the considerations of the Network members and would thus enable defendants or complainants to take cognisance of the arguments of the competition authorities and challenge them.

Finally, it is evident from the way case allocation is regulated that the Commission did not intend to make case allocation a legal procedure which would entail the right of the undertakings to be heard and culminate in a formal decision that could be challenged as such in a national or Community court. First, Regulation 1/2003 does not contain any substantive rules on case allocation. The allocation criteria and procedure are laid down in a Commission Notice and thus only constitute 'soft law'. They are regarded as merely providing orientations.[304] Moreover, paragraph 31 of the Network Notice explicitly provides that

> the allocation of cases between members of the network constitutes a mere division of labour . . . The allocation of cases therefore does not create individual rights for the companies involved in or affected by an infringement to have the case dealt with by a particular authority.

The Commission's position is based on the consideration that a case will only be assigned to an NCA that is well placed to handle it. This is normally the NCA of the Member State where the anti-competitive effects are felt, provided it can bring the infringement to an end.[305] That NCA would have been entitled, in any event, to commence *ex officio* proceedings.[306] In other words, the undertakings concerned were thus already potentially exposed to an investigation under the national system in question and thus could not, in any event, have prevented that NCA from opening proceedings. On this basis, it is only natural that the Commission

---

information duty. It is not foreseen that they be given the opportunity to make their views known prior to the (re)allocation.

[304] Dekeyser and Dalheimer, above n 16, 6.

[305] See para 8 of the Network Notice. See also Fingleton, above n 49, 338–9. Only where an anti-competitive agreement or conduct produces effects exclusively outside the territory of the Member State(s) where the parties are located will the NCA(s) in the affected Member State(s) not be in a position to end the infringement. Whether, in such a situation, the case can be allocated to the NCA of the Member State where the defendants are located without any effects being felt is doubtful, as most Member States seem to apply some sort of effects doctrine. See above n 11.

[306] See para 32 of the Network Notice. Interestingly, the statement that case reallocation 'does therefore not change the position of the parties', which was apparently contained in an early EU-restricted draft of the Network Notice (see Fingleton, above n 49, 339 and note 4 on 327), has nonetheless not been retained. In view of the enormous relevance of case allocation for the procedural rights of the defendants, the sanctions that they face and the legal position of complainants, such a statement would probably have provoked considerable criticism. However, see below in section III.E.2.b.

sees no need to involve the undertakings concerned in any way in the allocation process.

However, in view of the importance of the case allocation for the parties, in terms of applicable procedure, language and penalties, it seems unacceptable that parties are not even heard. To the extent that this is possible without jeopardising the success of the investigation, parties should therefore at least be given the opportunity to make their views known.

b. No Challengeable Act

Even if one regarded the allocation of a case as decision within the meaning of Article 249 EC, this decision would lack the requisite criteria to make it a challengeable act under Article 230 EC as it would not be of *direct* concern to the undertakings involved in the suspected infringement or third parties. The effects of a measure can only be considered to be direct where they are purely automatic and do not require any additional implementation.[307] However, since neither the Commission nor the Advisory Committee are empowered to assign or transfer cases to a particular authority, an allocation decision would in any event be non-binding and would thus not entail any obligation on the part of the competition authority concerned to open a procedure. Therefore, the effects of an allocation decision would only arise after the competition authority to which the case is attributed has actually initiated proceedings. The effects are thus not automatic, but require an additional implementing measure at national level.[308]

Another debatable issue is whether, in the case of reallocation, the 'decision' of the NCA stepping back and leaving the handling of the matter to another NCA could be challenged. This is a question of national law and, similar to the situation under Community law, will probably depend very much on the nature of the administrative act by which the national procedure is terminated. Where the NCA has to issue a formal decision terminating the procedure, it seems likely that a complainant whose complaint is thereby equally rejected can challenge the decision before a

---

[307] See, eg the judgments of the CFI in Joined Cases T–346/02 and T–347/02 *Cableuropa* [2003] ECR II–4251, para 65 and Case T–119/02 *Royal Philips Electronics v Commission* ('*Moulinex*') [2003] ECR II–1433, para 287.

[308] *Contra* L Parret, 'Judicial Protection after Modernisation of Competition Law' (2005) 32 *Legal Issues of Economic Integration* 339, 360, who pleads in favour of the possibility of judicial review of 'referral decisions' under Art 230 EC. However, Parret seems to neglect the fact that it is not the Commission which refers a case by decision, not even by informal act, to a particular NCA; rather, it is the NCA which 'decides' to take on a case and subsequently initiates proceedings, while, at the same time, all other Network members agree to refrain from investigating the same matter. See also above n 300.

national court.[309] An action brought by the company under investigation, on the other hand, would appear inadmissible as the termination of the procedure does not harm that company.[310]

Likewise, one may wonder whether the 'decision' of the NCA (to which a case has been reallocated) to open an investigation could be challenged by the undertaking concerned. This question is again governed by national law. However, in the light of the case law of the ECJ, which has ruled that the initiation of proceedings is a preliminary procedural step and as such cannot be subject to a separate judicial review,[311] it is doubtful that the opening of a national investigation itself can be appealed by the company under investigation. Rather, the company concerned will usually be compelled to await the (final) decision of the NCA and challenge the issue of case allocation indirectly in the context of the action directed against that latter decision.[312] On all accounts, the situation does not appear to be in any way different from the normal opening of an investigation under national law since, in view of the requirement of a material link, the NCA could have opened the case on its own motion.[313] Thus, the general national rules on judicial review will also be applicable here.

2. *Judicial Review of Article 11(6) 'Decisions'?*

The question arises whether the situation would be different where the Commission undertakes to remove a case from the jurisdiction of the NCAs, pursuant to Article 11(6) of Regulation 1/2003, by initiating proceedings itself. It has been argued that such an act of the Commission is a formal decision within the meaning of Article 249 (ex Article 189) EC as it has legal effects on the Member States. This would mean that the Commission's decision has to state the reasons in accordance with Article 253 (ex Article 190) EC and, more importantly, could be challenged by the Member States pursuant to Article 230 (ex Article 173) EC.[314] Finally,

---

[309] For the situation under Community law see Art 7(2) of the Implementing Regulation, para 35 of the Network Notice and paras 74–7 of the Notice on Complaints. It follows from these provisions that, under Community law, a complainant is entitled to a formal Commission decision susceptible to judicial review where the Commission does not intend to pursue the matter, but instead refers it to one or several NCAs and the complainant has not consented to such referral. Idot, above n 96, 324, para 8; Arts and Bourgeois, above n 40, para 45. The obligation incumbent on the Commission to reject complaints by formal decisions follows from established case law, notably the judgment of the ECJ in Case C–282/95 P *Guerin Automobiles v Commission* [1997] ECR I–1503, para 36.

[310] Wils, above n 221, para 119.

[311] See below n 332 and accompanying text.

[312] This is also the position of Arts and Bourgeois, above n 40, para 24, with regard to the situation under Belgian law (on the basis of the WEM 1999).

[313] Wils, above n 221, para 119.

[314] Van Der Woude, above n 38, 15; Arts and Bourgeois, above n 40, para 58; D Geradin and N Petit, 'Droit de la concurrence et recours en annulation à l'ère post-modernisation', GCLC Working Paper 06/05 (available at www.coleurop.be/content/ gclc/documents/ GCLC%20WP%2006-05.pdf), 9–10; Wils, above n 221, para 120.

individuals could have this decision reviewed by the CFI where they can demonstrate that it is of direct and individual concern to them. Since Article 81 or 82 proceedings are necessarily limited to a distinctive group of undertakings, the requirement of individual concern would in any event not be an issue where the act is challenged by the undertakings subject to the investigation. The condition of direct concern would be met if the initiation of proceedings by the Commission deprives the applicants of certain procedural rights which they would have enjoyed under the procedural rules of the NCA and for which the Commission procedure does not offer an equivalent.[315]

In this respect, reference has been made to the judgment of the CFI in the *Cableuropa* case, which concerned a Commission decision under Article 9(1) of the 1989 Merger Regulation referring the examination of a concentration to the Spanish competition authorities.[316] In *Cableuropa*, the CFI considered that the referral decision terminated the procedure under the EC Merger Regulation, thereby depriving the applicants of the possibility to exercise certain procedural rights which they derived from that regulation and precluding them from relying on the judicial protection that they would otherwise have enjoyed under Article 230 EC. On that basis, the CFI held that the referral was capable of affecting the legal situation not only of the parties to the concentration, but also that of third parties. That effect was direct, as the contested decision did not require any implementing measure but immediately established the Member State's competence to examine the concentration referred to it.[317]

It is doubtful, however, that this reasoning of the CFI in *Cableuropa* regarding the referral of concentrations under the Merger Regulation can be transferred to the allocation of cases under the Network Notice as there

---

[315] Van Der Woude, above n 38, 16. The example given by Van der Woude is a case where a company loses the advantage of contradictory proceedings before an independent judicial body. See also Siragusa, who submits that, in the absence of any harmonisation of the procedural rules applied by the Commission and the NCAs, private parties may appeal to the CFI a Commission decision withdrawing the competence from an NCA. M Siragusa, 'The Commission's Position within the Network: The Perspective of the Legal Practitioners' in Ehlermann and Atanasiu, above n 2, 255, 263.

[316] See above n 307. In the *Cableuropa* case, the relevant concentration had originally been notified to the Commission in accordance with the Merger Regulation. However, under the German clause applicable at that time (Art 9 of the 1989 Merger Regulation), the Commission could, in certain circumstances, refer a case to the competition authority of a Member State where the concentration concerned a distinct market within that Member State. The possibility of referrals still exists under the 2004 Merger Regulation. The relevant provisions have not only been streamlined in order to allow for a more fine-tuned and speedier allocation of cases, but the referral system has also been broadened in that the possibility of pre-notification referrals at the request of the merging parties has been newly introduced, as well as the possibility for the Commission to trigger the referral process, at the post-notification stage, of its own motion. See T Soames and S Maudhuit, 'Changes in EU Merger Control: Part 1' (2005) 26 *European Competition Law Review* 57, 59.

[317] See paras 54–68 of the judgment in *Cableuropa* (above n 307). See also paras 276–90 of the judgment in *Royal Philips* (above n 307).

are important differences between the two domains, ie the decentralised enforcement of Articles 81 and 82 EC and EC merger control.

a. No Formal Act of Referral or Pre-emption

The most obvious difference is the fact that Regulation 1/2003 does not provide for any referral or pre-emption decisions addressed to a member of the Network. Neither the Commission nor the Advisory Committee (or the ECN) can actually refer a case from the Commission to an NCA or vice versa in the sense that they cannot issue a formal and legally binding decision to the effect that a given case be handled by a particular competition authority.[318]

The Commission is indeed required to consult with the NCA concerned where it intends to take a case out of its jurisdiction,[319] but it is not intended that this dialogue results in a formal Commission decision addressed to the relevant Member State. The Commission has committed itself to explaining in writing the reasons for the application of Article 11(6) of Regulation 1/2003 to the NCA concerned and also to other Network members.[320] However, the wording of paragraph 55 of the Network Notice ('the Commission will explain the reasons . . . in writing'), which avoids the terms 'decision' and 'state the reasons' or 'statement of reasons',[321] clearly suggests that these written explanations will not have the character of a formal Commission decision. Moreover, the commitment to provide written explanations is laid down in a soft-law instrument only and as such does not create a legally binding obligation on the Commission. This is different where a concentration under the Merger Regulation is referred to an NCA. Article 9(1) of both the 1989 and 2004 Merger Regulations explicitly provides that such a referral by the Commission must be made 'by means of a decision notified . . . to the undertakings concerned and the competent authorities of the other Member States'.

Needless to say, the commitment to consult with the NCA(s) concerned is only made with regard to situations where an NCA is already acting on the case which the Commission intends to take on. In contrast, where the Commission is first to commence proceedings, there will usually be no consultation with NCAs and no explanations in writing. The Commission's opening of a procedure will nevertheless have the same effect, namely to

---

318 See above n 300.
319 See Reg 1/2003, Art 11(6), 2nd sentence.
320 See para 55 of the Network Notice, which corresponds to para 22 of the Joint Statement.
321 The French text reads: 'la Commission expose par écrit . . . les motifs d'application'; the German version states: ' so erläutert die Kommission . . . schriftlich ihre Gründe'; the Dutch text provides: 'dan licht de Commissie haar beweegredenen voor de toepassing van . . . toe'. The Italian wording is: 'la Commissione dovrà fornire per iscritto . . . le motivazioni dell'applicazione'. None of the language versions thus employs the same terms as those which are used in Art 253 EC.

relieve the NCAs of their competence to apply Article 81 or 82 EC to the same facts.

As a result, the written explanations provided by the Commission to the NCAs pursuant to paragraph 55 of the Network Notice constitute a simple act of communication which is part of the co-operation process between the Commission and the NCAs. Such explanations merely set out why the Commission envisages to initiate proceedings and thus have a purely informative character. They do not produce any legal effects[322] and therefore cannot form the basis of an action for annulment.[323]

b. No Exclusive Competences

Another important difference is the fact that, unlike Regulation 1/2003, the Merger Regulation creates a system of mutually exclusive spheres of application for EC and national (merger control) law, and also defines exclusive competences for the Commission and the NCAs. A concentration which has a Community dimension automatically comes within the ambit of the Merger Regulation and, as a consequence, will be scrutinised solely by the Commission in accordance with Community law procedures. Member States' authorities, on the other hand, exclusively apply national merger control laws and are only competent to assess concentrations without a Community dimension, ie cases which fall outside the scope of the Merger Regulation. It is thus excluded a priori that a given concentration is subject to both a national and a Community law procedure.[324] This means that it is precisely the referral decision of the Commission that creates the Member States' jurisdiction by taking a concentration with Community dimension out of the scope of the Merger Regulation and transferring the responsibility for its examination to the NCA. That NCA would not be competent to scrutinise a concentration with Community dimension if it were not for the referral decision.[325]

In contrast, Regulation 1/2003 establishes a system of concurrent jurisdiction where the Commission and the NCAs share the competence to apply EC competition law to the same facts. In this system, the allocation of cases is a question not of transferring competence, but merely dividing the work.[326] This means that any breach of Article 81 or 82 EC can

---

[322] The legal effect of depriving the NCAs of their competence to apply Art 81 or 82 EC occurs automatically through the formal act by which the Commission actually opens the proceedings, which is a preparatory act not subject to a separate appeal. See above section III.E.2.c.

[323] Cf Case 133/79 *Sucrimex* [1980] ECR 1299, paras 15–18, where it was held that the mere expression of an opinion is not an act of the Commission capable of being challenged under Art 173 (now Art 230) EC.

[324] Unless the assessment of parts of a case is formally referred to an NCA by way of a Commission decision under Art 9(1) of the Merger Regulation.

[325] Cf Gauer, above n 19, 7. See also para 276 of the judgment in *Royal Philips* (above n 307).

[326] Schaub, above n 2, 39.

theoretically come under the jurisdiction of either the Commission or one or several Member States' authorities all of whom apply the same substantive rules. However, when the infringement occurs, it is completely open which competition authority will act and consequently which procedural law—national or EC—will be applicable. Prior to the allocation of the case, defendants and complainants are therefore, in theory, subject to all the different procedural rules. By allocating the case to a particular authority, the relevant (national or EC) procedure is simply singled out from the number of potentially applicable procedural laws,[327] but—unlike a merger referral—the allocation does not establish the competence of the relevant authority as this competence is shared by all competition authorities.

Moreover, in contrast to the situation in merger control cases, the reallocation of a matter under Regulation 1/2003 and the Network Notice does not alter the basis for its assessment on substance. The relevant benchmark for evaluating the (il)legality of the agreement or practice, whether by the Commission or an NCA, is always Article 81 or 82 EC.[328] The possible parallel application, by NCAs, of national competition law has no impact on the outcome of the matter as it must be in line with the appraisal under Community competition law.[329]

Arguably, defendants and complainants are thus not deprived of any specific rights—unlike the parties in the *Cableuropa* cases—when it is agreed, within the Network, which competition authority will ultimately handle a certain case. Case allocation does therefore not alter the legal position of defendants or complainants, but rather defines it, as their procedural rights remain undetermined or unspecified until the case is eventually allocated, while the relevant substantive rules remain in any event the same. It is, however, settled case law that only measures which are capable of affecting the interests of the applicant 'by bringing about a distinct change in his legal position' are acts or decisions challengeable under Article 230 EC.[330]

---

[327] Cf Gauer, above n 19, 5, who even submits that, since companies are exposed by law to prosecution by a number of NCAs and the Commission, case allocation 'is only about removing some of these threats'.

[328] Arts and Bourgeois, above n 40, para 56 (p 39).

[329] An exception are cases dealing with unilateral conduct (Reg 1/2003, Art 3(2), 2nd sentence). However, this exceptional deviation from the general principle of supremacy cannot affect the correctness of the finding in principle.

[330] See, eg judgment of the ECJ in Case 60/81 *IBM v Commission* [1981] ECR 2639, para 9 and of the CFI in Case T–64/89 *Automec v Commission (Automec I)* [1990] ECR II–367, para 42. *Accord,* as concerns the position of the undertakings concerned and complainants, Arts and Bourgeois, above n 40, paras 62 and 66.

c. Initiation of Proceedings by the Commission

There is only one formal act that could be subject to judicial review, notably the initiation of proceedings by the Commission.

(1) The Position of Defendants and Complainants. The ECJ has held that the opening of a procedure is 'an authoritative act of the Commission, evidencing its intention of taking a decision', notably a negative clearance, exemption or prohibition decision.[331] However, in spite of being a formal act, the initiation of proceedings by the Commission is a preparatory measure and, as such, not open to challenge under Article 230 EC. This follows from the judgment of the ECJ in the *IBM* case, where it was expressly stated that neither the initiation of proceedings nor the statement of objections (SO) is a decision, within the meaning of Article 173 [now Article 230] EC, which may be the subject of an application for annulment. They must rather be regarded as necessary steps in a procedure involving several stages whose purpose it is to pave the way for the final decision and thus only constitute provisional measures preparatory to the (final) decision which represents their culmination.[332]

In this respect, it makes no difference whether the Commission takes a case out of the jurisdiction of a particular NCA or simply is the first to open the procedure. It is true that, like the referral decision under the Merger Regulation terminating the Commission procedure, the initiation of proceedings by the Commission leads to a change in the legal system to the extent that it brings to an end the national procedure before the NCA pursuant to Article 11(6) of Regulation 1/2003. However, in contrast to the situation under the Merger Regulation, the initiation of proceedings by the Commission under Regulation 1/2003 does not entail a transfer of competence from one authority to another. As the Commission's right to apply Articles 81 and 82 EC cannot be restricted in any way by a national procedure, the Commission is always entitled to adopt decisions under these provisions.[333] In other words, the undertakings concerned have no legal right to have their case treated by a particular authority (Commission or NCA)[334] and are therefore exposed to a possible Commission procedure

---

[331] Case 48/72 *Brasserie de Haecht* [1973] ECR 77, para 16. The case concerned the interpretation of Art 85 [now Art 81] and Reg 17. See also para 15 of the judgment in *IBM* (above n 330), where the ECJ held that the 'initiation of the procedure . . . is clearly marked by an act manifesting the intention to take a decision'.

[332] Paras 10–21 of the *IBM* judgment (above n 330).

[333] Judgment of the ECJ in *Masterfoods* (above n 16), para 48. This principle has not been changed by Reg 1/2003 (see para 79 of the judgment in *Wanadoo*, above n 37). Indeed, the new system gives NCAs jurisdiction to enforce the EC competition rules 'without in any way diminishing the power or the strategic leadership and supervisory role of the Commission'. Rizzuto, above n 37, 291.

[334] Arts and Bourgeois, above n 40, para 56.

at least for as long as the NCA procedure has not been terminated.[335] Moreover, the opening of the Commission procedure has no impact on the applicable substantive law. The change in the 'legal system' is thus limited to procedural aspects, even if these can be quite important for parties and complainants.

Lastly, the classification of the measure as preparatory and thus the possibility of an appeal against the initiation of proceedings cannot depend on whether or not an NCA has already dealt with the same matter prior to the Commission as this is a purely accidental element.[336]

(2) The Position of Member States. Admittedly, Member States might be in a different position than the parties subject to the investigation or complainants. No doubt the opening of a procedure by the Commission directly affects their legal position in that it terminates the allocation process to the detriment of the NCAs, which, pursuant to Article 11(6) of Regulation 1/2003, are automatically deprived of their right to deal with the same matter.[337] In relation to NCAs, the initiation of proceedings by the Commission could thus be considered 'the culmination of a special procedure' within the meaning of the *IBM* case law and thus an act which is amenable to an action for annulment.[338]

However, even though the ECJ has described the commencement of proceedings as a formal act,[339] this act will rarely have the character of a formal decision, ie a decision taken by the College of Commissioners. In practice, it is an internal act of the Commissioner responsible for competition who acts on the basis of delegated authority from the full Commission.[340]

Moreover, there is no obligation incumbent on the Commission to publish the formal commencement of proceedings in the Official Journal or elsewhere.[341] Even the undertakings concerned are often not notified

---

[335] Even beyond that point in time, the Commission claims the right to intervene and 'overrule' the decision of an NCA if that decision runs counter to a Commission decision or established case law. See above Chapter 1, section II.A.1.b(2).

[336] Arts and Bourgeois, above n 40, para 54.

[337] Cf Schnichels, above n 53, 119, who calls it a 'very drastic decision'.

[338] In para 11 of the *IBM* judgment (above n 330), the ECJ held that an exception from the general principle, whereby preparatory measures are not open for review under Art 230 EC, would apply where the provisional acts were at the same time 'the culmination of a special procedure distinct from that intended to permit the Commission or the Council to take a decision on the substance of the case'.

[339] See para 16 of the judgment in *Brasserie de Haecht* (above n 331). This is confirmed by Art 2(1) of the Implementing Regulation, which clearly contemplates some kind of formal act on the part of the Commission. C Kerse and N Khan, *EC Antitrust Procedure* (London, Sweet & Maxwell, 5th edn, 2005), para 2-078.

[340] Roth and Rose, above n 262, para 13.082.

[341] See Art 2(2) of the Implementing Regulation, which merely introduces a faculty to make public the initiation of proceedings. The practice under Reg 17 was not to publicise this formal step. The current practice is to publish a short notice on the Commission's website. Kerse and Khan, above n 339, para 2-080.

immediately. In this context, it is important to note that the opening of formal proceedings does not usually mark the beginning of the Commission procedure.[342] The Commission may exercise its investigatory powers before proceedings are formally instituted [343] and regularly does so. In fact, the time or moment when the parties must be informed of the Commission's 'decision' to initiate proceedings is not specified. Article 2(1) of the Implementing Regulation only provides that the decision to initiate proceedings must be taken no later than the date on which the statement of objections is issued.[344] In practice, the decision to commence proceedings is often taken just before the statement of objections is served on the parties. It is even permissible that the letter notifying the parties of the formal commencement of proceedings is sent together with the statement of objections.[345] In any event, the decision is not commonly communicated in a formal manner to the Member States or their NCAs.[346] They can thus only learn about the opening of a formal procedure by consulting the Commission's website, ie by actively searching for the information themselves, unless the Commission systematically provides this type of information to the ECN.[347]

The scope of Article 230 EC is not limited to the categories of measures listed in Article 249 EC. Any act which has binding legal effects on the applicant and is capable of affecting his interests can be challenged by way of an application for annulment.[348] Since the initiation of proceedings by the Commission puts an end to the Member States' jurisdiction, one may argue that Member States should be able to have the legality of that act reviewed by the ECJ pursuant to Article 230 EC.

---

[342] G-K De Bronett in Schröter *et al*, above n 11, Artikel 9 VO Nr 17, para 2. This was also the situation in the *Wanadoo* case, where the inspection was carried out prior to the formal opening of the matter (see paras 81 and 89 of the judgment, above n 37).

[343] Art 2(3) of the Implementing Regulation.

[344] Kerse and Khan, above n 339, para 2-080; Roth and Rose, above n 262, para 13.082.

[345] See the facts of the *IBM* case (para 2 of the judgment, above n 330). Similarly, in *Dyestuffs*, the ECJ rejected the argument that the Commission had infringed the relevant procedural rules by sending the applicants the statement of objections at the same time as it informed them of the initiation of proceedings. See the judgment of the ECJ in Case 57/69 *Azienda Colori Nazionali v Commission* [1972] ECR 933, paras 9–12. See also the Commission's standard SO cover letter reproduced in M Siragusa and C Rizza (eds), *EU Competition Law. Volume III Cartels and Horizontal Agreements* (Leuven, Claeys & Casteels, 2007), 269 (Annex 2.2).

[346] According to one author, however, the 'decision' must be served on the NCAs. See De Bronett, above n 342, Artikel 9 VO Nr 17, para 2.

[347] Even though Art 11(2) of Reg 1/2003 obliges the Commission to inform the NCAs of (new) cases by transmitting copies of the most important documents it has collected, that provision does not, in contrast to Art 11(3) of Reg 1/2003 (which lays down the inverse duty on the NCAs), specify the moment when such information has to be supplied.

[348] Established case law; see, eg para 9 of the *IBM* judgment (above n 330). In practice, a large variety of different acts have been acknowledged by the ECJ to produce legal effects and have thus been assimilated with a formal decision. For an overview of the relevant case law, see Geradin and Petit, above n 314, 4–6.

On the other hand, the fact that the decision to initiate proceedings produces legal effects vis-à-vis the Member States, it is submitted, does not remove its preparatory character, even in relation to the Member States.[349] Three arguments support this view. First, the legal effects follow directly and automatically from Article 11(6) of Regulation 1/2003. They are thus merely an inescapable 'side-effect' of a preliminary assessment of the matter by the Commission that leads it to form the intention to adopt a decision pursuant to Article 81 or 82 EC. It is this intention, nothing more, which is manifested by the institution of proceedings and the issuance, shortly afterwards, of the statement of objections. Secondly, the decision to open a formal procedure does not definitively lay down the position of the Commission. Even after commencing formal proceedings, the Commission can still close the matter for lack of Community interest in which case the Member States' jurisdiction revives.[350] Admittedly, this is an unlikely scenario, but it is not a priori excluded and thus underpins the provisional nature of the institution of proceedings.[351] Thirdly, it is doubtful that the decision can be regarded as

---

[349] Cf the distinction drawn by the ECJ in Case C–47/91 *Italy v Commission (Italgrani)* [1992] ECR I–4145, paras 26 and 27. The case concerns an action for annulment of a Commission decision to initiate the procedure provided for in Art 88(2) EC regarding the review of state aid.

[350] See, eg Case T–193/02 *Piau v Commission (FIFA)* [2005] ECR II–209, where the Commission, following a complaint by the applicant Mr Piau, initiated a procedure against the FIFA (Fédération Internationale de Football Association). In October 1999, the Commission sent FIFA a statement of objections alleging the incompatibility of its regulations with the Community rules on competition. However, in April 2002 the Commission decided to close the file. It considered that there was no longer any Community interest in continuing with the procedure as the relevant FIFA regulations had been amended, and it formally rejected Mr Piau's complaint.

[351] This aspect distinguishes our case from the state aid case cited above, where the action for annulment of a Commission decision to institute proceedings under the Treaty provisions on state aid was held admissible. In the latter case, the Commission had in fact opted for the procedure specifically designed for aid. The legal effects of the classification of the aid at issue as new rather than existing were considered to be definitive. Namely, the ECJ found that, in the case of new aid, it was impossible to regularise *ex post* aid measures of the Member State that had been carried out prior to the Commission's final decision. Even if the aid was ultimately declared compatible with the common market, those implementing measures which preceded the 'positive' Commission decision would still be deemed unlawful in that they were contrary to the prohibition to put the aid into effect before the Commission has approved it (EC Treaty, Art 88(3), last sentence). Similarly, if the relevant Member State respected the said prohibition and suspended payment of the aid, the possible adverse effects of this suspension on the undertakings concerned could not be remedied *ex post* either. It was in view of these (seemingly) irreversible consequences of the Commission's decision to institute an aid review procedure under Art 88(2) (ex Art 93(2)) EC that the ECJ considered the decision not simply a preparatory act, but a partly definitive measure, and declared the action for annulment admissible. See paras 28–30 of the judgment in Case C–47/91 (above n 349). It must be noted, though, that the ECJ did not follow the opinion of Advocate General W Van Gerven in the same matter. Van Gerven had proposed to reject the application as inadmissible (see para 19 of his joined opinion in Cases C–312/90 and C–47/91 [1992] ECR I–4117). In the same vein, Advocate General C Stix-Hackl, in a later case, did not find the arguments of the ECJ in *Italgrani* convincing. In her opinion in Case C–400/99 *Italy v Commission (Tirrenia)* [2001] ECR I–7303, again a state aid matter, she argued that the classification, by the Commission, of aid as new was neither constitutive nor definitive; such

the culmination of a special procedure *distinct from* that intended to permit the Commission . . . to take a decision on the substance of the case.[352]

This is, however, a requirement for allowing an exception to the general rule whereby preparatory measures are not actionable. Such an exception has been granted, for instance, with regard to decisions refusing confidential treatment of certain documents in competition matters, as such measures are definitive in nature and independent of any decision on the substance of the case.[353] These measures were adopted in the context of granting third parties access to the file, a procedure which is certainly connected with, but still separable from, the main proceedings. By contrast, the privation of Member States from their competence is a legal consequence which, pursuant to Article 11(6) of Regulation 1/2003, is automatically and intrinsically linked to the Commission's decision to open a formal procedure. In other words, it is a single preparatory measure which is primarily intended to pave the way for the final Commission decision but at the same time has legal effects for the Member States. Both aspects may be distinguishable. Nonetheless, these aspects are simply two sides of the same coin rather than the results of two distinct procedures.

In addition, there seems to be no reason why Member States, like undertakings, cannot be referred to challenging the final decision of the Commission. On the contrary, Member States enjoy a privileged status as applicants under Article 230(2) EC. Unlike natural or legal persons, they do not have to demonstrate that they are individually and directly concerned by the measure the legality of which they contest.[354] They do

---

classification could be reviewed by the court in the same way as the question of whether the measure at issue constituted aid at all. Consequently, the (incorrect) presumption of the Commission that the aid was new could also be remedied by challenging the final decision. An action for annulment of the decision to open an aid review procedure under Art 88(2) EC would thus be directed against a preparatory act and therefore would have to be declared inadmissible (paras 48–52 of her opinion).

[352] Para 11 of the *IBM* judgment (above n 330) (emphasis added). In this context, Geradin and Petit, above n 314, 9, incorrectly state that the Commission's decision to open a formal procedure automatically puts an end to any national procedure pending at that moment with regard to the same facts. However, the effect of Art 11(6) of Reg 1/2003 is only to relieve Member States of their competence without interfering directly with the procedure existent at national level. It is for NCAs themselves to take the steps necessary to comply with the legal consequences resulting from the Commission decision. This may include a formal or informal decision of the NCA to terminate the own proceedings and/or close the file. See Arts and Bourgeois, above n 40, para 54. See also Art 35(4) of Reg 1/2003, which provides that, where a Member State has established a dual enforcement system separating prosecution and adjudication, 'the effects of Art 11(6) shall be limited to the authority prosecuting the case *which shall withdraw its claim before the judicial authority* when the Commission opens proceedings and this withdrawal shall bring the national proceedings effectively to an end' (emphasis added). This confirms the view purported here.

[353] Para 20 of the judgment of the ECJ in *Akzo I* (above n 110).

[354] C Gaitanides in H von der Groeben and J Schwarze (eds), *Kommentar zum Vertrag über die Europäische Union und zur Gründung der Europäischen Gemeinschaft*, Band 4 (Baden-Baden, Nomos, 6th edn, 2004), Artikel 230, para 37.

not even have to prove a more general kind of legal interest in bringing the relevant proceedings (*allgemeines Rechtsschutzinteresse*). Such an interest is deemed to exist due to their institutional responsibility under the Treaty provisions.[355] Member States thus can seek the annulment of any binding act of a Community institution regardless of whether this act is of a general nature (eg directives and regulations) or constitutes an individual measure addressed to a natural or legal person (eg decisions). Consequently, they will always have the requisite *locus standi* to lodge an application for the annulment of a Commission decision concluding a particular cartel matter.[356] It is therefore submitted that there is no need to deviate from the general approach adopted by the ECJ in *IBM*.[357] The initiation of proceedings by the Commission is a preparatory act which as such is not actionable. Irregularities of the procedure and lack of competence, including the question of whether the Commission was right in assuming responsibility, thereby depriving Member States of the competence to handle the matter, must be raised in an action against the final decision.[358]

d. Conclusion

Altogether, it must be concluded that the (re)allocation of a case does not amount to a legal decision that could be subject to separate judicial review.[359] The same applies to the initiation of a procedure by the

---

[355] Gaitanides, *ibid*, Artikel 230 para 102; Lenaerts *et al*, n 218, para 7-061. This view is based, inter alia, on the judgment of the ECJ in Case 131/86 *United Kingdom v Council* [1988] ECR 905, para 6, where the ECJ explicitly held that Art 173(1) (now Art 230(2)) EC affords each Member State the right to bring an action for annulment 'without making the exercise of that right conditional on proof of an interest in bringing proceedings'.

[356] Cf Case 41/83 *Italy v Commission* [1985] ECR 873, concerning an action for annulment brought by the Italian Republic against a Commission decision finding that British Telecommunications had infringed Art 82 EC. The question of admissibility was not even raised.

[357] Cf paras 27–30 of the judgment in *Italgrani* (above n 349). In that case, the ECJ argued that the opening of state aid proceedings under Art 88(2) EC must be an actionable decision because otherwise the interests of the Member State would have not be sufficiently and adequately protected. According to the ECJ, certain effects of that decision (eg the classification as new aid and the suspensory effect resulting therefrom) could namely not be rectified *ex post* by annulment of the final decision.

[358] Kerse and Khan, above n 339, para 2-079, albeit without referring explicitly to the position of Member States. *Contra* Arts and Bourgeois, above n 40, para 58; Geradin and Petit, above n 314, 9–10; Schwarze and Weitbrecht, above n 269, 172, para 11; Van Der Woude, above n 38, 15; Wils, above n 221, para 120. In accordance with Art 230(2), actions can be brought, inter alia, on grounds of lack of competence and infringement of an essential procedural requirement. In support of their claims, Member States could thus plead that the Commission violated procedural rules and lacked competence since it disregarded the procedure and criteria for case allocation laid down in the Network Notice which, through administrative practice coupled with the requirements of equal treatment, have become binding on it. See Arts and Bourgeois, above n 40, para 60.

[359] Cf Fingleton, above n 49, 339. Wils, above n 221, para 120. Similarly, Siragusa, above n 315, 264–5, considers that laying down the allocation criteria in a non-binding 'soft-law' instrument reduces the possibility of claims based on incorrect case allocation.

Commission which, pursuant to Article 11(6) of Regulation 1/2003, has the automatic effect of depriving the NCAs of their competence.

Case allocation under the Network Notice is an informal process based on a common understanding among the members of the Network that a particular authority will act. It does not culminate in a formal allocation or referral decision, even in the event that the Commission takes a case out of the jurisdiction of an NCA. The allocation of a case is thus merely a preparatory measure and as such can only be challenged indirectly to the extent that it is reflected in the final decision (or a decision on interim measures) of the competition authority ultimately handling the case.[360] In the context of a judicial review of that (final) decision, the court will also assess whether the competition authority that adopted the decision was competent to act on the matter.

Where the competition authority (NCA or Commission) stepping back, in spite of the reallocation, has to close its own procedure by a formal decision, that decision will usually be challengeable as well. The issue of jurisdiction and case allocation might then be examined incidentally in the course of the judicial review of that decision.[361] Such a review would obviously not extend to the question of whether the competition authority to which the case has been reallocated was indeed competent, but would at least allow to verify whether the competition authority closing the case was right in refraining from any further investigation and leaving the enforcement to another member of the Network. Admittedly, Article 13 of Regulation 1/2003 provides a strong argument in favour of any competition authority which closes a file after having 'referred' the case to another competition authority in the EU.[362] However, depending on the procedural rights of complainants under the relevant national law, the decision may be vitiated for other reasons.

---

[360] Cf judgment of the ECJ in *IBM* (above n 330), para 12.

[361] In France, for instance, the Conseil de la concurrence is obliged to issue a formal decision if it has been seized by an undertaking and the case is subsequently reallocated to another competition authority. See Idot, above n 99, 325, para 83.

[362] See Arts and Bourgeois, above n 40, para 45. According to them, it would seem that decisions based on Art 13 Reg 1/2003 could only be challenged successfully if that provision was itself incompatible with superior Community law. The question of whether the mere reference to Art 13 of Reg 1/2003 and the fact that another authority is dealing with the matter is, as such, sufficient ground for rejecting a complaint was in fact the subject matter of an action for annulment brought by the European Association of Euro-Pharmaceutical Companies against a Commission decision rejecting several complaints that the applicant had lodged on the basis of Art 82 EC (see Case T–153/06 *EAEPC v Commission*, application of 13 June 2006; [2006] OJ C178/38). The application has, however, been withdrawn.

IV. EVALUATION

As Marsden writes, 'concurrency can be a very messy business'.[363] Therefore, in a system of parallel competences such as that set up by Regulation 1/2003, firm rules on the division of labour are critical. Work sharing and thus case allocation is a prerequisite for efficient enforcement, as unnecessary duplication of procedures leads to the needless wasting of resources and an unwarranted increase of costs for both the authorities and the companies involved.

At the same time, the allocation of a case to a particular NCA (or the Commission) has important consequences for the companies concerned in terms of the applicable procedural rules, including such fundamental aspects as rights of defence, access to file, legal privilege and language requirements. After all, companies face authorities from 27 national jurisdictions and the Commission, all of which operate different national procedures.

Against this background, and considering that the Community legal order is based on the rule of law,[364] the allocation process should be transparent, predictable and subject to judicial review. However, the allocation rules do not live up to these expectations. First, allocation is based on mere guidelines, the relevant criteria being laid down in a legally non-binding Commission notice. Secondly, there are no justiciable decisions of the Commission or the Network attributing cases to a particular authority. Case allocation is in fact a process of finding a voluntary understanding between the Network members about who is going to do the work and who is going to abstain from acting.

The third, and perhaps the most striking, shortcoming is the fact that the entire process is designed as a strictly internal matter between the Network members. As far as case allocation is concerned, neither Regulation 1/2003 nor the Network Notice give any standing to the undertakings concerned. Allocation takes place in the 'closed circle' of the ECN, which denies private undertakings any recognition as actors.[365] This is probably less grave for the undertakings concerned, ie the companies to whom the decision is addressed, who have *locus standi* to raise any procedural irregularities, including issues of case allocation in an action for annulment brought against the final Commission decision pursuant to Article 230(4) EC. On the other hand, the impossibility of challenging the case allocation separately before a final decision is rendered forces the parties to put up

[363] P Marsden, 'Inducing Member State Enforcement of European Competition Law: A Competition Policy Approach to "Antitrust Federalism"' (1997) 18 *European Competition Law Review* 234, 235.

[364] Art 6(1) EU Treaty.

[365] A Weitbrecht, 'The Network of Competition Authorities—How Will It Work in Practice: Remarks from a Practitioner' in Geradin, above n 53, 123, 128.

with the procedural rules and language requirements of the NCA throughout the entire procedure, which may put them at a disadvantage (compared to the rules of other NCAs) and may also be costly and burdensome.

Complainants, in turn, may even be left without appropriate remedy at all.[366] This is likely to be the case where, according to the applicable national rules, an NCA stepping back may reject the complaint and close the file by simple letter, ie without resorting to the adoption of a formal decision. Unlike the Community law system,[367] national regimes which allow for an informal treatment of complaints often do not afford complainants an official status and role in the proceedings. In any event, informal acts such as a simple letter will, in all likelihood, not be considered a measure that is susceptible to judicial review. The rights which complainants enjoy under Community law, in particular the right to have their complaint rejected by a formal, actionable decision, are not applicable in proceedings conducted by an NCA in accordance with the national procedural rules.[368]

The current solution chosen for the 'division of labour'[369] between the NCAs and the Commission may serve the interests of the authorities in that it is flexible and open, but it lacks the fundamental requirements of predictability, justiciability and transparency to the detriment of companies and individuals. In a Community based on the rule of law, this is hardly acceptable.

---

[366] Arts and Bourgeois, above n 40, para 70.

[367] See Art 7(2) and 23(1) of Reg 1/2003 and Arts 5–9 of the Implementing Regulation.

[368] P Oliver, 'Le règlement 1/2003 et les principes d'efficacité et d'équivalence' (2005) 41 *Cahiers de Droit Européen* 351, 374.

[369] Para 31 of the Network Notice.

4

Information Exchange and Administrative Assistance in the Course of an Investigation—The Free Movement of Evidence

P URSUANT TO ARTICLE 12(1) of Regulation 1/2003, NCAs and the Commission 'have the power to provide one another with and use in evidence any matter of fact or law, including confidential information'. In addition, Article 22(1) of Regulation 1/2003 entitles NCAs to carry out inspections in their own territory 'on behalf and for the account' of another NCA.[1]

Both provisions constitute cornerstones of the decentralised enforcement of Community competition law. First, they allow NCAs and the Commission to exchange between each other principally any kind of evidentiary material. Secondly, they make it possible for NCAs to assist each other in the collection of evidence. The second rule is equally essential as, without Article 22(1) of Regulation 1/2003, it would not be possible for an NCA to initiate the search for evidence located outside its own territory. These powers are not simply an expression of the general spirit of the Network in that they create opportunities for real work sharing; they are a precondition for decentralised enforcement, since they ensure that a single NCA can effectively investigate and punish an infringement even in cases where the relevant data and evidence is partly to be found outside its own territory. The provisions are thus indispensable if one seriously wants to abide by the principle that cases should be dealt with by a single authority as often as possible.[2]

I. THE LEGAL FRAMEWORK

Article 12 is one of the most significant provisions of Regulation 1/2003

---

[1] Similarly, pursuant to Art 22(2) of Reg 1/2003, the Commission can request NCAs to undertake inspections in their territory which the Commission considers necessary.
[2] See recital 18 of Reg 1/2003. See also para 26 of the Network Notice.

for both the competition authorities in the EU and the undertakings concerned. It provides the legal basis for a broad information exchange, including confidential information, between the Commission and the NCAs, as well as between the latter. While Article 12(1) of Regulation 1/2003 states the general principle, paragraphs 2 and 3 of that provision lay down certain procedural safeguards aimed at protecting the legitimate interests of the companies concerned, their managers, directors and staff.

A. Right to Share Information—Article 12(1) of Regulation 1/2003

1. *Free Circulation of Information*

Article 12(1) of Regulation 1/2003 covers two important aspects of administrative co-operation between the competition authorities in the EU. First, it grants all competition authorities, ie the Commission and the NCAs, the power to provide each other with any matter of fact or law, whether confidential or not, that they have collected for the purpose of applying Article 81 or 82 EC. Any kind of information may be transmitted. This can include general information on particular markets or sectors,[3] but also proprietary company documents, statements and business data in electronic or paper form. There is no exception for confidential data. Both non-confidential and confidential information may be exchanged in the same way, notwithstanding any national rules to the contrary. The right to share information allows the transfer of the relevant data from the Commission to the NCAs and vice versa, as well as the transmission from one NCA to another.[4] Article 12(1) is in fact one of the few, if not the only, provisions of Regulation 1/2003 where both the vertical and horizontal aspects of co-operation among competition authorities in the EU are covered by one and same rule and thereby put on an equal footing. On the other hand, it must be noted that Article 12(1) of Regulation 1/2003 (again) only establishes a right, not a duty. Not even in relation to the Commission is there an explicit obligation of NCAs to forward information which they have in their possession.[5]

---

[3] Such information may either be in the possession of the NCA the assistance of which has been requested or even publicly available, but more difficult to retrieve for a foreign NCA that is not familiar with the markets and local companies in the Member State of the transmitting NCA.

[4] Paras 26 and 27 of the Network Notice. See also Explanatory Memorandum, 21.

[5] It has, however, been suggested that the provision should be read, in conjunction with Art 10 EC, as imposing an obligation on the Commission and the NCAs to furnish the information which another Network member requires. K Dekeyser and E De Smijter, 'The Exchange of Evidence within the ECN' (2005) 32 *Legal Issues of Economic Integration* 161, 164–5. At the same time, however, the authors concede that such a duty would not be unlimited. In my view, there may be situations where, in accordance with Art 10 EC and the relevant case law, a Network member is under a duty to provide another Network member with a particular piece of

Secondly, the provision not only permits Network members to exchange the relevant information between each other, it also gives the receiving competition authority the right to use in evidence that information even if it is confidential in nature. Information exchanged pursuant to Article 12 of Regulation 1/2003 may therefore include non-confidential or confidential data and information which the receiving authority requires to prove the infringement. The provision can be expected to play a predominant role in relation to the transmission of evidentiary material.

Since information sharing is a key element for collaboration, this rule constitutes a major step towards an ever closer co-operation between competition authorities in the EU both at the vertical and the horizontal level.[6] It sets aside the *Spanish Banks* doctrine, which prevented NCAs from using confidential information that they had received from the Commission as evidence in a national procedure and from sharing such confidential information with other NCAs. Article 12(1) of Regulation 1/2003 equally prevails over any national provision that would preclude an NCA from transmitting confidential information that it has in its possession to another (foreign) authority.[7] Any evidence or other piece of information regarding the application of Articles 81 and 82 EC can thus circulate freely within the Network.[8]

2. *Administrative Assistance—Article 22(1) of Regulation 1/2003*

Where an NCA carries out an inspection or other fact-finding measure (eg request for information, interview) on behalf and for the account of another NCA, the second sentence of Article 22(1) of Regulation 1/2003 stipulates that the information collected shall also be exchanged and used in accordance with Article 12 of that Regulation. Consequently, the exchange of evidence and other (confidential) data follows the same rules irrespective of whether the information was already in the possession of the transmitting authority or has been collected specifically upon the request of the receiving authority pursuant to Article 22(1) of Regulation 1/2003.[9]

---

information (case-by-case analysis), but it probably goes too far to generally interpret Art 12 of Reg 1/2003 *juncto* Art 10 EC as containing an obligation to exchange information.

[6] Cf Art 11(1) of Reg 1/2003.

[7] Dekeyser and De Smijter, above n 5, 163 and 173; M Van Der Woude, 'The Modernization Paradox: Controlled Decentralization', paper for the IBC's 10th Annual Advanced Competition Law Conference, Brussels, 6 and 7 November 2003, 12. See also recital 16 of Reg 1/2003 and para 27 of the Network Notice.

[8] M Bloom, 'Exchange of Confidential Information among Members of the EU Network of Competition Authorities: Possible Consequences of a Relatively Broad Scope for Exchange of Confidential Information on National Procedural Law and Antitrust Sanctions' in C-D Ehlermann and I Atanasiu (eds), *European Competition Law Annual 2002: Constructing the EU Network of Competition Authorities* (Oxford, Hart Publishing, 2003), 391.

[9] K Dekeyser and D Dalheimer, 'Co-operation within the European Competition Network— Taking Stock after 10 Months of Case Practice', paper for the conference 'Antitrust Reform in

It should be noted, however, that the transmitting authority has to act in accordance with its own powers of investigation when carrying out fact-finding measures on behalf of another NCA. It therefore depends on the national laws of the Member State in whose territory the inspection takes place whether the evidence can be lawfully collected. Equally, the question of whether the authority granting assistance is at all entitled, in terms of proportionality of the measures, to conduct an on-the-spot investigation at the business premises of a particular company or search the private premises of an employee is governed by the applicable law in the Member State of origin. Where the transmitting authority is required to demonstrate a certain level of suspicion in order to be permitted to search business premises or private homes, the NCA requesting assistance has to furnish sufficient information for the transmitting authority to establish the probable cause according to the standards applicable in the Member State where the inspection is to be conducted. The fact that a lower threshold would apply in the Member State of the authority requesting assistance is irrelevant.[10] Similarly, the national law of the NCA carrying out the inspection determines whether a search warrant is required.

Moreover, it is important to know that the provision of administrative assistance lies in the full discretion of the NCA that has been asked to render such assistance. Article 22(1) of Regulation 1/2003 merely creates the possibility for NCAs to co-operate in fact-finding measures, but does not establish a duty of NCAs to grant assistance if so requested by another NCA. An NCA is thus free to decline such a request.[11]

Evidently, problems will occur where the collection of evidence that has already been transmitted to another NCA is vitiated by procedural irregularities in the Member State of origin. This issue will be discussed below.[12]

B. Limitations on the Use of Information—Article 12(2) and (3) of Regulation 1/2003

The basic principle is that any matter of fact or law, whether or not it is of a confidential nature, can circulate freely within the Network and can be

Europe: A Year in Practice', organised jointly by the International Bar Association (IBA) and the European Commission, Brussels, 9–11 March 2005, 11.

[10] Dekeyser and Dalheimer, above n 9, 12. Cf also Van Der Woude, above n 7, 13.

[11] See D Reichelt, 'To What Extent Does the Co-operation within the European Competition Network Protect the Rights of Undertakings?' (2005) 42 *CML Rev* 745, 765. See also Chapter 1, n 378 and Chapter 2, n 159. On the question of whether an NCA is obliged to transmit the information collected to the other NCA once it has agreed to carry out fact-finding measures on behalf of that other NCA, see below n 206 and accompanying text and also above n 5.

[12] See below section II.B.2.

used as evidence by the NCAs as well as by the Commission in a procedure regarding the enforcement of Article 81 or 82 EC.[13]

However, in order to grant a minimum level of protection not only to companies subject to an investigation, but also to the individuals concerned, Regulation 1/2003 contains a number of procedural safeguards. In fact, Article 12(1) and (3) of Regulation 1/2003 limits the use in evidence of information circulating in the Network in three respects.

1. Application of (National) Competition Law—Article 12(2) of Regulation 1/2003

The first sentence of Article 12(2) of Regulation 1/2003 explicitly provides that information exchanged between Network members shall only be used in evidence for the purpose of applying Articles 81 and 82 EC. Pursuant to the second sentence of Article 12(2) of Regulation 1/2003, the information may also be used for the enforcement of national competition law provided that the latter is applied in the same case and in parallel to Article 81 or 82 EC.

These limitations appear to be self-evident, given that Regulation 1/2003 pertains only to the enforcement of Articles 81 and 82 EC and the parallel application of national competition law. Other areas of law, in particular merger control rules, are excluded from the scope of Regulation 1/2003.[14] Consequently, the responsibilities of the ECN under Regulation 1/2003 are also restricted to matters regarding the implementation of these two Treaty provisions or national competition law. It would seem excluded that the Network deals with and shares information relating to other matters. However, depending on the relevant national rules, NCAs, being members of the Network and having access to the information circulated, may also be entrusted with the implementation of other (national) laws (eg unfair trade practices, public procurement).[15] Such NCAs could be inclined to use information that they obtained through the Network for enforcement activities outside the scope of Articles 81 and 82 EC or national competition law. The first sentence of Article 12(2) of Regulation 1/2003 therefore is more than a mere clarification.

Pursuant to the second sentence of Article 12(2) of Regulation 1/2003, the use of exchanged evidence for the application of national competition law is only permitted where the national rules are applied in parallel to Community competition law. This requirement becomes relevant in cases that are initially investigated under Article 81 or 82 EC and national

---

[13] C Swaak and M Mollica, 'Clementie en de modernisering van de EG-mededingingsregels' (2005) 8 *Markt & Mededinging* 36, 39.

[14] See the title of Reg 1/2003, recital 9 and Art 3(3) of Reg 1/2003.

[15] The French DGCCRF, for instance, not only has responsibilities in the field of competition law, but also has to ensure the fairness of commercial practices and the protection of consumers.

competition law but are later pursued only under national law because there is no effect on intra-Community trade. In such a situation, the information obtained via the Network can only be used to justify the initiation of the national proceedings in accordance with the *Spanish Banks* doctrine, not as (direct) evidence to prove the infringement of national competition law.[16]

The second sentence of Article 12(2) of Regulation 1/2003 places the use of exchanged evidence in relation to national competition law infringements under a further condition. The provision states that the parallel application of national competition law may not lead to a different outcome. This condition is particularly relevant where unilateral conduct is concerned. Specifically, NCAs can apply stricter national laws and impose sanctions for unilateral conduct which, under Article 82 EC, is not prohibited.[17] However, as follows from Article 12(2) of Regulation 1/2003, they may not do so on the basis of information which was exchanged in the Network. The question arises whether this also applies to the NCA which originally collected the evidence. Is evidence generally excluded from being used in a procedure regarding unilateral conduct that is illegal only under national law once the evidence has transited through the Network?[18] There is, however, no reason to shield a company or individual from punishment by the NCA that collected the evidence in the first place. That NCA could have imposed sanctions in any event and independently of the fact that the evidence circulated in the Network.

As concerns Article 81 EC cases, by contrast, the condition of the same outcome has no additional significance. NCAs are prohibited from the outset to apply national competition law to Article 81 cases if the parallel application of the national provisions leads to a different result, be it stricter or more lenient than the outcome under Article 81.[19]

Undertakings and individuals are thus effectively protected against the use of evidence that has been obtained through the Network for the application of sanctions which the relevant NCAs could not have imposed on the basis of Article 81 or 82 EC.

[16] Bloom, above n 8, 400. Swaak and Mollica, above n 13, 40. As concerns the *Spanish Banks* doctrine see above Chapter 3, n 165.

[17] Reg 1/2003, Art 3(2), 2nd sentence. With regard to cartels or concerted practices, Art 12(2) only reinforces the general rule resulting from Reg 1/2003, Art 3(2), 1st sentence and the supremacy principle, namely that national law may be neither stricter nor more lenient than Community law. See R Smits, 'The European Competition Network: Selected Aspects' (2005) 32 *Legal Issues of Economic Integration* 175, 181. On this convergence rule see above Chapter 1, section II.B.2.b.

[18] Cf C Gauer, 'Due Process in the Face of Divergent National Procedures and Sanctions', paper for the conference 'Antitrust Reform in Europe: A Year in Practice', organised jointly by the International Bar Association (IBA) and the European Commission, Brussels, 9–11 March 2005, 11 and 15 (regarding the over-protection of leniency applicants).

[19] This follows from Art 3(2) of Reg 1/2003 and the principle of supremacy of EC law. See also above Chapter 1, section II.B.2.b.

2. *Terms of the Original Mandate—Article 12(2) of Regulation 1/2003*

The first sentence of Article 12(2) of Regulation 1/2003 further limits the use in evidence of exchanged information to 'the subject matter for which it was collected by the transmitting authority'. This is an important principle, and was already enshrined in Regulation 17, limiting the use of information acquired by the Commission under that regulation.[20] The principle has now been extended to NCAs.[21] The wording of the provision moreover reflects the ECJ's case law regarding the former Article 20(1) of Regulation 17. It follows from the ECJ's ruling in *Dow Benelux* that the purpose restriction of that old provision had to be read in conjunction with the Commission's obligation, resulting from Article 14(3) of Regulation 17, to specify not only the purpose, but also the subject matter of an investigation.[22] The announced scope of the investigation of the NCA that originally gathered the information will therefore determine the extent to which that same information can be used by other Network members as evidence against a company or individual.

The scope of the investigation will normally be defined in the decision ordering the investigatory measures. In this regard, it must be noted that the Commission is required to specify the purpose of a request or the subject matter and purpose of an inspection it wishes to conduct pursuant to Articles 18(2) and (3), 20(3) and 21(2) of Regulation 1/2003.[23] According to the case law of the ECJ, this means that the Commission, while not being required to disclose all relevant information at its disposal, must nevertheless clearly indicate the presumed facts which it intends to investigate. The ECJ has pointed out that this obligation is a fundamental guarantee of the rights of defence.[24] It can therefore generally be assumed that all decisions of NCAs ordering an investigation will equally define the scope, ie the subject matter and purpose, of the inquiry. It is thus in the light of the original NCA decision ordering the investigation that the lawfulness of the use in evidence of information obtained by an NCA through the Network must be assessed. In other words, an NCA using evidence that it has received in the course of an investigation from various Network members must apply a sort of 'country of origin' principle in relation to each piece of evidence. It is not the scope of its own investi-

[20] Art 20(1) of Reg 17 read: 'Information acquired . . . shall be used only for the purpose of the relevant request or investigation.'
[21] Gauer, above n 18, 12 note 40.
[22] Paras 17–18 of the judgment in Case 85/87 *Dow Benelux* [1989] ECR 3137. On the purpose and subject matter restriction, see also Reichelt, above n 11, 779–80.
[23] Reg 17 had similar provisions, namely Arts 11(3) and 14(2). These rules are said to reflect the general prohibition of so-called 'fishing expeditions'. Swaak and Mollica, above n 13, 40 note 19.
[24] Para 41 of the judgment of the ECJ in Joined Cases 46/87 and 227/88 *Hoechst v Commission* [1989] ECR 2859.

gation that is relevant, unless it has gathered the information itself, but the subject matter of the NCA's inquiry in the territory of the Member State where the information originates. That subject matter determines whether the exchanged information can be used as evidence in the procedure conducted by the receiving NCA.

As a result, information collected on a suspected infringement relating to specific companies, products and geographical markets cannot later be used in a procedure that is conducted against the same companies, but concerns, for instance, other products or geographical markets.[25] On the other hand, the undertakings concerned need not be fully identical in both proceedings provided that the proceedings of the receiving authority concerns the same products and agreements or standard contracts as the investigation of the transmitting authority.[26]

Moreover, NCAs and the Commission are not completely barred from using information exchanged in the Network in any way outside the scope of the original investigation: they can use such information as circumstantial evidence, ie they may rely on information stemming from an earlier inquiry in order to justify the initiation of a new inquiry having a different scope. This follows from the principles developed by the ECJ in *Dow Benelux* and *Spanish Banks*.[27] In such a case, the relevant information merely serves as a basis for the NCA's evaluation, whether or not it is expedient to open a further investigation relating to a different subject matter. The information is thus not used for its evidentiary, but rather its informatory, value.[28] If sanctions are applied at the end of the new investigation, these will be imposed exclusively on the basis of evidence that has been collected in the course of the second investigation. The principle that information may only be used for the subject matter for which it was collected is therefore not infringed in these cases.

[25] Swaak and Mollica, above n 13, 40.

[26] D Schnichels, 'The Network of Competition Authorities: How Will It Work in Practice?' in D Geradin (ed), *Modernisation and Enlargement: Two Major Challenges for EC Competition Law* (Antwerp, Intersentia, 2004), 112. The example provided by Schnichels are parallel investigations of certain vertical restraints in standard contracts. While the supplier concerned would be the same in all proceedings, the customers may vary. The same would seem to apply where a certain cartel is investigated and the receiving authority directs its proceedings against other or additional cartel members than the transmitting authority.

[27] See para 19 of the ECJ's judgment in *Dow Benelux* (above n 22) and para 39 of the judgment in Case C–67/91 *Dirección General de Defensa de la Competencia v Asociación Española de Banca Privada and others* ('*Spanish Banks*') [1992] ECR I–4785. An exception only applies where the information circulated in the Network results from a leniency application. In that case, it may not even be used as circumstantial evidence. See above Chapter 3, section III.C.1.

[28] Swaak and Mollica, above n 13, 40.

3. Particular Safeguards for Individuals—Article 12(3) of Regulation 1/2003

The use of information is further restricted with regard to the sanctions that NCAs may impose on natural persons using evidence that they have obtained through the Network.

a. Rationale

When NCAs enforce Article 81 or 82 EC in accordance with Regulation 1/2003, the applicable procedures and sanctions are still determined by national law. All national systems as well as the Community law system provide for some kind of pecuniary sanctions to be imposed on legal persons. While there are certainly differences in the level of fines that undertakings can attract and their legal qualification (eg administrative, criminal), the differences between the various systems do not appear so important that they would seriously compromise procedural fairness if evidence to be used against a legal person is exchanged among the Network members. The underlying rationale of Regulation 1/2003 is that all national systems and the Community law rules guarantee an equivalent standard of protection of the rights of defence of undertakings.[29]

However, this equivalence cannot be assumed where individuals are concerned. There are fundamental differences in the applicable sanctions on individuals for infringement of Articles 81 and 82 EC. While some jurisdictions do not provide for any sanctions for natural persons (eg Community law), others allow for administrative fines to be imposed on individuals (eg France, Germany, Ireland, Spain). In some Member States company officials such as managers, directors or other employees may even be charged with criminal offences (eg France, Ireland, UK). These divergencies presumably correspond to differences in the procedural rights granted to individuals as there is generally a certain correlation between the available sanctions and the standard of protection of the rights of defence. In jurisdictions where individuals face criminal or even custodial sanctions, the level of protection is likely to be significantly higher than in jurisdictions where natural persons can incur only administrative fines or cannot be prosecuted at all.[30]

---

[29] Recital 16 of Reg 1/2003. Cf also Gauer, above n 18, 16. However, as Y Van Gerven, 'Regulation 1/2003: Inspections ("Dawn Raids") and the Rights of Defence' in C Baudenbacher (ed), *Neueste Entwicklungen im europäischen und internationalen Kartellrecht (Dreizehntes St. Galler Internationales Kartellrechtsforum 2006)* (Basel, Helbing & Lichtenhahn, 2007), 355, has rightly pointed out, it must be doubted that this assumption is correct. There are also many examples of discrepancies between national protection standards in regard to the rights of defence of undertakings (see also below section II.C.1.a).

[30] C Gauer, 'Does the Effectiveness of the EU Network of Competition Authorities Require a Certain Degree of Harmonisation of National Procedures and Sanctions?' in Ehlermann

The most significant examples in this respect are probably the privilege against self-incrimination and the right to remain silent, which are guaranteed by Article 6 ECHR[31] and therefore are certainly applicable in Member States where natural persons face criminal punishment for violations of Articles 81 and 82 EC. They should also probably be enjoyed by individuals in Member States where merely administrative fines can be imposed on them. In this context, it must be noted that Article 6 ECHR only applies in proceedings involving the determination of a 'criminal charge'. It is, however, settled case law of the ECtHR that the terms 'criminal offence' and 'criminal charge' used in Article 6 ECHR have an autonomous meaning.[32] Moreover, the ECtHR has held that these words describe a substantial rather than a formal concept, and the question of whether a procedure has indeed a criminal character consequently depends on the realities and not on the appearances of the matter.[33] On the basis of this case law, the punitive and deterrent aspects of financial penalties may justify the conclusion that violations of competition law, even where they can only be punished by administrative fines, must in fact be regarded as criminal offences within the meaning of Article 6 ECHR.[34]

By contrast, the Community law system, which solely provides sanctions for undertakings, does not acknowledge the right to silence and grants only limited protection against self-incrimination. Specifically, the Commission can compel the undertakings concerned to co-operate actively in the investigation, thereby forcing its employees and other staff members to answer certain factual questions or hand over incriminating documents. This

and Atanasiu, above n 8, 187, 199. Cf also W Wils, 'The Reform of Competition Law Enforcement—Will it Work?', Community Report for the FIDE XXI Congress, Dublin, 2–5 June 2004, in D Cahill (ed), *The Modernisation of EU Competition Law Enforcement in the EU—FIDE 2004 National Reports* (Cambridge, Cambridge University Press, 2004) (available at SSRN: http://ssrn.com/abstract=1319249), 661, para 197.

[31] See the judgment of ECtHR of 17 December 1996 in the case of *Saunders v United Kingdom* Reports/Recueil 1996-IV, 2044, para 68: 'The Court recalls that, although not specifically mentioned in Art 6 of the Convention, the right to silence and the right not to incriminate oneself are generally recognised international standards *which lie at the heart of the notion of a fair procedure* under Art 6' (emphasis added).

[32] Apparently, the Court of Human Rights considered the autonomous nature of these concepts for the first time as early as 1968, notably in the case of *Neumeister v Austria* (judgment of 27 June 1968 Publications Series A no 8, para 18), where it referred to the term 'charge' 'as this word is understood within the meaning of the Convention'. See W Overbeek, 'The Right to Remain Silent in Competition Investigations: The Funke Decision of the Court of Human Rights Makes Revision of the ECJ's Case Law Necessary' (1997) 22 *European Competition Law Review* 127, 130.

[33] Judgment of the ECtHR of 27 February 1980 in the case of *Deweer v Belgium* Publications Series A no 35, paras 42–4; see also judgments of the ECtHR of 21 February 1984 in the case of *Öztürk v Germany* Publications Series A no 73, para 50, and of 25 February 1993 in the case of *Funke v France* Publications Series A no 256, para 44.

[34] See further below Chapter 6, section I.A.1.b.

means that individuals can only decline to provide directly incriminating answers.[35]

The carefully balanced system of sanctions and procedural safeguards which exists within each national legal order may be distorted where evidence is freely exchanged and used against individuals by authorities from different Member States that apply diverging standards of protection when collecting such evidence.[36] Therefore, Regulation 1/2003 puts certain restrictions on the use of exchanged information as evidence against natural persons. The purpose of these restrictions is to ensure that the legal position of individuals is not undermined through the unlimited exchange of evidentiary material between Network members.

b. Use of Exchanged Information Against Individuals—Article 12(3) of Regulation 1/2003

(1) First Alternative—Symmetry[37] of Sanctions. The basic principle enshrined in the first indent of Article 12(3) of Regulation 1/2003 is that exchanged evidence may only be used to impose sanctions on natural persons where the laws in the Member State of the transmitting authority foresee sanctions for an infringement of Articles 81 and 82 EC which are 'of a similar kind' to those that the receiving authority intends to impose. In that case, the procedural safeguards for individuals under the two national systems concerned are again presumed to be equivalent.[38]

The term 'sanctions of a similar kind' has not been defined in Regulation 1/2003. It can be assumed, however, that a main distinction must be drawn between custodial sanctions on the one hand and financial penalties on the other. Irrespective of the qualification of the latter in the relevant national system[39], these two types of sanctions are certainly not similar.[40] Even though the Network Notice apparently differentiates only between these

---

[35] See Art 20(2)(e) of Reg 1/2003 and the judgment of the CFI in Case T–112/98 *Mannesmannröhren-Werke v Commission* [2001] ECR II–729, paras 62–7. See also para 28 (c) of the Network Notice. On the different approach of the ECJ and ECtHR to this privilege and the divergent interpretations of Art 6 ECHR given by both courts, see P Willis, '"You have the right to remain silent . . .", or do you? The privilege against self-incrimination following Mannesmannröhren-Werke and other recent decisions' (2001) 22 *European Competition Law Review* 313. See also below section II.C.1.a(2).

[36] Cf A Burnside and H Crossley, 'AM&S, AKZO and Beyond: Legal Professional Privilege in the Wake of Modernisation', paper for the conference 'Antitrust Reform in Europe: A Year in Practice', organised jointly by the International Bar Association (IBA) and the European Commission, Brussels, 9–11 March 2005, p 1. Cf also Explanatory Memorandum, 21.

[37] The expression has been borrowed from B Perrin, 'Challenges Facing the EU Network of Competition Authorities: Insights from a Comparative Criminal Law Perspective' (2006) 31 *EL Rev* 540, 547.

[38] Para 28 (c) of the Network Notice.

[39] It is conceivable that pecuniary sanctions are regarded as criminal penalties or merely as administrative fines falling outside the scope of (national) criminal law.

[40] Para 28(c) of the Network Notice.

two categories, notably 'sanctions which result in custody and other types of sanctions such as fines . . . and other personal sanctions', one may consider that a third category of penalties exists which is not similar to either of the two first-mentioned categories. These would be disciplinary measures such as the disqualification of company directors[41] or the suspension of certain civil rights. The facts that these measures restrict the personal freedom of the individual concerned and also carry a strong moral message, with potential damage to reputation, clearly distinguish them from purely financial penalties and make them more akin to custodial sanctions. It is therefore submitted that pecuniary sanctions and disciplinary measures should not be grouped together. Instead, one should regard disciplinary measures as being personal sanctions of a separate kind.

It follows that, pursuant to the first indent of Article 12(3) of Regulation 1/2003, the receiving NCA may only impose financial sanctions on the basis of exchanged evidence against individuals where the transmitting NCA could do the same[42] and that disciplinary measures may only be taken

---

[41] This cartel law sanction is possible, for instance, in the UK under the Company Directors Disqualification Act 1986. Sweden has also introduced a similar penalty recently. The amendments to the Swedish competition law that entered into force on 1 November 2008 provide for a new type of sanction, a so-called trading prohibition (näringsförbud; see Section 3 § 24 of the Swedish Competition Act), which can be imposed on managing directors and board members who have engaged in serious cartel infringements for a period of up to 10 years. See H Andersson and E Legnerfält, 'The New Swedish Competition Act' (2008) 29 European Competition Law Review 563.

[42] It is submitted that the conclusion drawn by Perrin, above n 37, 555, is not correct. Perrin develops a model whereby he distinguishes between two groups of NCAs, notably those which can impose custodial sanctions (Estonia, Ireland, Slovakia and the UK) and those which cannot. He then purports that evidence transferred from the first group is only admissible in the second group of Member States 'if it has been collected with 'the same level of protection of the rights of defence" (see point 3 'Possible Network gap' of his outline). However, the point of reference for determining the symmetry of sanctions should, in my view, be the country of destination. The question therefore is whether the sending NCA can impose the same sanctions as the receiving NCA, not the other way round. Since the laws of all those Member States which foresee custodial sanctions also provide for pecuniary sanctions (fines) on individuals (see the table presented by Perrin, above n 37, 552–4), evidence stemming from those four countries will generally be admissible in all other Member States. It is thus not necessary to resort to the second alternative of Art 12(3) of Reg 1/2003 (discussed in the following paragraph of the body text), which makes the admissibility of the exchanged evidence dependent on the equivalence of protection of defence rights in the Member States involved. This result also seems to be logical. A system providing for custodial sentences, given that this is a serious intervention and authorities operate in the criminal law sphere sensu stricto, will presumably have a higher standard of protection of defence rights than a system including only fines, at least not a lower one. Obviously, the latter type of sanctions (fines) may, under national law, also be classified as 'criminal' (in that case the level of protection can be expected to be at least equal), but they are often only regarded as administrative offences. By contrast, imprisonment is arguably always qualified as a criminal sanction (see W Wils, 'Is Criminalization of EU Competition Law the Answer?' (2005) 28 World Competition 117, 118). As concerns Perrin's next conclusion (see point 4 'Network gap' of his outline, idem, 555), I agree that information forwarded from a Member State other than Estonia, Ireland, Slovakia and the UK is in any event inadmissible as evidence in any of those four Member States for the purpose of imposing a custodial sentence (see the following paragraph of the body text). In my view, it is also unlikely to be admissible, under the second alternative of Art 12(3) of Reg 1/2003, for the purpose of inflicting a pecuniary sanction because, as submitted, the

by the receiving NCA if the transmitting NCA equally has the power to take such measures. Finally, the receiving NCA may only order the imprisonment of a person where the laws of the transmitting NCA also provide for custodial sanctions.

(2) Second Alternative—Equivalence of Protection. Where both systems, ie the laws of the transmitting authority and of the receiving authority, do not provide for similar kinds of sanctions, the procedural safeguards for individuals might differ significantly. However, even in the case of divergent sanctions the use of transferred evidence against a natural person is not precluded at the outset. The second indent of Article 12(3) of Regulation 1/2003 provides that the exchanged information may still be used against an individual provided, however, that

> the information has been collected in a way which respects the same level of protection of the rights of defence of natural persons as provided for under the national rules of the receiving authority.

It is important to note that the application of custodial sanctions, ie a sentence of imprisonment, on the basis of evidence that the prosecuting NCA has obtained through the Network is not permitted under this alternative even if the level of protection in the Member State where the evidence was collected could be considered identical to that applicable in the Member State of the receiving NCA. In other words, custodial sanctions can only ever be imposed under the first alternative of Article 12(3) of Regulation 1/2003, namely where the laws of both the transmitting and the receiving authority provide for this type of punishment of individuals in relation to violations of Article 81 or 82 EC.[43]

Assessing whether two NCAs from different Member States offer the same level of protection of the rights of defence is likely to be a complex and thus very difficult exercise. Not only is the notion of 'same level of protection' a vague concept; the fact that the standard of protection is not generally considered to be equivalent where the laws of the relevant Member States foresee different kinds of sanctions for individuals suggests

standard of protection in Estonia, Ireland, Slovakia and the UK is supposedly higher than in all other Member States.

[43] This limitation follows directly from Art 12(3) of Reg 1/2003, which reads: 'Information exchanged pursuant to paragraph 1 can only be used in evidence to impose sanctions on natural persons where:

- the law of the transmitting authority foresees sanctions of a similar kind in relation to an infringement of Article 81 or Article 82 of the Treaty or, in the absence thereof,

- the information has been collected in a way which respects the same level of protection of the rights of defence of natural persons as provided for under the national rules of the receiving authority. *However, in this case, the information exchanged cannot be used by the receiving authority to impose custodial sanctions*' (emphasis added).

that the condition will rarely be met.[44] In any event, the assessment requires a thorough comparative analysis, probably preceded by extensive research into the foreign legislation, which should not be limited to the statutory language. This is a resource-intensive and time-consuming exercise.[45] Ultimately, whether both systems guarantee the same level of protection (equivalence) must be evaluated on a case-by-case basis.[46]

Case-specific or Abstract Analysis of the Defence Rights. In this context, the question arises whether the equivalence of the protection should be evaluated *in abstracto*, on the basis of the safeguards provided generally in the laws of the transmitting NCA, or *in concreto*, namely by looking at the manner in which the evidence was actually collected by the transmitting NCA in the specific case.

The wording of the second indent of Article 12(3) of Regulation 1/2003 seems to suggest that a case-specific analysis is indeed required. The provision refers to the 'way in which the information has been collected' rather than to the applicable law of the Member State gathering the information.[47] It thereby implies that the relevant test is not whether, as a matter of law, the procedural rules of the transmitting NCA grant an equal level of protection, but whether the NCA, in the course of the investigation, de facto respected the same level of protection. This would mean that the receiving NCA has to know exactly which procedural rights the transmitting NCA actually conceded when it carried out the fact-finding measures at issue. However, such a case-specific analysis would be very difficult to make in practice.

Applying a case-specific test would allow an NCA to request the assistance of another NCA that theoretically has lower protection standards without being barred, at the outset, from using the collected information subsequently against an individual. It is even conceivable that the NCA

---

[44] Cf A Riley, 'EC Antitrust Modernisation: The Commission Does Very Nicely—Thank You! Part One: Regulation 1 and the Notification Burden' (2003) 24 *European Competition Law Review* 657, 611. Obviously, the requirement would be fulfilled where the NCA with the more severe sanctions and therefore the higher protection of individuals forwards evidentiary material to the NCA of a Member State where individuals are less protected. (NB: The point of reference is the sanction that the receiving authority intends to impose, ie the receiving NCA sets the minimum standard.) However, in such a case the relevant information can usually already be exchanged under the first indent of Art 12(3) of Reg 1/2003, since both systems are likely to provide for some sort of financial penalties for natural persons and would thus be considered to have sanctions of a similar kind.

[45] Cf A Kist, 'Exchange of Information: Scope and Limits Seen from the Perspective of Competition Authorities' in Ehlermann and Atanasiu, above n 8, 355, 357 and 360; Perrin, above n 37, 556.

[46] Gauer, above n 18, 16.

[47] See also para 28 of the Network Notice: 'If on the other hand, both legal systems do not provide for sanctions of a similar kind, the information can only be used if the same level of protection of the rights of the individual has been respected *in the case at hand* (see Article 12(3) of the Council Regulation)' (emphasis added).

which intends to use the evidence could 'instruct' its colleague agency to grant the individual concerned specific procedural rights (eg inform them that they have the right to remain silent) just in that particular case in order to ensure that the level of protection of the transmitting NCA meets the own standards. However, it is far from certain whether an NCA would accept being 'directed' in such a way by a colleague agency.[48] Moreover, the person concerned is likely to argue that, irrespective of the instructions and the way the transmitting NCA actually proceeded, the transmitting NCA cannot really grant a higher level of protection than that required by its own laws since it is not familiar with the procedural rules of the 'instructing' NCA. It is also doubtful whether an NCA could be trusted not to use all the powers it has been vested with in order to obtain as much information as possible on the investigated matter. The individual concerned, whether a suspect or a third party who is interrogated or whose premises are searched,[49] is likely to consider that the NCA might at any moment fall back on its 'residual' rights as provided for in its own procedural laws. With this perceived threat hanging over him, he could be inclined to co-operate to a greater extent than he would have been required to under the standards of the receiving NCA. Instructing another NCA therefore does not seem an appropriate way of guaranteeing that both the transmitting and receiving NCAs respect the same level of protection of the rights of defence.

Finally, applying a case-specific test also has the disadvantage that the receiving NCA would be burdened with the task of verifying whether the transmitting NCA has properly applied its own rules. Even where, on the basis of the abstract law, both NCAs guarantee the same level of protection of the rights of defence, the requirement of equivalence would not be fulfilled if the transmitting NCA has de facto collected the evidence in a way that infringes its own procedural rules. However, it is not the purpose of the second indent of Article 12(3) of Regulation 1/2003 to ensure that evidence that has been gathered illegally by one NCA is not used by others. If one considers the three stages at which protection could be granted to the individuals concerned,[50] it is evident that Article 12 of Regulation

---

[48] Receiving such directions would always imply that the 'directing' NCA regards the protection standards of the transmitting NCA as inferior compared to its own rules. This may be a (politically) quite sensitive issue.

[49] It is submitted that the term 'rights of defence' as used in Reg 1/2003, Art 12(3), second indent, covers not only the proper rights of defence of the individual who is being prosecuted, but also the rights of other natural or legal persons that are affected by the investigation, eg because they are interrogated or requested to supply certain documents or their premises are searched. It seems justified to also include the rights of such third parties since, in order to fully guarantee the fairness of the procedure, the suspect must have the right to invoke any procedural irregularities that have occurred in the course of the investigation of which he is the subject.

[50] The three relevant stages are information gathering, exchange of information and use of exchanged information. Reichelt, above n 11, 750.

1/2003 only governs the last stage in that it only deals with the 'use in evidence' of (confidential) information; it does not cover the question of whether that evidence was legally collected. The legality of the investigative measures is to be controlled solely by the competent authorities and courts in the country of origin, ie in the Member State of the transmitting NCA.[51]

The Process of Evaluation. For the above reasons, it is submitted that, in spite of the wording of the second indent of Article 12(3) of Regulation 1/2003, the question of equivalence must be evaluated by comparing the abstract rules governing the collection of information in the receiving and transmitting Member States, albeit taking into account which of the available procedures was followed by the transmitting NCA in the instant case.[52] This means that the receiving NCA must have a profound knowledge of the transmitting NCA's procedural rules—otherwise the analysis will be flawed.

This requirement of knowing and analysing the foreign procedural rules constitutes a significant hurdle. Can one really expect an NCA to have detailed knowledge of the procedures followed by its 26 colleague agencies or to have the manpower to research this? How can an NCA find out about the applicable rules if the relevant text is only available in a language that is not commonly understood and no (reliable) English translation exists? Moreover, the bare words of the law may not always be sufficient to fully grasp the methods and practices actually applied by the NCA in question even where these conform precisely with the legal rules. The study of the relevant administrative practice and case law may also be necessary.[53] However, an NCA can hardly be expected to obtain advice from an outside counsel or independent institute specialised in comparative law in order to

---

[51] Dekeyser and Dalheimer, above n 9, 12.

[52] See W Weiß, 'Grundrechtsschutz im EG-Kartellrecht nach der Verfahrensnovelle' (2006) *Europäische Zeitschrift für Wirtschaftsrecht* 263, 267–8. In Germany, for instance, the competition investigation is assimilated to a criminal procedure where the BKartA intends to impose a fine *(Bußgeldverfahren)*. However, the BKartA can also conduct a simple administrative procedure *(reines Verwaltungsverfahren)* in which criminal law guarantees are not applicable. See R Bechtold, *Kartellgesetz (Kommentar)* (Munich, Verlag CH Beck, 3rd edn, 2002), Vorbemerkung § 54 no 1 and § 59 no 2. Similarly, in Community law a distinction could be made between proceedings initiated by the Commission with a view to establishing an infringement and imposing a fine pursuant to Art 23(2) of Reg 1/2003 and other types of procedures, such as those aiming at the withdrawal of the benefit of block exemption (Art 29(1) of Reg 1/2003) or relating to sectoral inquiries (Art 17 of Reg 1/2003). In the UK, the OFT has different types of inspection procedures at its disposal (which require different forms of authorisation). See P Collins, 'Some Background Notes on the Investigative Powers of the Competition Authorities', paper for the 2006 EU Competition Law and Policy Workshop, European University Institute/RSCAS, Florence, available at www.eui.eu/RSCAS/research/Competition/2006(pdf)/200610-COMPed-Collins.pdf (accessed January 2009), 1, 3.

[53] See above n 45 and accompanying text.

ascertain the applicable procedural rules in the Member State of the transmitting NCA.

The second hurdle is the need to compare and evaluate the laws of the receiving and transmitting NCAs and to make an appraisal as to whether the level of protection guaranteed in both systems can be considered to be the same. This is probably an even thornier problem than the first. Regulation 1/2003 does not contain a definition or explanation of the term 'same level of protection'. The Network Notice also provides no guidance in this respect, even though it deals extensively with the exchange of confidential information pursuant to Article 12 of Regulation 1/2003.[54] It may be true that, due to the need to respect the rights of defence, ie the fairness of the procedure as guaranteed by Article 6 ECHR, which all 27 Member States have to respect, the rules and solutions applied by all NCAs are very similar and the 'variations, if any, are not of such a nature to impede the correct functioning of the . . . network'.[55] However, to conclude that the level of protection of the rights of defence is therefore essentially identical in all Member States would not only be overhasty and perfunctory, but would also deprive the second indent of Article 12(3) of Regulation 1/2003 of any significant meaning.

For instance, under German law, violations of the competition rules cannot be punished with criminal charges (except for bid rigging) as they merely constitute regulatory offences (*Ordnungswidrigkeiten*). Nonetheless, where the BKartA investigates a matter with the purpose of imposing a fine (so-called *Bußgeldverfahren*) it is bound by the German code of criminal procedure (Strafprozessordnung—StPO) and the suspect essentially enjoys the same rights as a person facing criminal charges.[56] However, whether this would be sufficient to consider that the level of protection of the rights of defence under German law is the same as under the laws of Member States such as the UK or Ireland, where individuals face criminal (custodial) sanctions for the breach of competition rules, is doubtful. In reality, procedural rules are far more complex than they may appear at first sight, and the devil often is in the details. Even where Article 6 ECHR defines certain requirements, possible solutions can be so diversified[57] that it is hardly possible to provide an exhaustive list. Moreover, Article 6 ECHR only establishes a common minimum standard. Procedural rules may in fact be different, for instance, with regard to the following issues:

- requirement of and conditions for obtaining prior judicial

---

[54] Paras 26–28 of the Network Notice.

[55] L Idot, 'A Necessary Step Towards Common Procedural Standards of Implementation for Articles 81 & 82 EC without the Network' in Ehlermann and Atanasiu, above n 8, 211, 215.

[56] See § 46(1) *Ordnungswidrigkeitengesetz* (law on regulatory offences) (OWiG). See also Bechtold, above n 52, § 59 no 2.

[57] See below n 332 and accompanying text.

authorisation for inspections, which, moreover, may vary depending on whether the search concerns business or non-business premises;

- right of parties to consult a lawyer of their choice and duty of the authority to conduct searches and/or interrogations only in the presence of a lawyer;
- supervision of the investigation by a prosecutor, the scope of his responsibility and the duty to take into account inculpatory and exculpatory evidence;
- use of language in the procedure and the right to (free) interpretation;
- methods of questioning, presence of a judge during interrogation of suspects, power to interrogate third parties;
- right to (free) legal assistance;
- timing and scope of access to the file;
- applicability (to legal persons) and scope of the privilege against self-incrimination;
- duty of co-operation of persons other than the suspect; right for such persons to refuse to give evidence (eg family members of the suspect).

The above non-exhaustive list of examples shows that a large number of very detailed rules have to be evaluated. Identical rules will seldom be found. This raises the question of how similar procedural rules must be to justify the conclusion that they offer equivalent rights of defence for the suspect and thus provide the same level of protection. Such an evaluation is particularly difficult to make where the rights of third parties, ie persons other than the suspect, are at issue, which—albeit indirectly—also benefit the suspect.[58] For example, is it a material difference if business premises can be inspected without prior judicial authorisation during normal business hours in the Member State where the evidence originates while, in the Member State of the receiving NCA, a search warrant is always required? Sometimes, differences between national rules will be fairly subtle, which means that they are not easy to detect and are difficult to appraise even where they all serve the same purpose, namely to preserve the fairness of the procedure.[59]

---

[58] See above n 49. The privilege is also known as the principle *nemo tenetur prodere seipsum*.

[59] Academic discussions, within the legal order of a Member State, regarding the applicable provision or its exact scope may add to these problems. Under German law, for instance, it is unclear whether the inspection of business premises must be conducted in accordance with Art 102 StPO, which defines the requirements for searching the dwellings of the accused, or Art 103 StPO, which determines the conditions under which third-party premises may be searched. However, there are considerable differences between the thresholds imposed by both provisions. See P Meyer and S Kuhn, 'Befugnisse und Grenzen kartellrechtlicher Durchsuchungen nach VO Nr 1/2003 und nationalem Recht' (2004) 54 *Wirtschaft und Wettbewerb* 880, 883–4. Similarly, there is some debate about the question of whether the company under investigation may request that the search be conducted in the presence of its legal counsel. *Idem*, 887.

The Privilege against Self-incrimination and the Requirement of Equivalence of Protection. Potential difficulties in establishing the exact (foreign) rules and evaluating their equivalence can be illustrated, for instance, by the privilege against self-incrimination, one of the basic elements of the rights of defence and a fundamental principle of the fair trial guarantee enshrined in Article 6 ECHR,[60] which applies at least in those Member States where violation of the competition rules can result in criminal sanctions.[61]

The question of equivalence of this privilege becomes particularly relevant where an NCA seeks to use against an individual information that has been collected by the Commission. Since the Commission does not have the power to impose (criminal) sanctions on natural persons and does not therefore grant individuals an absolute right to remain silent,[62] it has been suggested that evidence stemming from the Commission can never be used against individuals.[63] This consideration is probably based

---

[60] See above n 31.

[61] Criminal sanctions, albeit in different shades, for a breach of Community competition law are currently provided for by the domestic rules of Ireland, the UK, Estonia (in all three cases including fines for individuals and imprisonment); France, Cyprus, Slovak Republic (while the applicable sanctions in these three countries are mainly non-criminal fines on companies, imprisonment is exceptionally possible); Denmark, Malta (in both, only financial penalties for undertakings, which are, however, of a criminal nature); Greece (criminal fines for individuals); and Germany and Austria (imprisonment specifically only for bid-rigging). See Wils, above n 42, 130. On the more general question of whether competition law proceedings which are not formally part of the criminal law sphere but at the end of which severe sanctions may be imposed qualify as criminal proceedings within the meaning of Art 6 ECHR, see below Chapter 6, section I.A.1.b.

[62] The ECJ already held in *Orkem* that the Community competition rules (at that time Reg 17) do not expressively provide for a right to remain silent. Judgment of the ECJ in Case 374/87 *Orkem v Commission* [1989] ECR 3283, paras 27–8. See also above n 35. Under the Community law procedure, companies are hence only protected against direct self-incrimination. In para 30 of the judgment in *Orkem*, the ECJ even went as far as to state that neither the wording of Art 6 ECHR nor the decisions of the ECtHR indicates that the provision upholds the right not to give evidence against oneself. This dictum of the ECJ has obviously been 'overridden' by the judgment of the ECtHR in *Funke* (above n 33) and particularly *Saunders* (above n 31). Another question, of course, is whether undertakings, ie corporate bodies, can avail themselves at all of the privilege under Art 6 ECHR. While some authors contend that there is no case law indicating that Art 6 ECHR would embody an equally broad right of silence for legal persons (W Wils, 'The EU Network of Competition Authorities, the European Convention on Human Rights and the Charter of Fundamental Rights of the EU' in Ehlermann and Atanasiu, above n 8, 433, 455), others submit that the case law of the Strasbourg institutions makes no difference between natural and legal persons. The privilege would hence also be applicable to undertakings. See Willis, above n 35, 315 note 9; G Stessens, 'The Obligation to Produce Documents versus the Privilege against Self-incrimination: Human Rights Protection Extended Too Far?' (1997) 22 *EL Rev* HRC 45, 61. In any event, the ECJ itself has also held that, as a matter of principle, Art 6 ECHR 'may be relied upon by an undertaking' in competition law proceedings (para 30 of the judgment in *Orkem*). Yet the EU courts at Luxembourg have apparently not seen any reason to revise their case law in the light of the ECtHR's interpretation of Art 6 ECHR, but instead have, by and large, circumvented the ECHR issue. See further below n 76.

[63] Swaak and Mollica, above n 13, 41. See also W Wils, *Principles of European Antitrust Enforcement* (Oxford, Hart Publishing, 2005), para 519.

on the assumption that national laws providing sanctions for individuals must in any event also provide the procedural guarantees of Article 6 ECHR irrespective of the qualification of the sanction under national law; in other words, even where the sanction is considered to be purely administrative, Article 6 ECHR would require the NCAs concerned to grant natural persons the right to remain silent.[64] Hence, NCAs would principally be precluded from using against individuals information collected by the Commission. It should be noted, though, that the exact scope of this privilege, which has been the object of a number of decisions of both the Community courts and the ECtHR, has not yet been defined precisely.[65]

On the one hand, it is relatively clear that Community law currently does not recognise a right to silence in competition proceedings. On the contrary, parties under investigation can be compelled to produce documents and disclose certain factual information even if this information will later be used to establish that they have used unlawful conduct. Only answers to directly incriminating (so-called 'leading') questions, ie answers that would involve the confession of an infringement on the part of the undertaking concerned, can be declined.[66] On this basis, Community law seems to afford significantly less protection than Article 6 ECHR, which, according to the case law of the ECtHR, includes the right to remain silent, ie the right to decline answering 'leading' and 'factual' questions.[67] At the same time, it is settled case law that fundamental rights form an integral part of the general principles of Community law the observance of which the Community courts have to ensure, and the rights guaranteed by the ECHR have special significance in this respect.[68] This raises the question of

---

[64] See above n 33.

[65] On the historical background of this 'first order principle', see M O'Boyle, 'Freedom from Self-incrimination and the Right to Silence: a Pandora's Box?' in P Mahoney, F Matscher, H Petzold and L Wildhaber (eds), *Protection des droits de l'homme: la perspective européenne/ Protecting Human Rights: The European Perspective. Mélanges à la memoire de/Studies in memory of Rolv Ryssdal* (Köln, Carl Heymanns Verlag, 2000), 1021, 1021–2.

[66] Paras 35 of the judgment of the ECJ in *Orkem* (above n 62) and paras 65–7 of the judgment of the CFI in *Mannesmannröhren-Werke* (above n 35). Since a company can only act through its employees and agents, the right to decline answers to certain questions must in practice be conferred upon the individuals making statements on behalf of the company. See Willis, above n 35, 315 note 9. However, the privilege can only be claimed to the extent that the answers would (directly) incriminate the company under investigation, not the individual that is being questioned.

[67] Van Gerven, above n 29, 344. See further above n 31.

[68] The first time that the ECJ stated that fundamental rights form part of the general principles of law protected by the court (albeit, at the time, without explicit reference to the ECHR) was in its judgment in Case 11/70 *Internationale Handelsgesellschaft v Einfuhr- und Vorratsstelle für Getreide* ([1970] ECR 1125, para 4). In safeguarding these rights, the Luxembourg courts draw inspiration from the constitutional traditions common to the Member States. International treaties for the protection of human rights on which the Member States have collaborated or of which they are signatories equally provide guidelines (see Case 4/73 *Nold v Commission* [1974]

whether the approach taken by the Community courts is at all compatible with the requirements of EU law, not to mention the spirit of the ECHR.[69] Arguably, this case law will have to be revised.[70]

ECR 491, para 13). In this respect, the ECHR evidently is of particular significance. For an overview of the development of the ECJ's jurisprudence on the protection of fundamental rights as general principles of Community law and the relevance attributed in this context to the ECHR, see J-P Puissochet, 'La Cour européenne des droits de l'homme, la Cour de justice des Communautés européennes et la protection des droits de l'homme' in Mahoney *et al*, above n 65, 1139, 1140–3.

[69] The case law of the CFI is based, inter alia, on the consideration that the ECHR, while being of particular significance for the general principles of Community law, cannot be relied upon directly before the Community courts because the EU is not a signatory of the ECHR. See paras 59–60 of the judgment CFI in *Mannesmannröhren-Werke* (above n 35). Hence, the CFI does not recognise the scope and meaning of the guarantees of Art 6 ECHR as interpreted by the ECtHR, but instead gives preference to its own interpretation of that provision. This position appears not only incompatible with the spirit of the ECHR (see K Lenaerts and E De Smijter, 'A "Bill of Rights" for the European Union' (2001) 38 *CML Rev* 273, 296 and below n 70), but also seems to contradict the findings of the ECJ in *Orkem* (above n 62), where it was held that Art 6 ECHR '. . . may be relied upon by an undertaking subject to an investigation relating to competition law.' Willis, above n 35, 319. For a critical analysis questioning the compatibility of the current system with Art 6 ECHR, see also G Hogan, 'The Use of Compelled Evidence in European Competition Law Cases' in B Hawk (ed), *2004 Proceedings of the Fordham Corporate Law Institute* (New York, Juris Publishing, 2005), 659.

[70] Weiß, above n 52, 265, who points out that a revision of this case law is particularly required since the Commission's investigative powers have even been broadened by Reg 1/2003. See also B Vesterdorf, 'Legal Professional Privilege and the Privilege against Self-incrimination: Recent Developments and Current Issues' in B Hawk (ed), *2004 Proceedings of the Fordham Corporate Law Institute* (New York, Juris Publishing, 2005), 701, 730, who seems to take a similar position. Moreover, Art 27(2) of Reg 1/2003 explicitly states that the defence rights of the parties shall be fully respected in proceedings before the Commission. Apart from these circumstances, the arguments of the CFI in *Mannesmannröhren-Werke* are all the more questionable since Art 6(2) of the Treaty on European Union (TEU) explicitly states that the EU shall respect the fundamental rights 'as guaranteed by' the ECHR, which would include the interpretation given to them by the ECtHR. See Lenaerts and De Smijter, above n 69, 296, who submit that, since the ECtHR interprets the guarantees of the ECHR *ex tunc*, the case law of the ECtHR forms an integral part of the meaning and scope of these guarantees. The ECJ and the CFI would thus be obliged to take over the interpretations of the ECtHR. In the same vein, Van Gerven, above n 29, 344, postulates that 'it is probably time to openly acknowledge that the ECJ must respect the case law of the Strasbourg Court'. See also Overbeek, above n 32, 132, who would find it 'most peculiar' if the ECJ was to have a different view of fundamental rights than the ECtHR 'which was specifically called into being with the aim of interpreting' these guarantees. The ECJ itself seems to refer to the actual status, within the Community legal order, of the Strasbourg case law only at rare occasions (see S Douglas-Scott, 'A Tale of Two Courts: Luxemburg, Strasbourg and the Growing Human Rights Acquis' (2006) 43 *CML Rev* 629, 649), for instance, at para 29 of the judgment in Case C–94/00 *Roquette Frères* [2002] ECR 9011, where it noted that '[f]or the purposes of determining the scope of that . . ., regard must be had to the case-law of the European Court of Human Rights subsequent to the judgment in Hoechst'. In general, the ECJ seems however to reserve the possibility of giving its own diverging interpretation of HR Convention rights. In my view, it is not only peculiar, but both legally and politically unacceptable, that the Luxembourg courts adopt interpretations of fundamental rights guaranteed by the ECHR which depart from the interpretations of such rights given by the ECtHR. Indeed, the validity of Lenaert's and De Smijter's argument appears to have been confirmed by the CFI in a recent judgment regarding, inter alia, the question of whether, in cartel matters, the presumption of innocence—presumption emanating from Art 6(2) ECHR—must be taken into account (see judgment of 8 July 2004 in Joined Cases T–67/00, T–68/00, T–71/00 and T–78/00 *JFE Engineering and others v Commission* [2004] ECR II–2501). Referring in particular

On the other hand, as a matter of Convention law, the precise extent of the privilege against self-incrimination[71] is not entirely clear.[72] The interpretations of this privilege given by the ECtHR in *Funke* and *Saunders* seem to be diverging. In *Funke*, the ECtHR ruled that a suspect cannot be compelled to procure documents which the authorities believe must exist albeit without being certain, ie the suspect may not be pressed to provide evidence of offences which he allegedly committed as he would thus be forced to contribute to his own incrimination.[73] It seems to follow from this decision that, under Article 6 ECHR, a person is not only entitled to refuse the provision of directly incriminating information, but may also

to the judgments of the ECtHR in *Öztürk* (above n 33) and *Lutz* (Judgment of the ECtHR of 25 August 1987 in the case of Lutz Publication Series A vol 123, 4), the CFI ruled that '[g]iven the nature of the infringements in question and the nature and degree of severity of the ensuing penalties, the principle of the presumption of innocence applies in particular to the procedures relating to infringements of the competition rules applicable to undertakings that may result in the imposition of fines or periodic penalty payments' (see para 178 of the judgment in *JFE Engineering*). Furthermore, recital 37 of Reg 1/2003 refers expressly to the ECHR. Finally, as mentioned, Art 52(3) of the EU Charter provides that those rights of the EU Charter which correspond to rights of the ECHR must be understood to have the same scope and meaning as under the ECHR. Indeed, Arts 47(2) and 48 of the EU Charter correspond to Art 6 ECHR. The fair trial guarantee of Art 47(2) of the EU Charter provides even wider protection. See P Lemmens, 'The Relation between the Charter of Fundamental Rights of the European Union and the European Convention on Human Rights—Substantive Aspects' (2001) 8 *Maastricht Journal of European and Comparative Law* 49, 65–6. Certainly, the normative value of the EU Charter, which neither forms part of the Treaties nor constitutes an act of secondary legislation but is a 'solemn proclamation' of three Community institutions, is still doubtful. In practice, however, it is likely, over time, to have legal effects similar to the EC Treaty provisions. Lenaerts and De Smijter, above n 69, 298. See also B De Witte, 'The Legal Status of the Charter: Vital Question or Non-Issue?' (2001) 8 *Maastricht Journal of European and Comparative Law* 81, 86, who suggests that the question of the legal force of the EU Charter might become a non-issue to the extent that the Charter rights will be recognised as constituents of the general principles of Community law. (NB: As yet there seems to be no case law of the ECJ relying directly on the EU Charter. W Wils, 'Powers of Investigation and Procedural Rights and Guarantees in EU Antitrust Enforcement: The Interplay between European and National Legislation and Case-law', (2006) 29 *World Competition* 3, 18. See also A Riley, 'The ECHR Implications of the Investigation Provisions of the Draft Competition Regulation' (2002) 51 *ICLQ* 55, 87 note 152a, who states that so far the EU Charter has been referred to in a single judgment of the CFI only, but, at the same time, points to the potential of the EU Charter to influence existing rights.) Art 52(3) of the EU Charter and Art 6(2) TEU could (and should) therefore prompt the CFI and the ECJ to reconsider their jurisprudence. See Willis, above n 35, 319 note 32. See also below n 76, in particular, the reference to Vesterdorf (*idem*).

[71] The relation between the right to silence and the privilege against self-incrimination is not determined uniformly. See O'Boyle, above n 65, 1023. In the present document, the term 'privilege against self-incrimination' is used to describe the general concept, ie the freedom from being compelled to contribute to one's own conviction, which may or not encompass the right to remain silent. The latter right is thus regarded as the narrower notion, as a possible element of the privilege against self-incrimination, a privilege which (also) includes other aspects.

[72] O Einarsson, 'EC Competition Law and the Right to a Fair Trial' (2006) 25 *Yearbook of European Law* 555, 563, noting that 'with regard to the right to silence things are by no means clear', including the question to what extent corporate entities can avail themselves of this right.

[73] Para 44 of the judgment of the ECtHR in *Funke* (above n 33). The case concerned an investigation by the French customs authorities, which can require a suspect not only to provide information but also to produce documents.

decline the submission of purely factual information and documents since the latter might be used to prove the case against him.[74] In *Saunders*, however, the ECtHR held that the right not to incriminate oneself is primarily concerned with respecting the will of a suspect to remain silent. The ECtHR therefore distinguished between material obtained through the use of compulsory powers, which exists independently of the will of the suspect (eg documents acquired pursuant to a warrant, blood and urine samples), and documents obtained through methods of coercion (eg transcripts of interviews, testimonial declarations and other written statements). Only the latter category would fall within the privilege.[75] On this basis, *Saunders* would be narrower than *Funke* as it does not acknowledge an absolute right to withhold incriminating documents.[76] Moreover, as yet

[74] Willis, above n 35, 315. This reading seems to have been confirmed, at least partly, by *Saunders* (above n 31), where the ECtHR noted that testimony 'which appears on its face to be of a non-incriminating nature' might later be used by the prosecution in support of its case, eg by using it to contradict other statements of the accused. Therefore, the privilege against self-incrimination could not be limited to plain admissions of wrongdoing or directly incriminating remarks. At the same time, the ECtHR emphasised that it is for the prosecution to prove their case against the accused without compelling the accused to contribute to his conviction. On this basis, the privilege is closely connected with the presumption of innocence. See paras 71 and 68 of the judgment in *Saunders* (above n 31). Regarding the interpretation of *Funke* (above n 33), see also Stessens, above n 62, HRC 55–6. Stessens points out that the ruling in *Funke* must be seen in the light of the fact that the French authorities had requested the production of documents without being certain of their existence, and concludes that *Funke* (above n 33) does not support the view that every compulsory production of incriminating documents infringes the privilege against self-incrimination. He submits that *Funke* must rather be understood as a prohibition of 'fishing expeditions'.

[75] Para 69 of the judgment of the ECtHR in *Saunders* (above n 31). Mr Saunders had been interviewed several times during a non-judicial investigation conducted by inspectors of the Department of Trade and Industry ('DTI'). Answering the questions put to him by the DTI inspectors was compulsory and the refusal to do so was subject to severe punishment (fines and imprisonment). The ECtHR held that the use of transcripts of these interviews in the subsequent criminal proceedings against Mr Saunders violated the right not to incriminate oneself.

[76] See J Venit and T Louko, 'The Commission's New Power to Question and its Implications on Human Rights' in B Hawk (ed), *2004 Proceedings of the Fordham Corporate Law Institute* (New York, Juris Publishing, 2005), 675, 695; A Riley, 'Saunders and the Power to Obtain Information in Community and United Kingdom Competition Law' (2000) 25 *EL Rev* 264, 275. *Saunders* (above n 31) is, however, wider than *Orkem* (above n 62). Willis, above n 35, 316. The ECtHR, in *Saunders*, namely recognised that the privilege against self-incrimination is not confined to directly incriminating answers, but also applies to mere information on questions of facts and even to seemingly exculpatory remarks, since such testimony might later be used in support of the case of the prosecution, eg by citing them to contradict other statements of the accused or to otherwise undermine his credibility. See para 71 of the judgment in *Saunders* (above n 31); see also above n 74. Yet in *PVC II*, a judgment delivered after the ECtHR had handed down its decisions in *Funke* (above n 33) and *Saunders*, the CFI was completely silent on the Art 6 ECHR issue. It neither examined the scope of the guarantee nor discussed the question of whether or not the provision could be invoked in competition cases before the Community courts (in particular in the light of the *Öztürk* case). The CFI simply stated that the recognition of an absolute right of silence would constitute an undue hindrance to the Commission in the fulfilment of its task of enforcing the competition rules. See para 448 of the judgment of the CFI in *PVC II* (Joint Cases T–305–7, 313–16, 318, 325, 328, 329/94 and 335/94 *Limburgse Vinyl Maatschappij and others v Commission* [1999] ECR II–931). The position of the CFI is all the more disputable since the ECtHR, in *Saunders*, explicitly rejected the argument that the

it has not expressly been ruled by the ECtHR that the privilege applies equally to natural and legal persons, although it seems unlikely, on the basis of existing case law of the ECtHR applying the fair trial guarantee of Article 6 ECHR also to corporate entities, that the court would deny legal persons protection altogether under the privilege against self-incrimination.[77]

Yet another question is as of when a person can benefit from protection under Article 6 ECHR, ie from which stage of a competition law procedure (investigation, prosecution, trial) can the privilege against self-incrimination be invoked. According to its wording, Article 6 ECHR begins to apply as soon as a person is 'charged' with a criminal offence. The case law of the ECtHR at first sight seems to suggest that the privilege could only be relied upon after the Commission's statement of objections or a similar document of an NCA setting out the accusations has been served upon the party concerned.[78] In *Deweer*, the ECtHR notably defined the term 'charge' as the '*official notification* given to an individual by the competent authority of an allegation.'[79] More generally, it results from the case law of the ECtHR that the point at which Article 6 ECHR begins to apply may not be an uncertain, vaguely defined moment, but must rather be clearly marked by some sort of formal occurrence.[80]

complexity of an offence and the vital public interest in the investigation of such offences and the punishment of persons responsible could justify 'a marked departure . . . from one of the basic principles of a fair procedure' (see para 74 of the judgment in *Saunders*, above n 31). Similar arguments had already been deployed by the ECtHR in *Funke*, where it was held that the special features of customs law could not justify an infringement of the privilege against self-incrimination (para 44 of the judgment, above n 33). On the evasion manœuvre of the CFI in *PVC II*, see Willis, above n 35, 317. On the difficulties to reconcile *PVC II* with the *Saunders* judgment, see also I Forrester, 'Modernisation of EC Competition Law' in B Hawk (ed), *1999 Proceedings of the Fordham Corporate Law Institute* (New York, Juris Publishing, 2000), 181, 226. B Vesterdorf, above n 70, 716, however, notes that the ECJ, on appeal in the *PVC II* case, took a much more conciliatory position than the CFI, emphasising the relevance of the case law of the ECtHR for the interpretation of the guarantees enshrined in the ECHR. Vesterdorf even observes a general trend of the EU courts to base themselves increasingly on the case law of the ECtHR. Indeed, the ECJ, in *PVC II*, seemed to have endorsed the parties' argument that 'since *Orkem*, there have been further developments in the case-law of the European Court of Human Rights which the Community judicature must take into account when interpreting fundamental rights'. However, since there was no element of coercion present, this could not, in the view of the ECJ, lead to a different outcome in the case at hand. See paras 274–80 of the judgment in Joined Cases C–238, 244, 245, 247, 250–2 and 254/99 P *Limburgse Vinyl Maatschappij and others v Commission* ('*PVC II*') [2002] ECR I–8375. Nonetheless, in Case C–301/04 P *Commission v SGL Carbon* [2006] ECR I–5915, the ECJ once again confirmed its earlier jurisprudence reinforcing the idea that, after all, *Orkem* (above n 62) remains good law (paras 33–50, in particular 40–3). Van Gerven, above n 29, 346.

[77] See Einarsson, above n 72, 563 and 582. In fact, the ECtHR has even accepted to afford corporations the protection by fundamental rights the intrinsic nature of which would seem to exclude their application to legal persons. See below n 260 and accompanying text.

[78] Riley, above n 76, 270 note 45.

[79] Emphasis added. Para 46 of the judgment in *Deweer* (above n 33).

[80] For instance the issue of an order to close the business premises of a merchant (paras 9 and 46 of the judgment in *Deweer*, above n 33); the service of a warrant (judgment of 15 July 1982

On the other hand, the ECtHR has also ruled that the applicability of Article 6 ECHR does not depend on the formal institution of criminal proceedings which would give the person concerned the official status of *accusé*. The provision namely aims at protecting a person throughout the entire process and may well therefore be applicable at the pre-trial stage. As a consequence, the moment from which Article 6 ECHR becomes relevant must be determined not merely on the basis of formal criteria, but by using a substantive test.[81] One should also consider that the HR Court has mostly discussed this issue with a view to establishing whether the 'reasonable time' limit stipulated by Article 6(1) ECHR had been exceeded, ie from quite a different angle than the one considered here.[82] It can therefore be argued that, in competition proceedings, the privilege must be observed from the moment when the investigatory procedure is started, which can be long before the issue of the statement of objections.[83] On this basis, the relevant moment would be marked by the communication of the (formal) decision ordering an inspection or requesting information from certain undertakings in relation to a suspected infringement or even by the sending of an informal information request, as such acts imply an allegation, albeit yet unproven, that a violation has been committed.[84] Even a warning letter, which the ECJ

in the case of *Eckle v Germany* Publications Series A no 51, para 75); the request to lift parliamentary immunity (judgment of 19 February 1991 *Frau v Italy* Publications Series A no 195, para 14). See also para 74 of the judgment in *Eckle*, where the Court of Human Rights rejected the applicant's argument that the relevant moment was the date on which a complaint had been lodged against him because 'the complaint . . . did not lead to any formal measures of inquiry being ordered'. Cf further para 46 of the judgment in *Deweer* (above n 33), where the ECtHR generally defined the term 'charge' employed by Art 6(1) ECHR as 'the official notification given to an individual of an allegation that he has committed a criminal offence'.

[81] Paras 42–4 of the judgment of the ECtHR in *Deweer* (above n 33). In that case, the Court of Human Rights held that Art 6(1) ECHR applied from the moment that the applicant was faced with what the ECtHR called 'a prelude' to criminal proceedings. *Idem*, para 45.

[82] See D Harris, M O'Boyle and C Warbrick, *Law of the European Convention on Human Rights* (London, Butterworths, 1995), 171. Besides, the Court of Human Rights has looked at this issue very much on a case-by-case basis, which makes it difficult to draw any general conclusions from its jurisprudence.

[83] Para 109 of the opinion of Advocate General J Kokott in Case C–105/04 P *FEG and TU v Commission* [2006] ECR I–8725. Admittedly, her considerations also concern a case where the expiration of the reasonable period was at issue; however, they show how the case law of the ECtHR regarding the term 'charge' can be applied to EC competition matters. See also Overbeek, above n 32, 130. Overbeek bases his view essentially on the *Deweer* case. However, in *Saunders*, the ECtHR held that Art 6 ECHR was not applicable to the preparatory investigations which were carried out by tax inspectors and the results of which might later be used by other authorities (see para 67 of the judgment in *Saunders*, above n 31). Nonetheless, Overbeek's position seems sustainable as the ECtHR's approach is likely to be different where the investigative and the adjudicative functions are performed by the same authority, as in the case of the Commission, or where the preparatory investigation is immediately and specifically directed at the subsequent prosecution and conviction, albeit by another body. In such cases, Art 6 may be applied to the pre-trial stage. Cf Riley, above n 76, 274–5.

[84] See para 110 of the opinion of Advocate General J Kokott in *FEG* (above n 83). According to the Advocate General, a request for information addressed to the company under

regards as an investigative measure,[85] could be considered to imply an accusation and thus trigger the application of Article 6 ECHR.[86]

It follows from the above that, in many cases, differences between national laws regarding the privilege against self-incrimination may in fact simply reflect different interpretations of one and the same provision, namely Article 6 ECHR.[87] In such situations, not permitting the use of exchanged evidence against an individual seems unjustified since both systems, in spite of their apparent differences, aim at guaranteeing the fairness of the procedure as required by Article 6 ECHR. On the other hand, considering the divergencies between *Saunders* and *Funke*, it may be difficult to argue that both systems effectively provide the same level of protection and that the use against individuals, by one NCA, of evidence that was gathered by another NCA is not contrary to the second indent of Article 12(3) of Regulation 1/2003. Finally, an evaluation may be difficult to make because the legal situation in one of the relevant Member States is unclear, leading to uncertainty as to the applicable standard of comparison.[88]

investigation is comparable to an initial questioning of a suspect, and an inspection of the company's premises is comparable to a search of the suspect's dwelling.

[85] See para 49 of the judgment in *FEG and TU* (above n 83). A warning letter consequently forms the beginning of (the first stage of) a Commission procedure under Reg 17 or 1/2003. See further above nn 80 and 83.

[86] By contrast, the Community courts seem to consider Art 6 ECHR plainly inapplicable during the entire phase of the administrative procedure before the Commission merely because the Commission is not a 'tribunal' within the meaning of that article. (NB: Art 6 ECHR 'only' gives right to 'a fair and public hearing . . . by an independent and impartial *tribunal*'.) See F Zampini, 'Convention européenne des droits de l'homme et droit communautaire de la concurrence (1999) *Revue du Marché commun et de l'Union européenne* 628, 636 and 646, who does obviously not question this view. However, the position is hardly compatible with the spirit of the HR Convention. The very fact that the Commission does not qualify as a 'tribunal' within the meaning of Art 6 ECHR does not exclude the applicability of that provision, but rather raises the question of whether companies should not be given the opportunity to have their case heard and decided by a true tribunal. D Waelbroeck and D Fosselard, 'Should the Decision-making Power in EC Antitrust Procedures be Left to an Independent Judge?—The Impact of the European Convention on Human Rights on EC Antitrust Procedures' (1994) 14 *Yearbook of European Law* 111, 116. Whether the review of Commission decisions in antitrust matters by the CFI can remedy any deficiencies, in terms of Art 6 ECHR, of the earlier proceedings before the Commission is disputable. *Pro* Zampini, *ibid*, 641–3; *contra* Waelbroeck and Fosselard, *ibid*, 133. The issue here is whether the CFI has the requisite power, ie full jurisdiction. See further below Chapter 5, section III.B.2.

[87] Cf D Waelbroeck, '"Twelve Feet All Dangling Down and Six Necks Exceeding Long." The EU Network of Competition Authorities and the European Convention on Fundamental Rights' in Ehlermann and Atanasiu, above n 8, 465, 474–5. They do not necessarily reveal violations of the principles enshrined in the ECHR. See E Ameye, 'The Interplay between Human Rights and Competition Law in the EU' (2004) 25 *European Competition Law Review* 332, 338, referring to the Commission's Green Paper of 19 February 2003 on procedural safeguards for suspects and defendants in criminal proceedings throughout the European Union (COM(2003) 75 final). See also below n 286.

[88] Such an uncertainty can be illustrated by the position, under German law, regarding the protection of legal persons against self-incrimination. It is undisputed that, in criminal proceedings, an accused is not required to actively co-operate in a search, but only has to tolerate

Conclusion. Distilling all of the above, it is submitted, the NCA will have to make a value judgment. However, can we expect the receiving NCA, which has requested the assistance of the transmitting NCA and presumably needs the relevant evidence to prove its case, to make a fair judgment?

The application of the second indent of Article 12(3) of Regulation 1/2003 is also likely to raise enormous practical difficulties which may turn out to be almost insurmountable obstacles for the receiving NCA on which it is incumbent to verify whether the equivalence requirement is met prior to using against a natural person evidence that it has obtained from another NCA whose laws do not allow similar kinds of sanctions against individuals. At the least, the difficulties might discourage NCAs to have recourse to the second indent of Article 12(3) of Regulation 1/2003. On this basis, it seems unlikely that this provision will play an important role in practice.

C. Protection of Confidential Information

Establishing the right of Network members to share confidential information constitutes an unprecedented step. The national laws of most Member States prohibited NCAs from divulging confidential data to their counterparts in other Member States. Only few national authorities (eg the NMa and the Danish competition authority) have been empowered to transmit confidential information to foreign authorities. However, the transmission was usually subject to a number of strict conditions or principles, such as reciprocity and/or sufficient assurance that the receiving NCA would protect the confidentiality of the data.[89] Generally, authorities could exchange confidential information at the international level only if they obtained a voluntary waiver from the undertakings concerned permitting them to depart from their professional secrecy obligation.[90]

The above restrictions show that the protection of confidential infor-

---

it passively (*Duldungspflicht*), and also has an absolute right to remain silent. Since cartel investigations conducted with a view to imposing a fine (*Bußgeldverfahren*) are subject to the *Strafprozesordnung*, as a matter of principle, these rules also apply in competition cases. However, there is much debate about the question of whether legal persons can in fact invoke the right to remain silent, and the case law of the Federal Constitutional Court (Bundesverfassungsgericht) on this issue does not seem to be consistent. Meyer and Kuhn, above n 59, 891–2.

[89] See the examples quoted by Bloom, above n 8, 394–6, and further illustrations of the exchange rules of the Dutch Competition Act by Kist, above n 45, 359–60.

[90] As regards information exchange with authorities beyond the EU, this is still the case. This also applies, for instance, in respect of the co-operation taking place within the ECA or on the basis of bilateral agreements with countries outside Europe. A Burnside and Y Botteman, 'Networking amongst Competition Agencies' (2004) 10 *International Trade Law & Regulation* 1, 3; A Burnside and H Crossley, 'Co-operative Mechanisms within the EU: A Blueprint for Future Co-operation at the International Level' (2004) 10 *International Trade Law & Regulation* 25, 26.

mation is a serious concern. Evidently, the freedom now enjoyed by NCAs may not lead to situations where the protection of confidential information is lost due to the fact that the information has been exchanged and disclosed within the ECN. NCAs and the Commission must be obliged to protect the confidentiality of information obtained through the Network in the same way as if they had gathered it themselves.[91]

1. Legal Standard

The central norm regarding the protection of confidential information is Article 28(2) of Regulation 1/2003, which lays down the professional secrecy obligation. It is, however, not entirely clear what information exactly is covered by that provision.

a. The Obligation of Professional Secrecy

The general obligation of professional secrecy is enshrined in Article 287 (ex Article 214) EC. However, this provision only binds Commission officials and members of other Community institutions. Therefore, Article 28(2) of Regulation 1/2003 extends the professional secrecy obligation to officials and servants of the NCAs, as well as other persons working under their supervision.[92] Moreover, Article 28(2) of Regulation 1/2003 covers not only information collected and transferred by the Commission, but any information 'acquired or exchanged pursuant to this Regulation'. This means that all information circulating in the Network is protected under that provision regardless of whether it has been gathered by the Commission or an NCA.[93]

The wording of Article 28(2) of Regulation 1/2003 is very similar to its predecessor, Article 20(2) of Regulation 17. Under Regulation 17, the professional secrecy obligation was predominantly relevant to the vertical exchange of documents between the Commission and the members of the Advisory Committee, as the Commission was already obliged, under Regulation 17, to provide the Member States with copies of the most important documents it had collected with a view of applying Article 81 or 82 EC. This is still an important aspect of the secrecy obligation.[94] In addition, however, the new provision in Regulation 1/2003 aims

[91] Issues regarding legal professional privilege (sometimes also referred to as attorney–client or lawyer–client privilege) will be discussed further below (see below section II.C.1.a(1)).

[92] Moreover, the provision applies to officials and servants of other authorities of the Member States.

[93] Gauer, above n 18, 11. See also S Martinez Lage and H Brokelmann, 'The Possible Consequences of a Relatively Broad Scope for Exchange of Confidential Information on National Procedural Law and Antitrust Sanctions ' in Ehlermann and Atanasiu, above n 8, 405, 407.

[94] Dekeyser and Dalheimer, above n 9, 13.

equally at protecting information that is exchanged horizontally, ie information emanating from national investigations and being transmitted by an NCA.

It has been noted earlier that 'professional secrecy' is a Community concept, as its notion is based on Article 287 EC.[95] Therefore, it must be interpreted and applied uniformly within the EU. Theoretically, any information which has transited through the Network therefore enjoys the same level of protection throughout the EU. In practice, however, this may be difficult to realise. While providing an abstract common standard, Article 28(2) of Regulation 1/2003 lacks a definition of the type of information or even the categories of documents which actually come within the ambit of the non-disclosure rule. It simply states that information 'of the kind covered by the obligation of professional secrecy' may not be disclosed, but the scope of this concept remains unclear.[96] The exact level of protection therefore ultimately depends on the question of what information is considered as confidential in each of the jurisdictions. It is possible that, in this respect, NCAs and the Commission apply different concepts.[97]

b. Information Covered by the Secrecy Obligation

The question therefore remains of knowing what information is covered by the professional secrecy obligation. The distinction between disclosable and non-disclosable information becomes particularly relevant where an authority has to grant access to a file, since at this moment it must definitely be decided what information may be communicated to persons outside the ECN. Some guidance on the scope of the professional secrecy obligation may be derived from the Commission's Notice on Access to File

---

[95] See above Chapter 3, n 100 and accompanying text. See also Dekeyser and De Smijter, above n 5, 169.

[96] M Van Der Woude, 'Exchange of Information within the European Competition Network: Scope and Limits' in Ehlermann and Atanasiu, above n 8, 369, 374; Burnside and Crossley, above n 90, 30. As Smits, above n 17, 182, notes, the provision has indeed a 'somewhat tautological wording' in that it states that information which is protected under the rule of professional secrecy should be kept secret.

[97] Divergencies may exist, for instance, because national rules on disclosure within the national administration or access of interested parties or the public to documents held by public authorities are different. Cf Van Der Woude, above n 96, 383, Waelbroeck, above n 87, 478, and Kist, above n 45, 358. That the notion of confidentiality is not the same in all Member States is also admitted by Gauer, above n 30, 197. Nevertheless, she argues that the level of protection under Art 28(2) of Reg 1/2003 will be the same throughout the Community. See also Dekeyser and Dalheimer, above n 9, 13, who suggest that, as subsets of the notion of professional secrecy, the terms 'confidential information' and 'business secrets' form part of the common standard defined by Art 28 of Reg 1/2003. This is similar to Bloom, above n 8, 392. But see, on the other hand, the examples provided by Bloom, above n n 8, 395, of certain disclosure rights of national authorities, in particular in the Nordic countries. The Nordic co-operation agreement mentioned by Bloom entails, for instance, the risk that (confidential) information circulating freely in the ECN, may get in the hands of authorities outside the ECN (eg Iceland, Norway).

and the relevant case law of the EU courts. The Notice on Access to File, which relates essentially to the rights of undertakings to whom the Commission has addressed a statement of objections, ie undertakings under investigation,[98] generally distinguishes between accessible and non-accessible documents. Only the latter category is of interest here. There are essentially two different types of non-accessible documents, namely internal documents and documents containing business secrets or other confidential information.[99]

---

[98] Paras 3 and 4 of the Notice on Access to File. Therefore, the principles set out in the Notice are mostly not applicable where third parties (eg complainants) request access to the file. Paras 29–34 of the Notice on Access to File, however, contain a few specific rules for complainants and other involved parties. Generally, the procedural rights of third parties are more limited (see below section I.C.1.c and n 132). On the other hand, complainants may always invoke the right of public access to documents under Reg (EC) No 1049/2001 of the European Parliament and of the Council of 30 May 2001 regarding public access to European Parliament, Council and Commission documents ([2001] OJ L145/43) in order to obtain access to parts of the competition authority's file (see H Gilliams and L Cornelis, 'Private Enforcement of the Competition Rules in Belgium' (2007) 2 *TBM-RCB* 11, para 74; E De Smijter, 'Het Groenboek van de Commissie omtrent schadevorderingen wegens schending van de Europese mededingingsregels' (2007) 2 *TBM-RCB* 3, 6 note 17). It should be noted, though, that Reg 1049/2001 provides for a number of exceptions to the right of public access (see Art 4 of Reg 1049/2001) which seem to be broader than the exceptions laid down in the Notice on Access to File. Obviously, both sets of rules have quite a different finality. While the purpose of Reg 1049/2001 is to grant the public, ie any citizen or resident of the EU, the widest access possible to documents of the EU institutions in accordance with Art 255 EC in order to enhance the transparency of the Community's decision-making, the Notice on Access to File seeks to safeguard the rights of defence of the undertakings under investigation (see para 1 of the Notice). It is thus not surprising that, given the particular importance of the rights of defence, the rules of the Notice on Access to File are more advantageous, as far as the undertakings under investigation are concerned, in that they limit the possible exceptions to business secrets and internal documents. However, Reg 1049/2001 can be understood as guaranteeing the minimum level of openness of the EU institutions. This means that other, possibly more specific, rules on access to documents must be in conformity with Reg 1049/2001 and cannot, in any event, deprive anyone of access rights which he has under Reg 1049/2001, certainly not persons with a particular interest in the matter (cf the judgment of the CFI in Case T–123/99 *JT's Corporation v Commission* [2000] ECR II–3269, para 50 (regarding the former inter-institutional Code of Conduct on public access; see below n 118) and M De Leeuw, 'The Regulation on Public Access to European Parliament, Council and Commission Documents in the European Union: Are Citizens Better Off?' (2003) 28 *EL Rev* 324, 330). It would indeed be awkward if persons could gain access to documents under Reg 1049/2001 even though they may not have any kind of personal interest in knowing those documents, while persons who definitely have a specific (legitimate) interest in inspecting the Commission's file, such as complainants in competition matters, are declined access by the institution on the basis of other provisions. Cf A Leopold, 'Die Kartellbehörden im Angesicht der Informationsfreiheit' (2006) 56 *Wirtschaft und Wettbewerb* 592, 594. Therefore, it is submitted that complainants cannot be refused access to a file on the basis of the Implementing Regulation and/or the Notice on Access to File where such refusal could not also be based on Reg 1049/2001. On the relationship between the general access rules under Reg 1049/2001 (*lex generalis*) and the more specific rules in competition matters (*lex specialis*), see also below n 120.

[99] See paras 12–14 and 17–20 of the Notice on Access to File. See also para 86 of the judgment in Case T–353/94 *Postbank v Commission* [1996] ECR II–921, where the CFI held that the professional secrecy obligation covers both business secrets and (other) confidential information, and the judgment in T–198/03 *Bank Austria Creditanstalt v Commission* [2006] ECR II–1429, para 29.

(1) Business Secrets. Article 287 EC, which enshrines the general confidentiality obligation, refers in particular to 'information about undertakings, their business relations or their cost components'. Considering these examples, the CFI, in *Postbank*, found that the professional secrecy obligation covers information which, by reason of its content, falls within the category of business secrets and continued to describe 'business secrets' as

> information of which not only the disclosure to the public but also the mere transmission to a person other than the one that provided the information may seriously harm the latter's interest.[100]

Paragraph 18 of the Notice on Access to File provides a number of examples of information which, on the basis of the Postbank case, would qualify as business secrets. These examples include information relating to the undertaking's know-how, production secrets and processes, market shares, and customer lists.[101] One could therefore define business secrets as any kind of commercially relevant information the disclosure of which to any person outside the undertaking could harm the interests of that undertaking.[102]

It is, however, important to note that, on the basis of the CFI's findings in *Postbank*, documents can be confidential 'as against' specific individuals or companies if their disclosure just to those individuals or companies would damage the undertaking's interests. This may be the case, for instance, where certain business data could not be communicated to competitors without harm for the relevant undertaking, while disclosing them to customers would not raise particular concerns. Information might also be regarded as non-confidential in relation to defendants, while it is considered inaccessible for complainants.[103] Documents may thus enjoy either relative protection or absolute protection depending on whether only their disclosure to particular persons is barred or whether their release to anyone other than the company which provided the information is

---

[100] Judgment of the CFI in *Postbank* (above n 99), para 87.

[101] The former notice apparently did not take account of the judgment in *Postbank,* which had been handed down only shortly before the Notice was published. Instead, s IA1 of the 1997 Notice on Access to File proclaimed that, while the notion of 'business secrets' had not yet been fully defined, the relevant case law would suggest that the term should be construed in a broad sense.

[102] It goes without saying that (former) business secrets no longer need to be protected if they are in the public domain or if, due to the passage of time, they are no longer commercially important. On this basis, the Commission usually considers information on sales, turnover and market shares that is older than 5 years as no longer being confidential. Para 23 of the Notice on Access to File.

[103] Van Der Woude, above n 96, 375. See also para 29 of the judgment in *Bank Austria* (above n 99), where the CFI draws a distinction between protection afforded (to information covered by the professional secrecy obligation) in relation to persons that have a right to be heard in the context of the proceedings at hand (and thus a right to be granted access to the file) and protection afforded in relation to the general public. See further below section I.C.1.c.

precluded. In both cases, disclosure to the public, ie to persons who are not parties to the procedure (undertakings under investigation or third parties such as complainants or interveners) is, however, generally excluded.[104]

(2) (Other) Confidential Documents. In *Bank Austria*, the CFI held that '[t]he sphere of information covered by the obligation of professional secrecy extends beyond business secrets of undertakings'.[105] This category thus includes confidential information other than business secrets. Confidentiality can be claimed for any kind of sensitive information the disclosure of which could significantly harm the legitimate interests of a person or company.[106] These are in particular private data, such as the names of complainants or informants who wish to remain anonymous, and other information which would make it possible to uncover their identity.[107] Under the 1997 Notice on Access to File, documents which form part of a company's property and for which confidentiality has been claimed were also expressly classified as confidential. The example quoted by the Commission for such proprietary company documents was a market study commissioned by an undertaking.[108] This rule has not been reiterated in the revised notice. Paragraph 11 of the 2005 Notice on Access to File even provides that the results of 'a study commissioned in connection with proceedings' are accessible. However, the provision seems to apply only to studies commissioned by the Commission.[109] Moreover, it acknowledges that precautions may be necessary in view of intellectual property rights. Therefore, it is submitted that a company can still claim confidential treatment for studies, reports or similar documents commissioned by it to the extent that they have been acquired for personal/internal use only and are not publicly available. Like any other request for confidentiality, such a claim must be substantiated.[110]

(3) Internal Documents. Internal documents enjoy protection since they constitute confidential agency information (as opposed to confidential business information).[111] The category of internal documents mostly consists of drafts, memos and opinions. It also includes consultations with

---

[104] For exceptions, see below section I.C.1.c.

[105] Judgment in *Bank Austria* (above n 99), para 29.

[106] See para 19 of the Notice on Access to File and recital 13 of the Implementing Regulation.

[107] See para 19 of the Notice on Access to File and para 34 of the judgment in Case 145/83 *Adams v Commission* [1985] ECR 3539, where the ECJ pointed out that Art 214 (now Art 278) covers not only information stemming from companies, but also information supplied by natural persons and accompanied by a request for confidentiality in order to protect the anonymity of that person. The category of confidential information further includes military secrets (para 20 of the Notice on Access to File).

[108] Section I.A.2 of the 1997 Notice on Access to File.

[109] See para 14 of the Notice on Access to File.

[110] Para 22 of the Notice on Access to File.

[111] Cf Burnside and Botteman, above n 90, 8.

other Commission departments and, more importantly, correspondence with other public authorities concerning the case. Finally, minutes of meetings with individuals or undertakings are considered to be for internal use only unless the person has agreed the minutes.[112] These are all documents which relate to the procedure itself and, by their very nature, cannot be used by the Commission as evidence against the undertaking under investigation.[113] Moreover, the Commission, like other EU institutions, considers it indispensable that its departments and officials can express themselves freely on ongoing matters. Finally, the disclosure of such documents could violate the secrecy of the Commission's deliberations.[114]

On the basis of these considerations, the Commission used to regard the exclusion of internal documents from the category of accessible material as justified.[115] The principle that internal documents, including communications between Network members, are inaccessible has now also been enshrined in the third sentence of Article 27(2) of Regulation 1/2003 and been reiterated in Article 15(2) of the Implementing Regulation. Both provisions further specify that

> [i]n particular, the right of access shall not extend to correspondence between the Commission and the competition authorities of the Member States, or between the latter, including documents drawn up pursuant to Articles 11 and 14.[116]

It also follows from the above that written observations which the Commission forwards to an NCA in relation to a particular case are excluded from the right of access to the file. The third sentence of Article 27(2) of Regulation 1/2003 explicitly refers to documents drawn up in accordance with Article 11 of Regulation 1/2003. Pursuant to Article 11(4) of Regulation 1/2003, an NCA has to inform the Commission of the envisaged course of action prior to taking a final decision. Obviously, where necessary, the Commission will comment on the NCA's proposal either orally or in writing. This follows inter alia from paragraph 46 of the Network Notice, which complements Article 11(4) of Regulation 1/2003

---

[112] This provision probably aims at interviews conducted and recorded by the Commission and with the consent of the interviewee pursuant to Art 19 of Reg 1/2003.

[113] Paras 12 and 15 of the Notice on Access to File.

[114] Cf s I.A.3 of the 1997 Notice on Access to File. The need to protect the effectiveness of the EU institutions' decision-making process by guaranteeing the secrecy of their deliberations, including internal documents drawn up for such deliberations, is also recognised by Reg 1049/2001. See recitals 6, 11 and the 2nd subparagraph of Art 4(3) of Reg 1049/2001. The rationale underlying this exception, from the principle of public access, for internal documents laid down in Art 4(3) of Reg 1049/2001 is the need for a free 'space to think' common to all institutions. F Schram, 'Openbaarheid van Europese bestuursdocumenten' (2003) *Nieuw juridisch weekblad* 582, para 18; De Leeuw, above n 98, 335.

[115] Section I.A.3 of the 1997 Notice on Access to File.

[116] Reg 1/2003, Art 27(2), 4th sentence. The wording of Implementing Regulation, Art 15(2), 2nd sentence is virtually identical.

by providing that the Commission may make written observations before the adoption of the national decision. Such written observations, it is submitted, are documents drawn up pursuant to Article 11 and therefore enjoy the same protection as any other inter-agency correspondence or other internal document.[117]

In principle, the right of Community institutions to refuse disclosure of certain internal documents has been confirmed by the CFI in *Carlsen*. Even though that case concerned access of the public to several documents in the Council's possession, it can still be regarded as recognising more generally the legitimate interest of Community institutions in maintaining the confidentiality of their proceedings and the secrecy of their internal communications. In that case, the President of the CFI found that the disclosure of internal documents, notably written opinions of the Community institutions' legal services, may undermine the protection of the public interest in that it may have a negative effect on the functioning of the institutions and the stability of the Community legal order, which are matters of public interest.[118] Importantly, the President, in an *obiter dictum*, also noted that the characterisation of a document as internal 'is not, in principle, sufficient to ensure confidential treatment', ie to deny the public's right to access it.[119] This latter consideration seems to suggest that the institution must demonstrate for each internal document why its disclosure would adversely affect the functioning of the institution: the mere classification as 'internal' does thus not in itself justify an exception from the right of access. On this basis, the third sentence of Article 27(2) of Regulation 1/2003 must be interpreted restrictively. The provision, it is submitted, cannot be relied upon to generally exclude access to any piece of correspondence between Network members irrespective of its subject matter or content.[120] On the other hand, it arguably provides a valid legal

[117] See further below Chapter 5, section III.A.

[118] *See the order of the President of the CFI in Case T–610/97 R Carlsen and others v Commission* [1998] ECR II–485, paras 46–8. The Council decision which was the subject of the *Carlsen* case was taken on the basis of the then applicable non-binding inter-institutional Code of Conduct concerning public access to Council and Commission documents (93/730/EC [1993] OJ L340/41). Since 2001, the rules on public access to documents of the Community institutions have been laid down in a binding regulation, notably Reg 1049/2001. Art 4(2) of Reg 1049/2001, which expressly precludes access of the public to 'legal advice' documents subject to a public-interest test, is said to have been inspired by the ruling in *Carlsen*. De Leeuw, above n 98, 334. In addition, Art 4(3) of Reg 1049/2001 contains an explicit exception regarding documents for 'internal use', equally subject to a public-interest test.

[119] Para 45 of the Order in *Carlsen* (*ibid*).

[120] Cf Schram, above n 114, para 32 (regarding refusal of access to documents which could be relevant to a potential procedure against a Member State for failure to fulfil its obligations). Communications on uncontroversial matters, such as purely organisational or informatory questions, will evidently not be of much interest for the parties. On the other hand, the *obiter dictum* of the CFI's President may be seen as a kind of warning. The Commission and NCAs should apply that provision with care and should be aware that there is no general rule to the effect that internal documents are under no circumstances accessible. This view appears to be confirmed by the (later) case law of the CFI, which has consistently held that the application of

basis for withholding observations submitted in respect of contemplated decisions of Network members, as well as written/electronic communications regarding the allocation of cases.[121]

(4) Relevance for National Proceedings. The above rules and principles were specifically developed in relation to hearings and access to the file in Commission proceedings. The conduct of proceedings before NCAs, by contrast, is governed by national rules. However, if professional secrecy is a Community concept, the interpretation of this concept, as it results from the above classifications, must be uniform throughout the Member States. Moreover, the importance of the above principles suggests that they must be applied generally in all proceedings relating to the application of

one of the exceptions to the right of public access requires, in principle, a concrete, individual examination of each of the documents referred to in the request for access (see, eg the judgment of the CFI in Case T–2/03 *Verein für Konsumenteninformation v Commission* [2005] ECR II–1121, paras 69–71). This may be particularly relevant with regard to opinions of the Commission's legal service, which the Commission classifies as internal documents within the meaning of Art 27(2) of Reg 1/2003, thereby intending to exclude, by definition, access to them. Interestingly, in a recent judgment concerning the application of Reg 1049/2001, the CFI ruled that legal advice provided by the Council's legal service comes within the ambit of Reg 1049/2001, Art 4(2), third indent, which contains an exception for 'court proceedings and legal advice'. The CFI noted that this exception would not only cover legal advice drawn up in the context of court proceedings, since this type of advice would already be included in the exception relating to court proceedings, but also legal opinions provided for other purposes (judgment of the CFI in Case T–84/03 *Turco v Council* [2004] ECR II–4061, para 65). The CFI thereby excluded the application of the exception, under Art 4(3) of Reg 1049/2001, relating specifically to internal documents. Obviously, in competition matters, access to file by the parties to the proceedings is primarily governed by Reg 1/2003, the Implementing Regulation and the Notice on Access to File in so far as these acts contain specific arrangements for persons with a particular interest in the proceedings (see para 29 of the judgment of the CFI in *Bank Austria* (above n 99), where the court noted that, in competition matters, the professional secrecy obligation otherwise imposed on Community officials is mitigated in favour of persons on whom the applicable procedural rules confer a right to be heard). Indeed, in para 2 of its Notice on Access to File, the Commission states that the specific right of access pursuant to Art 27 of Reg 1/2003 and Art 15 of the Implementing Regulation is 'distinct from the general right to access' under Reg 1049/2001. However, none of the specific rules applicable in competition proceedings includes a provision dealing explicitly with documents containing legal advice. The Commission is therefore bound to apply the internal document exception if it wants to bar access of the parties to legal advice documents in competition matters. On the other hand, concerning the relation between the rules on public access to documents laid down in Reg 1049/2001 and rules on access to file contained in other legislative acts dealing with specific matters (eg customs law), the CFI has held that *lex specialis* does not set aside *lex generalis*. Rather, the most favourable provision shall apply as the rules are designed to ensure the widest access possible (see the judgment of the CFI in *JT's Corporation* (above n 98), para 50). On this basis, Reg 1049/2001 as interpreted by the Community courts may, after all, have an impact on the interpretation of the provisions on access to file applicable in competition matters. Cf De Leeuw, above n 98, 330.

[121] This will mostly concern observations submitted by the Commission in accordance with para 46 of the Network Notice in respect of an envisaged national decision, but theoretically also includes comments provided by NCAs in regard of a pending national or Commission decision. The term 'internal document' can undoubtedly be understood to include not only working documents drawn up by the relevant institution (eg the Commission) itself, but also documents received by it from an outside body (eg an NCA) in relation to the decision-making process. See De Leeuw, above n 98, 335.

Community competition law irrespective of whether these are national proceedings or proceedings before the Commission.[122] This is particularly true for the guarantee to protect business secrets, which could be considered a general principle of Community law.[123] It is equally important that officials of the Commission and the NCAs can express themselves freely and without the fear that a later disclosure of their comments, drafts or opinions could undermine the authority's position.[124] At the same time, the fact that certain documents or parts thereof are regarded as non-communicable has a significant impact on the fair trial guarantee since it restricts the right of access to the file, a right which is an essential precondition for making known one's views and thus for effectively exercising the right to be heard.[125] Consequently, like the Commission, all NCAs must grant confidential treatment to documents containing business secrets. Similarly, all NCAs must observe the principle that the category of internal documents, which, in accordance with Article 27(2) of Regulation 1/2003, specifically comprises correspondence exchanged between the members of the ECN, is covered by the professional secrecy obligation and generally may not be disclosed either to the public or to the parties of infringement proceedings.[126]

---

[122] See J Temple Lang, 'European Community Constitutional Law and the Enforcement of Community Antitrust Law' in B Hawk (ed), *1993 Proceedings of the Fordham Corporate Law Institute* (New York, Juris Publishing, 1994), 525, 547, who submits that, by virtue of Art 10 EC, NCAs when applying Community competition law have to observe the same confidentiality rules as the Commission. He bases his view on the judgment in the *SEP* case (Case T–39/90 *Samenwerkende Elektriciteits-Produktiebedrijven (SEP) v Commission* [1991] ECR II–1497, para 57), where the CFI noted: 'The Member States are bound, by virtue of the duty of co-operation laid down in Article 5 [now Art 10] of the Treaty, to take all measures necessary for the fulfilment of their obligations, the obligations in question in the present case being those arising from Article 20 [of Reg 17].'

[123] See para 28 of the judgment in Case 53/85 *Akzo v Commission (Akzo I)* [1986] ECR 1965, where the ECJ, after referring to Arts 19(3) and 21 of Reg 17, which obliged the Commission to have regard to the legitimate interest of undertakings in the protection of their business secrets, stated that these provisions, albeit dealing with particular situations, 'must be regarded as the expression of a general principle which applies during the course of the administrative procedure'. The case law of the ECJ further suggests that Member States have to observe general principles of Community law, in particular fundamental rights principles, when they implement Community legislation. See paras 17–19 of the judgment in Case 5/88 *Wachauf v Bundesamt für Ernährung und Forstwirtschaft* [1989] ECR 2609 and J Temple Lang, 'Community Constitutional Law: Art 5 EEC Treaty' (1990) 27 *CML Rev* 645, 654–6. For further references to case law, see K Lenaerts and Van Nuffel, *Constitutional Law of the European Union* (London, Sweet & Maxwell, 2nd edn, 2005), 17-067. For the various (dogmatic and pragmatic) reasons supporting this position see Temple Lang, above n 122, 531–3.

[124] The so-called 'space to think' (K Dekeyser and M Jaspers, 'A New Era of ECN Co-operation' (2007) 30 *World Competition* 3, 10) which is also recognised by Reg 1049/2001 (see De Leeuw, above n 98, 335).

[125] See K Lenaerts and J Vanhamme, 'Procedural Rights of Private Parties in the Community Administrative Process' (1997) 34 *CML Rev* 531, 545. In Community law terminology, the expression 'rights of defence' is commonly used to replace the notion of 'the right to a fair trial', which includes the right to be heard. See *idem*, 534.

[126] Cf also recital 15 of Reg 1049/2001, where, referring to the principle of loyal co-operation, the Council and the EP point out that Members States should not hamper the

c. Relation to Other Provisions

It is evident that the obligation of professional secrecy is not an absolute principle. There are a number of provisions which allow derogation from this principle, in particular Articles 12(1) and 27(2) of Regulation 1/2003 and the rules on access to the file.

The system of close vertical and horizontal co-operation established by Regulation 1/2003 and the Network Notice is based on the principle that case-related information, including confidential information, must be able to circulate freely within the Network. This principle is clearly expressed in Article 12(1) Regulation 1/2003. Article 28(2) of Regulation 1/2003 is 'without prejudice' to Article 12 of Regulation 1/2003. The application of the latter provision is thus reserved and Article 12 of Regulation 1/2003 may consequently derogate from the principle of professional secrecy.[127] This simply means that the secrecy obligation does not apply to the inter-agency relations between the competition authorities in the EU when exchanging information in accordance with Article 12 of Regulation 1/2003. A Network member cannot therefore oppose an information exchange within the ECN by referring to the confidential nature of the document or parts thereof.[128] On the other hand, Article 28(2) of Regulation 1/2003 does apply in relation to any (legal or natural) person or institution outside the ECN (including other national authorities, such as sectoral regulators and ministries) to which confidential information may principally not be disclosed.[129]

---

proper application of that regulation and should respect the security rules of the EU institutions. Arguably, an NCA that disregards the confidential nature of internal documents, stemming from the Commission or another NCA, would violate Art 10(2) EC, which obliges Member States not to jeopardise the attainment of the objectives of the EC Treaty. Cf Martinez Lage and Brokelmann, above n 93, 415–16 (with regard to the confidential nature of attorney–client communications). As concerns internal Commission documents, unauthorised disclosure would more specifically violate the duty not to interfere with the operation of the Community institutions, duty equally derived from Art 10 EC. See J Temple Lang, 'The Core of the Constitutional Law of the Community—Article 5 EC' in L Gormley (ed), *Current and Future Perspectives on EC Competition Law—A Tribute to Professor M.R. Mok* (London, Kluwer Law International, 1997), 41, 60.

[127] See Van Der Woude, above n 96, 380.

[128] An exception would only apply where another Network member must be regarded as 'third party' because it is commercially active (eg as stakeholder in a competing firm). In that rather exceptional and probably even unrealistic case, the undertaking concerned could invoke the confidential nature of certain documents 'as against' the relevant NCA (so-called SEP proviso). See further below section II.A.2.a, in particular nn 164 and 166.

[129] Swaak and Mollica, above n 13, 39. Accordingly, German law, for instance, provides specifically that the BKartA, albeit being required to co-operate with certain other authorities such as the German Federal Bank and supervisory bodies in the media and financial services sectors, is not entitled to pass on information which it has obtained through the Network to such authorities. It is noteworthy, however, that a similar restriction has not been included with regard to co-operation between the BKartA and sectoral regulators, with which information, including personal data and business secrets, may equally be exchanged. In view of the above considerations, the legality of the latter rules must be doubted.

Furthermore, there is an important general exception to the professional secrecy obligation. Pursuant to the fifth sentence of Article 27(2) of Regulation 1/2003, the Commission cannot be precluded from disclosing information if this is necessary to prove an infringement. The public interest in terminating and punishing violations of Articles 81 and 82 EC is obviously regarded as of a higher ranking than the legitimate private interest of the undertaking (or individual) concerned in protecting its business secrets or other confidential data. Paragraph 28(a) of the Network Notice reiterates this principle and suggests that the exception is inherent to the Community concept of 'professional secrecy obligation'. On this basis, it would also apply to NCAs where they need to divulge information in order to prove an infringement of the Community competition rules.[130]

Finally, the professional secrecy obligation is mitigated in relation to complainants and other interested third parties on whom Regulation 1/2003 confers specific rights in the course of the administrative proceedings before the Commission, in particular the right to be heard.[131] However, it follows from the case law of the Luxemburg courts that companies under investigation (defendants) and third parties such as complainants are not in the same procedural situation. While defendants are generally entitled to full disclosure of the Commission's file (with the exception of business secrets), the rights of third parties in the administrative procedure are more limited.[132] It must therefore be decided on a case-by-case and document-by-document basis which party must be granted access to which documents. In this process, the legitimate interest of companies in the protection of their business secrets and other confidential information must be balanced against the right of third parties (including complainants) to be heard and the requirements of due process and sound administration. Only insofar as it is necessary for the proper conduct of the investigation may information covered by the professional secrecy obligation be divulged to third parties. Since business secrets are afforded very special protection, they may not under any circumstances be disclosed to third parties, ie complainants, informants and other companies which are not the subject of the investigation.[133]

---

[130] See Gauer, above n 18, 12.

[131] Para 29 of the judgment of the CFI in *Bank Austria* (above n 99).

[132] See the judgment of the ECJ in Joined Cases 142 and 156/84 *BAT and Reynolds v Commission* [1987] ECR 4487, paras 19–20, and the judgment of the CFI in Case T–17/93 *Matra Hachette v Commission* [1994] ECR II–595, para 34. Also contrast Art 15 of the Implementing Regulation (access to the file for the parties under investigation) with Art 13(2) of the Implementing Regulation (hearing of persons other than the parties under investigation). The defendants' right of access to the file is only restricted in relation to business secrets and confidential data of other undertakings and internal documents.

[133] Judgment of the ECJ in *Akzo I* (above n 123), paras 27–8.

2. *Procedure*

Mutual trust of all Network members in the professional handling of confidential data[134] communication is a pre-condition for the effective use of the powers granted to NCAs under Article 12 of Regulation 1/2003.[135] In order to ensure the security of document transfer and guarantee that confidential information is actually treated as such, Member States have created the position of a so-called 'authorised disclosure officer' (ADO). The ADO is an official of the NCA who is specifically responsible for sending and receiving confidential information.[136] ADOs generally communicate by encrypted e-mail, though other secure forms of transmission may also be used. The technical standard of encryption is the same as that applied by the Commission when forwarding documents to the Member States for the purpose of consulting the Advisory Committee.[137]

In practice, this means that the exchange of confidential information in the ECN is systematically channelled through the ADOs, ie the relevant documents are always sent from the ADO of the transmitting NCA to the ADO of the receiving NCA.[138] The first takes care of the adequate protection of the document, while the second arranges for the forwarding to the relevant officials within his or her agency. This way of proceeding, ie central dispatching and central receipt of confidential data, means that each case handler or case team has to indicate which documents or parts of a document may not be disclosed to persons or institutions outside the ECN and mark the document accordingly.[139] Only after a document (or parts thereof) has been classified as confidential can it be handed over to the ADO for transmission to one or several other Network members.

3. *Leniency Applications*

Leniency applicants obviously have a particular interest in ensuring that information which they supply to one Network member will not be used against them by another Network member. Since not all competition authorities in the EU practice leniency and the existing programmes differ widely, potential leniency applicants are likely to fear that the free circu-

---

[134] Confidential data here is meant to comprise the three categories of non-communicable documents mentioned earlier (business secrets, confidential documents and internal documents).

[135] S Hossenfelder, 'Erste Erfahrungen des Bundeskartellamtes mit dem Behördennetzwerk' in X, *FIW-Schriftenreihe Band 206. Schwerpunkte des Kartellrechts 2004* (Köln, Carl-Heymanns-Verlag, 2006), 1, 8.

[136] Schnichels, above n 26, 113.

[137] Dekeyser and Dalheimer, above n 9, 14.

[138] *Ibid.*

[139] However, the classification of a document or parts thereof as confidential is not binding for the receiving authority, which applies its own procedural rules. See below in this section II.A.2.b.

lation of evidence in the ECN may harm their interests and, consequently, might be dissuaded from coming forward. Such a deterrent effect might ultimately jeopardise the efficiency of leniency programmes in general. Therefore, special rules have been developed in order to protect the confidentiality of information provided in the framework of leniency applications. It should be noted, though, that the relevant rules again are not laid down in a binding legal instrument. Instead of incorporating certain guarantees for leniency applicants in Regulation 1/2003, the Commission has chosen to include them only in the Network Notice.[140]

As concerns the initial case report, matters resulting from leniency applications are not treated differently from other cases. The new case must be notified to the Commission and the information is generally also transmitted to all other Network members under the condition that they may not use such information against the applicant, not even as intelligence justifying the initiation of their own proceedings.[141]

With regard to the further exchange of evidentiary material, pursuant to Article 12 of Regulation 1/2003, in the course of an investigation the Network Notice puts a number of restrictions on the Network members. The basic principle is that information stemming from a leniency application will only be forwarded to other competition authorities with the applicant's consent. Importantly, this principle applies not only with regard to information voluntarily submitted by the applicant himself, but also in respect of any other information which is subsequently collected by the relevant competition authority and which the authority could not have gathered if it was not for the leniency application.[142]

There are, however, two exceptions to the basic principle: namely, the applicant's consent is not required where the applicant has applied to both authorities, ie the transmitting and the receiving authority, for leniency

---

[140] The dubious legal value of the special regime governing the exchange of leniency information has been emphasised by C Swaak and M Mollica, 'Leniency Applicants Face to Modernization of EC Competition Law' (2005) 26 *European Competition Law Review* 507, 514–15, who even suggest that an NCA could decide to disregard these principles and, instead, rely directly on Art 12 of Reg 1/2003, which does not stipulate any exceptions for information stemming from leniency applications and thus would not preclude the NCA from disclosing such information to other Network members. Admittedly, the issue is of little practical relevance, since all NCAs have undersigned a written statement, in accordance with para 72 of the Network Notice, acknowledging the principles of that notice, in particular those regarding leniency applications, and declaring explicitly that they will abide by them. NCAs are therefore unlikely to depart from the rules protecting leniency applicants.

[141] See para 39 of the Network Notice. The fact that initial case reports, including cases of leniency applications, are generally distributed to all Network members results from the fact that all NCAs have provided a written commitment pursuant to para 72 of the Network Notice (see above n 140 and Chapter 3, section III.c.1).

[142] Para 40 of the Network Notice. However, it is not required that the applicant provide his consent to each single transfer of information. Rather, where the applicant has consented to the exchange of voluntarily submitted information, this consent is deemed to also cover the transfer of information that is collected later as a result of the leniency application. Moreover, the consent cannot be withdrawn.

regarding the same infringement;[143] and the applicant's consent is equally dispensable where the receiving authority specifically guarantees, in writing, that it will not use the transmitted information and any other information collected thereafter to impose sanctions on the leniency applicant and other persons covered by the favourable treatment under the relevant leniency programme or their respective (former) employees. Moreover, the written commitment must include the guarantee that all other authorities to which the information may subsequently be transmitted by the receiving authority will equally respect that guarantee.[144]

These two exceptions evidently do not allow for the free circulation of information throughout the entire Network.[145] They entitle a competition authority to forward information only to those individual Network members which have either themselves received a leniency application from the same applicant regarding the same infringement or which have explicitly declared that they would respect the immunity of the applicant and certain other legal and natural persons defined in the Network Notice. Thus, the above principles make it possible that immunity available under a particular leniency programme is transferred together with the information. The receiving authority is bound, either under its own leniency programme or by virtue of its written commitment, to grant immunity to the applicant. This means that de facto immunity can be obtained in other Member States, even those which do not operate a leniency programme. Similarly, applicants may be completely protected from sanctions even if they are not the first to claim leniency and thus would not qualify for full immunity under the programme of the receiving authority.[146] In this respect, the situation for potential applicants has certainly improved. There is no doubt that the Network members are sensitive to the question of how the efficiency of existing leniency programmes can best be protected in the modernised system.[147] Whether all potential adverse effects resulting from the authorities' right to exchange evidence are indeed fully compensated for by the above principles[148] is, however, doubtful.

First, information exchange between two (or more) authorities that have

---

[143] Para 41(1) of the Network Notice.

[144] Para 41(2) of the Network Notice. This latter alternative enables Network members to transmit information stemming from leniency applications to colleague agencies which do not operate leniency programmes and with which a leniency application therefore could not have been filed. S Blake and D Schnichels, 'Schutz der Kronzeugen im neuen EG-Wettbewerbsrecht' (2004) 15 *Europäische Zeitschrift für Wirtschaftsrecht* 551, 553, suggest that, in practice, only this latter alternative will play an important role as applicants are unlikely to provide their consent and there is hardly any need for authorities, both having received leniency applications, to exchange evidence.

[145] Unless the respective written guarantees have been provided by all Network members.

[146] See Blake and Schnichels, above n 144, 553, in particular note 29.

[147] This sensitivity is also documented by the Model Leniency Programme, which the ECN launched in September 2006. See above Chapter 3, section III.C.2.

[148] This is, however, the position of Dekeyser and Dalheimer, above n 9, 16.

both received leniency applications is easily possible without there being any guarantee for the applicant that immunity will actually be granted by the receiving authority.[149] The condition making the exchange of information permissible without the applicant's consent is that an application has also been lodged with the receiving authority, not that leniency has been obtained in the Member State of the receiving authority.[150]

Secondly, applicants are likely to be put under considerable pressure to consent to an information exchange. Paragraph 40 of the Network Notice explicitly states that the Network members 'will encourage leniency applicants to give such consent'. This intention clearly indicates that the competition authorities consider it crucial to be able to exchange evidence in leniency cases. If authorities warmly recommend or even strongly advise that the applicant should consent to an information exchange, the impression might be created that they will effectively take into account his (un)willingness to follow their suggestion when evaluating the co-operativeness of the applicant, which, in turn, may have an impact on the reward, if any, he would be entitled to under the respective leniency programme.[151] On this basis, applicants appear to be almost compelled to give their consent.

Finally, uncertainties remain in view of the non-binding nature of the principles being enshrined in the Network Notice only, rather than in Regulation 1/2003. Whether the written declarations of the Network members pursuant to paragraph 72 of the Network Notice can adequately allay the resulting concerns of potential whistleblowers is still an open question.[152]

II. AREAS OF CONCERN

The above description has revealed that, in spite of the safeguards enshrined in Article 12 of Regulation 1/2003, the broad exchange of information, in particular evidentiary information, in the course of an investigation and the possibility of an almost unlimited administrative

---

[149] A simple reason why the applicant could be refused (full) immunity by the receiving authority could be the fact that he was not the first to come forward in that particular Member State. In view of the divergencies between the leniency programmes in the EU, there may be many more reasons why an applicant, despite parallel applications, may in fact be granted immunity in one Member State but not in another (eg preclusion of amnesty for instigators or ringleaders; see further above Chapter 3, section III.c.2).

[150] This fact may particularly cause concern where a case is reallocated altogether to another authority. See Burnside and Crossley, above n 90, 29.

[151] For instance, under the Commission's leniency programme, an undertaking only qualifies for immunity if it fully co-operates, on a continuous basis and expeditiously, throughout the entire procedure. See para 12(a) of the 2006 Leniency Notice.

[152] See A Burnside and H Crossley, 'Co-operation in Competition: A New Era?' (2005) 30 *EL Rev* 234, 240.

assistance may compromise the legal position of the undertakings concerned. Some of the prime concerns raised in this context are the lack of transparency of the information flow, the question of how the due process of the information gathering can be guaranteed and the fear that the free circulation of evidence may lead to an erosion of protection standards in the EU.

A. Transparency

While it is uncertain whether the transparency principle has yet reached the status of a general and justiciable principle of Community law, it surely constitutes a value whose fundamental importance, in the Community legal order, has increased considerably over the last decade.[153] Its most advanced feature is the right of (public) access to documents, which, as far as documents of the Council, the Commission and the EP are concerned, is now codified in Article 255 EC.[154] The right of access to documents has further been included in Article 42 of the EU Charter. Transparency thus serves as a tool for judicial oversight and can certainly be used to evaluate Community norms.[155]

Except for the obligation to provide the Commission with an initial case report and to inform the Commission prior to the adoption of a final decision, the co-operation mechanisms of Regulation 1/2003 and in particular the provisions on horizontal co-operation grant discretionary powers to the NCAs but do not establish any obligations. Even the assistance in fact-finding is a purely facultative measure. Moreover, Regulation 1/2003 does not stipulate any information duties in relation to the companies under investigation. The only exception to this rule is the obligation to inform the undertakings concerned, pursuant to paragraph 34 of the Network Notice, of the reallocation of a case.[156] This means that only the exchange of information which is actually contained in the initial case report and the forwarding of the draft decision or draft statement of objections can effectively be anticipated by the companies concerned;[157]

---

[153] P Craig and G De Búrca, *EU Law. Text, Cases and Materials* (Oxford, Oxford University Press, 3rd edn, 2003), 392 and 395. By contrast, K Lenaerts, 'In the Union We Trust': Trust-enhancing Principles of Community Law' (2004) 41 *CML Rev* 317, 321, considers that transparency has definitely evolved into a general principle of Community law.

[154] The provision was introduced in 1999 by the Amsterdam Treaty. However, it lacks direct effect (see Case T–191/99 *Petrie v Commission* [2001] ECR II–3677, paras 34–5). In fact, modalities, conditions and limits for the exercise of this right are laid down in Reg 1049/2001.

[155] See P Craig and G de Búrca, *EU Law. Text, Cases and Materials* (Oxford, Oxford University Press, 4th edn, 2007), 567.

[156] This is not an obligation *sensu stricto* since it is not enshrined in the Regulation itself, but only mentioned in the Commission's notice.

[157] Reichelt, above n 11, 766. However, even here, the undertakings will not know whether any further information is in fact being exchanged. Art 11(4) of Reg 1/2003 provides that, at the

for the rest, they are left in the dark. The flow of information between the Network members during an ongoing investigation remains an entirely internal and discretionary process from which the companies concerned are completely excluded. They are usually not even informed of the mere fact that information is exchanged and therefore are unable to control the extent to which the authorities share in particular confidential information. This may, however, undermine their rights of defence. The lack of transparency is difficult to reconcile with the requirement of procedural fairness *sensu lato*. It is probably not practicable to inform undertakings generally of each instance of information exchange. However, there are at least two critical situations that deserve particular attention.

1. Transfer of a (Complete) Case File

Where a case is reallocated within the initial allocation period,[158] the competition authority stepping back may transfer the relevant case file to the authority to which the case has been reallocated in accordance with Article 12(1) of Regulation 1/2003. If this transfer takes place before the first formal investigative measure, it will usually not raise concerns. The transmitting authority will not yet have gathered many information and the availability of confidential data, if any, will still be quite limited. However, if the case is reallocated only after the first formal investigative measure has already been carried out (eg because the Network has only been informed of the case *ex post*), the amount of data, including confidential information, assembled in the case file may be much more important. The same would be true where the case is exceptionally reallocated after the initial allocation period because the known facts have changed materially.[159] Similarly, an NCA may decide to terminate or suspend its proceedings or reject a complaint pursuant to Article 13 of Regulation 1/2003 because another NCA is dealing with the same matter. Arguably, such a decision may still be taken at a later stage of the proceedings. Also in this case, the transfer of the case file to the other NCA conducting the parallel investigation is possible.[160]

The above examples demonstrate that there are a number of conceivable situations where an NCA that terminates or intends to terminate its own proceedings forwards information to another NCA (or the Commission)

---

request of the Commission, the acting NCA has to provide it with additional documents. These may also be made available to other NCAs. The precise extent of the information exchange under Art 11(4) of Reg 1/2003 will thus not be transparent to the companies. *Idem*, 761.

[158] Para 18 of the Network Notice.

[159] See para 19 of the Network Notice. One possible reason for such a material change is that the fact that intra-Community trade is affected only emerges after a certain amount of information and evidence has already been collected. See Kist, above n 45, 362.

[160] See para 23 of the Network Notice.

regarding a suspected infringement about which it has already gathered a significant amount of data and information. The collected material may include both circumstantial and direct (inculpatory) evidence, but also documents that may exculpate the company under investigation.[161] In this context, it is important to note that it is not for the competition authorities to judge whether a particular document must be qualified as an exculpatory document that could be used in an undertaking's defence. Therefore, the company under investigation has a right to have full access to the file so as to be able to properly prepare its defence and make its views known on all documents which are in the possession of the competition authority.[162]

It follows from the above that, where a case file is transmitted from one Network member to another, the undertaking concerned has a right to a complete transfer of the file. Therefore, the entire case file, including all documents and data that have been collected, must be forwarded whether or not the transmitting authority considers them to be of any exonerating value. It is a principal requirement of procedural fairness that exculpatory evidence is not lost as a result of an (incomplete) exchange of information even where the transmitting authority does not regard the particular information as relevant for the companies' defence.[163]

2. Transmission of Confidential Information

Since undertakings are not generally informed of the exchange of information taking place within the ECN, they are deprived of the opportunity to indicate to the receiving authority whether they consider certain (parts of) documents included in the exchange to be confidential because they contain business secrets or other commercially sensitive information the disclosure of which could harm the undertaking's interests. Undertakings simply have to rely on the transmitting NCA to properly mark confidential information, classify the relevant documents accordingly and use the correct way of transmission (eg encrypted e-mail) without having any possibility of verifying whether their legitimate confidentiality interests have been adequately protected. The same applies to complainants or other informants who wish to remain anonymous.

---

161 Van Der Woude, above n 96, 385.

162 See the judgment of the CFI in Case T–30/91 *Solvay v Commission* [1995] ECR II–1775, paras 81–3. The Commission has taken this case law into account. It follows from para10 (see in particular at note 13) of the Notice on Access to File that access to the file is not limited to documents which the Commission regards as relevant to or useful for an undertaking's defence. Indeed, access will be granted to 'all documents making up the Commission's file . . . with the exception of internal documents, business secrets of other undertakings, or other confidential information'. Lenaerts, above n 153, 328, considers that Art 27(2) of Reg 1/2003 on access of the parties concerned to the Commission file is inspired by the principle of equality of arms.

163 Van Der Woude, above n 96, 385. The possibility of transferring entire case files is recognised by the Commission on p 21 of the Explanatory Memorandum.

a. The SEP Scenario

The importance for an undertaking of knowing what business data is in fact transmitted to whom, even where communication takes place between public entities, may be illustrated by the *SEP* case. The case concerned the refusal of the Netherlands public electricity utilities SEP to provide copies of its gas supply contract with Statoil the disclosure of which the Commission had requested in the course of an investigation under Regulation 17. SEP argued that the subsequent transmission of the documents which contained highly confidential business information to the competent national authorities, in particular to the Netherlands administration, would compromise its commercial interests since the Netherlands State was controlling Gasunie, SEP's other main supplier of gas.[164] Even though the CFI considered that such an issue was likely to arise whenever an investigation concerns the commercial relationship between a public undertaking and a private company,[165] it must be noted that the SEP scenario actually represents a fairly exceptional, if not unique, situation. Since the time of the *SEP* case, all Member States have established independent competition authorities, and risks of confusion as to competence in respect of competition matters and state-owned companies no longer exist. It is therefore unlikely that this particular problem will recur.[166]

---

[164] Pursuant to Art 10 of Reg 17, the Commission has the duty to transmit copies of the most important documents collected in an infringement procedure to the competent authorities of the Member States. The CFI found, however, that the observance of the confidentiality of the relevant documents, particularly in relation to Gasunie, was sufficiently guaranteed by the professional secrecy obligation in Art 20 of Reg 17 and consequently dismissed the claim by which SEP had sought to have the Commission's decision ordering the production of the Statoil contract annulled. Para 53 of judgment of the CFI in *SEP* (above n 122). On appeal, the ECJ upheld the judgment of the CFI, albeit ruling that Art 20 of Reg 17 did not effectively avert the risk that the Member States' authorities would take into consideration, in one way or another, the information they received from the Commission. The ECJ therefore found that the Commission's obligation under Art 10 of Reg 17 to forward documents to national authorities may be limited where the confidential nature of certain documents 'as against' a particular authority has been raised and that argument is not irrelevant. See Case C–36/92 P *SEP v Commission* [1994] ECR I–1911, paras 27–37. The ECJ's reasoning in *SEP* is based largely on the judgment in *Spanish Banks* (above n 27), where it was held that the Member States' authorities, while being prohibited from directly relying on information they have received from the Commission in national procedures, are not required to completely disregard such information. They may still use it indirectly as circumstantial evidence.

[165] See para 57 of the CFI's judgment in *SEP* (above n 122). The CFI even noted that such situations arise very frequently in practice.

[166] Gauer, above n 18, 13. On the *SEP* case see also Reichelt, above n 11, 772–6, who argues that the SEP proviso still applies to any information exchange with an NCA that is commercially active. Martinez Lage and Brokelmann, above n 93, 414, equally submit that the SEP proviso is still good law as it is based on the general principles of Community law which could not be amended by secondary legislation. In my view, however, their submission is unlikely to be of any practical relevance.

b. The 'Country-of-destination' Principle

Where, subsequent to the transmission of information within the ECN, the receiving authority makes information from its file available to private parties, ie persons outside the Network (eg in the context of granting access to the file), it must ensure that business secrets and other confidential information are sufficiently protected against arbitrary disclosure.

Under the Community law procedure, the Commission may disclose information covered by the professional secrecy obligation only to the extent that such disclosure is necessary for the proper conduct of the investigation. In any event, business secrets may not be disclosed to third parties.[167] While it is for the Commission alone to decide whether or not a particular document contains business secrets, the undertaking concerned must be given the opportunity first to state its views before the Commission takes a decision and secondly to challenge the Commission's (negative) decision prior to its implementation in order to prevent the disclosure of the documents in question (the so-called AKZO procedure).[168] In practice, persons (including the undertakings under investigation, complainants and other third parties) are invited to indicate which documents or passages in documents they regard as constituting business secrets or other confidential information belonging to them and identify the companies with regard to whom such information must be considered as confidential.[169]

Neither Regulation 1/2003 nor the Implementing Regulation, or indeed the Network Notice, stipulates any similar rules with regard to national proceedings before an NCA. However, Article 28(2) of Regulation 1/2003 extends the professional secrecy obligation to the NCAs. In other words, NCAs are bound by the Community concept of professional secrecy when they conduct proceedings with a view to applying Article 81 or 82 EC.[170] Moreover, Member States have to observe the general principles of Community law when they implement Community rules.[171] Since the ECJ has held that the legitimate interest of undertakings in the protection of their business secrets is a general principle of the administrative procedure

---

[167] An exception applies according to Reg 1/2003, Art 27(2), 5th sentence and para 28(a) of the Network Notice, where the disclosure is necessary in order for the Commission or an NCA to prove an infringement.

[168] Paras 27–9 of the judgment of the ECJ in *Akzo I* (above n 123). See also para 38 of the ECJ's judgment in *SEP* (above n 122).

[169] See Art 16(2) and (3) of the Implementing Regulation. Companies are regularly asked to substantiate their claim for confidentiality in writing and provide non-confidential versions of the relevant documents.

[170] Para 28(a) of the Network Notice. See also Reichelt, above n 11, 775.

[171] See, eg para 19 of the judgment in *Wachauf* (above n 123) and further above n 123.

in competition matters,[172] NCAs have to provide, *mutatis mutandis*, a guarantee equivalent to that operated by the Commission.

The questions of course arise, with regard to documents exchanged within the ECN, of when and with which competition authority the undertaking concerned has to lodge its request for confidential treatment. These questions are particularly relevant given that the undertaking concerned, due to the lack of transparency, will often not be aware of the fact that a specific document is being circulated within the Network and will therefore not know which authority will ultimately make (evidentiary) use of the document, include it in its case file and deal with any requests for access to the file in relation to that document. An undertaking that wishes to claim confidential treatment for its business secrets or other sensitive information should therefore preferably make this request at the time when it first submits the relevant document. Alternatively, in particular where the document is seized during an on-the-spot investigation, the request must be lodged as soon as possible after the seizure if it cannot be made during the inspection. It must be addressed to the competition authority which first obtains the document, ie the authority which has requested the information or carried out the inspection in the first place, regardless of whether that authority conducts the investigation on its own behalf or on behalf and for the account of another NCA.[173]

It is, however, for the receiving (or second) authority, ie the authority ultimately using the document in its procedure, to assess the merits of such request. Consequently, there is no need for the transmitting authority to decide on the validity of the claim for confidentiality before forwarding the information.[174] Only in the exceptional case that the transmitting authority has already taken a decision with regard to the confidentiality of a particular document will it inform the receiving authority accordingly. That decision is not binding on the receiving authority, however, unless it is a

---

[172] See above n 123. See also Art 287 EC, where reference is made to information about undertakings, their business relations and their cost components.

[173] Where the fact-finding measures are carried out on behalf of another authority, the undertaking concerned can probably anticipate to whom the information will be transmitted because the applicable procedural rules will normally require the subject matter and purpose of the inspection to be specified. Reichelt, above n 11, 766. However, even in that situation it appears safer to address any confidentiality claim to the first authority so as to make sure that the request is directly attached to the relevant document.

[174] Gauer, above n 18, 11; Dekeyser and De Smijter, above n 5, 168. There seems to be a slight contradiction between the submission that 'professional secrecy' is a Community concept which must be interpreted and applied uniformly and the proposition that decisions regarding the confidentiality of documents or the simple classification of documents as confidential, by the transmitting NCA, are not binding for the receiving NCA. However, since each NCA has to ensure due process in accordance with its proper national rules and the international law principles of state sovereignty and non-interference prevent the extraterritorial application of national rules, national acts of classification or NCA decisions concerning the confidentiality of documents cannot oblige any authorities other than that which made the decision or act.

Commission decision.[175] Any other approach would significantly impede the free circulation of evidence in the Network as any disagreement between the undertaking and the first authority on the merits of the claim would likely prevent that authority from sharing the information with other Network members. Such a situation would not only unduly hamper the investigation conducted by the receiving authority,[176] but ultimately also risk emptying Article 12 of Regulation 1/2003 of its content.[177]

In practical terms, this means that, where a potentially confidential document is exchanged in the Network, the transmitting authority has to make sure that an existing request for confidential treatment is transferred together with the document.[178] Therefore, any confidentiality claim must always be attached immediately to the relevant document so that both document and confidentiality request will automatically be transmitted together. This obligation incumbent on the transmitting authority is of course crucial, since any omittance of the duty may lead to an irrevocable loss of the protection, if any, granted or to be granted to the confidential (parts of the) document.

Similarly, in the rare case that an authority has already decided on the request for confidentiality, that decision should be transmitted together

---

[175] Gauer, above n 18, 12; Dekeyser and De Smijter, above n 5, 168 note 19. However, para 16 of the Notice on Access to File seems to suggest that the Commission, in general, is prepared to respect the assessment made by the transmitting authority in respect of the confidentiality of a document. That provision, which specifically deals with access, granted by the Commission, to documents originating from Member States (or EFTA countries), states that '[t]he Commission will consult the entity submitting the document prior to granting access to identify business secrets or other confidential information'. Similarly, establishing the position of an ADO implies that, where an NCA classifies a document as confidential, the other Network members will endeavour to pay due regard to that classification and will not gratuitously depart from the (preliminary) evaluation of the transmitting NCA. Otherwise, it would make little sense to create this function as the ADO will usually be involved in the transmission process only if the Commission or the NCA in the Member State of origin has previously considered the document to contain confidential information.

[176] Cf Kist, above n 45, 360, who points to the fact that exchanging (confidential) information often is a time-consuming exercise and that companies should be precluded from unduly hindering an investigation by opposing an information exchange. Such impediment would be particularly undesirable where the first authority has in fact requested the relevant information or conducted the inspection on behalf and for the account of the second authority pursuant to Art 22(1) of Reg 1/2003.

[177] Applying a 'country-of-destination' principle in this context may force the undertaking from which the document originates and which requested confidential treatment to litigate in a foreign Member State, in which it may not even have a subsidiary or branch office. Martinez Lage and Brokelmann, above n 93, 414. However, since it is for the case-handling NCA to grant access to its file, it would simply be impractical to have the dispute about whether or not a particular document must be treated as confidential and thus as inaccessible decided by the transmitting authority which is not involved in the process of granting access to the file. Solving the confidentiality issue in direct contacts between the receiving authority and the undertaking or individual claiming confidentiality is more efficient and, moreover, is in line with the principle that each NCA conducts the procedure in accordance with its own national rules (including the national provisions on access to the file).

[178] Gauer, above n 18, 11.

with the relevant document. As pointed out, a (positive) decision is, however, not binding on the receiving authority. Nonetheless, it is submitted that, as a matter of principle, the receiving NCA should not deviate from the positive assessment of the transmitting NCA granting confidentiality. Conversely, where the applicant and the authority are not in agreement as to the confidential nature of the document or certain parts of it (eg because the request for confidential treatment has been denied by the authority), the transmitting authority may also inform the receiving authority of such dispute.[179]

In any event, it is for the receiving authority to apply an AKZO-type of procedure, unless it intends to honour the confidentiality status already awarded by the transmitting authority.[180] In other words, the receiving authority must afford the undertaking claiming confidentiality the opportunity to make known its views before adopting a negative decision, ie a decision refusing confidential treatment. Moreover, effective remedies must be available that allow the undertaking to have the authority's assessment reviewed before the decision is implemented and the information actually disclosed. These principles would also imply that the receiving authority has to inquire, if necessary via the transmitting authority, with the undertaking or person from whom a document originates whether a confidentiality request has or will be made if such a request has not been transmitted together with the document.[181]

In my view, a fairer solution, which would equally provide more legal certainty, would be that all NCAs and the Commission mutually recognise each other's confidentiality regime.[182] Clearly, the possibility for an NCA (and the Commission) to reclassify documents it has received via the Network is not favourable to the way competition procedures are perceived in terms of fairness and equity. Such mutual recognition could be coupled with the adoption of common criteria or standards for the classification of documents according to the three categories mentioned above

---

[179] Cf para 27 of the Network Notice in relation to the question of whether the legality of the information gathering has been or still might be contested. In that case, the transmitting authority may (and should) inform the receiving authority of the contestation.

[180] This does not mean that an NCA has to reveal the origin (place of seizure/delivery) of a document during the stage at which the investigation is still kept secret. Only when the NCA is about to grant access to the file, ie in a phase when the investigation is no longer conducted covertly, is the NCA obliged to verify whether there are any confidentiality issues and, in the case given, apply the AKZO procedure prior to disclosing the content of a document.

[181] This unwritten obligation does not alter the fact that it is safer for persons wishing to claim confidentiality to lodge the request at the same time as the relevant document is handed over to the authority so that the request can be attached to and transferred with the document. This way of proceeding minimises the risk that a (justified) confidentiality claim is accidentally ignored. In practice, these concerns are accommodated. Where confidential information is exchanged, the relevant document is transmitted together with a standard covering letter from the sending authority indicating the origin of the document and providing a warning as to its confidential contents.

[182] See Kist, above n 45, 364; Martinez Lage and Brokelmann, above n 93, 409.

(business secrets, other confidential documents, internal documents). The Commission's Notice on Access to File could serve as a basis for the development of these criteria. Even if such common criteria were adopted, their application and interpretation would probably still lead to diverging results in practice.[183] However, the existence of common standards would certainly increase the willingness of NCAs and the Commission to acknowledge each other's decisions regarding the confidential nature of individual documents.[184] On this basis, a positive decision by the transmitting authority regarding the confidential nature of a document would be binding for the receiving authority. Moreover, once a confidentiality status has been awarded, that status would be preserved throughout the Network. In this way, an erosion of confidentiality standards in the EU could at least partly be prevented.[185]

Nonetheless, in spite of the lack of transparency of the information exchange in the Network, it can be concluded that undertakings are adequately protected against the improper disclosure of business secrets and other confidential data to persons outside the ECN (including sectoral regulators and Ministries) provided that the companies make their views known in good time and that confidentiality requests are never separated from the relevant document, but always transmitted therewith. Moreover, the potential interest of each NCA to obtain information from its colleague agencies, combined with the fact that, pursuant to Article 12 of Regulation 1/2003, the transmission of information is a pure faculty, not an obligation, indirectly imposes some pressure upon NCAs to respect confidentiality claims or classifications of the transmitting authority. Otherwise, the receiving authority risks being regarded as unreliable or unco-operative in this respect, and being blacklisted and hence omitted from future exchanges.[186] Lastly, the mere fact that the Network members agreed to install the position of an ADO through whom the exchange of confidential

---

[183] Martinez Lage and Brokelmann, *ibid*. On the other hand, the adoption of a definition of the notion 'professional secrecy' is unlikely to be of much practical use as is it would either have to be formulated in very general and abstract terms to cover all possible cases or would have to be extremely detailed with the associated risk of inflexibility. See Dekeyser and Dalheimer, above n 9, 13; Burnside and Crossley, above n 90, 30.

[184] The Commission's Notice on Access to File and the existing case law already provide ample indications as to what categories of documents may qualify as confidential. See Lenaerts and Vanhamme, above n 125, 541. Bringing together these rules and principles, which are spread over different cases and legislative acts, in a single document would still be a useful exercise. Such a compendium would be more concise and transparent, and therefore more easily accessible. Moreover, in terms of legal certainty, it could be stated explicitly that the standards apply for both Commission and national proceedings involving the application of Art 81 or 82 EC.

[185] There is evidently a risk that decisions of the transmitting authority confirming the confidential nature of certain documents or data will be ignored if the receiving authority has lower protection standards, whereas decisions refusing confidential treatment might be used as arguments against the parties' confidentiality request if the standards of the receiving authority tend to be higher.

[186] Schnichels, above n 26, 114.

information is channelled and whose very existence presupposes that information is already classified prior to its transmission implies that NCAs and Commission are in principle willing to respect each other's classifications and that they will generally abstain from reclassifying documents received from other Network members.

As concerns the treatment of confidential information intra-agency, it would seem to follow from the judgment of the CFI in *SEP* that releasing confidential information at random to innumerous persons even within an NCA, such as to officials of other departments not involved in the enforcement of Article 81 or 82 EC, may violate the undertaking's rights.[187] The dissemination of information within each competition authority—and this includes both the Commission and the NCAs—must therefore be limited to those persons who are actually working on the specific case and those who are more generally taking care of co-operation and communication with other Network members, in particular those officials who have been entrusted with receiving and/or dispatching documents in respect of the ECN (eg the ADOs).

B. Judicial Control of Information Gathering

Article 12 of Regulation 1/2003 deals only with the exchange of and the use in evidence of information, not with its collection. Moreover, no limitations are imposed on the exchange procedure. The restrictions provided for by Article 12 of Regulation 1/2003 exclusively concern the subsequent use of the exchanged information and relate either to the subject matter of the proceedings or the applicable sanctions. Compliance with national rules governing the information gathering is therefore not a prerequisite for the exchange. This raises the question how undertakings can effectively be protected against the use, by the receiving authority, of evidentiary material that has been obtained in an illegal manner by the transmitting authority.

---

[187] See para 56 of the judgment (above n 122): 'In the present case . . . the provisions of Art 20 [of Reg 17] would prevent not only the disclosure of information relating to that contract outside the administrative directorate concerned but also the circulation of such information within the directorate itself'. In my opinion, this conclusion can be drawn regardless of whether the NCA in question is commercially active. It is based on the simple consideration that the more widely confidential information is dispersed, the higher the risk that it will accidentally leak to the public. See Waelbroeck, above n 87, 478 ('the sheer multiplication of the authorities . . . increases greatly the risk that disclosures of confidential information to third parties will be made'). This is particularly true if the persons to whom the information is forwarded are not involved in the relevant procedure and might therefore lack the sensitivity of realising the confidential nature of the information.

1. The 'Country-of-origin' Principle

The collection of documents and other information and, in particular, the conduct of inspections are regulated solely by the applicable national laws of the NCA carrying out the fact-finding measures. Paragraph 4 of the Network Notice makes it quite clear that each Network member remains fully responsible for ensuring due process in all cases it is dealing with. At the same time, Article 12 of Regulation 1/2003 does not limit the exchange and evidential use of information in view of any procedural irregularities that might have vitiated the information gathering. On the contrary, that provision, together with the Network Notice, indicates that the (possible) violation of national procedural rules governing the collection of information does not exclude a later transmission of that information and its use by the receiving authority. Paragraph 27 of the Network Notice, which deals with the exchange of information under Article 12 of Regulation 1/2003, provides that the NCA transmitting evidence may, but does not have to, inform the receiving NCA about the question of whether the legality of the information gathering has been or still might be challenged.[188] In other words, NCAs (and the Commission) are technically entitled, without formal restriction, to transmit any information they have gathered and to use any information they have received from other Network members irrespective of whether the collection of that information is potentially illegal.[189]

This finding seems to be at odds with the general principle of any state founded on the rule of law[190] that only legally collected evidence can be used against a person. Most Member States' laws will impose some kind of restrictions on the use of evidence that has been obtained in violation of mandatory rules.[191] The rights of defence would in fact seriously be curtailed if authorities could use in evidence, against an undertaking or individual, information that was subsequently determined, in the Member State of origin, to have been assembled illegally.

On the other hand, it is evident that only the Member State where the

---

[188] Para 27 of the Network Notice also states that the question of whether information was gathered in a legal manner by the transmitting authority is determined on the basis of the law applicable to that authority. These two sentences imply that the legality of the information gathering is not a relevant issue in the context of information exchange, at least not in the sense that it would exclude the exchange of the evidence at hand.

[189] Reichelt, above n 11, 751.

[190] The rule of law is one of the general principles of law common to all Member States. See Art 6(1) of the TEU (Treaty on European Union, also known as the Maastricht Treaty, [1992] OJ C191/1; for the consolidated version, see [2002] OJ C325/1).

[191] For the Commission procedure, see Case 46/87 R *Hoechst v Commission* [1987] ECR 1549 para 34. By way of example, for German criminal law, see L Meyer-Goßner, *Strafprozessordnung, Kommentar* (Munich, CH Beck, 48th edn, 2005), Einl no 55–57a. For Belgian criminal law, see R Verstraeten, *Handboek Strafvordering* (Antwerpen, Maklu, 4th edn, 2005), paras 1812–25.

information was collected can effectively control whether all relevant rules of procedure have been duly respected since only the authorities and courts in that Member State are familiar with those rules. It would not only hamper the functioning of the ECN, but also undermine mutual trust and respect among the Network members, if the receiving authority were to usurp the right to assess the conformity of the investigative measures with the laws of the transmitting authority.[192] Moreover, it would seem contrary to the principle of state sovereignty if one Member State were to judge the legality of measures taken by the public bodies of another Member State.[193]

In this context, it has been suggested that a distinction must be drawn between judicial review of the 'legality of the foreign evidence' (*rechtmatigheid van in het buitenland verzamelde bewijs*) and judicial review of the 'legality of the information gathering' (*rechtmatigheid van de onderzoekshandeling*). On the basis of Belgian jurisprudence developed with regard to criminal law cases, the authors argue that the national judge who has been seized to review the final decision of the receiving NCA may also assess the legality of the evidence collected by the transmitting NCA (ie the legality of the foreign evidence). By carrying out this review, the legality of the information gathering as such would only be scrutinised incidentally. Moreover, the review would be done on the basis of the law applicable in the Member State of the transmitting NCA with full respect to that Member State's sovereignty.[194] However, this line of argument is not entirely convincing.

In my view, the distinction between legality of evidence and legality of information gathering is a very formalistic construction which will often be difficult to sustain. When considering the legality of the evidence, the national judge de facto also reviews the lawfulness of the manner in which

---

[192] See Reichelt, above n 11, 752 and 779. Cf also E David, 'Cooperation Among National Authorities in the European Competition Network' (2008) *e-Competitions* No 22157, 1, paras 18–19, pointing to the rich case law in certain domains which makes any assessment of legality a complex exercise.

[193] Under the general rules of public international law, every sovereign state is required to respect the acts of other sovereign states and thus will not subject foreign acts of state to judicial review by its own courts (so-called act-of-state doctrine; see A Verdross and B Simma, *Universelles Völkerrecht* (Berlin, Duncker & Humblot, 3rd edn, 1984), § 1178). Admittedly, the relations between Member States are governed predominantly by Community law principles rather than by traditional international law (see Lenaerts and Van Nuffel, above n 123, 1-013). However, where public law demands respect for the acts of foreign states, this should apply a fortiori to acts of Member States adopted in the Community law sphere where relations tend to be closer, where Member States are subject to the same rules and principles, and where the national courts can refer questions regarding the application of the law to a supranational court (the ECJ). In such a context, it is even more natural that states will show mutual trust and respect for each other.

[194] 'Bovendien toetst de rechter de handeling van de toezendende autoriteit incidenteel aan het recht van de lidstaat van de autoriteit met volledige eerbiediging van de soevereiniteit van de lidstaat'. D Arts and K Bourgeois, 'Samenwerking tussen mededingingsautoriteiten en rechtsbescherming: enkele bedenkingen' (2006) 1 *TBM-RCB* 26, para 88.

the foreign evidence was obtained.[195] In this context, it is of little merit that the legality of the foreign authority's investigative measure is not reviewed directly, but only incidentally. In my view, even an indirect control of foreign investigations by the national judge encroaches upon the sovereignty of the Member State in whose territory the evidence was collected since even an incidental evaluation ultimately entails a judgment on the legality of the foreign investigative measure (the *onderzoekshandeling*).

Moreover, the case law to which the above authors refer does not seem to fully support their views. In the judgment cited, the Belgian court of last resort (Hof van Cassatie) clearly considered that it was not for the Belgian judge to assess the lawfulness or unlawfulness of the foreign investigative measure, in that case a criminal investigation conducted in France, using French law as a yardstick.[196] The Hof van Cassatie accepted that the national judge should only decide whether the foreign evidence, even if it had been collected in accordance with the applicable French law, could be relied upon in the Belgian proceedings or whether this would be contrary to the requirements of the ECHR. However, this evaluation is quite different from the (incidental) legal review of the information gathering suggested by the authors quoted above. The review accepted by the Hof van Cassatie on the basis of the ECHR sought to establish whether there was an incompatibility with the domestic *ordre public* of which higher-ranking international norms such as the ECHR form a part. It concerns the admissibility, in the Belgian proceedings, of the evidence collected in a foreign state rather than the question of whether the information gathering was in conformity with the foreign state's law.[197] By contrast, an (incidental) legal review of the information gathering would

---

[195] Cf Verstraeten, above n 191, para 1788: 'De onrechtmatigheid van een bewijs vindt zijn oorsprong in de manier waarop het bewijs werd verkregen.' In other words, the legality of the evidence cannot be established without determining whether the evidence was obtained in a legal manner. A useful distinction, by contrast, is that between the legality of the foreign information gathering and the admissibility of the evidence in the domestic procedure. While the first can only be reviewed by the courts of the Member State whose NCA collected the evidence (ie the transmitting NCA), the latter is to be judged on the basis of the procedural law of the Member State whose NCA seeks to use in evidence that particular piece of information (ie the receiving authority). Both aspects are independent of each other. Examples are a personal diary or the records of a lie detector the collection of which may be perfectly legal in one Member State, but which probably cannot be used in evidence according to the laws of another Member State. See also below n 197.

[196] Hof van Cassatie, judgment of 12 October 1993, AC 1993, 829: 'Overwegende dat het niet strijdig is vast te stellen, eendeels, dat de Belgische rechter de al dan niet wettelijkheid van een in het buitenland ingesteld gerechtelijk onderzoek niet heeft te beoordelen'.

[197] The Hof van Cassatie (*ibid*) namely ruled: 'Overwegende dat een vreemde wet die het afluisteren . . . toelaat niet strijdig is met de Belgische openbare orde voor zover die vreemde wet in overeenstemming is met onder meer de bepalingen van het EVRM'; and further '[d]at de appelrechters niet beoordelen "de conformiteit aan het EVRM . . . van een in Frankrijk verricht gerechtelijk onderzoek", maar wel de *aanwendbaarheid* in een Belgisch strafproces van een in het buitenland, zij het in het raam van een dergelijk onderzoek, verkregen bewijs;' (emphasis added).

have to be based on the domestic laws and procedures of the Member State to which the transmitting authority belongs and thus would directly interfere with that Member State's sovereign rights.

Finally, control by the Member State of the receiving authority would also cause difficulties in practical terms. Courts and authorities in that Member State lack both the legal and factual background to judge whether the laws of the transmitting authority have fully been observed. Therefore, it is exclusively for the Member State of origin to exercise control over the legality of the information gathering.[198]

On the other hand, this approach does not exclude the possibility that there may be situations where the courts in the country of the receiving authority should be entitled to refuse evidence stemming from another Member State, ie to consider it inadmissible. As suggested in the above-cited judgment of the Hof van Cassatie, it may be incompatible with the *ordre public* or other fundamental principles to admit a particular (foreign) piece of evidence in the national proceedings. Where these rules are considered imperative so that they would override the principle of free movement of evidence, the national judge may regard the evidence as illegal according to the domestic laws of the receiving Member State, and consequently reject it.[199] However, this option must be limited to very exceptional cases in order not to undermine the general principle of the 'free movement of evidence'. Moreover, the judge in the receiving Member State must refrain from reviewing, directly or indirectly, the manner in which the evidence was collected. The question of admissibility of foreign evidence should thus only be raised where there are general (fundamental) objections against the type or form of evidence which persist regardless of whether the evidence was gathered in a lawful or unlawful fashion.[200]

2. Five Unwritten Basic Safeguards

It must be ensured that the transmission of information does not deprive undertakings (or individuals) of their rights of defence. They must still be given the opportunity to effectively contest the legality of the investigative

---

[198] It must be noted that, according to more recent case law, the Belgian judge in criminal matters also seems to be under an obligation to establish, on the basis of the applicable foreign rules, whether the foreign information was collected in a legal manner prior to admitting it as evidence in Belgian court proceedings. See Verstraeten, above n 191, paras 1788 and 1801. However, in view of the 'country of origin' principle, which, it is submitted, is implied in Reg 1/2003, it would be incompatible with the superior rules of Community law to adopt the same approach, in Belgian competition proceedings regarding the application of Art 81 or 82 EC, in respect of evidence that has been obtained from another NCA or the Commission.

[199] Cf Weiß, above n 52, 267. He refers to GWB, s 50a(3), last sentence, according to which the BKartA still has the duty to comply with prohibitions on the use of evidence that are based on constitutional principles.

[200] See above n 195.

measures which are of concern to them.[201] This is an essential requirement of procedural fairness, and it is most unfortunate that Regulation 1/2003 does not deal at all with this issue while the Network Notice only mentions its randomly.[202]

Since the exchange as such cannot be challenged, certain safeguards must be installed, mostly applicable after the exchange has taken place, in order to adequately protect the parties' rights in case that illegally obtained information is circulating in the Network. It is therefore submitted that, despite the failure of Regulation 1/2003 to lay down written rules in this respect, the following five basic rules must be applied.

First, where information is forwarded to the Network, the Member State of origin, ie the Member State where the information was originally collected, and the authority which collected it must be indicated on the relevant documents. This is an important safeguard ensuring transparency. Only if exchanged documents are earmarked in this way can the under-takings or individuals concerned effectively learn that a certain piece of evidence has been circulated in the Network and know where the information gathering can be challenged.

Secondly, a (legal or natural) person wishing to contest the legality of the information gathering always has the right to address an application to the competent authorities or courts of the Member State where the information originates. This rule applies regardless of whether the information has been forwarded to one or several other NCAs or the Commission. The right inevitably correlates with the principle that legality control is exercised (only) in the Member State of origin.

Thirdly, in order to prevent the above right from becoming an empty shell, the receiving authority must be precluded from using the information obtained via the Network where it is subsequently determined to have been collected illegally in the Member State of origin. In other words, the illegality of an investigative measure renders the information derived from it unusable for any Network member.[203] The relevant documents must be removed from the case file of the receiving authority or authorities[204] and be destroyed or returned to the persons who provided them. In any event, the parties concerned must be informed of the removal of the evidence.

Fourthly, where the legality of the information gathering is already being contested at the moment of transmission, the transmitting authority must inform the receiving authority about such contestation.[205] Similarly, where

[201] Gauer, above n 18, 13.

[202] See the above-mentioned para 27 of the Network Notice, which states that 'the transmitting authority may inform the receiving authority whether the gathering of the information was contested or could still be contested'.

[203] See Gauer, above n 18, 13; cf also Van Gerven, above n 29, 352.

[204] Dekeyser and Dalheimer, above n 9, 12.

[205] This possibility is foreseen in para 28 of the Network Notice. However, it does not establish an obligation. See above n 202.

the legality of the investigative measure is challenged subsequently, ie after the evidence has been transmitted, that factor should always be communicated to the receiving authority or authorities. This is a simple formality which increases transparency and allows the receiving authority to take into account that the evidence it has obtained may ultimately have to be excluded from the proceedings. In addition, the first authority must be considered as having a duty to refuse the transfer of information to the second authority if the illegality of the information gathering has definitively been established before the information could actually be forwarded.[206] Admittedly, the latter obligation is not fully in line with the wording of Article 12 of Regulation 1/2003, which does not provide any restriction for the actual transmission of information; however, to guarantee an adequate and effective protection of the rights of defence, it seems more efficient to prevent the exchange of information which, in any event, could not be used by the receiving authority. If one allowed that authority to take cognisance of the unusable evidence, this would entail the risk that the receiving authority, building on this knowledge, would further investigate the matter, thereby making (indirect) use of the illegally obtained information.[207] A prohibition to transfer such evidence in the first place provides better protection and is therefore preferable.

[207] *Contra* Reichelt, who contends that an NCA which has (formally) agreed to assist another NCA in fact-finding pursuant to Art 22(1) of Reg 1/2003 foregoes its discretionary powers under Art 12(1) of Reg 1/2003 and is in fact obliged to forward any information it has collected to the NCA which requested the assistance. See Reichelt, above n 11, 765–6 (with reference to Van Der Woude, above n 96, 379 and Kist, above n 45, 366) and also above n 5. It must be noted, though, that Van Der Woude only raises the question without deciding it. Moreover, on the same page, he also points to the fact that Art 12(1) of Reg 1/2003 does not establish a duty and that an NCA thus cannot be compelled to forward information to another NCA. In my view, there is no reason why this qualification should change if Art 12 is applied in conjunction with Art 22 of Reg 1/2003. Similarly, Kist concludes that, since Art 12 of Reg 1/2003 does not lay down an obligation, the NCA 'may still decide not to pass on the information'. Moreover, the contributions of Van Der Woude and Kist are based on the draft text of Art 22(1) which stated: 'It *shall* transmit the information collected to the requesting authority in accordance with Article 12 of this Regulation' (emphasis added). (See Art 21(1) of the Draft Regulation.) However, this wording has not been maintained, and the actual text of Art 22(1) of Reg 1/2003 ('Any exchange and use of the information collected shall be carried out in accordance with Article 12 of this Regulation') leaves open the possibility that there will be no information exchange at all. The sentence is a simple reference to Art 12 of Reg 1/2003 intended to ensure that the safeguards of that provision are always respected regardless of whether the exchanged evidence has been collected by the transmitting authority at the request of another NCA or out of its own motion. Therefore, Reichelt's position does not appear convincing.

[207] Cf C Dekker, 'Op welk moment wordt het legal privilege geschonden?' (2005) *Nederlands tijdschrift voor Europees recht* 12, 14, who rightly points to the fact that authorities are likely to make indirect use of illegally obtained documents, even if that information is later removed from the file, in that the mere knowledge of those documents may induce them to make more inquiries and search for further evidence and may also influence the interpretation of other evidential material. This may be true even if officials only skim over the relevant documents perfunctorily. Burnside and Crossley, above n 36, 11. Cf also para 39 of the judgment in *Spanish Banks* (above n 27) and para 29 of the appeal judgment in *SEP* (above n 122). In both these cases the ECJ noted that, where information which they may not use as (direct) evidence has been disclosed to NCA officials, these officials are nonetheless not required to undergo acute amnesia.

Fifthly, where the legality of the information gathering is disputed, the (national) court called upon to decide on the lawfulness of the final decision of the receiving authority (eg a prohibition decision or a decision imposing fines) should, if possible, stay its proceedings and await the decision of the judge in the Member State of origin who has been engaged to scrutinise the collection of evidence. This kind of division of labour again corresponds to the principle that the legality control of the information gathering is exercised (only) by the courts in the Member State of origin.

This may lead to certain delays in the proceedings before the first court, ie the court that deals with the lawfulness of the receiving authority's decision. Where the proceedings in the Member State of origin concerning the collection of evidence take a considerable amount of time (eg because an appeal has been lodged against the first decision), a total halt to the proceedings in the first court may not be practicable. On the other hand, a decision of that court which does not take into account the (possible) illegality of a certain piece of evidence might seriously curtail the rights of defence of the undertakings concerned. In such a situation, the legitimate interest of the undertakings to protect their rights of defence and the (general) interest to have a court decision within a reasonable time must be weighed against each other. First, the judge should carefully consider whether the piece of evidence the legality of which is disputed in another procedure is a key element on which his decision depends or whether he can possibly reach a judgment without relying on it. If it is indeed a crucial piece of evidence, the judge should try to contact the authority or national court in the other Member State with a view to ascertaining how long those proceedings are likely to take and whether there is any possibility of speeding them up. If it is not feasible for the judge to await the foreign decision on the legality of the evidence, he may consider to give a ruling anyway. However, it is submitted that a court should abstain from rendering a judgment which would depend on a certain piece of evidence whose legality has not definitively been established if the judgment could not be appealed further, ie where there would be no judicial remedy under national law against the court's ruling regarding the final decision of the receiving authority.

Even if these five principles are observed, it is still doubtful that no irreparable harm is caused by the transfer of illegally collected information.[208] As noted, the mere fact that an authority has knowledge of the existence of certain (inculpatory) evidence, even if that evidence is later removed from the case file, may provide valuable insight and may thus have an impact on the way in which that authority conducts its investigation and on the conclusions drawn by it. On this basis, it would certainly

[208] This is, however, the position taken by Gauer, above n 18, 13.

be fairer to solve any issues relating to the legality of the fact-finding measures before the information or evidence resulting from these measures is actually circulated in the Network.[209] However, such a prior control would not be practicable. It would considerably delay the exchange of information between Network members and thus risk jeopardising the entire functioning of the ECN. The above suggestions of unwritten safeguards therefore present a workable compromise.

C. Differences in Procedural Rights and Guarantees

In the *Spanish Banks* case, the ECJ emphasised that Member States, even where they enforce Community competition law, do so in accordance with their respective national rules.[210] It is, however, well known that procedural guarantees and protection standards in competition proceedings vary widely across Member States. Despite these discrepancies, the Commission has always maintained that the harmonisation of national procedures is not necessary for the implementation of the present reform.[211] Commission officials frequently refer to the common minimum level of protection that is guaranteed by the ECHR and to which all Member States are signatories.[212] Whether these minimum standards together with the fairly limited safeguards of Article 12(3) of Regulation 1/2003 (regarding exclusively sanctions against individuals) are indeed sufficient to ensure that procedural rights and guarantees are not weakened or undermined due to an information exchange within the ECN is more than doubtful.

1. The Problem

Procedural rights and investigative powers in competition proceedings are not uniform throughout the EU. They not only vary from Member State to Member State, but often also differ significantly from the Community law system. At the same time, evidence can circulate freely within the Network. Thus a Network member can obtain evidence which it could not have lawfully collected itself pursuant to the own procedural rules because its investigatory powers are more limited than those of other Network

---

[209] Cf Van Der Woude, above n 96, 386.
[210] See paras 31 and 32 of the judgment in *Spanish Banks* (above n 27).
[211] Explanatory Memorandum, 12.
[212] Wils, above n 30, para 207; E Paulis and E De Smijter, 'Enhanced Enforcement of the EC Competition Rules since 1 May 2004 by the Commission and the NCAs', paper for the conference 'Antitrust Reform in Europe: A Year in Practice', organised jointly by the International Bar Association (IBA) and the European Commission, Brussels, 9–11 March 2005, 8. It is also worth noting that recital 37 of Reg 1/2003 explicitly states that the regulation acknowledges the fundamental rights and principles as recognised by the EU Charter and should therefore be interpreted and applied with respect to those rights and principles.

members or because its national regime grants a higher degree of protection to the persons concerned.[213] This inevitably raises the question of whether the present rules on information exchange should be interpreted more restrictively or even modified (*de lege feranda*) in order to prevent competition authorities from circumventing procedural limitations imposed on them by national or Community law.

a. Divergent Standards of Protection

In order to fully grasp the issues and concerns resulting from different procedures and protection standards across the EU, it seems worthwhile to briefly recapitulate some of the most outstanding procedural guarantees in anti-trust investigations. It is beyond the scope of this book to provide an exhaustive list of all existing procedural guarantees in the framework of competition law investigations. However, there are at least three areas of procedural safeguards which can serve as examples illustrating clearly the varying degrees of protection afforded by Member States and at Community level, namely the law of legal privilege, the right against self-incrimination and the principle of inviolability of the home. These differences add to the discrepancies existing in the field of leniency which have been discussed earlier.[214]

(1) Legal Professional Privilege. Probably the most prominent example of diverging protection standards in the EU are the rules on legal (professional) privilege, or lawyer–client privilege.[215] Legal privilege can be described as a rule of law according to which private communications between lawyer and client may not be subject to forced disclosure in judicial or administrative proceedings.[216] They are thus protected against

---

[213] See Wils, above n 30, paras 210–12 and Gauer, above n 18, 13–14.

[214] Above Chapter 3, section III.C.2.

[215] It has recently been the subject of much debate, not only in view of the possible effects of modernisation on legal privilege, but also against the background of two orders of the CFI and the ECJ in the *Akzo/Akcros* case, which revived academic discussions on the scope of this privilege, namely the order of the President of the CFI in Joined Cases T–125/03 R and T–253/03 R *Akzo Nobel and Akcros Chemicals v Commission* [2003] ECR II–4771 and the order of the President of the ECJ of 27 September 2004 in Case C–7/04 P(R) *Commission v Akzo Nobel and Akcros Chemicals* [2004] ECR I–8739. See, eg T Kapp and A Roth, 'Fällt eine weitere Beschränkung des europarechtlichen Legal Privilege?' (2003) 49 *Recht der Internationalen Wirtschaft* 946; C Seitz, 'Unternehmensjuristen und das Anwaltsprivileg im europäischen Wettbewerbsverfahren—Wandel in der europäischen Rechtsprechung?' (2004) 15 *Europäische Zeitschrift für Wirtschaftsrecht* 231, 233–5; E Gippini-Fournier, 'Legal Professional Privilege in Competition Proceedings before the European Commission: Beyond the Cursory Glance' in B Hawk (ed), *2004 Proceedings of the Fordham Corporate Law Institute* (New York, Juris Publishing, 2005), 587, in particular 621–56. See also A Andreangeli, 'Joined Cases T–125/03 and 253/03, AKZO Nobel Chemicals Ltd v Ackros Chemicals Ltd v Commission' (2008) 19 *European Business Law Review* 1141, with references also to older literature on the subject (at note 1).

[216] Gippini-Fournier, *ibid*, 590.

inspection and confiscation by public authorities. In common law countries, the privilege is conferred in view of the legal position of the client, while in civil law countries it is rather seen as an aspect of the general principle of confidentiality covering the relation between lawyer and client and is secured by rules on professional conduct. Nevertheless, in both common and civil law jurisdictions, the concept often operates in a similar way.[217]

However, the scope of the concept varies considerably across the EU. In most Member States and at the Community level, the privilege only covers communications between companies and their external legal advisers, while in some other Member States it also extends to communications with in-house lawyers (Belgium, Greece, Ireland, UK).[218] In yet a third group of Members States, the concept is essentially unknown (eg Germany, France, Czech Republic).[219] By way of examples, the situation at the Community level, in Germany and in the UK are described hereafter.

Since the ECJ's judgment of 1982 in *AM&S*, it has been established that, in competition investigations conducted at the Community level, written communications between a (corporate) client and its external counsel are privileged.[220] The Commission may not inspect, seize or use in evidence such material provided that three conditions are fulfilled. First, the communications have been made after the initiation of proceedings for the purpose of and in the interest of the client's defence. Earlier communications are, however, privileged to the extent that they are related to the subject matter of the proceedings. Secondly, the communications have been

---

[217] Burnside and Crossley, above n 36, 3. The reason for the different approach is that, in common law jurisdictions, parties to judicial proceedings are generally obliged to disclose all relevant documents. Communications between lawyer and client are exempted from this rule in order to allow parties to seek legal advice and prepare their defence without having to fear that details of these will be revealed later. In civil law countries, such protection is usually not necessary as there are no equivalent disclosure obligations. *Ibid.* On the different rationale underlying the concept of legal privilege, see Gippini-Fournier, above n 215, 595–621. On policy reasons, see also various examples of decisions of different appellate courts (inter alia UK, US and Canada) cited by Lord Scott in *Three Rivers District Council and others v Governor and Company of the Bank of England*, Opinions of the Lords of Appeal [2004] UKHL 48, paras 30 *et seq.*

[218] K Dekeyser and C Gauer, 'The New Enforcement System for Articles 81 and 82 and the Rights of Defence' in B Hawk (ed), *2004 Proceedings of the Fordham Corporate Law Institute* (New York, Juris Publishing, 2005), 549, 569. It should be noted, though, that Belgian law is frequently quoted as an example of a broad concept of legal privilege that also covers in-house counsel. However, the position with regard to in-house lawyers does not seem to be entirely clear. For a different view, see Gippini-Fournier, above n 215, 655.

[219] See Burnside and Crossley, above n 36, 5.

[220] Correspondence exchanged between a company and its legal department (in-house counsel) are thus excluded from protection under the Community law concept of legal privilege. In the past, the Commission has relied on evidence relating to in-house lawyers in at least two cases. See the examples quoted by J Faull, 'In-house Lawyers and Legal Professional Privilege: A Problem Revisited' (1998) *Columbia Journal of European Law* 139, 140. The recent *Akzo/Akcros* case (see above n 215 and below nn 233 and 234) has brought this issue again to the forefront.

prepared by an independent lawyer, ie a lawyer who is not linked to the client by virtue of an employment contract. Thirdly, the lawyer is entitled to practice in one of the Member States and is subject to the relevant rules of professional conduct.[221] Similar concepts of privilege apply in many of the EU's Member States (eg Italy, Sweden, Spain, Netherlands).[222]

Under German law, a very limited concept of legal privilege applies. As a general rule, communications between an external lawyer and client are not afforded any legal protection and may thus be subject to inspection and confiscation unless they are located at the lawyer's premises. The reason for this limited protection is that, pursuant to the applicable provisions of the code of criminal procedure (Strafprozessordung), exemptions from confiscation apply only where the relevant correspondence is in the possession (*Gewahrsam*) of the lawyer himself, but not in the possession of the client.[223] On this basis, communications between the in-house lawyer, who is also admitted to the bar (the so-called Syndicusanwälte), and the company employing him seem to be protected where the documents are kept in the lawyer's office.[224] By way of exception, communications located at the client's premises are privileged only where they specifically concern his defence against a criminal or regulatory offence (so-called *echte Verteidigerpost*). This requires proceedings against the client to have already been initiated and the lawyer to have actually been retained as defence

---

[221] Judgment of the ECJ in Case 155/79 *AM&S Europe Limited v Commission* [1982] ECR 1575, paras 21–5. Subsequently, in *Hilti*, the CFI held that the principle of legal privilege also extends to internal notes of a company which are confined to reporting the mere content of legal advice obtained from an external counsel, ie advice which, on its part, would be covered by the privilege. Order of the CFI in Case T–30/89 *Hilti v Commission* [1990] ECR II–163, para 18. The requirement that the lawyer must not be linked to the company by way of an employment contract would seem, however, to be contrary to the standards of legal privilege as established by the HR Court. See Andreangeli, above n 215, 1152.

[222] See Burnside and Crossley, above n 36, 5. Gippini-Fournier, above n 215, 651, even notes a certain trend in Member States towards alignment with the *AM&S* standards.

[223] § 97 para 2, sentence 1, StPO. M Buntscheck, 'Anwaltskorrespondenz—Beitrag zur geordneten Rechtspflege oder "tickende Zeitbombe"' (2007) 57 *Wirtschaft und Wettbewerb* 229, 233.

[224] T Kapp, 'Vertraulichkeit der Anwaltskorrespondenz im Kartellverfahren' (2003) 53 *Wirtschaft und Wettbewerb* 142, 143. However, protection to in-house legal advice is only granted to the extent that the documents are in the sole possession (*alleiniger Gewahrsam*) of the in-house counsel, meaning that other members of staff have no access to them. Buntscheck, *ibid*, 238–9. *Contra* Dekeyser and Gauer, above n 218, 569, who argue that, also under German law, in-house lawyers are not covered by the rules on legal privilege. They refer to a decision of the Bundesgerichtshof (order of the BGH of 18 June 2001—AnwZ(B) 41/100 (2001) 54 *Neue Juristische Wochenschrift* 3130–1), where it was held that the activities performed by an in-house counsel for his employer are not regarded as typical activities of an independent lawyer who is a member of a liberal profession and collaborates in the administration of justice (*unabhängiges Rechtspflegeorgan*). It should be noted that the exemption from confiscation under § 97 StPO is linked to the right of certain professionals such as doctors, lawyers, notaries and defence counsel to refuse testimony (*Zeugnisverweigerungsrecht*) enshrined in § 53 StPO. Whether this latter provision extends to in-house counsel is unclear. See Meyer-Goßner, above n 191, § 53 no 15.

counsel (*bestehendes Verteidigerverhältnis*).[225] By contrast, general type of legal advice in the possession of the client that is not related to a pending judicial procedure is not protected.[226] Correspondence with external counsel that is kept at the offices of the company under investigation, as well as communications emanating from an in-house lawyer but (also) in the possession of other employees, can therefore be examined, seized and used in evidence by German authorities.[227] In practice, this means that companies can effectively avail themselves of a kind of legal privilege only where the premises of their (external) counsel are inspected.[228]

Under the UK's Competition Act 1998, the requirement to produce documents does not extend to privileged communications, ie communications between a professional legal adviser and his client and communications that relate to judicial proceedings and would be protected from disclosure.[229] Since the term 'professional legal adviser' is understood to include both qualified lawyers who are employed by companies and those practising in their own right, legal privilege effectively covers written communications between a corporate client and external (independent) lawyers as well as in-house counsel advice. Legal privilege under UK competition law thus affords more extensive protection than under Community law in terms of the professionals to whom it applies.[230] UK law also seems to adopt a broader approach as to the type of advice that is covered. In a recent opinion, the House of Lords confirmed that the scope of 'legal advice privilege' is not confined to advice relating to the conduct of litigation. Communications plainly advising the client as to what should reasonably be done in a given legal context, including merely presentational advice, also qualify for that privilege.[231]

---

[225] Kapp, above n 224, 143; Buntscheck, above n 223, 234; Meyer-Goßner, above n 191, § 53 no 13 in conjunction with § 97 no 37. (NB: Under German law, violations of the competition rules are regulatory offences.)

[226] Meyer and Kuhn, above n 59, 888. On the different approach and interpretation, under German and Community law, as regards the 'connection' (*Zusammenhang*) that must exist between the lawyer–client communication and the proceedings initiated against the client, see Kapp and Roth, above n 215, 947–8.

[227] It must be noted, however, that there is still some debate about the exact scope of protection granted to lawyer–client communications under German law, protection that could be considered as constituting a kind of 'legal privilege'. See Meyer and Kuhn, above n 59, 888; Bechtold, above n 52, § 59 no 12. See also the judgments of two German courts discussed by Kapp, above n 224, 143–5. In particular, the position regarding in-house counsel is unclear. See above n 224.

[228] Buntscheck, above n 223, 234.

[229] R Whish, *Competition Law* (London, LexisNexis, 5th edn, 2003), 367. UK law in fact distinguishes between 'legal advice privilege', which is afforded to lawyer–client communications made for the purpose of obtaining or providing legal advice, and 'litigation privilege', which covers communications made between a lawyer or a client and a third party with respect to pending or expected litigation. Burnside and Crossley, above n 36, 6.

[230] Whish, *ibid*, 367.

[231] See Opinions of the Lords of Appeal in *Three Rivers* (above n 217), paras 34–8 (with reference to *Balabel v Air India* [1988] 1 Ch 317). By contrast, the ECJ has limited the scope of

The above examples demonstrate the extent to which protection standards regarding lawyer–client communications differ between Member States. As concerns proceedings conducted by the Commission, the ruling in *AM&S* is still the cornerstone of the law of legal privilege and a number of Member States have aligned their respective national rules with these standards.[232] It had been hoped by many that the recent *Akzo/Akcros* case, which relates to a dispute over the scope of legal privilege that arose during a surprise inspection carried out by the Commission, would prompt the Luxembourg courts to revisit the problem and possibly overrule the existing case law. Some statements made by the President of the CFI in an order regarding interim measures for which Akzo had applied in that case had indeed suggested that a reconsideration of the ECJ's approach in *AM & S* might be imminent.[233] However, these hopes have not been fulfilled. On 17 September 2007 the CFI rendered its judgment in the main proceedings, dismissing Akzo's claim that the personal scope of legal privilege should be construed or extended so as to also cover in-house counsel.[234] The CFI essentially held that:

legal privilege under Community competition law to written communications made after the initiation of the administrative procedure and 'earlier written communications which have a relationship to the subject matter of that procedure'. Para 23 of the judgment in *AM&S* (above n 221). See also Burnside and Crossley, above n 36, 13–14.

232 Gippini-Fournier, above n 215, 658 and 651. Another question is whether the German system (and other national systems denying legal privilege to communications with independent lawyers) is compatible with Community law.

233 The *Akzo/Akcros* case essentially concerns an application for annulment of a Commission decision rejecting the applicants' request to treat as privileged certain documents which the Commission had seized in the course of an investigation relating to suspected anti-competitive practices by Akzo and several other companies. Akzo had applied for interim measures in order to have that decision, which also stated the Commission's intention to include in its case file and/or to examine the documents at issue, suspended. The President of the CFI, ruling on the interim injunction, partly granted the request for provisional confidential treatment. Of particular interest regarding the definition of the scope of legal privilege is para 98 of that Order (above n 215): 'The President [of the CFI] considers that the applicants' plea raises very important and complex questions concerning the possible need to extend, to a certain degree, the scope of professional privilege as currently delimited by the case-law.' The President of the CFI further noted at para 125 of the Order that the evidence adduced by the applicants 'appears prima facie to be capable of showing that the role assigned to independent lawyers of collaborating in the administration of justice by the courts, which proved decisive for the recognition of the protection of written communications to which they are parties (*AM&S v . . .*), is now capable of being shared, to a certain degree, by certain categories of lawyers employed within undertakings on a permanent basis where they are subject to strict rules of professional conduct'. These considerations seemed to signal a certain openness towards a broader interpretation of the concept of legal privilege. However, on appeal, the President of the ECJ annulled the CFI's order and rejected Akzo's preliminary application in its entirety, albeit essentially for lack of urgency, which is a pre-condition for granting interim relief (see paras 36–44 of the order of 27 September 2004 in Case C–7/04 P(R); above n 215).

234 Joined Cases T–125/03 and T–253/03 *Akzo Nobel and Akcros Chemicals v Commission* [2007] ECR II–3523. At the time of finalising this manuscript (February 2009) the appeal against the CFI's judgment (Case C–550/07 P) is still pending before the ECJ.

in-house lawyers and outside lawyers are clearly in very different situations, owing, in particular, to the functional, structural and hierarchical integration of in-house lawyers within the companies that employ them.[235]

It further ruled that:

> abolishing, in the context of the modernisation of Community competition law, the notification system, and consequently conferring on undertakings under Regulation No 1/2003 greater responsibility in assessing whether their conduct is lawful in the light of Article 81(3) EC, are not directly relevant to this problem area.[236]

Moreover, the personal scope of legal privilege, as defined in *AM & S*, was found not to form 'a real obstacle preventing undertakings from seeking the legal advice they need'.[237] The Commission was therefore right to exclude communications with the applicant's in-house lawyer from the protection of legal privilege. In any event, there seems to be no uniform or even clearly majoritarian evolution, at the Member State level, to extend legal privilege to in-house counsel.[238] Divergencies are likely to persist.[239]

---

[235] Para 174 of the judgment (above n 234).

[236] Para 172 of the judgment (above n 234).

[237] Para 173 of the judgment (above n 234). The CFI noted that even if the current enforcement rules 'may have increased the need for undertakings to examine their conduct and to define legal strategies in respect of competition law with the help of a lawyer who has in-depth knowledge of the particular undertaking and of the market in question, the fact remains that such exercises of self-assessment and strategy definition may be conducted by an outside lawyer in full co-operation with the relevant departments of the undertaking, including its internal legal department. In that context, communications between in-house lawyers and outside lawyers are in principle protected under LPP [legal professional privilege], provided that they are made for the purpose of the undertaking's exercise of the rights of defence.' Thus, the CFI simply referred undertakings to the possibility of obtaining external legal advice, albeit with the participation of their in-house lawyers, if they wished such advice to benefit from the protection under the legal privilege concept. This is a disappointing 'strategy proposal', apparently stemming from a dim view of the role and performance of in-house lawyers who, in reality, would be more than able to provide the requisite legal advice on their own responsibility were it not for the Court's refusal to recognise that their communications benefit from legal privilege as well.

[238] Gippini-Fournier, above n 215, 654; Dekeyser and Gauer, above n 218, 569–70. See also para 170 of the judgment of the CFI in *Akzo/Akcros* (above n 234). Yet, the appropriateness of the distinction made by the ECJ between external lawyers, whose communications are shielded from disclosure, and in-house counsel, who are denied the benefit of legal privilege, is widely debated among legal commentators. There are quite a few writers who submit, at least with regard to in-house counsel who are members of the local bar or law society and thus subject to the ethical rules of the profession and monitoring by the competent supervisory body, that the distinction is not or no longer adequate. See, eg A Andreangeli, 'The Protection of Legal Professional Privilege in EU Law and the Impact of the Rules on the Exchange of Information within the European Competition Network on the Secrecy of Communications between Lawyer and Client: One Step Forward, Two Steps Back?' (2005) 2 *The Competition Law Review* 31, 39–42. Andreangeli points, inter alia, to the changing role and increasing importance of in-house counsel, in particular against the background of modernisation, which requires self-assessment and self-compliance of companies. In-house counsel indeed appear to be best placed to provide the requisite legal assistance. *Idem*, 39. Obviously, in *Akzo/Akcros*, the CFI did not endorse these arguments.

[239] Another question is whether Member States can apply national rules on legal privilege which lag behind the Community standard (such as the German rules) when they enforce Arts 81

(2) Privilege against Self-incrimination. Another telling example of diverging standards are the rules regarding the privilege against self-incrimination and the right to remain silent.

It has already been pointed out that the case law of the ECtHR regarding the safeguards against self-incrimination does not seem to be entirely consistent. Variations in the national protection standards may thus merely result from different interpretations of the relevant case law of the ECtHR and do not necessarily reflect disregard of the principles enshrined in the ECHR.[240] Nonetheless, there appear to be considerable differences between the approaches of the Community and national laws.

As concerns the Commission's power to ask questions, there are principally three different types of queries that the Commission can conduct. First, the Commission can question an undertaking informally, ie by way of simple letter, or by formal request, ie on the basis of a Commission decision. In the latter case, the undertaking is, in principle, required to answer the questions.[241] Secondly, during an on-the-spot investigation, the Commission can ask for oral explanations on documents that are being inspected or on other facts.[242] Supplying incorrect, incomplete or misleading answers or no information at all can attract fines of up to 1% of the undertaking's annual turnover.[243] Where an undertaking, partially or

and 82 EC. Case law suggests that Member States, when acting in the Community law sphere, are in any event bound to respect the general principles of Community law even if they otherwise apply their national procedural rules. See para 19 of the judgment in *Wachauf* (above n 123) and Temple Lang, above n 123, 654–5. Arguably, this expression of the supremacy rule, together with the fact that the ECJ, in *AM&S* (para 23 of the judgment, above n 221), considered legal privilege to be an essential corollary of guaranteeing full exercise of the rights of the defence, ie as an intrinsic element of a fundamental principle of Community law, would prevent Member States from providing less protection to lawyer–client communications in proceedings regarding the application of Community competition law. Cf Bechtold, above n 52, § 59 no 12. On this basis, it has been argued that the BKartA has to interpret and apply German rules on legal privilege in conformity with Community law, ie it has to grant at least the same level of protection as under the *AM&S* doctrine of the ECJ when it implements Arts 81 and 82 EC. T Kapp and M Schröder, 'Legal Privilege des EG-(Kartell-)Verfahrensrechts: Ist § 97 Abs. 2 Satz 1 StPO gemeinschaftsrechtswidrig?' (2002) 52 *Wirtschaft und Wettbewerb* 555, 561. Buntscheck, above n 223, 241.

240 See above n 87 and below n 286.

241 See Art 18(1)–(3) of Reg 1/2003. The duty to answer formal requests for information coincides with the general obligation imposed on undertakings, pursuant to Art 20(4) of Reg 1/2003, to submit to inspections that have been ordered by Commission decision.

242 Art 20(2)(e) of Reg 1/2003. The answers may be recorded. Compared to the relevant provision of Reg 17, the Commission's power to interrogate persons on the spot has been extended or, at least, clarified. Under Reg 17, there was some uncertainty as to whether the Commission could only ask questions relating to books and records found during the on-site inspection or whether it could also request more general explanations on the facts and circumstances of the case being investigated. C Kerse, *EC Antitrust Procedure* (London, Sweet & Maxwell, 3rd edn, 1994), para 3-058; Riley, above n 44, 608. See also Chapter 1, n 75.

243 Where the person interrogated during an on-site inspection has been picked by the Commission and was not authorised to speak on behalf of the company, that company may not be fined unless it has failed to rectify, within a time limit set by the Commission, the explanations provided by that (unauthorised) person. Seemingly, Reg 1/2003 draws a distinction between

totally, refuses to answer a formal request, the Commission can, moreover, impose periodic penalty payments in order to compel it to provide the requested information.[244] In all of the above situations, the undertaking is consequently required to answer—correctly and completely—the Commission's questions. In this respect, recital 23 of Regulation 1/2003 makes it clear that the undertaking may not decline to reply even if the information can subsequently be used to establish that the undertaking used illegal anti-competitive conduct. It is important to note that this principle equally applies with regard to the production of documents which the Commission can ask for either in response to a written request for information or during an inspection, ie documents must also be disclosed even if they constitute evidence against the company under investigation.

Recital 23 of Regulation 1/2003 in fact reflects settled case law of the Community courts. In *Orkem*, the ECJ held that the far-reaching duty of active co-operation only reaches its limits where the undertaking would have to provide the Commission

> with answers which might involve an admission on its part of the existence of an infringement which it is incumbent upon the Commission to prove.[245]

Under Community law, an unconditional right to silence for undertakings thus is not recognised.[246] In practice, this means that company representatives and members of staff cannot elect to remain completely silent. They have to respond to factual questions, even if this will lead them to confess their personal involvement in the investigated infringement. By contrast, they can decline answers which would directly incriminate the company they are working for.[247] Statements provided by employees in the course of

representatives and other staff members. While explanations of representatives are apparently imputed directly to the company and, in the event that the information supplied by the representative is incorrect or misleading, can immediately attract a fine to be imposed on the relevant company (NB: no fines can be imposed on individuals by the Commission), explanations of staff members can be rectified, ie the Commission first has to give the undertaking the opportunity, within a certain time limit, to correct, amend or supplement answers provided by a member of staff and may only impose a fine after that time limit has expired without the company having rectified those explanations (see the first and second indents of Art 23(1)(d) of Reg 1/2003 and Art 4(3) of the Implementing Regulation). On this differentiation between (official) company representatives and other (unauthorised) personnel see Vesterdorf, above n 70, 727–8.

[244] See Arts 23(1)(b)–(d) and 24(1)(d) of Reg 1/2003. A third possibility exists pursuant to Art 19(1) of Reg 1/2003, which empowers the Commission to interview any legal or natural person in order to collect information on the subject matter of the investigation, provided the person consents to such an interview. This power has (also) been newly introduced by Reg 1/2003. However, there are no penalties for providing incorrect, incomplete or misleading information in the course of an interview conducted under this provision. Whish, above n 229, 264.

[245] Para 35 of the judgment in *Orkem* (above n 62); see also para 67 of the judgment in *Mannesmannröhren-Werke* (above n 35).

[246] Dekeyser and Gauer, above n 218, 560.

[247] In *Mannesman-Röhrenwerke*, for instance, a distinction was made between 'purely factual information' on certain meetings of a suspected cartel, including the names of participants,

an antitrust investigation, in particular during dawn raids, could therefore be regarded as having a coerced rather than a voluntary character.[248]

Under German law, the scope of the protection against self-incrimination is again determined by the applicable rules of criminal procedure. As noted earlier,[249] persons only have to passively tolerate a search (*Duldungspflicht*). There is no obligation of active co-operation, a rule that is considered to result from the general principle that no one may be forced or induced to incriminate or testify against himself (the *nemo tenetur* principle).[250] This principle, which is considered to provide extensive protection, also applies in cartel investigations conducted with a view to imposing fines (*Bußgeldverfahren*). Natural persons, such as company directors and other members of staff, therefore enjoy an absolute right to silence. They can simply refuse to answer questions.[251] However, it is still being disputed whether legal persons can invoke the *nemo tenetur*

which was not held to be incriminating so that the undertakings were obliged to provide it, and information regarding the purpose of such meetings, which the undertakings were entitled to decline (see para 6 of the judgment, read in conjunction with paras 70 and 71, above n 35). However, requiring an employee to disclose the identity of persons attending cartel meetings means that he may be forced to admit his own participation in the illegal practices at issue, while not—according to the CFI—incriminating the undertaking. This is important to note, since statements initially given to the Commission may find their way—through exchange of information—to NCAs whose rules provide for (criminal) sanctions on individuals. In this situation, the safeguards laid down by Art 12(3) of Reg 1/2003 become crucial to protecting the individual. *Contra* Vesterdorf, above n 70, 729, who doubts that such a situation will often arise since an admission by an individual to the effect that he personally participated in a breach of the competition rules would, in most instances, also incriminate the company itself so that the answer could be declined. However, in my opinion, in view of the above differentiation made by the CFI in *Mannesman-Röhrenwerke*, the situation does not appear unlikely, but rather typical.

[248] See Hogan, above n 69, 668. *Accord* also Vesterdorf, above n 70, 728, albeit only with regard to statements of representatives and other authorised personnel (for the distinction between authorised and unauthorised staff, see above n 243). The individual who refuses to supply (complete) information cannot be fined: sanctions can only be imposed on the relevant company. However, the duty of loyalty towards the employer combined with the fear of penalties being applied against it may indirectly put considerable pressure on the staff. Also the psychological pressure companies can exert on their employees, eg by threatening to fire unco-operative staff members, should suffice to qualify statements made by employees during Commission investigations as compelled evidence. See Venit and Louko, above n 76, 689. Moreover, as Vesterdorf, above n 70, 729–30, admits, reality is much more complex than we can imagine. Therefore, many other psychological constraints can affect persons who are interrogated on the spot in the context of an unpleasant surprise inspection which, after all, may entail serious (economic) consequences for the entire company, including its staff. An exception would apply, however, with regard to statements provided during an interview conducted pursuant to Art 19 of Reg 1/2003 since, in this case, the person interviewed has voluntarily submitted to the interrogation; moreover, no sanctions can be imposed, either on the individual or the company, for supplying incorrect, incomplete or misleading information. Venit and Louko, above n 76, 688. Also Vesterdorf, above n 70, 727.

[249] See above n 88.

[250] Meyer and Kuhn, above n 59, 891. See also Meyer-Goßner, above n 191, Einl no 29a.

[251] See StPO, § 136(1), 2nd sentence, read in conjunction with § 163a(3) StPO and § 46(2) OWiG. Pursuant to StPO, § 136(1), 2nd sentence, the suspect (*der Beschuldigte*) must be advised 'dass es ihm nach dem Gesetz freistehe, sich zu der Beschuldigung zu äußern oder nicht zur Sache auszusagen'. He only has to answer questions regarding his identity (*Angaben zur Person*).

principle. In a judgment of 1997, the Bundesverfassungsgericht ruled that the guarantee against self-incrimination, being based on the constitutional principle of human dignity, cannot apply to legal persons.[252] However, the case law of the Bundesverfassungsgericht does not appear to be entirely consistent. Moreover, the 1997 judgment does not seem to take proper account of the fact that, at least as far as competition law infringements are concerned, legal persons are equally exposed to quasi-criminal sanctions. The situation with regard to undertakings therefore remains unclear.[253]

In competition proceedings conducted by the BKartA, the protection against self-incrimination afforded to natural persons is thus more far-reaching than under Community law as individuals have the right to remain silent. Moreover, the German standard is in stark contrast to that of some other Member States, such as France and Greece, which seemingly deny persons any protection against self-incrimination in administrative competition proceedings.[254]

Finally, it cannot be excluded that, applying the standards of the ECHR, legal persons must also be granted the right to silence. Even though, at present, no case law of the ECtHR expressly confirms that the right to silence, which is part of the fair trial guarantee enshrined in Article 6(1) ECHR, applies to legal persons, such a conclusion is not a priori precluded.[255] In fact, existing case law of the Strasbourg institutions tends to show that corporate bodies can equally claim the protection of the fundamental rights of the ECHR,[256] including the fair trial guarantee.[257] In a number of judgments, the ECtHR has recognised that legal entities can exercise certain rights typically enjoyed by natural persons, such as the right of respect for the home, as guaranteed by Article 8 ECHR,[258] and the right to freedom of expression, as guaranteed by Article 10 ECHR.[259] There is one case which arguably deserves to be cited literally

---

[252] BVerfGE 95, 220, 242.

[253] See Meyer and Kuhn, above n 59, 892. The basic approach of German competition law is that it is the directly responsible individual who is to be charged for violations of the competition rules. Theoretically, sanctions against legal persons are supposed to be the exception rather than the rule, and undertakings can only be fined where the specific conditions of § 30(1) OWiG are fulfilled, which requires in particular the act of an authorised company representative (meaning essentially that the infringement must legally be imputable to the undertaking). In practice, however, fines are frequently imposed on the corporations involved. Cf Bechtold, above n 52, § 81 no 40.

[254] This appears at least to have been the case at the time of the *Orkem* judgment (1989). In some other Member States (eg Belgium), the situation is unclear. See the opinion of Advocate General Darmon in *Orkem* (above n 62), paras 97–111, in particular 105, 108 and 110.

[255] See Stessens, above n 62, 61. On the diverging case law of the ECtHR regarding the exact scope, *rationes materiae*, of the right to silence, see above nn 74 and 76 and accompanying text.

[256] See Venit and Louko, above n 76, 692.

[257] Einarsson, above n 72, 582.

[258] Judgment of the ECtHR of 16 April 2002 in the case of *Sociétés Colas and others v France* Reports/Recueil 2002-III, 105, para 41.

[259] Judgment of the ECtHR of 26 April 1979 in the case of *Sunday Times v UK* Publications Series A no 30, paras 45, 67, 68.

in this context. In *Autronic v Switzerland*, the ECtHR also applied Article 10 ECHR on the freedom of expression to a corporation. It notably held that:

> In the Court's view, neither Autronic AG's legal status as a limited company nor the fact that its activities were commercial nor the intrinsic nature of freedom of expression can deprive Autronic AG of the protection of Article 10 (art. 10). The Article (art. 10) applies to 'everyone', whether natural or legal persons.[260]

Thus, even the intrinsic nature of a fundamental right cannot prevent that right from being applied for the benefit of a legal person. Finally, in its opinion in the *Stenuit* case, the European Commission on Human Rights ('HR Commission') explicitly took the position that Article 6 ECHR is applicable to corporations if they face charges that are considered criminal within the meaning of the ECHR.[261]

(3) Inviolability of the Home. Procedural safeguards during competition proceedings also differ considerably with regard to the inviolability of the home. Differences concern the level of justification or degree of suspicion required to permit a search, the question of what kind of premises can be searched (eg business premises, private homes, third-party premises) and whether a prior judicial authorisation (search warrant) is needed.

The investigative powers of the Commission as regards on-site inspections are laid down in Articles 20 and 21 of Regulation 1/2003. Pursuant to these provisions, the Commission can carry out inspections of business premises and private homes. It has a right to enter those premises, examine business-related books and records which are kept there, take copies of them and, where necessary, seal business premises or books and records located there. Where the inspection has been ordered by formal decision,[262] the undertaking concerned is obliged to submit to the inspection and to actively co-operate, ie it has to hand over books and records at the Commission's request.[263] The decision must specify the subject matter and purpose of the investigation. This is not merely a

---

[260] Judgment of the ECtHR of 22 May 1990 in the case of *Autronic AG v Switzerland* Publications Series A no 178, para 47.

[261] Opinion of the HR Commission of 30 May 1991 in the case of *Société Stenuit v France* Publications Series A no 232-A, para 66. Since the relevant French legislation was subsequently modified, the applicant withdrew its complaint and the ECtHR struck the case from the list without considering its merits. It is noteworthy, however, that the ECtHR has meanwhile implicitly confirmed the applicability of Art 6 ECHR in respect of the modified French competition procedure (judgment of the ECtHR of 14 October 2003 in the case of *Lilly France v France*, Application no 53892/00; not included in the Reports/Recueil). Thus, nothing really suggests that the ECtHR would refuse to follow the approach of the HR Commission in *Stenuit*.

[262] Pursuant to Art 21(1) of Reg 1/2003, the inspection of non-business premises must always be ordered by decision, while the inspection of business premises can also be conducted on the basis of a simple written authorisation provided that the undertaking concerned voluntarily submits to the inspection. See Whish, above n 229, 265.

[263] See Art 20(4) of Reg 1/2003. The provision does not apply with regard to private homes.

formality but a fundamental requirement, as it enables undertakings to assess the scope of their obligation to co-operate.[264] The possibility for the Commission to impose fines for refusal or failure to provide complete records and periodic penalty payments in order to compel the undertaking concerned to submit to the inspection underpins the duty of active co-operation.[265]

While the above inspection rights of the Commission include a general power of search, ie the right to seek for items of information which are not yet known or fully identified, they do not permit the Commission to obtain access to premises or furniture by means of physical force.[266] Therefore, under Community law, a search warrant is not required unless the Commission requires the assistance of the police or other national enforcement bodies of the Member State concerned in order to overcome the opposition of the undertaking.[267] The Commission also needs a search warrant where it intends to enter private dwellings, which, in any event, may not be inspected without prior judicial authorisation of the relevant Member State.[268]

Similarly, under German law, the BKartA is entitled to inspect both business premises and private dwellings.[269] This includes the right to inspect third-party premises, ie premises which are occupied by a person who is not suspected of an offence. The relevant provisions have different requirements regarding the requisite level of suspicion. Third-party premises may only be inspected if certain facts justify the conclusion that the items searched for (eg business records) are located at these premises. By contrast, the premises of the suspect can be searched on the basis of a mere assumption that evidentiary material might be found

---

[264] Para 29 of the ECJ's judgment in *Hoechst* (above n 24).

[265] Arts 23(1)(c) and 24(1)(e) of Reg 1/2003. Again, these provisions do not apply where the inspection relates to non-business premises. Wils, above n 70, 8.

[266] C Kerse and N Khan, *EC Antitrust Procedure* (London, Sweet & Maxwell, 5th edn, 2005), para 3-052. This follows in fact from paras 27 and 31 of the judgment of the ECJ in *Hoechst* (above n 24).

[267] Provided that, under the applicable national law, such police assistance may only be rendered with authorisation of the judiciary. Art 20(6) and (7) of Reg 1/2003. These rules essentially codify the *Hoechst* judgment of the ECJ (see in particular paras 31–4 of the judgment; above n 24). Interestingly, in para 18 of the *Hoechst* judgment, the ECJ explicitly rejected the possibility that the scope of Art 8(1) ECHR, which guarantees the inviolability of the home, could be extended to business premises, again a ruling which has been 'overturned' by later case law of the ECtHR (see above n 258).

[268] Art 21(3) of Reg 1/2003. While the undertakings' duty to submit to an inspection and the Commission's powers to seal premises or books are not applicable in respect of private homes, the rules on assistance to be granted by national (police) agents (Art 20(5) and (6) of Reg 1/2003) have explicitly been declared applicable in the case of inspection of non-business premises. See Art 21(4) of Reg 1/2003.

[269] See § 102 StPO (*Durchsuchung beim Verdächtigen*) and § 103 StPO (*Durchsuchung bei anderen Personen*).

there.[270] However, in both cases, a search warrant is required.[271] It is undisputed that the inviolability of the home, which is guaranteed by Article 13 of the German Federal Constitution, also applies to business premises.[272]

It might appear that German and Community law, in this respect, are not tremendously different. However, under Community law, the Commission is not only entitled to inspect and even search business premises without having obtained prior judicial authorisation provided the undertaking does not oppose it; it can also compel undertakings under threat of fines or periodic penalty payments to submit to the inspection.[273] The combination of these powers is quite remarkable, certainly in the light of the judgments of the ECtHR in *Niemitz* and *Sociétés Colas*, from which it clearly follows that the safeguards of Article 8 ECHR regarding the inviolability of the home can also be invoked by legal persons with regard to their business premises.[274]

There seem to be a few national jurisdictions where the situation is comparable to that under Community law. In the UK, for instance, officers of the OFT can enter business premises without a warrant pursuant to

[270] There is, however, some dispute in the legal literature about whether the inspection of business premises must be conducted in accordance with § 102 StPO or § 103 StPO. See Meyer and Kuhn, above n 59, 883.

[271] § 105(1) StPO. The powers of the BKartA, pursuant to § 59(2) GWB, to enter business premises and request the production of business records, do not apply in so-called *Bußgeldverfahren*, but only in administrative proceedings which do not have the objective of imposing fines. Bechtold, above n 52, § 59 no 4. Moreover, § 59 GWB distinguishes between simple inspections (*Einsichtnahme und Prüfung*) and real searches (*Durchsuchungen*). In the latter case, § 59(4) GWB also requires the existence of a search warrant.

[272] Meyer and Kuhn, above n 59, 884.

[273] Obviously, under German law, undertakings can always submit voluntarily to an inspection. The main difference between Community law and the German system lies in the fact that, under German law, undertakings cannot be forced to submit to an inspection unless the authority presents a search warrant. Moreover, they are not obliged to assist the officials. There is no duty, on their part, to hand over records or other documents, or to provide information. They have a right to remain completely inactive, thereby forcing the NCA de facto to search for the relevant items itself. By contrast, under Community law, the company under investigation has to co-operate actively. This, according to the Commission, even includes the duty to assist officials in finding the information they want. The undertaking thus has to do more than just granting full access to its offices, filing cabinets and PCs. Whish, above n 229, 265. On this basis, simple passiveness could be considered as opposition, and thus attract fines pursuant to Arts 23(1)(c)and 24(1)(e) of Reg 1/2003.

[274] Judgment of the ECtHR of 16 December 1992 in the case of *Niemitz v Germany* Publications Series A no 251-B, paras 27–33. In *Niemitz*, the ECtHR ruled that protection of the 'home' under Art 8 ECHR extends to a lawyer's office. For *Sociétés Colas* (relating to the application of Art 8 ECHR to legal persons), see above n 258. This latter case concerned dawn raids carried out—without prior judicial authorisation—by officials of the French DGCCRF in the context of a cartel investigation. The ECtHR held that there was infringement of Art 8 ECHR. Recently, both judgments have been confirmed as concerning the protection of the business premises of corporations under Art 8 ECHR. See the judgment of the ECtHR of 15 July 2003 in the case of *Ernst and others v Belgium*, Application no 33400/96, para 109. In that judgment (para 116), the ECtHR also emphasised the need of a judicial authorisation to indicate precisely the cause and scope of the search.

Section 27 of the Competition Act 1998. A written authorisation of the OFT is sufficient.[275] The authorised officer who has no warrant may nonetheless require any person to produce documents which are considered to be relevant to the investigation (eg minutes of meetings, diaries of directors, invoices), provide explanations of a document produced and indicate the location of specified documents.[276] However, Section 27 of the Competition Act 1998 does not confer the power to actually search offices, desks or filing cabinets, or to use force. Where this is necessary, a judicial warrant must be obtained pursuant to Section 28 of the Competition Act 1998, a provision which grants the right of forcible entry.[277] The inspection of non-business premises always requires a warrant.[278]

The situation is similar in Belgium. Pursuant to Article 44 §3 No 2 WEM 2006, both the members of the Competition Service and the Auditors are empowered to conduct searches of business premises. This power includes the right to use force. For such searches, they only need to obtain the prior written authorisation of the President of the Raad.[279]

Under the laws of the Netherlands, the protection standards seem to be even lower. The officials of the NMa have far-reaching inspection rights: namely, they may enter all premises except for private dwellings without the resident's consent and without judicial authorisation.[280] They are not

---

[275] The power includes the right to inspect third-party premises, but excludes private dwellings. See paras 4.2 and 4.3 of OFT Guideline 404 regarding powers of investigation (December 2004), available at http://www.oft.gov.uk/shared_oft/business_leaflets/ca98_guidelines/oft404.pdf (accessed February 2009). Usually, the occupier of the premises must be notified in writing at least two working days in advance of the inspection. The notification must specify the subject matter and purpose of the investigation, as well as the offences that may be committed if a person fails to comply. Pursuant to s 27(2) of the Competition Act 1998, a prior notification is dispensable in certain circumstances, in particular where the premises to be inspected are or were occupied by the company under investigation. Paras 4.3, 4.4 and 4.7 of OFT Guideline 404. See also Whish, above n 229, 363. Where dawn raids are carried out, the latter case is likely to be the rule rather than the exception.

[276] Para 4.5 of OFT Guideline 404 (*ibid*).

[277] Whish, above n 229, 364–5.

[278] Para 4.2, read in combination with para 5.1 of the OFT Guideline 404. *Contra* Whish, above n 229, 364, who, referring to the definitions in s 59(1) of the Competition Act 1998, submits that s 27 of the Competition Act 1998 also applies to private premises if they are used for an undertaking's affairs or business records are kept there.

[279] By contrast, the search of private dwellings of company directors, managers and staff requires prior authorisation through a judicial warrant issued by an independent court (*juge d'instruction*). In all cases of a search (*huiszoeking*), the relevant officials must also be in possession of a specific assignment/order (*opdrachtbevel*), in addition to the President's authorisation, issued by the Auditoraat and indicating the subject matter and purpose of the search (see WEM 2006, Art 44 §3, penultimate subparagraph).

[280] B Van Reeken and S Noë, 'Competition Law in the Netherlands', in F Vogelaar, J Stuyck, B Van Reeken (eds), *Competition Law in the EU, Its Member States and Switzerland, Volume I* (The Hague, Kluwer Law International, 2000), 417, 474; Waelbroeck, above n 87, 474. To enter domestic premises, the officials require the occupant's consent. M Araujo, 'The Respect of Fundamental Rights within the European Network of Competition Authorities' in B Hawk (ed), *2004 Proceedings of the Fordham Corporate Law Institute* (New York, Juris Publishing, 2005), 511, 524.

even required to present a written authorisation, but merely have to carry proof of their identity. This means that NMa officials can effectively search offices and other business premises without having to specify, in advance, the subject matter and purpose of the investigation.[281] Moreover, they are entitled to seal business premises and objects, request police assistance and impose administrative fines for the refusal to co-operate.[282] These broad powers of investigation enable the NMa to conduct, de facto, so-called 'fishing expeditions'.[283] This is in stark contrast to most Member States' jurisdictions, which generally prohibit such expeditions.[284]

However, despite these discrepancies, it cannot be presumed a priori that in each case the system with the lower standard is incompatible with the ECHR.[285] Apart from the fact that the equilibrium between public powers and individual (defence) rights plays an important role, the differences are not necessarily linked to a disregard for the ECHR principles on the part of the legal systems affording less protection. Many disparities simply result from different interpretations of the articles of the ECHR and the case law of the ECtHR.[286]

---

[281] See A Knijpenga, 'Chapter 12. The Netherlands' in M Holmes and L Davey (eds), *A Practical Guide to National Competition Rules across Europe* (The Hague, Kluwer Law International, 2004), 237, 247.

[282] Van Reeken and Noë, above n 280, 474.

[283] See Van Der Woude, above n 96, 383. In practice, however, this risk seems to have been minimised as the NMa has committed itself to inform the undertakings concerned of the purpose and subject matter of the investigation. Moreover, the NMa is obliged to draw up, prior to the conduct of an inspection, an internal document which sets out in writing the purpose and subject matter of the measure and its proportionality in relation to the degree of suspicion entertained by the NMa. When the parties are granted access to the file, at a later stage of the procedure, this document must be made available to them.

[284] Arguably, the prohibition of 'fishing expeditions' could equally be regarded as a principle of Community competition law. See Van Der Woude, above n 96, 383. See also above n 23. It could even be said to be a requirement of the ECHR. See above n 274. In this context, it should also be noted that, pursuant to Art 8(2) ECHR, interferences by a public authority with the inviolability of the home are only allowed if they are in accordance with the law and are necessary for the protection of certain general interests, such as public safety. However, it is difficult to see how the observance of these requirements can be controlled if the NCA can proceed to search premises without determining beforehand (in a decision, authorisation or request for a warrant) the subject matter and purpose of that search.

[285] Even though it might be argued that, in those countries where a judicial warrant is dispensable, such as the Netherlands, the concomitant absence of an inspection decision which precisely indicates the subject matter and purpose of the inspection would entail a breach of Art 8 ECHR. See P Huber, 'De nieuwe inspectiebevoegdheden in VO 1/2003' (2004) 10 *Nederlands tijdschrift voor Europees recht* 84, 86. See also above n 274.

[286] See Van Gerven, above n 203, 347, who cites the example of the Dutch rules regarding on-the-spot investigations and the approach taken by the NMa towards the judgment of the ECtHR in *Sociétés Colas* (above n 258). The NMa seemingly argues that the NMa's right to enter business premises without judicial warrant does not violate the principles established by the ECtHR since the investigative powers of its inspectors are less intrusive than in the case decided by the ECtHR.

b. The Resulting Concern

The modernisation process has left the national procedural rules, which are to be applied when NCAs enforce Articles 81 and 82 EC, essentially untouched.[287] This means that significant procedural divergencies continue to exist, as has been illustrated by the above examples. However, Regulation 1/2003 hardly takes into account this lack of harmonisation. Certainly, Article 12(3) of Regulation 1/2003 seeks to ensure that information is not used against individuals without due respect for the person's human rights guarantees. However, the fact that the scope of this provision is limited to individuals suggests that undertakings are expected to tolerate the unlimited use, against them, of any evidentiary material circulating freely within the Network, ie material being transferred from one Network member to another, regardless of whether it has been legally obtained in the first place and whether the receiving authority, on its part, could have legally collected it.[288] This situation raises the question of whether undertakings do not deserve better protection of their rights of defence.[289] Procedural guarantees, it is submitted, create legitimate expectations, on the part of the undertakings, that their rights will not be undermined, if they benefit from a higher level of protection in one Member State or under Community law, by an unrestricted exchange of evidence with other Member States or the Commission. These legitimate expectations may not be curtailed.

(1) The Risk of Erosion. When drafting the modernisation proposal, the Commission deliberately chose not to harmonise the procedural rules of the Member States applicable to competition proceedings. This was considered unnecessary for the implementation of the reform.[290] Why should we then be concerned about the diverging procedural rules and

---

[287] The only attempt to bring national procedural rules closer to each other is the determination of the type of decisions that NCAs can take when enforcing Community competition law. Namely, Art 5 of Reg 1/2003 requires all Member States to empower their respective national authorities to adopt the catalogue of decisions listed in that provision (ie prohibition decisions, decisions on interim measures, decisions accepting commitments and decisions imposing fines). This rule was necessary to align the decisional powers of the NCAs (and the content of such decisions) with those of the Commission in order to guarantee effective enforcement at Member State level. See p 12 of the Explanatory Memorandum. See further above Chapter 1, section II.B.1.d.

[288] See Araujo, above n 280, 528.

[289] It is noteworthy that as long ago as 1998, Faull, above n 220, 144–5, addressed the concern resulting from the exchange of confidential material between jurisdictions with different legal privilege concepts, although his remarks concerned the international plan, not the situation within the EU. He suggested that future bilateral agreements between the US and the Community would have to deal with this issue to the extent that they would provide for the exchange of confidential information.

[290] The Commission repeatedly stated that there would be no need 'to embark on a full-scale harmonisation' of national procedures. See, eg p 12 of the Explanatory Memorandum.

protection standards? Would the straightforward answer not simply be that any information or evidence that has been legally collected by an NCA can be transmitted without restriction inside the ECN and can therefore legally be used by any other NCA (or the Commission) unless the conditions of Article 12(2) and (3) of Regulation 1/2003 are not met?[291] Indeed, some authors argue that information which was legally collected in one Member State can legally be used in any other Member State against undertakings regardless of whether the procedural guarantees applicable in the latter State grant a higher level of protection.[292] However, with all due respect, this approach seems to overly simplify matters[293] and the result can hardly be regarded as satisfactory, certainly not in a legal system which is deemed to be governed by the rule of law.[294]

Indeed, according to its wording, Article 12 of Regulation 1/2003 does not restrict the exchange of legally collected information, including evidentiary material, in any way.[295] Consequently, a Network member may pass on any information that it has collected in accordance with its own rules of procedure. Correspondingly, the receiving authority may use that information against an undertaking irrespective of whether it could have itself gathered the information by its own means.[296] The only restrictions imposed by Article 12(3) of Regulation 1/2003 concerning the use of evidence by the receiving authority namely concern such use against

---

[291] On the basis of the wording of Art 12 of Reg 1/2003, Network members may even provide each other with illegally obtained information, as that provision places no restrictions on the transmission of information. The validity of this approach is indirectly confirmed by para 27 of the Network Notice, which provides that Network members may inform each other if the legality of the information gathering has been contested in the Member State of origin. Besides the fact that the Network Notice as such is not a binding instrument, one may be surprised that this paragraph stipulates a mere faculty and does not even attempt to impose some kind of obligation on the Member States or the Commission. Moreover, it is concerned with information aspects only, rather than with conditions limiting or excluding the transfer of evidence. It can therefore be concluded that, on the basis of the law as its stands, the illegality of the information gathering does not prevent the information from being passed on, not even where the illegality has definitively been established. But see my arguments and conclusions above in section II.B.2.

[292] See Gauer, above n 18, 13–14; Dekeyser and De Smijter, above n 5, 171; and Wils, above n 62, 454–6 (except where the higher protection standard reflects a requirement of the ECHR). The underlying rationale would be that the rights of defence of undertakings are considered as being sufficiently equivalent throughout the EU. See recital 16 of Reg 1/2003. This approach is also taken in practice. For instance, OFT Guideline 404 purports that the OFT may use documents collected by the NCA of another Member State where such documents are not privileged, even if these documents would be inadmissible under the UK rules on legal privilege (see para 6.3 of the OFT Guideline, n 275).

[293] Cf Araujo, above n 280, 525.

[294] See above n 190.

[295] See Dekeyser and De Smijter, above n 5, 161–2. Arguably, the principle of unlimited information exchange even applies in the case of information that has been gathered illegally. See above nn 188 and 189 and accompanying text.

[296] See Dekeyser and De Smijter, above n 5, 171.

individuals.[297] However, where an NCA intends to impose sanctions on a legal person, it has literally unlimited power to use evidence furnished by other Network members.[298] This means, for instance, that the BKartA could use against a company information that it has obtained from the Commission and which the BKartA could not itself have collected due to the privilege against self-incrimination applicable under German law. Similarly, the OFT could deploy evidence that would benefit from in-house counsel legal privilege under UK law but which was collected and forwarded by a Network member not bound by that privilege.[299]

Such a strict reading of Article 12 of Regulation 1/2003 may have serious and quite undesirable consequences. First, it may induce NCAs, which are unable to collect certain information, to circumvent the safeguards applicable under their own rules by requesting NCAs in Member States with lower protection standards (or the Commission) or more intrusive investigatory powers to collect that information on their behalf pursuant to Article 22(1) of Regulation 1/2003. Such a move towards 'taking advantage of the "weakness" of foreign legislation'[300] represents a kind of 'forum shopping' on the part of public authorities which would seriously damage the fairness of the procedure as perceived by the undertakings concerned. Secondly, even where there is no explicit request for information gathering directed from one Network member to another and thus no (deliberate) attempt to circumvent the member's own national standards, the mere fact that evidence can be transferred from a jurisdiction with a lower level of protection to one with a higher level of protection means that the higher protection may effectively be lost.[301] Thirdly, the repeated loss of higher protection implies that protection standards in the EU will gradually erode. Ultimately, the jurisdiction with the lowest level of protection might impose its standards across the whole of the EU.[302] The desire to establish ever-closer co-operation within the ECN and therefore facilitate the exchange of information cannot, in my view, justify the deterioration of the protection standards which are instrumental for, or closely related to, one of the most fundamental safeguards in Community law, the right of defence. Effective enforcement and the

---

[297] But even in this context, the (il)legality of the information gathering, surprisingly enough, is of no relevance.

[298] Van Gerven, above n 29, 354.

[299] In fact, para 6.3 of OFT Guideline 404 (above n 275) makes explicit reference to this scenario, stating that the OFT 'could be sent the communications of in-house lawyers . . . by an NCA from another Member State where the communications of such lawyers are not privileged'.

[300] Martinez Lage and Brokelmann, above n 93, 416.

[301] Van Gerven, above n 29, 353, describes this phenomenon as 'export' of looser standards of protection. Conversely, where the issue is the confidential treatment of certain information, it is the transfer of that information from a jurisdiction with high protection standards to a jurisdiction with lower standards that entails the risk that the higher protection will be lost. See the example given by Van Der Woude, above n 96, 383.

[302] Martinez Lage and Brokelmann, above n 93,416; Van Der Woude, above n 96, 383.

principle of 'free movement of evidence' are certainly legitimate claims, but must not be used to deprive legal and natural persons of fundamental guarantees.

(2) The Human Rights Dimension of Procedural Divergency. The potential loss of higher protection standards is not only alarming because the procedural fairness as such guaranteed by Article 6 ECHR might be at stake. More importantly, all procedural safeguards discussed above are rooted, one way or another, in the ECHR.

It was pointed out earlier that the privilege against self-incrimination and the right to silence are elements of the fair trial guarantee of Article 6 ECHR, a guarantee which occupies a central position in the ECHR, reflecting the fundamental principle of the rule of law.[303] The right to silence and the right not to incriminate oneself, in turn, are considered as generally recognised international standards which lie at the heart of the notion of a fair procedure.[304] Even though the privilege has been the subject of a number of judgments of the ECtHR, its precise scope, under the ECHR, remains somewhat unclear.[305] There is no case law of the ECtHR explicitly recognising the applicability of the privilege against self-incrimination to corporate bodies. On the other hand, the case law does not preclude a priori the privilege from being applied in favour of legal persons. It thus does not exclude companies suspected of an infringement of Article 81 or 82 EC from invoking the privilege against self-incrimination and the right to silence under Article 6 ECHR.[306]

As noted, the inviolability of the home is guaranteed by Article 8 ECHR.[307] However, the provision does not afford an absolute right. Interference by public authorities with the exercise of this right is justified if the requirements of Article 8(2) ECHR are fulfilled, ie the interference must have a legitimate aim, and must be 'in accordance with the law' and 'necessary in a democratic society'.[308] In this context, the ECtHR has consistently held that, despite the existence of a certain margin of discretion for the signatory states, the exceptions must be interpreted

---

[303] See para 55 of the judgment of the ECtHR in *Sunday Times* (above n 259).

[304] Above n 31. The privilege against self-incrimination has been considered as filling a gap in the Convention's right to a fair trial that has not been closed by Protocol No 7 to the ECHR, which includes a number of additional guarantees in respect of the criminal process. However, it is not an absolute right, and the question of whether a particular interference is indeed in breach of Art 6 ECHR must be evaluated on the basis of the proceedings in the relevant case taken as a whole. Harris *et al*, above n 82, 214; C Ovey and R White, *Jacobs & White, The European Convention on Human Rights* (Oxford, Oxford University Press, 3rd edn, 2002), 177.

[305] See above section I.B.3.b.

[306] Andreangeli, above n 238, 37.

[307] In the terms of the ECHR, Art 8 guarantees everyone's 'right to respect for his private and family life, his home and his correspondence'.

[308] The latter criterion essentially establishes a proportionality test. Harris *et al*, above n 82, 291.

narrowly. This means, in particular, that the measures must be strictly proportionate to the legitimate aim pursued and that the relevant legislation and practice must provide adequate and effective safeguards against abuse.[309] Based on these principles, the case law of the ECtHR suggests that, where the entry to and search of a home is at issue, a system of prior judicial authorisation will usually be needed in order for the above criteria to be satisfied.[310] Moreover, Article 8 ECHR is one of those provisions for which the ECtHR has clearly acknowledged that they also apply to companies.[311] Indeed, the ECtHR has not only held that Article 8 ECHR applies in the economic sphere in that it also protects individuals in respect of the premises which they use to carry out their professional or business activities,[312] but has explicitly ruled that the guarantee extends to legal entities: it namely includes 'the right to respect for a company's registered office'.[313] Undertakings that are being raided by an NCA can without doubt avail themselves, with regard to their business premises, of the protection afforded by Article 8 ECHR.[314]

---

[309] See paras 47–9 of the judgment of the ECtHR in *Sociétés Colas* (above n 258).

[310] See, eg para 57 of the judgment in *Funke* (above n 33), where the ECtHR held that the searches at issue were in violation of Art 8 ECHR, emphasising the lack of any requirement of a judicial warrant. Wide and broadly framed powers will usually not pass the test as they do not provide guarantees against arbitrary use and do not allow for close scrutiny of the relevant measures. See Harris *et al*, above n 82, 339. Cf also Riley, above n 70, 74–7. Relying on the case of the ECtHR, Riley notes that a judicial warrant is not necessarily required. However, a legal regime that operates without prior judicial authorisation would have to provide other extensive safeguards against arbitrary interference such as notice, mandatory presence of a lawyer and/or an independent observer. Riley considers the safeguards existing at Community level (eg requirement of a motivated formal Commission decision) as insufficient and concludes that the Commission's inspection powers under Art 20 of Reg 1/2003 are likely to be incompatible with Art 8 ECHR. Doubts regarding the compatibility of the Community law system with Art 8 ECHR are also voiced by Ameye, above n 87, 341 and Waelbroeck and Fosselard, above n 86, 138.

[311] P Roth, 'Ensuring that Effectiveness of Enforcement Does not Prejudice Legal Protection: Rights of Defence. Fundamental Rights Concerns', paper for the 2006 EU Competition Law and Policy Workshop, European University Institute/RSCAS, Florence; available at www.eui.eu/RSCAS/research/Competition/ 2006(pdf)/200610-COMPed-Roth.pdf (accessed January 2009), 1, 6.

[312] See paras 27–33 of the judgment of the ECtHR in *Niemitz* (above n 274) regarding the application of Art 8 ECHR to the law offices of a private practitioner. However, at the same time, the ECtHR indicated that the powers of public authorities to interfere may be more far-reaching where business rather than private premises are concerned (para 31 of the same judgment).

[313] See para 41 of the judgment of the ECtHR in *Sociétés Colas* (above n 258).

[314] As for the applicability of Convention rights at Community level, see above nn 69 and 70. For the sake of clarity, it should be noted that the judgment of the ECJ in Hoechst, where it was held that the protective scope of Art 8 ECHR could not be extended to business premises (see above n 267), was already handed down in 1989, ie prior to the rulings of the ECtHR in *Niemitz* and *Sociétés Colas*. Nonetheless, Reg 1/2003, Art 20, paras 6–8 clearly codifies the case law of the ECJ as established in *Hoechst* and further developed in *Roquette Frères*. See J Schwarze and A Weitbrecht, *Grundzüge des europäischen Kartellverfahrensrechts* (Baden-Baden, Nomos, 1st edn, 2004), 60 para 21; Riley, above n 70, 59 and 65. In particular, the provision sanctions the principle that there is no automatic requirement of prior judicial authorisation. A search warrant

With regard to legal privilege, the situation is less clear. The ECHR does not expressly recognise the right of a client to communicate privately with his defence lawyer. Moreover, in legal writings, one can find different foundations for this privilege. Legal privilege has been regarded, inter alia, as a public policy instrument in that it fosters increased compliance with the law, thereby contributing to the administration of justice. Specifically, it allows people to consult lawyers in full privacy without having to be afraid that their communications might subsequently be disclosed and thus permits them to obtain proper legal advise.[315] An alternative view is to regard the privilege as emanating from the fundamental right to privacy, in which case it would enjoy protection under Article 8 ECHR.[316] The ECtHR has chosen yet another approach, and has considered the confidentiality of lawyer–client communications to be part of the fair trial guarantee enshrined in Article 6 ECHR. The leading case in this respect appears to be *S v Switzerland*,[317] a case concerning surveillance by the Swiss authorities of meetings between a lawyer and his detained client.[318] The ECtHR held that

> an accused's right to communicate with his advocate out of hearing of a third person is part of the basic requirements of a fair trial in a democratic society and follows from Article 6 para. 3 (c) . . . of the Convention.

It argued that a lawyer's assistance would lose much of its usefulness if he were unable to communicate with his client in private and receive confidential instructions from him, whereas it is the purpose of the Convention to grant rights that are practical and effective.[319] There are, however, a

is only required where the company concerned actually or potentially opposes the inspection ordered by the Commission (in the latter case, it merely is a precautionary measure) and the national law prescribes the existence of a judicial warrant. The provision also expressly limits the scope of the judicial review that can be carried out by the national judge prior to the enforcement of the inspection decision, thereby excluding de facto any substantial rigorous pre-inspection control. Riley, above n 70, 75–7. The compatibility, with Art 8 ECHR, of the Commission's power to conduct surprise inspection the lawfulness of which can only be controlled effectively a posteriori (by the CFI) is quite doubtful. See J Temple Lang and C Rizza, Analysis of 'The Ste Colas Est and Others v France case. European Court of Human Rights Judgment of April 16, 2002' (2002) 23 *European Competition Law Review* 413, 416.

[315] So-called utilitarian rationale. See Gippini-Fournier, above n 215, 598. This concept is based on the assumption that legal advise will be more accurate if the lawyer has been fully informed about all relevant facts and circumstances, which, in turn, requires that the client has been completely frank and open.

[316] So-called privacy rationale. See Gippini-Fournier, above n 215, 607.

[317] Gippini-Fournier, above n 215, 613.

[318] See the judgment of the ECtHR of 28 November 1991 in the case of *S v Switzerland* Publications Series A no 220.

[319] Para 48 of the judgment in *S v Switzerland* (*ibid*). There are later judgments of the ECtHR confirming that communications between legal advisers and clients must be afforded full secrecy in order to allow clients to obtain adequate legal representation and advice and thus full and effective access to the courts. More generally, the ECtHR considers lawyers to have a special status in the democratic society in that they function as intermediaries between the public and the courts and thus play a central role in the administration of justice. See the judgment of the

number of other judgments of the ECtHR in which legal privilege was based on Article 8 ECHR.[320] The main difference between both approaches lies in the fact that Article 6(3) ECHR generally applies only from the moment that charges have been brought. An application of the guarantee during the preliminary investigation phase is possible, depending on the particular features of the relevant proceedings, but application at the pre-investigation stage would seem to be excluded since no right to counsel arises at that moment under Article 6(3) ECHR.[321] In any event, like the privilege against self-incrimination and the inviolability of the home, legal professional privilege also finds a basis in the Convention.

These examples illustrate that some important procedural safeguards protecting the interests of suspected or accused persons and sometimes of third parties in competition proceedings emanate from fundamental rights which are guaranteed by the ECHR. The same will be true for many other procedural rights that might be affected by an unrestricted and uncontrolled exchange of information among Network members.[322]

ECtHR of 21 March 2002 in the case of *Nikula v Finland* Reports/Recueil 2002-II, 45, para 45. See further Andreangeli, above n 238, 32–5. Similarly, in *AM&S* (para 23 of the judgment; above n 221), the ECJ regarded unhindered legal communications between lawyer and client as instrumental to the effective exercise of the rights of defence.

[320] See, eg the judgment of the ECtHR of 25 March 1992 in the case of *Campbell v United Kingdom* Publications Series A no 233. The case concerned interception and censorship, by UK prison authorities, of correspondence between an inmate and his legal adviser. The ECtHR held that a prisoner's correspondence with his lawyer is, in principle, privileged under Art 8 ECHR (para 48 of the judgment). Interestingly, the ECtHR also emphasised the general interest in ensuring that any person who wishes to consult a lawyer can do so under conditions which favour full and uninhibited discussions (para 46 of the judgment), an argument which seems to be inspired by the consideration that legal privilege serves the administration of justice. *Campbell* may be distinguished from *S v Switzerland* (above n 318) in that the latter case concerned interference with oral communications, while in the former the authorities actually tampered with letters exchanged between a prisoner and his solicitor, ie correspondence, which is explicitly mentioned in Art 8 ECHR and primarily refers to written communications (Ovey and White, above n 304, 248). The *Niemietz* case (above n 274), which concerned a breach of Art 8 ECHR (even though the ECtHR also referred to Art 6 ECHR when discussing encroachment on professional secrecy), is sometimes also quoted in connection with lawyer–client privilege. See, eg Harris *et al*, above n 82, 345. For further references to legal privilege cases relying on Art 8 ECHR rather than Art 6 ECHR, see Gippini-Fournier, above n 215, 613 note 71.

[321] See Gippini-Fournier, above n 215, 615–17. (Arguably, in competition matters, Art 6 ECHR applies from the moment that an investigation has been commenced and, more precisely, from the moment that the decision ordering an inspection is notified to the undertakings concerned; see further above n 84 and accompanying text.) This would mean that general legal advice which has not been provided in respect of an ongoing investigation is not privileged under Convention terms. This conclusion would further signify that legal privilege under the case law of the ECJ, namely *AM&S*, goes beyond the requirements of the Convention to the extent that Community law protects certain communications passed between lawyer and client prior to the commencement of an investigation. *Idem*, 619–20.

[322] See, eg the protection of the confidentiality of information provided to public authorities which could come within the ambit of Art 8 ECHR or Art 1 Protocol 1 ECHR. Wils, above n 62, 456.

Two observations are to be made with regard to this finding. First, the human rights dimension clearly underpins the seriousness of the problem. We are dealing not just with an undesirable side effect of Article 12 of Regulation 1/2003, but with a problem affecting some of the most important rights that a person can enjoy in a democratic society. The adequate protection of human rights, in particular those guaranteed by the ECHR to which all current Member States of the EU are signatories, is one of the central issues of modern society.[323] In this respect, it can make no difference whether the persons concerned are individuals or corporate bodies since, as was shown above, legal persons are not excluded from such protection under the ECHR. The prominent role that fundamental rights play in ensuring the legality and fairness of proceedings under Articles 81 and 82 EC is also recognised by the ECJ and the CFI. Indeed, both courts attach great importance to the rights of defence of undertakings—the Community law term for the fair trial guarantee[324]—as is illustrated by ample case law seeking to secure the rights of defence in cartel proceedings, case law which can only partly be cited here.[325]

Secondly, the assumption that the ECHR sets the relevant minimum standard is not as such decisive. Indeed, it has been argued that an information exchange would only be excluded where the standard of protection in the jurisdiction of origin actually lags behind the requirements of the Convention. Where the degree of protection granted in the jurisdiction of destination goes beyond the standards set by the ECHR, a transfer of information from another authority having a lower standard, but still complying with the Convention, would thus be perfectly acceptable.[326] However, this approach seems to neglect a key element of the determination of the appro-

---

[323] This even applies to democratic countries such as the EU Member States whose legal systems are governed by the rule of law and which are deemed to fully abide by the fundamental rights enshrined in the Convention.

[324] See above n 125.

[325] Since the 1980s, applicants in competition matters before the ECJ (and later the CFI) have regularly invoked Convention rights. One of the earliest cases in this respect is *National Panasonic*, an application of 1979 in which the applicant company relied on Art 8 ECHR in order to question the legality of a Commission decision ordering an on-site investigation (Case 136/79 *National Panasonic v Commission* [1980] ECR 2033, paras 17–20). See Riley, above n 70, 61–2. In recent years, human rights issues have increasingly been raised. From 1995 until about 2004, there were approximately 30 competition cases before the Luxemburg courts in which defendants sought to challenge Commission decisions on the basis of human rights. See Ameye, above n 87, 333. Ameye observes, however, that both the ECJ and the CFI tend to recourse to procedural or formal flaws, thereby avoiding a decision in favour of the human rights defence. Similarly, in an article published in 1994, Waelbroeck and Fosselard (above n 86, 114) noted that, until then, the ECJ had systematically dismissed all pleas based on an alleged violation of Art 6 ECHR.

[326] Wils, above n 62, 455–6. If applied strictly, this approach could mean that evidence stemming from the Commission is largely excluded from being used in any national competition procedures because, arguably, the Community law procedure, in many respects, falls short of the ECHR standards. See Riley, above n 70, 85, who submits that 'it would not be unreasonable . . . to take the view that, at least in respect of the competition procedures, the protection of Convention rights within the Community legal order is theoretical and illusory'.

priate protection standards: that attention must be paid to the fact that, within each legal system, there normally exists an equilibrium between the powers of public authorities and the (defence) rights of persons affected by public interference. In other words, the competition authority's armoury ultimately determines the availability of defence rights and other fundamental guarantees for the undertakings and, if applicable, the individuals concerned. The standard of protection will presumably be higher where the competition authority has more intrusive investigatory powers and more serious sanctions at its disposition.[327] At the same time, competition investigations are complex matters[328] and equilibrating the related public 'investigative' powers and private (defence) rights is a complicated exercise. With the help of many detailed rules, public powers and private rights are carefully balanced.[329] Each set of national rules thus forms a kind of 'closed system' which keeps the procedure within the boundaries of the fair trial guarantee of Article 6 ECHR. This delicate balance existing within a given system will be upset where the different national systems interact.[330] The complexity of each system, which increases if sanctions on individuals are

---

[327] Cf Gauer, above n 30, 199; Wils, above n 30, para 197. The issue is not, however, limited to the balance between the nature of the penalties and the fair trial guarantees (notably the privilege against self-incrimination). See Wils, above n 30, para 209. Other (intrusive) powers of the competition authorities, in particular in connection with dawn raids, may also trigger broader defence rights.

[328] An instructive example for the complexity of rules is the variety of investigatory powers accorded to the OFT. These rules not only include different powers (procedures), from which the OFT can choose, when it wants to attend premises in order to obtain information, but also the possibility of using directed surveillance and civil informants (so-called covert human intelligence sources, or CHIS). See Collins, above n 52, 3–4. Another example is provided by David, above n 192, paras 57 and 58, regarding the French law where the power to seize and inspect electronic documents is normally subject to certain requirements, such as speciality, which have then been relaxed by case law in relation to dawn raids.

[329] See Araujo, above n 280, 524, who uses a constitutional law term and describes this phenomenon as 'a given set of checks and balances'. For instance, in contrast to the Commission, the French competition authority (DGCCRF) does not have the power to send out written requests for information, but it can summon to its offices staff members of the undertakings concerned. On the other hand, the right to be heard is organised in two phases—not just in a single phase, as under Community law. See Idot, above n 55, 217 and 215. Under German law, the situation is different again. Written requests for information can be addressed to the companies under investigation, but it is uncommon for their staff members to be summoned to the offices of the BKartA. Access to file is in practice handled in a remarkably flexible way, the parties effectively having access to the BKartA's dossier at all stages of the procedure and thus being able to make their views known at all times. These examples probably do not signal a superior level of protection in one or the other jurisdiction, but clearly demonstrate that, within each legal system, numerous detailed provisions together form a sophisticated and complex set of rules which must be considered as a whole. See also P Lowe, 'Preventing and Sanctioning Anticompetitive Conduct: Effective Use of Administrative and Criminal Sanctions, Leniency Programmes and Private Action in the EU' in B Hawk (ed), *2006 Proceedings of the Fordham Corporate Law Institute* (New York, Juris Publishing, 2006), 87, 94, who notes that sanctions 'do not exist in a vacuum', but that their nature and severity are interlinked with other aspects of the procedure, such as investigative powers, standard of proof and procedural safeguards.

[330] Burnside and Crossley, above n 36, 1; Weiß, above n 52, 268;

involved,[331] and the risks associated with the interplay between different legal systems is highlighted by the solution offered by the UK competition rules for protecting the right of individuals not to incriminate oneself. Under UK law, the OFT can address general requests for information to individuals, which they have to answer, and can also compel them to give an explanation of particular documents. However, UK authorities are precluded from using any such statement as evidence against that individual in criminal proceedings for the UK criminal cartel offence.[332] The efficiency of this protection is put at risk if the response is transmitted to another Network member which can impose sanctions on individuals in the 'normal' competition proceedings, such as the BKartA.[333] It is therefore submitted that the unrestricted exchange of evidentiary material between NCAs with diverging procedures and protection standards risks compromising the overall fairness of the procedure.

This means that, even if the lower level of protection in the Member State of origin is still compatible with the requirements of the Convention, it is hardly acceptable that an NCA circumvents the better protection existing under its own rules by obtaining evidence through the Network which it could not have gathered itself.[334] Therefore, the distinction between, on the one hand, differences in the level of protection reflecting requirements of the ECHR and, on the other hand, differences that are due to a level of protection exceeding the standards of the ECHR[335] does not serve any useful purpose.

NCAs and the Commission should always abstain from using in evidence information that has been gathered by another authority whose protection standards lag behind the authority's own standards; not to do so would call

---

[331] Lowe, above n 329, 94.

[332] The example has been taken from Roth, above n 311, 13.

[333] It is not clear whether Art 12(3) of Reg 1/2003 would effectively preclude the BKartA from using the response in evidence against the individual concerned as it could claim that both the UK and the German system provide for 'sanctions of a similar kind' for natural persons, notably criminal sanctions in the UK and quasi-criminal sanctions (*Ordnungsstrafen*) in Germany. Cf Roth, *ibid*, 13.

[334] Cf Araujo, above n 280, 528. *Contra* Wils, above n 70, 24, who maintains that, in view of the safeguards of Art 12(3) of Reg 1/2003, the problem only concerns legal persons and the only example of a potential circumvention of rights to be found is that of legal privilege. In my view, however, the issue is far more complex than this simple statement since each national procedure consists of an elaborate and carefully balanced system of investigatory powers and defence rights which vary in many details and must be considered as a whole (see also above n 327). Moreover, differences in protection standards are not always connected with the type of sanctions available and are therefore not necessarily reflected in Art 12(3) of 1/2003. This is recognised by Wils himself. See Wils, above n 30, para 209. For instance, protective rules may also result from non-competition-type legislation, such as data protection laws (see the example of Austria quoted by Perrin, above n 37, 557). Admittedly, such norms do not create defence rights *sensu strict*; however, since they may ultimately protect the persons under investigation, they should also be taken into account (see also above n 49). In any event, Art 12(3) of Reg 1/2003 protects only individuals, not companies.

[335] See Wils, above n 62, 455–6.

into question the procedural fairness established by it's own domestic system.[336] One must not forget that '[p]rocedure is thus not an end in itself, but a guarantee for a balanced decision'.[337]

(3) Perceived Discrimination. It has been argued that the problem of discrepancies between national procedures, including the sanctions available, existed before Regulation 1/2003. Application of the same law and co-operation between NCAs and between NCAs and the Commission under the new enforcement system would only make these differences more apparent.[338] However, it is submitted that the issue to be addressed here is not simply one of 'outer appearance'; a number of elementary factors have changed.

Admittedly, the fact that NCAs enforce EU competition law in accordance with their own—often diverging—procedural rules is not new. In this respect, the situation prior to the adoption of Regulation 1/2003 was in no way different. On the other hand, it is also well known that, before 1 May 2004, NCAs hardly ever applied Articles 81 and 82 EC. In many Member States, the authorities were not even empowered to enforce Community competition law.[339] Those who had the power mostly preferred to confine their proceedings to the application of their own national competition law, with which they were obviously more familiar. They often took recourse to Article 81 or 82 EC only in cases where domestic law did not allow them to condemn the relevant anti-competitive practices, for instance, because the national competition rules provided for sectoral exemptions.[340] In this respect, however, things have changed drastically. Not only have all NCAs been vested with the power to enforce Articles 81 and 82 EC, but they are also effectively obliged, pursuant to Article 3 of Regulation 1/2003, to apply these Treaty provisions whenever the inter-state trade criterion is fulfilled. The ultimate aim of the Commission, of course, is to have a much larger number of enforcement decisions than previously taken at national level. These two features, in particular the legal obligation of Member States' authorities to apply Community competition law, puts the problem of diverging national procedures into a different light.

---

[336] Cf Burnside and Crossley, above n 36, 20, who sharply criticise the co-operation provisions under Reg 1/2003, in particular the rights of exchange under Art 12, submitting that they might 'make a mockery of national procedural rules'. However, this would not solve the problem that evidence collected by the Commission might be precluded from being used by NCAs as the procedural rules of the Community in competition matters do not (always) comply with the ECHR standards. See above n 326.

[337] Lenaerts and Vanhamme, above n 125, 569.

[338] Gauer, above n 30, 199.

[339] In 1999, when the White Paper was published, seven of the 15 then-Member States had not empowered their competition authorities to enforce Arts 81 and 82 EC. See para 94 of the White Paper.

[340] See A Klimisch and B Krueger, 'Decentralised Application of EC Competition Law: Current Practice and Future Prospects' (1999) 24 *EL Rev* 463, 466–7.

The possibility of exchanging information and, in particular, evidentiary material did not exist prior to 1 May 2004. On the contrary, the *Spanish Banks* doctrine precluded both the Commission and NCAs from providing each other with evidence which they had gathered in relation to particular proceedings. The fact that now, under Regulation 1/2003, evidence collected under different protection standards may be circulated among Network members is another important element which distinguishes the current situation from that under the former enforcement system.

Finally, companies and their lawyers are all the more sensitive to the problem of diverging national standards because, as shown above, the matter overlaps with that of ensuring proper protection of fundamental rights, in particular the fair trial guarantee (rights of defence).

In view of these features, it is submitted, the issue of procedural diversity nowadays has a qualitatively and fundamentally different relevance than it used to have under the previous enforcement system. For companies under investigation, the situation under Regulation 1/2003 therefore turns out to be quite different from the situation prior to the reform. While NCAs increasingly apply Community competition law, procedural diversity continues to exist. Under the old regime, companies and, where applicable, individuals had to cope with different procedures and faced different sanctions. Such differences must be accepted and are acceptable to the extent that NCAs apply only national competition rules which have been enacted by national parliaments and can vary from Member State to Member State. However, where the same substantive law, notably Articles 81 and 82 EC, is enforced, albeit by public bodies from different Member States, continued procedural diversity is difficult to justify and double standards are likely to be perceived as blunt discrimination.[341] Why should companies understand and accept being prosecuted according to diverging rules and standards, even though they have infringed one and the same substantive provision laid down in the same (supranational) 'code of law', notably the EC Treaty? Where these procedural differences also lead to substantive differences in outcome, undertakings will regard the rules all the more as being genuinely unfair.[342] Moreover, even within the same Member State, two companies may be subject to unequal standards as the level of protection, for instance in the case of legal privilege, will in fact depend on whether the NCA collected the evidence itself or obtained it

---

[341] See Idot, above n 55, 216 and 221. The prohibition of any form of discrimination is a general principle of Community law which must be respected not only by the Community institutions, but also by the Member States when applying Community law. K Lenaerts, 'Respect for Fundamental Rights as a Constitutional Principle of the European Union' (2000) 6 *Columbia Journal of European Law* 1, 7.

[342] As I Forrester, 'Diversity and Consistency: Can They Cohabit?' in Ehlermann and Atanasiu, above n 8, 341, 343, puts it, where identical rules are applied, 'discrepancies of approach and of outcome are therefore not the same as the normal patterns of legal diversity which characterise Europe'.

through the Network from another NCA affording a different degree of protection. Such differential treatment amounts to discrimination.[343] There is no obvious explanation for these discrepancies except for the fact that the Commission considered it superfluous to harmonise national procedures. But it is precisely the validity of this consideration which is called into question by the above analysis.

2. Possible Solutions

As we have seen, strict application of the country of origin principle—as it appears to have been enshrined in Article 12 of Regulation 1/2003—may entail a creeping erosion of protection standards. The question here is not one of compatibility with Regulation 1/2003, particularly its Article 12, but one of credibility of the public bodies responsible for competition law enforcement and trust of those subject to Regulation 1/2003 in the proper administration of justice. Albeit formally in conformity with Article 12 of Regulation 1/2003, the unlimited exchange of evidence between enforcers committed to different protection standards is likely to be perceived as inherently and profoundly unfair by firms and individuals subject to competition investigations. This may undermine the confidence of those concerned in the objectives and value of anti-trust law, hamper competition advocacy and ultimately jeopardise the willingness of companies and staff members to abide by the competition rules. There appear to be at least three different ways to address the problem of too broad and unrestricted an exchange of evidence between Network members and the potential loss of protection standards associated therewith.

Probably the most obvious way of addressing the problem, at least with regard to legal certainty and practicability, would be to harmonise national competition procedures insofar as the application of Articles 81 and 82 EC is concerned. Arguably, an EU directive (or even a regulation) pursuing this objective could be passed on the basis of Article 83 EC,[344] which gives the Council a wide mandate to adopt 'any appropriate regulations or directives to give effect to the principles set in Articles 81 and 82'. However, this option also seems to be the most difficult solution in terms of political feasibility as currently a political consensus for such a far-reaching act of Community legislation in the field of competition law is highly unlikely.

Other writers have suggested that, in order to prevent the emergence or application of different standards, the substantial law to be applied should be Community law. In addition, national (procedural) rules should be enacted to regulate, inter alia, the rights of parties concerned to be heard prior to the transmission of information, the obligation to issue a motivated

---

[343] Andreangeli, above n 238, 47–8.
[344] Martinez Lage and Brokelmann, above n 93, 417.

decision regarding the transfer of information and safeguards against the inappropriate disclosure of confidential information.[345] However, these proposals not only appear to be impracticable, but also seem to run counter to the objectives and spirit of Regulation 1/2003. There can be little doubt that the legislator intended not to have the exchange of information and evidence based on formal transmission decisions. On the contrary, by setting up the ECN and linking all Network members by a common Intranet, the Commission deliberately chose to create a co-operation system which allows its participants to communicate in a speedy and informal way without having to resort to legal procedures and formal decision-making. The parties are not formally involved in this process.[346] It would also unduly hinder co-operation within the ECN if the Network members were required to adopt, prior to each information exchange, a formal transmission decision which could then be challenged before the national courts. Such a scenario would entail a number of further questions regarding, for instance, the right to be heard, effective judicial remedies (including the question of a suspensive effect) and the right of appeal. To deal with all these issues would make efficient co-operation virtually impossible.

There may be other solutions that are less strict and formal, thereby allowing Network members to maintain a swift co-operation mechanism. The ultimate goal of such an option should be that the highest protection standard will always prevail.[347] In other words, NCAs and the Commission should systematically refrain from using in evidence information that has been collected by another competition authority in accordance with rules which only provide a lower degree of protection than their own laws. To

[345] Araujo, above n 280, 525–6.

[346] This follows, for instance, from the fact that Reg 1/2003 does not stipulate the actual process of exchanging information or documents. Recital 15 of Reg 1/2003 simply states that it is necessary to set up 'arrangements for information and consultation' and that '[f]urther modalities for the co-operation within the network will be laid down and revised by the Commission', ie by informal instruments such as notices and guidelines. Similarly, recital 4 of the Network Notice provides: 'Consultations and exchanges within the network are matters between public enforcers and do not alter any rights or obligations arising from Community or national law for companies.' See also above Chapter 3, section III.E.1.a and section II.A in this chapter. This result may be regrettable, but reflects the current legal situation.

[347] See Van Der Woude, above n 7, 13. In contrast to the solution proposed here, Van der Woude suggests (similar to Araujo, see above n 345 and accompanying text) that the transfer of information be based on a decision challengeable before an independent body. In his view, safeguards are only effective if their implementation is subject to judicial control. Cf also the OECD's Best Practices for the formal exchange of information between competition authorities in hard-core cartel investigations, available at www.oecd.org/dataoecd/1/33/35590548.pdf (accessed February 2009). At points II.B.4 and C.2 of these Best Practices, the requesting authority is required to respect its own privilege against self-incrimination and not to use information that would be covered by legal professional privilege according to the rules of the requesting jurisdiction, while the transmitting (requested) authority is required to apply always its own rules on legal professional privilege. The Best Practices thus aim to ensure that the higher standard will effectively prevail.

implement this rule, it is necessary to compare, in each case, the protection standards of the transmitting and receiving authorities. In order to ease the burden of such a comparison, it would be useful to establish a matrix showing the most important investigative powers of the NCAs of all 27 Member States and the Commission, as well as the rights of companies under investigation.[348] On the basis of such a matrix, each NCA could relatively quickly establish whether protection standards in a particular Member State lag behind the own standards and thus whether a particular document originating in that Member State could effectively be used by it as evidence. The filtering of exchanged evidentiary material could be further facilitated by the establishment, at the level of NCAs (and possibly the Commission), of so-called 'taint teams', who are specifically trained to exercise the necessary comparative analysis of the applicable protection standards. These taint teams would comprise only officials who are not part of the relevant case team and would thus have a more neutral stance towards the (non-)admissibility of certain pieces of information as evidence.[349] This system obviously also requires that all information and documents circulating in the Network are marked in such a way that it is possible to identify not only the person or company which submitted or handed over the material, but also the competition authority which obtained or collected it in the first place. Such a procedure would also enhance transparency by allowing the parties, once they have gained access to the file, to take cognisance of the origin of all evidentiary material in the file of the acting competition authority. This, in turn, would enable them to challenge the use of any transferred pieces of evidence on the grounds of circumvention of the protection standards applicable in the Member State of destination. Given the lack, in Regulation 1/2003, of any binding rules that guarantee the observance of higher protection standards, this approach may, for the time being, represent a workable and acceptable compromise until such time as the Commission and Member States are willing to strike

---

[348] Such a matrix should certainly contain information regarding the following aspects: powers regarding on-site inspections (duty of co-operation, forced entrance, requirement of judicial warrant, proportionality, level of suspicion, presence of a lawyer), power to interrogate individuals/staff, privilege against self-incrimination, legal professional privilege, access to file and protection of confidential information. This list is by no means exhaustive. A first step in the direction of providing such information are the 'Results of the questionnaire on the reform of Member States (MS) national competition laws after EC Regulation No 1/2003'. This document, which shows the (lack of) convergence of the national and Community procedural rules in table form, is available on the ECN's website (http://ec.europa.eu/competition/ecn/documents.html). However, it provides little detail on the investigatory powers and no information on defence rights.

[349] See International Competition Network, Cartels Working Group (Subgroup 1), 'Co-operation between competition agencies in cartel investigations', report to the ICN Annual Conference, Moscow, May 2007 (Luxemburg, Office for Official Publications of the European Communities, 2007), 24.

a new path and consider harmonisation of the procedures to be applied with respect to the enforcement of Articles 81 and 82 EC.[350]

This does not necessarily mean 'full-scale harmonisation' of all relevant procedural rules, an approach that the Commission has clearly rejected in the past.[351] The Commission and Member States could start by agreeing on (a minimum of) certain fundamental rules and principles which are to be applied in all competition proceedings regarding Articles 81 and 82 EC.[352] These common rules could provide a sufficient basis to make it possible that, for the rest, Member States mutually recognise each others' standards as equivalent. The principle of mutual recognition could be combined with an 'anti-abuse clause' which would preclude an NCA from invoking the equivalence rule where that NCA has resorted to evidence gathered by another NCA for the sole purpose of circumventing stricter domestic rules concerning the collection of evidence.[353] Such a system of minimum harmonisation coupled with mutual recognition would not only make the exchange and use in evidence of information pursuant to Article 12 of

---

[350] Admittedly, Van der Woude's suggestion (see above n 347) is preferable in the sense that it would improve the effectiveness of the principle that the highest protection standard should prevail. The need to adopt a formal transmission decision would oblige the transmitting authority to refuse the transfer of information where the standards of the receiving authority are lower and would also facilitate judicial review. However, as noted above, the requirement of such a formal decision seems hardly compatible with Reg 1/2003. Moreover, the system proposed here has the advantage that judicial control of the transfer and use of evidence will be in the hands of the same judge who is called upon to review the legality of the prohibition decision, while in Van der Woude's scenario, the transmission decision would be reviewed by the courts in the Member State of origin and the prohibition decision by the courts in the Member State of destination of the relevant evidence. In terms of efficiency, the latter solution is therefore less convenient.

[351] See p 12 of the Explanatory Memorandum.

[352] *Contra* S Meiklejohn, 'You Can't Legislate Perfection: The Virtues of Experimentation in the Design of Antitrust Enforcement Regimes' in B Hawk (ed), *2003 Proceedings of the Fordham Corporate Law Institute* (New York, Juris Publishing, 2004), 55, 70, who does not consider it undesirable to have procedural divergence. He submits that 'rather than viewing . . . variations in competition law as complications that must be eliminated, we should view them as opportunities for productive experimentation' (this is sometimes also referred to as 'systems competition'). It seems that Meiklejohn considered mainly the (multiple) application of varying merger control regimes at international level (outside the EU). In my view, within the ambit of Arts 81 and 82 EC and under the 'common umbrella' of the enforcement system set up by Reg 1/2003, the time for experimentation has expired as this would undermine legal certainty, coherence and the rights of undertakings within the EU.

[353] Cf the judgments of the ECJ in Case 229/83 *Edouard Leclerc and others v SARL 'Au blé vert' and others* [1985] ECR 1 and Case 33/74 *van Binsbergen v Bestuur van de Bedrijfsvereniging voor Metaalnijverheid* [1974] ECR 1299. In both cases, the ECJ based its ruling on some sort of anti-abuse principle. It found that Member States may in fact restrict certain freedoms resulting from the EC Treaty (in those cases the free movement of goods (*Leclerc*) and the freedom to provide services (*van Binsbergen*)) where the relevant activity has been organised in such a way that it has a cross-border element and thus falls within the scope of those EC Treaty provisions for the sole purpose of avoiding the application of certain mandatory national rules which would otherwise have governed the exercise of the activity.

Regulation 1/2003 easier[354] and more reliable, but would also certainly increase the perceived fairness of national procedures.

III. CONCLUSION

This chapter has outlined the articles of Regulation 1/2003 on the exchange of information focusing on the horizontal exchange of evidence between NCAs. It has been demonstrated that Regulation 1/2003, in particular Article 12, puts virtually no limits on the transmission of information, thus creating the basis for a 'free movement' of evidence within the Network.

From the perspective of the authorities, this may be desirable; from the undertakings' point of view, the free circulation of evidence is certainly less welcomed. In view of the large discrepancies between the various national procedures, an unrestricted exchange of evidence and other information may entail a loss of protection or a fading of protection standards at the expense of the undertakings concerned. These adverse consequences do not concern pure formalities, but affect fundamental guarantees such as the right to a fair hearing (rights of defence) protected by the ECHR. Moreover, the transfer of evidence collected under one legal order to another legal order may also disturb the delicate balance of rights and duties existing within a given legal system. It is precisely this balance, however, ie the careful weighing of investigatory powers of the authority and defence rights of the person subject to the procedure, which guarantees the overall legality and fairness of the proceedings. It therefore seems necessary to further clarify and limit the right of competition authorities in the EU to exchange and use evidence in competition matters while recognising the necessity for NCAs (and the Commission) to co-operate with regard to fact-finding in order to ensure effective enforcement of the EC competition rules.

The following rules and principles have been elaborated. Where a case is reallocated and the file transferred to another NCA (or the Commission), the authorities should abide by the principle that, in all cases, the entire dossier is transmitted, including any possibly inculpatory as well as exculpatory evidence.

As concerns the protection of confidential information, it is submitted that two aspects are crucial and should always be observed by the authorities. First, a confidentiality request must always be attached to and transmitted together with the relevant document. Secondly, where the receiving authority intends to reject the request or to disregard confidentiality which has already been awarded by the transmitting authority, it must

---

[354] For instance, the evaluation of the equivalence of protection standards in individual cases required under Reg 1/2003, Art 12(3), second indent would become redundant.

apply an AKZO-type of procedure, meaning that it must give the person concerned the opportunity to make his/her views known and, should the case arise, to have a negative decision of the NCA reviewed before the information is actually released. Companies are therefore called upon to submit any confidentiality claims as early as possible, ideally at the moment when they submit the relevant piece of information.

A judicial review of the information gathering may only be carried out by the courts of the Member State where the information was collected ('country of origin' principle) as it is the domestic law of that Member State which determines the applicable procedural guarantees and hence the legality of the investigative measure. Enabling the courts in the Member State of the receiving authority to adjudicate on the question of whether the sending authority has observed the relevant procedural rules would mean forcing a judge to apply foreign rules he is not familiar with. It would also mean the right to judge the legality of acts of foreign state bodies could be usurped. This would not only run counter to the principle of state sovereignty, but also undermine mutual trust between the members of the ECN. However, in order to minimise the risk that illegally collected evidence is circulated between and eventually also used by Network members— whether directly or indirectly—certain unwritten safeguards must be respected. First, information may not be transmitted where it has definitively been established beforehand that the information was obtained in an illegal manner. Secondly, where the lawfulness of the information gathering is being disputed after the transfer of the information to another Network member, the sending authority must inform the receiving authority of such a dispute. Thirdly, a Network member which is in possession of foreign information that has been gathered by the sending authority illegally is prohibited from using that information in evidence. Instead, it has to remove the relevant documents from its case file and destroy them or return them to the person who provided them. Finally, in order to make the 'free movement' of information more transparent and allow persons to challenge the information gathering at the right place, the origin of documents exchanged in the ECN, including the identity of the authority which collected them in the first place, must always be indicated on the document.

The discrepancies that exist between the procedural rules and safeguards of the 27 Member States and the Commission procedure pose a major risk to the standards of legal protection of individuals and undertakings. This is a particularly severe problem as many of the protection standards can be linked to fundamental guarantees of the ECHR by which all Member States are bound. Moreover, in a system such as that established by Regulation 1/2003, where all agencies apply the same substantive rules rather than different national laws, operating diverging standards may seriously compromise the credibility of the authorities and the public enforcement system which, in turn, may undermine the respect of those subject to the law and their willingness to observe the rules.

In order to avoid a complete erosion of these standards, all Network members and the Commission should abide by the principle that the highest protection standard always prevails. In other words, information must not be forwarded if it appears that the receiving authority, by requesting the exchange, consciously or unconsciously bypasses its own domestic standards. To facilitate comparison of different legal orders, a matrix should be established which lists the most important investigatory powers of all NCAs and the Commission, together with the rights of defence of the persons subject to the investigation, including the position of third parties (ie persons other than the undertakings concerned who may become involved in the procedure, such as persons who could be interviewed or whose dwellings could be searched). It may still be difficult to establish, in each individual case, the higher standard. However, if such efforts are not made, the standards of protection in the EU will inevitably fade over time.

Ultimately, some kind of minimum harmonisation of the national procedural rules, possibly coupled with a system of mutual recognition of protection standards, may have to be envisaged. It would certainly have benefited the facilitation of the information exchange, the safeguard of high protection standards and the confidence of undertakings in the fairness of competition proceedings under Regulation 1/2003 had the Commission acknowledged the need for some form of (limited) harmonisation of national procedures from the beginning of the modernisation process and made corresponding proposals.

5

Consultation Prior to Final Decision Taking

ONE MECHANISM WHICH is designed to guarantee uniformity of the interpretation and consistent application of EC competition law is the obligation incumbent on each NCA to inform the Commission of the envisaged course of action prior to adopting a final decision.

I. THE PRINCIPLES

Article 11(4) of Regulation 1/2003 provides that, at least 30 days before taking certain types of decisions, NCAs shall notify the Commission of the proposed measure.

A. NCA Decisions Subject to Prior Consultation

1. The Relevant Types of Final Decisions

In accordance with the wording of Article 11(4) of Regulation 1/2003, the informatory duty only applies in relation to prohibition decisions, commitment decisions and decisions withdrawing the benefit of a block exemption. It thus does not cover decisions on interim measures. As a consequence, interim measures can be adopted by NCAs without it being necessary for the Commission to be consulted beforehand. The reason for this is probably that such decisions are supposed to be of a provisional nature and thus would not definitively rule on the question of whether or not Article 81 or 82 EC has been infringed. Therefore, the Commission obviously did not consider it necessary to supervise national decisions on interim measures with a view to ensuring consistency. Divergencies from the Commission's decision practice or existing case law of the Luxemburg courts can still be remedied in the final decision.

On the other hand, decisions accepting commitments are included in the list of national measures of which the Commission must be notified in advance. Similar to decisions ordering interim measures, commitment decisions under Article 9 of Regulation 1/2003 contain no definite finding as to the existence of an infringement prior to the commitment, nor the absence of an infringement following the commitments.[1] They simply state that 'there are no longer grounds for action'. This principle should apply *mutatis mutandis* to commitment decisions adopted by NCAs since, for most if not all NCAs (and the Commission), it is a new tool, first introduced by Regulation 1/2003, and should therefore be applied in accordance with that regulation. Moreover, a commitment decision which effectively states that, after the implementation of the commitments offered by the undertakings concerned, the agreement or practice does not violate Article 81 or 82 EC would come close to a positive decision. However, not only are NCAs excluded from adopting positive decisions,[2] but also this approach would potentially allow companies to circumvent the abolition of the notification system: namely, they could seek to obtain the blessing of the NCA through a twisted use of the instrument of commitment decisions. Like commitment decisions adopted by the Commission, commitment decisions taken at the national level will therefore not make a conclusive finding as to the existence or non-existence of an infringement. They cannot preclude other competition authorities (including the Commission) from taking a negative decision in respect of the same agreement or practice.[3] However, there are binding for the authority that adopted them and thus definitely close to the relevant procedure.[4]

Against this background, it is rather surprising that the Commission does not deem it necessary to monitor the adoption of interim measures by NCAs, while it regards the supervision of national decisions accepting commitment as indispensable. Admittedly, interim measures are adopted for a limited period of time only, ie until a decision in the main proceedings has been reached. However, in this respect, they are similar to commitment decisions which can be adopted for a specific period pursuant to Article 9(1) of Regulation 1/2003. Moreover, the assumption that interim measures represent only a provisional arrangement of the matter is a theoretical, but not always realistic, position. De facto interim measures can

---

[1] Recital 13 of Reg 1/2003. See also p 18 of the Explanatory Memorandum and C Gauer, D Dalheimer, L Kjolbye and E De Smijter, 'Reg 1/2003: A Modernised Application of EC Competition Rules' (2003) (Spring) *Competition Policy Newsletter* 3, 5.

[2] See above Chapter 1, section II.B.1.d(1).

[3] Not even a Commission decision accepting commitments is binding for NCAs (or national courts). Recital 13 of Reg 1/2003. See also S Hossenfelder and M Lutz, 'Die neue Durchführungsverordnung zu den Artikeln 81 und 82 EG-Vertrag' (2003) 53 *Wirtschaft und Wettbewerb* 118, 122.

[4] Pursuant to Art 9(2) of Reg 1/2003, proceedings that were concluded with a commitment decision can only be reopened if the relevant facts have changed (or if the decision was based on incorrect or incomplete facts in the first place, or if the companies do not comply with it).

have quite a definite character.[5] It would therefore have been more logical had the Commission also included interim measures in the category of decisions of which it must have been informed beforehand.

2. Decisions on Fines

On the other hand, it is curious that decisions imposing fines or other penalties are not listed in Article 11(4) Regulation 1/2003 and thus seemingly could be taken without prior consultation of the Commission. This may appear surprising at first sight. In most cases, however, the decision on fines will be combined with a prohibition decision; in other words, the decisions imposing sanctions and ordering that the infringement be brought to an end will be contained in one and the same act and will thus be subject to the consultation procedure. Where this is not the case (ie where the penalties are imposed by a separate decision), the decision on penalties will only be taken after a decision has been issued establishing the existence of an infringement. In the latter scenario, the Commission may consider monitoring the choice of sanctions and, where appropriate, the amount of fines imposed by an NCA in a particular case to be nonessential, so long as it has been consulted in respect of the infringement decision before the decision on penalties was taken. This would make sense as the need to ensure consistency exists with regard to the findings on the substance of case, rather than with regard to the penalties applied at the national level for a particular infringement. Moreover, in view of the large divergencies between the sanctions available in the Member States, it would hardly be possible to seek EU-wide consistency in terms of penalties imposed by NCAs.

In practice, however, there appears to be a common understanding in the Network that consultation pursuant to Article 11(4) of Regulation 1/2003 should also take place on decisions imposing fines or other penalties. This understanding is deduced *a contrario* from the wording of paragraph 48 of the Network Notice, which lists, under the term 'other types of decisions'—ie those not falling within the scope of Article 11(4) Regulation 1/2003—only decisions rejecting complaints, terminating an investigation or ordering an interim measure, but makes no mention of decisions on fines.[6] This approach seems to be backed by the preparatory

---

[5] If, for instance, in a refusal-to-supply case under Art 82 EC, the allegedly dominant company is ordered by preliminary injunction to deliver the requested goods to the applicant, the supply of the goods is in fact definite until the time when the ruling in the main proceedings is issued.

[6] W Wils, 'The Reform of Competition Law Enforcement—Will it Work?', Community Report for the FIDE XXI Congress, Dublin, 2–5 June 2004, in D Cahill (ed), *The Modernisation of EU Competition Law Enforcement in the EU—FIDE 2004 National Reports* (Cambridge, Cambridge University Press, 2004, 661. L Idot, 'Le nouveau système communautaire de mise en oeuvre des articles 81 et 82 CE (Règlement 1/2003 et projets de textes d'application)' (2003) 39

documents of Regulation 1/2003. The Explanatory Memorandum published together with the Draft Regulation states that Article 11(4) 'establishes a consultative obligation regarding all decisions by Member States' authorities aimed at terminating *or penalising* an infringement'.[7] The relevant part of the draft Article 11(4) is identical to the text that was eventually adopted by the Council.

There is no doubt that NCAs can voluntarily assume an informatory duty with regard to decisions on fines. In view of the wording of Article 11(4) of Regulation 1/2003, however, it is submitted that there is no formal consultative obligation in respect of national decisions which impose fines without, at the same time, ruling on the existence of an infringement of Article 81 or 82 EC. This is relevant for Member States which operate a dual enforcement system whereby the right to issue prohibition decisions, on the one hand, and the power to impose fines, on the other, are vested in two separate bodies. The body solely imposing fines can adopt its decisions without prior consultation of the Commission. This may be important in terms of preserving independence and impartiality in the event that the relevant body is a court.[8]

B. The Stance of the Commission—'Qui tacit . . .'

It is important to note that informing the Commission pursuant to Article 11(4) of Regulation 1/2003 does not trigger a consultation process *sensu stricto*: there is no obligation on the part of the NCA to obtain the Commission's (explicit or implicit) approval before adopting the final decision. In fact, the Commission is not even required to respond in any way to the proposal forwarded by the NCA.[9] This means that the NCA can proceed to issue the envisaged decision if the Commission does not formulate any objections or simply does not react at all provided the 30-day period has expired.[10] Where the NCA wishes to deviate substantially from the initially proposed and notified course of action, it is obliged to reconsult the Commission.[11]

Cahiers de Droit Européen 283, 329, para 96, who argues that, in spite of the 'clumsy drafting' of Art 11(4) of Reg 1/2003, it is difficult to see why decisions on fines would not be included in the scope of that provision.

[7] Emphasis added. P 21 of the Explanatory Memorandum.

[8] In Sweden, for instance, the KKV is entitled to rule on the existence of an infringement and issue injunctions, while fines can only be imposed by the Stockholm District Court. In Austria, the Oberlandesgericht Wien (Vienna Court of Appeal) acts as central cartel court (Kartellgericht) and decides on the termination of infringements and the imposition of fines.

[9] Hossenfelder and Lutz, above n 3, 123.

[10] Para 46 of the Network Notice.

[11] K Dekeyser and D Dalheimer, 'Co-operation within the European Competition Network—Taking Stock after 10 Months of Case Practice', paper for the conference 'Antitrust Reform in Europe: A Year in Practice', organised jointly by the International Bar Association

If the Commission deems it necessary to comment on the draft decision, it can make written (or oral) observations.[12] The Commission seems to make ample use of this possibility and provides extensive commentaries on individual cases even where it does not disapprove of the contemplated NCA decision.[13] It remains to be seen whether the Commission will continue this practice on a long-term basis in spite of its often deplored scarce resources. In any event, there is no formal obligation on the part of the NCA to take account of the Commission's comments. The observations are not issued in the form of a Commission decision and therefore are not binding on the NCA.[14] In theory, the NCA is thus free to adopt the decision as it has been proposed in the first place.

In practice, the Commission has considerable leverage over NCAs in view of its right of evocation under Article 11(6) of Regulation 1/2003. Where substantial disagreement on the appropriate course of action persists even after intensive discussions between the Commission and the NCA concerned, the Commission can always pull in the case, thereby relieving the NCA of its competence to act on the matter. Even if this right is only exercised as *ultima ratio* in the event of major divergencies which threaten to compromise the consistent application of Article 81 or 82 EC, the mere existence of this Commission power is likely to put sufficient pressure on the NCAs to induce them to adhere to the Commission's viewpoint.[15]

However, from a formalistic perspective, Article 11(4) of Regulation

---

(IBA) and the European Commission, Brussels, 9–11 March 2005, 1, 9. C Gauer, 'Due Process in the Face of Divergent National Procedures and Sanctions', paper for the conference 'Antitrust Reform in Europe: A Year in Practice', organised jointly by the International Bar Association (IBA) and the European Commission, Brussels, 9–11 March 2005, 1, 17.

[12] Para 46 of the Network Notice. Reactions are in practice also given in more informal ways (eg by telephone or possibly e-mail). See Dekeyser and Dalheimer, above n 11, 10; B Lasserre, 'Le Conseil de la concurrence dans le réseau communautaire' 2005/No 3 *Concurrences—RDLC* 42, 47.

[13] See S Hossenfelder, 'Erste Erfahrungen des Bundeskartellamtes mit dem Behörden-netzwerk' in X, *FIW-Schriftenreihe Band 206. Schwerpunkte des Kartellrechts 2004* (Köln, Carl-Heymanns-Verlag, 2006), 1, 5: 'Das Bundeskartellamt stellt fest, dass die Kommission sich bislang die Zeit nimmt, jeden Einzelfall zu kommentieren. Zu inhaltlichen Differenzen ist es zwischen Bundeskartellamt und Kommission nicht gekommen.' It is quite astonishing that the Commission deems it necessary to comment on the Bundeskartellamt's draft decisions, given the fact that the Bundeskartellamt, in general terms, is one of the oldest and most experienced competition authorities in Europe and, moreover, one of the few NCAs to have applied Arts 81 and 82 EC already in the past. Lasserre, at the time President of the French Conseil de la concurrence, notes that where the Commission exceptionally made written observations, they did not present a firm or irrevocable position. Lasserre, above n 12, 47. It seems that the observations of the Commission often concern the question of whether the effect-on-trade criterion is fulfilled which is the essential requirement for applying Art 81 or 82 EC.

[14] J Steenbergen and M Van Der Woude, 'EU-mededingingsrecht na 1 mei 2004: Verordening 1/2003' in (2004) 52 *Sociaal-Economische Wetgeving* 192, 199.

[15] See A Jones and B Sufrin, *EC Competition Law* (Oxford, Oxford University Press, 1st edn, 2001), 1027; Steenbergen and Van Der Woude, *ibid*, 199. See also Stockmann's comment quoted above Chapter 2, n 11.

1/2003 does not impose a consultative obligation on NCAs in the narrow sense of the term, but a mere informatory duty.

II. THE INFORMATION PROCEDURE

In order to inform the Commission properly, NCAs shall provide the Commission with a summary of the case and, if possible, the draft decision. Further details and some practicalities of this information requirement are laid down in the Network Notice.

A. What is Transmitted to the Commission?

Article 11(4) of Regulation 1/2003 states that NCAs shall provide the Commission with a case summary, the envisaged decision 'or, in the absence thereof, with any other document indicating the proposed course of action'. The wording is deliberately open so as to accommodate the divergent procedural frameworks existing at national level. Accordingly, Member States are not obliged to provide the Commission with a copy of the draft decision in order to fulfil the information requirement; they are free to select any other type of document, provided that it sets out the intended course of action. Consultation at the stage of the statement of objections is thus possible.[16]

This option is of particular relevance for Member States with dual enforcement systems, where the adjudicative function is performed by a court or administrative tribunal.[17] These Member States may want to exclude the adjudicative body from the consultation process with the Commission in order to preserve the impartial and independent character of that body. In that case, forwarding the draft decision of the relevant court or tribunal would not be an option. Instead, the consultation duty can, for instance, be fulfilled by providing a copy of the document that the investigating and/or prosecuting body intends to submit to the adjudicating body.[18]

---

[16] C Gauer, 'Does the Effectiveness of the EU Network of Competition Authorities Require a Certain Degree of Harmonisation of National Procedures and Sanctions?' in C-D Ehlermann and I Atanasiu (eds), *European Competition Law Annual 2002: Constructing the EU Network of Competition Authorities* (Oxford, Hart Publishing, 2003), 187, 190. See also Gauer, above n 11, 17.

[17] But also Member States with an integrated authority may choose to start the consultation procedure on the basis of the draft statement of objections. In fact, the NMa has opted for this alternative.

[18] Wils, above n 6, para 184. Surprisingly, the Austrian legislator has opted for appointing precisely the judicial body, namely the Kartellgericht, as competition authority within the meaning of Art 11(4) of Reg 1/2003 thereby compelling it to forward drafts of its judgments to

In practice, the Commission is informed by transmission of a copy of the draft decision, the statement of objections or the draft statement of objections.[19] Pursuant to the fourth sentence of Article 11(4) of Regulation 1/2003, the NCAs have to make additional documents available where the Commission considers this necessary for an adequate assessment of the case.

In this context, it has been questioned whether the Commission will actually be in a position to prevent an inconsistent application of Articles 81 and 82 EC merely on the basis of the information forwarded by NCAs under Article 11(4) of Regulation 1/2003. One may indeed wonder whether a case summary and the draft decision are sufficient for the Commission to uncover divergencies in a field of law where facts play such a pre-eminent role for the evaluation.[20] On the one hand, the Commission can always request the NCA concerned to provide further explanations on the case and forward additional factual information, including documents, if it feels that the information transmitted initially does not suffice for it to assess the case properly. On the other hand, these options are unlikely to be exercised unless the case summary and the draft decision itself trigger questions or raise doubts as to the compatibility of the intended decision with the EC competition rules or existing case law. Ultimately, it is therefore possible that the Commission will detect only fairly obvious inconsistencies, namely those which are noticeable without in-depth knowledge of the entire case file.[21]

B. How is the Information Circulated in the ECN?

Since, in contrast to the initial case report, draft decisions and (draft) statements of objections are likely to contain a large amount of confidential data, they are not forwarded via the ECN's Intranet. In practice, NCAs transmit the relevant documents either through secure e-mail (encryption) or by other secure means of transport. Usually, the (draft) text of the

the Commission. See § 83(1) no 1 KartG 2005. Similarly, in Belgium, the adjudicative body (Raad voor de Mededinging) has recently changed its practice. While, in the past, it used to forward a summary of the report drawn up by the investigative body (Reporters Unit; now Auditoraat) to the Commission, it now communicates the own draft decision (*projet de decision*) pursuant to Art 11(4) of Reg 1/2003. The reason apparently is that the submission of the above summary report leads to problems in the event that the Raad does not endorse the preliminary assessment made by the investigative body. In such a situation, the consultation procedure would arguably have to be repeated. Yet the Austrian and Belgian practice raise concerns under Art 6 of the ECHR. See below section III.B.

[19] Dekeyser and Dalheimer, above n 11, 9.
[20] Steenbergen and Van Der Woude, above n 14, 199.
[21] *Ibid*, 199.

decision or statement of objections is only sent to the Commission, not circulated generally in the Network.[22]

This does not mean, however, that the other Network members are not informed. The third sentence of Article 11(4) of Regulation 1/2003 entitles NCAs to share the information provided to the Commission with other NCAs.[23] Indeed, it had initially been envisaged that draft decisions (or statements of objection), like initial case reports, would be forwarded to all members of the Network. However, this approach turned out to be impractical (it would probably have led to an excess of information and documents circulating in the Intranet or ECN) and was therefore abandoned. Instead, the other NCAs are provided with basic data about the case in computerised form as well as a meaningful abstract of the intended decision. To this end, the ECN has developed certain requirements for summarising the envisaged decision.[24]

Moreover, the ECN has created an electronic standard form by which NCAs notify the other Network members of the actual termination of a particular procedure. Even though Regulation 1/2003 does not impose any obligation in this respect, there is a common understanding among all Network members that such notification is desirable.[25] This is in line with the Joint Statement, which provides that Network members shall inform each other of the termination of all cases that have been notified to the Network in accordance with Article 11(2) or (3) of Regulation 1/2003.[26]

The asymmetric way in which the Commission and NCAs are informed of proposed national decisions raises again the question of whether the procedure chosen is adequate to allow NCAs to effectively exercise the rights they have been afforded under Regulation 1/2003. This concerns in particular the right, enshrined in Article 14(7) of Regulation 1/2003, to request that cases dealt with by an NCA be included in the agenda of the

---

[22] Dekeyser and Dalheimer, above n 11, 10.

[23] D Reichelt, 'To What Extent Does the Co-operation within the European Competition Network Protect the Rights of Undertakings?' (2005) 42 *CML Rev* 745, 762–3, submits that the right of an NCA informing the Commission, pursuant to Art 11(4) of Reg 1/2003, to share that information with other NCAs is limited to those NCAs which are dealing with the same case. However, neither the wording of the provision nor its purpose, which is to ensure the consistent enforcement of Arts 81 and 82 EC, supports this view. It is probably true that the Commission bears the ultimate responsibility for safeguarding consistency in the application of the Community competition rules. However, NCAs which are not dealing with the same case can equally contribute to these efforts. They might be handling or have handled cases that raise similar or comparable issues and therefore have an interest in closely following the course of action of the NCA informing the Commission. They could even provide useful comments. M Widegren, 'Consultation among Members within the Network', in Ehlermann and Atanasiu, above n 16, 419, 423. There appears to be no valid reason to restrict the information exchange under Art 11(4) of Reg 1/2003 to the Commission and certain selected NCAs. See also below n 27. For practical reasons, however, the amount of information transmitted to other NCAs prior to the final decision taking is limited.

[24] Hossenfelder, above n 13, 3. Dekeyser and Dalheimer, above n 11, 10.

[25] Hossenfelder, above n 13, 3.

[26] Para 24 of the Joint Statement.

Advisory Committee. It is a prerequisite for the exercise of this right that each NCA has proper knowledge of the decisions envisaged by other NCAs.[27] However, since it is for the Commission to ensure overall uniform interpretation and consistent application of Articles 81 and 82 EC, the review of national measures by other NCAs should be limited to uncover possible divergencies with existent decisions or ongoing cases of the reviewing NCA. It is important, however, that not only the Commission, but also NCAs are informed of the planned decision at an early stage as they are under an obligation, derived from Article 10 EC, to avoid taking decisions which would conflict with an existing NCA decision.[28] Receiving a summary of the draft decision together with the computerised form of basic case data would seem sufficient for an NCA to carry out an initial screening and assess whether the case might raise issues of consistency or require a coordinated approach with own cases.[29] Where an NCA feels that it requires more detailed information to finally assess the question of (possible) inconsistencies with its own matters, it can obtain additional information or even the full text of the intended decision upon request.

Finally, the issue of the proper language of communication has to be broached once again. In view of the above rights of NCAs regarding the Advisory Committee's agenda, it is important that information on proposed national decisions is circulated in a language which is understood by at least most, if not all, NCAs: forwarding the information only in the official language of the transmitting NCA would often not be suitable. However, neither Regulation 1/2003 nor the Network Notice give any implications as to which language should be used or how the language would be determined.[30] English has apparently been recognised by Network members as the most commonly understood language, and consequently the practice is to provide information on the computerised form as well as the descriptive summary of the intended decision in English.[31] Since, under Article 11(4) of Regulation 1/2003, the complete text of the draft decision or documents from the case file are not generally circulated in the Network, this practice should not pose any particular problem. However, the question arises of which language such documents should be

---

[27] On this basis, the position taken by Reichelt (above n 23) that Art 11(4) of Reg 1/2003 does not allow for a broad horizontal exchange of information is hardly defendable.

[28] See below Chapter 6, section II.C.

[29] Cf Widegren, above n 23, 422 and 424.

[30] In view of the relevance of the language for mutual understanding in the Network and the possibility of NCAs exercising their rights and actively participating in the discussions held in the ECN or the Advisory Committee on individual cases, it is astounding that the language issue is not mentioned in Reg 1/2003, the Network Notice or the Joint Statement. Cf M Wezenbeek-Geuke, 'Het voorstel voor een verordening van de Raad betreffende de uitvoering van de mededingingsregels van de artikelen 81 en 82 van het verdrag' [2001] *Nederlands tijdschrift voor Europees recht* 17, 25.

[31] Hossenfelder, above n 13, 4.

provided in if an NCA requests their transmission. In accordance with the principle that the authority which formulates the request should take care to use the appropriate language,[32] it would not be for the transmitting authority but for the receiving authority to prepare a translation of the requested documents into its own language if necessary.

III. THE POSITION OF PARTIES AND COMPLAINANTS

A. The Problem—Secrecy of Network Correspondence

There can be no doubt that certain observations of the Commission have a significant impact on the outcome of national proceedings. In view of the Commission's leverage, it is likely that NCAs take due account of the comments made by it. Theoretically, the Commission's observations may influence not only the amount of fines, but also the type of decision.[33] At the same time, it should be noted that observations are submitted at a late stage of the procedure, namely shortly before the NCA adopts the final decision. At this time, the parties and complainants, if any, will already have been given the opportunity to make their views known. However, having regard to the possible impact of the Commission's observations on the national decision, the question arises whether the parties should be heard again in the event that the Commission submits observations on the NCA's draft decision in order to fully guarantee the rights of defence. This seems particularly relevant to those NCAs which have the character of an independent and impartial tribunal within the meaning of Article 6 ECHR.[34]

It is clearly not the intention of the Commission that the undertakings concerned be informed of its opinions and given the opportunity to comment on them. Regulation 1/2003 does not contain any provision affording the parties the right to have knowledge of comments submitted by the Commission or any other Network member on a proposed decision of an NCA. On the contrary, the fourth sentence of Article 27(2) of Regulation 1/2003 explicitly excludes correspondence between the members of the Network, 'including documents drawn up pursuant to Articles 11 and 14' from the right of access to the file.[35]

Article 27 of Regulation 1/2003 only covers access to the Commission's file, while access to the NCAs' files is regulated by national law. It can be argued, however, that Article 27(2) of Regulation 1/2003 must also be

---

[32] *Ibid.*

[33] It is possible, for instance, that, following the Commission's reaction, the will NCA decide to impose fines while it had initially intended to issue a mere prohibition decision.

[34] See above n 8.

[35] See also Art 15(2) of the Implementing Regulation.

applied *mutatis mutandis* by NCAs when granting access to their own files, otherwise the principles enshrined in that provision could be easily circumvented and the protection of internal documents and Network correspondence afforded by Regulation 1/2003 would ultimately be lost. Moreover, Article 28(2) of Regulation 1/2003 obliges both the Commission and Member State officials to respect the principle of professional secrecy by forbidding them to disclose any

> information acquired or exchanged by them pursuant to this Regulation and of the kind covered by the obligation of professional secrecy.

Arguably, not only facts and evidence, but also other types of correspondence between the ECN members, including Commission opinions pursuant to Article 11(4) of Regulation 1/2003, constitute information within the meaning of Article 28(2) of Regulation 1/2003 and may therefore not be disclosed by NCAs to the extent that they are covered by the duty of professional secrecy. The rules on professional secrecy aim to protect not only the private interest of the undertakings involved in the case, but also the public interest pursued by the competition authorities concerned. Having regard to the confidentiality of Network correspondence established by Article 27(2) of Regulation 1/2003, it must therefore be considered that observations made by the Commission or other NCAs in the context of the consultation procedure under Article 11(4) of Regulation 1/2003 are covered by the obligation of professional secrecy.[36]

It follows from the above that NCAs may not communicate such observations to the undertakings concerned or to other interested parties, including complainants. In accordance with the supremacy of Community law, any national provision to the contrary would be inapplicable. Consequently, the companies and possibly natural persons subject to the investigation are de facto precluded from submitting on their part comments on those observations. It is doubtful, however, whether this is in line with the requirements of Article 6 ECHR.[37]

B. The Impact of Article 6 ECHR—The Right to Adversarial Proceedings

Article 6 ECHR guarantees the right to a fair trial, a right which holds a prominent place in a democratic society.[38] According to the case law of the

---

[36] Cf Gauer, above n 11, 17. See also above Chapter 4, section I.C.1.b(3).

[37] See Steenbergen and Van Der Woude, above n 14, 199, who argue that undertakings concerned and other interested parties must be given the opportunity to express their views on the Commission's opinion before the NCA adopts a final decision.

[38] Judgment of the ECtHR 27 February 1980 in *Deweer v Belgium* Publications Series A no 35, para 44.

ECtHR, one of the key features of the concept of a fair trial is the principle of 'equality of arms' and the right to adversarial proceedings.[39] As pointed out earlier, Member States are required to act in conformity with the principles of the ECHR when enforcing Community competition law.[40] Moreover, equality of arms can also be considered a general principle of Community law[41] which Member States consequently have to observe when they act in the Community law sphere.

1. Submissions of Third Parties

The right to adversarial proceedings

> means in principle the opportunity for the parties to a criminal or civil trial to have knowledge of and comment on all evidence adduced or observations filed, even by an independent member of the national legal service, with a view to influencing the court's decision.[42]

In other words, the notion of an adversarial process requires that all relevant material, including observations or documents submitted by a third party, be made available to both parties, the prosecutor/plaintiff and the defendant. As a consequence, the ECtHR has held this right to be infringed where an advocate general or similar officer intervenes in judicial proceedings and delivers an opinion intended to advise and accordingly influence the court without communicating his submissions to the parties and giving them the opportunity to reply to them. Examples are the advocate general before the Portuguese Supreme Court and the *procureur-generaal* before both the Hooge Raad in the Netherlands and the Belgian Hof van Cassatie. The ECtHR reached these conclusions despite the fact that the advocate general is usually not regarded as being a party to the proceedings, in view of the important part played by him in the proceedings and the nature of his submissions, which make it impossible to consider his opinion as neutral.[43]

---

[39] Judgment of the ECtHR of 28 August 1991 in the case of *Brandstetter v Austria* Publications Series A no 211, para 66.

[40] Above Chapter 3 III.D.1.

[41] K Lenaerts, 'In the Union We Trust': Trust-enhancing Principles of Community Law' (2004) 41 *CML Rev* 317, 325, basing himself on para 83 of the judgment of the CFI in Case T–30/91 *Solvay v Commission* [1995] ECR II–1775. According to Lenaerts, even Art 27(2) of Reg 1/2003 on access of the parties concerned to the Commission file is inspired by the principle of equality of arms (*idem*, 328).

[42] Judgment of the ECtHR of 20 February 1996 in the case of *Lobo Machado v Portugal* Reports/Recueil 1996-I, 195, para 31. Similarly, the CFI held in *Solvay* that the general principle of equality of arms presupposes that, in a competition case, the knowledge which the undertaking concerned has of the file used in the proceeding is the same as that of the acting competition authority (para 83 of the judgment; above n 41).

[43] See the judgment of the ECtHR in *Lobo Machado* (*ibid*), paras 29–31. This case concerned submissions of the Advocate General before the Portuguese Supreme Court. The ECtHR has

A similar problem exists with regard to the opinion of the Advocate General before the ECJ, which is submitted only after closure of the written procedure and brings to an end the oral procedure. Thus, even though the Advocate General makes his submissions in open court, the parties do not have the opportunity to submit observations in response to the opinion expressed by him. In contrast to the rulings of the ECtHR cited above, the ECJ considers that this is not in conflict with Article 6 ECHR. In *Emesa Sugar v Aruba*, the ECJ held that the above case law of the ECtHR was not transposable to the opinion delivered before the ECJ by the Advocate General.[44] The ECJ emphasised that the Advocate General could exercise his duties in full impartiality and total independence without being subject to any authority—that is, that he was not entrusted with the defence of any particular interest. His opinion would not form part of the proceedings between the parties, but rather would open the stage of deliberation. Moreover, in the event that the Advocate General submitted additional arguments which had not been debated between the parties, the ECJ could reopen the oral procedure.[45] However, it is doubtful whether this ruling is really consistent with above judgments of the ECtHR.[46] The ECJ admitted that the Advocate General takes part in the process by which the ECJ reaches its judgment.[47] This is the crucial point. Irrespective of whether one qualifies him as impartial and independent,[48] the Advocate General presents (legal) arguments that assist the ECJ in reaching a decision.[49] Their purpose thus is to influence the ECJ. If this were not the case, the system would make no sense. The argument that the opinion is an

rendered conforming judgments in cases regarding the role and submissions of the procureur général in criminal and civil proceedings before the Belgian Cour de cassation, the procureur-generaal before the Hooge Raad of the Netherlands and the avocat général at the French Cour de cassation. See judgments of the ECtHR 30 October 1991 in *Borgers v Belgium* Publications Series A no 214, 21, paras 24–9; of 20 February 1996 in the case of *Vermeulen v Belgium* Reports/Recueil 1996-I, 224; paras 29–33; 27 March 1998 in the case of *JJ v The Netherlands* Reports/Recueil 1998-II, 603, paras 42–3; 31 March 1998 in the case of *Reinhardt and Slimane-Kaïd v France* Reports/Recueil 1998-II, 640, para 105.

[44] Order of the ECJ of 4 February 2000 in Case C–17/98 *Emesa Sugar v Aruba* [2000] ECR I–665, para 16.

[45] Paras 11, 12, 14 and 18 of the Order in *Emesa Sugar* (*ibid*).

[46] The Order in *Emesa Sugar* has been criticised by a number of authors, recently by N Marsch and A-C Sanders, 'Gibt es ein Recht der Parteien auf Stellungnahme zu den Schlussanträgen des Generalanwalts? Zur Vereinbarkeit des Verfahrens vor dem EuGH mit Art. 6 I EMRK' (2008) 43 *Europarecht* 345. For more references see K Lenaerts and P Van Nuffel, *Constitutional Law of the European Union* (London, Sweet & Maxwell, 2nd edn, 2005), 10-080 note 306, who endorse the criticism.

[47] Para 15 of the Order in *Emesa Sugar* (above n 44).

[48] In some of the cases of the ECtHR mentioned earlier, the relevant officer was also considered impartial and independent. Moreover, by publicly recommending which arguments of the parties should be allowed or dismissed, the Advocate General will naturally and legitimately be regarded by the parties as taking sides with one or the other of them. See the judgment of the ECtHR of 7 June 2001 in *Kress v France*, Report/Recueil 2001-IV, 1, paras 81–2.

[49] Para 13 of the Order in *Emesa Sugar* (above n 44).

element of the deliberations rather than part of the adversarial proceedings does not alter the opinion's objective.[50] It is precisely during the deliberations that judges discuss and form opinions. The theoretical possibility of reopening the oral procedure, which in practice is rarely ever used, cannot, in my view, remedy the shortcoming of the principle procedural rule, which does not afford parties the opportunity to respond to the Advocate General's opinion.[51] In the light of the case law of the ECtHR on the principle of equality of arms, the ECJ's order in *Emesa Sugar* therefore seems incompatible with Article 6 ECHR.[52]

If the Commission submits observations on a decision contemplated by an NCA, this will in most, if not all, cases be done with a view to influencing the NCA's final decision[53] in order to maintain consistency in the enforcement of Articles 81 and 82 EC. On this basis, observations of the Commission which are issued in the framework of the consultation process pursuant to Article 11(4) of Regulation 1/2003 are undoubtedly comparable to the kind of submissions considered by the ECtHR in the above judgments.[54] In this context, it is interesting to note that the task of the avocat général at the French Cour de cassation, which formed the subject matter of one of the cases cited above, is to render a kind of 'second opinion'. He namely performs his work after having received the report and the draft judgment of the reporting judge. The avocat général does not argue the prosecution's case, but basically seems to comment on the recommendations of the reporting judge. Where he does not concur with these recommendations, he will trigger a debate.[55] His role is thus virtually the same as that performed by the Commission when submitting comments on an envisaged national decision pursuant to Article 11(4) of Regulation 1/2003.

[50] Moreover, in the light of the judgment of the ECtHR in *Kress* (above n 48, paras 77–80), this position is difficult to sustain as the Advocate General at the ECJ is not a member of the trial bench or even a judge, and does not attend the deliberations. Marsch and Sanders, above n 46, 359.

[51] Marsch and Sanders, above n 46, 360.

[52] Marsch and Sanders, above n 46, 360; cf also S Douglas-Scott, 'A Tale of Two Courts: Luxemburg, Strasbourg and the Growing Human Rights Acquis' (2006) 43 *CML Rev* 629, 643: 'the Strasbourg court seems to be indicating that there might be a right to comment on the ECJ Advocate General's opinion under Art 6(1) ECHR'.

[53] See above Chapter 1, n 201 and accompanying text.

[54] W Wils, 'The EU Network of Competition Authorities, The European Convention on Human Rights and the Charter of Fundamental Rights of the EU' in Ehlermann and Atanasiu, above n 16, 459. When ruling that the parties should have had access to the observations submitted by the Advocate General of the Portuguese Supreme Court, the ECtHR referred, inter alia, to the fact that the purpose of those observations was to assist the national Supreme Court and ensure that its case law was consistent. See para 28 of the judgment in *Lobo Machado* (above n 42); paras 29 and 31 of the judgment in *Vermeulen* (above n 43); and para 42 of the judgment in *JJ v The Netherlands* (above n 43). The Commission, it appears, pursues a very similar goal, namely the uniform and coherent application of EC competition law, when commenting on national draft decisions.

[55] See paras 73–5 of the judgment in *Reinhardt and Slimane-Kaïd* (above n 43).

2. Distinction between Non-judicial Bodies and 'Courts of the Classic Kind'

On the other hand, the ECtHR has also held that the prosecution and punishment of minor offences, which are nevertheless 'criminal' within the meaning of Article 6 ECHR, by non-judicial bodies (eg administrative authorities or professional disciplinary bodies) rather than courts of law is not inconsistent with the ECHR. However, the ECHR requires in such cases that the person concerned can challenge the decision of the non-judicial body before an independent and impartial tribunal which has full jurisdiction and offers all the safeguards of Article 6 ECHR.[56] Importantly, this kind of two-step system is not permitted for ordinary (traditional) judicial benches. The ECtHR has made it clear that 'courts of the classic kind', at all levels of jurisdiction, have to provide the guarantees of Article 6 ECHR and a breach of these guarantees at a lower court cannot be remedied by the fact that the proceedings before the appeal court comply with the requirements of the ECHR.[57]

Consequently, procedures before NCAs such as the BKartA, Autorità Garante or OFT, which are genuine administrative bodies and therefore do not fall within the category of tribunals of the 'classic kind', do not have to meet the standards of Article 6 ECHR in every respect. Therefore, this type of NCA can adopt final decisions without having to afford the undertakings the opportunity to comment on any observations it might have received from the Commission provided that the decision is subject to a comprehensive review by a court of law in an adversarial trial fulfilling all conditions laid down by Article 6 ECHR.

The situation is different with regard to NCAs of Member States that have incorporated the bifurcated model. In these Member States, the

---

[56] Judgments of the ECtHR of 23 June 1981 in the case of *Le Compte, Van Leuven and De Meyere v Belgium* Publications Series A no 43, para 51; 10 February 1983 in the case of *Albert and Le Compte* Publications Series A no 58, para 29; and 21 February 1984 in the case of *Öztürk v Germany* Publications Series A no 73, para 56.

[57] According to the Court of Human Rights, Art 6(1) ECHR concerns above all courts of first instance. It does not even require the existence of appeal courts. However, where a contracting state chooses to set up courts of further instance, those courts must equally provide the guarantees of Art 6(1) ECHR. Moreover, the possibility of appeal proceedings does not free the trial courts from the obligation to meet the requirements of Art 6(1) ECHR. The opposite result would run counter to the purpose of having several levels of jurisdiction, which namely is to reinforce judicial protection. Judgment of the ECtHR of 26 October 1984 in the case of *De Cubber v Belgium* Publications Series A no 46, para 32. Arguably, the ECJ applies a similar distinction with regard to the possibility of referring questions to the ECJ for a preliminary ruling pursuant to Art 234 EC. According to its case law, not all judicial bodies that may be considered courts under the national system of a Member State also qualify as courts for the purposes of Community law, notably Art 234 EC. Such courts must fulfil certain essential requirements (see para 29 of the judgment of the ECJ in Case C–53/03 *Syfait and others vs GlaxoSmithKline* [2005] ECR I–4609. The ECJ thereby seems to distinguish between the classic type courts, which are fully independent and form part of the Member States' judiciary, and tribunals, which are (closely) linked to the executive branch and as such are more akin to an administrative body.

adjudicative body often has the character of an independent and impartial tribunal (eg the Stockholm District Court, the Kartellgericht in Austria, criminal courts in the UK and Ireland which are involved in the enforcement of Articles 81 and 82 EC, possibly the Raad voor de Mededinging in Belgium and the Conseil de la concurrence in France[58]). According to the case law of the HR Court cited above, this latter type of NCA must satisfy the requirements of Article 6(1) ECHR. In view of the comparable nature of observations filed by the Commission under Article 11(4) of Regulation 1/2003 and opinions submitted by the Advocate General in certain national court proceedings, there is little doubt that the undertakings concerned, in competition procedures before such NCAs, must be given the opportunity to reply to the Commission's observations. Where the Commission has indeed filed observations, the relevant NCA must therefore inform the undertakings accordingly, provide them with a copy of the observations and fix an appropriate time limit within which the undertakings may submit comments.[59] Failure to do so would vitiate the procedure and could lead to the annulment of the NCA's decision on appeal.

Admittedly, it is unlikely that the Commission would introduce new facts or documents to the procedure.[60] Consequently, there can hardly be a question of new evidence being adduced. This would happen only in the rare event that the Commission had certain data or reports in its possession which may be relevant to the assessment of the case and which it had not yet communicated to the NCA concerned. It is, however, conceivable that the Commission's opinion contains important new legal arguments which have not yet been put forward by any of the parties to the proceedings. Moreover, the case law of the ECtHR is quite clear on this point. The fair trial guarantee of Article 6 ECHR and, more precisely, the principle of equality of arms require that the parties be given the opportunity to comment on every document in the court's file even when, in the court's view, it does not present any new fact or argument.

---

[58] As concerns the two latter enforcement bodies, it is certainly open to discussion whether they are in fact 'courts of the classic kind'. However, in view of their composition, their formal independence from the executive and the role they fulfil within the dual enforcement system, there are good reasons to regard them as tribunals within the meaning of Art 6 ECHR.

[59] Cf paras 67–8 of the judgment in *Brandstetter* (above n 39), where it is emphasised that not only must parties be given the hypothetical possibility of inspecting the file, including any observations received by the court, and reacting to it, but courts must also 'ensure that the other party will be aware that observations have been filed and will get a real opportunity to comment thereon'. In other words, the guarantee of adversarial proceedings requires the court to actually inform the parties of all submissions lodged in respect of the pending case and afford them sufficient time to reply to them.

[60] See K Dekeyser and M Jaspers, 'A New Era of ECN Co-operation' (2007) 30 *World Competition* 3, 10.

Only the parties to a dispute may properly decide whether this is the case; it is for them to say whether or not a document calls for their comments.[61]

3. Avoidance of Disclosure of the Commission's Observations

The obligation, arising from Article 6 ECHR, for NCAs which are traditional judicial bodies to communicate observations received from the Commission to the undertakings concerned can only be evaded where the consultation process pursuant to Article 11(4) of Regulation 1/2003 takes place between the Commission and the investigating/prosecuting body within the Members State's dual system (eg on the basis of the statement of objections or the draft application to the adjudicative body). The investigating/prosecuting body could then take into account the observations of the Commission without having to disclose them to the companies under investigation—the reason being that this body cannot be considered a tribunal within the meaning of Article 6(1) ECHR.

Furthermore, the adjudicative body, which by contrast is considered a tribunal within the meaning of Article 6 ECHR, will not base its findings directly on the Commission's observations, if at all. The observations will be considered only to the extent that they are reflected in the (final) application by which the prosecuting body requests the tribunal to adjudicate on the suspected infringement. That application must evidently be communicated to the undertakings concerned, which must be given the opportunity to respond to it. In this way, the guarantees of Article 6(1) ECHR would be observed without there being any need to disclose the actual submission of the Commission to the undertakings.

As concerns Member States with a dual enforcement system, consultations between the investigating/prosecuting body and the Commission before the adoption of the statement of objections would not result in an infringement of Article 6(1) ECHR even where the Commission's observations are not communicated to the undertakings concerned. However, where the adjudicative body deems it necessary to consult with the Commission on the basis of the general rules governing co-operation between the Commission and NCAs,[62] Article 6(1) ECHR requires the NCA (adjudicative body) to inform the undertakings concerned of any submissions made or opinions expressed by the Commission, whether

---

[61] Judgment of the ECtHR of 18 February 1997 in the case of *Nideröst-Huber v Switzerland* Reports/Recueil 1997-I, 101, para 29. The judgment concerns a civil litigation case. However, the Court of Human Rights has consistently held that the requirements derived from the right to adversarial proceedings under Art 6(1) ECHR are the same for both civil and criminal cases (see, eg para 28 of the same judgment; para 31 of the judgment in the *Lobo Machado* case (n 42); cf also para 30 of the judgment in *Albert and Le Compte* (n 56)).

[62] See Art 11(5) of Reg 1/2003, which provides that NCAs may consult the Commission on any case involving the application of EC competition law.

orally[63] or in written form, and afford them the possibility to comment on them.[64]

IV. CONCLUSION

In order to ensure coherence and consistency, an NCA must inform the Commission of the envisaged decision prior to the conclusion of a procedure (Article 11(4) of Regulation 1/2003). Depending on whether the Member State has an integrated or a dual enforcement system, this obligation may be fulfilled, for instance, by providing the Commission with the draft decision (integrated model) or the draft application to be submitted to the adjudicative body (dual system). If, on the other hand, it is the adjudicative body itself which consults with the Commission, problems may arise.

Such adjudicative bodies may be considered tribunals within the meaning of Article 6 ECHR. On this basis, the right to an adversarial procedure and the principle of 'equality of arms', which are aspects of the fair trial guarantee enshrined in Article 6 ECHR, would require the adjudicative body of the Member State to inform the undertakings concerned of the Commission's observations, if any, and afford them the opportunity to make their views known. However, this appears to be incompatible with Article 27(2) of Regulation 1/2003 and Article 15(2) of the Implementing Regulation by virtue of which correspondence between Network members is included in the category of 'internal documents' to which the parties concerned a priori have no access. In Member States operating a dual enforcement system, the obligation to inform the Commission prior to final decision taking must therefore be assumed by the investigating/prosecuting body rather than the adjudicative body in order to avoid violation of the ECHR.

---

[63] See paras 13 and 33 of the judgment of the ECtHR in *Vermeulen* (n 43).
[64] *Contra* Dekeyser and Jaspers, above n 60, 10.

6

Particular Issues of Parallel Proceedings

WHILE REGULATION 1/2003 and, more particularly, the allocation principles laid down in the Network Notice[1] seemingly aim to ensure that cases are assigned, as often as possible, to a single authority, Regulation 1/2003 does not exclude a priori parallel[2] proceedings being conducted by several NCAs.[3] This possibility of parallel actions at the national level obviously raises a number of issues. The most significant seems to be the question of whether the principle of *ne bis in idem* precludes the imposition of multiple fines by several Member States on the same persons regarding the same infringement.[4] Since, in any

[1] See in particular recital 18 of Reg 1/2003 and para 7 of the Network Notice.

[2] Unless indicated otherwise, the term 'parallel' is used here in a broad sense, covering both concurrent/simultaneous proceedings (ie proceedings that coincide in terms of the time at which they are conducted) and successive proceedings (ie situations where a second procedure is instituted after a first procedure regarding the same infringement has already been terminated).

[3] S Hossenfelder in U Loewenheim, K Meessen and A Riesenkampff (eds), *Kartellrecht, Kommentar, Band 1: Europäisches Recht* (Munich, CH Beck, 2005), VerfVO Art 5, para 9; C Arhold, 'Die Reform der europäischen Wettbewerbsaufsicht aus praktischer Sicht' (2005) 40 *Europarecht* (Beiheft 2), 119, 134; W Weiß, 'Grundrechtsschutz im EG-Kartellrecht nach der Verfahrensnovelle' (2006) *Europäische Zeitschrift für Wirtschaftsrecht* 263, 266. See also paras 12–13 of the Network Notice. Whether the drafters of the Network Notice envisaged parallel proceedings being conducted against the same persons is, however, unclear. A Klees, 'Der Grundsatz *ne bis in idem* und seine Auswirkungen auf die Zusammenarbeit der Kartellbehörden im European Competition Network (ECN)' (2006) 56 *Wirtschaft und Wettbewerb* 1222, 1229 note 58. In any event, where a case has effects in more than three Member States, it is in principle for the Commission to initiate proceedings in accordance with the 'three-plus' rule (see para 14 of the Network Notice). However, the Commission is under no obligation to take on such cases. Its discretionary powers, including considerations of Community interest and enforcement priorities, permit it to decline cases even if the suspected infringement presumably affects competition in more than three Member States. See also above Chapter 3, nn 19 and 282 and accompanying text.

[4] Until recently, the question of applicability of *ne bis in idem* (or double jeopardy) on parallel national antitrust proceedings had attracted little attention in the legal literature. However, the decentralisation of EC competition law enforcement coupled with the obligation of NCAs to apply Arts 81 and 82 EC is likely to result in increased enforcement activities at the national level. This new situation has made the issue of *ne bis in idem* more topical. R Nazzini, 'Some Reflections on the Dynamics of the Due Process Discourse in EC Competition Law (2005) 2 *The Competition Law Review* 5, 5; E Paulis and C Gauer, 'Le règlement n° 1/2003 et le principe du ne bis in idem' 2005/No 1 *Concurrences—RDLC* 32, para 6. U Soltész and J Marquier,

event, parallel proceedings in respect of the same infringement but directed against different persons (eg different members of the same cartel) are permitted, a group of further issues imposes itself which concern the Member States' obligations under Article 10 EC. The questions to be discussed in this respect are (i) whether the general duty of loyalty obliges NCAs engaged in parallel procedures to avoid diverging national decisions, which would lead to a kind of de facto binding effect of national decisions on other NCAs: and (ii) whether the effects of national decisions adopted under Regulation 1/2003 must be confined to the domestic territory of the relevant NCA. The latter includes at least two aspects, namely whether anti-competitive effects outside the domestic territory may be taken into account by NCAs and whether national decisions applying Articles 81 and 82 EC are enforceable in other Member States.

I. THE PRINCIPLE OF *NE BIS IN IDEM*

The principle of *ne bis in idem* is enshrined in both the ECHR and the EU Charter of Fundamental Rights. The existing case law of the ECJ seems to suggests, however, that *ne bis in idem* is not applicable in the case of parallel cartel proceedings being conducted by several Member States against an international cartel as the different national procedures have different objectives in that they aim to protect different interests.

Nonetheless it is submitted that Member States are now precluded from imposing parallel fines on the same undertakings with regard to the same infringement. This principle must apply, at least, to the extent that NCAs take into account the effects of the relevant anti-competitive conduct outside the own territory. The latter approach, it will be argued in the second part of this chapter, is a necessary and logic step of decentralised enforcement, entirely consistent with the objective expressed in recital 18 of Regulation 1/2003 that cases should be handled by a single authority and with Article 10 EC.

A. The Concept

The principle that no one may be tried or punished twice for the same offence (*ne bis in idem*), sometimes also referred to as the rule against

---

'Hält "doppelt bestraft" wirklich besser?—Der *ne bis in idem*-Grundsatz im Europäischen Netzwerk der Kartellbehörden' (2006) 17 *Europäische Zeitschrift für Wirtschaftsrecht* 102. See also W Wils, 'The Principle of "Ne Bis in Idem" in EC Antitrust Enforcement. A Legal and Economic Analysis' (2003) 26 *World Competition* 131, 144.

double jeopardy,[5] is guaranteed by several international instruments, the most important of which, for the present analysis, seem to be the ECHR and the EU Charter.

1. Article 4 of Protocol No 7

The rule against double jeopardy is stipulated in Article 4(1) of Protocol No 7 to the ECHR, which introduced a number of additional rights in relation to criminal proceedings.[6]

a. Scope of the Principle

The *ne bis in idem* principle prohibits the repetition of criminal proceedings which have been concluded by a final acquittal or conviction, ie a decision which can no longer be appealed. The principle only applies, according to the wording of Article 4(1) of Protocol No 7, if the second procedure were to take place under the jurisdiction of the same state as the first one.[7] While the outcome of the first procedure is irrelevant, meaning that protection against double jeopardy is afforded no matter whether the first decision was a conviction, an acquittal or even a (formal) discontinuation of the proceedings,[8] Article 4(1) of Protocol No 7 does not preclude

[5] In English criminal law, the principle is transposed into a plea of *autrefois aquit* respectively *autrefois convict*. See, eg Nazzin, above n 4, 10. Paulis and Gauer, above n 4, para 21, contend that there is a difference between *ne bis in idem* and 'double jeopardy'. However, the discrepancies described by them cannot strictly be linked to the expressions used. Rather, they result from differences between the underlying concepts, which, in turn, are largely, but not always, consistently reflected in the terminology. While European writers tend to use the latin expression, the term 'double jeopardy' seems more frequent in US law context. In this book, both terms are used interchangeably.

[6] Protocol 7 was signed by 10 states in November 1984 and entered into force on 1 November 1988. According to C Ovey and R White, *Jacobs & White, The European Convention on Human Rights* (Oxford, Oxford University Press, 3rd edn, 2002), 195, the paucity of the case law of the ECtHR in respect of the *ne bis in idem* principle is explained by the fact that only few states have ratified Protocol 7. This position does not seem entirely justified: on 1 January 2006, the Protocol had been ratified by a total of 39 states, with only five states joining later than 2002 (ie the year of publication of the 3rd edn of *Jacobs & White*). By way of comparison, the ECHR itself has been ratified by 46 states. It must be noted, however, that five EU Member States, namely Belgium, Germany, the Netherlands, Spain and the UK have still not (yet) ratified Protocol No 7, the UK being the only one which also has not signed it (status: 12 February 2009; see the updated list of Council of Europe treaty ratifications available at www.conventions.coe.int/Treaty/Commun/ListeTableauCourt.asp?MA=3&CM=16&CL=ENG).

[7] Art 4(1) of Protocol No 7 reads: 'No one shall be tried or punished again in criminal proceedings under the jurisdiction of the same State for an offence for which he has already been finally acquitted or convicted . . .'

[8] This follows from the wording of the article, which explicitly refers to both persons having been acquitted or convicted. In the decision of 3 October 2002 in the case of *Zigarella v Italy* Reports/Recueil 2002-IX, 291, 297, the ECtHR confirmed that the 'provision applies even where the individual has merely been prosecuted in proceedings that have not resulted in a conviction. In criminal cases the *non bis in idem* principle applies whether the person has been convicted or not.' The case concerned two sets of charges brought against the applicant for

the reopening of a case if there is evidence of new or newly discovered facts. Moreover, the *ne bis in idem* guarantee does not shield persons from being subject, with regard to the same conduct, to several kinds of procedures (eg criminal and civil liability procedures).[9]

b. Penal Character of Competition Law Proceedings

Article 4(1) of Protocol No 7 only applies to the extent that the relevant procedure is of a criminal nature. Presumably, the term 'criminal' used in this provision has the same meaning as in Article 6 ECHR.[10] The case law of the ECtHR regarding the interpretation of the notion 'criminal' in Article 6 can therefore be applied *mutatis mutandis* to Article 4 of Protocol No 7.

With regard to Article 6, the ECtHR has consistently held that the term 'criminal' has an autonomous meaning.[11] As a consequence, the classification of a particular offence, under national law, as non-criminal is irrelevant when it comes to the question of whether the procedure must be regarded as being of a criminal nature within the meaning of the Convention.[12] Otherwise, the signatories could easily escape their obliga-

---

breaching town planning laws. After the applicant had obtained building permissions for the relevant construction works, the first set of proceedings was concluded by a judgment holding that there was no cause to continue the proceedings as there was no longer any offence. The application was directed against the second set of proceedings, but was held to be ill-founded since the Italian court had terminated the second proceedings as soon as it had learned of the fact that the applicant had already been tried for the same offence.

[9] See Art 4(2) of Protocol No 7.

[10] D Harris, M O'Boyle and C Warbrick, *Law of the European Convention on Human Rights* (London, Butterworths, 1995), 569. The presumption seems to be indirectly confirmed by the judgment of the ECtHR of 23 October 1995 in the case of *Gradinger v Austria* Publications Series A vol 328-C, as well as the other cases relating to the application of Art 4 Protocol No 7, which all concerned a combination of criminal conviction and administrative sanction. See Paulis and Gauer, above n 4, para 47; Wils, above n 4, 134. In paras 35 and 36 of the judgment in *Gradinger*, the ECtHR held, with regard to the applicability of Art 6 (1) ECHR, that the national proceedings at issue, despite falling within the administrative sphere, 'may be classified as "criminal" for the purposes of the Convention'. In paras 48 *et seq*, the ECtHR then assessed indeed the alleged violation of Art 4 Protocol No 7 without questioning the applicability *ratione materiae* of that provision. This omission implies that the earlier qualification of the national proceedings as 'criminal' within the meaning of Art 6 ECH, in the view of the HR Court, was sufficient to render Art 4 Protocol No 7 applicable.

[11] The first case in which the ECtHR implied that the term 'criminal charge' should be understood to have an autonomous meaning was the judgment of 27 June 1968 in *Neumeister v Austria* Publications Series A no 8. In the *Engel* case, the ECtHR for the first time referred explicitly to the autonomy of the concept 'criminal'. See the judgment of the ECtHR of 8 June 1976 in the case of *Engel and Others* Publications Series A no 22, para 81. This has become settled case law. See also, in particular, the judgment of 21 February 1984 in *Öztürk v Germany* Publications Series A no 73, paras 48–50.

[12] It is not the national label which is decisive, but the true character of the procedure. X De Mello, 'Droit de la concurrence et droits de l'homme' (1993) 29 *Revue Trimestrielle de Droit Europeen* 601, 615. However, the statement often made that the domestic classification is altogether irrelevant is not entirely correct. In fact, the autonomy of the concept operates in only

tions under the Convention simply by proclaiming, at their discretion, that a certain offence has a disciplinary, administrative or similar character, but not a criminal one.[13]

In *Engel*, the ECtHR also indicated the relevant criteria which must be taken into consideration when assessing the character of an offence. The ECtHR began with the domestic classification, which could obviously be no more than be a starting point as it only has a formal and relative value. The very nature of the offence (irrespective of the characterisation under the national law) was regarded as being of greater importance. Finally, the ECtHR considered the severity of the penalty at issue.[14] In *Bendenoun*, a case which concerned penalties incurred under the French tax code, the ECtHR further elaborated on the relevant criteria. The court notably relied on four cumulative factors. In the first place, the ECtHR considered the scope of the relevant provision noting that the tax surcharges at issue had been imposed on the basis of a general rule applying to all citizens (in their capacity as tax payers), not just to 'a given group with a particular status'. Further, in addition to the severity already mentioned in *Engel*, the ECtHR analysed the nature and purpose of the penalty, pointing to the fact that the surcharges were meant to be a punishment rather than pecuniary compensation, and that they were also intended to have a deterrent effect.[15]

On the basis of these criteria, there can be hardly any doubt that fines imposed by the Commission for infringements of Article 81 or 82 EC must be considered criminal charges within the meaning of Article 6 ECHR.[16] The relevant provisions, including in particular Article 23 of Regulation

---

one way. Where national law classifies an offence as criminal, that classification is indeed decisive and automatically renders Art 6 ECHR applicable. The ECtHR will not exercise any control in this respect and will not question such 'positive' classification. Only where there is no such classification under national law must it be determined autonomously whether the offence is nonetheless criminal in the sense of Art 6 ECHR. See para 81 *in fine* of the judgment in *Engel* (above n 11).

13 The most prominent example in this respect is certainly Art 23(5) of Reg 1/2003, which reads: 'Decisions [imposing fines] taken pursuant to paras 1 and 2 shall not be of a criminal law nature.' The same provision was already contained in Reg 17 (see Art 15(4) thereof). As will be argued below, this formal proclamation cannot distract from the fact that, for the purposes of the HR Convention, infringement procedures under Reg 1/2003 and the Implementing Regulation constitute, in essence, criminal law procedures.

14 Para 81 of the judgment in *Engel* (above n 11).

15 Judgment of the ECtHR of 24 February 1994 in the case of *Bendenoun v France* Publications Series A no 284, para 47. The ECtHR further explained that none of the four factors was decisive on its own, but, taken together, they would make the charge at issue a criminal one within the meaning of Art 6 ECHR (*ibid*).

16 In fact, Waelbroeck and Fosselard had reached this conclusion in their article of 1994 (D Waelbroeck and D Fosselard, 'Should the Decision-making Power in EC Antitrust Procedures be Left to an Independent Judge?—The Impact of the European Convention on Human Rights on EC Antitrust Procedures' (1994) 14 *Yearbook of European Law* 111, 123). See further W Wils, 'La compatibilité des procédures communautaires en matière de concurrence avec la Convention Européenne des Droits de l'Homme' (1993) 32 *Cahiers de Droit Européen* 329, 333–4; J Schwarze, 'Rechtsstaatliche Grenzen der gesetzlichen und richterlichen Qualifikation von Verwaltungssanktionen im europäischen Gemeinschaftsrecht' (2003) 14 *Europäische*

1/2003, are of general application in that they apply to all economic actors. Their objective clearly is both punitive and deterrent[17], the latter purpose having a double function, notably general deterrence and specific deterrence (*Generalprävention* and *Spezialprävention*).[18] Moreover, the amount of fines that can be incurred by undertakings under Community competition law certainly is substantial, the possible maximum fine being fixed at no less than 10% of a company's aggregate global turnover.[19] Finally, as

---

Zeitschrift für Wirtschaftsrecht 261, 268. See also I Forrester, 'Modernisation of EC Competition Law' in B Hawk (ed), *1999 Proceedings of the Fordham Corporate Law Institute* (New York, Juris Publishing, 2000), 181, 221, who finds it 'difficult to avoid the conclusion'; and A Riley, 'The ECHR Implications of the Investigation Provisions of the Draft Competition Regulation' (2002) 51 *International and Comparative Law Quarterly* 55, 67, who calls it an 'inescapable conclusion'. According to Y Van Gerven, 'Regulation 1/2003: Inspections ("Dawn Raids") and the Rights of Defence' in C Baudenbacher (ed), *Neueste Entwicklungen im europäischen und internationalen Kartellrecht (Dreizehntes St. Galler Internationales Kartellrechtsforum 2006)* (Basel, Helbing & Lichtenhahn, 2007), 326, 343, it can even 'be safely concluded that a competition procedure can be qualified as a "criminal" matter in the sense of the Convention.' Similarly, L Idot, 'Le futur "règlement d'application des articles 81 et 82 CE": chronique d'une révolution annoncée' (2001) 177 *Recueil Dalloz* 1370, 1374, notes that it is no longer disputed that infringement proceedings under Community competition law fall within the scope of criminal law in the sense of the HR Convention. Also, the Advocates General at the ECJ and CFI tend to recognise the criminal law character of sanctions imposed for competition infringements. See, eg Advocate General Léger in Case C–185/95 P *Baustahlgewebe v Commission* [1998] ECR I–8417. At para 31 of his opinion, Léger notes that '[i]t cannot be disputed . . . that, in the light of the case-law of the European Court of Human Rights and the opinions of the European Commission of Human Rights, the present case involves a "criminal charge".' The case related indeed to Commission proceedings under Art 82 EC. See further Advocate General Vesterdorf in *Polypropylene*, where he considers that 'competition cases of this kind are in reality of a penal nature' (joined opinions of the Advocate General of 10 July 1991 in the Case T–1/89 *Rhône-Poulenc v Commission and other cases (Polypropylene)* [1991] ECR II–867, para II.A. (991). In the same tenor, Advocate General Darmon, in *Woodpulp II*, describes Commission decisions imposing fines for competition law infringement as being 'manifestly of a penal nature' (opinion of the Advocate General of 7 July 1992 in Joined Cases C–89, 104, 114, 116, 117 and 125–129/85 *Ahlström and others v Commission (Woodpulp II)* [1993] ECR I–1307, para 451).

[17] This follows, inter alia, from the Commission's annual reports on its competition policy (see, eg XXVIIIth Report on Competition Policy 1998, paras 2 and 3; XXXIst Report on Competition Policy 2001, 4) and the Guidelines on the Calculation of Fines. Moreover, in the Cartonboard cases, the Commission repeatedly invoked the right to raise at any time the general level of fines in order to ensure their deterrent effect. See, eg para 349 of the judgment of the CFI in Case T–352/94 *Mo och Domsjö AB v Commission* [1998] ECR II–1989, para 254 of the judgment of the CFI in Case T–347/94 *Mayr-Melnhof v Commission* [1998] ECR II–1751 and para 108 of the judgment in Joined Cases 100–103/80 *Musique Diffusion and others v Commission (Pioneer)* [1983] ECR 1825. See also Waelbroeck and Fosselard, above n 16, 123 and F Zampini, 'Convention européenne des droits de l'homme et droit communautaire de la concurrence (1999) *Revue du Marché commun et de l'Union européenne* 628, 634.

[18] Para 4 of the 2006 Guidelines on the Calculation of Fines. See also M Zuleeg, 'Criminal Sanctions Imposed on Individuals as an Instrument of Enforcement of European Community Law' in C-D Ehlermann and I Atanasiu (eds), *European Competition Law Annual 2001: Effective Private Enforcement of EC Antitrust Law* (Oxford, Hart Publishing, 2003), 453, 461.

[19] One of the largest penalties ever incurred by a single undertaking was the fine of €497 million imposed in 2004, after five years of extensive investigation, on the US software company Microsoft for abuse of a dominant position on the market for PC operating systems (Art 82 EC). See the press release of 24 March 2004 (IP/04/382). Previously, in 2001, the Commission had imposed a cumulative fine of €462 million on the Swiss company Hoffman-La Roche for its

follows from the case law of the ECtHR, the classification of the fines imposed under the first two paragraphs of Article 23(5) of Regulation 1/2003 as non-criminal is irrelevant.[20] In this respect, it should also be noted that the classification under Community law is not related to ECHR issues at all, but merely seems to be inspired by the fact that the Community has no (general) competence in criminal law matters.[21]

---

participation and instigative role in the vitamins cartels (press release IP/01/1625 of 21 November 2001). Even though these amounts are truly outstanding, there have been many other cases in which the Commission has applied impressively huge sanctions, albeit smaller than the two cited above. For instance, in 2002, the Japanese videogames maker Nintendo was penalised with a fine of €149 million for colluding to impede exports from low-priced to high-priced countries. In the same spirit, the Commission had previously imposed fines of ECU 102 million on Volkswagen (1998) and almost €72 million on DaimlerChrysler (2001) for obstructing parallel trade by their motor vehicle dealers within the Community. See the press releases of 28 January 1998 (IP/98/94), 10 October 2001 (IP/01/1394) and 30 October 2002 (IP/02/1584). And there are more examples of such mammoth fines. See J Schwarze, 'Les sanctions imposées pour les infractions au droit européen de la concurrence selon l'article 23 du règlement n° 1/2003 CE à la lumière des principes généraux du droit' (2007) 43 Revue Trimestrielle de Droit Europeen 1, 2–3. Obviously, it is hardly possible to fix an absolute amount of fine which would surely turn the penalty—formally characterised as administrative sanction—into a criminal one. However, the enormous amounts to which the Commission resorted in recent years certainly provide additional arguments for classifying the sanctions under Reg 1/2003 as criminal within the meaning of Art 6 ECHR That is to say, the magnitude of the fines simply underpins that their purpose is punishment and deterrence of potential (re)offenders. See Schwarze, above n 16, 267–8.

[20] R Smits, 'The European Competition Network: Selected Aspects' (2005) 32 Legal Issues of Economic Integration 175, 183 and 186.

[21] See O Einarsson, 'EC Competition Law and the Right to a Fair Trial' (2006) 25 Yearbook of European Law 555, 567–8; Schwarze, above n 19, 9 and 24; F Vogelaar, 'Interface: EC and Dutch Competition Law—In Which Fields or Areas Would the Netherlands Still Have Autonomous Regulating Powers?' in Obradovic and N Lavranos (eds), Interface between EU Law and National Law (Groningen, Europa Law Publishing, 2007), 185, 196. The ECJ reconfirmed in Case C–176/03 Commission v Council [2005] ECR I–7879, para 47, that, '[a]s a general rule, neither criminal law nor the rules of criminal procedure fall within the Community's competence'. However, the Community may have a kind of 'annex competence' to introduce criminal penalties in a field of law which does fall within its competence if a criminal sanctioning system is necessary to guarantee the full effectiveness of Community measures adopted in that specific field (see para 48 of the judgment and further below n 113). While that judgment has been confirmed by the ECJ in Case C–440/05 Commission v Council (Shipping pollution) [2007] ECR I–9097, some key questions regarding the Community's criminal law competence have not been answered by the ECJ. See S Peers, 'The European Community's Criminal Law Competence: The Plot Thickens' (2008) 33 EL Rev 399. There is, inter alia, considerable debate about the question whether the reasonings of the ECJ in Case C–176/03 and the Shipping Pollution case are restricted to environmental policy or could be applied in other fields of Community policy. See A Dawes and O Lynskey, 'The Ever-longer Arm of EC Law: The Extension of Community Competence into the Field of Criminal Law' (2008) 45 Common Market Law Review 131, 140–3. While it is true that the ECJ in both cases expressly linked its statements to environmental protection measures, there is, in my view, no reason why this logic could not be extended to other policy areas provided that the Community has the power to enact binding legislation and the relevant measures are essential to the fulfilment of the Community's tasks and the achievement of the Treaty objectives. Therefore, it is submitted that, on the basis of these judgments (Case C–176/03), it can well be argued that the Community legislator has the power to introduce genuine criminal sanctions for the infringement of Arts 81 and 82 EC, at least at the Community level (ie to the extent that the provisions are enforced by the

While the ECJ has not yet ruled explicitly that proceedings regarding the infringement of Community competition law involve criminal charges, it seems nonetheless to have accepted implicitly that, in terms of the HR Convention, fines imposed under Regulation 17 (or now Regulation 1/2007) come within the ambit of criminal law.[22] The same reasoning would apply to national proceedings regarding violations of Article 81 or 82 EC, where, in accordance with domestic law, such violations are subject to extensive financial penalties.[23]

The decision of the HR Commission in *Société Stenuit* provides strong support for these findings.[24] The case is of particular relevance as it relates to a fine imposed on a company under French competition law for engaging in bid rigging with regard to a public tender. The HR Commission held that this fine was criminal in nature.[25] There are two

Commission), in order to guarentee the effectiveness of these provisions. Regardless of the judgment in Case C–176/03, Wils even reaches the conclusion that, given the wide mandate of Art 83(1) EC and applying a teleological interpretation, that provision alone would provide a sufficient legal basis for the Council to criminalise infringements of the Community competition rules (W Wils, 'Is Criminalization of EU Competition Law the Answer?' (2005) 28 *World Competition* 117, 157). If such legislation existed, this would imply that criminal punishment is deemed necessary to ensure compliance with Arts 81 and 82 EC and achievement of the Treaty objectives (Art 3(1)g EC). Arguably, the Community could then also require the Member States to introduce criminal penalties for violations of the Community competition rules. Cf F Vogelaar, 'Criminalisering van het mededingingsrecht: trendy of noodzaak?' (2005) 54 *Ars Aequi* 1015, 1017–18.

[22] Wils, above n 21, 121. Indeed, in Case 374/87 *Orkem v Commission* [1989] ECR 3283, the ECJ acknowledged that such proceedings fall within the scope of Art 6 ECHR and thus indirectly recognised that sanctions under Reg 17 (now Reg 1/2003) are of a criminal nature. Para 30 of the judgment in *Orkem* reads: 'As far as Art 6 of the European Convention is concerned, *although it may be relied upon by an undertaking subject to an investigation relating to competition law*, it must be observed that . . .' (emphasis added). See also the judgments of the ECJ in Case C–199/92 P *Hüls v Commission (Polypropylene)* [1999] ECR I–04287, para 149–50 (application of the presumption of innocence in competition proceedings; here the ECJ even refers to the judgment of the ECtHR in *Öztürk*, above n 11) and Joined Cases C–238, 244, 245, 247, 250–2 and 254/99 P *Limburgse Vinyl Maatschappij and others v Commission (PVC II)* [2002] ECR I–8375, para 59 (application of the principle of *ne bis in idem* in a competition matter)—both judgments with explicit reference to the relevant criminal law guarantees of the ECHR (Art 6(2) ECHR and Art 4(1) of Protocol No 7 respectively); and the judgment of the CFI in *JFE Engineering and others v Commission* [2004] ECR II–2501. Thus, P Roth, 'Ensuring that Effectiveness of Enforcement Does not Prejudice Legal Protection: Rights of Defence. Fundamental Rights Concerns', paper for the 2006 EU Competition Law and Policy Workshop, European University Institute/RSCAS, Florence; available at www.eui.eu/RSCAS/research/Competition/2006(pdf)/200610-COMPed-Roth.pdf (accessed January 2009), 5, even asserts that the ECJ now has effectively recognised the criminal law nature of competition proceedings.

[23] Wils, above n 4, 133; De Mello, above n 12, 628.

[24] Waelbroeck and Fosselard, above n 16, 121–2. See also De Mello, above n 12, 628, who presumes that the ECtHR would endorse the reasoning of the HR Commission in its opinion of 30 May 1991 in *Société Stenuit v France* Publications Series A no 232-A.

[25] Para 65 of the opinion of the HR Commission in *Société Stenuit* (*ibid*). Unfortunately, the case was settled before it reached the ECtHR. On the other hand, the opinion of the HR Commission of 1990 in *M&Co* (Decision of 9 February 1990, application no 13258/87; Decisions and Reports 64 (1990), 138) had already implied that Art 6 ECHR was applicable to proceedings regarding violations of (Community) competition law. See W Peukert, 'The Importance of the European Convention on Human Rights for the European Union' in P

important considerations in the Commission's opinion. First, the HR Commission observed that the aim of the relevant French legislation was to maintain free competition on the domestic market and that it thus served the 'general interests of society normally protected by criminal law'.[26] Secondly, as concerns the nature and severity of the penalty, the HR Commission noted that the fine which had actually been imposed on the applicant, in itself, was not negligible. More importantly, however, the Commission emphasised that the maximum fine which companies could incur under the relevant French legislation, notably 5% of the annual turnover, revealed 'quite clearly that the penalty in question was intended to be deterrent'.[27]

Applying these two criteria to Articles 81 and 82 EC and the relevant Community regulations, it becomes obvious that the characterisation of Community competition law cannot be any different from that of French competition law. The aim of the Community competition rules is to ensure, in the general interest of the public, the prevalence of unrestricted and undistorted competition within the Community.[28] At the same time, the Commission is entitled to impose severe fines for infringements of these rules. The maximum amount of a fine under Community law (10% of the annual aggregate worldwide turnover) is even larger than under the relevant French law and thus shows all the more that the objective of the rules is not only to punish, but also to deter (potential) offenders. Last but not least, the fact that the pecuniary sanction, imposed under Article 23(2) of Regulation 1/2003, cannot be converted into a custodial sentence is irrelevant for the purposes of its classification under the ECHR.[29]

At first sight, the recent decision of the ECtHR in *OOO Neste St Petersburg* seems to call into question the above conclusions.[30] In this case, the ECtHR ruled that the applicants—several Russian companies that had been accused of violations of the Russian competition law by engaging in concerted practices with the aim to increase fuel prices—had not been 'charged with a criminal offence' within the meaning of Article 6 ECHR

Mahoney, F Matscher, H Petzold and L Wildhaber (eds), *Protection des droits de l'homme: la perspective européenne/Protecting Human Rights: The European Perspective. Mélanges à la memoire de/Studies in memory of Rolv Ryssdal* (Köln, Carl Heymanns Verlag, 2000), 1107, 1113. See also De Mello, above n 12, 627, who considers it as probably the most important point of the decision in *M&Co* that, referring to *Öztürk*, above n 11, the HR Commission notes that '[f]or the purpose of the examination of this question it can be assumed that the anti-trust proceedings in question would fall under Article 6 (Art. 6) had they been conducted by German and not by European judicial authorities'.

[26] Para 62 of the opinion of the HR Commission in *Société Stenuit* (above n 24).
[27] *Ibid*, para 64.
[28] See recitals 1 and 9 of Reg 1/2003.
[29] Judgment of the ECtHR of 23 July 2002 in the case of *Janosevic v Sweden* Reports/Recueil 2002-VII, para 69.
[30] See Paulis and Gauer, above n 4, para 48.

and consequently declared the application inadmissible.[31] A careful reading of the decision reveals, however, that the main purpose of the proceedings at issue was the restoration of competition and the prevention of further disturbances of competition. They did not, in the HR Court's view, predominantly aim at punishing and deterring offenders. This followed, inter alia, from the fact that the federal government agency which is in charge of enforcing the Russian competition law (Antimonopoly Commission) can impose (administrative) fines on companies only for obstruction of the investigations, not for violations of the substantive competition rules. The proceedings initiated by the Antimonopoly Commission were thus quite distinct from criminal proceedings, which, moreover, could only be instituted by a public prosecutor in order to establish the criminal responsibility of individuals (eg company managers), not corporate bodies such as the applicants. Moreover, regarding the nature of the offence and the criterion that, in order to qualify as criminal, an offence must be of universal application, the ECtHR held that 'freedom of market power is a relative, situational value . . .'.[32] Lastly, the powers of the Antimonopoly Commission[33] were considered to belong to the regulatory sphere. The types of decision which this authority could adopt, in particular the confiscation of profits and the compulsory break-up of the company, albeit being binding on the offenders, were namely found to constitute a pecuniary compensation for damages rather than a punishment.[34]

In view of these decisions, the applicability of Article 6 ECHR in the context of antitrust proceedings should not be taken for granted, but must be carefully considered for each national system and, within each national system, for the various types of procedures that an NCA can conduct.[35] On the other hand, the peculiarities of the case also demonstrate that the Russian antitrust proceedings that were at the bottom of the ECtHR's decision in *OOO Neste St Petersburg* are quite different from the competition procedures in the EU, where these are intended to lead to the application of penalties for the infringement of substantive antitrust provisions.[36] In practice, competition authorities usually have both repressive

---

[31] Decision of the ECtHR of 3 June 2004 in the case of *OOO Neste St Petersburg and others v Russia*, Application no 69042/01.

[32] P 10 of the online version of the decision (above n 31).

[33] Pursuant to the relevant Russian laws, the Anti-Monopoly Commission essentially has the power to conduct investigations, issue cease-and-desist orders and orders to remove the consequences of violations, restore the previous situation, confiscate the illegally gained profits and divide the offender company. Further, it can impose fines for non-compliance with such orders.

[34] P 10 of the online version of the decision (above n 31).

[35] See B Lasserre, 'Le Conseil de la concurrence dans le réseau communautaire' 2005/No 3 *Concurrences—RDLC* 42, 50, para 43 and Paulis and Gauer, above n 4, para 48.

[36] All Member States' competition rules provide for fines to be imposed on undertakings for violations of substantive provisions. See M Bloom, 'Exchange of Confidential Information among Members of the EU Network of Competition Authorities: Possible Consequences of a

and more administrative functions,[37] Thus, some proceedings, such as the withdrawal of the benefit of a block exemption (see Article 29 of Regulation 1/2003) or procedural penalties (eg fines for not responding (fully or timely) to an information request), may not qualify as 'criminal' within the meaning of the ECHR.[38] However, if proceedings aim at the imposition of more or less serious fines, they arguably enter the criminal sphere as defined by the ECtHR. Thus, on the basis of the distinction between regulatory and repressive powers which underlies the decision of the ECtHR, the OOO *Neste St Petersburg* case arguably does not cast doubt on the conclusion that antitrust procedures in the EU, which can lead to the imposition of severe sanctions for breaches of substantive law provisions, are of a criminal nature.[39] Finally, as concerns the allegedly relative and situational value of free competition, the findings of the HR Court are in stark contrast to the prevailing approach in the EU.[40] Not only has the

Relatively Broad Scope for Exchange of Confidential Information on National Procedural Law and Antitrust Sanctions' in C-D Ehlermann and I Atanasiu (eds), *European Competition Law Annual 2002: Constructing the EU Network of Competition Authorities* (Oxford, Hart Publishing, 2003), 389, 396 (and the table on p 403). (Luxemburg used to operate an abuse control system whereby undertakings could only be fined for breaches of individual prohibition decisions. However, in 2004, a new Competition Act, directly inspired by Arts 81 and 82 EC and Reg 1/2003, entered into force and replaced the former system.) Moreover, in 2001, all but three Member States (Austria, the Netherlands, Portugal) could apply substantial penalties, the possible maximum fine being expressed in percentages of the undertaking's annual turnover. See the table provided by I Maher, 'Networking Competition Authorities in the European Union: Diversity and Change' in Ehlermann and Atanasiu, *idem*, 223, 232. Since the 2002 amendments, the Austrian competition law also provides for fines of up to 10% of the annual turnover (see F Höpfel and R Kert, 'Country Analysis—Austria' in G Dannecker and O Jansen (eds), *Competition Law Sanctioning in the European Union* (The Hague, Kluwer Law International, 2004), 305, 336). The same is true for Portugal (see Art 43(1) of the Portuguese Competition Act (Law No 18/2003)) and the Netherlands (see Art 57(1) Mededingingswet NL). The Dutch legislator even considered raising the maximum percentage to 25%. Such sanctions clearly have a punishing and deterrent effect.

[37] N Jalabert-Doury, 'Competition Authorities and Art 6 ECHR: The Odd OOO Neste Case' (2005) *Revue de Droit des Affaires Internationales/International Business Law Journal* 207, 231.

[38] Procedural sanctions do not really punish an undertaking; rather, they aim to compel it to comply with a decision of the competition authority. It is thus doubtful that they are of a criminal nature within the meaning of the ECHR

[39] Einarsson, above n 21, 571–2 and Roth, above n 22, 5 note 21. Another question is whether the ECtHR was right in considering that confiscation of profits or the break-up of a company, which, from the undertaking's perspective, seem fairly repressive measures, nonetheless belong to the regulatory sphere. See Jalabert-Doury, above n 37, 214. It would certainly have benefited the persuasiveness of the HR Court's decision had it at least considered whether, in spite of their prima facie compensatory effect, such orders could be classified as sanctions. (T Kuck, 'Die Anerkennung des Grundsatzes *ne bis in idem* im europäischen Kartellrecht und seine Anwendung in internationalen Kartellverfahren' (2002) 52 *Wirtschaft und Wettbewerb* 689, 697, for instance, seems to consider confiscation of profits as a form of pecuniary sanction.) In any event, given that the ECtHR did not qualify the skimming of profits and structural remedies as sanctions, the judgment in *Neste* certainly does not stand in the way of applying Art 6 ECHR (under its criminal head) to competition proceedings the purpose if which clearly is to punish and deter (re)offenders by imposing severe (administrative) fines or even criminal sentences. Soltész and Marquier, above n 4, 102 note 4; Jalabert-Doury, above n 37, 216.

[40] See Jalabert-Doury, above n 37, 215.

Commission emphasised that cartels can never be viewed favourably as they operate at the expense of consumers, competitiveness and innovation, and thus constitute 'a veritable cancer in an open, modern market economy',[41] but moreover the ECJ has held that Community competition rules are part of the *ordre public*.[42]

It follows from the above that competition proceedings conducted by the Commission with the objective of imposing fines as well as national proceedings for the violation of Articles 81 and 82 EC, which provide for similar penalties, constitute criminal proceedings for the purposes of Article 6 ECHR.

2. EU Charter of Fundamental Rights

The EU Charter equally enshrines the rule against double jeopardy.[43] Namely, Article 50 of the EU Charter provides that no one shall be tried or punished again for an offence for which he/she has already been finally acquitted or convicted. Like Article 4 of Protocol No 7, the rule of the EU Charter is also confined to criminal proceedings. Both provisions thus correspond almost exactly, but with one exception. In Article 50 EU Charter, the words 'under the jurisdiction of the same State' have been replaced by the term 'within the Union'. Thus, while Article 4 of Protocol No 7 prohibits a second trial from taking place only within the same state as the first prosecution, Article 50 EU Charter broadens the territorial scope of the guarantee and applies to the European Union as a whole, thus establishing the principle of an EU-wide *ne bis in idem*. It consequently precludes a second trial not only in the same Member State as the first one, but also in any other Member State of the EU. In other words, for the purposes of the *ne bis in idem* principle, the Member States are treated as a single jurisdiction under the EU Charter.[44]

Since the EU Charter is not a simple copy of the ECHR, the drafters of the EU Charter have taken care to ensure harmony and consistency between the two sets of rules. The purpose is for the ECHR to become the standard of interpretation and that protection under the EU Charter does

---

[41] The Commission's XXXIst Report on Competition Policy 2001, 4 (foreword by Commissioner Mario Monti).

[42] Preliminary ruling of the ECJ in Case C–126/97 *Eco Swiss v Benetton* [1999] ECR I–3055, paras 36–7.

[43] On the question of whether or not the EU Charter has any legal force, see below section I.D.1.

[44] The rule is said to correspond to the 'acquis in Union law', as reflected inter alia in Arts 54–8 of the Convention implementing the Schengen Agreement of 14 June 1985, [2000] OJ L239/19 ('Schengen Convention'). See p 45 of the explanations relating to the Charter prepared by the Bureau of the Convention, which drafted the EU Charter, document CONVENT 49 of 11 October 2001 (CHARTE 4473/00), available at www.europarl.eu.int/charter/pdf/04473_en.pdf (accessed February 2009) ('Explanations to the EU Charter').

not, in any event, fall behind the level of protection offered by the Convention. Article 52(3) EU Charter therefore provides that Charter rights which correspond to rights guaranteed by the Convention shall have the same meaning and scope as those Convention rights. The guarantees of the ECHR thus determine the minimal content of fundamental rights in the EU. However, the EU Charter may provide more extensive protection.[45]

Apart from the above-mentioned difference relating to the territorial ambit, Article 50 EU Charter therefore has the same meaning and scope as Article 4(1) of Protocol No 7,[46] which arguably includes the broad interpretation given by the ECtHR to the notion 'criminal'.

B. Rationale

In general terms, the principle of *ne bis in idem* is the expression of a natural requirement of equity and justice protecting suspects and accused against double punishment for the same offence, which would appear unnecessary, ie disproportionate in legal terms, and unfair if one considers the main objectives of sanctions (deterrence, punishment and sometimes compensation).[47] At the same time, the principle provides legal certainty for the person prosecuted no matter whether he or she has been convicted or acquitted.[48]

The above consideration, ie mere protection of the individual against repeated prosecution and punishment, seems to be one of at least three rationales supporting the existence of the *ne bis in idem* principle at the national level. The other two are respect for judicial decisions (principle of

---

[45] On the general relation between EU Charter and Convention and the drafting of the relevant articles of the EU Charter, see P Lemmens, 'The Relation between the Charter of Fundamental Rights of the European Union and the European Convention on Human Rights—Substantive Aspects' (2001) 8 *Maastricht Journal of European and Comparative Law* 49, 50–4.

[46] Lemmens, *ibid*, 66. See also p 45 of the Explanations to the EU Charter.

[47] F Schoneveld, 'Cartel Sanctions and International Competition Policy: Cross-border Co-operation and Appropriate Forums for Cooperation' 26 (2003) *World Competition* 433, 436. Schoneveld also points to the dangers of excessive sanctions in antitrust matters, namely the (financial) weakening of certain market players which, in turn, may trigger mergers, take-overs or alliances and thus ultimately reduce competition. *Idem*, 453–4. Even at the level of fines operated by the Commission (alone), ie in cases where there is no allegation of double or excessive sanctioning, inability of the firms to pay and imminent insolvency sometimes appears to be an issue. W Wils, 'Does the Effective Enforcement of Arts 81 and 82 EC Require not only Fines on Undertakings but also Individual Penalties, in particular Imprisonment?' in Ehlermann and Atanasiu, above n 18, 411, 424–5. On the proportionality aspect, see also the opinion of Advocate General Ruiz-Jarabo Colomer in Joined Cases C–187/01 and C–385/01 *Gözütok and Brügge v Commission* [2003] ECR I–1345, para 50.

[48] Para 49 of the opinion of Advocate General Ruiz-Jarabo Colomer in *Gözütok and Brügge* (*ibid*).

res iudicata) and the idea that a state's criminal claim (*ius puniendi*) extinguishes once it has been used (*Strafklageverbrauch* or *Erledigungsprinzip*).[49]

From an economic perspective, the rationale underlying the rule against double jeopardy could be described as the attempt to enhance efficient law enforcement.[50] In this sense, the prohibition of double punishment and double prosecution essentially has five purposes. First, it helps to prevent overpunishment. Secondly, it creates incentives for efficient prosecution, meaning that, in view of the fact that they do not have a second shot, authorities are induced to apply the optimal level of care when preparing and conducting a prosecution. Thirdly, the *ne bis in idem* principle aims at minimising costs by avoiding multiple procedures. Fourthly, it provides incentives for the various authorities responsible for the prosecution and punishment of the relevant offences to coordinate their actions and distribute their work efficiently. Finally, the rule also reduces the risk of an abuse of powers in that it prevents mischievous multiple prosecutions.[51]

C. Relevant Case Law on the Application of *Ne Bis in Idem*

1. *Interpretation of the Principle by the Court of Human Rights*

The most relevant case concerning the interpretation of the double jeopardy rule by the HR Court appears to be the judgment of 29 May 2001 in the case of *Franz Fischer v Austria*.[52] That case concerns two separate proceedings and two convictions, pronounced by an administrative authority and a regional court against the applicant for driving under the influence of alcohol, on the one hand, and causing death by negligence while being intoxicated, on the other.

The ECtHR noted that the mere fact that a single act constitutes several offences would not be contrary to Article 4 of Protocol No 7. However, relying on the wording of Article 4 of Protocol No 7, which does not actually refer to the notion of 'same offence', the ECtHR found

[49] See C Van Den Wyngaert and G Stessens, 'The International *non bis in idem* Principle: Resolving Some of the Unanswered Questions' (1999) 48 *ICLQ* 779, 780–1. Cf also para 88 of the opinion of Advocate General Ruiz-Jarabo Colomer in Case C–213/00 P *Italcementi v Commission* [2004] ECR I–123: '. . . since that duplication of penalties entails an unacceptable repetition in the exercise of the right to punish'. Advocate General Mayras in Case 7/72 *Boehringer Mannheim v Commission* [1972] ECR 1281, 1293, rather sees *ne bis in idem* principal as a means of recognising the *res iudicata* status of final criminal decisions.

[50] Wils, above n 4, 136.

[51] For a more detailed analysis of these economics see Wils, above n 4, 136–40.

[52] Application no 37950/97 (not included in the Reports/Recueil). Two earlier judgments of the ECtHR interpreting Art 4 of Protocol No 7—the judgments in *Gradinger* (above n 10) and *Oliveira v Switzerland* (judgment of 30 July 1998, Reports/Recueil 1998-V, 1990)—had been ambiguous and contradictory. The *Franz Fischer* judgment reconciles both. Wils, above n 4, 134.

that it should not confine itself to asserting whether a person has been tried or punished twice for nominally different offences. What was actually decisive in the case was that the applicant had been tried and punished twice for two offences which did not differ in their essential elements.[53] The HR Court thus distinguished this case from the *Oliveira* case, where it had found no violation of Article 4 of Protocol No 7, in that the essential elements of the relevant offences in the *Oliveira* case did not overlap.[54]

The first important conclusion to be drawn from the *Fischer* case therefore is that Article 4 of Protocol No 7 is infringed not only when a person is tried or punished twice for offences which are nominally the same, but also when the essential elements of the two offences overlap.[55]

The judgment identifies another significant aspect of the double jeopardy rule. The ECtHR rejected the argument that there could be no violation of Article 4 of Protocol No 7 because the applicant's second punishment, a prison term, had been reduced by one month, a period which was considered equivalent to the fine paid under the first sentence. The HR Court emphasised that the principle of *ne bis in idem* was not limited to the right not be punished twice, but extended to the right not to be prosecuted twice. Therefore, the reduction granted in relation to the second conviction could not alter the finding that Mr Fischer had actually been tried twice for essentially the same offence.[56]

The second central point of the judgment in *Fischer* is thus that the application of Article 4 of Protocol No 7 cannot be circumvented simply by taking into account the first sentence and deducting it from the second. Such a kind of setting-off arrangement (*Anrechnungsprinzip*) does not preclude a violation of the double jeopardy rule as that rule prohibits not only multiple punishment, but also multiple prosecution. An earlier final

---

[53] Paras 25 and 29 of the judgment in *Fischer* (above n 52).

[54] See para 27 of the judgment in *Fischer* (above n 52). In the *Gradinger* case, the ECtHR had found a violation of Art 4 Protocol No 7 because both relevant decisions (a conviction and an acquittal) were based on the same conduct. In addition, as the ECtHR noted in *Fischer*, the essential elements of the offences at issue in the *Gradinger* case overlapped.

[55] Interestingly, this also seems to be the approach of UK law, where a claim of double jeopardy, in order to be successful, requires that both offences have 'the same essential ingredients'. See the citation of the relevant case law provided by Schoneveld, above n 47, 451. By contrast, in the context of EU law, notably Art 54 Schengen Convention, the ECJ has considered the only relevant criterion to determine whether the *ne bis in idem* principle applies to be the 'identity of the material acts, understood in the sense of the existence of a set of concrete circumstances which are inextricably linked together'. Para 36 of the judgment of the ECJ in Case C–436/04 *Van Esbroeck* [2006] ECR I–2333. It must be noted, though, that the wording of Art 54 Schengen Convention differs from the wording of Art 4 Protocol No 7 in that the first provision refers to 'the same acts' while the latter uses the expression 'offence', thereby implying that, under the ECHR, the legal qualification of the acts cannot be totally disregarded. See paras 27–8 of the aforementioned judgment in *Van Esbroeck*.

[56] Para 30 of the judgment in *Fischer* (above n 52).

judgment thus constitutes an absolute bar to any further criminal charges being brought against the same person.[57]

2. (Non-)Application of the Principle by the Community Courts in International Cartel Matters

There are a number of cases in which the Community courts had to deal with the question of whether undertakings could be subject to multiple proceedings and multiple fines for the infringement of antitrust rules based on the same set of facts.

a. Walt Wilhelm: Emergence of the Setting-off Rule

In 1969, the ECJ had to rule on the question of whether the Community competition rules and national competition law could be applied concurrently to the same facts against the same undertakings. In its famous *Walt Wilhelm* judgment, the ECJ decided in favour of the concurrent applicability of both sets of rules. At the same time, however, the ECJ reiterated the principle of supremacy of Community law,[58] stating that the application of national competition law might not lead to results which would be incompatible with measures taken in implementation of Community competition law as this would prejudice the uniform application, throughout the Community, of Articles 81 and 82 EC and ultimately jeopardise the attainment of the objectives of the Treaty.[59]

The ECJ justified its conclusion that Community and national competition law can be applied in parallel to the same facts essentially by arguing that both sets of rules pursue different aims:

> Community law and national law consider cartels from different points of view. Whereas Articles 85 regards them in the light of obstacles which may result for trade between Member States, each body of national legislation proceeds on the basis of the considerations peculiar to it and considers cartels only in that context.[60]

---

[57] W Wils, 'The EU Network of Competition Authorities, the European Convention on Human Rights and the Charter of Fundamental Rights of the EU' in Ehlermann and Atanasiu, above n 36, 433, 451. This would also exclude the possibility of commencing a second procedure the mere purpose of which is to determine that the undertaking concerned has infringed the competition rules without imposing a fine at all.

[58] The supremacy principle or, in the words of the ECJ, 'the precedence of Community law' (*la préeminence du droit communautaire*), was first proclaimed by the ECJ in Case 6/64 *Costa v ENEL* [1964] ECR 585, 594 (English special edition).

[59] Paras 3–6 of the judgment in Case 14/68 *Walt Wilhelm v Bundeskartellamt* [1969] ECR 1. These principles are now, at least partly, enshrined in Arts 16(2) and 3(2) of Reg 1/2003. As to the curious fact that the latter provision only lays down that national competition law may not be stricter than Community law, but does not codify the more obvious rule resulting from the principle of supremacy, notably that national law may not be more lenient than Community law, see above Chapter 1, section II.B.1.c.

[60] Para 3 of the judgment in *Walt Wilhelm, ibid*. See also para 11 of the same judgment ('two parallel proceedings pursuing different ends').

The ECJ thereby excluded the applicability of the *ne bis in idem* principle in the relation between national and Community competition law.[61] As concerns the issue of double punishment, the ECJ conceded, however, that if such parallel procedures were to lead to the imposition of consecutive sanctions

> a general requirement of justice . . . demands that any previous punitive decision must be taken into account in determining any sanction which is to be imposed.[62]

This statement has generally been interpreted as requiring, in the case of two consecutive procedures, the second authority to deduct from the fine it intends to impose the amount of the first penalty (the so-called *Anrechnungsprinzip*/setting-off rule).[63]

Ever since this judgment, it had been common ground that the same agreement or conduct could 'in principle, be the object of two sets of parallel proceedings', one before the Commission under Article 81 or 82 EC and one before an NCA under national law.[64] This position has, however, become doubtful in view of the obligation of NCAs, under Article 3(1) of Regulation 1/2003, to also apply Community competition law in all cases where they apply national competition law and the effect-on-trade criterion is fulfilled. Indeed, some authors emphasise that NCAs can apply national competition law only in conjunction with Articles 81 and 82 EC in cases with an inter-state trade effect and, consequently, argue that where NCAs are relieved of their competence to apply Community competition law pursuant to Article 11(6) of Regulation 1/2003 because the Commission has initiated proceedings, they would equally be deprived of the right to apply national competition law. In other words, in all cases which have an effect on intra-Community trade, national competition law can no longer be applied on a stand-alone basis.[65] It is therefore possible that the situation which the ECJ faced in

---

[61] H Schröter in H Schröter, T Jakob and W Mederer (eds), *Kommentar zum Europäischen Wettbewerbsrecht* (Baden-Baden, Nomos, 1st edn, 2003), 154 para 125.

[62] Para 11 of the judgment in *Walt Wilhelm*, above n 59.

[63] See Kuck, above n 39, 692; J Schwarze and A Weitbrecht, *Grundzüge des europäischen Kartellverfahrensrechts* (Baden-Baden, Nomos, 1st edn, 2004), 154 para 25; E-J Mestmäcker and H Schweitzer, *Europäisches Wettbewerbsrecht* (Munich, CH Beck, 2nd edn, 2004), §21 para 34. The duty of the Commission to set off the amount of a fine incurred under the national law of a Member State against the sanction to be imposed under Community competition law was again pronounced (incidentally) by the ECJ in 1972 in *Boehringer*, above n 49, para 3: 'In fixing the amount of a fine the Commission must take account of penalties which have already been borne by the same undertaking for the same action, where penalties have been imposed for infringements of the cartel law of the Member State and, consequently, have been committed on Community territory.'

[64] Para 3 of the judgment in *Walt Wilhelm*, above n 59.

[65] See Chapter 1, n 280 and accompanying text.

Walt Wilhelm will no longer occur under the new enforcement regime established by Regulation 1/2003.[66]

b. Double Prosecution by the Commission: The PVC II Case

Yet another question is whether the *ne bis in idem* principle precludes the Commission from resuming proceedings and imposing penalties on undertakings where a first negative decision regarding the same facts has been annulled. This was the situation the ECJ had to deal with in the *PVC* case. In 1988 the Commission had imposed fines on several PVC producers for infringement of Article 81. That decision was then annulled by the ECJ on procedural grounds. Following the annulment, the Commission simply readopted the same decision in 1994, this time observing the relevant procedural requirements, and reimposed the same fines as in the first decision.

The ECJ held that the *ne bis in idem* principle, which it found to be a fundamental principle of Community law,[67] only prohibits a fresh in-depth assessment of the same alleged offence. According to the ECJ, it does not, however,

> preclude the resumption of proceedings in respect of the same anti-competitive conduct where the first decision was annulled for procedural reasons without any ruling having been given on the substance of the facts.[68]

The second *PVC* decision of the Commission, adopted in 1994, was thus upheld.

The *PVC II* judgment appears to represent a fair compromise between the need to protect persons against double jeopardy and the public interest in not allowing serious violations of (competition) rules to remain unpunished.[69] Only in cases where the annulment is merely due to procedural flaws and no consideration is given to the question of whether the relevant

---

[66] See Schwarze and Weitbrecht, above n 63, 154 para 27, who argue that there is no more room for the parallel application of national competition law where the Commission has already penalised the anti-competitive conduct on the basis of Community competition law.

[67] The recognition, albeit implicit, of *ne bis in idem* as a fundamental principle of Community law in fact goes back to 1967, notably to the ruling of the ECJ in Joined Cases 18 and 35/65 *Gutmann v Commission* [1967] ECR 61 (English special edition), two staff cases concerning repeated disciplinary proceedings against the applicant, an official of the European Atomic Energy Community. Mr Gutmann had lodged an application for annulment of the second disciplinary measure pleading violation of the principle *non bis in idem*. Observing that, because of the vagueness of the contested decision as to its factual grounds, it was unable to distinguish the facts of that decision from those which gave rise to the first disciplinary measure, the ECJ held that it could not be excluded that both proceedings had indeed been initiated on the basis of the same set of facts (p 66 of the judgment). As a result, the contested decision had to be annulled.

[68] Paras 61–2 of the judgment of the ECJ in *PVC II* (above n 22).

[69] Wils, above n 4, 141, justifies the result by applying the economic rationale underlying the *ne bis in idem* principle.

facts and evidence establish the alleged offence is the Commission entitled to resume proceedings and readopt the decision as, in such circumstances, the annulment cannot be considered an acquittal.

On the other hand, the ruling implies that the *ne bis in idem* principle precludes the Commission from readopting a decision where it has been annulled for other reasons, notably for lack of evidence. Where the court considers the evidence adduced by the Commission to be insufficient to establish the existence of an illegal agreement or conduct and, as a consequence, annuls a negative decision, the annulment would appear to be equivalent to an acquittal and would thus bar the Commission from commencing a second procedure.[70] The judgment of the ECJ in *PVC II* therefore has often been interpreted as generally recognising the applicability of the *ne bis in idem* principle in Community competition law.[71]

c. Concurrent Sanctioning by the Community and Third Countries

One of the earliest competition matters in which the question of double jeopardy arose is the *Boehringer* case of 1972. The German company Boehringer Mannheim had been fined by the Commission for infringement of Article 81 EC. In a later procedure, a US court also imposed a fine on that company for infringement of the US federal antitrust law. The Commission rejected Boehringer's request to deduct the amount of the fine paid in the US from the fine imposed under Community law. The ECJ confirmed the Commission's refusal, emphasising that, even though both decisions appeared to be based partly on the same facts, they did not relate to identical actions and the convictions were thus different in scope.[72]

Since that judgment, the globalisation of markets resulting, inter alia, from the promotion of international trade by the World Trade Organization (WTO) and the increasing opening up of domestic markets for foreign commerce[73] has created a situation where the effects of both legal and illegal commercial behaviour rarely remain within the national

---

[70] Wils, above n 4, 142.

[71] See, eg Kuck, above n 39, 690; Schwarze and Weitbrecht, above n 63, 153 para 25; Mestmäcker and Schweitzer, above n 63, §21 para 33.

[72] The ECJ noted that the conviction under Community law had been directed primarily against an agreement for the division of the common market and certain agreed restrictions of the production of synthetic quinidine, while the US conviction related to agreements on quinquina bark, the acquisition and division of American strategic stocks, and the application of high selling prices on the US market. Paras 5 and 6 of the judgment in *Boehringer* (above n 49).

[73] On various causes of this recent phenomenon of increasing economic interdependence (*weltwirtschaftliche Verflechtung*), which is now commonly described as 'globalisation', see E Kantzenbach, 'Globalisierung und Wettbewerb—einige Anmerkungen' in A Fuchs, H-P Schwintowski and D Zimmer (eds), *Wirtschafts- und Privatrecht im Spannungsfeld von Privatautonomie, Wettbewerb und Regulierung. Festschrift für Ulrich Immenga zum 70. Geburtstag* (Munich, CH Beck, 2004), 213, 216–17.

boundaries of a single state or even a larger region, such as a language area. More and more often, anti-competitive agreements or conduct by powerful firms have a huge geographical reach;[74] indeed, the effects of antitrust violations may even be felt worldwide. Some of the recent international antitrust matters, such as the *Vitamins, Lysine* and *Graphite Electrodes* cartels and the *Microsoft* case, are good examples of this phenomenon. The companies involved in these cartels were often subject to parallel antitrust proceedings both in the EU and in third countries, notably the US and Canada.[75]

In both the *Lysine* and *Graphite Electrodes* cases, the parties challenged the Commission decision inter alia on the ground that the imposition of further sanctions by the Commission in addition to those which had already been exacted by the US and Canadian antitrust authorities was in breach of the rule against double jeopardy.[76]

The parties essentially argued that it would follow from *Boehringer* that the Commission, when determining the fine to be imposed under Article 81 EC, was under a duty to take account of the sanctions already applied in the US and Canada since, according to the parties, the facts complained of by the Commission, on the one hand, and by those third country authorities, on the other hand, were identical.[77]

However, the CFI rejected the applicants' arguments entirely. Recalling the judgment in *Walt Wilhelm*, which recognised the possibility of having the same infringement subject to two sets of parallel proceedings and concurrent sanctions pursuing different aims, it held that

> . . . the principle non bis in idem cannot, a fortiori, apply in the present case because the procedures conducted and penalties imposed by the Commission on the one hand and the American and Canadian authorities on the other clearly pursued different ends. The aim of the first was to preserve undistorted competition within the European Union and the EEA, whereas the aim of the second was to protect the American and Canadian markets.[78]

---

[74] R Whish, *Competition Law* (London, LexisNexis, 5th edn, 2003), 427.

[75] See L Ritter and D Braun, *EC Competition Law, A Practitioner's Guide* (The Hague, Kluwer Law International, 3rd edn, 2004), 1141. The cases mentioned are but some of the most prominent antitrust violations with a worldwide dimension that were detected, prosecuted and punished in recent years.

[76] See paras 76 *et seq* of the judgment of the CFI in Case T–224/00 *Archer Daniels v Commission* ('*Lysine*') [2003] ECR II–2597 and paras 130 *et seq* of the CFI's judgment of 24 April 2004 in Joined Cases T–236, 239, 244–246, 251 and 252/01 *Tokai Carbon and others v Commission* ('*Graphite Electrodes*') [2004] ECR II–1181.

[77] This interpretaion of the *Boehringer* judgment had initially also been defended in an earlier edition of P Roth and V Rose (eds), *Bellamy & Child. European Community Law of Competition* (Oxford, Oxford University Press, 4th edn, 1993), para 12-094.

[78] Para 90 of the judgment in *Archer Daniels* (above n 76) and para 134 of the judgment in *Tokai Carbon* (above n 76). It is interesting to note that the findings of the CFI regarding the *ne bis in idem* issue in *Archer Daniels* and *Tokai Carbon* are, to a large extent, literally the same. On this point, the later judgment (*Tokai Carbon*) seems to consist mainly of a 'cut-and-paste'

The CFI further considered that it could not be deduced from *Boehringer* that the Commission is effectively required to set off an earlier penalty imposed by the authorities of non-member States if the facts alleged by those authorities are the same as the facts underlying the Commission decision.[79] Moreover, the CFI found that, even if such an obligation, on the part of the Commission, to set-off the first sanction could be inferred *a contrario* from the judgment in *Boehringer*, it would have been for the undertakings concerned to prove that the facts of the relevant proceedings were actually the same. However, the applicants had not shown

> that the penalty imposed in the United States related to application of the cartel or its effects other than in the United States . . . and in the EEA in particular, an extension which, moreover, would have clearly encroached on the territorial jurisdiction of the Commission. That observation applies equally to the judgment handed down in Canada.[80]

Despite the fact that the relevant cartels in both cases operated on a global basis, the CFI essentially denied that the *ne bis in idem* principle could have any bearing on international antitrust cases where parallel proceedings are conducted against the cartel members and concurrent penalties imposed on the same undertakings for their participation in the same worldwide anti-competitive agreement or conduct. Not even the setting-off rule, which in *Boehringer* still appeared as a possible solution for attenuating the effects of multiple sanctions, seems to be a real option anymore.

D. Applicability of the *Ne Bis in Idem* Principle to Multiple National Proceedings under Article 81 or 82 EC

In view of the above case law, the question remains whether the *ne bis in idem* principle protects individuals and undertakings from being prosecuted and/or punished more than once within the Community, albeit by different Member States' authorities, under Article 81 or 82 EC for the same anti-competitive agreement or conduct.[81]

exercise. Whether this exercise really embraces all the arguments that the various applicants in that matter submitted to the court is an open question.

[79] According to the CFI, the ECJ merely considered the identity of the facts as a precondition for a possible set-off, albeit without deciding that, in the case of identical facts, the first penalty must be deducted from the second. Paras 95–8 of the judgment in *Archer Daniels* (above n 76) and paras 139–40 of the judgment in *Tokai Carbon* (above n 76).

[80] Paras 101–3 of the judgment in *Archer Daniels* (above n 76) and para 143 of the judgment in *Tokai Carbon* (above n 76). Cf also para 6 (*in fine*) of the judgment in *Boehringer* (above n 49).

[81] The issue of multiple fines being imposed on the basis of a parallel application of national competition law (by an NCA) and Community competition law (by the Commission) can be neglected here as this situation seems to be purely hypothetical. First, as has been pointed out earlier, many authors and in particular Commission officials contend that national competition

1. The EU Charter

The most obvious solution would be to rely on Article 50 of the EU Charter, since that provision extends the scope of the *ne bis in idem* guarantee to the territory of the European Union. Under this rule, the fact that the relevant proceedings are conducted by authorities of different Member States and are thus not taking place within the same state would not preclude the application of the guarantee. The rule against double jeopardy as enshrined in the EU Charter would therefore protect undertakings, which have been punished by the NCA of a given Member State for the infringement of Article 81 or 82 EC, from being subject to further national proceedings, initiated by NCAs of other Member States, equally with the aim of enforcing Article 81 (or 82) EC in respect of the same facts.[82] However, the EU Charter formally has no binding legal force as it has not yet been integrated into the EC or EU Treaty. It is not a formal Community act, but a solemn proclamation of three Community institutions.[83]

Whether the guarantees enshrined in the EU Charter can be considered to form part of the *acquis communautaire* is still being disputed. According

---

law can no longer be applied on a stand-alone basis in cases where there is an effect on intra-Community trade (see above Chapter 1, n 280). Moreover, NCAs could not in any event adopt a decision that would deviate from the Commission's assessment of the matter (except for Art 82 cases). On this basis, it is fair to conclude that national competition law has been largely marginalised and only retains an independent function for cases with merely regional or local scope, ie in respect of agreements or conduct which do not meet the effect-on-trade criterion. A Fuchs, 'Kontrollierte Dezentralisierung der europäischen Wettbewerbsaufsicht' (2005) 40 *Europarecht* (Beiheft 2), 77, 79. Secondly, in practice, NCAs are unlikely to claim the right to apply national competition law with regard to an infringement which is being prosecuted or has already been prosecuted and punished by the Commission given the de facto restraints of many NCAs resulting from (too) limited financial means and scarce human resources.

[82] Wils, above n 4, 146. The conclusion is self-evident unless one argues that concurrent proceedings conducted by different states or under different jurisdictions do not concern the same offence because each NCA takes account only of the domestic effects of the infringement. On this latter point, see, eg the considerations of the Community courts in *Boehringer* (above n 49, para 6), *Archer Daniels* (above n 76, para 103) and *Tokai Carbon* (above n 76, para 143). Cf also the Commission in *Vitamins* [2003] OJ L6/1, para 773, where it bluntly rejected the parties' argument that it should have taken into account the sanctions imposed on them by the US and Canadian authorities: 'it is in any case untrue that the Commission was intending to sanction it for the same facts as the US courts had . . . In the same way, the US antitrust authorities only exercise jurisdiction to the extent that the conduct has . . . effect on US commerce.' However, these arguments are difficult to sustain where the relevant authorities apply nominally the same provision (a fact which distinguishes the hypothetical case discussed here from the aforementioned decisions and court rulings). Moreover, Commission and Community courts seem to neglect the fact that the finding of a violation of Art 81 does not depend on certain effects having actually materialised in the territory of the EU (since Art 81 prohibits already agreements and practices which have as their object a restriction of competition; Schröter, in Schröter *et al*, above n 61, 126 para 65). See Wils, above n 4, 146.

[83] See the judgment of the CFI in Joined Cases T–377/00, T–379/00, T–380/00, T–260/01 and T–272/01 *Philip Morris and others v Commission* [2003] ECR II–1, para 122. See further above Chapter 3, n 224 and the accompanying text.

to some authors, the Charter is in fact part of the *acquis communautaire*. These authors maintain that the Member States' reluctance to integrate the fundamental guarantees into the Treaties had only political, rather than legal, reasons.[84] Other writers argue, however, that the deliberate and express choice of the Member States to make the Charter not a formal part of the Treaties and thus not to afford it binding legal force may not be circumvented by regarding the Charter as part of the *acquis communautaire*.[85] In any event, the preamble of the Explanations to the EU Charter states that the EU Charter

> reaffirms . . . the rights as they result, in particular, from the constitutional traditions and international obligations common to the Member States.

The constitutional traditions common to the Member States, in turn, form one of the sources of the general principles of Community law.[86] Indeed, the principle *ne bis in idem* is recognised, in one way or another, in almost all Member States.[87] There can thus be little doubt that the prohibition of double sanctions and double proceedings is a rule common to the legal traditions of the Member States and therefore a general principle of Community law. This has been explicitly acknowledged by the Community judicature[88] and is indirectly confirmed by the fact that the rule has been incorporated in the EU Charter.[89]

---

[84] Rather than being unwilling to accept the binding force of the guarantees, the Member States simply feared that they might give the wrong political signal by formally inserting the Charter in the EU legal order, namely that the EU would develop into some kind of 'superstate', or that extensive discussions on the Charter would overshadow other (more) important matters on the agenda of the Intergovernmental Conference. See K Lenaerts and E De Smijter, 'A "Bill of Rights" for the European Union' (2001) 38 *CML Rev* 273, 299. Cf, however, E Pache, 'Die europäische Grundrechtscharta—ein Rückschritt für den Grundrechtsschutz in Europa?' (2001) 36 *Europarecht* 475, 486, who believes that the lack of legal enforceability of the EU Charter provides a strong negative signal to EU citizens that overrides the positive symbolic value of its proclamation and concludes: 'Die Charta ist ebenso ein offensichtliches Dokument des fortbestehenden Dissenses der Mitgliedstaaten über die Finalität der europäischen Integration.'

[85] See Schwarze, above n 16, 517; Kuck, above n 39, 690.

[86] See K Lenaerts and Van Nuffel, *Constitutional Law of the European Union* (London, Sweet & Maxwell, 2nd edn, 2005), 17-068. On this basis, one could indeed argue that the Charter rights are binding.

[87] Schwarze and Weitbrecht, above n 63, 153 para 24; Van Den Wyngaert and Stessens, above n 49, 780; M Fletcher, 'Some Developments to the *ne bis in idem* Principle in the European Union: Criminal Proceedings Against Hüseyn Gözütok and Klaus Brügge' (2003) 66 *MLR* 769, 770.

[88] See, eg para 130 of the judgment in *Tokai Carbon* (above n 76).

[89] See the preamble to the EU Charter: 'This Charter *reaffirms*, with due regard for the powers and tasks of the Community and the Union and the principle of subsidiarity, the rights as they result, in particular, from the constitutional traditions and international obligations common to the Member States.' On this basis, the EU Charter does not add new rights, but simply makes existing rights (more) visible. K Lenaerts and M Desomer, 'Het EVRM en de Europese Unie' in P Lemmens (ed), *Uitdagingen door en voor het EVRM* (Mechelen, Wolters Kluwer, 2005), 177, 219.

However, Article 50 of the EU Charter considerably broadens the scope of the *ne bis in idem* principle in that it prohibits double punishment and double prosecution within the whole of the European Union.[90] It thus considers all Member States of the EU to form a single unitary jurisdiction. In this respect, the EU Charter clearly departs from the traditional approach, which is reflected both in the national laws of the Member States and in the ECHR. Historically, the *ne bis in idem* principle applies nationally, ie protection against double jeopardy is usually granted only in relation to two proceedings being conducted in one and the same state.[91] While the recognition of *res iudicata* to foreign national judgments is more frequent in common law legal systems, it is still rather exceptional for civil law jurisdictions to incorporate an international *ne bis in idem*.[92] Moreover, there seems to be no common approach regarding the scope and application of the national *ne bis in idem*.[93] Discrepancies concern, for instance, the definition of the *idem* (*idem factum* or legal *idem*) and the *bis* (prohibition of double prosecution or only anti-cumulation of sanctions) and the applicability to legal persons. Where a legal *idem* is required, this is sometimes determined by the scope of the offence and sometimes by the identity of the legal values protected.[94]

[90] Cf A Vitorino, 'La Charte des droits fondamentaux de l'Union européenne' (2002) *Revue du Droit de l'Union Européenne* 27, 59: 'Il s'agit là d'une valeur *ajoutée* significative de la Charte' (emphasis added).

[91] Nazzini, above n 4, 11–12. J Vervaele, 'Joined Cases C–187/01 and C–385/01, Criminal proceedings against Hüseyin Gözütok and Klaus Brügge, Judgment of the Court of Justice of 11 February 2003, Full Court, [2003] ECR I–5689' (2004) 41 *CML Rev* 795, 801.

[92] Such an exception is Art 68 of the Penal Code (Wetboek van Strafrecht) of the Netherlands, which stipulates that the double jeopardy prohibition applies not only where a first judgment has been rendered by a domestic court, but also in case of a foreign judgment, and thus provides for an international *ne bis in idem*. Van Den Wyngaert and Stessens, above n 49, 783, Vervaele, *ibid*, 804. Similar rules are said to exist in Spain and France. See T Eilmansberger, '"Ne bis in idem" und kartellrechtliche Drittstaatssanktionen' (2004) 15 *Europaisches Wirtschafts- und Steuerrecht* 49, 51. See also the comparative analysis of the national rules of the then six Member States made by Advocate General Mayras in *Boehringer* (above n 49), 1295–6. This comparison shows that only the Netherlands law includes a true international *ne bis in idem*, while the laws of Belgium and France provide for a limited international *ne bis in idem*: namely, foreign judgments are not a bar to exercise jurisdiction if the relevant offence has been committed in Belgium or France. According to Mayras's analysis of 1972, German and Italian law, in contrast, do not recognise the preclusive effect of foreign criminal judgments at all. However, Eilmansberger, *idem*, 51, quotes Germany and Italy as examples of countries acknowledging the duty to take into account foreign sanctions (*Anrechnungsprinzip*). According to the relevant case law, the German rule against double jeopardy, which has the rank of a fundamental right (see Art 103(3) of the German Constitution—Grundgesetz), includes the duty to take into account previous sanctions that have been inflicted for the same wrongdoing, while it does not recognise an absolute preclusive effect of foreign judgments. See L Meyer-Goßner, *Strafprozessordnung, Kommentar* (Munich, CH Beck, 48th edn, 2005), Einl no 177.

[93] In para 78 of her opinion in Case C–467/04 *Francesco Gasparini and others* [2006] ECR I–9199, Advocate General E Sharpston states: 'there is no single, truly common definition of what precisely that principle means, what exactly the scope is'.

[94] See J Vervaele, 'The Transnational *ne bis in idem* Principle in the EU Mutual Recognition and Equivalent Protection of Human Rights' (2005) 1 *Utrecht Law Review* 100, 100–1. On the variables of the *ne bis in idem* principle, see also Eilmansberger, above n 92, 50.

In view of the significant difference between the scope of Article 50 EU Charter and domestic provisions on the *ne bis in idem* principle and the divergencies between the various national interpretations, it seems difficult to sustain the view that Article 50 EU Charter embodies a (constitutional) principle common to the Member States. In my view, it appears at least premature to regard the guarantee of a Union-wide *ne bis in idem* as an expression of 'the constitutional traditions common to the Member States' and a general principle of Community law.[95]

Moreover, despite the fact that the EU Charter has been predicted to potentially play a major role in the interpretation of Community law,[96] there is to date hardly any case law of the Community courts drawing directly on its articles.[97]

Only recently has the ECJ, for the first time, effectively relied on the EU Charter. In a judgment of 27 June 2006, concerning an application for partial annulment of a Council directive, the ECJ directly referred to several articles of the EU Charter.[98] In response to the submission of the Council that the application should not be examined in the light of the EU Charter as it does not constitute a source of Community law, the ECJ noted that

---

[95] It is worth noting, though, that there are binding provisions applicable in specific fields of Union law which equally extend the scope of the *ne bis in idem* principle to the entire territory of the European Union, including notably Art 54 of the Schengen Convention. This is the first time a multilateral convention has established an international *ne bis in idem* principle which has the character of an individual right *erga omnes*. Vervaele, above n 91, 805.

[96] See J Schwarze, 'Der Grundrechtsschutz für Unternehmen in der Europäischen Grundrechtecharta' (2001) 12 *Europäische Zeitschrift für Wirtschaftsrecht* 517, 517–18, who submits that the EU Charter, on the basis of its mere existence and despite its non-legally binding character, could shape the further development of EU law. Schwarze mentions a number of Advocates General who have explicitly referred in their conclusions to guarantees of the EU Charter. Similarly, Pache, above n 84, 486, contends that the Charter will indirectly serve as a source of law in that it will provide guidance to the Community courts when they determine the constitutional traditions common to the Member States. See also Lenaerts and De Smijter, above n 84, 298; Riley, above n 16, 87 note 152a; J Callewaert, 'Het EVRM en het communautair recht: een Europese globalisering?' (2001) *Nederlands tijdschrift voor Europees recht* 259, 265.

[97] Schwarze, above n 96, 518, quotes several opinions of Advocates General, but in fact no judgments. Similarly, Lenaerts and Desomer, above n 89, 221, and W Wils, 'Powers of Investigation and Procedural Rights and Guarentees in EU Antitrust Enforcement: The Interplay between European and National Legislation and Case-law' (2006) 29 *World Competition* 3, 18, mention two judgments of the CFI, but no judgment of the ECJ. In contrast, some case law of the HR Court cites the EU Charter. Notably, in the judgment of 11 July 2002 in the case of *Christine Goodwin v UK* Reports/Recueil 2002, 588, para 99, the ECtHR relied inter alia on the wording of Art 9 ('Right to marry and right to found a family') of the EU Charter in order to determine the essence of the fundamental right to marry as enshrined in Art 12 of the HR Convention. The EU Charter seems to share the destiny of Sleeping Beauty, waiting for Prince Charming (ie the formal incorporation into the Treaties or the ratification of the Treaty establishing a Constitution for Europe) to wake her up. (The metaphor has been borrowed from Vitorino, above n 90, 63.)

[98] See para 58 of the judgment in Case C–540/03 *European Parliament v Council* [2006] ECR I–5769. The case concerns an application for annulment of certain provisions of Council Directive 2003/86/EC on the right of family reunification [2003] OJ L251/12.

[w]hile the Charter is not a legally binding instrument, the Community legislature did, however, acknowledge its importance by stating, in the second recital in the preamble to the Directive, that the Directive observes the principles recognised not only by Article 8 of the ECHR but also in the Charter. Furthermore, the principal aim of the Charter, as is apparent from its preamble, is to reaffirm 'rights as they result, in particular, from the constitutional traditions and international obligations common to the Member States, the Treaty on European Union, the Community Treaties, the [ECHR], . . .

Arguably, this line of reasoning could also be applied here. Indeed, Regulation 1/2003, like many other Regulations adopted since the proclamation of the EU Charter, equally refers to the Charter and contains a clear commitment to respect rights enshrined therein:

This Regulation respects the fundamental rights and observes the principles recognised in particular by the Charter of Fundamental Rights of the European Union. Accordingly, this Regulation should be interpreted and *applied* with respect to those rights and principles.[99]

However, there are two important factors which distinguish the present situation from the above-mentioned case regarding the Council directive on family reunification (*EP v Council*). First, in *EP v Council*, the relevant fundamental rights—Article 8 of the ECHR and Article 7 of the EU Charter—have virtually the same wording and scope. By contrast, the wording of Article 50 of the EU Charter departs from the wording of its counterpart in the ECHR in that the EU Charter affords a broader, ie EU-wide, protection against double jeopardy. This discrepancy concerns an essential aspect of the norm, notably its scope. It follows that Article 50 of the EU Charter is not a simple copy of Article 4 Protocol No 7. Moreover, recognition of an international *ne bis in idem* is seldom to be found in the legal systems of the Member States. Article 50 of the EU Charter thus cannot be considered to reflect the constitutional traditions or international obligations common to the Member States, which could, however, be said about Article 7 of the EU Charter, which repeats Article 8 of the ECHR almost word for word.[100] It is also important to note that the deviation is crucial with regard to the question raised here, ie the permissibility of multiple sanctions imposed by authorities of different Member States.

Secondly, in *EP v Council*, the ECJ relied upon the EU Charter when reviewing the lawfulness of the Council directive, which was directly challenged by the applicant. In other words, what was at stake was the

---

[99] Emphasis added. Recital 37 of Reg 1/2003.

[100] The only difference between Art 8 ECHR and Art 7 EU Charter is that in the latter article the term 'correspondence', which is used in the ECHR, has been replaced by the notion of 'communications' in order to exclude any doubts as to the protection of modern forms of 'correspondence', such as electronic mail. This is, however, a purely formal modification, as Art 8 of the ECHR also covers communications other than traditional mail. Lemmens, above n 45, 57 note 39.

validity of the directive itself, which, in one of the recitals, had explicitly referred to the EU Charter. In this context, it seems logical that the ECJ drew on the fundamental rights of the EU Charter and regarded them as part of the rules in the light of which it had to assess the legality of the contested Community act.[101] After all, it was the Council which adopted the directive at issue and which has also committed itself (together with EP and Commission) to comply with the principles of the EU Charter by solemnly proclaiming it.

In the present case, the possible unlawfulness does not concern the Community act (Regulation 1/2003) as such,[102] but rather concerns an act of a Member State. Namely, it is the relevant NCA decision, imposing a second sanction on an individual or a company, that could be incompatible with the EU Charter. This decision was adopted in accordance with national procedures and thus was based on domestic law as well as the EC Treaty provisions on competition. Here, Regulation 1/2003, and even more so the legally non-binding EU Charter, can at best be of incidental relevance. Moreover, apart from the fact that it is not a formal legal instrument of the Community or the Union, it is uncertain to what extent the EU Charter, having been promulgated and endorsed by the Community institutions, could be binding for the NCAs of the Member States.[103] Member States are bound to respect the general principles of Community law where they implement Community rules.[104] However, as argued above, an EU-wide *ne bis in idem* cannot be considered as yet to form part of the general principles of Community law. The EU Charter is therefore unlikely

---

[101] On this technique of invoking and using as a yardstick legally non-binding instruments ('Fediol-technique') see Case 70/87 *Fediol v Commission* [1989] ECR 1781, paras 18- 22 (regarding the invocability of certain provisions of the GATT) and K Lenaerts and T Corthaut, 'Of birds and hedges: the role of primacy in invoking norms of EU law' (2006) 31 *EL Rev* 287, 301–2.

[102] In my view, the legality of Reg 1/2003 itself would be contestable only if it was impossible to interpret it in a way consistent with the requirements of the EU Charter and the application of Reg 1/2003 would thus necessarily involve an infringement of the fundamental rights enshrined in the Charter. See para 22 of the judgment in Case 5/88 *Wachauf v Bundesamt für Ernährung und Forstwirtschaft* [1989] ECR 2609. By contrast, in the pre-cited case *EP v Council* (Case C–540/03), above n 98, the ECJ held in para 23 of the judgment that 'a provision of a Community act could, in itself, not respect fundamental rights if it required, or expressly or impliedly authorised, the Member States to adopt or retain national legislation not respecting those rights'. The two approaches seem to be irreconcilable. If one endorses the latter approach (judgment in *EP v Council*), one would have to conclude that Reg 1/2003 violates the EU Charter in that it does not entirely preclude parallel proceedings by several Member States, but clearly leaves open the possibility of two or three NCAs investigating and punishing the same infringement, and thus 'impliedly authorises' such parallel action in defiance of Art 50 EU Charter (see inter alia Art 13 of Reg 1/2003 (only optional suspension or termination of a parallel procedure) and paras 5 and 12–13 of the Network Notice).

[103] See Roth, above n 22, 4.

[104] See, eg para 105 of the judgment of the ECJ in *EP v Council* (above n 98) and para 19 of the judgment in *Wachauf* (above n 102).

to have direct legal implications for national decisions, even where such measures ultimately implement EC law.[105]

Taking everything into consideration, it must be concluded that both the legal effect and the material impact of the EU Charter on the Community legal order, at least as concerns the recognition of an international *ne bis in idem* as part of the fundamental guarantees of Community law, remains doubtful. Even if one accepts that the Community institutions are de facto bound by the EU Charter inasmuch as the Community acts which they adopt explicitly refer to the Charter,[106] it is unclear whether this approach implies that the Member States' authorities are equally bound when adopting national measures in the implementation of such acts. In view of all these uncertainties, it may appear unrealistic, but not entirely excluded, that companies can successfully invoke the *ne bis in idem* principle laid down in Article 50 EU Charter where, after having been convicted (or acquitted) on the basis of Article 81 or 82 EC, they are subject to further antitrust proceedings conducted in one or more other Member States with regard to the same facts.

2. Article 54 Schengen Convention

Another possibility would be to apply Article 54 Schengen Convention,[107] which equally offers a Community-wide *ne bis in idem* guarantee. However, it would seem that this provision cannot be relied upon directly in the context of Community competition law.

The Schengen Convention of 1990 implements the Schengen Agreement of 1984, an agreement which was originally concluded by only five Member States as part of an intensified, but at the time still purely inter-

---

[105] The only way to get around this problem, it would seem, is to submit that the relevant national rules, on which the NCA decision is based, in turn, are incompatible with superior Community law, notably Reg 1/2003, insofar as that this regulation must be interpreted, in the light of the EU Charter, as excluding a priori that parallel sanctions be imposed by different NCAs on the same persons for the same infringement. An argument for this approach can be found in recital 37 of Reg 1/2003, which states that 'this Regulation should be interpreted *and applied* with respect those rights and principles' recognised by the EU Charter (emphasis added). However, the invocability of EU norms in indirect judicial review procedures at the national level remains problematic. See Lenaerts and Corthaut, above n 101, 302–9.

[106] According to Advocate General J Kokott, it must be taken into account in competition proceedings that the Commission is bound to comply with the EU Charter because of its solemn commitment and also in view of recital 37 of Reg 1/2003. See note 59 of her opinion in Case C–105/04 P *FEG and TU v Commission* [2006] ECR I–8725.

[107] Art 54 reads: 'A person whose trial has been finally disposed of in one Contracting Party may not be prosecuted in another Contracting Party for the same acts provided that, if a penalty has been imposed, it has been enforced, is actually in the process of being enforced or can no longer be enforced under the laws of the sentencing Contracting Party.' Art 55 Schengen Convention provides the possibility for Schengen states to make reservations limiting the scope of the EU-wide *ne bis in idem* principle.

governmental, form of co-operation.[108] The purpose of the Schengen Agreement[109] was the gradual abolition of checks at the common borders of the participating states. The Schengen Convention thus fell outside the scope of the Community Treaties and, initially, even outside the context of the EU Treaty. The Amsterdam Treaty did incorporate the Schengen *acquis*; however, only parts of the Schengen *acquis* were incorporated as Community law, while other parts 'merely' became Union law.[110]

In fact, it was the Maastricht Treaty of 1992 which integrated police and judicial co-operation into the institutional framework of the EU, placing it under title VI of the EU Treaty, headed 'Provisions on co-operation in the fields of justice and home affairs', the so-called third pillar. Since the Amsterdam Treaty, however, police and judicial co-operation under the third pillar has been confined to criminal matters, while co-operation in civil matters has been 'communitarised' and brought within the sphere of the EC Treaty.[111] This means that, despite its incorporation into Union law, police and judicial co-operation in criminal matters (PJCC) still remains outside the ambit of the Communities.

There can be little doubt that Article 54 of the Schengen Convention relates to PJCC given that *ne bis in idem* is a traditional criminal law principal. Article 54 is therefore still a third pillar provision, falling outside the area of the Community policies and, more particularly, outside the scope of the common rules on competition. This is confirmed by the Council decision which determines the legal basis for each of the provisions of the Schengen *acquis*. According to that decision, the legal basis for Article 54 of the Schengen Convention are Articles 31 and 34 EU Treaty, which deal with judicial co-operation in criminal matters and the competences of the Council in this field.[112] By contrast, the introduction and imposition of sanctions for infringements of EC competition law by the

---

[108] A Tchorbadjiyska, 'Joint Cases C–187/01 and C–385/01 Gözütok and Brügge (E.C.J. February 11, 2003) 2003 E.C.R. I–1345' (2004) 10 *Columbia Journal of European Law* 549, 550.

[109] [2000] OJ L239/13. The original five Schengen states were Belgium, Germany, France, Luxemburg and the Netherlands. By the time the Amsterdam Treaty entered into force, all other Member States except for Ireland and the UK had joined the Schengen Convention. Lenaerts and Van Nuffel, above n 86, 2-017. The UK and Ireland have, however, opted to participate in certain provisions of the Schengen *acquis*, including Art 54 of the Schengen Convention. See Fletcher, above n 87, 772 (with references to the relevant Council decisions). The EU-wide *ne bis in idem* thus applies in all Member States, including the 12 new Member States which acceded in May 2004 and January 2007. See p 8 of the Commission Green Paper of 23 December 2005 on Conflicts of Jurisdiction and the Principle of *ne bis in idem* in Criminal Proceedings (COM(2005) 696 final; 'Green Paper on Criminal Jurisdiction').

[110] Lenaerts and Van Nuffel, above n 86, 3-020.

[111] *Ibid*, 2-016 and 3-015, in particular note 57.

[112] Annex A of the Council decision of 20 May 1999 determining, in conformity with the relevant provisions of the Treaty establishing the European Community and the Treaty on European Union, the legal basis for each of the provisions or decisions which constitute the Schengen *acquis* ([1999] OJ L176/17).

Community or the Member States, even if these are of a criminal or quasi-criminal nature, must be regarded as a measure annexed to the enforcement of Articles 81 and 82 EC and the implementation of Regulation 1/2003. The relevant sanctioning regime thus cannot be considered separately from those provisions and therefore falls within the scope of the EC Treaty.[113] Applying Article 54 of the Schengen Convention in the context of EC competition law enforcement would thus blur the lines between the different pillars as organised by the Amsterdam Treaty.

Moreover, the introduction of the Community-wide *ne bis in idem* rule in Article 54 of the Schengen Convention is closely linked to the security issues arising from the abolition of border controls, which, in turn, made closer co-operation among the Schengen states necessary in order to combat crime and create a common area of freedom, security and justice. The provision is thus predominantly related to the right of free movement of persons.[114] By contrast, corporate bodies, at which the competition rules are primarily directed, enjoy the freedom of establishment. While it is nowadays certainly also easier for companies to expand illegal activities beyond the borders of a given Member State, this phenomenon is not related to the removal of (physical) border controls.

Finally, the fact that Article 54 of the Schengen Convention is a third pillar provision also implies that it applies only to criminal offences *sensu stricto*. The broad meaning given to the term 'criminal' by the ECtHR in

---

[113] This view is supported by a recent judgment by which the ECJ annulled Council Framework Decision 2003/80/JHA, ie a measure adopted under the third pillar, in accordance with Art 47 EU and the principle that acts under the EU Treaty may not encroach upon the powers conferred by the EC Treaty upon the Community (see *Commission v Council*, above n 21). The Framework Decision had laid down a number of particularly serious environmental offences in respect of which Member States were required to introduce criminal penalties. It thus clearly had the purpose of protecting the environment, one of the essential objectives of the EC Treaty. The ECJ therefore ruled that, in view of its aim and content, the measure could have been properly adopted on the basis of Art 175 EC, the relevant provision for the implementation of the Community's environmental policy (see para 51 of the judgment). The ECJ thus assumed a kind of 'implied power' or 'annex competence' of the Council to regulate and harmonise the criminal law sanctions applicable in a specific policy field for which it may also enact substantive rules where such penalties are considered necessary to ensure that those substantive rules are effectively observed. See T Eilmansberger, 'The Green Paper on Damages Actions for Breach of the EC Antitrust Rules and Beyond: Reflections on the Utility and Feasibility of Stimulating Private Enforcement Through Legislative Action' (2007) 44 *CML Rev* 431, 440–1. On this basis, appropriate sanctioning mechanisms, whether adopted at national or Community level, which aim to ensure compliance with substantive Community rules, it would seem, form part of the same area of Community law as those substantive rules and, generally, are not subject to the provisions on PJCC under the third pillar, even if the sanctioning mechanisms have a criminal law character.

[114] Vervaele, above n 91, 807–8; paras 59–60 of the opinion of Advocate General Ruiz-Jarabo Colomer in Case C–150/05 *van Straaten v Netherlands* [2006] ECR I–9327. See also para 38 of the judgment of the ECJ *Gözütok and Brügge* (above n 47). The provisions regarding police and judicial cooperation essentially constitute flanking measures, the main objective of the Schengen Convention being the elimination of checks on the movement of persons within the Schengen area. Tchorbadjiyska, above n 108, 550.

the context of interpreting Article 6 ECHR, it is submitted, cannot be transposed to the Schengen rule. The interpretation applied by the ECtHR is prompted and justified by the aim to provide an effective and comprehensive guarantee. At first sight, adopting the autonomous approach of the HR Court within the EU in order to extensively protect EU citizens and possibly also companies might appear justified. However, this would mean disregarding the internal structure of the Union and the varying competences of the Community institutions in respect of each of the three pillars. The provisions relating to PJCC deal with a very specific field of Union law which must be distinguished from the second pillar (common foreign and security policy) and, more particularly, from the first pillar, including the articles on Community policies of which the competition rules from part. The provisions of the third pillar are intended to facilitate co-operation between the Member States with regard to the prevention, detection and prosecution of criminal offences. They are concerned with infringements of national rules (as opposed to Community rules), which, under the applicable domestic law, qualify as criminal. Typical examples are terrorism, trafficking in persons, illicit drug trafficking and fraud.[115] These examples show that, for the purposes of defining the scope of the PJCC, a classical notion of criminal law must be applied, which, moreover, respects the domestic classification.[116] Therefore, Article 54 of the Schengen Convention cannot be invoked in matters which, according to the relevant national law, do not belong to the criminal law sphere.[117]

For the above reasons, Article 54 of the Schengen Convention does not apply *ratione materiae* in the context of the enforcement of Articles 81 and 82 EC unless the relevant national procedures are actually qualified as criminal under domestic law.

---

[115] See Art 29 EU Treaty.

[116] This would exclude administrative and even quasi-criminal proceedings dealing with administrative wrongdoings or regulatory offences, even though the latter may entail severe sanctions. See the distinction made by Zuleeg, above n 18, 453.

[117] See M Wasmeier and N Thwaites, 'The Development of *ne bis in idem* into a Transnational Fundamental Right in EU Law: Comments on Recent Developments' (2006) 31 *EL Rev* 565, 575, who consider that extending the scope of Art 54 of the Schengen Convention to administrative proceedings would constitute 'another "quantum leap" after lifting the principle to the transnational level'. Cf also Nazzini, above n 4, 12. This does not exclude the protection of individuals who are subject to competition proceedings by Art 54 Schengen Convention where, in terms of domestic law, such proceedings are indeed of a criminal nature (eg Ireland, UK). Cf also Wils, above n 47, 448, implying that a strict distinction must be drawn between true criminal antitrust sanctions introduced as part of the Community's competition policy under Art 83 EC and third pillar provisions.

3. 'Old' Case Law of the Community Courts—New Situation under Regulation 1/2003

None of the aforementioned judgments actually deals with the new type of situation with which parties might be confronted more regularly under Regulation 1/2003, namely the parallel enforcement of Article 81 (or 82) EC against the same undertakings with regard to the same facts by two or more NCAs. The case law discussed above is therefore of only limited value. Nonetheless, the cases may provide some more general arguments and guidance.

a. The PVC II Case

The question of multiple prosecution of the same firms by several NCAs under Community competition law is different from the repeated prosecution of a company by the same authority, which was at issue in *PVC II*. In that sense, the case must clearly be distinguished from the question raised here. However, in its *PVC II* judgment, the ECJ expressly acknowledged that the *ne bis in idem* guarantee is a fundamental principle of Community law which, as a matter of principle, is applicable in competition matters.[118] Thus, whether or not the sanctions that can be imposed for violations of competition law are qualified, under the applicable national system, as criminal, the *PVC II* case makes it clear that both Commission and NCAs have to observe the rule against double jeopardy when they prosecute and punish infringements of Article 81 or 82 EC.

b. The Judgment in Walt Wilhelm

Similarly, *Walt Wilhelm* is not exactly pertinent as that case only deals with the concurrent application of national and Community competition law. It does not address the issue of multiple application of the same rules, ie Article 81 or 82 EC, by two or more NCAs with respect to one set of facts.[119]

Moreover, the approach of the ECJ, which may have been justified in 1969, appears to be less convincing now. The ECJ based its ruling in

---

[118] Para 59 of the judgment of the ECJ in *PVC II* (above n 22).

[119] Cf Wils, above n 16, 351, who argues that the parallel application of Art 81 and national law, which was at issue in the *Walt Wilhelm* case (above n 59), falls outside the ambit of the *ne bis in idem* principle because both procedures concern different infringements (*des infractions distinctes*). In a later publication, however, the same author questions the lawfulness of the setting-off rule. There, Wils considers that national and Community competition law appear to cover the same essential elements, which, in the light of the test developed by the ECtHR in *Fischer*, would render the compatibility, with the *ne bis in idem* principle, of double prosecution under both sets of rules 'highly doubtful'. Wils, above n 4, 143. Cf also Advocate General L Geelhoed in *Graphite Electrodes*, who submits that, 'strictly speaking, Walt Wilhelm does not deal with the issue of ne bis in idem' (para 50 of his opinion in Case C–308/04 P *SGL Carbon v Commission* [2006] ECR I–5977).

particular on the consideration that Regulation 17 had created a 'special system of the sharing of jurisdiction between the Community and the Member States with regard to cartels'.[120] However, this system has been changed significantly by Regulation 1/2003. Due to the principle of concurrent jurisdiction, which underlies Regulation 1/2003, and the duty imposed on NCAs to apply the Community rules, the Commission and NCAs share the responsibility to enforce Community competition law. National competition law, according to many, can no longer be applied on a stand-alone basis in cases which affect inter-state trade.[121] There are also strict conflict rules so that, in any event, the application of the national competition rules cannot have an outcome that is different from the application of Community competition law. Finally, it must be noted that the national competition rules of many Member States are closely modelled upon or even a direct copy of Articles 81 and 82 EC. In view of this considerable degree of convergence,[122] it is questionable whether one can still maintain that national and Community competition law have different objectives which, in turn, could justify the conduct of parallel proceedings.[123]

Also in the light of the judgment of the ECtHR in *Fischer*, it is doubtful whether the ECJ's ruling in *Walt Wilhelm* could still be upheld.[124] In *Fischer* the ECtHR held that the *ne bis in idem* principle excludes double sanctions not only where the offences are nominally the same, but also where their essential elements are identical or overlap. Even though national and Community competition law appear to pursue slightly different ends,[125] in that the first aims at protecting competition on the

[120] See para 11 of the judgment in *Walt Wilhelm*, above n 59.

[121] See above Chapter 1, section II.B.1.b(1), particularly note 280, and above n 66. At least, it is unlikely that, in practice, it will often be applied where the Commission has already taken a decision on the matter, since its application cannot in any event lead to a different result than the application of the Community competition rules.

[122] See para 107 of the opinion of Advocate General Tizzano in Case C–397/03 P *Archer Daniels v Commission* [2006] ECR I–4429: 'In that connection, it should be pointed out that since the Court delivered its judgment in Walt Wilhelm (more than 30 years ago) the degree of interdependence and integration of Community and national systems for safeguarding competition on which that judgment was based has significantly increased, in particular with the decentralisation of the application of Community antitrust law introduced by the recent Regulation No 1/2003.'

[123] This was, however, one of the main arguments of the ECJ in *Walt Wilhelm* (see para 11 of the judgment, above n 59). Also according to Advocate General Geelhoed, that case law has largely been superseded since Reg 1/2003 came into force (see para 50 note 23 of his opinion in *SGL Carbon*, above n 119). *Accord* J Bourgeois, '*Ne bis in idem* and Enforcement of EEA Competition Rules' in M Monti, N von und zu Liechtenstein, B Vesterdorf, J Westbrook and L Wildhuber.(eds), *Economic Law and Justice in Times of Globalisation/Wirtschaftsrecht und Justiz in Zeiten der Globalisierung. Festschrift for Carl Baudenbacher* (Baden-Baden, Nomos, 2007), 313, 316 (relying on the ECJ's judgment in *SGL Carbon*).

[124] See Wils, above n 4, 143; Kuck, above n 39, 693–4.

[125] Or, as the ECJ puts it, Community and national competition law 'consider cartels from different points of view' (para 3 of the judgment in *Walt Wilhelm*, above n 59).

respective domestic market while the second predominantly seeks to eliminate or prevent obstacles to trade between Member States,[126] the essential elements of the relevant offences overlap.[127] In both cases, the rules are ultimately meant to ensure that competition, be it in the whole or a specific part of the Community (ie the territory of a Member State), is not distorted by anti-competitive agreements or conduct.[128] The overlap between the essential elements of national and Community antitrust rules is all the more obvious where the national provisions are modelled upon Articles 81 and 82 EC, as is the case in most, if not all, Member States.[129]

---

[126] In order to enhance market integration. Cf R Wesseling, *The Modernisation of EC Antitrust Law* (Oxford, Hart Publishing, 2000), 32. See also para 5 of the judgment in *Walt Wilhelm*, above n 59.

[127] Wils, above n 4, 143, argues that Arts 81 and 82 EC contain an additional element, notably the effect-on-trade criterion, but otherwise appear to cover the same ground as national competition law. This view seems to be indirectly confirmed by Art 3(2) and (3) of Reg 1/2003. While Art 3(2), 1st sentence provides that the application of national competition law may not lead to a different outcome than the (parallel) application of Community competition law, Art 3(3) stipulates that this concordance rule does not apply with regard to the application of national laws 'that predominantly pursue an objective different from that pursued by Arts 81 and 82 of the Treaty'. This implies that national competition provisions are considered to have essentially the same objective as Community competition law. Otherwise, ie if national competition law were considered to have a purpose totally different from that of Community competition law, Member States could apply their national competition rules, in accordance with Art 3(3) of Reg 1/2003, without regard to overall coherence, notably when the result would not coincide with that under the Community rules. This was evidently not the intention of the drafters of Art 3 of Reg 1/2003. See also Eilmansberger, above n 92, 50 note 7, and 53.

[128] See Kuck, above n 39, 694, Bourgeois, above n 123, 316 and Advocate General Ruiz-Jarabo Colomer in case *Italcementi* (above n 49), para 91: 'The unity of the legal right to be protected is beyond doubt. In the arrangement designed to ensure free competition, it is not possible to speak, within the European Union, of separate spheres, the Community sphere and the national spheres, as though they were watertight compartments. Both sectors seek to protect free and open competition in the common market, one contemplating it in its entirety and the other from its separate components, but the essence is the same.' In that case, the applicants had challenged the imposition of multiple fines by the Commission and the Autorità Garante on the same companies. (The Advocate General opined, however, that the fines related to different agreements and thus did not concern the same facts.) It is noteworthy that, in relation to Art 54 Schengen Convention, both Advocate General Ruiz-Jarabo Colomer and the ECJ found in *Van Esbroeck* that the application of the *ne bis in idem* rule does neither depend on the legal qualification nor the identity of the legal interest protected (paras 46–7 and paras 31–2 of the judgment in *Van Esbroeck*, above n 55) thereby seemingly rejecting the considerations of said Advocate General in *Italcementi* and also in *Gözütok and Brügge* (para 56 of his opinion, above n 47). On this discrepancy, see further below at n 251.

[129] The 10 new Member States, which joined the EU in May 2004, have copied Arts 81 and 82 EC (almost) verbatim. Most other Member States equally relied closely on the wording of the Community provisions. H Sauter, 'Die Globalisierung der Wettbewerbsbehörden durch die Erweiterung der Europäischen Union' in A Fuchs, H-P Schwintowski and D Zimmer (eds), *Wirtschafts- und Privatrecht im Spannungsfeld von Privatautonomie, Wettbewerb und Regulierung. Festschrift für Ulrich Immenga zum 70. Geburtstag* (Munich, CH Beck, 2004), 351, 356. With its seventh amendment act (7. GWB-Novelle), even Germany, which for a long time maintained a distinction between horizontal and vertical agreements (the first being prohibited with no general exemption clause available and the latter being subject to abuse control only) has now aligned its national cartel rules with Community law. Sections 1 and 2 para 1 GWB

On this basis, the findings of the ECJ in *Walt Wilhelm* appear incompatible with the HR Court's ruling in *Fischer*. Even the solution suggested by the ECJ—declaredly inspired by general considerations of equity and intended to attenuate the consequences of dual procedures—cannot alter this conclusion.[130] The HR Court explicitly rejected the possibility of avoiding a violation of the double jeopardy rule by the operation of some kind of setting-off system as Article 4 Protocol No 7 safeguards not only the right not to be punished twice but also the right not to be tried twice.[131] The *ne bis in idem* principle thus prohibits not only a cumulation of penalties, but also any repetition of proceedings. On this basis, the earlier of the two decisions should have been considered an absolute bar to any further investigation.

On the other hand, *Walt Wilhelm* does contain some noteworthy elements. First, the permissibility of parallel proceedings and double sanctions regarding one set of facts has been justified, inter alia, by the special division of jurisdiction between the Commission and NCAs with regard to cartels which existed under Regulation 17.[132] However, this

correspond almost literally to Art 81(1) and (3). See M Lutz, 'Schwerpunkte der 7. GWB-Novelle' (2005) 55 *Wirtschaft und Wettbewerb* 718, 719. (On the 7. GWB-Novelle in general see also R Bechtold, 'Die Entwicklung des deutschen Kartellrechts seit der 7.GWB-Novelle (Juli 2005 bis Oktober 2007)' (2007) 60 *Neue Juristische Wochenschrift* 3761). A similar move has been made by the Austrian legislator. Under the new cartel act (KartG 2005), the substantive cartel provisions of the Austrian law are now largely, albeit not fully, harmonised with Community law. See J Barbist, 'Austria Goes Europe—Major Reform in the Austrian Competition System' (2005) 26 *European Competition Law Review* 611, 611–12.

[130] See Vervaele, above n 91, 806.

[131] See paras 29 and 30 of the judgment in *Fischer* (above n 52). The position of the ECtHR, excluding that the *ne bis in idem* principle could be satisfied by a reduction of the second penalty, is strongly supported by Advocate General Ruiz-Jarabo Colomer in *Italcementi* (at para 96 of his opinion, above n 49) as '[t]hat principle is not a procedural rule which operates as a palliative for proportionality when an individual is tried and punished twice for the same conduct, but a fundamental guarantee for citizens'. *Contra* apparently C Kerse and N Khan, *EC Antitrust Procedure* (London, Sweet & Maxwell, 5th edn, 2005), 7-074–7-075, who submit that the set-off rule developed by the ECJ in *Walt Wilhelm* will also apply where more than one NCA enforce Community competition law with regard to the same facts 'provided fines are not imposed twice for exactly the same conduct'. What is meant with 'exactly the same conduct', however, remains unclear. Moreover, where the current conduct is not the same, there would be no need to apply the set-off rule as the *ne bis in idem* principle would not preclude a second sanction anyway.

[132] Para 11 of the judgment in *Walt Wilhelm*, above n 59. Mestmäcker and Schweitzer, above n 63, §21 para 34. See also Eilmansberger, above n 92, 54, who emphasises that it was not the obligation to take into account the earlier sanction, but the possibility of having parallel procedures and dual sanctions (under Community and national law) which the ECJ accepted in view of the special division of powers between the Commission and the NCAs. Only as a consequence of this dualism was the obligation to set off the fines established on grounds of justice and equity. Eilmansberger criticises the CFI on this account which, in *Archer Daniels* (paras 99–100, above n 76) seemingly misinterpreted *Walt Wilhelm* (above n 59) by finding that an obligation to take into account earlier fines could not be accepted in relation to third countries because there exists no such special division of jurisdiction between the Community and third states.

argument no longer seems valid where both authorities involved have the power to apply the same substantive rules and thus share the same competence. As the Commission has repeatedly stated, the allocation of cases under Regulation 1/2003 is a matter of dividing the accruing work, not one of attributing competence. Therefore, *Walt Wilhelm* does not support the view that multiple national proceedings under Article 81 or 82 EC regarding the same facts are permissible.

Secondly, the fact that the ECJ apparently felt an urge to give way to 'a general requirement of natural justice'[133] in order to mitigate the effect of dual sanctions in favour of the parties concerned seems to indicate that it was not at ease with the consequences resulting from its own interpretation of Regulation 17 and the coexistence of national and Community competition law.[134] That the ECJ, as a last resort, had to turn to such an argument in order to re-establish the overall fairness of the system, in my view, echoes the weakness of its reasoning. Again, *Walt Wilhelm* cannot be relied upon to justify dual national procedures and sanctions, even if one is set off against the other, where both procedures apply Articles 81 and 82 EC to the same facts.

c. *The* Lysine *and* Graphite Electrodes *Cases*

Neither are the judgments in *Archer Daniel* (lysine cartel) and *Tokai Carbon* (graphite electrodes cartel) pertinent. Those cases concern the parallel application of Community competition law and the competition law of third countries, whereas the present issue is the parallel application of the same set of rules by several NCAs.

Moreover, these decisions are not entirely convincing. As in the *Vitamins* case, *Archer Daniel* and *Tokai Carbon* concern worldwide cartels formed on the basis of global anti-competitive arrangements.[135] Nonetheless, both the Commission and the CFI bluntly refused to even consider more closely the possible application of the *ne bis in idem* principle, arguing that the Commission, on the one hand, and the US and other third country authorities, on the other hand, had applied their antitrust rules only with regard to the effects of the cartel on the respective EU or national territory.[136] In each case, however, the series of acts or course of conduct underlying the infringement of the Community competition rules were regarded as constituting 'a single continuing infringement'.[137] The same series of acts or

---

[133] Para 11 of the judgment in *Walt Wilhelm*, above n 59.

[134] Cf Kuck, above n 39, 692.

[135] See para 567, fourth indent, of the Commission decision in *Vitamins* (above n 82), para 69 *et seq* of the Commission decision in *Lysine* [2001] OJ L152/24 and para 106 of the Commission decision in *Graphite Electrodes* [2002] OJ L100/1.

[136] See above n 82.

[137] Para 106 of the Commission decision in *Graphite Electrodes* (above n 135), para 238 of the Commission decision in *Lysine* (above n 135) and also para 560 of the Commission decision in

course of conduct, it would seem, also formed the basis of the conviction in other jurisdictions. Furthermore, even though the Commission formally based its decision on the assumption that the relevant geographical market comprised the whole of the EEA, it considered the market to be virtually worldwide in scope.[138] These considerations inevitably led to the conclusion that, in case of global cartel arrangements relating to a worldwide product market, the acts underlying the infringement form an indivisible whole.[139] On this basis, the antitrust procedures conducted by the Commission and third countries actually concern offences whose essential elements are largely overlapping, if not identical. In the light of the rulings in *Fischer, Walt Wilhelm* and *Boehringer*, such similarity warrants close consideration of the *ne bis in idem* principle or, at least, the setting-off rule proclaimed by the ECJ.[140]

This assessment cannot be altered by the fact that each authority

Vitamins (above n 82), albeit in the latter case the Commission considered that there were distinct infringements for each of the vitamin products.

[138] See para 69 of the Commission decision in *Vitamins* (above n 82) and para 14 of the decision in *Graphite Electrodes* (above n 135). It is less clear, though, in the *Lysine* case (see para 297 of the decision, above n 135).

[139] Cf para 36 of the judgment in *Van Esbroeck* (above n 55), where the ECJ ruled that 'identity of the material acts' is to be 'understood in the sense of the existence of a set of concrete circumstances which are inextricably linked together'.

[140] See Eilmansberger, above n 92, 54–5 and Ritter and Braun, above n 75, 89 note 600, and 1141. In this context, it should be noted that considerations of natural justice and equity, which in fact led the ECJ in *Walt Wilhelm* to 'create' the setting-off rule, must also be applied in relation to non-member countries (Eilmansberger, above n 92, 53). Cf also Advocate General Geelhoed, who considers that it was the 'territorial overlap' that furnished a valid ground for applying the setting-off rule in *Walt Wilhelm* (see para 50 of his opinion in *SGL Carbon*, above n 119). As concerns the interpretation of the judgment in *Boehringer*, it seems difficult to sustain that the ruling does not imply the existence of a duty, on the part of the Commission, to deduct the earlier sanction inflicted by third countries from the amount of the later fine to be imposed under Community law. Why would the ECJ consider the identity of the offences at issue, if it did not intend to attach any consequences to the (possible) finding that such identity was in fact established? See Roth and Rose, above n 77, para 12-094. The reasoning of the CFI in *Archer Daniels* and *Tokai Carbon* (see above n 76), in my view, is evasive and not compelling. However, on appeal, the CFI's ruling in *Archer Daniels* (above n 122) has been confirmed by the ECJ. More recently, the ECJ has also upheld the CFI's finding regarding double jeopardy in the *Graphite Electrodes* cases (see the judgment in *SGL Carbon*, above n 119). In *Archer Daniels*, the ECJ held that the fines imposed by the Commission, on the one hand, and by non-member countries, on the other, sought to sanction the implementation of the cartel in different territories and that the relevant facts were therefore not identical (paras 68–72 of the appeal judgment, above n 122). The ECJ, in particular, rejected the argument that the Commission took account of the worldwide turnover of the appellants in calculating the fine and, for this reason, should have deducted the amounts already paid to the US and Canadian authorities and calculated on the basis of the turnover in those countries. In the court's view, 'the worldwide turnover was used only to determine the relative size of the undertakings concerned in order to take account of the effective capacity of those undertakings to cause significant damage' (para 74 of the appeal judgment). This is a formalistic and hardly convincing argument. By considering in its calculation the offenders' worldwide turnover, the Commission effectively also takes into account the turnover generated outside the EU and thus the profits resulting from the cartel activities in non-member countries (see also below n 141). There is consequently at least a substantial overlap of the relevant facts.

contends to impose sanctions in respect of the effects of the cartel only in its own territory.[141] The existence of an infringement of Article 81 EC does not require any effects to have actually materialised on the market if the relevant agreement or concerted practices clearly have an anti-competitive aim.[142] Therefore, the anti-competitive arrangement or conduct which qualifies as agreement or concerted practice within the meaning of Article 81 and, as such, marks the existence of an antitrust violation (*Tatbestands-mäßigkeit der Handlung*) must be distinguished from the effects actually or potentially resulting therefrom.[143] In other words, penalties are applied,

---

[141] See, eg para 773 of the *Vitamins* decision (above n 82). Interestingly, the Commission's method for setting the fine can also be understood as indicating just the contrary. This was particularly obvious in the fining policy practiced until 1998, when the Commission still used to calculate fines as a percentage of an undertaking's annual (worldwide) turnover in the products concerned. Wils, above n 47, 422. The methods applied from 1998 until recently were not based on turnover percentages, but instead used a lump sum as the starting point for the fine. However, under the 1998 Guidelines on the Calculation of Fines, the turnover still served as an important element in evaluating the effective economic capacity of offenders and thus in determining the overall amount of the fine (see para 1.A of the 1998 Guidelines). Indeed, from the fact that the Commission assessed the relative importance of each of the offenders in the *Vitamins* case on each relevant market 'on the basis of their respective *worldwide* product turnover' (para 681 of the decision in *Vitamins*, above n 82 (emphasis added)), a US commentator deduces that the Commission really considered 'the worldwide cartel overcharge' when calculating the fine. See C Sprigman, 'Fix Prices Globally, Get Sued Locally? US Jurisdiction over International Cartels' (2005) 72 *University of Chicago Law Review* 265, 285. See also Soltész and Marquier, above n 4, 105. In other words, by using worldwide proceeds as a reference, the Commission effectively takes account not only of the EU-wide, but also the global effects of a cartel. *Contra* ECJ on appeal in *Archer Daniels*, para 74 (above n 122). It must be noted that, in 2006, the Commission revised its guidelines for setting fines. Under the new terms, the basic amount of the fine will be determined by reference to the value of sales of goods or services to which the infringement relates within the EEA (see paras 12 and 13 of the 2006 Guidelines on the Calculation of Fines). However, para 18 of the same guidelines provides that, where the geographic scope of an infringement extends beyond the EEA and the sales within the EEA do not properly reflect the weight of the undertaking concerned, the Commission may use the undertaking's share of the larger (worldwide) market as a factor to determine the individual sales value which, in turn, serves as reference for the basic amount. Also under the 2006 Guidelines on the Calculation of Fines, worldwide proceeds are thus at least indirectly taken into account.

[142] This is established case law since Joined Cases 56 and 58/64 *Consten and Grundig v Commission* [1966] ECR 299, 342 (English special edition). Soltész and Marquier, above n 4, 105. See also Roth and Rose (eds), *Bellamy and Child. European Community Law of Competition* (Oxford, Oxford University Press, 6th edn, 2008), para 2.075 and Schröter *et al*, above n 61, 223, para 92 and 259, para 139 (with further references).

[143] See Klees, above n 3, 1226; Eilmansberger, above n 92, 54–5, who points out that the effects of a cartel are only relevant to determine jurisdiction, but are not in itself the reason that a fine is imposed. This also seems to be the approach in US antitrust law. See Sprigman, above n 141, 273, who notes that '[i]t is the price-fixing agreement itself, and not the individual "transactions", that is unlawful', ie the acts by which the fixed prices are applied and the anti-competitive agreement is ultimately implemented are not a requisite for the finding of an antitrust offence. Admittedly, differentiating between the offence and its effects will be more difficult where the illegal conduct does not consist of a restrictive agreement, but of concerted practices. However, concerted practices can also have as their object the restriction of competition and the unlawful acts (eg exchange of sensitive business data) and their effects, ie the impact of those acts on the actual price formation, can be distinguished. And the market behaviour of the companies resulting from the concertation is still distinct from the effects, if

first and foremost, for the acts which give rise to the relevant infringements, not for the (economic) effects of the offence on the market.[144] Moreover, the effects of, and thus the harm inflicted by, a worldwide cartel on a particular national market are not independent from the effects on other markets.[145] Against this background, it seems difficult to break down the continuing illegal action, on the basis of its effects, into different offences that can then be prosecuted and punished separately in different jurisdictions.[146] Moreover, it is debatable whether the amount of fines can be calculated exactly in relation to the effects of the illegal conduct in a specific territory (eg as a proportion of the difference between the cartel prices and the prices that would have prevailed in the absence of the cartel). In practice, a precise quantification of the financial gains arising from the illegal cartel activity is not feasible.[147] The relevant territorial effects will rather be used as a more general element of consideration in the assessment of the fine which is also evident from the Commission practice.[148] Overlaps are thus not excluded.

The rule against double jeopardy commonly applies only within the same jurisdiction. Moreover, excluding multiple prosecution and punishment of worldwide cartels in different jurisdictions may be politically undesirable as each state seeks to enforce its own rules in order to maintain an effective level of deterrence.[149] Since there is no guarantee that other

---

any, of that behaviour on the market. See Schröter *et al*, above n 61, 258, para 138; Roth and Rose, above n 142, para 2.050.

[144] See Wils, above n 4, 146. *Contra* apparently ECJ in *Boehringer* (above n 49), para 6. The amount of the penalty may depend inter alia on the economic effects, if any, that the illegal conduct actually had. The reason is that the sanction must be proportionate to the gravity of the infringement, which, in turn, is determined, inter alia, by reference to the actual impact on competition, ie the concrete effects on the market, including the scope of the market affected and the harm suffered by the economy. This shows, however, that the effects of a cartel are just one of various criteria applied in calculating the fine, but not the reason why a penalty is imposed at all. See s 1.A of the 1998 Guidelines on the Calculation of Fines and paras 19–23 of the 2006 Guidelines on the Calculation of Fines. See also the opinion of Advocate General Ruiz-Jarabo Colomer in one of the appeals against the judgment of the CFI in the *Cement* cases, notably C–204/00 P *Aalborg Portland v Commission* [2004] ECR I–123, paras 98–101.

[145] Sprigman, above n 141, 276, wrote with regard to the global vitamins cartel that: 'harm inflicted on US markets cannot be "independent" of foreign harm. The domestic harm would not have occurred but for the globalization of the cartel.' Effects thus also appear to be indivisible.

[146] Or, to use the Commission's own words, it would be 'artificial to sub-divide the individual actions into separate infringements as it is clear that the actions were undertaken in the context of an overall common plan pursuing the same anti-competitive purpose' (para 237 of the decision in *Lysine*, above n 135).

[147] See C Ryngaert, 'Zaak C–289/04, Showa Denko KK t. Commissie, "Grafietelektroden"' (2006) 54 *Sociaal-Economische Wetgeving* 441, 442; Advocate General L Geelhoed in his opinion in Case C–289/04 P *Showa Denko v Commission* [2006] ECR I–5859, para 57. See also W Wils, 'Optimal Antitrust Fines: Theory and Practice' (2006) 29 *World Competition* 183, 207.

[148] See paras 12, 13 and 18 of the 2006 Guidelines on the Calculation of Fines and further above n 141.

[149] See Schoneveld, above n 47, 446, in relation to the extended jurisdiction of US courts in international cartel matters.

countries' sanctions are sufficiently deterrent, the efficiency of a state's cartel policy could be put at peril by the strict application of the double jeopardy rule at the international level.[150] At the same time, however, national antitrust rules and concepts, combined with the extraterritorial application of these rules, do not fit world markets. Enforcement of national competition rules against non-national participants in global cartels may even be perceived as illegitimate.[151]

Whether firms are indeed deterred ultimately depends on the applicable as well as the applied sanctions.[152] In theory, the goal of guaranteeing an effective deterrent can be achieved by enforcement through a single authority provided it has the power to impose sufficiently large fines or other forms of severe punishment which effectively dissuade potential (re)offenders. Coordinating sanctions in international cartel matters may involve significant complexities and challenges;[153] however, such bureaucratic difficulties, it is submitted, are not a valid reason for denying legal and natural persons a priori the benefit of the fundamental principle *ne bis in idem* or at least mitigation of the sanction through application of the setting-off rule. Moreover, one might argue that enforcement by a single authority reduces the extent of coordination required.

Globalisation of cartel matters and the problem of multiple enforcement of antitrust rules against worldwide cartels are relatively new phenomena which deserve closer attention and probably more innovative solutions.[154] Indeed, the persuasiveness of the decisions in *Vitamins*, *Lysine* and *Graphite Electrodes* would have benefited had the Commission and the CFI discussed more extensively the scope and implications of the rule against

---

[150] Ryngaert, above n 147, 443. Waiving unilaterally the state's (sovereign) right to punish violations of the domestic laws would certainly be considered unacceptable where such waiver is not based on the principle of reciprocity. See B Kotschy, 'L'application du principe non bis in idem aux ententes internationales—point final dans une discussion trentenaire?' (2006) *Revue du Droit de l'Union Européenne* 712, 721–2.

[151] Cf E Fox, 'International Antitrust and the Doha Dome' (2003) 43 *Virginia Journal of International Law* 911, 924. Fox even speaks of double illegitimacy where national antitrust rules exempt export cartels and are thus indifferent to harm caused to non-domestic consumers, but at the same time disregard the interest of foreign sovereigns by attempting to penalise anti-competitive conduct taking place abroad (eg import cartels); *idem*, 920.

[152] Each fine has the dual purpose of punishing the relevant illegal conduct and being exemplary at the same time. Para 97 of the opinion of Advocate General Ruiz-Jarabo Colomer in *Aalborg Portland* (above n 144).

[153] Schoneveld, above n 47, 435. Fox proposes the adoption, at global level, of a kind of framework directive laying down the basic substantive antitrust rules (which every state would then implement in its own terms) coupled with certain choice of law principles so that, in the case of global antitrust matters, a given set of national rules 'would be applied to the entire affected geographic area as if the entire affected area were within the borders of the nation whose law is applied'. Fox, above n 151, 928.

[154] See, eg Fox, above n 151, 925–32, who suggests a system of global antitrust governance, ie world rules (which could take different forms, such as a complete antitrust regime, framework measures, or a co-operative protocol), with the WTO as the competent forum.

double jeopardy, including the case law of the ECtHR as well as the judgment in *Boehringer*, which in my view implies a setting-off obligation.

4. HR Convention—Construing Article 4 Protocol No 7

It has already been pointed out that antitrust proceedings under Articles 81 and 82 EC, whether conducted by the Commission or by an NCA, for the purposes of Article 4 Protocol No 7 are of a criminal nature.[155] Furthermore, for Article 4 Protocol No 7 to apply, there must be identity of three elements: namely, the offender, the subject matter (comprising the relevant facts and the offence)[156] and the state concerned must all be the same in both relevant proceedings.

The requirement that the state which intends to put the person on trial a second time must be the state in which he or she was convicted or acquitted first clearly seems to exclude the applicability of the *ne bis in idem* principle to parallel proceedings conducted by two or more NCAs of different Member States. However, the case law of the HR Courts supports the view that, having regard to the current level of European integration and the special regime for the enforcement of Community competition law, Article 4 Protocol No 7 is amenable to a dynamic interpretation. The notion 'under the jurisdiction of the same State' could then be interpreted as referring to the EU at large at least insofar as the implementation of Regulation 1/2003 is concerned.

a. Identity of the Offender

The identity of the offender is beyond doubt where both proceedings are directed against the same company or companies. The requirement is obviously also fulfilled where the same individual(s) are subject to multiple proceedings.

With regard to the question of whether undertakings, as opposed to natural persons, can invoke the *ne bis in idem* principle, it must be noted that there is no case law explicitly applying Article 4 Protocol No 7 to

---

[155] See above section I.A.1.b.

[156] On the question of whether the '*idem*' relates to the offence or the facts, ie whether there must be identity of the charge or only the factual circumstances, see Van Den Wyngaert and Stessens, above n 49, 789–94. It is submitted here that both elements, the offence and the underlying facts, must be taken into consideration in order to determine whether there is an '*idem*'. This follows from the case law of the ECtHR, which, eg in *Fischer*, at several instances notes that the applicant was tried twice 'on the basis of one act' (see paras 25 and 29 of the judgment, above n 52) and in addition considers whether the relevant offences were sufficiently similar (see also above n 55 and below nn 163, 169 and 251). The solution suggested by Van Den Wyngaert and Stessens, above n 49, 793, namely that *ne bis in idem* does not apply where the offences are not same, no matter that the relevant facts may be identical, and that 'harsh consequences . . . can be softened' through the *Anrechnungsprinzip*, is clearly contrary to Art 4 Protocol No 7 as interpreted by the ECtHR in *Fischer*. See above n 131.

companies. However, in view of the existing judgments and opinions applying other provisions of the ECHR, particularly Article 6 ECHR, to legal entities,[157] in can be concluded that, as a matter of principle, companies can avail themselves of the guarantees of the ECHR to the extent that, in terms of content, these guarantees are susceptible to protecting not only human beings, but also corporations.[158] Since companies, whether or not they are incorporated, can be subject to criminal proceedings and thus can incur criminal sanctions within the meaning of the HR Convention in the same way as natural persons, there is little doubt that they are also afforded protection under the *ne bis in idem* guarantee of Article 4 Protocol No 7.[159]

Problems regarding the identity of the parties only arise if, for instance, the first procedure concerns one or more companies while the second is conducted against individuals (eg staff members of the companies punished first). In this case, the proceedings relate actually to different entities, notably legal persons on the one hand and natural persons on the other, no matter whether the individuals concerned are employees of the undertakings which were prosecuted first. Therefore, in this scenario, there is no identity of parties and double jeopardy issues do not arise.[160] Similarly, the *ne bis in idem* guarantee obviously does not apply if several Member States prosecute and punish different (corporate) members of the same cartel.

Exceptionally, the *ne bis in idem* guarantee may apply where the first procedure concerns not an incorporated firm, but an individually owned company or partnership without legal personality. In such a situation, the individual owner or owners would be personally liable for the fines imposed on the firm and would thus face double jeopardy if, in a second procedure, they were charged as individuals.[161]

---

[157] See the judgment of the ECtHR in *Lilly France* (judgment of 14 October 2003, application no 53892/00) and the opinion of the HR Commission in *Société Stenuit* (above n 24) concerning the application of Art 6 ECHR to antitrust procedures conducted against companies incorporated under French law as well as the opinion of the HR Commission in *M&Co* (above n 25), which implicitly recognises the applicability of Art 6 ECHR in favour of a limited partnership. See further the judgment of the ECtHR in *Sociétés Colas and others v France* Reports/Recueil 2002-III, 105 (regarding Art 8 ECHR) and the judgment of 26 April 1979 in *Sunday Times v UK* Publications Series A no 30 (regarding Art 9 ECHR).

[158] Application to corporations would be excluded, for instance, where the right to marry (Art 12 ECHR) or the respect for family life (Art 8 ECHR) are concerned.

[159] De Mello, above n 12, 617–18, who maintains this view on the basis of a broad interpretation of the term 'victim' in the former Art 25 (now Art 34) ECHR. Cf also Schwarze, above n 96, 519 with regard to the fair trial guarantees of the EU Charter.

[160] Zuleeg, above n 18, 462; Schwarze and Weitbrecht, above n 63, 154 para 27; Nazzini, above n 4, 10.

[161] See Zuleeg, above n 18, 462. This seems to be a fairly hypothetical case though. In approximately 100 decisions in which the Commission imposed fines under Reg 17, it apparently never addressed a single decision to an individual in his capacity as operator/owner of a business having no legal personality. See Wils, above n 47, 413. The reason is probably that, in particular because of the *de minimis* concept, but also in view of the effect-on-trade criterion, a

Finally, the question arises of whether the *ne bis in idem* guarantee protects undertakings that are members of an industry or trade association against prosecution where that association has already been prosecuted and punished. Under Community law, the members of an association can be held liable for the payment of a fine imposed on the association unless they have not implemented the relevant decision of the association and have distanced themselves from it or were not even aware of its existence.[162] On this basis, they would indirectly be punished twice if the double jeopardy rule did not apply. On the other hand, an association and its members are different legal entities. Thus, formally, there is no identity of the offender. That the member undertakings, de facto, may have to pay a fine twice results from the fact that they usually finance the activities of that association by means of monetary contributions and, as a consequence, are also liable for the payment of its debts. In other words, members do not pay double fines, but simply contribute to the association's funds in order to cover its liabilities. It is therefore submitted that the *ne bis in idem* guarantee does not provide protection where parallel proceedings are conducted against an association of undertakings and its members.

b. Identity of the Subject Matter—The Idem

The wording of Article 4 Protocol No 7 further requires that the second trial concerns 'an offence for which he [the accused] has already been finally acquitted or convicted'. The term 'offence' seems to embrace a factual and a legal element.[163]

(1) Identity of Facts. A double jeopardy issue only arises where a person is prosecuted twice in relation to the same act or conduct. In other words, there must be identity of the facts which form the basis of the trial. By contrast, where several (unrelated) acts are concerned, Article 4 Protocol No 7 does not shield the person who committed these acts from being subject to two different trials for each of the acts and the offences which they constitute.[164]

firm must have a certain financial size and volume of business in order for its activities to come within the ambit of the Community competition rules. It is quite uncommon for companies of this magnitude not to be incorporated.

[162] See Art 23(4) of Reg 1/2003.

[163] By contrast, Art 54 Schengen Convention has a different wording that seems to exclude any relevance of the legal qualification of a wrongdoing. Accordingly, the ECJ has held that the existence of an *idem* under Art 54 Schengen Convention depends exclusively on the identity of the concrete facts. See above n 55.

[164] An example would be a person who drives under the influence of alcohol from to A to B and, a couple of months later, again drives a car under the influence of alcohol from A to B. Even if at both occasions the person uses the same car and the same route, both incidents would constitute separate acts (*Realkonkurrenz*) and could be prosecuted consecutively in two different procedures.

The question of whether the incidents at hand resulted from the same conduct has apparently never been an issue in the cases decided by the ECtHR. In both *Gradinger* and *Fischer*, for example, the ECtHR seems to have taken it for granted that causing a traffic accident, which leads to the death of a person, while driving a car under the influence of alcohol constitutes a single act.[165] In the *Oliveira* case, driving on a road covered with snow, sliding, colliding with another vehicle and causing injury to the driver of that vehicle was equally regarded as one act.[166] This means that an activity which stretches over a certain period of time and has various consequences can be considered a single act.[167] The decisive point seems to be the natural contiguity between the various elements which are inextricably linked together and thus form a single act.[168]

(2) Significance of the Legal Qualification. The term 'offence' clearly has a legal dimension. The ECtHR has given a broad interpretation to this notion and ruled that the *ne bis in idem* principle is not confined to cases where a person is tried twice for nominally the same offence, but also extends to cases where a person is tried twice for different offences based on one act if 'such offences have the same essential elements'.[169]

Similarly, Advocate General Ruiz-Jarabo Colomer, in *Italcementi*, opined that the *ne bis in idem* principle applies where the relevant procedures, based on the same facts, aim to protect 'a single legal right'.[170] In the Advocate General's view, it is thus not the formal denomination of a wrongdoing, but rather the legal value underlying the provision, that is decisive in determining the identity of two charges within the meaning of the double jeopardy rule. This approach is close, if not identical, to the one adopted by the ECtHR, which would need to consider the legal interest protected when analysing the essential elements of an offence.[171]

---

[165] See paras 7–9 and 55 of the judgment in *Gradinger* (above n 10) and paras 7–9 and 29 of the judgment in *Fischer* (above n 52).

[166] See paras 7 and 26 of the judgment in *Oliveira* (above n 52).

[167] This does not mean that the same conduct or act cannot constitute various offences (*Idealkonkurrenz/concours idéal d'infractions*) which, moreover, is not contrary to Art 4 Protocol No 7. In such a case, the greater penalty usually absorbs the lesser one. See para 25 of the judgment in *Fischer* (above n 52) and para 26 of the judgment in *Oliveira* (above n 52).

[168] See also the definition given by the ECJ in *Van Esbroeck* for the term 'the same acts' in Art 54 Schengen Convention: 'identity of the material acts, understood in the sense of the existence of a set of concrete circumstances which are inextricably linked together' (para 36 of the judgment; above n 55). Similarly, the ECJ has accepted that a series of acts can constitute a single infringement of Art 81 or 82 EC if they are closely linked, eg because the undertakings act in the pursuit of one economic aim or the various factual elements are part of an overall common plan. See above Chapter 3, n 274.

[169] Para 25 of the judgment in *Fischer* (above n 52). See further above section I.C.1.

[170] Para 89 of his opinion in *Italcementi* (above n 49).

[171] Eilmansberger, above n 92, 53. See, however, the different approach adopted in relation to Art 54 of the Schengen Convention by both Advocate General Ruiz-Jarabo Colomer himself and the ECJ in *Van Esbroeck* (above n 55). These findings are, however, essentially based on the

The above considerations and arguments concerning the identity of the offence seem to be of only marginal relevance here since, in our hypothetical case, the NCAs enforce a uniform set of substantive rules, notably Article 81 or 82 EC. In other words, they apply nominally the same provisions. There can thus be no doubt about the identity of the offence.[172]

However, critics will argue that there is no identity of the protected right or interest since each NCA will impose fines only for the effects of the infringement on its respective territory. There is namely a common understanding among the members of the Network that no competition authority will impose sanctions for effects outside its own territory.[173] Alternatively, opponents of the applicability of the double jeopardy rule will contend, for the same reason (ie that each NCA only considers the domestic effects), that multiple national sanctions, albeit relating to the same unlawful agreement or conduct, are not based on the same facts.[174]

It is submitted that these arguments cannot be accepted. First, as has been pointed out earlier, the effects of a breach of Article 81 or 82 EC are irrelevant for the finding of an infringement.[175] The geographically limited perspective of the NCAs cannot hide the fact that the territorial scope of the effects is not a substantive, but purely an incidental, element in that it has no impact on the existence of a violation of the law and does not even change its nature.[176] It only has relevance for the intensity of the wrongdoing and may thus influence the magnitude of the fine or other

consideration that, unlike the ECHR and the EU Charter, both of which employ the term 'offence', the Schengen Convention adopts a purely fact-based approach with regard to the denomination of the '*idem*'. See above n 55.

[172] Soltész and Marquier, above n 4, 105. See also Bourgeois, above n 123, 316 and para 157 of the opinion of Advocate General Sharpston in *Gasparini* (above n 93): 'In such circumstances, the legal interest protected is, by definition, already established by the EC competition rules; and is one and the same for the whole Community.'

[173] Paulis and Gauer, above n 4, para 19; Arhold, above n 3, 133. Cf also K Ritter in U Immenga and E-J Mestmäcker (eds), *Wettbewerbsrecht, Band 1. EG/Teil 2. Kommentar zum Europäischen Kartellrecht* (Munich, CH Beck, 4th edn, 2007), Art 5 VO 1/2003, para 7, who submits that NCAs may only adopt the measures which are necessary to restore competition in the domestic territory.

[174] Paulis and Gauer, above n 4, paras 44–5. They rely on the judgment of the ECJ in *Boehringer* (para 6 of the judgment, above n 49), where the ECJ noted: 'In any case the argument whereby the action penalized consists in the cartel agreement itself and not in its application cannot be accepted.' This approach has been followed by the CFI: see, eg the judgments in *Archer Daniels* (above n 76, paras 101–3) and *Tokai Carbon* (above n 76, para 143). The ruling of the CFI in *Archer Daniels* has been confirmed on appeal by the ECJ (see above n 122). The ruling in *Tokai Carbon* was not appealed. See also Kotschy, above n 150, 717, who argues that the ECJ (in *Archer Daniels*) defined the *idem* in such a way that there will be no *idem* (of facts) in competition matters where the respective proceedings relate to the territories of different states.

[175] See above section I.D.3.c.

[176] The geographically limited perspective of the NCA seems to be inspired by the effects doctrine. However, this doctrine is relevant only for the question of whether a particular NCA has jurisdiction over the matter, but in principle has no bearing on the scale of the penalties to be applied once jurisdiction has been ascertained. See Arhold, above n 3, 135 note 55.

punishment.[177] Therefore, where the same anti-competitive agreement or conduct is prosecuted and penalised concurrently by two or more NCAs, the relevant facts underlying the infringement are identical no matter whether, in each procedure, the effects of the infringement are taken into account only to a limited (not overlapping) extent, namely insofar as they occurred on the domestic territory of the respective NCA.[178]

Secondly, the approach of the ECJ in *Walt Wilhelm*, whereby concurrent proceedings and concurrent sanctions under two sets of rules (Community and national competition law) are permissible because each set of rules considers cartels from a different angle,[179] is not transferable to the present case. It is doubtful whether this position is at all sustainable. Advocate General Ruiz-Jarabo Colomer has been quite firm on this point and clearly stated that, in his view, the Commission and the NCA protect the same legal right even if one applies Community law and the other national law because, within the common market in which free competition must be ensured, one cannot speak of 'separate spheres, the Community sphere and the national spheres as though they were watertight compartments'. The Advocate General further noted:

> Both sectors seek to protect free and open competition in the common market, one contemplating it in its entirety and the other from its separate components, but the essence is the same.[180]

---

[177] See para 94 of the opinion of Advocate General Ruiz-Jarabo Colomer in *Italcementi* (above n 49).

[178] Ritter and Braun, above n 75, 80. They see as the only possible exception a matter concerning several distinct national markets. However, in such a case, there would either be separate agreements or practices for each of the national markets and thus no '*idem*' or, where the conduct on all relevant markets is covered by a common purpose and an overall plan, the continuing acts implementing this plan together would constitute a single (indivisible) infringement which would again lead to an identity of the underlying facts. See also Wils, above n 4, 146; Soltész and Marquier, above n 4, 105.

[179] Para 3 of the judgment in *Walt Wilhelm*, above n 59.

[180] Para 91 of the opinion of Advocate General Ruiz-Jarabo Colomer in *Italcementi* (above n 49) and further at para 97, note 71 of the same opinion, which reads: 'I disagree with that approach since, as I have just pointed out, the national authorities and the Commission supervise the same values when they punish the same conduct by applying competition law, whether national or Community.' *Accord* P Cramer and P Pananis in Loewenheim *et al*, above n 3, §82 para 87 and Eilmansberger, above n 92, 53. Eilmansberger even submits (in note 39 of his article) that *Walt Wilhelm* has actually been overruled by the judgment of the ECJ in *Aalborg Portland*. According to Eilmansberger, while the ECJ rejected the applicability of the ne bis in idem rule on account of the particular circumstances of that case, notably because the national and Community procedures concerned different fact situations, it implicitly acknowledged, as a matter of principle, the applicability of the ne bis in idem principle in competition matters pursued by the Commission and a Member State (see paras 338–40 of the judgment in Joined Cases C–204, 205, 211, 213, 217 and 219/00 P *Aalborg Portland and others v Commission* [2004] ECR I–123). However, in Joined Cases C–295–298/04 *Manfredi v Loyd and others* [2006] ECR I–6619, para 38, the ECJ recently reiterated the phrase from *Walt Wilhelm* that Community competition law and national competition law consider restrictive practices from different points of view.

These latter considerations relate to the parallel application of Community and national competition law.[181] They are all the more true if both 'sectors' involved (notably the NCAs conducting parallel proceedings) apply Community competition law,[182] albeit each of them considering predominantly a 'separate component' of the common market (the domestic territory). Moreover, the ECJ in *Walt Wilhelm* explicitly noted that

> the acceptability of a dual procedure of this kind follows in fact from the special system of the sharing of jurisdiction between the Community and the Member States with regard to cartels.[183]

However, this system has been changed drastically by Regulation 1/2003 introducing the *exception légale* with regard to Article 81(3) EC, creating a system of parallel competences and defining quite precisely the relationship between national and Community competition law.[184] On this basis, the considerations of the ECJ in *Walt Wilhelm* no longer appear to be valid.

In any event, it would certainly not be justifiable to follow the approach developed by the ECJ in *Walt Wilhelm* in relation to cases where both authorities apply Community competition law, ie the same set of substantive rules. In this scenario, it is evident that the repeated procedures would protect the same legal right.[185]

While it may be true that, in each individual case, the acting NCA will mainly be concerned with safeguarding and/or restoring effective competition within its own territory, it cannot be denied that the primary purpose of the Community rules applied in both proceedings is to eliminate obstacles to trade between Member States, thereby maintaining free and undistorted competition in the common market in accordance with Article

---

[181] The Advocate General's point of view is clearly supported by the fact that the majority of the Member States have national competition laws which are closely modelled upon Arts 81 and 82 EC. Many have even copied the EC Treaty provisions almost literally—just leaving out the interstate trade element (compare eg Art 81(1) EC with Art 2 §1 of the Belgian Competition Act (WEM 2006) ,which reads: 'Sont interdits, sans qu'une décision préalable soit nécessaire à cet effet, tous accords entre entreprises, toutes décisions d'associations d'entreprises et toutes pratiques concertées qui ont pour objet ou pour effet d'empêcher, de restreindre ou de fausser de manière sensible la concurrence sur le marché belge concerné ou dans une partie substantielle de celui-ci et notamment ceux qui consistent à: . . .') Even Germany—probably the Member State with the longest history of an 'independent' national competition regime—has recently (7. GWB-Novelle) given up its traditional distinction between horizontal and vertical agreements and introduced legislation which repeats Art 81(1) EC almost verbatim (see s 1 GWB). Likewise, all new Member States which acceded to the EU since 2004 have national competition provisions that are very similar or even identical to Arts 81 and 82 EC. K Cseres, 'The Interface between EC Competition Law and the Competition Laws of the New Member States: Implementation or Innovation?' in D Obradovic and N Lavranos (eds), *Interface between EU Law and National Law* (Groningen, Europa Law Publishing, 2007), 203, 220–1. See also above n 129.
[182] Arhold, above n 3, 137.
[183] Para11 of the judgment in *Walt Wilhelm*, above n 59.
[184] See Art 3 of Reg 1/2003.
[185] Soltész and Marquier, above n 4, 105. See also para 157 of the opinion of Advocate General Sharpston in *Gasparini* (above n 93), quoted above at n 172.

3(g) EC.[186] Each NCA applying Community competition law must pursue this objective since Member States are under a legal duty to comply with Regulation 1/2003 and to ensure that Articles 81 and 82 EC are effectively enforced.[187] The identity of the goal pursued is pivotal. In this respect there may be no difference in result between a procedure conducted by the Commission and a national procedure.[188]

Finally, as will be argued below, NCAs can and should also penalise offenders with regard to the effects that their illegal agreement or behaviour produces in the territory of other Member States.[189] This is a prerequisite for the efficient enforcement of the Community competition rules and thus fully in line with the spirit of Regulation 1/2003, which promotes the objective that cases should be handled, to the largest extent possible, by a single authority.[190] If an NCA does not take account of the

---

[186] Arguably, the following line of arguments will still be sustainable after the Reform Treaty, as approved by the European heads of state or government during the informal Lisbon summit in October 2007 ('Lisbon Treaty'), will have entered into force. While the maintenance of a system of undistorted competition will no longer form one of the Union's (explicit) fundamental fields of activity (subpara (g) will be deleted from the current Art 3(1) EC), Protocol No 6, which is to be annexed to the EU Treaty, states that the contracting parties consider that the term 'internal market as set out in Article 3 of the Treaty on European Union includes a system ensuring that competition is not distorted'. It is very likely that this protocol will play an important role for the interpretation of the new Art 3 EU Treaty (see Lenaerts and Van Nuffel, above n 86, 17-061), in particular since the protocols will be an integral part of the Treaties (see Art 51 of the amended EU Treaty) and, after ratification, thus will bind the Member States in the same way as actual Treaty provisions (J Steenbergen, 'Het mededingingsbeleid en het Verdrag van Lissabon' (2008) 56 *Sociaal-Economische Wetgeving* 136, 138). Moreover, Art 3(1)(b) of the amended EC Treaty (which will be renamed 'Treaty on the Functioning of the European Union') confers exclusive competence on the Union for establishing the competition rules necessary for the functioning of the internal market. Therefore, in legal terms, it seems that little will change. Steenbergen, *ibid*, 143. For a more sceptical view, however, on the future role of competition in the EU under the Lisbon Treaty, see A Weitbrecht, 'From Freiburg to Chicago and Beyond—the First 50 Years of European Competition Law' (2008) 14 *European Competition Law Review* 81, 88. For a pessimistic view, see A Riley, 'The EU Reform Treaty and the Competition Protocol: Undermining EC Competition Law' (2007) 28 *European Competition Law Review* 703, 706–7, who believes that the proposed amendment will be detrimental to the further development of EC competition law.

[187] Soltész and Marquier, above n 4, 106, and Kuck, above n 39, 694. See also E Paulis, 'Latest Commission Thinking and Progress on the Modernisation of Regulation 17' in X, *European Competition Law: A New Role for the Member States/Droit européen de la concurrence: un nouveau rôle pour les Etats membres* (Brussels, Bruylant, 2001), 15, 17, where he unequivocally states: 'It [decentralised application] requires a culture where National Competition Authorities, like the Commission, when applying EC law, behave like authorities which take care of the Community interest . . .' Cf also para 91 of the opinion of Advocate General Ruiz-Jarabo Colomer in *Italcementi* (above n 49), quoted above.

[188] Cf J Temple Lang, 'European Community Constitutional Law and the Enforcement of Community Antitrust Law' in B Hawk (ed), *1993 Proceedings of the Fordham Corporate Law Institute* (New York, Juris Publishing, 1994), 525, 584, who suggests that NCAs should be regarded as 'arms of the Community when they apply EC antitrust law (just as every national judge is also a Community law judge) . . .'

[189] In other words, the common understanding between the NCAs is not consistent with the spirit of Reg 1/2003 and Art 10 EC. See below section II.D.

[190] Soltész and Marquier, above n 4, 106; Arhold, above n 3, 133. The objective of having each case treated, if possible, by a single authority is laid down in recital 18 of Reg 1/2003 and restated in para 7 of the Network Notice.

effects of an infringement outside its own territory, this may lead to underpunishment, with the consequence that one or more other NCAs must repeat the procedure in order to be able to impose additional fines and thus achieve, through the summation of the individual sanctions, an adequate punishment.[191] If, on the other hand, all effects are sanctioned by a single national decision, there is a priori no need and thus no justification for parallel procedures.[192]

c. Single State or Jurisdiction Requirement

A literal reading of Article 4 Protocol No 7 suggests that the guarantee prohibits double punishment and double prosecution only where they occur within the same state. The *ne bis in idem* principle under Article 4 Protocol No 7 is thus meant to operate only within the domestic legal order of each of the contracting states. This is also evident from the case law of the HR Court.[193] This approach seems to exclude prima facie the application of the *ne bis in idem* principle to parallel competition proceedings conducted by the NCAs of different Member States.

However, regarding the effectiveness of the guarantees of the HR Convention, on the one hand, and the state of integration of the Community, in particular with respect to competition law enforcement, on the other, a dynamic interpretation of the ECHR and a rethinking of the concept of territoriality might be required. This would allow the legal scope of Article 4 Protocol No 7 to be expanded so as to cover any repetition of proceedings in the EU as a whole. For the purposes of Article 4 Protocol No 7, the EU would then have to be considered as constituting a unitary jurisdiction.

(1) Dynamic Interpretation. The ECtHR has consistently held that the HR Convention is 'a living instrument which must be interpreted in the light of present-day conditions'.[194] It goes without saying that the same must hold true for the Protocols to the HR Convention. This means that developments that have taken place since the HR Convention or its Protocols were drafted and signed must be taken into consideration when interpreting their provisions.

Moreover, the ECtHR has demonstrated in the past its willingness to take into account the particularities of the Community legal order and to have due regard to the fact that the Community is not a traditional interna-

---

[191] Wils, above n 4, 146. Soltész and Marquier, above n 4, 105 are sceptical about this argument, however.
[192] On this basis (but only on this basis), Paulis and Gauer, above n 4, para 44, agree that the *ne bis in idem* guarantee constitutes a bar to parallel procedures conducted by other NCAs.
[193] Vervaele, above n 94, 102.
[194] See, eg para 39 of the judgment of 18 February 1999 in *Matthews v UK* Reports/Recueil 1991-I, 251.

tional organisation but a supranational organisation *sui generis*.[195] At the same time, however, the ECtHR is committed to ensure that Member States do not evade their obligations under the ECHR simply because they have transferred certain sovereign powers to the Community.[196] Thus, when interpreting Community law, the ECtHR does so from the perspective of the objectives of the HR Convention.[197] This is entirely in line with another guiding principle, also resulting from established case law of the ECtHR, notably that the HR Convention 'is intended to guarantee rights that are not theoretical or illusory, but practical and effective'.[198]

A good example of this Community-oriented or even Community-friendly approach of the ECtHR is the judgment in *Matthews*, in which the court held that the European Parliament could be conceived as the legislature (in Gibraltar and the Community) within the meaning of Article 3 Protocol No 1.[199] As the ECtHR noted at the outset,

> [t]he mere fact that a body [the European Parliament] was not envisaged by the drafters of the Convention cannot prevent that body from falling within the scope of the Convention.

It further recalled that 'the word "legislature" . . . has to be interpreted in the light of the constitutional structure of the State in question'[200] before analysing carefully the relevant provisions of Community law and, more particularly, the new role and accrued powers of the European Parliament in the legislative process since the Maastricht Treaty.[201] In this context, the HR Court also made allowance for the supremacy principle, which it

[195] The *sui generis* nature of the Community legal order has been acknowledged by the ECJ as early as 1963 in its judgment in *van Gend & Loos* [1963] ECR 1, 12. See also Opinion 1/91 of the ECJ regarding a draft agreement for the creation of the European Economic Area (EEA), [1991] ECR I–6079, para 1, third subpara: 'The Community treaties established a new legal order . . .'

[196] See above Chapter 3, nn 236 and 237 and accompanying text.

[197] I Canor, 'Primus inter pares. Who is the ultimate guardian of fundamental rights in Europe?' (2000) 25 *EL Rev* 3, 13.

[198] See, eg para 34 of the judgment in *Matthews*, above n 194.

[199] Art 3 Protocol No 1 provides that the contracting states must 'hold free elections at reasonable intervals . . . which will ensure the free expression of the opinion of the people in the choice of the legislature'.

[200] Paras 39 and 40 of the judgment in *Matthews*, above n 194. Evidently, in 1950, ie before the existence of the European Communities, the drafters of the HR Convention could not have been thinking of the European Parliament. Also Protocol No 1 which was signed by the six old Member States (Belgium, France, Germany, Italy, Luxemburg, Netherlands) already in 1952, was actually drafted at a time when the European Parliament had not yet been created. At the same time, however, the peoples of a large number of European countries were still deprived of free elections. See para 3 of the joint dissenting opinion of Judges Freeland and Jungwiert in the *Matthews* case (n 194). (Both Judges dissented as they considered that the European Parliament, lacking an essential power in their view intrinsic to the notion of 'legislature', notably the right to initiate legislation, could not properly be regarded as a legislature in the true sense, in any event not with regard to Gibraltar.)

[201] This analysis necessitated an appraisal of the internal structure of the EU and the essential elements of the division of powers between the different institutions. Canor, above n 197, 13.

described as an 'inherent aspect of EC law'[202], and the *sui generis* nature of the European Community'.[203] Finally, the ECtHR concluded that 'the European Parliament represents the principal form of democratic, political accountability in the Community system'.[204] Further,

[It] is sufficiently involved in the specific legislative processes leading to the passage of legislation under Articles 189b and 189c of the EC Treaty, and is sufficiently involved in the general democratic supervision of the activities of the European Community, to constitute part of the 'legislature' of Gibraltar for the purposes of Article 3 of Protocol No 1.[205]

Another illustrative case is *Pafitis v Greece*,[206] a matter concerning the question of whether the preliminary ruling procedure under Article 234 (ex Article 177) EC should be taken into account to assess whether the length of proceedings in a national court of a Member State must be regarded as excessive and thus contrary to the fair trial guarantee of Article 6 ECHR, which entitles everyone to 'a hearing within a reasonable time'. In the relevant case, the competent Greek court had stayed proceedings pending the outcome of its reference to the ECJ. Several matters had therefore been prolonged by more than two and a half years.[207] The ECtHR was in fact very brief on the question of whether that prolongation was a material factor in determining the duration of the national court proceedings for the purposes of Article 6 ECHR. Observing that only delays imputable to the relevant judicial authorities could be taken into account, the ECtHR noted that it could not

... however, take this period into consideration in its assessment of the length of each particular set of proceedings: even though it may at first sight appear relatively long, to take it into account would adversely affect the system instituted by Article 177 of the EEC Treaty and work against the aim pursued in substance in that Article.[208]

---

[202] Para 41 of the judgment in *Matthews*, above n 194.
[203] *Ibid*, para 48.
[204] *Ibid*, para 52.
[205] *Ibid*, para 54.
[206] Judgment of the ECtHR of 26 February 1998 in the case of *Pafitis and others v Greece* Reports/Recueil 1998-I, 436.
[207] Between 1986 and 1994, the applicants in the *Pafitis* case had brought several civil actions against the Bank of Central Greece challenging the lawfulness of certain capital increases of that bank. The proceedings were delayed and adjourned numerous times for various reasons, inter alia on account of a one-year strike by the members of the Athens bar and because the Greek district court seized with these matters in 1993 had referred some questions to the ECJ for a preliminary ruling and reserved its decision until delivery of the ECJ's judgment. The ECJ gave its ruling only in 1996.
[208] Para 95 of the judgment in *Pafitis* (above n 206). On the terminology, see R Lawson, 'Europees Hof voor de Rechten van de Mens, Pafitis t Griekenland' 1998 *Sociaal-Economische Wetgeving* 220, 222, who contends that, by switching from 'attributable to the state' to 'imputable to the relevant judicial authorities', the ECtHR really narrowed down the

This judgment may be criticised for not considering whether the Member States' responsibility to ensure expeditious trials as required by Article 6 ECHR continues after they have transferred to the ECJ the sole competence to interpret and annul Community legislation.[209] This question should also have been discussed in view of the later findings in *Matthews*, and the answer would probably have been in the affirmative. On this basis, and contrary to the implicit findings of the court in *Pafitis*, the lengthy procedure of the preliminary reference to the ECJ under Article 234, which significantly contributed to the delays of the national proceedings, may have been attributable to Greece after all and thus should have been taken into consideration.[210]

However, despite this criticism, like the *Matthews* case, *Pafitis* tends to underpin the readiness of the ECtHR to adopt a dynamic approach and make allowance for the specificities of Community law.[211] And there are other examples of such a Community-friendly interpretation of the ECHR by the ECtHR.[212] In *Piermont v France*,[213] the applicant, a German environmentalist and member of the EP, had been expelled from French

responsibility of the contracting states: where courts cannot control the delays, the relevant state automatically cannot be held liable even though the situation may in fact be due to the state's negligence in not properly organise the court system. In my view, the words 'imputable to the relevant judicial authorities' (para 93) were used by the ECtHR as equivalent to the term 'attributable to the state'. In para 96 of *Pafitis*, the ECtHR noted that the delays caused by the lawyers' strike could not be 'attributed to the State' and finally concluded (in para 97) that both the delays due to the preliminary reference and those linked to the lawyers' strike were beyond the jurisdiction of the domestic courts and would therefore be disregarded.

[209] Cf Lawson, above n 208, 222–3, with references to a number of earlier judgments of the ECtHR. Lawson argues that, according to the case law cited, the Contracting Parties have the duty to organise their legal systems in such a way that they comply with the requirements of Art 6 ECHR. This would apply, *mutatis mutandis*, to the organisation of the reference procedure set up by the Member States under Art 234 EC. Criticism is also voiced by Peukert, above n 25, 1118–19, who doubts that the system instituted by Art 234 could be adversely affected by applying the requirement of speediness to it, since that system, like Art 6 ECHR, aims itself at improving judicial protection.

[210] The judgment in *Pafitis* implies that Members States cannot be held liable for the fact that, due to an ever increasing caseload of the Community courts, preliminary rulings are very lengthy procedures causing considerable delays to national court proceedings. This finding seems to be contrary to the reasoning of the ECtHR in *Matthews*, where it considered that '[t]he Convention does not exclude the transfer of competences to international organisations provided that Convention rights continue to be "secured". Member States' responsibility therefore continues even after such a transfer' (para 32 of the judgment, n 194). Similar considerations can be found in the judgment of the ECtHR of 18 February 1999 in the case of *Waite and Kennedy v Germany*, Report/Recueil 1999-I, 393, para 67.

[211] This is the positive aspect of the judgment in *Pafitis*, which pays deference to the autonomy of the Community legal order and honours the fact that preliminary reference rulings have an essential role to play within the Community system. Lenaerts and Desomer, above n 89, 205.

[212] A number of further examples are given by B Daiber, 'Durchsetzung des Gemeinschaftsrechts durch den EGMR?' (2007) 42 *Europarecht* 406, who contends that the ECtHR not only reviews indirectly Community law but, by interpreting the ECHR in the light of Community law, sometimes even goes as far as virtually ensuring its effective enforcement (*idem* 408–9).

[213] Judgment of 27 April 1995 in the case of *Piermont v France* Publications Series A no 314.

Polynesia (one of France's overseas territories, or OTs) and banned from re-entering that territory because of her participation in an anti-nuclear demonstration during the local election campaign. The ECtHR found that this interference with the applicant's right to freedom of expression, guaranteed by Article 10 of the ECHR, could not be justified on the basis of Article 16 of the ECHR, which authorises the signatories of the ECHR to impose restrictions on the political activity of aliens. While rejecting the argument based on her European citizenship because, at the time in question, the Treaties did not yet recognise such citizenship, the ECtHR held that the applicant's

> possession of the nationality of a member State of the European Union and, in addition to that, her status as a member of the European Parliament do not allow Article 16 (art. 16) of the Convention to be raised against her, especially as the people of the OTs take part in the European Parliament elections.[214]

In other words, for the purposes of Article 16 of the ECHR, the applicant could not be considered an 'alien' despite the fact that she did not have the nationality of the contracting state which expelled her. This interpretation of the term 'alien' indicates that the Community cannot, in any circumstances, be subdivided into its constituent parts, ie the single Member States, but must be regarded as a unified whole.

In a more recent judgment, the ECtHR took a similar approach towards the interpretation Article 8 of ECHR, taking into account the freedom of movement guaranteed by Community law and, more particularly, the obligations imposed on Member States as regards the right of entry and residence of nationals of other Member States, and found a violation of the HR Convention right.[215] The applicant in that case, Ms Mendizabal, was a Spanish national who had been residing in France since 1975. From 1990, she had repeatedly been given residence permits for short periods of three months only. The ECtHR recalled that Article 8 of the ECHR did not guarantee the right of persons to enter and reside in a state the nationality of which they do not possess or the right to obtain a particular type of residence permit there,[216] but then considered that the case in question warranted a different approach:

> La Cour considère toutefois qu'il s'impose, dans la présente requête, d'avoir une approche différente : en effet, le point essentiel tient à la qualité de ressortissante communautaire de la requérante, qui . . . tirait directement du droit communautaire . . . le droit de séjourner en France et de se voir délivrer une

---

[214] *Ibid*, para 64.
[215] Judgment of 17 January 2006 in the case of *Mendizabal v France*, Application no 51431/99, para 68.
[216] *Ibid*, paras 65 and 66.

« carte de séjour de ressortissant d'un Etat membre de la communauté économique », d'une durée de cinq ans.[217]

There is thus clearly a certain interdependence and interaction between the Community and the ECHR legal spheres. They can no longer be regarded as two separate, hermetically closed systems.[218] Not only is the ECHR a source of inspiration for the Community courts when developing and interpreting (the general principles of) Community law and a key reference for the protection of fundamental rights within the sphere of Community law,[219] but likewise Community law can influence the scope and meaning of the guarantees of the ECHR[220] as well as the conditions for lawful state interference with these rights.[221]

It should also be noted that the possibility of applying a dynamic interpretation of international legal instruments such as the ECHR is implicitly foreseen by the Vienna Convention on the Law of Treaties. To the extent that the dynamic approach aims at furthering the objectives of the ECHR in that it secures a kind of *effet utile* of the fundamental rights enshrined therein, it is in conformity with Article 31(1) of the Vienna Convention, which lays down general rules of interpretation.[222] The article provides that, while having regard to the ordinary meaning of the words, a treaty shall be interpreted 'in the light of its object and purpose'. Moreover, Article 31(3)(c) of the Vienna Convention allows for any additional rules of international law applicable as between the parties to be taken into account. This would include other international agreements concluded between them, such as the EC Treaty and the EU Treaty.[223]

---

[217] Para 67 of the judgment in *Mendizabal* (above n 215).

[218] J-P Puissochet, 'La Cour européenne des droits de l'homme, la Cour de justice des Communautés européennes et la protection des droits de l'homme' in Mahoney, F Matscher, H Petzold and L Wildhaber (eds), *Protection des droits de l'homme: la perspective européenne/ Protecting Human Rights: The European Perspective. Mélanges à la memoire de/Studies in memory of Rolv Ryssdal* (Köln, Carl Heymanns Verlag, 2000), 1139, 1140; Callewaert, above n 96, 266.

[219] K Lenaerts, 'Respect for Fundamental Rights as a Constitutional Principle of the European Union' (2000) 6 *Columbia Journal of European Law* 1, 9.

[220] The latter fact is illustrated not only by *Matthews* and *Pafitis*, but also by the ruling in *Goodwin*, where the ECtHR discussed the institution of marriage in order to assess the scope of the fundamental right to marry as guaranteed in Art 12 of the HR Convention. In this context, it referred to the corresponding article of the EU Charter, which, in contrast to the provision of the HR Convention, does not contain any reference to 'men and women'. On this basis, the ECtHR concluded that the very essence of the applicant's right to marry had been impaired because the relevant provisions of UK law denied the applicant, a post-operative male-to-female transsexual, legal recognition of her changed gender, thereby depriving her of the right to marry a man, ie a person of her present opposite sex (paras 100–1 of the judgment in *Goodwin*, above n 97).

[221] As illustrated inter alia by the judgment in *Piermont* cited above (n 213). See also Daiber, above n 212, 410 *et seq.*

[222] A Potteau, 'Observations à l'arrêt Matthews c le Royaume-Uni' (1999) 10 *Revue Trimestrielle des Droits de l'Homme* 873, 891.

[223] See Potteau, *ibid*, 892; A Berramdane, 'La Cour européenne des droits de l'homme juge du droit de l'Union européenne' (2006) *Revue du Droit de l'Union Européenne* 243, 256. Cf also

Finally, interpreting Article 4 Protocol No 7 ECHR as recognising, in the framework of Community competition law enforcement, an international *ne bis in idem* principle is not excluded by the fact that, according to the intentions of the contracting parties, the application of the principle at the international level is to be governed by other international instruments.[224] Indeed, there are a number of international conventions concluded under the auspices of the Council of Europe (eg relating to extradition or validity of criminal judgments) which include an international *ne bis in idem*. However, these conventions deal with the problem of double jeopardy only within a classic intergovernmental setting. In the case of extradition, for instance, double jeopardy may provide a valid ground for a state to refuse co-operation, ie not to extradite a person, in order to prevent further prosecution elsewhere. The prohibition thus applies solely in the case of co-operation between two sovereign states with regard to a particular matter, ie where there is a requesting state and a requested state. The international *ne bis in idem* enshrined in these conventions therefore produces protective effects merely *inter partes* rather than *erga omnes*,[225] and does not establish an individual right against double jeopardy in transnational matters.[226] The scope and objective of those conventions is thus entirely different from Article 4 Protocol No 7 with the interpretation advocated here. Moreover, the application of *ne bis in idem* in the context of other conventions is sometimes limited by broad exceptions so that, in practice, protection of the individual by these conventions is rather fragmentary.[227]

The case law of the ECtHR thus permits a dynamic interpretation of the notion 'within the jurisdiction of the same state' which has due regard to the particularities of Community (competition) law.

(2) Unity of the EU Legal Order and the Wording of the ECHR. There are a number of elements supporting the view that, within the EC/EU, the territoriality concept must be redefined which would imply that the relevant 'state' territory within the meaning of Article 4 Protocol No 7 must be defined as the EU in its entirety. For the purposes of Article 4 Protocol No 7, the EU would thus form a single unitary jurisdiction.

European integration has led to the emergence of 'a unique international

---

para 150 of the judgment of the ECtHR of 30 June 2005 in *Bosphorus Hava Yollari Turizm v Ireland*, Application no 45036/98.

[224] See para 27 of the Explanatory Report to Protocol No 7 to the ECHR, available at http://conventions.coe.int/Treaty/EN/Reports/HTML/117.htm.

[225] The prohibition is applicable only to the state that passed judgment. Therefore, other states remain free to extradite and, moreover, can prosecute and punish the person where they get hold of him/her without extradition. H Schermers, 'Non Bis In Idem' in F Capotorti, C-D Ehlermann, J Frowein and others (eds), *Du droit international au droit de l'intégration. Liber Amicorum Pierre Pescatore.* (Baden-Baden, Nomos, 1987), 601, 609.

[226] Vervaele, above n 94, 104.

[227] See Schermers, above n 225, 609.

construction'.[228] In an integrated, borderless Europe, in which all EU citizens enjoy the right of free movement, it seems unacceptable that a person can be prosecuted or even punished repeatedly for the same act under the jurisdiction of different Member States, in particular where the double jeopardy is due to the fact that the person has exercised its right of free movement.[229] The fundamental principles of legal certainty and justice, it would seem, require that an offender in the Union, after having been tried and convicted (or acquitted) once in one Member State, does not have to fear for ever to be repunished or reprosecuted for the same act in another Member State.[230]

These considerations are largely based on aspects of humanity[231] and the idea that individuals must not be deterred from moving freely within the Union.[232] This would imply that they predominantly apply to natural persons as opposed to legal persons. However, one should not forget that economic integration has always been a motor for and cornerstone of a more extended and intensified European integration, starting from the objective of establishing a common market, as proclaimed at the very beginning of the integration process by Article 2 of the former EEC Treaty, and later the internal market envisaged in Article 14 EC (ex Article 7a EC), finally culminating in the wish to create 'an ever closer union among the peoples of Europe' (Article 1 EU) which, in the medium term, should become 'an area of freedom, security and justice' (Article 2 EU).[233]

EC competition law, in turn, aims to promote such economic integration by creating a level playing field and thus is one of the cornerstones of the Union's legal order.[234] Therefore, economic operators, including corporations and other legal persons which exercise or benefit from the economic freedoms guaranteed by the EC Treaty (free movements of goods, services and capital, freedom of establishment), it is submitted, cannot be deprived

---

[228] The formulation of Advocate General Sharpston in para 81 of her opinion in *Gasparini* (above n 93).

[229] See V Mitsilegas, 'The Constitutional Implications of Mutual Recognition in Criminal Matters in the EU' (2006) 43 *CML Rev* 1277, 1300.

[230] Schermers, above n 225, 602 and 604. The very existence of Art 54 Schengen Convention confirms the general acceptance of his view, at least as regards the Schengen area.

[231] See Schermers, above n 225, 604: 'it would be inhuman to leave offenders for ever in fear'.

[232] This also appears to be the main reason for introducing Art 54 Schengen Convention, a provision clearly linked to the abolition of borders and the free movement rights. See para 33 of the judgment in van *Esbroeck* (above n 55) and para 32 of the judgment of the ECJ in Case C–496/03 *Miraglia* [2005] ECR I–2009.

[233] And, indeed, M Fletcher, 'Extending "Indirect Effect" to the Third Pillar: the Significance of Pupino?' (2005) 30 *EL Rev* 862, 875, considers this goal of creating an area of freedom, security and justice a 'cross-pillar objective', ie an objective which is not strictly limited to the third pillar, but is valid in all three pillars.

[234] See para 36 of the judgment in Case C–126/97 *Eco Swiss v Benetton* [1999] ECR I–3055: '. . . Art 85 [now Art 81] of the Treaty constitutes a fundamental provision which is essential for the accomplishment of the tasks entrusted to the Community and, in particular, for the functioning of the internal market'.

the protection which is afforded to individuals. If these economic operators are subject to multiple prosecution and punishment for the same offence in several Member States, their confidence in the rule of law, a principle explicitly recognised in Article 6(1) EU as one of the principles on which the Union is founded, would be undermined. On this basis, it seems only fair that legal persons are protected against double jeopardy in the same way as natural persons with regard to whom this protection seems to be an indispensable element of European integration.

Moreover, a system such as that of concurrent jurisdiction established by Regulation 1/2003, by which the authorities of different states (plus the Commission) are vested with equal powers to enforce the same supranational provisions vis-à-vis private parties, was not and could not have been envisaged by the drafters of Article 4 Protocol No 7, which was opened for signature in 1984. Here, the analogy to the *Matthews* case becomes evident. The drafters were naturally focusing on repeated prosecution of an individual under the criminal laws of the same state.[235] This also explains why the explanatory memorandum to Protocol No 7 states that the international application of the principle is 'adequately covered' by a number of international conventions, such as the European Convention on Extradition of 1957. However, such international instruments are not an appropriate means of regulating the relations between the Member States with regard to the implementation of the Community's antitrust rules, which is characterised by special features and, moreover, does not belong to the sphere of classic criminal law enforcement which these international conventions intend to address.

All these considerations[236] could lead to the conclusion that the Union should be considered as a single area with a unitary jurisdiction rather than an accumulation of 27 separate jurisdictions of its Member States.[237] On this basis, Article 4 Protocol No 7 would exclude a Member State from putting a person—natural or legal—on trial again for the same offence for which the person has already been prosecuted and convicted (or acquitted) in another Member State. This interpretation could, however, also be considered as *contra legem* in that it runs counter to the express wording of Article 4 Protocol No 7. By including the requirement 'under the juris-

---

[235] Since that time, globalisation has changed the world in many respects and has also 'internationalised' crimes. Typical examples are the increased emergence of organised crime, money laundering and international trafficking in persons. The number of criminal matters involving a foreign element has thereby supposedly risen significantly so that the question of an international *ne bis in idem* is certainly much more topical now than it was in 1984. See Van Den Wyngaert and Stessens, above n 49, 779 and 803–4.

[236] Further arguments for a unitary approach specifically in the field of Community competition law are set out below (below section I.D.5).

[237] See Mitsilegas, above n 229, 1309. See also the quotes from the decisions of a regional Czech court cited by M Petr, 'The Ne Bis In Idem Principle in Competition Law' (2008) 29 *European Competition Law Review* 392, 396.

diction of the same State', the drafters of the Protocol clearly wanted to exclude the possibility that the ECtHR could interpret the provision as also covering double prosecution or punishment under different legal orders.[238] On the other hand, the existing level of integration in the EC, which constitutes a legal order *sui generis*, and the fact that the Union is striving to become an area of freedom, security and justice, were obviously far from the drafters' minds in 1984. At the same time, it is acknowledged that the ECHR is a living instrument the interpretation of which must be adapted to the present circumstances. Nonetheless it is doubtful whether, even in the context of Community (competition) law enforcement, the ECtHR would be ready to adopt such a progressive interpretation of the term 'under the jurisdiction of the same State' as suggested above.

5. Ne Bis in Idem as a 'Propriae Naturae' Principle Within Community Law

The ECJ has explicitly acknowledged that *ne bis in idem* is a fundamental principle of Community law.[239] Arguably, *ne bis in idem* could therefore be understood to form an autonomous or *propriae naturae* principle of Community law like many other general principles developed by the ECJ. Irrespective of the uncertainties surrounding the legal value of the EU Charter and the question of whether Article 54 Schengen Convention could be applied in the present context, the scope and exact meaning of this key concept would thus be defined, refined and developed by the Community judicature.[240] This would allow the definition of the principle to be adapted to the particular features of the supranational context in which it is applied.[241]

This approach appears justified bearing in mind that the Community (EC) is not just an international organisation in the traditional sense, but is a supranational organisation which has created a legal order *sui generis*[242] governing the relations between its members and envisaging a dynamic integration, in both economic and legal terms, of its Member States.[243] The EU, together with the two European Communities, ie the EC and the European Atomic Energy Community, certainly constitutes a unique inter-

---

[238] Cf Schermers, above n 225, 608.

[239] Para 59 of the judgment in *PVC II* (above n 22).

[240] Para 80 of the opinion of Advocate General Sharpston in *Gasparini* (above n 93).

[241] See para 81 of the opinion of Advocate General Sharpston in *Gasparini* (above n 93). On this basis, it is submitted, the *ne bis in idem* principle, albeit being inspired by the constitutional traditions common to the Member States (see Art 6(2) EU), is not strictly dependent on them. The concept, including its territorial ambit, can therefore be adjusted to the requirements of the specific legal context in which it is invoked.

[242] Para 12 of the judgment in *van Gend & Loos*, above n 195.

[243] See Lenaerts and Van Nuffel, above n 86, 1-013. The Community legal order does not only govern the relations between the Member States, but also their relations with the Community institutions, the relations between those institutions and the relations between the Community and individuals.

national construction.[244] Moreover, since the Maastricht Treaty, the process of European integration has gained a more political dimension. The Member States are called upon to create an ever-closer union.[245] The most important element in this context is probably the acknowledgment that the Union is founded on the principle of 'the rule of law' (*Rechts-staatlichkeit*),[246] which underpins the particular importance of the legal (as opposed to economic or political) aspects of the integration process.

a. The Basic Idea

If *ne bis in idem* thus is an autonomous principle of European law, not only Article 4 Protocol No 7, to which the ECJ specifically referred in *PVC II*, would serve as a legal reference: inspiration should also be drawn from Article 50 EU Charter and Article 54 Schengen Convention, which can be regarded as an indication of a trend, within the Union's legal order, to afford the concept a transnational dimension and protect persons against double jeopardy within the territory of the EU as a whole.[247] The approach to regard *ne bis in idem* as an autonomous principle would also seem to imply that the interpretation given to the concept must be same in all areas of Community/Union law.[248] This would require reconciliation of the apparent inconsistency in the case law of the ECJ regarding the definition of the *idem*.[249] In *Van Esbroek*, the ECJ held that, with regard to Article 54 Schengen Convention, the only relevant criterion is 'the identity of the material acts',[250] while, in the context of EC competition law, in the *Cement* case (*Aalborg Portland*) the ECJ ruled that the principle would not apply unless there also was a 'unity of the legal interest protected'.[251]

---

[244] See para 81 of the opinion of Advocate General Sharpston in *Gasparini* (above n 93).

[245] See Art 1(2) EU Treaty: 'This Treaty marks a new stage in the process of creating an ever closer union among the peoples of Europe . . .'

[246] Art 6(1) EU. Also with regard to the EC, it has explicitly been recognised that it is 'a Community based on the rule of law' (*Rechtsgemeinschaft*). See Judgment of the ECJ in Case 294/83 *Les Verts v European Parliament* [1986] ECR 1339, para 23.

[247] Due the *propriae naturae* character of the principle under EC/EU law, the fact that *ne bis in idem* as recognised in the domestic legal orders of most Member States only covers purely national situations is not a hindrance to extending, in the supranational context of Community competition law enforcement, the scope of the principle so as to cover also transnational situations. See also above n 241.

[248] Para 101 of the opinion of Advocate General Sharpston in *Gasparini* (above n 93). According to Sharpston, this conclusion follows from Art 6 EU being applicable to all pillars under the EU Treaty.

[249] *Ibid*, para 156.

[250] See para 36 of the judgment in *Van Esbroeck* (above n 55).

[251] Para 338 of the judgment in *Aalborg Portland* (above n 180) reads: 'As regards observance of the principle *ne bis in idem*, the application of that principle is subject to the threefold condition of identity of facts, unity of offender and unity of the legal interest protected.' The difference in approach between *Van Esbroeck* and *Cement* can probably be explained by the fact that Art 54 Schengen Convention uses the words 'for the same acts', while both Art 4 Protocol No 7 and Art 50 EU Charter, which may have inspired the ECJ in the *Cement* case, employ the

On the other hand, it must be recalled that, while the Maastricht Treaty of 1992 establishing the European Union created a legal link between the Communities and supplementary policies and forms of co-operation of the EU, these subsist as different integration paths.[252] The pillar structure of the Union's legal order has also been maintained following the Amsterdam Treaty of 1997.[253] The Communities continue to exist as separate organisations. While the same institutions (Commission, EP, Council) exercise the powers conferred upon them by the various Treaties, these powers remain different under each Treaty.[254] And not only competences, but also procedures and legal instruments differ depending under which Treaty or in which field of the Union's policies (eg PJCC or common foreign and security policy) the institutions act.[255] Moreover, (legislative) powers vary depending on the applicable legal basis even within a particular pillar, for instance under the EC Treaty.[256]

As a consequence of these differences in powers and legal instruments, the degree of integration is not the same in all fields of Community/EU law. There can be little doubt that the legal integration of the Member States (through the existence/adoption of common legal rules or through approximation or harmonisation of national laws) is much more advanced in some areas than in others.[257] This 'state of the Union', it is submitted, justifies the viewpoint that the definition of a fundamental principle can be adapted to the particular conditions in the field in which it is applied. Moreover, Article 50 EU Charter only lays down the minimum standard.[258] Thus, a

---

term 'for the same offence'. See also above nn 128 and 171. For an attempt to reconcile both approaches see para 157 of the opinion of Advocate General Sharpston in *Gasparini* (above n 93).

[252] Lenaerts and Van Nuffel, above n 86, 3-012 and 3-014.

[253] *Ibid*, 3-019.

[254] *Ibid*, 1-011, describe this phenomenon as 'organisational unity and functional diversity'.

[255] This includes differences in the powers of the Community courts to exercise supervision on the legality of the acts adopted and compliance of the Member States with the relevant provisions of Community/Union law. See Lenaerts and Van Nuffel, above n 86, 3-015.

[256] *Ibid*, 5-013.

[257] An example is consumer protection, where national laws have gradually become more and more aligned through various harmonisation directive and regulations. In the field of competition law, Member States even apply a uniform set of rules (Arts 81 and 82 EC), albeit in addition to the existing national rules. However, the latter have de facto also been largely approximated. By contrast, (substantive) criminal law still remains an almost absolute prerogative of the national legislator. Under Art 31 EU, only certain common actions regarding judicial co-operation in criminal matters can be taken. However, the exact scope of this provision is disputed. See Mitsilegas, above n 229, 1304–6.

[258] It is therefore permissible that, under Art 54 of the Schengen Convention, a purely factual approach has been taken as regards the definition of the *idem*, while in competition matters the ECJ (probably inspired by Art 50 EU Charter, which refers to the 'same offence' and thus seems to require an *idem crimen*; see above n 251) takes into account the legal interest protected, as the first approach (*idem factum*) is more favourable from the perspective of the accused. See Wasmeier and Thwaites, above n 117, 574.

fundamental principle does not necessarily have the same content and scope across all fields of EC/EU law.[259]

b. The Features of the New Enforcement System under Regulation 1/2003

On this basis, *ne bis in idem*, as a fundamental principle of Community law, must be defined, at least in the field of EC competition law enforcement,[260] as having a transnational scope and thus protecting legal and natural persons in the Community as whole. The special features of this area of law justify considering the Community, in this context, as a single legal order or unitary jurisdiction.[261]

First, it is important to note that we are dealing here with the parallel application, by several NCAs, of the same substantive rules, notably Article 81 or 82 EC. In my view, this is a crucial element clearly distinguishing this case from all of the case law available to date in which the Community Courts considered the possible application of the *ne bis in idem* principle.[262] The relevance of this differentiation has implicitly been acknowledged by the ECJ in its recent judgment on appeal in *Graphite Electrodes*. The ECJ notably considered the (in)applicability of the *ne bis in idem* principle in international cartel matters where, parallel to the Community, non-member states exercise their powers. As it noted,

> [i]n that regard, the exercise of powers by the authorities of those States responsible for protecting free competition under their territorial jurisdiction meets requirements specific to those States. The elements forming the basis of other States' legal systems in the field of competition not only include specific aims and objectives but also result in the adoption of *specific substantive rules* . . .[263]

It then went on to state that,

---

[259] *Contra* Sharpston, at para 103 of her opinion in *Gasparini* (above n 93): 'I cannot see how a core element of a fundamental principle could vary substantially in its content depending on whether *ne bis in idem* is being applied under Art 54 of the CISA or generally as a fundamental principle of Community law' (for example, within competition law). On the other hand, Sharpston also notes, at para 81 of the same opinion, that the definition should be 'adapted to the particular features of the supranational context in which it is to apply'.

[260] As concerns the question of whether this criminal law principle is applicable in competition proceedings see above section I.A.1.b.

[261] Obviously, if one adheres to the view of Advocate General Sharpston quoted above at n 259, one could argue that, in view of the explicit wording of Art 54 Schengen Convention (and Art 50 EU Charter) and given the requirement of coherence, *ne bis in idem* in Community/EU law must in any event be considered to apply also in transnational situations. Cf also Fletcher, above n 233, 877, who sees it as one of the significances of the *Pupino* ruling of the ECJ (judgment in Case C–105/03 *Maria Pupino* [2005] ECR I–5285) that it offers a potentially more coherent legal framework for the creation of an area of freedom, security and justice.

[262] With the exception of *PVC II* (above n 22), where the repeated application (after annulment of the first Commission decision) of the same provisions of Community competition law to the same undertakings in respect of the same facts was at issue.

[263] Emphasis added. Para 29 of the judgment in *SGL Carbon* (above n 119).

[o]n the other hand, the legal situation is *completely different* where an undertaking is caught exclusively—in competition matters—by the application of Community law and the law of one or more Member States on competition, that is to say, where a cartel is confined exclusively to the territorial scope of application of the legal system of the European Community.[264]

It follows from these considerations that the distinction between matters involving third countries and matters involving only the EU and its Member States is all the more pertinent where the issue is not—as in *Walt Wilhelm*—the parallel application of different rules (Community and national law), but the multiple application of Community law, ie the repeated application of the same set of substantive rules.

Secondly, one must have regard to the special character of the enforcement system set up by Regulation 1/2003. This system, it is submitted, has three essential features which justify the conclusion that the territories of the Member States form a unitary jurisdiction. These features are: the principle of concurrent jurisdiction; the case allocation rules coupled with the objective to have each case treated by a single authority; and the requirement of close co-operation between the members of the ECN. These elements in fact underpin the *sui generis* nature of the Community.[265]

Taking these three essential elements together, it becomes clear that Regulation 1/2003 has created a decentralised but integrated system whereby each single NCA to which a case is allocated basically replaces the Commission as the enforcement agency for the entire Union. This latter aspect is implied by the fact that cases shall only be allocated to an authority which can effectively bring to an end the infringement.[266] The existence of a case allocation system, albeit one based on non-binding rules, also minimises the risk that the application of the *ne bis in idem* on a Union-wide basis will lead to accidental or even arbitrary results. The allocation principles help to ensure that cases are assigned to an appropriate competition authority which can react adequately to the infringement.[267]

---

[264] Emphasis added. *Ibid*, para 30.

[265] Cf in this context the considerations of the CFI in *Tokai Carbon* (para 136 of the judgment, above n 76), where it held that, in the absence of any specific provision in an international convention or any rule of public international law preventing authorities or courts of different states from prosecuting and punishing the same person for the same facts twice, '[s]uch prohibition could arise today only through very close international co-operation leading to the adoption of common rules'. This is exactly what Reg 1/2003 seeks to establish: common rules and close co-operation between the Member States.

[266] Para 8 subpara 2 of the Network Notice. Allocation to several NCAs shall only take place in exceptional cases.

[267] Cf Commission Green Paper on Criminal Jurisdiction, 3. In that Green Paper, the Commission considers it a prerequisite for the application of the *ne bis in idem* principle in the EU that a system for allocating criminal matters to an appropriate jurisdiction is put in place. And even though the title might suggest something else, the Green Paper on Criminal Jurisdiction deals in fact 'only' with the question of how such an allocation system could be fashioned, while

Moreover, under Articles 81 and 82 EC, each NCA, like the Commission, has to pursue the goal of restoring effective competition in the common market.

> A very original system has thus been created, in which the Commission and the authorities of the Member States . . . in practice jointly safeguard freedom of competition within the Community.[268]

At the same time, Article 13 of Regulation 1/2003 allows other NCAs to suspend or close cases regarding the same facts, thereby promoting the objective of having each case dealt with by a single authority. In such an integrated system, where all authorities are empowered to apply the same substantive law, and which is, moreover, based on close co-operation of the enforcers, it would be simply unacceptable if a person (legal or natural) could be repeatedly subject to prosecution for the same acts.[269]

The requirement that the competition rules shall be applied in close co-operation (Article 11(1) of Regulation 1/2003) is an essential element in the evaluation of the enforcement system in terms of double jeopardy. It is in the context of international co-operation agreements that an international *ne bis in idem* is sometimes accepted.[270] Such agreements generally require a large degree of mutual trust between the signatories and acknowledgement of the functioning of the other parties' criminal justice systems.[271] It is precisely this aspect which strongly militates for a

the issue of *ne bis in idem* as such is addressed only marginally in a short passage at the end of the document (see s 3, 8–9). Interestingly, the mechanism proposed by the Commission for allocating jurisdiction in criminal proceedings is very similar to the system established by Reg 1/2003 and the Network Notice. Notably, the proposal provides, inter alia, for information duties, consultation/discussion between the national bodies concerned in order to determine the 'best placed' jurisdiction and the 'ability to refrain from initiating a prosecution, or to halt an existing prosecution, on the mere ground that the same case is being prosecuted in another Member State' (cf Art 13 of Reg 1/2003). The Commission even submits that it is not necessary to have binding rules at EU level for such arrangements whereby national bodies agree (voluntarily) that one abstains from taking action while another proceeds with the case. See ss 2.1 and 2.2 (pp 4–5) of the Green Paper on Criminal Jurisdiction. The facts that the allocation principles laid down in the Network Notice are non-binding and that there is no formal obligation for NCAs, under Art 13 Reg 1/2003, to close or suspend their proceedings if another NCA is dealing with the same infringement are thus not reasons to deny the applicability of *ne bis in idem* in competition matters on a EU-wide basis. On the Green Paper on Criminal Jurisdiction see further M Fletcher, 'The Problem of Multiple Criminal Prosecutions: Building an Effective EU Response?' (2007) 26 *Yearbook of European Law* 33 (with particular focus on questions regarding the *ne bis in idem* guarantee) and Wasmeier and Thwaites, above n 117, 575–8.

[268] Para 107 of the opinion of Advocate General Tizzano in *Archer Daniels* (n 122).

[269] See para 121 of the opinion of Advocate General Ruiz-Jarabo Colomer in *Gözütok and Brügge* (above n 47). The same view was already expressed in 1987 by Schermers, above n 225, 602.

[270] See the examples provided by Van Den Wyngaert and Stessens, above n 49, 784–6.

[271] Van Den Wyngaert and Stessens, above n 49, 804. See also para 92 of the judgment of the CFI in *Archer Daniels* (above n 76) and paras 119–25 of the opinion of Advocate General Ruiz-Jarabo Colomer in *Gözütok and Brügge* (above n 47), albeit both in relation to the Schengen Convention. The ECJ confirmed the views expressed by the Advocate General in

Community-wide *ne bis in idem*.[272] Co-operation in the ECN takes place 'on the basis of equality, respect and solidarity'. Moreover, the Member States have declared that, despite the existing differences in their enforcement system, they 'nonetheless mutually recognize the standards of each other's system as a basis for cooperation'.[273] This implies a certain degree of mutual trust of the Member States in their enforcement systems. Last but not least, the common 'competition culture' of the Member States, which the Commission has consistently evoked in order to justify its decision to do away with the centralised enforcement system of Regulation 17,[274] comes into play here. There is thus no justification for Member States not respecting and taking into consideration other NCAs' decisions and thus completely denying the effect of *res iudicata*.[275] The *ne bis in idem* principle is just a corollary of this respect and consideration.[276]

Gözütok and Brügge (see para 33 of the judgment, above n 47). There can be no doubt that Reg 1/2003 together with the Network Notice leads to the creation of very close relations between the NCAs.

[272] The importance of the mutual trust element in the considerations of the ECJ in the Schengen cases, which ultimately justify an EU-wide *ne bis in idem*, has also been emphasised by Advocate General Sharpston. However, in her view, mutual trust is not unlimited and does not extend so far as to provide a sensible basis for applying the principle to all national decisions discontinuing criminal proceedings, eg not to those relying, without any substantive assessment of the offence, on a time-bar (see paras 105–9 of her opinion in *Gasparini*; above n 93).

[273] Paras 7 and 8 of the Joint Statement.

[274] See, eg para 4 of the executive summary of the White Paper, 9 of the Explanatory Memorandum and recital 1 of Reg 1/2003. Paulis, above n 187, 23. However, a number of authors have expressed doubts as to whether such a common competition culture is indeed already existent within the Community. *Contra* the assumption that, at this stage, there exists a competition culture in the EU is M Van Der Woude, 'De herziening van het Europese mededingingsrecht en de gevolgen daarvan voor de nationale rechter' (2002) 50 *Sociaal-Economische Wetgeving* 176, 184. See also E Mohr Mersing, 'The Modernisation of EC Competition Law—The Need for a Common Competition Culture' in B Hawk (ed), *1999 Proceedings of the Fordham Corporate Law Institute* (New York, Juris Publishing, 2000), 259, 267, who submits that the emergence of a 'true common competition culture' requires prior alignment of the national antitrust regimes with the Community competition rules.

[275] The conclusion is not invalidated by the fact that the Explanatory Memorandum states on p17 that NCA decisions have no legal effects in foreign Member States as this statement, in my view, only precludes that a national decision is automatically enforceable outside the territory of the NCA which adopted it (see below nn 366 and 367 and accompanying text). However, actively enforcing a foreign decision and (passively) respecting that matters have definitively been settled by abstaining from prosecuting, re-evaluating and punishing again the same infringement, it is submitted, are two different things. The lack of automatic enforceability of NCA decisions in foreign jurisdictions therefore does not preclude that Member States are held to recognise and honour the *res iudicata* effect of decisions adopted by other NCAs.

[276] Para 125 of the opinion of Advocate General Ruiz-Jarabo Colomer in *Gözütok and Brügge* (above n 47). See also Fletcher, above n 87, 773. Moreover, Fletcher (*ibid*, 774) points out that, in the framework of the Schengen Convention, harmonisation or approximation of the national criminal law procedures was not required in order for the *ne bis in idem* rule to become applicable. This argument applies *mutatis mutandis* to the field of EC competition law enforcement where a harmonisation of national procedures has explicitly been considered as unnecessary (see p 12 of the Explanatory Memorandum).

Lastly, it is a general requirement of natural justice, certainly within a given legal system (here the Community system of competition law), to protect persons against being penalised twice on the basis of the same facts:

> It would be inherently unfair and contrary to the principles on which the construction of a United Europe rests if, in order to protect a certain legal principle, a person could be punished in several Member States for committing the same acts.[277]

> De integratie vereist wederzijdse hulp, welke onwaarschijnlijk is zonder wederzijds vertrouwen in de respectieve rechtssystemen en zonder wederzijdse erkenning van beslissingen die zijn gegeven in een waarachtig 'gemeenschappelijk huis' van fundamentele rechten.[278]

It is thus submitted that, for the purposes of Community competition law enforcement, the 27 Member States of the EU form one unitary jurisdiction.[279] In this context, the territorial ambit of the *ne bis in idem* guarantee must therefore be defined as comprising the whole of the EU.[280]

---

[277] Para 58 of the opinion of Advocate General Ruiz-Jarabo Colomer in *Gözütok and Brügge* (above n 47).

[278] Para 61 of the opinion of Advocate General Ruiz-Jarabo Colomer in *van Straaten* (above n 114).

[279] Arguably, the *ne bis in idem* principle could also apply where Community competition law and national competition law are applied in parallel (ie the situation which was at issue in *Walt Wilhelm*). The reason is that the system for the sharing of competences between Community and Member States which prevailed at the time of the judgment in *Walt Wilhelm* has changed significantly. Today, there is a considerable degree of interdependence and integration of Community and national systems for safeguarding competition. Convergence between the systems is increasing steadily. This is not only a result of Reg 1/2003 and its detailed conflict rules, but also of a de facto harmonisation between national and Community rules, as many Member States have modelled their domestic competition laws on Arts 81 and 82 EC. See also above n 122 and the accompanying text.

[280] See Soltész and Marquier, above n 4, 107, and Schwarze and Weitbrecht, above n 63, 155 para 29, who apply a Community law-based *ne bis in idem* principle. Cf also Wils, above n 4, 146 and A Burnside and H Crossley, 'Co-operative Mechanisms within the EU: A Blueprint for Future Co-operation at the International Level' (2004) 10 *International Trade Law & Regulation* 25, 26, who rely on Art 50 EU Charter. Finally, G Dannecker, 'Die Neuregelung der Sanktionierung von Verstössen gegen das EG-Kartellrecht nach der Verordnung (EG) 1/2003 des Rates vom 16. Dezember 2002 zur Durchführung der in den Art. 81 und 82 des Vertrages niedergelegten Wettbewerbsregeln' in Fuchs *et al*, above n 129, 61, 67–8, seems to favour a direct application of Art 54 of the Schengen Convention. *Contra* Petr, above n 237, 395–6, and Advocate General Mayras in *Boehringer* (above n 49), 1294, who had explicitly opined, on the basis of a comparative analysis of the national rules of the then six Member States, that the *ne bis in idem* principle was only valid within a particular legal system. By contrast, Advocate General Ruiz-Jarabo Colomer is of the opinion that the decisive factor is not whether the penalties are imposed under one legal system or under several legal systems (para 56 of his opinion in *Gözütok and Brügge*, above n 47), and he adds that '[t]oday, Advocate General Mayras' position [in *Boehringer*] would be untenable because it conflicts with the wording of Art 54 of the Convention' (para 59 of the opinion). In my view, the provisions of the Schengen Convention cannot be applied directly in the context of EC competition law enforcement. See above section I.D.2.

6. *Types of Decisions that Bar Further Proceedings*

Finally, with regard to competition proceedings, one needs to consider which types of decision can trigger the application of the *ne bis in idem* guarantee. In particular, the question arises whether commitment decisions and non-action decisions equally provide protection against a second procedure under the double jeopardy rule. Since Article 50 EU Charter and Article 4 Protocol No 7 essentially have the same wording and the ECJ also draws inspiration from the ECHR, both provisions and the relevant case law of the ECtHR and the ECJ need to be taken into account.

At the outset, it is important to recall that Article 4 Protocol No 7, Article 50 EU Charter and Article 54 Schengen Convention only apply once the first proceedings have been concluded by a final conviction or acquittal.[281] This means that, while the result of the proceedings is irrelevant,[282] a *ne bis in idem* effect can only be attached to a decision that can no longer be appealed.

As a consequence, parallel proceedings in two or more Member States are possible for as long as none of the procedures has resulted in a final decision. Several NCAs may thus simultaneous investigate the same infringement. Only when one NCA has disposed of the matter by an unappealable decision, ie a decision against which there are no further ordinary remedies, are the other NCAs obliged to discontinue their proceedings.[283] This is certainly contrary to the interest of the 'accused', who has to duplicate the efforts to defend himself, may have to deal with different procedural rules and languages, and will likely be forced to mandate several lawyers. However, such a situation can hardly be avoided in cases with cross-border elements which lead more than one Member State to assume jurisdiction. Article 13 of Regulation 1/2003, which makes it possible for NCAs to suspend or close their proceedings for the mere reason that another NCA is dealing with the case, intends and may indeed help to avoid such a situation. It should be noted, though, that the provision does not impose an obligation on NCAs to discontinue proceedings in the case of parallel actions in several Member States.[284]

---

[281] Art 54 Schengen Convention uses a slightly different wording than the other two provisions. It does not employ the terms 'finally acquitted or convicted', but requires that the first 'trial has been finally disposed of'.

[282] See above n 8.

[283] Wils, above n 57, 449; Burnside and Crossley, above n 280, 28 and 31; E Ameye, 'The Interplay between Human Rights and Competition Law in the EU' (2004) 25 *European Competition Law Review* 332, 339.

[284] See para 22 of the Network Notice.

Further, the types of decision that, within the catalogue of decisions that NCAs may adopt pursuant to Article 5 of Regulation 1/2003, can have a *ne bis in idem* effect must be determined.[285]

a. Decisions Imposing Fines

There can be no doubt that decisions of an NCA imposing fines on an undertaking or individual conclude criminal proceedings with a 'conviction' within the meaning of Article 4 Protocol No 7 or Article 50 EU Charter. Such decisions therefore constitute a bar to investigations by other NCAs regarding the same infringement once they have become unappealable.[286]

b. Mere Prohibitions

The situation is slightly different if the NCA only prohibits (the continuation of) the relevant agreement or practice, albeit without imposing a fine on the undertakings concerned.[287] In such a case, the NCA has made an adjudication on the merits of the case. However, it considers the established infringement not sufficiently grave to justify the application of penalties, for instance because the offenders could not have been aware of the unlawfulness of their conduct due to a lack of precedents or an unexpected change in the competition policy. Therefore, mere prohibitions are also decisions finally disposing of the case and, in that sense, clearly constitute a conviction, albeit without punishment.[288]

Nonetheless, it has been argued that prohibition decisions can only qualify for the application of the *ne bis in idem* rule if they are the result of proceedings which have initially been instituted by the competition authority with a view to imposing penalties.[289] It is possible that such decisions aim primarily at restoring effective competition rather than at punishing the companies concerned and therefore appear to be of a purely administrative nature not entering the criminal law sphere.[290]

The proposition to distinguish between the initial purpose of the proceedings cannot be accepted, however, as it neglects two essential elements of Article 4 Protocol No 7 (and Article 50 EU Charter). First, the ECtHR has explicitly ruled that the outcome of the procedure is irrelevant.

---

[285] It is self-evident that decisions ordering interim measures cannot have a *ne bis in idem* effect as they do not contain a definitive assessment of the case but only seek to provide a provisional solution to the competition issues encountered.

[286] Wils, above n 57, 449; Paulis and Gauer, above n 4, para 60.

[287] In the terminology of Reg 1/2003, Art 5, first indent, these are decisions 'requiring that an infringement be brought to an end'.

[288] Wils, above n 57, 449–50.

[289] Paulis and Gauer, above n 4, para 66.

[290] *Ibid*, paras 65 and 66.

The guarantee applies even if a person has merely been prosecuted in proceedings which have not led to a conviction.[291] Mere prohibitions contain the finding of an infringement while exculpating the offenders from any guilt. They thus form a 'mixed species' combining elements of both conviction and acquittal, and should therefore not be excluded from the scope of the provision. Secondly, both Article 4 Protocol No 7 and Article 50 EU Charter expressly[292] prohibit any repetition of proceedings. Even where the competition authority initially does not intend to penalise the investigated agreement or practice, there can be no doubt that the undertakings concerned are subject to a severe procedure. They will have to defend their position or at least to argue their case. Moreover, there always remains an uncertainty as to the outcome of the matter since the competition authority may ultimately still decide that the infringement, after all, calls for the imposition of fines. Even though the fear and risk of being penalised may be reduced in these cases, the burden for the parties is comparable whether or not the competition authority has announced, as from the beginning, its intention to apply sanctions. The question of whether a prohibition decision triggers the *ne bis in idem* effect thus cannot depend on the originally proclaimed intention of the acting authority. Therefore, mere prohibition decisions equally constitute a bar to further investigations, prosecutions and penalties regarding the same infringement.[293]

The same considerations apply where an NCA decides to withdraw the benefit of a block exemption pursuant to Article 29(2) of Regulation 1/2003 (unless of course the withdrawal is coupled with a decision on fines) as well as to decisions imposing only a symbolic fine.

c. Article 13 Decisions

Pursuant to Article 13 of Regulation 1/2003, NCAs and the Commission may suspend proceedings pending before them and reject complaints for the mere reason that another NCA is dealing with the same matter. Such decisions cannot, however, provide any bar to prosecutions in other Member States. First, a decision based on Article 13, ie on the sole consideration that another NCAs has taken on the case, does not contain any ruling on the substance of the case. It can therefore not be equated to a conviction or acquittal.[294] Secondly, attaching a *ne bis in idem* effect to

---

[291] P 297 of the judgment of the ECtHR in *Zigarella* (above n 8).

[292] Both provisions employ the words '[n]o one shall be liable to be *tried* or punished again' (emphasis added).

[293] Wils, above n 57, 450.

[294] See para 62 of the judgment of the ECJ in *PVC II* (above n 22). Cf also para 30 the judgment of the ECJ in *Miraglia* (above n 232), where the ECJ held that a decision not to pursue the prosecution and to close the case 'on the sole ground that criminal proceedings have been

Article 13 decisions would run counter to the objective of that provision the purpose of which is that a single competition authority pursues the matter while all others refrain from taking action in respect of the same agreement or conduct. In other words, those authorities which step back shall certainly not block the (only) other authority acting on the case to investigate and, if necessary, penalise the infringement.

d. Positive Decisions

Article 10 of Regulation 1/2003 provides for a new type of instrument: so-called positive decisions which contain a finding that Articles 81 or 82 EC are not applicable to a particular agreement or practice because it either falls outside the ambit of Article 81(1) (respectively Article 82 EC) or is covered by Article 81(3). These decisions have also been called 'non-infringement decisions', which makes it even more obvious that they essentially constitute an acquittal.[295]

Nonetheless, it has been suggested that this type of decision—as in the case of mere prohibitions—should be differentiated according to the initially signalled purpose of the procedure and to accord the *ne bis in idem* effect only to positive decisions which terminate proceedings that were originally commenced with a view to imposing sanctions.[296] However, these arguments must be rejected for the same reasons as above. Since positive decisions, in contrast to exemption decisions of the 'old style', will not be issued at the parties' request but only on the Commission's own initiative, the undertakings concerned are subject to an involuntary investigative procedure. Moreover, positive decisions contain an adjudication on the merits of the case, notably a finding of inapplicability, and are thus tantamount to an acquittal. Lastly, even though they will be issued only in the public interest to clarify the law and ensure its consistent application,[297] positive decisions will be understood by the parties to provide legal certainty as to the lawfulness of their conduct. It would plainly be unfair and contrary to the principles of legitimate expectations if other authorities

initiated in another Member State against the same defendant and in respect of the same acts' does not constitute a decision finally disposing of the case within the meaning of Art 54 of the Schengen Convention. The view is also shared by Van Den Wyngaert and Stessens, above n 49, 798, who base themselves on the relevant provision of the Penal Code of the Netherlands.

295 Wils, above n 57, 450.

296 Paulis and Gauer, above n 4, para 67. It should be noted that the discussion is largely hypothetical, since NCAs are not empowered to issue positive decisions. See above Chapter 1, section II.B.1.d(1). At the horizontal level, the problem of double jeopardy with regard to this type of decision is thus not raised. In the vertical relation between Commission and NCAs, it is unlikely that the issue will arise as the initiation of proceedings by the Commission prevents NCAs from investigating the same case anyway under Community competition law (Art 11(6) of Reg 1/2003) and the NCAs' right to apply national competition law on a stand-alone basis in this situation is disputed (see Chapter 1, n 280 and accompanying text).

297 See Art 10 and recital 14 of Reg 1/2003.

could reopen a case and investigate the same matter a second time. These considerations cannot be altered by the fact that recital 14 of Regulation 1/2003 states that positive decisions are only of a declaratory nature; they are formal Commission decisions, and as such are binding on NCAs and have precedence in accordance with Article 249 EC and Article 16 of Regulation 1/2003.[298]

e. Non-action Decisions

The situation with regard to non-action decisions is more complex. Pursuant to Article 5(2) of Regulation 1/2003, NCAs may adopt decisions to the effect that 'there are no grounds for action on their part' because, on the basis of the available information, the conditions for a prohibition are not fulfilled. As discussed in Chapter 1, the exact legal nature and effect of non-action decisions remain unclear.[299] Where they are issued as formal decisions and equally contain a statement of reasons, they can hardly be distinguished from positive decisions. Moreover, in such a case they contain, at least de facto, an adjudication on the merits of the case, since the NCA has to justify why Article 81 or 82 EC is not applicable. This seems to lead to the conclusion that non-action decisions are also tantamount to an acquittal.

On the other hand, the inapplicability of the competition rules is not a constituent of the operative part of the decision. This is probably the only—and certainly the most important—difference between non-action decisions and positive decisions. The wording of Article 5(2) of Regulation 1/2003 also suggests that non-action decisions are based on a preliminary or summary examination of the information which is in the NCA's possession at the relevant time rather than on an in-depth investigation and assessment of all information that is potentially available on the matter. In other words, the NCA finds that the material in front of it does not justify a further investigation of the case, but at the same time (implicitly) reserves the right to reopen the case should it be presented with further evidence.[300] On this basis, non-action decisions are more of a procedural nature. They appear to constitute a provisional closing of the case and thus cannot be equated to an acquittal. They can therefore not entail any *ne bis in idem* effect.[301]

---

[298] This is also conceded by Paulis and Gauer, above n 4, para 67. On the binding effect and the supremacy of positive decisions, see above Chapter 1, section II.A.1.a(2).

[299] I have called these decisions non-action decisions to distinguish them from positive decisions pursuant to Art 10 of Reg 1/2003. Except for formalistic aspects, the actual difference is not clear. See above Chapter 1, section II.B.1.d(1).

[300] Cf the wording of the relevant provision of the German Competition Act, GWB § 32c, sentences 2 and 3 (cited above at Chapter 1, n 331).

[301] Wils, above n 57, 450. Cf also Van Den Wyngaert and Stessens, above n 49, 798.

f. Commitment Decisions

Decisions accepting commitments also raise questions about whether they bar further proceedings and penalties in accordance with the principle of *ne bis in idem*. Pursuant to Article 9(1) of Regulation 1/2003, commitment decisions shall only state that 'there are no longer grounds for action'. On this basis, they could be placed on an equal footing with non-action decisions. Recital 13 of Regulation 1/2003 moreover specifies that they shall not conclude 'whether or not there has been or still is an infringement'. Thus, commitment decisions are different from positive decisions in that they do not seem to contain any determination as to the merits of the case. This absence of a definite evaluation would deprive them of a *ne bis in idem* effect.[302]

On the other hand, it is appears that the purpose of commitment decisions after all is to terminate the relevant proceedings. The remedies offered by the undertakings involved must meet the concerns of the Commission, and the possibility of reopening the case is limited to a number of specific situations enumerated in Article 9(2) of Regulation 1/2003. These considerations tend to equate commitment decisions to final convictions or acquittals. This view seems to be supported by the judgment of the ECtHR in *Gözütok and Brügge*, where it was held that Article 54 of the Schengen Convention applies to out-of-court settlements, even if they are made without the involvement of the court, between the defendant and the public prosecutor.[303] Commitment decisions essentially draw up a kind of settlement agreement reached between the undertakings concerned and the Commission and make the offered remedies binding on the undertakings.

However, there are two significant differences between commitment decisions and the type of out-of-court settlements which were at issue in the cited judgment of the ECJ.[304] First, it is apparent from *Gözütok and Brügge* that a decisive element in the ECJ's assessment was the fact that, under the applicable national law, a settlement between defendant and prosecutor had the effect of definitely barring further prosecution.[305] By

---

[302] This is indeed the position taken by Paulis and Gauer, above n 4, para 61.

[303] Para 48 of the judgment (above n 47) reads: 'the answer to the questions must be that the *ne bis in idem* principle laid down in Art 54 of the CISA also applies to procedures whereby further prosecution is barred, such as the procedures at issue in the main actions, by which the Public Prosecutor in a Member State discontinues, without the involvement of a court, a prosecution brought in that State once the accused has fulfilled certain obligations and, in particular, has paid a certain sum of money determined by the Public Prosecutor.'

[304] Paulis and Gauer, above n 4, para 61.

[305] Nazzini, above n 4, 14. In the cases giving rise to the preliminary references, criminal proceedings against the accused had been discontinued by the relevant public prosecutor's office in return for the payment of a certain sum determined by the prosecutor. In para 30 of its judgment (above n 47), the ECJ held that 'where, following such a procedure, further prosecution is definitively barred, the person concerned must be regarded as someone whose

contrast, Regulation 1/2003 does not explicitly provide that Article 9 decisions constitute a bar to further proceedings. On the contrary, Recital 13 of Regulation 1/2003 provides that commitment decisions are without prejudice to the powers of competition authorities and courts of the Member States.[306] Moreover, the additional wording that 'such decision shall terminate the proceedings', which was included in Article 9(2) of the Draft Regulation, was removed in the final version of Regulation 1/2003.[307]

Secondly, in accordance with recital 13 of Regulation 1/2003, commitment decisions are only adopted in cases in which the Commission did not envisage imposing fines. The condition clearly suggests that the remedies that are made binding upon the undertakings by a commitment decision are not intended to function as a penalty.[308] This distinguishes the remedies under Article 9 of Regulation 1/2003 from the pecuniary compensation accepted by the defendants in return for the discontinuance of the prosecution in *Gözütok and Brügge*. In the latter case, the amounts paid by the accused were considered to penalise their allegedly unlawful conduct.[309]

It must be concluded that commitment decisions cannot be placed on the same footing as the out-of-court settlements which were at issue in *Gözütok and Brügge* and therefore cannot be equated to a conviction or acquittal within the meaning of Article 4 Protocol No 7 or Article 50 EU Charter. Commitment decisions do not entail a *ne bis in idem* effect.[310]

7. The Position of Complainants

At first sight, the application of the *ne bis in idem* principle to parallel national proceedings may adversely affect the position of complainants. It may seem to better fit their interests if a second procedure, albeit limited to the finding that the competition rules have been infringed (ie excluding the imposition of a second fine), remains possible. However, such an approach

case has been finally disposed of for the purposes of Art 54 of the CISA in relation to the acts which he is alleged to have committed'.

[306] This implies that commitment decisions are not binding for national authorities and courts, which are thus free to make their own evaluation as to whether there really was an infringement in the past and whether it has actually been remedied through the commitments. See M Busse and A Leopold, 'Entscheidungen über Verpflichtungszusagen nach Art. 9 VO (EG) Nr. 1/2003' (2005) 55 *Wirtschaft und Wettbewerb* 146, 151. Cf also the German rule, whereby s 33(4) GWB, which makes decisions of the BKartA binding on domestic courts that are seized in follow-on damages actions, does not apply to commitment decisions of the BKartA. See E Rehbinder in U Loewenheim, K Meessen and A Riesenkampff (eds), *Kartellrecht, Kommentar, Band 2: GWB* (Munich, CH Beck, 2006), §32b para 14.

[307] For this reason, the argument submitted by Wils, above n 57, 451, is no longer valid.

[308] Paulis and Gauer, above n 4, para 61.

[309] Para 29 of the judgment in *Gözütok and Brügge* (above n 47).

[310] Paulis and Gauer, above n 4, para 61; *contra* Eilmansberger, above n 92, 52.

would be incompatible with the *ne bis in idem* guarantee as enshrined in Article 4 Protocol No 7 and Article 50 of the EU Charter since both provisions clearly preclude not only a second sanction, but also a second procedure where the first has resulted in a final conviction or acquittal.[311]

Moreover, a careful examination reveals that the rights of complainants are not unduly curtailed. Complainants have the right to freely choose the competition authority with which they wish to lodge a complaint.[312] This right is not in any way affected by the application of the *ne bis in idem* principle.[313] On the other hand, Article 13 of Regulation 1/2003 affords NCAs (and the Commission) the power to reject complaints for the sole reason that another authority is dealing with the matter. This power has been introduced independently of any double jeopardy issue and thus clearly shows that complainants, a priori, do not have a right for their complaint to be handled effectively by a particular NCA. Thus, they always run the risk that the authority which they have approached does not itself investigate the matter, but instead refers it to another NCA or the Commission.

Obviously, complainants may have a legitimate interest in gaining access to the file and, possibly, obtaining (copies of) certain documents to be able to prove the existence of an infringement if they are involved in or envisage private litigation before a civil court.[314] In Commission proceedings, the access right of complainants is largely governed by the provisions of Regulation 1049/2001 on public access to documents.[315] Theoretically, these rules could even be relied upon by potential litigants to gain access to documents originating from the Member States and forwarded to the Commission (eg draft decisions) as Regulation 1049/2001 covers all documents held by the three Community institutions (Commission, Council, EP) and thus applies not only to documents drawn up by the

---

[311] Both provisions state that '[n]o one shall be liable to be *tried* or punished again' (emphasis added). See also above n 131 and accompanying text.

[312] This is the only form of forum shopping that can theoretically occur under Reg 1/2003. See above Chapter 3, n 155 and accompanying text.

[313] It cannot be excluded, of course, that the double jeopardy rule may discourage a complainant to lodge a complaint with his 'preferred' authority if he knows that another NCA is already dealing with the matter. However, since the *ne bis in idem* guarantee only bars second proceedings from the moment that there is a final, unappealable decision, the conduct of parallel (simultaneous) proceedings as such is not excluded by that principle. On this basis, a complainant can always approach a second authority and thereby make an attempt to have the case ultimately decided by the NCA he prefers.

[314] H Gilliams and L Cornelis, 'Private Enforcement of the Competition Rules in Belgium' (2007) 2 *TBM-RCB* 11, paras 70–1. See also paras 67–8 of the judgment in Case T–353/94 *Postbank v Commission* [1996] ECR II–921.

[315] See Gilliams and Cornelis, *ibid*, paras 72–4. The Implementing Regulation and the Commission's Notice on Access to the File primarily deal with access of the undertakings under investigation and contain very few rules regarding access of third parties such as complainants. Under these rules, the latter only have a right to (a limited) access to the file where the Commission has informed them of its intention to reject the complaint. See also above Chapter 4, n 98.

Commission itself, but also to documents which it receives from other institutions, Member States, third countries, international organisations and private parties, including undertakings.[316] As a general rule, the Commission has to consult with the author before granting access to a third-party document, but ultimately retains discretion to decide whether it will effectively communicate the document or whether non-disclosure is justified on the basis of the exceptions laid down in Regulation 1049/2001.[317] However, with regard to documents originating from Member States, a specific exception rule applies allowing Member States to request that the institution not disclose their content without the prior consent of the Member State concerned.[318] The CFI has interpreted this rule as granting Member States an absolute veto right over the disclosure of documents authored by them but in the possession of a Community institution.[319] In practice, the possibility of obtaining access to Member State documents relating to competition matters via the Commission is thus unlikely to play any significant role.[320]

---

[316] See Art 2(3) of Reg 1049/2001. This means that the so-called 'authorship rule' contained in the formerly applicable Code of Conduct has been removed. M De Leeuw, 'Case Note on Cases C–41/00 P, Interporc Im- und Export GmbH v Commission of the European Communities; T–76/02, Mara Messina v Commission of the European Communities; Case T–47/01, Co-Frutta soc. coop. rl v Commission of the European Communities' (2004) 1 *CML Rev* 261, 274. According to that rule, Community institutions were not authorised to process requests for access to third-party documents even if the relevant documents were in the institution's possession, but instead had to refuse access to them as the authorship rule constituted an absolute and unqualified exception to the principle of transparency. Applicants were thus obliged to address their request directly to the third party that was the author of the document. See J Heliskoski and P Leino, 'Darkness at the Break of Noon: the Case Law on Regulation No. 1049/2001 on Access to Documents' (2006) 43 *CML Rev* 735, 769.

[317] See Art 4(4) of Reg 1049/2001 and para 56 of the judgment in Case T–168/02 *IFAW v Commission* [2004] ECR II–4135. Should the institution intend to grant access against the explicit will of the author, it must, however, inform him about possible remedies available to challenge the institution's decision. De Leeuw, *ibid*, 275. These principles would also apply where the Commission has been requested to disclose a document originating from an undertaking (eg a competitor of the applicant). However, in this event, the Commission would arguably be entitled (and obliged) to grant partial access in accordance with Art 4(6) of Reg 1049/2001 by providing a non-confidential version of the document in which all business secrets have been deleted. (Art 4(2) of Reg 1049/2001 notably justifies a refusal to grant access where disclosure of the document would undermine the protection of commercial interests of a private person.)

[318] Art 4(5) of Reg 1049/2001.

[319] M Maes, 'L'accès du public aux documents des Institutions de la Communauté européenne: vers une révision du règlement (CE) 1049/2001' (2007) *Revue du Droit de l'Union Européenne* 411, 419. In *IFAW v Commission* (above n 317), para 58, the CFI held that the special treatment granted to Member States (as compared to other third parties) under Art 4(5) of Reg 1049/2001 'would risk becoming a dead letter if the Commission were able to decide to disclose that document despite an explicit request not to do so from the Member State concerned'.

[320] See Heliskoski and Leino, above n 316, 776, who note that the improvement brought by the abolition of the authorship rule, 'insofar as it concerns Member State documents, remains rather small for any practical purposes'.

On the other hand, the domestic laws of almost all Member States provide for similar rights of public access to government documents as Regulation 1049/2001.[321] In some Member States, the right of public access is even of a constitutional nature.[322] In national proceedings, complainants can rely on those rules in the event that no specific provisions exist which also grant complainants access to competition dossiers.[323] Arguably, a request for access to the file can be lodged with all competition authorities in the EU regardless of the place of residence or registered office of the complainant (within the EU).[324] In the same vein, complainants can use an NCA decision in support of their civil claim before any national court in the EU. Even though national decisions formally have no binding legal force outside the Member State whose NCA adopted them,[325] they can have a strong persuasive value[326] and thus help the

---

[321] The only exception seemingly being Luxemburg. See De Leeuw, above n 316, 273 (who counts two exceptions, notably Germany and Luxemburg, among the old 15 Member States; however, Germany has meanwhile adopted a law on public access to government information; see below in this note). The recently acceded 12 Member States (with the exception of Cyprus and Malta) had enacted legislation in this field even prior to their accession to the EU. Germany and the UK were among the last countries in the EU to introduce legislation in this respect. See Maes, above n 319, 421. In Germany, the Informationsfreiheitsgesetz (Freedom of Information Act) only entered into force on 1 January 2006. The act also applies to documents held by the BKartA. A Leopold, 'Die Kartellbehörden im Angesicht der Informationsfreiheit' (2006) 56 Wirtschaft und Wettbewerb 592, 592.

[322] Eg Poland, Hungary and Czech Republic. See De Leeuw, above n 316, 273.

[323] In this respect, it should be noted that the right of access to documents held by the Community institutions under Reg 1049/2001 is unconditional, ie the applicant does not have to justify his/her request by demonstrating a specific (legitimate) interest in viewing the requested documents (Maes, above n 319, 417). The same applies to the access right under the German Informationsfreiheitsgesetz (Leopold, above n 321, 593).

[324] While Art 255 EU only provides for a right of access for EU citizens and EU residents, the right of access under Reg 1049/2001 is in practice granted to all natural and legal persons, ie also third country nationals or residents. Maes, above n 319, 417. As concerns national legislation on public access, the principle of non-discrimination (Art 12 EC) would seem to preclude that nationals of other Member States are refused access to documents on grounds of their nationality.

[325] And even within the same Member State, the question of the legal force of a final NCA decision vis-à-vis third parties, ie parties other than the undertakings to whom the decision is addressed, can be controversial because the principle of res iudicata is usually considered to apply only as between the parties. Cf the discussions of Gilliams and Cornelis, above n 314, paras 62–7, regarding decisions of the Belgian competition council (Raad voor de Mededinging). By contrast, under s 58A of the UK Competition Act, infringement decisions of the OFT are binding on national courts hearing actions for recovery of damages and other monetary claims arising out of a breach of UK or Community competition law. See A Komninos, 'Public and Private Antitrust Enforcement in Europe: Complement? Overlap?' (2006) 3 The Competition Law Review 5, 19, and R Nazzini, 'Parallel and Sequential Proceedings in Competition Law: An Essay on the Modes of Interaction between Community and National Law (2005) 16 European Business Law Review 245, 260 and 264. Equally, under German law, a civil court deciding on a follow-on damage action is bound by the relevant decision of the BKartA. Section 33(4) GWB even extends this binding effect, on civil courts, of a prohibition decision of the national cartel authority to decisions stemming from foreign NCAs or the Commission. On this provision see Lutz, above n 129, 728 and Rehbinder, above n 306, §33 para 60–1.

[326] They could, for instance, be regarded as creating a (rebuttable) presumption of fact. See Gilliams and Cornelis, above n 314, para 65 juncto para 68. In this sense see also M Siragusa,

complainant to prove his case even if the decision stems from a foreign NCA (that is, foreign in relation to the national court before which the civil matter is pending).[327]

E. Conclusion

One commentator describes a situation in which the same cartel case is investigated and sanctioned by more than one NCA as a 'legal nightmare' and calls upon the NCAs to take the basic principle of work sharing, notably the principle 'one case—one law—one authority', seriously.[328] The above analysis supports this view.

It militates in favour of applying the *ne bis in idem* principle in Community competition matters where the same illegal agreement or conduct is investigated and punished subsequently by several NCAs. The specificities of Community law, in particular the fact that the EC is 'a Community built on the rule of law', and the particular features of the enforcement system established by Regulation 1/2003, combined with the requirements of procedural fairness and equity, command that the *ne bis in idem* guarantee be applied also with respect to competition proceedings conducted in different Member States. A very important aspect in this context is the fact that all NCAs apply the same substantive law, notably Articles 81 and 82 EC. It seems to be an element of general justice that, on the basis of identical facts, the same substantive rule can be violated only once. This view is supported by Article 50 EU Charter, which, for the first time, acknowledges an international *ne bis in idem* covering the entire EU. Admittedly, the EU Charter is not a legally binding instrument, but it still can be seen as an indication that, in matters of Community law, a purely

'A Reflection on Some Private Antitrust Enforcement Issues', paper for the 2006 EU Competition Law and Policy Workshop, European University Institute/RSCAS, Florence, available at http://www.eui.eu/RSCAS/Research/Competition/2006(pdf)/200610-COMPed-Siragusa.pdf (accessed February 2009), 1, 6, who submits that judges will in practice regard the facts described in NCA decisions as proven unless the defendant can rebut them. On the other hand, Komninos, 'Effect of Commission Decisions on Private Antitrust Litigation: Setting the Story Straight' (2007) 44 *CML Rev* 1387, 1422–3, rightly points out that there is no pre-existing hierarchy between public and private enforcement decisions nor a general primacy of public over private antitrust enforcement. Both are independent of each other.

[327] Cf paras 67–8 of the judgment of the CFI in *Postbank* (above n 314), where it was held that the right of a national court to use information it has obtained from the Commission was intrinsically tied to the courts' duty to safeguard the rights which litigants derive from the direct effect of Arts 81 and 82 EC. These considerations must apply, *mutatis mutandis*, where the information (in form of a decision) is furnished not by the Commission, but by a foreign NCA. Cf also the aforementioned provision of German antitrust law (s 33(4) GWB), above n 325; and See also Roth and Rose, above n 142, para 14.087.

[328] T Tóth, 'EU Enlargement and Modernisation of Competition Law: Some National Experiences' in D Geradin (ed) *Modernisation and Enlargement: Two Major Challenges for EC Competition Law* (Antwerp, Intersentia, 2004), 367, 383.

national approach to the principles of *res iudicata* and *ne bis in idem* is no longer regarded as appropriate.

Alternatively, the whole of the EU must be regarded as a single jurisdiction for the purposes of applying Article 4 Protocol No 7, which equally lays down the *ne bis in idem* guarantee, albeit only at the national level. Indeed, the HR Court has not only interpreted the fundamental rights and guarantees of the ECHR and its Protocols in a dynamic way, but has also adopted a markedly Community-oriented approach in the past, for instance by regarding the European Parliament as legislature within the meaning of Article 3 Protocol No 1. The case law of the HR Court thus seems to sustain the view that the notion of 'under the jurisdiction of the same state' applied in Article 4 Protocol No 7 can be interpreted as covering the jurisdictions of all 27 current EU Member States.

Not all types of decisions that can be adopted at the end of a competition procedure constitute a bar to further proceedings: only decisions which have become unappealable and which, moreover, contain a conviction or acquittal, ie a definitive appraisal of the contested acts, can entail a *ne bis in idem* effect. These comprise decisions prohibiting a certain agreement or conduct and/or imposing fines and also positive decisions. The other types of decision provided for in Article 5 of Regulation 1/2003, in particular decisions accepting commitments and non-action decisions, as well as Article 13 decisions, rather give only a provisional assessment of the case, which implies that the acting NCA, and other competition authorities, preserve the right to take up the matter (again) and continue or institute proceedings. A *ne bis in idem* effect can therefore not be attached to these decisions.

The above approach to multiple proceedings, instituted by several NCAs with a view to enforcing Articles 81 and 82 EC in respect of the same facts, is a fair solution and one which would spare authorities, companies and their counsels a legal nightmare without unduly encroaching upon the position of complainants.

II. NCA DECISIONS AND THE DUTY OF LOYALTY

Article 10 EC enshrines one of the fundamental constitutional principles of Community law.[329] It imposes positive duties of action and negative duties

---

[329] See J Temple Lang, 'Article 5 of the EEC Treaty: the Emergence of Constitutional Principles in the Case Law of the Court of Justice' (1987) 10 *Fordham International Law Journal* 503, 504. In fact, some of the most important principles of Community law, such as the direct effect of directives (for an express reference to Art 10 EC see Case 190/87 *Kreis Borken v Moormann* [1988] ECR 4689, para 22) and the liability of Member States for failure to implement a directive (see Joined Cases C–6 and C–9/90 *Francovich and Bonifaci v Italy* [1991] ECR I–5357), are considered to have been based primarily on Art 10 EC. See J Temple Lang, 'The Duties of co-operation of national authorities and courts under Article 10 E.C.: two more

of abstention on the Member States.[330] The provision thereby aims to secure the full effectiveness of EC law throughout the Community and the attainment of the Treaty objectives which shall neither be frustrated by inactivity on the part of the Member States nor by national measures taken unilaterally by Member States.

In the context of decentralised application of Community competition law, the question arises of which implications this provision has for the rights and duties of NCAs when enforcing Articles 81 and 82 EC. In particular, one may wonder whether Article 10 EC obliges a Member State to recognise the legal force of a decision which has been adopted by the NCA of another Member State under Article 81 or 82 EC and Regulation 1/2003. In the case of parallel action by two or more NCAs regarding the same infringement, the second Member State may (also) have a duty to respect the foreign decision as regards its content and to avoid taking measures which would conflict with it on substance. Finally, whether NCAs can or even must impose sanctions in relation to the effects of the relevant infringement in the territory of other Member States must also be considered.

A.   Article 10 EC—The Principle of Loyalty

In express terms, Article 10 EC is directed only at Member States, which might suggest that the provision is a one-way street assigning duties solely to the Member States in favour of the Community. However, the ECJ has held that Article 10 EC governs the relations between the Community and the Member States in all directions in that it imposes on them mutual duties of loyal co-operation. This general principle has emerged from a long series of judgments.[331]

---

reflections' (2001) 26 *EL Rev* 84, 87. Above all, the ECJ relied upon Art 10 EC when it declared Community law to have 'precedence' over national law (see the judgment in *Costa v ENEL*, above n 58, 594). A von Bogdandy in E Grabitz and M Hilf (eds), *Das Recht der Europäischen Union. Kommentar. Band I* (Munich, CH Beck, State: 31st Supplement—October 2006), Art 10 no 4.

[330] Art 10(1) EC contains duties to act (*Handlungspflichten*) and Art 10(2) EC lays down a duty to abstain (*Unterlassungspflicht*). The ECJ often does not distinguish between the two parts of the provision. However, the qualification of an obligation as positive or negative duty, in many cases, is in fact a question of phrasing. For instance, the prohibition to discriminate (negative duty) can also be framed as obligation of equal treatment (positive duty). Von Bogdandy, *ibid*, Art 10 no 25.

[331] In 1997, Art 10 EC was relied upon in more than 200 cases. J Temple Lang, 'The Core of Constitutional Law of the Community—Article 5 EC' in L Gormley (ed), *Current and Future Perspectives on EC Competition Law—A Tribute to Professor M.R. Mok* (London, Kluwer Law International, 1997), 41, 44.

1. General Duties under Article 10 EC

Article 10 EC has a broad wording and thus is very wide in scope. Its vagueness has not, however, prevented the ECJ from deducing an extensive list of specific and sometimes even quite precise obligations from Article 10 EC.[332] In doing so, the ECJ has progressively developed the principle—going beyond the express words of Article 10 EC[333]—from a one-sided duty engaging only Member States to a four-dimensional, general principle of mutual loyalty and solidarity obliging the Member States and the Community institutions,[334] a principle which, moreover, must be regarded as the basis of the whole of the Community system.[335]

In German legal literature, the principle enshrined in Article 10 EC is commonly referred to as *Gemeinschaftstreue* and considered to be inspired by and akin to the concept of *Bundestreue* (*loyauté* or *fidélité fédérale*), a fundamental principle of German constitutional law.[336] While the ECJ prefers the terms 'loyal co-operation', 'sincere co-operation' or 'co-operation in good faith',[337] these differences in terminology do not seem to reveal any significant conceptual differences.[338]

---

[332] See Temple Lang, above n 331, 43. For an overview of the various obligations resulting from Art 10 EC see Temple Lang (1987), above n 329, 506–31 and M Lück, *Die Gemeinschaftstreue als allgemeines Rechtsprinzip im Recht der Europäischen Gemeinschaft* (Baden-Baden, Nomos, 1992), 1, 25–77. Broadly speaking, the duties can be grouped into three categories: the duty to implement Community law (including the duty to supplement Community action); the duty not to interfere with the operation of the Community legal order and the functioning of its institutions; and the duty to co-operate and assist each other (eg by supplying information). Cf Temple Lang, above n 331, 42.

[333] See Lück, *ibid*, 23; M Zuleeg in H von der Groeben and J Schwarze (eds), *Kommentar zum Vertrag über die Europäische Union und zur Gründung der Europäischen Gemeinschaft, Band 1* (Baden-Baden, Nomos, 6th edn, 2003), Artikel 10 EG, para 1.

[334] The leading case establishing this general, four-dimensional obligation is Case 230/81 *Luxembourg v EP* [1983] ECR 255. In para 37 of this judgment, the ECJ refers to 'the rule imposing on Member States and the Community institutions mutual duties of sincere cooperation, as embodied in particular in Article 5 [now Article 10] of the EEC Treaty'. In Case 44/84 *Hurd v Jones* [1986] ECR 29, para 38, the ECJ confirmed this approach by ruling that Art 10 EC 'is the expression of a more general rule imposing on Member States and the Community institutions mutual duties of genuine cooperation and assistance'. See also M Blanquet, *L'article 5 du traité CEE* (Paris, Librairie Générale de Droit et de Jurisprudence, 1994), 1, 414–15 (describing *la généralisation du principe*).

[335] That solidarity is the basis of the entire Community system was in fact already proclaimed in 1969 by the ECJ in Joined Cases 6 and 11/69 *Commission v France* [1969] ECR 523, para 16.

[336] M Zuleeg, 'Die föderativen Grundsätze der Europäischen Union' (2000) 53 *Neue Juristische Wochenschrift* 2846, 2846; A Hatje in J Schwarze (ed), *EU-Kommentar* (Baden-Baden, Nomos, 2000), Artikel 10 EGV, para 1. But also non-German authors compare the principle of loyalty with the *Bundestreueprinzip*. See, eg W Van Gerven and H Gilliams, 'Gemeenschapstrouw: Goede trouw in E.G.-verband' in (1989–1990) *Rechtskundig Weekblad* 1158, para 1, who regard the Community law principle as a variant of *Bundestreue* and consequently call it *gemeenschapstrouw*; Blanquet, above n 334, 371–2 and 408 *et seq*, who employs the term *fidélité communautaire*, and also V Constantinesco, 'L'article 5 CEE, de la bonne foi à la loyauté communautaire' in Capotorti *et al*, above n 225, 97.

[337] See Blanquet, above n 334, 412–13. The latter term illustrates that Art 10 EC can also be considered as a specific expression or variant of the well-known *bona fides* principle of public

The principle is four-dimensional since, in accordance with the case law of the ECJ, it governs the relations between the 'centre', ie the Community institutions, and the Member States in all directions. Not only must the Member States support the Community institutions in fulfilling their tasks,[339] the Community institutions are also under a duty to assist the Member States' authorities.[340] Moreover, the duties not only apply vertically, ie in the relation between the Member States and the Community, they also apply horizontally, as between the Member States.[341] Finally, it follows from the pre-cited case *Luxembourg v EP* that the Community institutions also owe duties of loyalty towards one another.[342]

As concerns fulfilment of the Member States' obligations under Article 10 EC, it is important to note that the provision binds all national authorities irrespective of their role within the domestic legal order of the Member States. In particular, the fact that a Member State has, say, a federal structure or has delegated powers to (quasi-)autonomous regions does not release it or the relevant decentralised bodies from the duties imposed by Article 10 EC. Thus, the principle of loyalty applies just as well to local, municipal and regional authorities as to (central) government bodies.[343]

---

international law, albeit adapted, in terms of scope and content, to the particularities and needs of the Community legal order and thus going beyond the *bona fides* obligations as acknowledged under traditional international law. Cf Constantinesco, above n 336, 101–2; Blanquet, above n 334, 404–5; Lück, above n 332, 80–5. Cf also Van Gerven and Gilliams, above n 336, paras 4–5, who even draw the parallel with the principle of *goede trouw* applicable to contractual relations under private law.

[338] See Lück, above n 332, 23; Zuleeg, above n 333, Artikel 10 EG, para 1.

[339] This follows directly from the wording of Art 10 EC.

[340] See para 17 and 18 of the order of the ECJ in Case C–2/88 Imm *Zwartveld and others* [1990] ECR I–3365 and also para 53 of the judgment in Case C–234/89 *Delimitis* [1991] ECR I–935.

[341] See para 36 of the judgment of the ECJ in Case 42/82 *Commission v France (Italian wine)* [1983] ECR 1013, where the ECJ bases itself on 'the duty of co-operation between Member States which is inherent in the Community system', albeit without expressly referring to Art 10 EC. In Case C–251/89 *Athanasopoulos v Bundesanstalt für Arbeit* [1991] ECR I–2797, para 57, which relates to co-operation between social security institutions of different Member States, the ECJ explicitly relies on Art 10 EC. See further Hatje in Schwarze, above n 336, Artikel 10 EGV, para 54.

[342] See paras 37 and 38 of the judgment in *Luxembourg v EP* (above n 334) and also judgment of the ECJ in Case C–65/93 *EP v Council* [1995] ECR I–643, para 23. Temple Lang, above n 331, 69. Lück, above n 332, 58, seems to overlook this last, inter-institutional aspect when he describes the obligations derived from Art 10 EC only as three-dimensional. Admittedly, the two latter functions of the principle are far less developed in the case law of the ECJ. See Van Gerven and Gilliams, above n 336, paras 3 (1160) and 7. Interestingly, Van Gerven and Gilliams point to a different kind of three dimensionality of the principle. In their view, the principle of *gemeenschapstrouw* embraces the following three elements: the duty to correctly perform all obligations and not to abuse own powers; the duty of loyal and active co-operation/assistance; and the duty of solidarity. *Idem*, para 3 (p 1160).

[343] J Temple Lang, 'The Duties of National Authorities under Community Constitutional Law' (1998) 23 *EL Rev* 109, 112–13. See also the judgment of the ECJ in Case 96/81 *Commission v Netherlands* [1982] ECR 1791, para 12.

In the same vein, the principle binds any national authority regardless of the types of power it exercises (legislative, executive or judicial). Therefore, administrative and regulatory authorities are subject to the requirements of Article 10 EC in the same way as national courts.[344] The provision even applies to private bodies to the extent that they have been vested with public powers.[345]

It goes without saying that Article 10 EC imposes duties on national authorities and national courts only insofar as they act within the Community law sphere. However, this sphere is entered not only when the Member States' authorities or courts implement Community law, but equally when they apply any provision of national law that is incompatible with Community law.[346] On the other hand, Article 10 EC is not applicable where national bodies act in the purely national law sphere.[347]

2. Specific Duties in the Field of Competition Law

It follows from the above that, as a matter of principle, NCAs are bound by the general principle of loyalty laid down in Article 10 EC when enforcing Articles 81 or 82 EC. However, that principle is of a complementary and subsidiary nature.

a. The Complementary Nature of Article 10 EC

The case law of the ECJ indicates that Article 10 EC does not create duties by itself, but generally has to be applied in combination with other, more

---

[344] For the duties of national courts, see in particular the judgments of the ECJ in Case 106/77 *Amministrazione delle Finanze v Simmenthal* [1978] ECR 629, para 21 (albeit without explicit reference to Art 10 EC) and in Case C–213/89 *The Queen v Secretary of State for Transport, ex parte: Factortame* [1990] ECR I–2433. See further J Temple Lang, 'The Duties of National Courts under Community Constitutional Law' (1997) 22 *EL Rev* 3, 3–18. In Case 103/88 *Fratelli Costanzo v Commune di Milano* [1989] ECR 1839, the ECJ extended this principle to administrative authorities by ruling that '[i]t would, moreover, be contradictory to rule that an individual may rely upon the provisions of a directive . . . before the national courts seeking an order against the administrative authorities, and yet to hold that those authorities are under no obligation to apply the provisions of the directive and refrain from applying provisions of national law which conflict with them. It follows that when the conditions under which the Court has held that individuals may rely on the provisions of a directive before the national courts are met, all organs of the administration . . . are obliged to apply those provisions.' See also Temple Lang, above n 343, 109–11. With regard specifically to NCAs, this approach has been confirmed in Case C–198/01 *Fiammiferi v Autorità Garante* [2003] ECR I–8055, para 50. On this latter judgment, see J Temple Lang, 'National Measures Restricting Competition, and National Authorities under Art 10 EC' (2004) 29 *EL Rev* 397.

[345] Temple Lang, above n 331, 42.

[346] In such a situation, Art 10 EC notably requires them to set aside the conflicting national rule. See para 21 of the judgment in *Simmenthal* (above n 344).

[347] Temple Lang, above n 331, 49.

specific, rules of Community law.[348] This also seems to follow from the wording of Article 10 EC.[349] Even if read in conjunction with the Community's tasks laid down in Article 3 EC the principle remains vague and does not seem to allow that concrete obligations are derived from it.[350]

The general objective of ensuring that competition in the internal market is not distorted (Article 3(g)) has been further concretised by Articles 81 *et seq.* Moreover, it is settled case law that Articles 81 and 82 EC, even though they are addressed to private undertakings, also create obligations for the Member States, precisely through the interposition of Article 10 EC.[351] Some ten years ago, the question was therefore raised whether, by virtue of Article 10 EC, NCAs have a general duty to actively enforce Community competition law when the occasion to do so arises and to end agreements and practices which are incompatible with Articles 81 and 82 EC.[352]

On the other hand, in the judgment in *Leclerc*, the ECJ found that

> as Community law stands, Member States' obligations under Article 5 [now Article 10] of the EEC Treaty, in conjunction with Articles 3(f) and 85 [now Article 81] *are not specific enough* to preclude them from enacting legislation of the type at issue . . .[353]

The relevant case law therefore appears to be slightly ambiguous on this point.

---

[348] Lenaerts and Van Nuffel, above n 86, para 5-047; Hatje in Schwarze, above n 336, Artikel 10 EGV, para 6; Zuleeg, above n 333, Artikel 10 EG para 2. Cf also para 7 of judgment of the ECJ in *Commission v Netherlands* (above n 343).

[349] See Temple Lang (2001), above n 329, 91; Art 10 EC states that Member States shall 'ensure fulfilment of the obligations arising out of this Treaty or resulting from action taken by the institutions of the Community'. It is also illustrated by the case law of the ECJ. See, eg the judgment in *Commission v Netherlands* (above n 343), para 7 (Art 10 EC combined with Art 211 (ex Art 155) EC; *Moormann* (above n 329), paras 22–4 (Art 10 EC read together with Art 249 (ex Art 189) EC) and Case 13/77 *GB-INNO v ATAB* [1977] ECR 2115, paras 29–32 (Art 10 EC in conjunction with Arts 3(f), 82 and 90 EC).

[350] Lück, above n 332, 165–6.

[351] See in particular the judgment in *GB-INNO v ATAB* (above n 349), paras 30–1; para 48 of the judgment in Case 66/86 *Ahmed Saeed Flugreisen and others v Zentrale zur Bekämpfung unlauteren Wettbewerbs* [1989] ECR 803. Temple Lang, above n 343, 116–17 (with further references).

[352] See Temple Lang, above n 331, 57–8, who argued that, in view of the judgments in *Ahmed Saeed* (which established a duty of non-competition authorities to apply Community competition law; *ibid*) and *Fratelli Costanzo* (where the ECJ established that national administrative authorities have in fact the same duties as national courts to apply sufficiently precise and unconditional provisions of directives; see above n 344), it would be odd if NCAs did not have a duty to use their powers to enforce Community competition law. He concluded that the only reason for any doubt on this point was that the Commission had in fact never suggested that NCAs have such a duty.

[353] Emphasis added. Para 20 of the judgment of the ECJ in Case 229/83 *Edouard Leclerc and others v SARL 'Au blé vert' and others* [1985] ECR 1. The national legislation at issue required the fixing, by the publisher or importer, of retail prices for books.

The issue has been settled in the meantime. Article 3 of Regulation 1/2003 imposes a duty on NCAs to apply Community competition law in all cases in which they apply national competition law and the trade between Member States is likely to be affected. The question of whether Article 10 EC, read in conjunction with Articles 81 and 82 EC, is precise enough to establish a duty on Member States to enforce Community competition law actively whenever the occasion arises has therefore become obsolete.[354]

b. The Subsidiary Nature of Article 10 EC

Moreover, since Article 10 EC enshrines the general principle, it operates as *lex generalis*. Thus, where provisions of primary (eg Article 86)[355] or secondary Community law (eg a directive)[356] impose concrete duties on the Member States, these specific rules prevail and Article 10 EC is inapplicable.[357]

Regulation 1/2003 specifies a wide range of different obligations which Member States have to meet in relation to the enforcement of Community competition law. In particular, the conflict rules laid down in Articles 3(2) and 16 of Regulation 1/2003, the information and consultation duties imposed by Article 11(2) –(5) of Regulation 1/2003, the rules on mutual assistance contained in Article 22 of Regulation 1/2003 and, finally, the obligation to designate the competent national authorities (Article 35(1) of Regulation 1/2003) can be regarded as special examples of the more general duty embodied in Article 10 EC.[358]

---

[354] Obviously, Art 3 of Reg 1/2003 does not oblige NCAs to enforce Art 81 or 82 EC in every single case that is brought to their attention. It leaves each NCA a broad margin of discretion to decide whether it wants to pursue a matter at all and thus to determine its own enforcement priorities.

[355] Art 86 (ex Art 90) is one of the EC Treaty provisions which has been regarded as a specific expression of the general duty enshrined in Art 10 EC. See the opinion of Advocate General W Van Gerven in Case C–48/90 *Netherlands v Commission* ('*Dutch PTT*') (Joined Cases C–48/90 and C–66/90) [1992] ECR I–565, para 37. Other examples are the second sentence of Art 30 (ex Art 36), Art 292 (ex Art 219) and the former Art 6(1) EEC Treaty. See Van Gerven and Gilliams, above n 336, para 6.

[356] Temple Lang, above n 331, 44–5 and 62, who submits that there is no need to rely on Art 10 EC if the directive details the relevant duty and that, in case of non-fulfilment, there is thus only breach of the directive, not of Art 10 EC. However, the ECJ seems often to quote both the general rule of Art 10 EC and the specific provision of secondary Community law. See, eg Case C–290/89 *Commission v Belgium* [1991] ECR I–2851, para 5; Case 141/78 *France v UK* [1979] ECR 2923, paras 8 and 12.

[357] Von Bogdandy, above n 329, Art 10 no 30; Temple Lang (2001), above n 329, 91. Cf also the judgment of the ECJ in Case C–18/93 *Corsica Ferries v Porto di Genova* [1994] ECR I–1783, para 18, where it was held 'that there can be no question of applying it [Art 10 EC] autonomously when the situation concerned is governed by a specific provision of the Treaty'.

[358] Cf para 47 of the judgment of the CFI in Case T–339/04 *France Télécom v Commission* ('*Wanadoo*') [2007] ECR II–521, where Art 20 of Reg 1/2003 is qualified as a clarification of the duty of loyal co-operation in the event of an inspection.

However, Regulation 1/2003 is silent on the relevance of national procedures and national decisions for the authorities of Member States other than the one in which the decision was adopted. The question of whether national decisions can have legal effects or practical implications for the authorities of Member States other than the one in which the decision was adopted is not dealt with by Regulation 1/2003.[359] Nor does Regulation 1/2003 address the question of what kind of sanctions should be applied by NCAs and how their size should be determined. Therefore, the issues raised above in the introduction to this section of the chapter (Section II) can and must be resolved by relying on Article 10 EC.

B. Duty to Recognise the Legal Force of Foreign NCA Decisions on a Case-by-case Basis

It is obvious that a principle such as that of loyalty and solidarity is built on mutual confidence and thus presupposes a considerable degree of mutual trust. Both Member States and Community institutions must trust that each of them will effectively observe the Community rules and will enforce them with a reasonable degree of efficiency.[360]

On the basis of these considerations, it is arguable that national decisions implementing Community law should have legal force in the entire Community. In view of the similarities between the loyalty obligations under Article 10 EC and the principle of *Bundestreue*, it has been suggested that Article 10 EC imposes a duty on Member States to automatically recognise the legal force of administrative acts of other Member States which have been adopted in the application of Community law.[361] This would mean that NCA decisions in the field of Community competition law would also be afforded Community-wide effect and would be enforceable in all Member States.

While it would certainly have been possible to incorporate a provision to that effect into Regulation 1/2003, which is a Council regulation adopted on the basis of Article 83 EC,[362] it was clearly not the intention of the

---

[359] The sole exception is Art 13 of Reg 1/2003, which gives NCAs the power to suspend proceedings or reject a complaint because another NCA is dealing with the same matter.

[360] J Temple Lang, 'The Duties of Cooperation of National Authorities and Courts and the Community Institutions under Art 10 EC Treaty', General Report for the XIX FIDE Congress, Helsinki, 1–3 June 2000, 394, who even draws the parallel with the principle of mutual recognition.

[361] A Bleckmann in H von der Groeben, H von Boeckh, J Thiesing and C-D Ehlermann (eds), *Kommentar zum EWG-Vertrag, Band 1 (Artikel 1-136)* (Baden-Baden, Nomos, 3rd edn, 1983), Artikel 5, paras 39–40; *accord* Blanquet, above n 334, 411. A Klimisch and B Krüger, "Decentralised application of EC competition law: current practice and future prospects" (1999) 24 *EL Rev* 463, 480, even suggest that, without recourse to Art 10 EC, NCA decisions applying Community law *ipso jure* have Community-wide effect.

[362] C-D Ehlermann, 'The Modernization of EC Antitrust Policy: A Legal and Cultural Revolution' (2000) 37 *CML Rev* 537, 551 and 572; see also Klimisch and Krüger, *ibid*, 481.

Community legislature to automatically attribute Community-wide legal force to all NCA decisions that implement Articles 81 and 82 EC. There are examples, albeit not many, of legislative acts of the Community which explicitly require national authorities to recognise and implement the decisions of other Member States in a specific field[363] or which expressly afford certain national measures Community-wide validity.[364] By contrast, Regulation 1/2003 does not contain a similar provision, nor does it address the question of recognition and enforcement of NCA decisions.[365] Moreover, in the context of discussing the possibility of decentralising the application of Article 81(3) EC, the White Paper explicitly states that a national decision is enforceable only within the territory of the NCA which adopted it.[366] Nothing in Regulation 1/2003 suggests that this approach has subsequently been abandoned. On the contrary, the Explanatory Memorandum restates that NCA decisions have no legal effect in foreign Member States.[367] The assumption of a territorial limitation of NCA decisions therefore underlies the decentralised system established by Regulation 1/2003.[368]

Against this background, it seems that obliging Member States to generally and automatically recognise the legal force of foreign NCA decisions would have required a clear and express provision in Regulation 1/2003.[369] Acknowledging such a far-reaching duty of automatic mutual

Indeed, Art 83(1) EC gives the Council a wide mandate to lay down any appropriate rules to give effect to the principles set out in Arts 81 and 82 EC.

[363] Eg Council Directive 2001/40/EC of 28 May 2001 on the mutual recognition of decisions on the expulsion of third country nationals [2001]OJ L149/34.

[364] Eg Art 2(3) of Council Reg (EEC) No 3911/92 of 9 December 1992 on the export of cultural goods [1992] OJ L395/1, which reads: 'The export licence shall be valid throughout the Community'. On various methods, applied in different areas of Community law, of vesting national decisions with trans-national effects see E Schmidt-Aßmann, 'Verwaltungskooperation und Verwaltungskooperationsrecht in der Europäischen Gemeinschaft' (1996) 31 *Europarecht* 270, 285–6 and 293.

[365] This has been criticised by a several writers who considered it desirable for national decisions enforcing Community competition law to be binding throughout the Community. See M Siragusa, 'A Critical Review of the White Paper on the Reform of the EC Competition Law Enforcement Rules' in B Hawk (ed), *1999 Proceedings of the Fordham Corporate Law Institute* (New York, Juris Publishing, 2000), 273, 289; Ehlermann, above n 362, 571.

[366] Para 60 of the White Paper.

[367] P 17 of the Explanatory Memorandum. See also Paulis, above n 187, 19.

[368] As concerns, however, *res iudicata* and *ne bis in idem*, see above n 275.

[369] J Basedow, 'Who will Protect Competition in Europe? From Central Enforcement to Authority Networks and Private Litigation' (2001) 2 *European Business Organizational Law Review* 443, 457. Admittedly, Basedow bases his conclusions also on considerations of public international law, which, it is submitted, cannot be applied directly to the relations between Member States in the Community law sphere. See below section II.D. On the different possibilities of how to make national decisions binding on the entire Community, including by way of regulation or multilateral treaty, see Siragusa, above n 365, 289–90, and Bundeskartellamt, *Praxis und Perspektiven der dezentralen Anwendung des EG-Wettbewerbsrechts*, Diskussionspapier für die Sitzung des Arbeitskreises Kartellrecht am 8. und 9. Oktober 1998, 29–30.

recognition through the 'loop way' of Article 10 EC would thus run counter to the implicit intentions of the Community legislator, who adopted Regulation 1/2003. It would also go beyond the *Cassis de Dijon* case law.[370] Finally, the existence of specific Community instruments providing for the recognition and enforcement, under certain conditions, of national acts, such as Regulation 44/2001, imply that a duty of automatic mutual recognition cannot be derived from Article 10 EC. Otherwise such specific legislation would be obsolete.

On the other hand, all NCAs have concurrent jurisdiction in EC antitrust matters. At the same time, Regulation 1/2003 and the Network Notice are guided by the spirit to also offer a one-stop shop in the case of national proceedings. The ultimate goal of the case allocation principles, combined with the rules on suspension of cases and rejection of complaints,[371] is to have each case, if possible, handled by a single authority. This objective is explicitly stated in recital 18 of Regulation 1/2003 and repeated, in slightly different terms, in paragraph 7 of the Network Notice.[372] Moreover, there is an institutionalised system of close co-operation which allows Network members to consult each other on individual cases and gives each NCA the theoretical possibility of commenting on decisions envisaged by other Network members.

Against this background, it would only seem fair if an NCA were obliged to honour the legal force of a decision adopted by another NCA and permit its execution, where necessary, on its own territory. In the present context, such an approach towards foreign acts would appear to be implied in the concept of loyalty and solidarity. It is therefore submitted that Article 10 EC, while not requiring Member States to automatically and mutually recognise the legal force of all foreign decisions which have been adopted to implement Article 81 or 82 EC,[373] can certainly be construed in such a

---

[370] Blanquet, above n 334, 411 note 250. In the leading *Cassis de Dijon* judgment the ECJ established the principle that, unless certain mandatory requirements (eg public health) justify a trade restriction, a product which is lawfully produced and marketed in one Member State may also legally be imported into and sold in all other Member States (Case 120/78 *Rewe v Bundesmonopolverwaltung für Branntwein* [1979] ECR 649, para 14: 'There is therefore no valid reason why, provided that they have been lawfully produced and marketed in one of the Member States, alcoholic beverages should not be introduced into any other Member State'.). However, the ECJ did not go as far as establishing mutual duties of the Member States to formally and automatically recognise the legal force of national (approval) decisions.

[371] Art 13 of Reg 1/2003.

[372] Which reads: 'network members will endeavour to reallocate cases to a *single* well placed competition authority as often as possible' (emphasis added). See also para 16 of the Joint Statement.

[373] See Lück, above n 332, 168–9. Cf also Schmidt-Aßmann, above n 364, 300–1, who emphasises that Community-wide effects of national administrative acts are based on the principle of recognition. Even though Schmidt-Aßmann sees different ways of achieving such recognition, eg by ordering the transnational effects in a legislative act of the Community (eg in a regulation) or by explicit confirmation of the Member States, he does seem to require some form of express and unequivocal declaration. This would exclude any automatism based on Art 10 EC.

way as to impose a duty on Member States to recognise the validity of foreign NCA decisions on a case-by-case basis. This means that recognition would take place only when a request is made by the Member State which adopted the decision and only by the NCA of the Member State to which the request is submitted. Such a request for recognition may be justified, for instance, where recognition is necessary to allow enforcement of the decision against a particular undertaking in the other Member State.[374] The recognition, it is submitted, can only be refused in exceptional circumstances, for instance if the Commission has 'overruled' the national decision.[375]

C. Duty to Avoid Conflicting Decisions

Another question is of course whether NCAs are bound, by virtue of Article 10 EC, to respect the contents of a national decision of another Member State applying Article 81 or 82 EC and to abstain from adopting a decision that would conflict with that other Member State's decision. This question could become relevant, for instance, if an NCA initially intends to punish a company which has participated in a restrictive agreement or practice that has already been investigated and held to be contrary to Article 81 by another NCA.[376] In such a case, would Article 10 EC

---

[374] Such recognition will be necessary in most of the cases, as NCA decisions have no Community-wide legal force and there are no general instruments to provide for the transnational recovery of fines imposed by national acts. Art 256 EC does not apply to the enforcement of national decisions, while Council Directive 76/308/EC on mutual assistance for the recovery of claims resulting from operations forming part of the system of financing the European Agricultural Guidance and Guarantee Fund, and of the agricultural levies and customs duties [1976] OJ L73/18, despite having a broad scope, does not cover public claims deriving from competition law sanctions. O Jansen, 'The System of International Co-operation in Administrative and Criminal Matters in Relation to Regulation 1/2003', CLaSF Working Papers Series, Working Paper 03, January 2004 (available at www.clasf.org/publications/workingpapers.htm, accessed February 2009), 1, 4 and 16. There are a number of EU agreements and international conventions which allow for co-operation between the contracting states in proceedings with transborder elements, including some which cover co-operation in the enforcement of decisions imposing financial penalties. However, the scope of these instruments is often restricted to criminal procedures or at least to matters that may lead to the involvement of criminal courts (eg Schengen Convention). See the overview given by Jansen, *ibid*, 18 *et seq* (some instruments are even specifically limited to road traffic offences). The confinement to criminal matters would seem to exclude their application in cases where fines for competition law infringements are imposed on undertakings (unless such pecuniary sanctions are qualified as criminal under the relevant national law as is the case, eg in Denmark; see above Chapter 4, n 61) and further in all Member States with purely administrative sanctioning systems (Jansen, *ibid*, 39). In addition, the relevant international conventions are often applicable only in a limited number of Member States and thus do not provide for a coherent Community-wide system, while the pre-Maastricht Community instruments have not been ratified at all (*idem*, 23 and 28).

[375] See para 102, subpara (2), of the White Paper and above Chapter 1, section II.A.1.b(2).

[376] One can imagine a situation where the NCA of Member State A has investigated an infringement and imposed fines on cartel members A1 and A2, both of which have their principal

preclude the second NCA taking up the matter from ultimately finding that the agreement was compatible with Community competition law after all?[377] This question, it is submitted, should normally be answered in the affirmative.

1. Duty to Pay Deference to Foreign NCA Decisions

The binding legal effects of a national decision enforcing Community competition law are limited to the territory of the Member State whose authority adopted it and, as has been submitted in the previous section, there is no general reciprocal duty on Member States to formally and automatically recognise the legal force of foreign NCA decisions. However, Community law must be applied uniformly throughout the entire EU. This has been stressed by the ECJ in numerous cases.[378] The principle of uniform application also holds true where Community law is implemented by the Member States in accordance with the procedural (and substantive) rules of their national laws.[379] In addition, Member States have a general duty, derived from Article 10 EC, not to take decisions which would run counter to a Community measure.[380] With regard to Commission decisions applying Articles 81 and 82 EC, as well as group exemption regulations adopted under Article 81(3) EC, this duty has explicitly been laid down in Articles 3(2) and 16 of Regulation 1/2003 for both NCAs and national courts.

At the same time, the ECJ has repeatedly ruled that the principle of loyalty enshrined in Article 10 EC also applies between the Member States.[381] Arguably, this implies that the duties imposed on Member States with regard to Commission decisions must also apply, *mutatis mutandis*, in relation to national decisions of other Member States.[382] Obviously, the

---

place of business in that Member State. This decision has subsequently prompted a second NCA, located in Member State B, where another member of the same cartel (company B3) is domiciled, to take up the matter and initiate proceedings against B3.

[377] The reverse case, that the first NCA holds an agreement or practice to be compatible with the EC competition rules while the second authority wants to condemn it, should not occur in practice as NCAs cannot adopt positive decisions but only non-action ,decisions which, in any event, do not bind other authorities. See below section II.C.2.

[378] See, eg para 4 of the judgment in *Walt Wilhelm*, above n 59 (specifically with regard to Community competition law); para 14 of the judgment in *Simmenthal* (above n 344); para 18 of the judgment in *Factortame* (above n 344); and para 15 of the judgment in Case 34/73 *Fratelli Variola* [1973] ECR 981.

[379] Joined Cases 205–215/82 *Deutsche Milchkontor and others v Germany* [1983] ECR 2633, para 17.

[380] Art 10 EC in fact operates as a general conflict and non-interference rule. J Temple Lang, 'Community Constitutional Law: Art 5 EEC Treaty' (1990) 27 *CML Rev* 645, 678.

[381] See the judgments in *Athanasopoulos* and *Italian wine*, both above n 341.

[382] Curiously enough, Temple Lang raised the question of 'how far findings of fact made by Community or *national* authorities applying Community law are binding or conclusive for *other authorities* applying Community law to the same facts' (emphasis added) as long ago as 1993, albeit without answering it. Temple Lang, above n 188, 568.

force of Commission decisions in the legal order of a Member State is and must be stronger than that of a national act of another Member State because Commission decisions benefit from the primacy of Community law. However, this does not mean that Member States can completely ignore national decisions of other Member States which have been adopted in the application of Community law.

This should be all the more so in a field such as Community competition law, which is characterised by the concurrent jurisdiction of the Commission and the Member States and by a sophisticated and institution-alised system of close co-operation, including (non-binding) arrangements for the allocation of cases. In particular, the mechanisms for (voluntary) mutual consultation, the possibility of providing administrative assistance to other NCAs and the right to exchange evidence with each other underline that Regulation 1/2003 has made the Commission and NCAs partners in a joint enterprise, the protection of undistorted competition in the Community in accordance with Article 3(g) EC. The NCAs could even be regarded as 'arms of the Community' when they apply Articles 81 and 82 EC.[383] It seems self-evident that in such a partnership each partner must pay careful attention to the decisions of the other partners. Moreover, the consultation mechanisms available in the Network give each NCA the opportunity to express its views on a contemplated decision of another NCA before it is actually adopted. All this supports the position that formal NCA decisions cannot be entirely disregarded by other Network members. NCAs must accord some deference towards foreign NCA decisions adopted in the same matter.[384]

Moreover, it follows from the case law regarding Article 10 EC that Member States, under certain circumstances, could be required not to act contrary to non-binding advice or opinions expressed by the Commission (eg in a legislative proposal).[385] On this basis, the fact that NCA decisions have no legal force outside the own territory of the NCA which adopted them and thus are not formally binding on other NCAs would not preclude that an NCA must have due regard to an existing decision of another NCA concerning the same facts and has to make all reasonable efforts to avoid any substantial conflict with such other decision.

Finally, it should be recalled that the enforcement system established by

---

[383] Cf Temple Lang, above n 188, 584.

[384] See I Forrester, 'Diversity and Consistency: Can They Cohabit?' in Ehlermann and Atanasiu, above n 36, 341, 352; J-P Schneider, 'Vollzug des Europäischen Wirtschaftsrecht zwischen Zentralisierung und Dezentralisierung—Bilanz und Ausblick' (2005) 40 *Europarecht* (Beiheft 2), 141, 146.

[385] Temple Lang, above n 331, 46. The leading case is *France v UK*, above n 356, where the ECJ held that Member States were required, by virtue of a non-binding Council resolution, to first consult the Commission and seek its approval before adopting certain measures in the fisheries sector (paras 7–9 of the judgment). The relevant resolution had suggested that Member States should proceed in this way.

Regulation 1/2003 should be based on mutual trust and confidence between all members of the ECN, and that these seem to be prerequisites for decentralisation and close co-operation between the NCAs and the Commission.[386] The Council and the Commission have confirmed that co-operation under Regulation 1/2003 is based on the equality, respect and solidarity of the Network members. In addition, Member States have mutually recognised the standards of each others' enforcement systems.[387] If these elements are indeed the foundations of the decentralised system, there is in principle no reason for any NCA to doubt the lawfulness and appropriateness of the decisions of the other Network members.[388]

It is therefore submitted that Article 10 EC, in conjunction with the principle of uniform application, precludes NCAs, when applying Community competition law, from simply ignoring the decision of another NCA in the same matter. NCAs are therefore obliged to pay some deference and therefore make all reasonable effort to abstain from adopting measures that would be inconsistent with the contents of other NCAs' decisions.[389]

Even though the operative part of a decision generally is the only part producing legal effects,[390] the obligation to observe the contents of a foreign NCA decision applies not only to the operative part, but equally to

---

[386] Cf Ehlermann, above n 362, 573.

[387] Paras 7 and 8 of the Joint Statement.

[388] This would also be in line with public international law (act-of-state doctrine; see above Chapter 4, n 193), although the relationships between Member States are of course governed predominantly by Community law principles. However, where public law demands respect for the acts of foreign states, this should apply a fortiori to acts of Member States adopted in the Community law sphere, albeit with the exception described hereafter.

[389] See the opinion of Advocate General Van Gerven in Case C–128/92 *HJ Banks v British Coal* [1994] ECR I–1209, para 60, where he noted: 'the duty of cooperation which . . . Art 5 of the EEC Treaty imposes on the national court (and which applies expressly to acts of the institutions) entails for the national court the obligation, in relation to a decision adopted by the Commission and relied upon or challenged by the parties before that court, to mitigate as far as possible in the interests of the Community the risk of a ruling that conflicts with that decision'. Since the duty of co-operation or loyalty, according to the case law of the ECJ, also applies horizontally in the relation between the Member States, these considerations are arguably also valid in relation to national acts (eg NCA decisions) implementing Community law. Cf also para 56 of the judgment in *Italian wine*, above n 341. That case concerned certain border checks of the French authorities regarding wine imported from Italy, in particular the refusal to accept the accompanying (Italian) documents and the requirement of systematic oenological analyses. It was, however, an established fact that controls were also carried out by the Italian authorities in order to protect consumers and the health of humans. On that basis, the ECJ held that '[t]he French authorities were under a duty to take into account the existence of those checks carried out in the country of origin of the wine'. Cf further Gilliams and Cornelis, above n 314, para 68, who seem to go even further. With regard to the question of legal force of foreign NCA decisions in subsequent private enforcement proceedings before national courts, they submit that 'the obligation of cooperation set out in article 10 EC as well as the more general prohibition on discrimination on the basis of nationality require national courts to accept the dictum of the aforementioned decisions, in as far as they relate to the application of articles 81 and 82 EC'. Cf also s 33(4) GWB, mentioned above at n 325.

[390] Judgment of the CFI in *Dutch Banks* [1992] ECR II–2181, para 31.

the findings (of fact and law) on which it is based.[391] Limiting the obligation solely to the operative part would not fully guarantee the uniform application of Community competition law. NCAs might still express conflicting views on the substance of the case, in particular on the legal assessment of the relevant facts, and thus compromise the uniformity of EC competition law throughout the Community.[392] Moreover, we are dealing with neither the formal legal effects of a foreign decision nor with the position of individuals who, under Community law, can challenge an act only to the extent that it adversely affects their interests.[393] Therefore, the general rule whereby a distinction must be made between the legally binding operative part and the non-binding grounds of a decision is not relevant here.

An exception to the principal rule that NCAs must make all reasonable efforts to avoid conflicting decisions may apply where the foreign NCA decision is manifestly wrong. Alluding to the ECJ's case law on the marginal review of complex economic appraisals made by the Commission,[394] mostly in competition matters, one can imagine that an NCA decision could be considered as 'manifestly wrong' where it is either based on an incorrect statement of facts or vitiated by a manifest error of appraisal or a misuse of power.[395] This case law is inspired by the consideration that, where the Commission must assess complex economic matters, it disposes of a considerable margin of appreciation which precludes the Community courts from substituting their own assessment for the Commission's appraisal.[396] The Community courts may, however, verify that no overt mistakes have been made. These considerations are also valid where the

---

[391] Cf A Riley, 'Beyond Leniency: Enhancing Enforcement in EC Antitrust Law' (2005) 28 *World Competition* 377, 387–8. Riley argues, in respect of private antitrust litigation, that both issues of law and findings of fact in Commission prohibition decisions cannot be relitigated, in national courts, by the addressees of such decisions where the decision has not been challenged at all or has been challenged unsuccessfully before the Community courts. His reasoning is based on a combination of Art 16(1) of Reg 1/2003 and the relevant case law of the ECJ, in particular the judgment in Case C–344/98 *Masterfoods* [2000] ECR I–11369 and the opinion of Advocate General Van Gerven in *Banks v British Coal* (above n 389), paras 58–61).

[392] Examples would be, for instance in cartel matters, different views of the NCAs involved as to whether a certain conduct amounts to an agreement or rather constitutes a concerted practice, whether or not a particular company acted as instigator or ringleader, or inconsistent assessments of the duration and gravity of an infringement.

[393] Cf Temple Lang, above n 188, 569–70. See also paras 31–2 of the judgment in *Dutch Banks* (above n 390), where it was held that an undertaking could not separately challenge the reasoning (legal assessment) of a decision by which the Commission had granted the requested negative clearance and whose operative part thus did not affect the legal position of the undertaking.

[394] See K Lenaerts and J Vanhamme, 'Procedural Rights of Private Parties in the Community Administrative Process' (1997) 34 *CML Rev* 531, 560.

[395] Cf the judgment of the ECJ in Case C–7/95 *John Deere v Commission* [1998] ECR I–3111, para 34.

[396] The relevant case law is based on the judgment of the ECJ in Case 42/84 *Remia v Commission* [1985] ECR 2545, para 34. See further K Lenaerts, D Arts and I Maselis, *Procedural Law of the European Union* (London, Sweet & Maxwell, 2006), para 7-154.

question arises whether an NCA must have due regard to a foreign national decision. Obviously, it would jeopardise both the conformity of the enforcement and the mutual trust between the Network members were NCAs to make a comprehensive review of every foreign NCA decision before concluding whether or not they have to respect its contents. On the other hand, an NCA cannot be forced, by virtue of Article 10 EC, to follow a decision which is (evidently) wrong and not formally binding on it. It is therefore submitted that limiting the exception (to the rule that the contents of foreign NCA decisions must be respected) to manifest errors of fact or law and misuse of power by the foreign NCA provides a workable compromise.

However, in a case where an NCA finds it difficult to comply with the duties under Article 10 EC because it considers a foreign national decision to be manifestly wrong, it should not simply defy the foreign act. Rather, the relevant case law relating to Article 10 EC suggests that the NCA should use the available procedures to co-operate and resolve the problem.[397] This applies in particular where there are uncertainties about the legal situation.[398] On this basis, an NCA that intends to adopt a decision conflicting with the decision of another NCA in the same matter should first consult that other NCA. This would follow from Article 10 EC read in conjunction with Article 11(1) and recital 15 of Regulation 1/2003, which lay down the general duty of close co-operation between all members of the ECN.[399] Such consultation between the NCAs involved can help to clarify the situation. It may forecome divergent interpretations of the relevant facts or the existing decision and reveal objective reasons explaining the difference in approach. If the NCAs do not succeed in overcoming the difficulties, they can always consult the Commission in accordance with Article 11(5) of Regulation 1/2003, which, it is submitted, would even include the possibility of requesting the Commission's opinion

---

[397] In Case 94/87 *Commission v Germany* [1989] ECR 175, para 9, the ECJ held: 'In such a case the Commission and the Member State concerned must respect the principle underlying Article 5 [now Article 10] of the Treaty, which imposes a duty of genuine cooperation on the Member States and the Community institutions, and must work together in good faith with a view to overcoming difficulties whilst fully observing the Treaty provisions . . .' See also Temple Lang, above n 380, 679. NCAs thus have to use the available consultation mechanisms in the ECN (eg have the case put on the agenda of the Advisory Committee pursuant to Reg 1/2003, Art 14(7), 1st sentence) and speak out before a national decision which they consider flawed is adopted.

[398] See paras 47 and 48 of the judgment in Case 7/71 *Commission v France* (*Euratom Treaty*) [1971] ECR 1003.

[399] Admittedly, the pre-cited case law (above n 397), of which the case *Commission v Germany* is only one example, is regarded as establishing a duty to consult the *Commission* (see Temple Lang, above n 331, 43 and 66–7). However, there is no reason why, within the ECN, the duty to co-operate in good faith in order to solve problems of consistency and uniformity should not create an obligation to (first) consult with the NCA whose national decision is allegedly flawed before engaging the Commission.

on the relevant questions of fact or law.[400] If the Commission expresses an opinion, this would evidently be without prejudice to the powers of the ECJ and would thus by no means affect the right of any national court seized to review the lawfulness of an NCA decision that is based on the EC antitrust rules to make a reference to the ECJ for a preliminary ruling in order to clarify issues of Community law.[401]

The approach suggested here evidently depends on the availability of the relevant national decisions in one or more commonly understood languages. Where the decisions of NCAs are essentially inaccessible for language reasons, conformity and consistency in the enforcement practice of NCAs will be difficult to achieve.[402] On the other hand, it cannot be required that all national decisions are systematically translated into all other Community languages as this would be an excessive burden, in terms of both costs and resources, on the responsible NCAs. However, it seems to be a fair compromise that a translation of a final decision, possibly in draft version, into one of the working languages can be commanded in the event that the case allocation process has revealed that two or more NCAs will be acting on the same matter and thus will have to take into account each others' decisions. The language to be chosen should be determined after consultation among the NCAs involved, and even a sharing of costs could be envisaged.[403] This would seem to be a workable solution. Alternatively, a centrally run database, similar to the existing database for national courts' judgments,[404] but containing summary translations of NCA decisions in one or two working languages (English, French or German), could be

[400] See Temple Lang, above n 343, 123. The procedure suggested here is in fact comparable to the possibility for national courts to ask the Commission's opinion on questions concerning the application of the Community competition rules (Art 15(1) of Reg 1/2003). Para 27 of the Commission Notice on co-operation between the Commission and the courts of the EU Member States in the application of Articles 81 and 82 of the EC [2004] OJ C101/54 ('National Courts Notice') explains that the Commission may be asked for its opinion on economic, factual and legal matters. See also para 53 of the judgment in *Delimitis* (above n 340). Cf further Temple Lang (1997), above n 344, 15, who argues, on the basis of Art 234 EC in conjunction with Art 10 EC, that national courts have a duty 'to take all reasonable steps to see that Community law is clarified and as far as possible uniformly applied'. The same argument can be applied, on the basis of Art 10 EC and Reg 1/2003, in particular Art 11(1) thereof, with regard to NCAs.

[401] Cf para 27 of the National Courts Notice.

[402] The fact that the existence of 23 official languages in the Community may jeopardise effective co-operation and consistency in the decision-making of NCAs and impair the precedence value (in respect of the particular infringement decided upon) of foreign national decisions has been highlighted by M Wezenbeek-Geuke, 'Het voorstel voor een verordening van de Raad betreffende de uitvoering van de mededingingsregels van de artikelen 81 en 82 van het verdrag' [2001] *Nederlands tijdschrift voor Europees recht* 17, 25.

[403] Cost sharing may be particularly appropriate where only one or two NCAs have to provide a translation, while the other authority (eg the OFT) has drafted its decision in the requested/working language anyway.

[404] See http://ec.europa.eu/competition/elojade/antitrust/nationalcourts/ (accessed February 2009).

envisaged. The provision of summary translations could again be limited to cases where parallel enforcement actions by several NCAs were commenced or contemplated.

2. *Types of Foreign NCA Decisions that Require Deference*

On the basis of the foregoing, the question arises of whether all types of national decisions have the effect of indirectly (ie via Article 10 EC) requiring some deference by foreign NCAs. It is submitted that this effect only results from negative decisions—meaning prohibitions and decisions imposing fines—to the extent that the latter also include a finding of illegality of the relevant agreement or practice. It does not, however, result from non-action decisions and commitment decisions. With regard to non-action decisions, it has expressly been stated that they only bind the authority which adopted them.[405] This can only mean that they do not bind the national courts of the same Member State[406] and, a fortiori, cannot impose a certain finding or conclusion on foreign courts and NCAs, not even via Article 10 EC.[407]

Similar considerations apply with regard to commitment decisions as such decisions do not include a definitive finding on the question of whether there has been or, after fulfilment of the commitment, still is a violation of the EC competition rules. A commitment decision simply states that there are no longer grounds for action.[408] As a consequence, such decisions cannot prejudice the powers of other NCAs or courts.[409] These rules have been developed for commitment decisions adopted by the Commission. However, since commitment decisions constitute a new type of instrument also for NCAs, the same principles are likely to apply in the event that commitments are made binding by NCAs.

Despite this formal approach, which excludes an authoritative force, via Article 10 EC, of foreign commitment and non-action decisions, both these types of measure can obviously have a strong persuasive value which can (duly) influence foreign NCAs (as well as domestic and foreign courts).[410]

---

[405] P 16 of the Explanatory Memorandum.

[406] Arhold, above n 3, 127.

[407] The same would apply with regard to interim measures as they contain merely a provisional assessment of the matter.

[408] Art 9(1) and recital 13 of Reg 1/2003.

[409] See recital 13 of Reg 1/2003.

[410] See W Wils, *The Optimal Enforcement of EC Antitrust Law. Essays in Law and Economics* (The Hague, Kluwer Law International, 2001), 139 note 84.

D. Duty to Apply Sanctions also for Extraterritorial Effects of an Infringement

There seems to be a common understanding between the Network members that no NCA will impose sanctions in relation to the effects of an anti-competitive conduct that have occurred outside its own territory.[411] However, in terms of efficiency of the decentralised enforcement system and effectiveness of Community law, it is doubtful that acting according to this understanding is appropriate.[412]

In fact, it is submitted that the principle of full effectiveness, combined with the requirements of uniformity and proportionality, not only allows NCAs but also requires them to penalise the effects of the illegal conduct in the territories of other Member States.[413] Where national law does not confer the necessary powers on the NCA, they can be derived from Community law. The principles of state sovereignty and territorial limitation of national acts, which are principles of public international law, do not form an obstacle to this approach.

1. National Implementation and the Problem of 'Underfining'

It was the clear objective of the Commission to create an enforcement system which would be more efficient than the previous system existing under Regulation 17. Decentralisation is not a purpose in itself, but a tool to increase the efficiency of enforcement[414] by involving more actors and

---

[411] This has been confirmed repeatedly by NCA officials at various conferences I have attended. See also above n 173. An example of this policy is the Dutch *Northsea Shrimp* case (*Noordzeegarnalen*, case no 2269 of 14 January 2003), which involved several Dutch companies and associations, but also some smaller German and Danish firms. The case was handled by the NMa, with the assistance of the BKartA and the Danish NCA during the fact-finding stage. The NMa ultimately imposed fines on all cartel participants, including the German and Danish companies, albeit only for the effects of the cartel in the Netherlands. See the 2003 Annual Report of the Dutch NCA (*Jaarverslag 2003 NMa en DTe*), 83, at point 7.3. See also Smits, above n 20, 185 and M Reynolds and D Anderson, 'Immunity and Leniency in EU Cartel Cases' (2006) 27 *European Competition Law Review* 82, 87 note 24.

[412] Reg 1/2003 itself is tacit on the question of whether NCAs can take into account the effects of an infringement in other Member States. W Wils, 'The Reform of Competition Law Enforcement—Will it Work?', Community Report for the FIDE XXI Congress, Dublin, 2–5 June 2004, in D Cahill (ed), *The Modernisation of EU Competition Law Enforcement in the EU—FIDE 2004 National Reports* (Cambridge, Cambridge University Press, 2004) (available at SSRN: http://ssrn.com/abstract=1319249), 661, para 130. This is certainly regrettable. Smits, above n 20, 185, who further notes that there is 'amazingly little commentary on this gap in enforcement' (*idem*, 184). However, as will be argued in this section, the gap can be bridged by applying the Community law principles of full effectiveness, uniformity, proportionality and equal treatment.

[413] Wils, *ibid*, para 134; see also L Pignataro, 'La riforma del diritto communitario della concorrenza: il regolamento n. 1/2003 sull'appplicazione degli articoli 81 e 82 del Trattato CE' (2003) 8 *Contratto e Impresa/Europa* 233. Doubts as to the compatibility of such a 'territorial limitation' of the penalisation are also expressed by Arhold, above n 3, 134.

[414] C-D Ehlermann, 'Implementation of EC Competition Law by National Anti-Trust Authorities' (1996) 17 *European Competition Law Review* 88, 90, who even speaks of 'maximisation of efficiency'.

freeing some of the Commission's resources so that the Commission can concentrate its enforcement activities on the most serious cartel violations.

However, if NCAs, whenever they impose sanctions for an infringement of the Community competition rules, only take into account the effects which have occurred in their own territory, the extraterritorial effects of the illegal behaviour will not be punished unless the NCAs of the other Member States affected, in turn, open proceedings and penalise the effects in their respective territories. Since the Community competition rules only apply if inter-state trade is affected, it is unlikely that there will be many infringements whose effects are confined to the territory of a single Member State.[415]

The current approach of the NCAs therefore inevitably leads either to a duplication of procedures or a situation where many undertakings which have been involved in antitrust violations will be 'underfined' because parts of their illegal conduct will remain unpunished.[416] Even though the first NCA to have conducted an investigation and penalised the offenders may assist the other NCAs that follow by providing information and evidentiary material, the multiplication of proceedings can hardly be considered an efficient way of enforcement.[417] It certainly is not consistent with the spirit of Regulation 1/2003, which explicitly proclaims, in recital 18, the objective 'that each case should be handled by a *single* authority'.[418] Nor is the regular underfining of competition law infringements an acceptable option as it would undermine the deterrent effect of sanctions and thus ultimately the effectiveness of EC competition law.

[415] See above Chapter 1, n 113 and the accompanying text.

[416] Cf Wils, above n 4, 146 and Forrester, above n 384, 351. Limiting sanctions to the domestic effects precludes NCAs from taking proper account of the real geographic scope and thus of the actual impact and seriousness of the infringement. In 2001, Wils, above n 47, 420–3, argued that, in economic terms, ie considering the potential gains from antitrust violations (based on certain estimates of the average overcharge and the likely duration of cartels, as well as the probability of detection and punishment), the current level of fines imposed by the Commission is considerably lower than what would be required to guarantee deterrence at least with regard to price cartels. In 2005, ie four years later, he reaffirmed these conclusions. Even supposing an increase in the detection rate (due inter alia to more efficient leniency programmes), the general level of fines would still be too low to effectively deter (potential) offenders. See Wils, above n 21, 139–40. To the extent that his evaluation is correct, the situation would be aggravated by the application of merely 'domestic' fines.

[417] Schermers, above n 227, 604. See also G DI Federico and P Manzini, 'A Law and Economics Approach to the New European Antitrust Enforcing Rules' (2004) 1 *Erasmus Law and Economics Review* 143, 155. Since duplication of procedures increases costs and inconvenience for the companies which have to defend themselves in different legal systems, probably using different languages and requiring legal advice from several counsels, it may even be considered contrary to the principle of proportionality. See Temple Lang, above n 188, 548.

[418] Emphasis added. Klees, above n 3, 1227; Arhold, above n 3, 133–4. Cf also Pignataro, above n 413, 264, who, referring to Art 35(1) of Reg 1/2003, highlights the obligation imposed on Member States to ensure effective compliance with Reg 1/2003. Despite the above considerations, it has been suggested that parallel national proceedings will have to be conducted precisely because of the territorial limitation of fines. S Hossenfelder in Loewenheim *et al*, above n 3, VerfVO Art 5, para 9.

Finally, this issue is also related to the question of *ne bis in idem*. To the extent that the fines imposed by an NCA take into account all effects of the infringement throughout the Community and thus remedy the entire wrongdoing, it is all the more obvious that a double jeopardy plea is justified if a second NCA subsequently initiates proceedings regarding the same infringement against the same undertakings.[419]

2. Effectiveness, Uniformity and Proportionality

The Community's laws and policies are mostly carried out by national authorities and national courts.[420] Member States therefore have an obligation to ensure that Community legislation is implemented and observed within their territory. In other words, Member States must give full force and effect to Community law within their domestic legal order. Moreover, Community law must be applied uniformly throughout the Union and in accordance with the principle of proportionality.

The cumulative effect of these requirements justifies the view that NCAs are under an obligation to take into account the impact of the anti-competitive conduct in the whole of the EU when determining the sanctions for an infringement of the Community competition rules. Limiting the sanctions to the domestic effects of the wrongdoing would fall short of a fully effective, uniform and proportional implementation of Article 81 or 82 EC.[421]

a. Full Effectiveness of Community Law and National Sanctions

Since the Commission's enforcement powers under the EC Treaty are fairly restricted, it is primarily for the Member States to ensure implementation of Community rules. Where Community law does not provide for common rules to this effect, the relevant national authorities act in accordance with their domestic procedural and substantive rules.[422] As we have seen, this also applies in the field of Community competition law despite the fact that the Commission has its own powers to enforce Articles 81 and 82 EC. Regulation 1/2003, while imposing an obligation on Member States to

---

[419] See above section I.D.4.b(2). To the extent that the first sanction imposed on an undertaking adequately punishes the wrongdoing, ie an optimal penalty has been applied, additional proceedings would obviously lead to 'overpunishment'. See Wils, above n 4, 136.

[420] See Hatje in Schwarze, Artikel 10 EGV, above n 336, paras 2 and 34. In fact, implementation of Community legislation by the Member States is the rule rather than the exception. In general, there is no direct Community administration. Antitrust law is one of the few exceptions (next to state aids) where the Community (through the Commission) has the power to apply Community rules in individual cases. See Ehlermann, above n 362, 575–6.

[421] Pignataro, above n 413, 264.

[422] Para 17 of the judgment in *Deutsche Milchkontor* (above n 379).

enforce Articles 81 and 82 EC, does not lay down the applicable procedure. NCAs therefore have to apply national implementation rules.

On the other hand, the application of national rules must not affect the scope and effectiveness of Community law.[423] By virtue of Article 10 EC, Member States must thus take all necessary measures to ensure that Community law is effectively complied with by everyone, public bodies as well as private parties, within their jurisdiction. Where Community rules require or prohibit a certain behaviour of individuals or companies—such as Articles 81 and 82 EC—the duty to guarantee the full effectiveness of Community law may even include an obligation for Member States to introduce and apply sanctions for an infringement of those rules.[424] As concerns breaches of EC competition law, this obligation follows from Article 10 EC *juncto* Article 5 of Regulation 1/2003. The latter provision brings about a very limited degree of harmonisation of the national procedural rules by listing the possible types of decisions which NCAs may adopt, including decisions imposing fines. However, the question of how such fines should be assessed is left to the national legislature. Moreover, Article 5 of Regulation 1/2003 explicitly empowers Member States to apply penalties other than fines that are provided for in their domestic laws.

In such cases, where Community law does not itself determine the penalty but instead refers for that purpose to the national laws, the choice of penalties remains at the Member States' discretion. That discretion is, however, limited by the requirement that the penalties must be 'effective, proportionate and dissuasive'.[425] In the context of EC competition law enforcement by NCAs, Member States can exercise this discretion not only in relation to the question of which penalties (eg monetary criminal sanctions, imprisonment) national legislation may arrange for in addition to the fines which are expressly mentioned in Regulation 1/2003, but also in respect to the determination of the magnitude of fines for which Regulation 1/2003 itself does not provide any parameter or guidelines.

The criteria used by NCAs to assess the amount of fines imposed for breaches of Community competition law must therefore be such as to guarantee that the fine is in any event effective, proportionate and

---

[423] Para 22 of the judgment in *Deutsche Milchkontor* (above n 379).

[424] Temple Lang, above n 380, 651. Cf also Case 68/88 *Commission v Greece* [1989] ECR 2965, paras 22–8, where Greece was convicted for failure to fulfil its obligations under Art 10 EC by omitting to prosecute and punish traders who had evaded certain agricultural levies which constituted own resources of the Communities, and Case C–326/88 *Anklagemyndigheden v Hansen* [1990] ECR I–2911, paras 11–18, where the introduction, by Denmark alone, of a system of strict criminal liability of the employer for infringements of the Community rules on the maximum daily driving period by drivers employed by him was considered a means of ensuring compliance with these rules and thus consistent with the relevant regulation.

[425] Settled case law. See para 24 of the pre-cited judgment in *Commission v Greece* and para 17 of the pre-cited judgment in *Hansen* (both *ibid*).

dissuasive. The emphasis here is on the dissuasive character of the fine.[426] This element was also accentuated by the ECJ in a preliminary ruling concerning the principle of equal treatment of men and woman in labour law matters. By its reference, the German *Arbeitsgericht* sought to establish whether the relevant Council directive required Member States to provide for specific sanctions against the employer in the event of discrimination on the grounds of sex regarding access to employment. The ECJ held that:

> Although . . . full implementation of the directive does not require any specific form of sanction for unlawful discrimination, it does entail that that sanction be . . . Moreover, it must also have a *real deterrent effect* on the employer. It follows that where a Member State chooses to penalize the breach of the prohibition of discrimination by the award of compensation, that compensation must in any event be adequate in relation to the damage sustained.[427]

Arguably, a national rule or policy of penalising only the domestic effects of an infringement of the Community competition rules would be inconsistent with the above requirements because it would not provide sufficient deterrence. A fine which is indifferent to the fact that the penalised anti-competitive conduct also had (adverse) effects outside the territory of the relevant Member State[428] and thus a priori could not be substantially higher than a fine for an equivalent violation of the national competition rules can hardly be expected to have a strong dissuasive effect on potential offenders of the Community antitrust rules.[429]

This kind of 'purely domestic' fine is not deprived of any deterrent effect and therefore could not be said to render Community competition law entirely ineffective. The question, in my view, is, however, whether the dissuasive force is sufficiently strong given the larger territorial scope of the adverse effects and thus the noticeable seriousness of the infringement compared to purely national matters. If the deterrent effect of a sanction in the form of a compensation depends on the compensation being adequate in relation to the damage sustained, the deterrent effect of a sanction in the form of a fine depends on the adequacy of its amount in relation to the scope and seriousness of the harm caused. Disregarding the extraterritorial effects of a violation of Article 81 or 82 EC would be tantamount to playing down the actual harm.

Furthermore, under Article 10 EC, Member States not only have a duty to disapply national rules which conflict directly with Community law, but also a duty to refrain from measures which interfere with the effectiveness

---

[426] The element of proportionality will be discussed below (see below section II.D.2.c).

[427] Emphasis added. Case 14/83 *von Colson and Kamann* [1984] ECR 1891, para 23.

[428] According to the common practice in the ECN, each NCA imposes fines only for the effects of the infringement in the own territory. See above n 173 and accompanying text.

[429] See also above n 416.

of Community law. In a long series of case law, the ECJ has used formulas such that Member States may not adopt or maintain measures 'which deprive Community law of its effectiveness' or 'which render Community law ineffective'.[430] A more recent judgment suggests that the relevant standard, at least in competition matters, is not the (complete) ineffectiveness of Community law, but the question of whether Community law is rendered 'less effective'.[431] In its 2003 judgment in the *Fiammiferi* case, the ECJ held that:

> Since a national competition authority such as the Authority is responsible for ensuring, inter alia , that Article 81 EC is observed and that provision, in conjunction with Article 10 EC, imposes a duty on Member States to refrain from introducing measures contrary to the Community competition rules, those rules would be rendered *less effective* if . . . the authority were not able to declare a national measure contrary to the combined provisions of Articles 10 EC and 81 EC . . .[432]

This approach also seems to fit better with another formula frequently used by the ECJ, notably that Community law must be given 'full effect' or must be 'fully effective'.[433] There is no full effectiveness where the effectiveness is impaired (though not entirely suspended).[434]

On this basis, fines imposed by NCAs for a breach of Community competition law must take into account the effects of the wrongdoing in all Member States concerned, not only in the Member State whose NCA imposes the fine, in order to create sufficient deterrence and thus guarantee the full effectiveness of Community law.[435]

---

[430] See, eg the judgments in *INNO v ATAB*, above n 349, para 31, and *Leclerc*, above n 353, para 14. For further references, see Temple Lang (2004), above n 344, 400.

[431] Temple Lang (2004), above n 344, 402. Cf also W Van Gerven, 'Of Rights, Remedies and Procedures' (2000) 37 *CML Rev* 501, 532–5, who pleads, in the context of the protection of rights of individuals derived from Community law, for applying an adequacy test rather than a test of minimum effectiveness as far as national remedial rules (not procedural rules *sensu stricto*) are concerned since the test of minimum effectiveness would not always guarantee sufficient judicial protection.

[432] Para 50 of the judgment in *Fiammiferi* (above n 344).

[433] See, eg paras 22 and 24 of the judgment in *Simmenthal* (above n 344); para 15 of the judgment in *van Colson and Kamann* (above n 427). See also Lenaerts and Van Nuffel, above n 86, 17-010.

[434] Cf also the judgment of the ECJ in *Fratelli Variola* (above n 378), according to which Member States are prohibited from adopting national legislation which reproduces the terms of an EC regulation because such reproduction conceals the Community law nature of the relevant rules and thus interferes with the exclusive jurisdiction of the ECJ under Art 234 EC. Certainly the incorporation into national law does not render the terms of the regulation as such ineffective.

[435] See Pignataro, above n 413, 264; Wils, above n 412, para 134.

b. Uniformity of Community Law, Equal Treatment and National Sanctions

It is settled case law that Community law must be applied uniformly throughout the Union.[436] In fact, the requirement of uniformity ensures that the implementation of Community law by the Member States does not lead to unequal treatment of citizens or companies.[437]

The risk of unequal treatment is most notably associated with the (non-binding) nature of the case allocation process. If NCAs, as a general rule, impose sanctions only for the domestic effects of a given infringement, adequate punishment of the offenders depends on whether, in each case, the NCAs of all Member States affected by the infringement take up the matter and impose sanctions since, arguably, only the sum of all individual national penalties would mark the full retribution. However, this scenario (parallel intervention of all relevant NCAs) is not only unlikely, it would also run counter to the spirit of Regulation 1/2003 and could, in any event, not be enforced as a rule.[438]

The purpose of the case allocation principles, combined with the rules on suspension of cases and rejection of complaints,[439] is to have each case preferably handled by a single authority.[440] On the other hand, recital 12 of the Network Notice leaves open the possibility of parallel action by two or three NCAs (or more) where action by a single NCA would not be suffi-cient to sanction the infringement adequately. However, since the

[436] The requirement of uniform application was already implied by the judgment in *Costa v ENEL*, above n 58, where it was in fact based on Art 10 (ex Art 5) EC (see p 594 of the judgment: 'The executive force of Community law cannot vary from one State to another in deference to subsequent domestic laws, without jeopardising the attainment of the objectives of Treaty set out in Art 5(2) and giving rise to the discrimination prohibited by Art 7.'). Later, it was explicitly postulated in para 4 of the judgment in *Walt Wilhelm*, above n 59. See further para 14 of the judgment in *Simmenthal* (above n 344) and Lenaerts and Van Nuffel, above n 86, 14-049.

[437] See para 17 of the judgment in *Deutsche Milchkontor* (above n 379); it was explicitly confirmed inter alia in Case C–290/91 *Peter v HZA Regensburg* [1993] ECR I–2981, para 8. See also the citation from *Costa v ENEL* (*ibid*). Equal treatment can also be seen as a basic element of the due process guarantee. Temple Lang, above n 188, 535.

[438] Moreover, the ultimate calculation of the adequate sanction, which must be reached through the addition of several individual sanctions, is rendered extremely difficult by the fact that the sanctioning systems of the Member States vary to a considerable degree both in terms of nature and severity of applicable sanctions (see the overview given by Bloom, above n 36, 396; see also Maher, above n 36, 232 and Roth and Rose, above n 142, 14.171). Obviously, deter-mining the adequate sanction, within each national system, is already a difficult task. However, the task would certainly be rendered far more difficult, if not impossible, if the diverging systems had to be combined in such a way that there was ultimately overall adequacy. The fact that, even if only one system is applied in each matter, there may be disparities in the treatment of comparable matters by different NCAs due to the divergencies existing between the national sanctioning systems must be accepted for as long as the sanctions applicable to an infringement of Community competition law have not been harmonised (see the judgment of the ECJ in *Hansen*, above n 424, para 15).

[439] Art 13 of Reg 1/2003.

[440] See recital 18 of Reg 1/2003 and para 7 of the Network Notice.

allocation principles are not mandatory and the Network cannot take binding allocation decisions, Network members cannot be obliged to investigate and punish an infringement. It ultimately depends on the discretion of each NCA whether it opens a case and strives to penalise the wrong-doers.[441]

On this basis, uniform enforcement and equal treatment, in terms of punishment, is difficult, if not impossible, to realise. An NCA which imposes a sanction only in relation to the domestic effects of the investigated infringement may assume that other NCAs will also act on the matter so that further sanctions will be inflicted on the offenders and full retribution will be achieved. In some cases this assumption may be correct, but in others it may not. An NCA has little, if any, influence on the enforcement policy of its colleague agencies and the way they exercise their discretion. It cannot compel other Network members to prosecute and punish a particular perpetrator.

Consequently, in some cases, the undertakings concerned will be adequately punished through the parallel action of all relevant NCAs. However, in other cases, the offenders will get away with a sanction which is considerable lower than what would have been adequate since the sole NCA imposing sanctions does not take into account the effects outside its own territory and the other NCAs whose territories are affected remain inactive. Moreover, even with regard to the same matter, some undertakings will be punished harder than others. If, for instance, in the case of an illegal cartel affecting Member States A and B, the NCA of Member State A chooses to prosecute and punish only those companies which have a registered office in its territory while the NCA of Member State B imposes sanctions on all cartel members irrespective of their principal place of business, some offenders may be punished once and others twice.[442]

---

[441] See recital 5 of the Network Notice: 'At the same time each network member retains full discretion in deciding whether or not to investigate a case.'

[442] Notably, those with no registered office in Member State A will be punished only once (by the NCA of Member State B). This example raises the question, of course, of whether NCAs can prosecute and punish undertakings which have no seat in its territory. Under public international law, the mere service of an official document (such as a subpoena or judgment of a court or an information request of the Commission) in a foreign state, without the permission of that state, is already considered a violation of its territorial sovereignty. A Verdross and B Simma, *Universelles Völkerrecht* (Berlin, Duncker & Humblot, 3rd edn, 1984), § 456. However, in the field of Community competition law, these rules have been relaxed. See Temple Lang, above n 188, 548. See also below section II.D.3.b. In my view, there is therefore no reason to assume that Member States, when applying Community competition law, cannot exercise jurisdiction over companies based in other Member States and impose sanctions on them. See Wils, above n 412, para 135. Whether such decisions can effectively be enforced is a separate question and, from a strictly legal perspective, depends on the formal recognition of the foreign act. See above section II.B. However, in practice, ie even without formal recognition, enforcement difficulties would probably not be very frequent. The Commission sometimes imposes fines on companies based in third countries and, apparently, these companies usually pay the fines. Similarly, one may expect companies within the EU to obey

Uniform implementation of EC antitrust law in terms of applied penalties would thus be compromised. Equal treatment of undertakings would depend on many factors that are beyond the control of a single NCA and could therefore become a rather accidental occurrence.

c. Proportionality of National Sanctions

The above considerations concerning the unjustified equal treatment of Community and national competition law cases also support the view that fines imposed by NCAs without having regard to the effects of a Community competition law infringement in other Member States are disproportionate in the sense that they are too low.

Proportionality is a well-established principle of Community law.[443] It means that state measures must not be disproportionate in relation to their purpose. The Community law concept of proportionality is largely based on the German doctrine (*Verhältnismässigkeitsgrundsatz*), which is the most fully developed in the EU.[444] Arguably, the principle thus requires that state action must be suitable and necessary to achieve the aim pursued and adequate in view of its objective (proportionality *stricto sensu*).[445] Traditionally, the requirement therefore functions as a tool for limiting government intervention in that it protects individuals against unduly restrictive or excessive state measures.[446] As concerns penalties, proportionality would thus primarily serve to cut back a sanction, not to challenge its low-level character. However, as a well-established general principle of Community law it forms part of the principles for judicial review and therefore can be used as a general yardstick for the evaluation of national

decisions which have been issued by a foreign NCA. Wils, above n 412, 46 note 213. Seemingly, the French Conseil de la concurrence recently imposed a fine of 120,000 Euro on a Belgian chocolate producer, obviously assuming that the company would comply with the foreign decision (see Conseil de la concurrence, décision n° 07-D-24 du 24 juillet 2007 relative à des pratiques mises en œuvre par le réseau Léonidas). (It is not clear whether the decision is addressed to the Belgian corporation or a French subsidiary.) See also the *Northsea Shrimp* case quoted above at n 411.

[443] P Craig and G de Búrca, *EU Law. Text, Cases and Materials* (Oxford, Oxford University Press, 4th edn, 2007), 544. See also J Schwarze, *Europäisches Verwaltungsrecht* (Baden-Baden, Nomos, 2nd edn, 2005), 690–1; Lenaerts and Van Nuffel, above n 86, 5-036 and Art 5, sentence 3 EC.

[444] Schwarze, *ibid*, LXXIV and 669; see also S Douglas-Scott, 'A Tale of Two Courts: Luxemburg, Strasbourg and the Growing Human Rights Acquis' (2006) 43 *CML Rev* 629, 657.

[445] Craig and De Búrca, above n 443, 545; Schwarze, above n 443, LXXV–LXXVI. In the German legal terminology, this latter requirement is called *Angemessenheit* or *Verhältnismässigkeit im engeren Sinne*. See Schwarze, *ibid*, 671. By contrast, Lenaerts and Van Nuffel, above n 86, 5-038–5-040, distinguish between only two steps of assessment, notably appropriateness and indispensability. This 'reduction' has little impact, if any, in practice. As Craig and De Búrca, *ibid*, point out, the ECJ in fact sometimes merges the second and the third element into one.

[446] See Craig and De Búrca, above n 443, 544. In German administrative law, it is also referred to as *Übermaßverbot*. Schwarze, above n 443, 670.

acts in the sphere of Community law.[447] On this basis, state measures can be regarded as disproportionate not only because they are excessive in relation to the objective pursued, but also because they are too lenient and therefore probably not very suitable to achieve the desired end.[448] This means that, in terms of proportionality, sanctions imposed under Community law must be sufficiently severe in relation to the seriousness of the offence, ie they must adequately punish the offender and at the same time deter others.

The territorial scope of the effects of a competition law infringement, in particular the actual harm caused to customers, suppliers or consumers, are usually an important element in assessing the gravity of the violation and determining the proper amount of a fine.[449] To achieve adequate punishment, the authority therefore has to take into account the geographical dimension of the infringement, which implies that it will normally have to differentiate between cross-border and purely national cases. Breaches of Article 81 or 82 EC usually affect traders and/or consumers in more than one Member State.[450] Accordingly, they will cover a larger territory, affect more persons and cause more harm than purely national law matters. Due to their larger market impact, they should be punished more severely than sole violations of national competition law which, by definition, have no (appreciable) cross-border effects and thus affect only persons within the territory of a single Member State.[451] If, however, NCAs fix fines or other sanctions in EC competition law matters without having regard to the effects outside their own territory, they neglect the real geographical dimension of the infringements and tend to apply inadequate sanctions.[452]

The non-consideration of the extraterritorial effects cannot be justified by referring to the possibility of parallel proceedings and parallel sanctions

---

[447] Craig and De Búrca, *ibid*, 545.

[448] The desired end being sufficient deterrence of potential offenders, proportionality is thus closely linked to the question of full effectiveness of Community law.

[449] See para 91 of the judgment of the ECJ in *Aalborg Portland* (above n 180), where the court, considering the criteria material to the setting of the fine, held: 'Objective factors such as the content and duration . . ., the extent of the market affected and the damage to the economic public order must be taken into account.' Cf also para 22 of the 2006 Guidelines on the Calculation of Fines, according to which the geographical scope of the infringements and the actual implementation are among the factors which the Commission will consider when setting the fine.

[450] Due to the requirement of an effect on inter-state trade.

[451] Obviously, it is possible that, in some Member States, the flat rate (eg turnover percentage or basic amount) applied in Community law matters, according to national law or administrative practice, is in fact higher than that used in national cases. Yet, on the basis of the NCAs' declared approach, a significant difference between the sanctions in the two situations seems excluded. Otherwise, it would have to be regarded as an indication that the NCAs do, after all, take into account the effects of a breach of Community competition law in other Member States.

[452] As will be shown below (below sections II.D.2.d and II.D.3), there are no legal restrictions preventing Member States from considering the extraterritorial effects of a violation of Art 81 or 82 EC when determining the appropriate sanction for such violation.

which could theoretically be inflicted by the NCAs of the other Member State(s) concerned. As shown above, the *ne bis in idem* principle bars this approach.[453] Moreover, where NCAs penalise infringements of national law, they are called to protect competition solely on the domestic market. However, when they impose sanctions for breaches of Community competition law, they act in the Community's interest[454] and thus ought to safeguard freedom of competition in the Community as a whole. The goal is different and therefore the sanction should be different. If the EC law infringement affects competition in several Member States, it is in those Member States that free and open competition must be restored. This applies, in my view, in particular where the relevant geographical market extends beyond the national boundaries of the Member State concerned because, in such a case, the wrongdoing can hardly be divided into a national and a foreign part. The differentiation between EC and national law cases must be reflected in the penalty.

It follows from the above that NCAs must take into account the extra-territorial effects of a breach of Community competition law.[455] They must generally apply stricter sanctions than in the event of a sole violation of national law the effects of which are essentially confined to the territory of a single Member State[456] in order to achieve adequate punishment and thus honour the principle of proportionality.

d. No Lack of Powers of NCAs

It might be argued that NCAs cannot take into account effects outside their own territory because national law does not empower them to do so. However, this argument must be rejected. The question of whether NCAs have the requisite power to penalise extraterritorial effects must be assessed

---

[453] See above section I.D.5.

[454] Paulis, above n 187, 17. Cf also D Smeets, 'Nouveau règlement européen en matière d'ententes et nouveau rôle du Conseil de la concurrence' (2004) 71 *DAOR* 21, 22, who submits that NCAs must pursue the same goal as the Commission when applying Community competition law; and A Schwab and C Steinle, 'Pitfalls of the European Competition Network – Why Better Protection of Leniency Applicants and Legal Regulation of Case Allocation is Needed' (2008) 29 *European Competition Law Review* 523, 529.

[455] Cf Schermers, above n 225, 611. Indeed, this seems to be the approach of the OFT under the UK sanctioning regime, where fines are calculated on the basis of the turnover generated in the relevant market, ie the (product and geographic) market that forms the subject of the infringement. Adjustments are made to avoid double punishment where the company has been fined elsewhere in the EEA. See J Killick, 'Is it Now Time for a Single Europe-wide Fining Policy? An Analysis of the Fining Policies of the Commission and the Member States', CLaSF Working Papers Series, Working Paper 07, December 2005 (available at www.clasf.org/publications/workingpapers.htm), 1, 14. This implies that the turnover achieved in the entire EEA normally is accounted for, which, in turn, means that the effects of the infringement (in form of additional proceeds) outside the UK are actually taken into consideration.

[456] See P Oliver, 'Le règlement 1/2003 et les principes d'efficacité et d'équivalence' (2005) 41 *Cahiers de Droit Européen* 351, 367–8. Cf also Schermers, above n 225, 604.

solely on the basis of Community law.[457] Both the system established by Regulation 1/2003 and the ECJ's case law militate in favour of the assumption that NCAs are entitled to determine sanctions in relation to the overall effects of an EC competition law infringement. Where a national provision regarding penalties exists that is susceptible to interpretation, NCAs thus have to interpret this rule extensively in the sense that it includes the possibility of imposing sanctions for extraterritorial effects or, to use the words of former Advocate General Van Gerven, they have to 'shape the remedies existing in their legal system in accordance with the requirements of Community law'.[458] But even where such interpretation of an existing provision does not appear possible, NCAs are not precluded from sanctioning the extraterritorial effects of a breach of the EC antitrust rules.

First of all, it should be recalled that Regulation 1/2003 has established a system of concurrent jurisdiction in which NCAs are called upon, in the same way as the Commission, to enforce Community competition law. Like the Commission, Member States can adopt decisions 'requiring that an infringement be brought to an end', as well as decisions imposing fines and certain other decisions.[459] The Joint Statement explicitly confirms that Member States have full parallel competences.[460] These principles already suggest that NCAs can fully remedy and punish distortions of competition in the common market.[461]

Secondly, it follows from the case law of the ECJ that, under certain circumstances, national authorities such as NCAs can exercise powers, derived from Community law in combination with Article 10 EC, which go beyond their formal powers under national law.[462] This conclusion can be drawn from a combination of the judgments in *Simmenthal*, *Factortame* and *Fratelli Costanzo*. In the preliminary ruling in *Simmenthal* (1978), the ECJ first established the requirement of full effectiveness of Community law and gave it priority over rules of national law which could impair this effectiveness.[463] The judgment in *Simmenthal* also implies that a national

---

[457] Wils, above n 412, para 134.

[458] W Van Gerven, 'Bridging the Unbridgeable: Community and National Tort Laws After Francovich and Brasserie' (1996) 45 *ICLQ* 507, 516. This statement is made in a different context, notably the adaptation of national judicial remedies to the need of providing effective legal protection for rights of individuals derived from Community law.

[459] Art 5 of Reg 1/2003.

[460] See paras 6 and 11 of the Joint Statement.

[461] Cf Monopolkommission, *Folgenprobleme der europäischen Kartellverfahrensreform*, 32. Sondergutachten (2001), para 59, where the Monopoly Commission argues that NCAs, like the Commission, should make an overall assessment (*Gesamtbetrachtung*) in the Community interest (*im europäischen Interesse*) and not only consider the effects of the competitive restriction in the own territory, ie the national interest.

[462] Temple Lang, above n 343, 127.

[463] Case 106/77 (above n 344). See Craig and De Búrca, above n 443, 311. The requirement of full effectiveness is in fact a corollary of the principle of supremacy of Community law. See Lenaerts *et al*, above n 396, 3-003.

court may exercise powers which it does not formally have under national law if this is necessary to give full force and effect to Community law.[464] Roughly ten years later, in *Fratelli Costanzo*, the ECJ expanded these principles to non-judicial authorities, ruling that all administrative bodies are under the same duty as national courts to apply the provisions of a directive if the conditions are fulfilled under which, according to the case law of the ECJ, individuals may rely upon such provisions before the national courts.[465] In other words, non-judicial bodies have to safeguard the rights individuals derived from Community law in the same way as national courts.

The above principles were further elaborated and built upon in 1990 in *Factortame*, a reference from the House of Lords.[466] The case concerned a (general) lack of power of English courts to suspend Acts of Parliament and grant interim injunctions against the Crown. The House of Lords considered, however, that provisional measures by a UK court were required in that matter in order to safeguard the rights of the applicants under Community law. The ECJ held that

> a court which in those circumstances would grant interim relief, if it were not for a rule of national law, is obliged to set aside that rule.[467]

Thus, the ECJ effectively again required a national court to grant a novel

---

[464] In that case, domestic law in fact prohibited the Italian court, which had turned to the ECJ, from deciding itself whether a national provision was unconstitutional (because it was incompatible with Community law) and instead required it to refer that question to the Italian constitutional court. However, the ECJ held that, in order to ensure the effectiveness of Community law, a national court is bound to refuse 'of its own motion to apply any conflicting provision of national legislation . . . and it is not necessary for the court to request or await the prior setting aside of such provision by legislative or other constitutional means'. Para 24 of the judgment in *Simmenthal* (above n 344).

[465] The applicant in *Fratelli Costanzo* (above n 344) had been excluded from a tendering procedure by decision of the competent municipal administration. The national court seized with the appeal against that decision considered the measure of the municipality to be illegal on the ground that it was based on a national decree, which was itself contrary to the applicable Community directive. It therefore referred to the ECJ the question as to whether the municipal authority was obliged to disregard the conflicting domestic provisions and give effect to the directive. The ECJ answered in the affirmative. See further above n 344.

[466] Above n 344.

[467] Para 21 of the judgment (above n 344). The question was triggered by a piece of legislation enacted by the UK in the fisheries sector in order to stop a practice known as 'quota hopping', legislation which was, however, considered to be contrary to certain EC Treaty provisions. Due to that legislation, the applicants in the main proceedings had been unable to re-register their fishing vessels and were thus deprived the right to engage in fishing activities. In the parallel matter (Case 246/89 R *Commission v UK* [1989] ECR 3125), the President of the ECJ had in fact granted an application of the Commission for interim measures ordering the UK to suspend the application of the contested national rules. The applicants in *Factortame* were therefore also seeking an interim relief before the courts of the UK. The ECJ recalled *Simmenthal* and the principle of full effectiveness of Community law, which would be equally impaired if a national rule could prevent a court seized with a dispute governed by Community law from granting the necessary interim relief.

remedy—that is, to exercise a power which it did not have under domestic law, not even in a comparable situation involving only national law.[468]

From the combination of these cases, it can be concluded that, where Community law, by virtue of Article 10 EC, imposes a duty (here the duty to impose sanctions also for extraterritorial effects of a breach of the Community competition rules) on national authorities, whether judicial or non-judicial, it also confers the requisite legal powers (of both a procedural and a substantive nature).[469] The lack of a provision, in the domestic laws of the Member States, explicitly empowering NCAs to take into account the effects of EC competition law infringements that have occurred outside their respective territory does not therefore prevent NCAs from effectively penalising such effects. NCAs can obtain these powers directly from Community law.

3. Sovereignty and Extraterritoriality

Under public international law, state sovereignty and thus the power to exercise public authority is, in principle, territorially limited.[470] Normally, states may thus not exercise jurisdiction with regard to persons or facts

---

[468] Temple Lang, above n 343, 127; Craig and De Búrca, above n 443, 312.

[469] Temple Lang, above n 343, 127–8. This conclusion does not sit easy with the principle of national procedural autonomy and the rule that Member States, subject to the principles of equivalence and practical possibility, are not required 'to create new remedies in the national courts to ensure observance of Community law' (see para 44 of the judgment in Case 158/80 *Rewe v HZA Kiel* (butter-buying cruises) [1981] ECR 1805). However, the apparent contradictions in the development of the ECJ's case law can be reconciled to a context-specific balancing approach, whereby the various interests concerned are weighed against each other. See Craig and De Búrca, above n 443, 320 *et seq.* Cf also Von Bogdandy, in Grabitz and Hilf, above n 329, Art 10 no 43, for whom the term 'procedural autonomy' is simply misleading since, even though, in terms of organisation, national bodies belong to the national administration, they functionally form part of the Community administration when they implement Community law. Similarly, Van Gerven, above n 431, 501–2, has suggested abandoning the term 'procedural autonomy' and replacing it with 'procedural competence' since this branch of law (ie national procedural rules), albeit falling primarily under the responsibility of the Member States, can also be affected by Community law.

[470] See A Cassese, *International Law* (Oxford, Oxford University Press, 2nd edn, 2005), 49; Verdross and Simma, above n 442, §§ 1019 and 1022. It should be noted that customary international law does not regulate or allocate jurisdiction as such; rather, it puts limits to the exercise of jurisdiction by a state, jurisdiction which itself is based on national rules. There are essentially four principles which are widely accepted, by the international community, as justifying the exercise of national jurisdiction (territoriality, nationality, the protective and universality principles). Verdross and Simma, above n 442, § 1183. Of these four, territoriality (together with nationality) seems to be the key principle. C Mavroidis and D Neven, 'Some Reflections on the Extraterritoriality in International Economic Law. A Law and Economics Analysis' in X (ed), *Mélanges en hommage à Michel Waelbroeck. Troisième partie. Droit de la concurrence, libre circulation et politiques communes* (Bruxelles, Bruylant, 1999), 1297, 1299–1300 and 1302. For a brief overview of these concepts see also W Van Gerven, 'EC Jurisdiction in Antitrust Matters: The Wood Pulp Judgment' in B Hawk (ed), *1989 Proceedings of the Fordham Corporate Law Institute* (New York, Juris Publishing, 1990), 451, 452–4.

outside their national frontiers as such extraterritorial application[471] of their laws is considered to encroach upon the sovereign rights of the other states. It is therefore frequently argued that a Member State can apply sanctions for violations of the Community competition rules only in respect of the effects of that infringement on its own territory.[472]

However, penalising the effects of a breach of EC competition law also in the territory of other Member States, it is submitted, does not infringe the sovereignty of those other Member States. First, taking into account the effects which a Community law infringement has in other Member States for the mere purpose of determining the adequate fine or other sanction does not constitute an exercise of extraterritorial powers *sensu stricto*. Secondly, the principles of public international law cannot directly and invariably be applied to intra-Community relations.

a. No Extraterritoriality Sensu Stricto

An exception to the territoriality principle is the rule that a state may exercise jurisdiction, ie pass binding legislation, with regard to facts occurring or conduct engaged in outside the own territory, but considered prejudicial to the state.[473] On this basis, it is widely, if not globally, accepted that a state can apply domestic antitrust rules to activities committed abroad and enforce them against any perpetrator of such rules if the effects of these activities are felt within the boundaries if its territory.[474] This is considered a form of extraterritorial application of national legislation.

However, where an NCA also considers the effects of an EC competition law infringement that have occurred outside the national boundaries of its

---

[471] The term 'extraterritoriality' is difficult to define. Mavroidis and Neven, above n 470, 1298. If one interpreted the territoriality principle in such a way as to also cover effects, on the domestic territory, of acts committed abroad (*idem*, 1300), it is submitted, there would be no question of extraterritoriality. Cf also Van Gerven, above n 470, 453, who classifies the effects doctrine as objective territoriality principle. However, the phrasing is, in my view, of less importance. What international law really is concerned with is a reasonable exercise of national jurisdiction (cf Mavroidis and Neven, above n 470, 1300). In other words, one needs to find plausible points of contacts which link the wrongdoing as closely as possible to the regulating state in order to limit the number of states that can assert jurisdiction and thus reduce the number of potential jurisdictional conflicts (Van Gerven, above n 470, 477–8).

[472] E Paulis and C Gauer, 'La réforme des règles d'application des articles 81 et 82 du Traité' (2003) 11 *Journal des tribunaux. Droit Européen* 65, para 58; D Waelbroeck, '"Twelve Feet all Dangling Down and Six Necks Exceeding Long." The EU Network of Competition Authorities and the European Convention on Fundamental Rights' in Ehlermann and Atanasiu, above n 36, 465, 472; Burnside and Crossley, above n 280, 31. Cf also J Temple Lang, 'Decentralised Application of Community Competition Law' (1999) 22 *World Competition* 3, 13 ('a national authority is obliged to consider only its national market') and above n 411.

[473] Cassese, above n 470, 49. Enforcement measures can, however, not be taken outside the own territory. *Idem*, 50.

[474] The so-called effects doctrine. See above Chapter 3, nn 11 and 42.

Member State for the sole purpose of determining the appropriate sanction,[475] which in most cases will be a pecuniary fine, this cannot simply be classified, in my view, as a case of strict extraterritoriality.

Indeed, the situation described here can be distinguished from the more 'classic' instances of extraterritoriality, where a state asserts jurisdiction over foreign acts and persons that have (almost) no territorial connection with the state,[476] for two reasons: the nature of the law applied and the existence of strong territorial links.

First of all, it is important to recall that, in our scenario, the NCA does not simply apply a national rule to an activity and an offender abroad who might be completely unaware (and justifiably so) of the obligations arising from the alien law. Even though the amount and calculation of the fine will be governed by provisions of national law, the decision of the NCA to actually impose a fine will primarily be based on Article 81 or 82 EC. The relevant norms are thus rules of a supranational legal order which, by definition, apply in the whole of the EU.[477] All citizens and companies located within the EU are subject to these rules and can thus not really be surprised if the rules are enforced against them.[478] Moreover, their applicability, in the territories of all 27 Member States, has been brought about with the express consent of these states either by conclusion of the EC Treaty in 1957 or by subsequent accession. There is a democratic legitimation for their application.

Secondly, the case allocation rules laid down in the Network Notice envisage that jurisdiction can be asserted only if a number of cumulative conditions are fulfilled. In addition to the effects of the infringement, which must be felt in the territory of the acting Member State,[479] the important criteria notably are the place of business of the undertakings concerned and the location of evidence. It is the requirement that the NCA which must be able 'to effectively bring to an end the entire infringement'[480] suggests that at least some of the undertakings concerned must be based in the territory of the NCA. Otherwise the relevant national decision

---

[475] Which must be effective, proportionate and dissuasive. See above n 425.

[476] See, eg the Helms-Burton Act, enacted by the US in 1996, which provided for sanctions against foreign companies purchasing certain property in Cuba, and the other examples quoted by Cassese, above n 470, 49–50.

[477] This factor is also stressed by Waelbroeck, above n 472, 472. Cf also Bundeskartellamt, above n 369, 29, regarding the question of whether NCA decisions should have Community-wide validity ('Greifen nationale Wettbewerbsbehörden Fälle nach EG-Kartellrecht auf, so wenden sie Recht an, auf das sich die Mitgliedstaaten der Gemeinschaft geeinigt haben und . . . wird damit die Rechtsordnung anderer Mitgliedstaaten nicht verletzt, sondern eine Entscheidnung im Rahmen der dort geltenden Gesetze getroffen').

[478] Whether the Community competition rules can be applied and enforced against companies located outside the EU is a quite different matter. The ECJ had to deal with this question in the famous *Woodpulp I* case (Joined Cases C–89, 104, 114, 116, 117 and 125–129/85 *Ahlström Osakeyhtiö and others v Commission* [1988] ECR 5193).

[479] Para 8 subpara 1 of the Network Notice.

[480] Para 8 subpara 2 of the Network Notice.

risks being enforceable only with difficulty, since it is has no EU-wide validity. As concerns, for instance, a cease-and-desist order against a foreign firm, the enforceability essentially depends on whether that firm voluntarily submits to the decision.[481] However, companies might be less inclined to co-operate in such a way if they feel that the acting NCA has no hold on them anyway because all firms involved in the matter are located outside its territorial reach. Moreover, where several of the undertakings concerned are based in the territory of the NCA, an order against them may actually prove sufficient to stop the illegal activities as a whole. Similarly, the condition that the NCA can gather the necessary evidence[482] seems to imply that at least some of the requisite information and documents are to be found in its territory. In addition, the acting NCA can always request the assistance of other Network members pursuant to Article 22(1) of Regulation 1/2003. However, where a large part or even all of the evidence must be collected abroad, the question arises whether the procedure is still efficient and thus compatible with the spirit of Regulation 1/2003. In view of the combination of both conditions, the location of the companies and the evidence, at least in part, in the domestic territory, it is likely that the relevant acts (eg conclusion of the restrictive agreement or engagement in a concerted practice) will also have been committed in the territory of the NCA which fulfils the requirements. Together, the three aforementioned criteria thus ensure that there are strong territorial links with the Member State whose NCA investigates and penalises a breach of Community competition law, provided, of course, that the NCA effectively observes the allocation principles of the Network Notice.[483]

It follows from the above that a clear distinction can be made between the elements of territoriality which justify that an NCA asserts jurisdiction in a particular case (jurisdictional nexus) and the ancillary extraterritorial aspects of the case, notably the effects of the infringement outside the national boundaries of the respective Member State. On this basis, the question of whether the NCA, when determining the sanction, takes into account whether the unlawful conduct also had effects in the territory of other Member States, ie whether it considers the real territorial scope of the infringement, becomes a purely adjectival rather than a substantive question. It affects neither the existence and nature of the infringement nor the jurisdiction of the acting NCA, but only the intensity of the

---

[481] As Wils, above n 412, para 135 has pointed out, even though Reg 1/2003 does not provide for any mechanism for the recognition and enforcement of foreign NCA decisions, it is not a priori excluded that an NCA addresses an order to a company in another Member State. In practice, enforcement problems in such cases are rare. See above n 442. See also below section II.D.3.b.

[482] Para 8 subpara 3 of the Network Notice.

[483] See para 9 of the Network Notice: 'The above criteria indicate that a material link between the infringement and the territory of a Member State must exist in order for that Member State's competition authority to be considered well placed.'

violation.[484] The extraterritorial effects are, it is submitted, nothing but a criterion for evaluating the seriousness of the wrongdoing and thus a mere element of calculation in the assessment of the fine. That calculation can hardly be considered to encroach upon the sovereign rights of the other Member States.[485]

b. The Permissive Rule

Finally, it can be argued that, in any event, the rules of public international law on state sovereignty and territoriality have been relaxed in the field of Community competition law by consent of the Member States and thus do not hinder NCAs in applying sanctions also for the extraterritorial effects of a breach of Articles 81 and 82 EC.

It follows from the case law of the ECJ that the Community treaties have established a legal order *sui generis* consisting of supranational rules characterised, in particular, by their primacy over national law. For the benefit of this new legal order, the Member States have limited their sovereign rights.[486] Despite the fact that these treaties were concluded in the form of an international agreement, the general principles of public international law which traditionally govern the relations between sovereign states can therefore not be applied to the intra-Community relations,[487] at least not indistinctively.

---

[484] See para 94 (*in fine*) of the opinion of Advocate General Colomer in *Italcementi* (above n 49): 'The test of the territorial extent of the unlawful conduct is not substantive, but adjectival, since it does not affect the nature of the infringement, but only its intensity'. See also above n 176.

[485] Cf also Ryngaert, above n 147, 443, who argues that even at the international level outside the EU there is no violation of the sovereignty of other states if a state imposes fines for extra-territorial effects of an antitrust violation since such intervention does not prevent the other states from applying their own armoury of sanctions ('Het opleggen van een kartelboete door één Staat verhindert andere Staten immers niet om hun eigen sanctie-arsenaal, ter verwezenlijking van hun eigen economische belangen, te blijven aanwenden.'). Ryngaert's view is based, inter alia, on the fact that there is no rule against double jeopardy at the international level, which, in turn, means that a state's right to punish (*ius puniendi*) is in principle not exhausted through punishments inflicted by other states. Within the EU, this may be different. As has been argued above (section I.D), both the ECHR and the EU Charter militate in favour of an EU-wide *ne bis in idem* in the field of Community competition law. On this basis, a Member State does in fact lose its right to punish if another Member State has already imposed a sanction in the same competition matter on the same offenders. However, this restriction of the sovereign right to exercise the *ius puniendi* is the consequence of an international treaty (EC Treaty) or convention (ECHR) or a 'solemn declaration' (EU Charter) which the Member States of the EU have chosen to sign or agreed to live up to. Moreover, the *ne bis in idem* principle precludes a second procedure and a second fine whether or not the NCA which imposes the first sanction effectively takes into account the effects outside its own Member State. It is in fact not the penalisation of extraterritorial effects but the voluntary recognition of a transnational *ne bis in idem* which entails the exhaustion of the Member States' *ius puniendi*.

[486] Judgment of the ECJ in *van Gend & Loos*, above n 195, 12; opinion of the ECJ of 14 December 1991—Opinion 1/91, para 1.

[487] Lenaerts and Van Nuffel, above n 86, 1-013; see also Schermers, above n 225, 605: 'Within the Community, sovereignty should not be an argument either way.'

More particularly in the field of competition law, there are a number of elements which suggest that the normal rules on extraterritoriality have been relaxed in such a way as to allow NCAs to exercise, to a certain extent, extraterritorial jurisdiction.[488] This includes, it is submitted, the right to penalise the effects of an infringement in other Member States and also the right to exercise jurisdiction over companies of other Member States.[489]

Indeed, by establishing a system of concurrent jurisdiction, Regulation 1/2003 has explicitly assigned the task to enforce the Community competition rules (also) to the Member States. By adopting this Council regulation, Member States have given their approval to the decentralised system. However, decentralisation is only an efficient way of enforcement if as many cases as possible are handled by a single authority. Regular duplication of procedures, which would be inevitable if NCAs could solely remedy the domestic part of the wrongdoing,[490] is therefore not a viable alternative. Nor is constant underpunishment. The right of NCAs to also penalise extraterritorial effects therefore seems inherent in the system, at least if one gives due consideration to the ultimate objective of Regulation 1/2003, which is to create a more efficient enforcement system.[491] Arguably, the Member States have therefore waived the right to object to the exercise of a fairly limited extent[492] of extraterritorial jurisdiction by NCAs when enforcing the EC Treaty rules on competition.[493] Obviously, such a waiver can be presumed only on the basis of a broad respect for the case allocation rules and, in particular, the requirement of a material link with the territory of the Member State whose NCA acts.

This approach is supported by the Joint Statement, in which the Member States explicitly declare that each of the Network members shall have 'full parallel competence'.[494] Moreover, the Network Notice provides that NCAs can designate one NCA as the lead institution where competition in several Member States is affected and no NCA can successfully deal with the case alone.[495] This is a form of particularly close co-operation. It especially confers a coordinating function on the lead authority, for instance in the event of parallel investigative measures by several NCAs, such as simultaneous dawn raids in several Member States,

---

[488] Cf Smits, above n 20, 187, who would find it 'peculiar' if doctrines derived from public international law were applied in the context of competition law enforcement in the internal market.

[489] See Temple Lang, above n 188, 548.

[490] Penalising only domestic effects is often insufficient because, due to the effect-on-trade criterion, most cases will affect more than one Member State.

[491] See Klees, above n 3, 1227.

[492] The extraterritorial aspects, if any, are fairly limited because there must in any event be a clear territorial link with the NCA's Member State. See above section II.D.3.a.

[493] Temple Lang, above n 188, 548.

[494] Para 11 of the Joint Statement; see also para 6 thereof.

[495] Para 13 of the Network Notice; see also para 18 of the Joint Statement.

which must be well planned and prepared to secure the surprise effect and thus guarantee the success of the operation.[496] But does the possibility of appointing a leader not also imply that the lead authority can act for the other NCAs, at least to some extent? Would that not mean that, while the other NCAs assist the lead institution in gathering the relevant information and collecting the necessary evidence, the lead authority can impose fines 'on their behalf'?[497] It is true that, pursuant to paragraph 13 of the Network Notice, each NCA remains responsible for conducting its own proceedings; but this does not necessarily mean that each national procedure has to be terminated with a decision prohibiting a certain conduct and imposing a sanction. Arguably, it is therefore possible to interpret the 'leading role' of the coordinating NCA as encompassing the right to remedy the effects of the entire infringement in the EU, including those which have occurred in other Member States, if this is the most efficient way to successfully conclude the case.[498]

Lastly, an argument can be made that the Network members, by allocating a case to a particular authority, give their approval to the exercise of limited extraterritorial powers by that particular NCA. This consent is given implicitly by all Network members in that they either do not oppose the NCA which originally notified the Network remaining in charge of the case or request the reallocation of the matter to another authority, reallocation which is then approved explicitly (by acceptance of the transfer of the matter) or tacitly (by non-opposition). In any event, if all Network members agree in some form, explicitly or implicitly, to the fact that a particular NCA takes on the case, this means, in view of the needs of efficiency and full effectiveness of Community law, that the relevant NCA can bring to an end the entire infringement and effectively remedy the wrongdoing. This approach, in turn, presupposes that the acting NCA can and will also penalise the effects outside its own territory,[499] an extraterritorial element which is therefore covered by the agreement of the Network members.

Arguably, this implicit approval or consent also comprises the permission, where necessary, to send the relevant decision by normal post directly to addressees located in the territory of another Member State. Admittedly, it seems that there is no general Community or international law instrument which would entitle a Member State to effect the service of documents issued by an administrative authority (eg a decision imposing fines) or a judicial body on persons residing or domiciled in another Member State directly through the post. The European Convention on the

---

[496] See para 13 of the Network Notice.

[497] See Waelbroeck, above n 472, 472.

[498] This may, for instance, be assumed where all or most of the companies involved have their seat in the Member State of the lead authority.

[499] Pignataro, above n 413, 264.

Service Abroad of Documents relating to Administrative Matters, which provides for such a simple service of documents on foreign persons through the normal post and could be used as a tool in competition matters by those Member States which have an administrative sanctioning system, has been ratified by only eight Member States.[500] The Schengen Convention in principle applies solely in the context of criminal punishment and covers administrative sanctions only to the extent that the relevant decision can give rise to proceedings before a criminal court. It thus cannot be relied upon by Member States with purely administrative sanctioning systems.[501] However, the principles of efficiency and full effectiveness would suggest that an NCA to which a competition case has been allocated has implicitly also been authorised to use direct transmission by normal post where it needs to serve a decision imposing fines on a person residing or having its seat in another Member State.

4. Exclusion of Purely 'National' Sanctions

Each of the above principles alone (full effectiveness, uniformity or equal treatment, proportionality) supports the view that purely national sanctions, ie sanctions which do not take into account extraterritorial effects of the wrongdoing, would fall short of important requirements of Community law. Their combination therefore justifies the conclusion that NCAs are not only entitled, but even under a duty, to penalise those effects which a breach of Community competition law has outside the boundaries of their own territory when they impose sanctions for such a breach.

Obviously, the shortcomings, in particular the problem of inequality of treatment, could be remedied through systematic parallel imposition of several national sanctions by the NCAs of all Member States affected by the relevant infringement. However, there are no mandatory rules or legal guarantees ensuring that all NCAs will effectively act against the perpetrators of an infringement which has affected customers, suppliers or consumers in their territory. Moreover, it would be against the objective of decentralisation and the spirit of Regulation 1/2003 to create an enforcement practice which is based, as a general rule, on parallel proceedings and thus on duplication of work.

Indeed, in 1993 it was still considered that 'the scope for avoiding all duplication of effort is limited under the Regulations at present'.[502] However, since that date, the situation has changed fundamentally. In fact, the three major reasons[503] given by Temple Lang to support his opinion no

---

[500] Jansen, above n 374, 7 and 17. The Member States that have ratified the convention are Austria, Belgium, Estonia, France, Germany, Italy, Luxembourg and Spain.

[501] See Jansen, above n 374, 31.

[502] Temple Lang, above n 188, 577.

[503] See Temple Lang, *ibid*, 577, the three bullet points at no 7.

longer exist. First, the transfer of confidential information is possible under Regulation 1/2003. Secondly, all NCAs have the requisite powers, under national law, to apply Articles 81 and 82 EC. Thirdly, both Commission and NCAs apply the same substantive rules and are thus guided by the same principles. National competition law plays only a subordinate role and can, in any event, never justify an outcome which is different from the solution dictated by Community law. Moreover, on the basis of Article 13 of Regulation 1/2003, all Network members can decline to deal with a matter on the grounds that another authority is dealing with it and, where this is not yet the case, they can try to have the case effectively transferred to another Network member.

The solution submitted here does not conflict with rules of public international law. The imposition of fines or other sanctions which, by their size, take into account that the wrongdoing which is penalised also had effects in the territory of other Member States either does not constitute an exercise of extraterritorial powers *sensu stricto* or is a legitimate form of extraterritoriality due to permission by the Member States concerned.[504]

Regulation 1/2003 has created a single integrated system for the enforcement of Articles 81 and 82 EC encompassing the idea of a one-stop shop principle. Moreover, the rules are to be applied in partnership. Full partnership requires mutual trust and equality of the participants[505] which must have the same rights and powers to enforce Community competition law. However, if the powers of the NCAs were curtailed by a strict application of traditional rules on (extra)territoriality, the Commission would in fact be obliged to deal itself with most of the cases.[506] This would be contrary to the very idea of decentralisation.

E. Conclusion

Article 10 EC enshrines the general principle of mutual loyalty and solidarity which applies between all actors under Community law and thus also between Member States. In the context of EC antitrust law enforcement, this general duty of loyalty leads to a number of specific obligations. In view of the special features of the new enforcement system, in particular the principle of concurrent jurisdiction, the sophisticated and institutionalised mechanisms for close co-operation, including (non-binding) arrangements for the allocation of cases and the possibility of commenting on envisaged decisions of other Network members, it is only fair to expect Member States and their NCAs to mutually respect each

---

[504] See Arhold, above n 3, 135 note 55.

[505] Cf para 7 of the Joint Statement.

[506] See Temple Lang, above n 188, 587. Unless, of course, one considers systematic multiplication of procedures or regular underpunishment as acceptable alternatives.

other's enforcement decisions. On this basis, NCAs are not free to completely disregard foreign NCA decisions, but instead have to make all reasonable efforts to avoid taking decisions that would conflict with the existing decision of another NCA in the matter. Moreover, in individual cases, they may be required, under Article 10 EC, to recognise the validity of a foreign NCA decision, thereby rendering it enforceable in their own territory. Finally, the spirit of Regulation 1/2003 and the Network Notice, which aim to offer a one-stop shop for competition matters also in the case of national proceedings, coupled with the general Community law principle that fines must be effective, proportionate and dissuasive, oblige NCAs to impose sanctions also for the extraterritorial effects of infringements of Article 81 or 82 EC, in order to prevent 'underfining'.

7

Conclusions—Is the ECN a Supermodel or an 'Anti-example'?

IT HAS BEEN suggested that this new kind of co-operative system established by Regulation 1/2003 for the enforcement of the Community competition rules and, in particular, the ECN could be 'a model for efficient management of the internal market in general',[1] that is, it could serve as an example for co-operation in other areas of Community law. With regard specifically to the field of antitrust law, the question has been raised whether the ECN could be 'a blueprint' for co-operation at the international level beyond the EU.[2]

If, however, competition law enforcement is a form of criminal justice within the meaning of the ECHR, as has been argued above,[3] it is submitted that the exchange of evidence should not be undertaken without a minimum level of harmonisation of the applicable procedural rules. In the absence of such harmonisation, mandatory rules may be circumvented and the delicate balance between investigatory powers and the rights of defence which keeps each national system within the limits imposed by the ECHR, and in particular Article 6 thereof, may be distorted to the detriment of the legal and natural persons whose adequate protection would thus be sacrificed.

It is further submitted that, despite the undoubtedly many positive aspects of this form of solidary implementation of EC Treaty provisions, the new system also increases the risk of an excessive fragmentation of enforcement systems, a tendency that is already visible now through the creation of a multitude of sector-specific networks and the coexistence

---

[1] See C-D Ehlermann, 'Implementation of EC Competition Law by National Anti-Trust Authorities' (1996) 17 *European Competition Law Review* 88, 90; D Gerber, 'The Evolution of a European Competition Law Network' in C-D Ehlermann and I Atanasiu (eds), *European Competition Law Annual 2002: Constructing the EU Network of Competition Authorities* (Oxford, Hart Publishing, 2003), 43, 64.

[2] See the article by A Burnside and H Crossley, 'Co-operative Mechanisms within the EU: A Blueprint for Future Co-operation at the International Level' (2004) 10 *International Trade Law & Regulation* 25, in particular 32.

[3] See above Chapter 6, section I.A.1.b.

of a large number of sectoral[4] supervisory and regulatory bodies with overlapping functions. This fragmentation may ultimately impede effective implementation of Community law and meaningful co-operation.

I. RECAPITULATION OF THE ABOVE ANALYSIS AND CONCLUSIONS

Before evaluating the co-operative enforcement system established by Regulation 1/2003 under more abstract aspects, it is useful to briefly recapitulate, on the basis of the analysis made in the previous chapters, the essential features and main shortcomings of the new system.

A. General

1. Concurrent Jurisdiction—A Unique Form of 'Joint' Administrative Execution

As a first general remark, it is worthwhile noting that Regulation 1/2003 marks a new form of administrative execution (*Verwaltungsvollzug*) in which a Community institution (the Commission) and Member States' authorities (the NCAs) fully share the responsibility of enforcing primary Community law (Articles 81 and 82 EC).

Traditionally, the execution of Community law was the responsibility of either the Member States or the Community (so-called *Trennungsprinzip*),[5] the rule being that the implementation of Community law is, in the first place, a matter for the Member States unless the task is explicitly assigned to a Community institution or body.[6] Direct enforcement by the Community itself, usually the Commission, and indirect enforcement by national bodies of the Member States could thus be clearly distinguished.[7]

Obviously, competition law enforcement always played a special role in this respect. It forms the only notable exception to the general rule according to which Community law is administered, in individual cases, by the Member States' authorities.[8] In the area of competition law, direct

[4] The terms 'sector' and 'sectoral' are used here not only to describe a division by industry sector such as telecommunication, banking, but also as a domain-oriented fragmentation based on a distinction between various fields of law (eg private law, criminal law, torts law, antitrust law).

[5] The term is used by J Schwarze (ed), *Europäisches Verwaltungsrecht* (Baden-Baden, Nomos, 2nd edn, 2005), CII.

[6] K Lenaerts and P Van Nuffel, *Constitutional Law of the European Union* (London, Sweet & Maxwell, 2nd edn, 2005), para 11-011. In this respect, the Community legal order shows elements of a federal system (executive federalism). *Idem*, para 14-047.

[7] Schwarze, above n 5, CI.

[8] C-D Ehlermann, 'The Modernization of EC Antitrust Policy: A Legal and Cultural Revolution' (2000) 37 *CML Rev* 537, 576.

enforcement through measures taken by the Commission was (and is) possible.[9] At the same time, enforcement in this field of law was governed by a sort of mixed system whereby, under Regulation 17, both the Community and the Member States were already responsible for the implementation of the EC Treaty rules on competition pursuant to Articles 84 and 85 EC. However, due to the lack of an express obligation on the Member States to actually enforce Articles 81 and 82 EC, the absence in many Member States of independent competition authorities (or the failure of some Member States to authorise their NCA to apply the EC competition rules) and the monopoly of the Commission to apply Article 81(3) EC, which existed under Regulation 17, this was more of a theoretic approach than a given reality. Competition law was therefore usually viewed (only) as an example of direct enforcement (*unmittelbarer Gemeinschaftsvollzug*) by the Commission.[10]

In that Regulation 1/2003 abolishes the Commission's exemption monopoly and explicitly obliges the Member States to enforce the EC competition rules, it has put full and equal responsibility on both the Community and the Member States for the implementation of these Treaty provisions. The Commission and NCAs really must join forces to guarantee the effective protection of free and undistorted competition in the Community in accordance with Articles 3(g), 81 and 82 EC. This system of full concurrent jurisdiction (or parallel competences) to apply the same substantive rules (EC Treaty provisions), using the same kind of enforcement measures (eg pecuniary sanctions), it is submitted, represents a unique form of 'joint' execution of Community law.

Joining forces not only suggests that parallel, individual measures will be taken by different bodies. It also means that there should be a large degree of solidarity among these bodies and hence that they have to co-operate. Indeed, the competences and duties imposed on the Commission and the NCAs are backed by rules and mechanisms which allow close co-operation, both vertically and horizontally, between Commission and NCAs. Against this background, the new model also confirms a more general trend in European administrative law which has more recently been observed in the legal doctrine: the previously clear division between direct and indirect

---

[9] J-P Schneider, 'Vollzug des Europäischen Wirtschaftsrecht zwischen Zentralisierung und Dezentralisierung—Bilanz und Ausblick' (2005) 40 *Europarecht* (Beiheft 2), 141, 146. Schneider also notes that direct execution is often regarded as a form of centralised enforcement, while indirect execution is assimilated with decentralisation. This classification, however, is not always correct (*idem*, 141). Regardless of the terminology, it can be stated that indirect (or decentralised) enforcement through the Member States' authorities is in fact the 'normal way' in which Community rules (outside the realm of competition law) have always been implemented. D Gerber and P Cassinis, 'The "Modernisation" of European Community Competition Law: Achieving Consistency in Enforcement—Part I' (2006) 27 *European Competition Law Review* 10, 10.

[10] See Schwarze, above n 5, CIII.

execution is more and more often replaced by different forms and degrees of administrative co-operation (*Verwaltungskooperation*).[11] The ECN is an example of such a novel form of administrative co-operation.[12] It is submitted that the ECN has the potential to develop into an elaborate and intensified form of administrative co-operation in that it embraces both horizontal and vertical co-operation, takes place on a long-lasting basis and in an institutionalised manner, and is based on detailed rules.[13] It can thus be distinguished from simple forms of co-operation on a selective basis (*schlichte punktuelle Zusammenarbeit*).[14] At the same time, it must be kept in mind that (intensified) co-operation also raises specific legal problems since, in a co-operative system, individual measures cannot be viewed in complete isolation.[15] As the previous chapters have shown, also in this respect, the ECN is a prominent example.

2. Flexibility and Pragmatism

The second general observation that can be made concerns the operation of the Network itself. Co-operation in the ECN is characterised by a high degree of flexibility and pragmatism. The Commission has always under-lined the need for flexible and rapid mechanisms.[16] It is thus no surprise that Regulation 1/2003 contains only a limited number of mandatory rules, most of which concern the vertical level, ie co-operation and consultation

[11] There exists a multitude of enforcement models in the different areas of Community law which all require some sort of collaboration between the Community and the Member States' authorities. These models no longer fit into the traditional categories of direct and indirect execution. Schneider, above n 9, 141. One of the first legal writers to provide a systematic analysis of existing forms of administrative co-operation apparently was E Schmidt-Aßmann, 'Verwaltungskooperation und Verwaltungskooperationsrecht in der Europäischen Gemeinschaft' (1996) 31 *Europarecht* 270, 289 *et seq*. The articles of Schneider and Schmidt-Aßmann also suggest that the variety of forms and models of administrative co-operation is steadily increasing.

[12] Schwarze, above n 5, CVII–CXI. See also Schneider, above n 9, 146. Obviously, administrative co-operation in the sphere of Community law as such is not a new phenomenon (Schmidt-Aßmann, *ibid*, 274). However, it is gaining importance. See Schwarze, above n 5, CII. Moreover, the co-operation models become more varied and complex, as also illustrated by the ECN.

[13] The advanced nature is demonstrated inter alia by the fact that the ECN is an interactive model in which all members of the Network may and shall respond to each other. Moreover, it provides a complex system of formalised multidirectional information exchange. See D Gerber, 'The Evolution of a European Competition network' in Ehlermann and Atanasiu, above n 1, 43, 53–4.

[14] See Schmidt-Aßmann, above n 11, 275 *et seq*. Obviously, there were contacts between the Commission and the NCAs before the establishment of the ECN. However, apart from the limited obligatory information process under Reg 17, these contacts were mostly sporadic and depended largely on personal relationships. See Gerber, *ibid*, 47. In his article, Gerber provides a good analytical overview of the development of what he calls 'the European competition law network' from the early years of European integration until the beginning of the modernisation process.

[15] Schmidt-Aßmann, above n 11, 274.

[16] See para 104 of the White Paper.

between the Commission and the NCAs. By contrast, horizontal co-operation between the NCAs is essentially based on facultative rules and thus largely depends on voluntary action by the NCAs. There is no formal obligation to notify other NCAs of new cases (see Article 11(3) of Regulation 1/2003), no strict obligation to provide administrative assistance at the horizontal level (see Article 22 of Regulation 1/2003) and no duty to inform other NCAs beforehand of the envisaged final decision (Article 11(4) of Regulation 1/2003). Moreover, the ECN is not mentioned in any of the Articles of Regulation 1/2003.[17]

Admittedly, details of the ECN and modalities of co-operation between the Network members are laid down in the Network Notice adopted by the Commission. However, such a Commission notice is not a formal, legally binding instrument. It may bind the Commission itself through general principles of law, such as equal treatment and legitimate expectations,[18] but it cannot legally oblige the Member States. While it is true that all NCAs have signed a statement by which they declare to abide by the principles laid down in the Network Notice,[19] the legal value of such a declaration that is made by a national authority rather than by the Member State remains unclear.

The most striking example of the lack of binding co-operation rules is probably the absence, in Regulation 1/2003, of any rules on the division of the workload, ie the allocation of cases among the Network members. Again, these rules can be found only in the non-binding Network Notice. The facultative character of these rules is even highlighted by the Network Notice itself, which notably states that 'each network member retains full discretion in deciding whether or not to investigate a case'.[20] In other words, all NCAs may do as they like.[21]

The ECN is a forum for discussion which provides a framework for co-operation and consultation between the competition authorities in the EU.[22] As such, it obviously has to offer a certain degree of flexibility. Nonetheless, the purely voluntary nature of many of the co-operative mechanisms in Regulation 1/2003 leads to a number of serious concerns. First, the horizontal dimension of the co-operation process seems to have been neglected. Even though there is a common understanding that

---

[17] The only reference to the ECN, albeit without use of the proper name, can be found in recital 15 of Reg 1/2003.

[18] See above Chapter 3, n 17.

[19] See para 72 of the Network Notice and the list of authorities that have signed the statement published on DG Comp's website.

[20] Para 5 of the Network Notice.

[21] This statement is evidently exaggerated. NCAs are, of course, bound (and possibly restrained) by their national laws and also subject to certain duties resulting from Art 10 EC; however, case allocation according to the rules of the Network Notice is a voluntary exercise, not a legal obligation.

[22] Para 1 of the Network Notice.

generally the same information is made available to all Network members so that Commission and NCAs should essentially have the same information level,[23] this practical approach cannot conceal the fact that, from a formal perspective, NCAs do not have the same rights as the Commission to obtain information, evidence or administrative assistance from other Network members. This inequality does not seem to fit with the co-operative nature of the system.[24] The second concern relates to the principle of legal certainty. In view of the vague, non-binding criteria for allocating cases, it is extremely difficult, if not impossible, for companies to predict which authority will ultimately handle a particular case. Yet the 'selection' of an authority has important consequences for the undertakings concerned in terms of applicable procedure (including rights of defence), language and penalties. The lack of predictability therefore is hardly compatible with the requirement of legal certainty.[25] This is all the more so since the companies under investigation have no say in the allocation process, which is a purely internal matter of the Network and thus a completely intransparent process for firms and individuals.[26]

B. Intranet Relations

As concerns the intranet relations, two main comments can be made. First, it is submitted that despite the co-operative nature of the ECN the Commission is the true 'ringleader' in this Network of public authorities. Consequently, there is a certain tension between the formal *pari passu* approach and the reality of the Network. Secondly, mutual information and consultation under the Network Notice may result in a large number of data constantly circulating in the Network which, in turn, may increase the administrative burden on the authorities, which somehow have to handle this huge amount of information. This raises efficiency concerns.

---

[23] See para 10 of the Joint Statement.

[24] See also below section I.B.1.

[25] As concerns the question of compatibility with Art 7 ECHR (legality, in particular predictability, of sanctions), see below section I.C.1.

[26] See para 4 of the Network Notice, which reads: 'Consultations and exchanges within the network are matters between public enforcers'. See also para 31 of the Network Notice, which describes case allocation as 'a mere division of labour'. The undertakings concerned are only informed at the end of the allocation process in the event that a case is indeed reallocated within the Network (para 34 of the Network Notice). The same applies to complainants. Clearly, case allocation also affects the (legal) position of complainants, who may see 'their' case being transferred to an authority with which they are not at all familiar in terms of procedure, language etc and which, above all, possibly does not grant the same rights to complainants as the one with which the complaint was originally lodged.

1. The Preeminent Role of the Commission

Co-operation in legal matters requires mutual respect and trust in the adequacy of each other's procedures, standards and enforcement measures. In other words, it presupposes a genuine partnership in which all partners are equal.[27] Accordingly, the Joint Statement provides that '[c]ooperation between the NCAs and with the Commission takes place on the basis of equality, respect and solidarity'. It further states that

> Member States accept that their enforcement systems differ but nonetheless recognise the standards of each other's system as a basis for cooperation.[28]

However, despite this official commitment, there is a noticeable tension between the formal co-operative *pari passu* approach and the hierarchical elements contained in Regulation 1/2003.

The first disparity between the Commission and the NCAs relates to the exchange of information. While the NCAs are obliged to provide certain information to the Commission, in particular information on new cases and summaries of contemplated final decisions (Article 11(3) and (4) of Regulation 1/2003), such informative duties do not exist in relation to other NCAs. Legally speaking, NCAs thus do not have a right to request such information. This is surprising since a proper allocation of cases (or rather an efficient division of work[29]) and a consistent and coherent application of EC antitrust law would seem to require that NCAs are aware of the matters handled and informed of the decisions envisaged by their counterparts in other Member States. In this context, it should be noted that Regulation 1/2003 does not exclude parallel proceedings, thus it may well be the case that several NCAs investigate and assess the same infringement. Similarly, the provision of administrative assistance—for example, the conduct of inspections or the carrying out of other fact-finding measures by one NCA on behalf and for the account of another NCA pursuant to Article 22(1) of Regulation 1/2003—is a mere faculty. No NCA is obliged to render this form of assistance to another NCA. By contrast, the Commission can require an NCA, pursuant to Article 22(2) of Regulation 1/2003, to undertake inspections which the Commission deems necessary or has ordered.

The second inequality concerns the position of the Commission vis-à-vis the NCAs. Apparently, the Commission does not fully trust the NCAs to perform a satisfactory job. It has gained certain surveillance rights, notably the right to be informed, 30 days in advance, of any prohibition or commitment decision contemplated by an NCA.[30] According to the

---

[27] Cf Schmidt-Aßmann, above n 11, 295.
[28] Paras 7 and 8 of the Joint Statement.
[29] See para 3 of the Network Notice.
[30] Art 11(4) of Reg 1/2003. This provision also applies where an NCA intends to withdraw the benefit of a block exemption.

Network Notice, this power includes the right to make written observations on the case, which would seem to include the possibility of suggesting how the matter should be decided by the NCA. Article 11(4) of Regulation 1/2003 thus gives the Commission a sort of interventionary power. Most importantly, however, the Commission has retained the right of evocation, which already existed under Regulation 17 and is now codified in Article 11(6) of Regulation 1/2003. The right to submit comments in individual matters, coupled with the right of evocation, means that the Commission effectively has a considerable degree of leverage. The implied threat to be relieved of their competence is likely to induce NCAs to follow the Commission's view.[31]

Altogether, the Commission thus has a preeminent position in the Network. It is not just a *primus inter pares*, but de facto ranks above the NCAs.[32] Arguably, granting the Commission this specific, superior role was necessary to ensure coherence and uniformity in the implementation of the Community's competition rules and thus prevent a renationalisation of competition law enforcement.

As concerns the 'ordinary' Network members, it must be kept in mind that there are clearly huge divergencies between the Members States and, as a consequence, between the NCAs in terms of history, political and legal traditions, practical experience in the field of (EC) competition law and financial resources. Due to these differences, the know-how and expertise, the available funds and ultimately the performance of the NCAs can vary to some extent, or may be perceived as being uneven, which, in turn, may lead to inequalities in the informal status of NCAs within the Network.[33] Such disparities should, however, diminish over time and eventually vanish all together.

2. Increased Complexity

An analysis of the evolution of co-operation between competition authorities in the EU from the early days of DG Comp (then still DG IV) until today shows that the interaction between the Commission and the NCAs

---

[31] See above Chapter 1, n 201. On the other hand, it must be noted that, as yet, no case has been reported in which the Commission actually exercised the right of evocation in an Art 11(4) situation. See above Chapter 1 n 205. This may, however, also be seen as proof that NCAs do indeed adopt the Commission's proposals (if it has made any).

[32] See Gerber, above n 13, 53 note 25, who compares the ECN to a ship and the role of the Commission in the ECN to that of the ship's commander. A Fuchs, 'Kontrollierte Dezentralisierung der europäischen Wettbewerbsaufsicht' (2005) 40 *Europarecht* (Beiheft 2), 77, 108 and 116, even describes the Commission as the controlling spider in the web ('*die alles kontrollierende "Spinne im Netz der europäischen Wettbewerbsbehörden"'*). The expression has probably been borrowed from M Van Der Woude, 'Exchange of Information within the European Competition Network: Scope and Limits' in Ehlermann and Atanasiu, above n 1, 377. See further above Chapter 1 nn 269 and 270.

[33] See Gerber, above n 13, 55.

has become much more complex than it used to be. Not only have the number of participants, now unified in the ECN, and the size of many individual authorities become significantly larger;[34] the amount of information available has also increased considerably and the information processes are more complex. Information circulating in the ECN on the one hand is more technical and specific, while on the other hand it is less targeted.

Compared to the previous rules, Regulation 1/2003 and the Network provide for more formalised information duties and rights. These rules also influence the characteristics of the information. Generally, the information transmitted will be case related and thus more specific and technical (eg initial case reports, abstracts of intended NCA decisions, documentary evidence).[35]

In addition, flow patterns and goal-orientation have changed. Under Regulation 17, information was often provided informally on an ad hoc basis (which is not really desirable) in order to meet particular needs. Moreover, information was primarily transmitted from the Commission to the NCAs and only to a very limited extent in the opposite direction. Exchange of information between the NCAs was essentially precluded due to the *Spanish Banks* doctrine. In contrast, in the ECN, information flows are often automatic and multidirectional. Each Network member is entitled to provide all other members with information, including confidential information and evidentiary material. A side effect of this multi-directionality is that the information received by individual Network members is less targeted. In the former system, the bulk of information was forwarded only if it was potentially relevant for the recipient. This is different in the ECN, where certain types of information, such as initial case reports and summaries of envisaged decisions, are sent to all Network members automatically, regardless of whether the matter potentially concerns them.[36] The standard of generally informing all members increases the effort required to actually review the information. Review of the received information is, however, a key factor. If the ECN is to have the desired effect on enforcement activities (proper case allocation, avoidance of unnecessary multiple proceedings, consistent and coherent decision making etc), that is, if the information is to shape decisional outcomes, and if NCAs are to play an influential role in this system, it is certainly not sufficient that they merely receive, process and store information. The above objectives can only be achieved if the information available in the Network is actually read and sorted, and its relevance for the activities of

---

[34] Gerber, above n 13, 51. The growing number of participants results from the expansion of the EU and from the creation of additional NCAs in those Member States which did not have an independent competition authority (eg Italy and the Netherlands).

[35] Gerber, above n 13, 55–6.

[36] *Ibid.*

the individual NCA (or the Commission) evaluated and, if necessary, taken into account.[37]

In view of the increased amount of information transmitted and the elevated complexity of information and information flows, the burden on the NCAs to properly administer the information circulating in the ECN has certainly become heavier. The general workload of the NCAs is further augmented by the fact that they may have to deal with a large number of different languages, which means that all officials have to be trained to understand (more) foreign languages and/or translations will have to be made by a separate translation service.[38] It is thus safe to assume that the NCAs will have to make available additional resources (compared to the situation before May 2004) in order to meet this new challenge.[39] As concerns the Commission, its overall administrative burden will probably not have increased. However, it is submitted that many, if not all, of the resources that the Commission intended to free by abolishing the notification/authorisation system and shifting part of the workload to the NCAs will actually be absorbed by new tasks it has to assume as a result of the increased information exchange, the need to monitor NCAs and national courts[40] and, possibly, the need to intervene in the proceedings before NCAs or national courts in order to safeguard the uniformity of EC competition law (eg as *amicus curiae*).[41] This raises the question of whether the new enforcement system is really as efficient as it has been purported to be.

---

[37] Cf Gerber, above n 13, 57. Gerber describes the desired effect as 'normative influence'. Obviously, the structure of the information, ie the question of whether it is easily accessible and understandable and thus more likely to be assimilated, also plays in important role in this context. *Idem*, 61.

[38] While the initial case report is submitted in standardised form in English, other information and documents circulating in the Network will usually be forwarded in the original language, which can be any of the 23 official languages of the EU. Co-operation without mutual understanding in the plain sense of the word does not seem possible. However, Reg 1/2003 and the Network Notice say nothing about how this language issue ought to be tackled. M Wezenbeek-Geuke, 'Het voorstel voor een verordening van de Raad betreffende de uitvoering van de mededingingsregels van de artikelen 81 en 82 van het verdrag' [2001] *Nederlands tijdschrift voor Europees recht* 17, 25.

[39] See G Di Federico and P Manzini, 'A Law and Economics Approach to the New European Antitrust Enforcing Rules' (2004) 1 *Erasmus Law & Economics Review* 143, 154.

[40] The obligations of NCAs to submit draft decisions (Art 11(4) of Reg 1/2003) and of national courts to forward judgments to the Commission (Art 15(2) of Reg 1/2003) would be useless if the Commission failed to make available resources to actually scan these documents. The administrative burden caused by the information exchange and the monitoring task should not, in my view, be underestimated. At the end of October 2007, approximately 800 new cases had been notified to the ECN and a total of 231 envisaged national decisions had been submitted to the Commission (aggregate figures since 2004). See the statistical data on the ECN's portal (above Chapter 2, n 121).

[41] See Di Federico and Manzini, above n 39, 155.

C. External Relations—The Position of Defendants and Complainants

The ECN certainly has an influence on the way NCAs operate.[42] The largest is undoubtedly the impact of this co-operative model on the undertakings under investigation and, to a lesser extent, the complainants. The central question is how a system which essentially allows for the free movement of confidential information and (incriminatory) evidence between public enforcement bodies of the Member States can adequately protect the rights of the undertakings and individuals concerned without harmonising the applicable procedural rules. This question is all the more pressing in areas where fundamental rights are affected. The main issue here are the rights of defence or, in the terminology of the ECHR, the fair trial guarantee enshrined in Article 6 ECHR.

There are essentially three stages of the procedure where the co-operation mechanisms provided for by Regulation 1/2003 become relevant: the beginning, when the proceedings are initiated; during the course of an investigation; and at the end, just before the proceedings are terminated.

1. Initiation of Proceedings

Pursuant to Article 11(4) of Regulation 1/2003, NCAs are to inform the Commission of the initiation of proceedings which involve the application of Community competition law. The protection of the confidential information is not the issue here, since the information exchanged at this early stage of the procedure, in the form of an initial case report, is still quite limited (names of the parties, industry sector/products concerned, territory potentially affected, type of infringement suspected, origin of the case). Apart from the fact that an investigation is pending against them, which even the authorities may want to keep secret at this stage, the dispersion of this information within the ECN does not raise confidentiality concerns from the perspective of the undertakings.

The crucial point in this initial phase is the (re)allocation of the case to a particular authority. This is of tremendous importance for the parties concerned because the applicable procedural rules, including those governing the rights of defence and the legal position of complainants, depend on this allocation. It also determines the sanctions available, which vary considerably across the Member States.

Nonetheless, this process is designed as a purely internal matter of the Network. Neither the undertakings concerned nor complainants are heard. The exchange of views between Network members on the case allocation

---

[42] See Gerber, above n 13, 59.

would fall within the category of internal Network correspondence which is a priori not accessible.[43] Finally and most importantly, there is no formal allocation decision since neither the ECN itself nor the Commission or an NCA can legally refer a case to a particular authority. As a consequence, the act of allocation as such, being a completely intransparent and informal occurrence, cannot be challenged by the parties.

The Network members intend to solve any reallocation issues within a period of two months, starting from the day the initial case report is submitted. Obviously, the formal involvement of the parties in the allocation process risks delaying the procedure considerably. However, the two-month period does not seem so short that it would exclude a priori any participation of the parties. Moreover, the two-month period is a guideline rather than a deadline, and thus could be extended if necessary.

The decision of the Commission to initiate proceedings also cannot be challenged, it has been submitted, in line with the judgment of the ECJ in *IBM*, because it is a preparatory measure, an intermediate step in a procedure involving several phases. Similar considerations are likely to apply with regard to national decisions initiating proceedings. The allocation of a case can thus only be challenged in the context of a judicial review of the final decision.[44]

In addition to the difficulty, if not impossibility, of having allocation 'decisions' reviewed, case allocation under the Network Notice raises concerns in terms of legal certainty, a fundamental principle which includes the requirement that sanctions be predictable. The allocation criteria are non-binding, vague and not always conclusive. It is therefore hard for undertakings to foresee which authority will handle a case and thus which penalty, from the diverse sanctioning systems of the Member States, may ultimately be applied.

On the basis of all these considerations, it has been submitted that the total lack of any rights for the parties in relation to the allocation process, even the right to make their views known, does not meet the standards to be expected of a Community based on the rule of law. Moreover, the unpredictability of the outcome of the allocation process seems to entail an infringement of Article 7 ECHR.[45]

2. Collaboration in the Course of an Investigation

The co-operation of authorities in the course of ongoing proceedings will regularly concern the exchange and use of confidential information and evidentiary material pursuant to Article 12 of Regulation 1/2003. Key

---

[43] Reg 1/2003, Art 27(2), sentences 3 and 4.
[44] See above Chapter 3, section III.E.1.6.
[45] See above Chapter 3, sections III.D and III.E.

issues in this context are the protection of confidentiality and the possible circumvention or erosion of protection standards, in particular in relation to defence rights which have the status of human rights or fundamental freedoms under the ECHR, such as the right against self-incrimination and the inviolability of the home.

a. Confidentiality

The professional secrecy obligation of Community officials, ie the duty not to disclose confidential information to persons outside one's own institution,[46] is laid down in Article 287 EC. By Article 28(2) of Regulation 1/2003, it has been extended to those officials of national authorities who are involved in the application of Community competition law and exchange or receive confidential information pursuant to Regulation 1/2003. However, the provision does not lay down what information is covered by the secrecy obligation. The question therefore arises which confidentiality standards are to apply and which authority can legally afford a document confidential status.

(1) The Standard. On the basis of Article 28(2) of Regulation 1/2003, any information circulating in the Network must enjoy the same level of protection regardless of whether it has been gathered and transmitted by the Commission or any of the NCAs. However, the Article does not define what type of information must be considered as confidential. In proceedings before an NCA, the determination of confidentiality therefore depends, as a matter of principle, on the applicable national law, which may vary from Member State to Member State. On the other hand, the notion of 'professional secrecy', being a Community law concept, must be applied uniformly throughout the Community. The question of disclosure mainly arises when an authority grants the parties access to the file. It has therefore been submitted that guidance may be sought from the Commission's Notice on Access to File.[47]

That notice distinguishes between accessible and non-accessible documents. The latter group comprises three categories of information, notably business secrets, other kinds of sensitive information and internal documents. It follows from the judgment of the ECJ in *Akzo I* that the protection of business secrets is a general principle of Community law. The preclusion of access to internal documents is explicitly laid down in Article 27(2) of Regulation 1/2003. These two principles thus also have to be observed by the Member States' authorities in the context of proceedings

---

[46] On the basis of the SEP scenario, it may exceptionally also be the case that certain information is confidential vis-à-vis specific persons and thus may not even be communicated randomly within the same institution. See above Chapter 4, n 187 and the accompanying text.

[47] See above Chapter 4, section I.C.1.b(4).

regarding the enforcement of Community competition law. As concerns other types of confidential information, NCAs should follow as closely as possible the rules and principles of the Notice on Access to File in order not to prejudice the uniform application of the professional secrecy obligation.

(2) The Procedure. Since access to file and confidentiality in NCA proceedings are governed by the provisions of national law, it is for the NCA granting such access and hence, in the case of transmitted information, for the receiving NCA to decide whether or not a certain document (or parts thereof) deserve protection ('country of destination' principle). However, given that confidential information can circulate freely in the Network, the person or company providing the information will rarely know by which authority that information will ultimately be used and thus is deprived of the opportunity to lodge a confidentiality request with the receiving authority.

In order to ensure that legitimate interests in preserving the confidentiality of certain information are nonetheless adequately protected, it has been submitted that the following principles must be respected by all Network members.

1. Confidentiality requests can always be lodged with the authority to which the information is initially supplied. It is in fact in the best interests of the parties to make such a request at the same time as the information is provided or, at least, as soon as possible thereafter.
2. The transmitting authority has to attach any confidentiality request to the relevant document and always has to transmit it together with that document. It is, however, not obliged to decide on the request as this is a matter for the receiving authority.
3. The receiving authority, in turn, has to apply the AKZO procedure, that is, it has to give the person from whom the document originates the opportunity to indicate which (parts of the) information it considers confidential before actually disclosing it. Accordingly, even if a confidentiality claim has not been transmitted together with the document, the receiving authority has to inquire if the person who provided the information (if necessary via the transmitting authority) intends to make any such claim.[48] Moreover, the receiving authority has to provide efficient remedies against a decision refusing to award the requested confidentiality status.
4. Finally, in the exceptional case that the transmitting authority has already decided on the request and has granted confidentiality, the

---

[48] Therefore, the origin of a document or any other information must always be shown. Ideally, both the original supplier of the information and the transmitting authority should be indicated.

receiving authority should not needlessly deviate from that decision. It is certainly not desirable that NCAs reclassify documents that have already been afforded confidentiality status as this would seriously compromise the (perceived) fairness of proceedings under Regulation 1/2003.

It has therefore further been submitted that a fairer solution for the above problem would be a mutual recognition, by all Network members, of each other's confidentiality regimes, possibly coupled with the adoption of certain common standards for the classification of documents. The three categories named in the Notice on Access to File could serve as a basis for the development of such standards.[49]

Finally, it should be noted that even if all NCAs and the Commission were to recognise each other's confidentiality standards and were also to agree to respect any confidentiality status already awarded by the transmitting authority, the system may not be entirely watertight. Problems may arise, for instance, where the NCA is required, on the basis of national law, to forward the entire case file, including confidential elements, to the national court seized to review the legality of the NCA's decision and that court will subsequently make that information available to the parties (eg a complainant whose complaint has been rejected or a company under investigation which doubts that the evidence in the authority's file really corroborates the allegations made against it) in accordance with a strict application of the principle of adversarial proceedings.[50] Similarly, confidentiality may be undermined if the NCA is obliged to disclose certain information it has received to other public agencies (eg tax authorities, securities supervision bodies, district attorney).[51]

b. Human Rights Issues

A second group of concerns that arise with regard to the free movement of evidence in the ECN are related to the adequate protection of the rights of defence, in particular those recognised by the ECHR.

(1) Background. In principle, all information circulating in the Network can be used in evidence by every Network member. Regulation 1/2003 puts

---

[49] See above Chapter 4, section I.C.1.b.

[50] This situation seems to have occurred in the Belgian system.

[51] See B Perrin, 'Challenges Facing the EU Network of Competition Authorities: Insights from a Comparative Criminal Law Perspective' (2006) 31 *EL Rev* 540, 558. Arguably, however, such national provisions would be incompatible with Art 12(2) of Reg 1/2003, which limits the use of transmitted information as evidence to the subject matter for which it was collected in the first place (and moreover to the enforcement of Arts 81 and 82 EC). NCAs would thus have to invoke the primacy of Community law to escape their obligations under the relevant domestic provision. Whether Art 12(2) of Reg 1/2003 also precludes the use of ECN information as intelligence in non-competition matters is unclear.

only a few limitations on this use. First, exchanged information can only be used for the subject matter for which it was collected (Article 12(3) of Regulation 1/2003). This depends on the terms of the original mandate. Normally, the scope of the mandate will be defined in the decision ordering the investigation.

Secondly, the use of transmitted evidence in proceedings against individuals (in contrast to legal persons) is restricted. According to the first alternative of Article 12(3) of Regulation 1/2003, evidence collected by another authority can be used against an individual if the national laws of the Member States of the transmitting authority and the receiving authority provide for similar kinds of sanctions (eg both systems provide for monetary penalties or both allow imprisonment). In the absence of a similar sanctioning system, the second alternative of Article 12(3) of Regulation 1/2003 provides that the transmitted information may only be used against an individual if it has been collected 'in a way which respects the same level of protection of the rights of defence of natural persons' as those rights applicable in the receiving Member State. Even though it has been submitted that the test is an abstract rather than a case-specific one, this equivalence requirement is extremely difficult to verify. It can hardly be expected for an NCA to be familiar with the procedural rules of its 26 colleague agencies. Moreover, comparing the two systems and making a well-founded judgement on the equivalence of protection afforded by both is a complex exercise. Each national law will consist of an elaborate, coherent system of detailed rules and principles which may be similar between Member States, but will hardly ever be identical. Neither Regulation 1/2003 nor the Network Notice gives any guidance as to how similar rules must be to justify the conclusion that they offer the same level of protection. In view of these practical difficulties, NCAs may be discouraged from using transmitted evidence if they would have to rely on the second alternative. In any event, the imposition of custodial sanctions is excluded under this alternative. Imprisonment of a person on the basis of exchanged evidence is therefore only possible if the laws of both the transmitting and the receiving authority provide for it.

(2) Concerns. While individuals thus are protected, albeit to a fairly limited extent, against the use of the evidence that is freely circulating in the ECN and has possibly been collected in accordance with rules that do not offer the same protection standards as those of the receiving authority, a similar guarantee does not exist for undertakings. Thus an NCA (or the Commission) may attempt to circumvent its own safeguards by requesting another Network member that only has to observe lower protection standards to collect the necessary evidence. No provision of Regulation 1/2003 or the Network Notice prevents an authority from using in

evidence, against a company, whatever information forwarded by an authority of a Member State whose procedural guarantees for defendants are more limited.[52]

With the help of three examples (inviolability of the home, right to silence/right not to incriminate oneself, professional legal privilege), it has been demonstrated how diverse procedural rules and safeguards can be. These differences can be fundamental or related to various details of the specific rule. At the same time, these examples illustrate that many procedural rights are rooted in the ECHR. Inviolability of the home and the privilege against self-incrimination are guaranteed by Article 8 and Article 6(1) ECHR respectively. Even professional legal privilege has been considered to have a basis in the ECHR, in either Article 6 or 8 ECHR. Fundamental rights thus play a key role in ensuring the legality and fairness of competition proceedings under Articles 81 and 82 EC.

Not only is the accidental circumvention of legally secured protection standards a serious concern; NCAs (or the Commission) may also be tempted to practice a kind of forum shopping.[53] They could deliberately undertake to benefit from lower protection standards, ie they could actively seek to obtain evidence from outside the own jurisdiction by asking a foreign agency to collect the relevant material on their behalf.[54] Such incidental circumvention of their own standards or even the blatant abuse of the rules on information exchange would not only undermine the position of defendants and the (subjective) confidence of the parties in the fairness of the proceedings; it may also ultimately lead to a notable erosion of protection standards. Above all, it could have serious repercussions on the equilibrium between the powers of public authorities and the procedural rights of persons affected by public interference. However, it is precisely this equilibrium, the delicate balance between the authority's armoury and the private person's defence rights, that keeps each national

---

[52] A well-known example often quoted in this context is that of the OFT, which can effectively circumvent the rule on legal privilege applicable in the UK if it succeeds in obtaining the required documents via the BKartA since, under German law, the concept of legal privilege is virtually unknown. The OFT has even announced that it would do so should the opportunity arise. See above Chapter 4, n 292.

[53] This does not appear to be an entirely hypothetical concern. In practice, horizontal exchange of evidentiary material seems to take place mostly following a request for assistance in fact-finding. In other words, the evidence exchanged was not already in the possession of the transmitting authority, but has specifically been gathered at the request of the receiving authority. It is also interesting to note, in this context, that the Belgian NCA recently carried out, for the first time, an inspection of private premises. Again, this was done at the request of another Network member. Whether these instances of mutual assistance involve any kind of forum shopping on the part of the requesting NCAs is unknown.

[54] At times, when huge amounts of business data and other internal company material are stored electronically and thus often accessible for a multitude of staff members at various offices of the firm across the EU (at least in the case of a company with EU-wide business activities, which is the type of company that is most likely to be involved in competition matters affecting trade between Member States), such a scenario does not appear purely hypothetical.

system in conformity with fundamental guarantees, such as those mentioned above, but which will be upset if different systems interact. The unrestricted exchange of evidentiary material between NCAs with diverging protection standards consequently risks compromising the overall fairness of the procedure.

It has therefore been suggested herein that NCAs and the Commission should systematically refrain from using in evidence information that has been collected by an authority whose laws provide for a lower degree of protection so as to ensure that the highest protection standard will always prevail. In order to facilitate the comparison of protection standards between the Member States, a matrix should be developed which shows the most important investigative powers of the NCAs of all 27 Member States and the Commission, as well as the rights of companies under investigation. In addition, so-called 'taint teams' could be set up. This approach may represent a workable and acceptable compromise for as long as Commission and Member States do not seem inclined to consider harmonisation of the procedures to be applied with respect to the enforcement of Articles 81 and 82 EC. Harmonising the procedural rules, at least certain basic rules and protection standards (eg right against self-incrimination, legal privilege, access to file, confidentiality), it is submitted, would, however, be the preferable solution as it would provide better guarantees against the circumvention of defence rights and a creeping erosion of protection standards. It would also be far more practical than the human resource-intensive comparison suggested above.[55]

c. Judicial Control of Information Gathering

Finally, the question of who is going to control the legality of the information gathering must be answered. Since each NCA applies its own procedural rules, fact-finding measures must be carried out in accordance with the laws of the Member State whose NCA conducts the fact-finding. Even if the information thereby assembled is later transmitted to other Network members, the benchmark for the legality of the information gathering is always the rule of the Member State where the information was collected. It is evident that the courts of that Member State are best qualified to review the legality of the fact-finding measure since they are familiar with the relevant laws. Moreover, if the NCA or the courts of the receiving Member State(s) were to usurp the right to assess the conformity of the extraneous information gathering within foreign laws, they would not only undermine mutual trust and respect among Network members, but also interfere with the sovereign rights of the Member State where the information was collected in the first place. It is thus always for the courts

---

[55] See above Chapter 4, section II.C.2.

in the Member State of the transmitting authority, ie the Member State where the information was collected, to review the legality of the information gathering (the 'country of origin' principle).[56]

However, in order to allow defendants to challenge the legality of the information gathering and effectively protect them against the use in evidence of information that was not legally collected, five unwritten safeguards, it has been submitted, should be respected by all Network members.[57]

1. The Member State of origin, ie the Member State where the information was collected, and the authority which collected it must be indicated on the relevant documents. This rule ensures transparency and makes it possible for defendants to address any complaint regarding the legality of the fact-finding to the competent courts or authorities.
2. A person wishing to contest the legality of the information gathering can and must lodge the application with the authorities or courts of the Member State whose NCA collected it regardless of whether the information has meanwhile been forwarded to one or more other Network members.
3. The receiving authority is precluded from using the information obtained via the Network where it has definitively been determined that the information was illegally collected in the Member State of origin. In other words, the illegality of an investigative measure renders the information derived from it unusable by any Network member.
4. Where the legality of the information gathering is already being contested at the time of transmission, the transmitting authority must inform the receiving authority about such contestation. Moreover, the transmitting authority must be considered as having a duty to refuse the transfer of information to other Network members if the illegality of the information gathering has definitively been established before the information could actually be forwarded. If the legality of the information gathering is only challenged after the evidence has actually been transmitted, that fact should also subsequently be communicated to the receiving authority.
5. In the case of a dispute about the legality of the information gathering, the (national) court called upon to decide on the lawfulness of the final decision of the receiving authority (eg a prohibition decision or a decision imposing fines) should, if possible, stay its proceedings and await the decision of the judge in the Member

---

[56] See para 27 of the Network Notice.
[57] See above Chapter 4, section II.B.2.

State of origin that has been seized to scrutinise the collection of evidence.

3. Termination of Proceedings

At the latest 30 days prior to the termination of its proceedings by a prohibition, a commitment decision or a withdrawal of a block exemption, the NCA has to inform the Commission about the envisaged course of action. Normally, this information duty can simply be fulfilled by forwarding the text of the draft decision together with a summary of the case.[58] Problems may arise, however, in Member States whose competition authority has a dual structure, that is, where investigative and adjudicative functions are assigned to separate bodies and the latter function is vested in a court of law or administrative tribunal. This is the case, for instance, in Sweden (Stockholm District Court), Austria (the Kartellgericht, which is the Vienna Court of Appeals) and Belgium (the Raad voor de mededinging is qualified as an administrative tribunal under national law).

Problems arise because the Commission has the right to make written observations with a view to influencing the outcome of the proceedings, for instance in order to ensure consistent application of the EC competition rules. However, such external influence on the decision-making of the adjudicative body may be incompatible with the requirements of independence and impartiality of a court of law, guarantees protected by Article 6(1) ECHR and the principle of separation of powers.[59] Even though the Commission's comments are formally not binding and may thus be disregarded by the court, the potential interference may damage the outward appearance of independence and impartiality to which the ECtHR attaches considerable importance. 'Justice must not only be done, it must also be seen to be done.'[60]

More importantly, the submission of comments by the Commission may be incompatible with one of the key features of the fair trial guarantee of Article 6(1) ECHR, notably the right to adversarial proceedings and the principle of 'equality of arms'. It results from these requirements that defendants must be given access to all evidence and observations filed, including third-party opinions, even if these originate from an independent

---

[58] See Art 11(4) of Reg 1/2003.

[59] Similar concerns may be raised where the Commission makes submissions as *amicus curiae* pursuant to Art 15(3) of Reg 1/2003.

[60] English law doctrine. The often quoted aphorism goes back to a dictum of Lord Chief Justice Hewart in the leading English criminal case *Rex v Sussex Justices, ex parte McCarthy* [1924] 1 KB 256, at 259; [1923] All ER 233, at 234. The ECtHR has repeatedly emphasised the public's increased sensitivity to the fair administration of justice and, as a result, the growing importance that must be attached to the outward appearances. See para 82 of the ECtHR's judgment in *Kress v France*, Report/Recueil 2001-IV, 1, and further the case law cited above at Chapter 2, n 111 and accompanying text.

body external to the court. However, pursuant to the fourth sentence of Article 27(2) of Regulation 1/2003, correspondence between the members of the Network 'including documents drawn up pursuant to Articles 11 and 14' are explicitly excluded from the right of access to the file. Consequently, an NCA (adjudicative body) that communicates the observations submitted by the Commission in the context of the consultation procedure under Article 11(4) of Regulation 1/2003 to the undertakings concerned would violate the Regulation. This conflict, it has been submitted, can only be avoided by arranging for the consultation procedure to be held between the investigating/prosecuting body and the Commission, rather than between the adjudicative body and the Commission, since the former body, not being a court of law, is not subject to the requirements of Article 6(1) ECHR.[61]

4. Parallel Proceedings

A further fundamental issue arising under Regulation 1/2003 and the Network Notice is the extent to which parallel national proceedings regarding the same matter are possible and what impact an NCA decision may have on the decision of another NCA concerning the same infringement.

a. Parallel Proceedings and the Issue of Ne Bis In Idem

Neither Regulation 1/2003 nor the Network Notice excludes the possibility of parallel proceedings being conducted by several NCAs with regard to the same infringement. However, where such parallel proceedings are directed against the same persons (identity of the offender) and the decisions are taken consecutively, that is, the second decision is adopted when the decision terminating the first procedure has become unappealable, the question arises whether the second punishment violates the *ne bis in idem* (or double jeopardy) guarantee.[62]

Ne bis in idem is a fundamental principle of Community law.[63] It is laid down in both the ECHR (Article 4 of Protocol 7) and the EU Charter (Article 50). However, protection against repeated prosecution and punishment is mostly only granted if both proceedings take place within

---

[61] See above Chapter 5, section III.B.2 and 3.

[62] The following considerations are based on the premise that competition law proceedings are criminal proceedings within the meaning of the ECHR (and EU Charter), which today seems to be virtually common ground. See above Chapter 6, section I.A.1.b.

[63] Para 59 of the judgment of the ECJ in *PVC II* (Joined Cases C–238, 244, 245, 247, 250–2 and 254/99 P *Limburgse Vinyl Maatschappij and others v Commission* [2002] ECR I–8375; para 26 of the judgment of the ECJ in Case C–308/04 P *SGL Carbon v Commission* [2006] ECR I–5977.

[64] See above Chapter 6, n 92 and para 34 of the judgment of the ECJ in *SGL Carbon, ibid.*

the same state. Thus, the *ne bis in idem* principle does not generally apply at international level,[64] a factor which would also exclude its applicability in the present context, notably parallel competition proceedings conducted in different Member States. However, there are a number of arguments supporting the view that parallel (consecutive) proceedings by NCAs against the same parties concerning the same infringement under Article 81 or 82 EC are precluded by the *ne bis in idem* guarantee.

First, Article 50 of the EU Charter explicitly provides EU-wide protection against double prosecution and punishment in that it provides that no one shall be tried or punished again for an offence for which he or she has already been finally acquitted or convicted 'within the Union'. There are still some uncertainties regarding the legal status and binding force of the EU Charter, though, as it has not yet been incorporated into the Treaties, but only constitutes a solemn proclamation.[65] On the other hand, recital 37 of Regulation 1/2003 expressly refers to the EU Charter and requires the Regulation to be interpreted and applied with respect to the principles enshrined within the EU Charter. It follows from a recent judgment of the ECJ[66] that such a reference to the EU Charter cannot simply be disregarded as it is a formal recognition, by the Community legislature, of the importance of the EU Charter. On this basis, it can be argued that Article 50 EU Charter can be used as a yardstick when assessing the permissibility of parallel action by several NCAs concerning the enforcement of Articles 81 and 82 EC and thus the implementation of Regulation 1/2003.[67]

Secondly, it appears that the ECtHR could interpret Article 4 of Protocol 7 (which, according to its wording, provides for only a national *ne bis in idem*) in a dynamic, Community-oriented way and accept that, in the field of Community competition law enforcement, the term 'jurisdiction of the same State' cannot be taken literally. Rather, the term must be understood to comprise the whole of the EU (ie all Member States form a single jurisdiction when enforcing Article 81 or 82 EC). In the past, the ECtHR has repeatedly taken an innovative stance when it came to the interpretation of the ECHR in a Community law context. In the *Matthews* case,[68] for instance, the ECtHR held that the European Parliament was to be considered as legislature in the Member States even though the EP did not even exist when the relevant provision of the ECHR guaranteeing free

---

[65] Obviously, the EU Charter can have binding force de facto, notably via the application of general principles of Community law, which, in turn, are largely derived from the often homonymic provisions of ECHR. However, this line of argument cannot be applied here since, with regard to the central aspect, the *ne bis in idem* principle of the EU Charter deviates from the ECHR. See above Chapter 6, section I.D.1.

[66] Case C–540/03 *European Parliament v Council* [2006] ECR I–5769.

[67] See above Chapter 6, section I.D.1.

[68] Chapter 3, n 231.

[69] See above Chapter 6, section I.D.4.c(1).

elections of the 'legislature' in all contracting states was signed. More examples for such Community-friendly interpretation of HR Convention rights by the ECtHR have been cited above.[69] The justification for such a dynamic interpretation can be found in the special enforcement regime created by Regulation 1/2003 which is characterised inter alia by concurrent jurisdiction of all competition authorities in the EU, application of the same substantive rules and close co-operation of the Network members in all questions, including case allocation.[70]

Thirdly, since the ECJ has explicitly acknowledged that *ne bis in idem* is a fundamental principle of Community law, it could also be considered to form an autonomous, or *propriae naturae*, principle of Community law.[71] On this basis, not only Article 4 of Protocol No 7, to which the ECJ specifically referred in *PVC II*, would serve as a legal reference. Above all, inspiration should be drawn from Article 50 EU Charter and Article 54 Schengen Convention, which can be regarded as indications of a trend, within the Union's legal order, to afford the concept a transnational dimension and protect persons against double jeopardy within the territory of the EU as a whole.

There are essentially three arguments which support this view. First, Member States are called upon to create an ever-closer union based on the 'the rule of law' (*Rechtsstaatlichkeit*), which underpins the particular importance of the legal aspects of the integration process. Secondly, it is submitted that Regulation 1/2003 has created a decentralised but integrated system whereby each single NCA to which a case is allocated basically replaces the Commission as the enforcement agency for the entire Union. Thirdly, and probably most importantly, a distinction must be made between international cartel matters, where the undertakings concerned are subject to several antitrust laws of different legal orders, and the present case, where the same substantive rules, notably Article 81 or 82 EC, are applied repeatedly to the same companies. In my view, this is a crucial aspect which clearly distinguishes the present case from all cases[72] in which the Community Courts have in the past considered the question of double jeopardy. Moreover, the relevance of this differentiation has been implicitly acknowledged by the ECJ in its recent appeal judgment in *Graphite Electrodes*.[73]

Finally, the argument that, in the case of parallel national proceedings, there is no *idem* because each NCA, when imposing a fine, only takes into account the effects of the infringement on the domestic territory, it has been submitted, must be dismissed. First, the existence of an infringement of Article 81 or 82 EC is independent of any actual effects of the restriction

[70] Chapter 6, section I.D.4.c(2).
[71] Chapter 6, section I.D.5.
[72] Except for the *PVC II* case (above n 63).
[73] *SGL Carbon* (above n 63).

or abuse on the market. Secondly, when NCAs enforce Community competition law, the purpose is to protect or restore effective competition in the common market. In other words, NCAs like the Commission must act in the interest of the entire Community.[74] On this basis, free competition in the Community cannot be divided into different (national) compartments and a geographically limited perspective of the NCAs as concerns the punishment of violations of the Community competition rules does not seem to be appropriate in relation to the ultimate goal of their enforcement measures.[75]

b. Parallel Proceedings and the Loyalty Obligation

(1) Duty to Remedy Extraterritorial Effects. The above considerations also imply that there is not only a right, but even a duty under Article 10 EC for NCAs to impose penalties not just for the domestic effects of an infringement, but for the effects in the entire Community, including extraterritorial effects. By virtue of Article 10 EC, Member States must thus take all necessary measures to guarantee that Community law is effectively complied with by everyone within their jurisdiction. Where necessary, such compliance must be ensured by means of penalties, which, in turn, must be effective, proportionate and dissuasive. At the same time, the objective of case allocation under Regulation 1/2003 and the Network Notice is to have each case, if possible, handled by a single authority.[76] These two goals, providing a one-stop shop for enforcement in the case of an NCA procedure and applying effective, proportionate and dissuasive sanctions, can only be achieved if NCAs can fully remedy and punish violations of the EC competition rules no matter whether the effects of the infringement extend beyond the boundaries of the own territory. It has therefore been submitted that NCAs must take into account the extraterritorial effects of a violation of the EC competition rules when imposing fines for such a violation.

General rules of public international law, such as state sovereignty and the territoriality principle, do not preclude this approach mainly for two reasons. First, the Community is not a traditional international organisation. It has created a legal order *sui generis* and the relations between Member States are thus not governed by the classic principles of public international law. These rules have been relaxed in the field of Community competition law by consent of the Member States and thus do not hinder

---

[74] See E Paulis, 'Latest Commission Thinking and Progress on the Modernisation of Regulation 17' in X, *European Competition Law: A New Role for the Member States/Droit européen de la concurrence: un nouveau rôle pour les Etats membres* (Brussels, Bruylant, 2001), 15, 17.

[75] See above Chapter 6, section I.D.5.b.

[76] Recital 18 of Reg 1/2003.

NCAs to apply sanctions also for the extraterritorial effects of a breach of Articles 81 and 82 EC. Moreover, by allocating (or not opposing the allocation) a case to a single authority, the Network members can be regarded to have implicitly agreed that this particular authority will remedy the entire effects of the infringement, whether these are purely internal or also extraterritorial. Secondly, taking into account the extraterritorial effects of a violation purely for the calculation of the penalty does not constitute an exercise of extraterritorial powers *sensu stricto*. An important difference to classic instances of extraterritoriality is the fact that NCAs do not 'impose' national rules on a foreign act and/or foreign offenders, but apply Community competition rules to which all persons doing business in the EU are subject and certainly all persons residing or having a place of business in the EU. Thirdly, the case allocation rules laid down in the Network Notice envisage that jurisdiction can be asserted only if a number of cumulative conditions are fulfilled. In addition to the effects of the infringement, which must be felt in the territory of the acting Member State, the important criteria are the place of business of the undertakings concerned and the location of evidence. There will thus be a strong material link with the territory of the acting NCA—a jurisdictional nexus.[77] Against this background, it becomes clear that considering the non-domestic effects of the violation for the sole purpose of calculating the actual amount of the fine (or computing another penalty) is just an additional element in the assessment (of the gravity) of the infringement helping the NCA to determine an appropriate (effective, proportionate and dissuasive) sanction.[78]

(2) Duty to Recognise and Respect Foreign NCA Decisions. Article 10 EC also has a horizontal dimension: it applies to the relations between Member States and obliges them to mutual loyalty and sincere co-operation to the extent that the Member States act in the Community law sphere. In view of the fact that Regulation 1/2003 gives full parallel competences to the NCAs, provides mechanisms for close co-operation (via the ECN), in particular as regards case allocation, and advocates the one-stop shop principle, it would seem a logical step that Member States mutually recognise each other's national decisions in the field of Community competition law. Such recognition would afford NCA decisions Community-wide legal validity and would render them enforceable in all Member States. This is certainly a desirable result as it would remove disparities in terms of legal force between national enforcement decisions and enforcement decisions taken by the Commission which are automatically valid in the entire EU. However, it appears that the possibility of an EU-wide validity

---

[77] See paras 8 and 9 of the Network Notice.
[78] See above Chapter 6, section II.D.

of national decisions was discussed in the preparation phase preceding the adoption of Regulation 1/2003 but ultimately rejected. In any event, the Explanatory Memorandum states explicitly that an NCA decision has no legal effect outside the territory of the Member State whose NCA adopted it.[79] It would thus run counter to the express intention of the Community legislature to construe Article 10 EC in such a way as to make national decisions taken in the context of Regulation 1/2003—through the 'loop way' of that Treaty provision—automatically enforceable in all Member States.

On the other hand, the special features of the enforcement regime set up by Regulation 1/2003 and further elaborated in the Network Notice provide strong arguments in favour of a duty of the Member States to recognise the legal force of foreign NCA decisions in individual cases at the request of the Member State which adopted the decision. This approach means that there is no automatism of the recognition and no general Community-wide validity. Rather, foreign decisions would be recognised only by the NCA of another specific Member State to which the relevant request is addressed. Recognition may be required where it is necessary, for instance, to allow enforcement of the decision against a particular undertaking in the other Member State and can only be refused in exceptional circumstances (eg if the Commission has 'overruled' the decision).[80]

Similarly, the loyalty obligation under Article 10 EC, combined with the central features of the new enforcement system and the characteristics of the ECN, militates in favour of a duty of the Member States to mutually respect each other's decisions and pay deference to them. On this basis, NCAs are obliged to make all reasonable efforts to avoid taking decisions that would conflict with the (unappealable) decision adopted by another NCA regarding the same infringement.[81]

II. HAVE THE RIGHTS OF UNDERTAKINGS BEEN SACRIFICED?

The above chapters, in particular Chapter 4.II, have shown that the almost unlimited exchange and use in evidence of information in competition proceedings in the EU raises a number of serious concerns. Many of these concerns result from the lack of harmonisation of the procedural rules of the Member States, which, even though they display considerable discrepancies, are nonetheless applicable where EC antitrust law is enforced by NCAs.

---

[79] P 17 of the Explanatory Memorandum. As concerns *res iudicata* and *ne bis in idem*, however, see above Chapter 6, n 275.

[80] See above Chapter 6, section II.B.

[81] Chapter 6, section II.C.

Already at the beginning of the modernisation process, ie shortly after the publication of the White Paper, Kon expressed the view that there would be no good reason why NCAs should follow separate procedures 'in matters as fundamental as powers of search and seizure, rights of inspection, rights of defence, . . .'.[82] The author was apparently thinking of enforcement disparities and the issue of legal certainty. To my mind, the existence of procedural divergencies, combined with the right to exchange probative (inculpatory) material, also puts the objective fairness of the procedure into question. Moreover, it may damage the perceived (subjective) fairness. Companies subject to an investigation and complainants may find discrepancies between the national procedures acceptable as long as each NCA only applies its own domestic competition law. However, where NCAs enforce the same substantive rules (Articles 81 and 82 EC), procedural divergencies, in particular with regard to investigative powers and defence rights, are difficult to justify.[83]

However, the Commission has not opted for harmonisation, but simply empowered NCAs (and the Commission) to exchange sensitive information and use it in evidence without aligning the applicable national rules of procedure. As concerns sanctions on undertakings, evidence can circulate freely in the Network and, pursuant to Article 12(1) of Regulation 1/2003, can be used against them without restriction.[84] This means that the receiving authority can base its accusation and punishment on whatever incriminating material it obtains through the Network regardless of whether the level of protection of the rights (of defence) of undertakings is much lower in the Member State which collected the evidence than in the Member State of the receiving authority. Under Regulation 1/2003, companies are left without remedy against such circumvention and erosion of protection standards.

In the case of penalties for individuals, Article 12(3) of Regulation 1/2003 lays down limitations on the use of exchanged evidence. However, these limitations only apply where the laws of the authorities involved do not provide for the same kind of sanctions. In other words, where both the sending and the receiving authority can impose the same type of penalties on individuals, these are equally left without protection against the use of evidence that was collected by the sending authority under less stringent rules than those which the receiving authority would have had to observe.

---

[82] S Kon, 'The Commission's White Paper on Modernisation: The Need for Procedural Harmonisation' in B Hawk (ed), *1999 Proceedings of the Fordham Corporate Law Institute* (New York, Juris Publishing, 2000), 233, 252.

[83] See L Idot, 'A Necessary Step Towards Common Procedural Standards of Implementation for Articles 81 & 82 EC without the Network' in Ehlermann and Atanasiu , above n 1, 211, 221.

[84] Except for the rule which limits the use to the subject matter of the investigation (Art 12(2) of Reg 1/2003).

As Advocate General Geelhoed noted in one of the recent cartel cases,

> the interplay between the fundamental rights of legal persons and competition enforcement remains a balancing exercise: at stake are the protection of fundamental rights versus effective enforcement of Community competition law.[85]

It should be added that balancing effective enforcement and fair trial guarantees is a complex process as national rules tend to be complicated,[86] and the emerging balance is a very delicate one which is unique to each national system. The exercise becomes even more difficult where several systems must be reconciled, and the equilibrium established within a given national system can easily be disturbed where diverging national systems interact. As a consequence, the requirements of the ECHR will probably no longer be satisfied. The example of the UK's solution to the protection of the right against self-incrimination described above highlights the risks for the overall fairness of the procedure associated with the interaction of non-harmonised systems.[87]

It seems that the Commission has underestimated the human rights dimension of the existing disparities between the procedural laws of the Member States. In a zestful effort to enhance the effectiveness of competition law enforcement by 'recruiting the help' of 27 other agencies[88] and making NCAs true enforcers of the EC competition rules, while at the same time according them the right to resort to evidence collected abroad, the Commission, it is submitted, has lost sight of the need to ensure that the fundamental rights of the parties, in particular the fair trial guarantee of the ECHR (or, in the terminology of the ECJ, the rights of defence) are not eroded. Arguably, the effective and adequate protection of certain fundamental rights has thus been sacrificed to putatively raise the efficacy of competition law enforcement in the EU.

III. FINAL CONCLUSION

Much can be said about the imperfections of the enforcement system and, more specifically, the co-operation framework (ECN) established by

---

[85] Para 67 of the opinion of Advocate General Geelhoed in Case C–301/04 P *Commission v SGL Carbon* [2006] ECR I–5915 (the Commission's appeal). Obviously, this statement also holds true where natural persons are subject to competition proceedings and face penalties for the infringement of competition rules.

[86] See, eg the various options that the OFT has if it wants to attend premises in order to obtain information. P Collins, 'Some Background Notes on the Investigative Powers of the Competition Authorities', paper for the 2006 EU Competition Law and Policy Workshop, European University Institute/RSCAS, Florence, available at www.eui.eu/RSCAS/research/Competition/2006(pdf)/200610-COMPed-Collins.pdf (accessed January 2009), 3.

[87] See above Chapter 4, section II.C.1.b(2).

[88] The expression has been borrowed from I Forrester, 'Diversity and Consistency: Can They Cohabit?' in Ehlermann and Atanasiu, above n 1, 341.

Regulation 1/2003 and the relevant Commission notices. The previous chapters, particularly Chapters 4 and 6, have undoubtedly revealed that the adequate protection of the (defence) rights of companies and individuals in national competition proceedings is at the heart of the concerns. These rights might be curtailed by the lack of binding allocation rules, the absence of a genuine one-stop shop principle and the possibility of a free flow of information and evidence in the Network. It could be argued that the Commission has not only underestimated these issues, but more importantly also overlooked the human rights dimension of the concerns, for many of the relevant (procedural) rights are indeed rooted in the ECHR. In a different context (that of effective judicial protection of Community law rights), it has been suggested that the key question to be usually answered by the competent national judge is whether the (procedural) rules of his own national legal order may override the Community law requirement of effective protection.[89] In the present context, it is submitted, the inverse question has to be asked: can the Community law requirements of a smooth functioning of the ECN and a seamless co-operation between the Network members[90] override the legal protection afforded by a national legal order to a company or individual involved in competition proceedings? It is submitted that this question should be answered in the negative and that the system therefore needs some 'technical' upgrading. At least some Community-wide procedural minimum standards which take proper account of the rights of defence should be established.[91] Moreover, the national sanctioning systems have to be approximated, otherwise the new system risks compromising the confidence of citizens and undertakings in the fairness of the procedures, the equality of treatment and the rule of law.[92] In addition, for practical purposes and the sake of clarity, there should be uniform rules allowing the service of documents on persons located in the territory of another Member State through normal post and facilitating the transnational enforcement of NCA decisions.[93]

On the other hand, the setting up of a platform for co-operation encompassing all relevant national authorities and the Commission is an undisputable achievement. The ECN marks an important shift away from the common inter-governmental approach towards co-operation which,

[89] S Prechal, 'Judge-made Harmonisation of National Procedural Rules: A Bridging Perspective ' in J Wouters and J Stuyck (eds), *Principles of Proper Conduct for Supranational, State and Private Actors in the European Union: Towards a Ius Commune. Essays in Honour of Walter Van Gerven* (Antwerpen, Intersentia, 2001), 39, 51.

[90] Which, admittedly, has the ultimate goal of ensuring effective enforcement of the EC Treaty rules on competition.

[91] See Fuchs, above n 32, 109.

[92] See Schneider, above n 9, 153.

[93] Cf O Jansen, 'The System of International Co-operation in Administrative and Criminal Matters in Relation to Regulation 1/2003', CLaSF Working Papers Series, Working Paper 03, January 2004 (available at www.clasf.org/publications/workingpapers.htm), 39–40.

until recently, used to govern collaboration in competition matters between agencies in the EU,[94] even though traditional instruments of public international law do not seem adequate where the relations between Member States in an integrated Europe are concerned.[95] The ECN has also certainly brought NCAs and their officials, as well as Community officials, closer to each other. The co-operation, which had already started prior to 1 May 2004, between those involved in the process has increased their knowledge about the legal systems, traditions and mentalities of other Member States. Regular meetings in person have enhanced mutual comprehension and appreciation. After all, the law must not only be obeyed, but also enforced by human beings. Co-operation between them will not work if they remain aliens to each other. The removal of psychological barriers and practical hurdles is probably as important as the removal of legal obstacles. It seems that growing mutual trust and confidence among all Network members have indeed replaced the atmosphere of distrust and reservation which was common in the early days of competition law.[96] In particular, informal contacts between officials of different authorities seem to occur much more frequently now and, at large, experiences with the new co-operation mechanisms appear to be viewed favourably.[97] It is to be hoped that, in this respect, NCAs and Commission have set an example the effects of which will spill over into other areas of Community law and policy.

[94] Outside the scope of Community law, states are generally still forced to resort to these instruments. Unless domestic law authorises the own competition agency to exchange (confidential) information, which is rarely the case, co-operation in antitrust matters can essentially be based only on bilateral dedicated competition agreements or informal ways of co-operation. However, both these avenues usually exclude the exchange of confidential information. (The only 'second generation' competition agreement, ie a competition-specific bilateral treaty which also permits the exchange of confidential information, currently in force is the Antitrust Mutual Enforcement Assistance Agreement (AMEAA) of 1999 between the US and Australia.) Few agencies can rely on non-competition specific bilateral agreements such as mutual legal assistance treaties. See International Competition Network, Cartels Working Group (Subgroup 1), 'Co-operation between competition agencies in cartel investigations', Report to the ICN Annual Conference, Moscow, May 2007 (Luxemburg, Office for Official Publications of the European Communities, 2007), 9, 13–18 and 23. Curiously, in 1997 Marsden still suggested that horizontal co-operation between Member States in competition matters should be made possible by way of bilateral co-operation agreements or a kind of multilateral code. See P Marsden, 'Inducing Member State Enforcement of European Competition Law: A Competition Policy Approach to "Antitrust Federalism"' (1997) 18 *European Competition Law Review* 234. Seemingly, at the time, Marsden did not consider it realistic that secondary Community legislation could be passed that would empower Member States to exchange confidential information.

[95] See Perrin, above n 51, 561 and 543, who notes that the exchange of information with NCAs of the Member States followed the same rules as the exchange with agencies from third countries 'almost as if the existence of the EU was of no consequence'.

[96] Cf the comment made by JP Slot, 'A View from the Mountain: 40 Years of Developments in EC Competition Law' (2004) 41 *CMLRev* 443, 473, regarding the flourishing international co-operation.

[97] This positive evaluation has been confirmed by several NCA officials with whom I spoke in the course of my research. See also International Competition Network, above n 94, 22, which equally describes the overall assessment by NCAs as favourable. It must be noted, though, that only six competition authorities (including DG Competition) responded to the questionnaire that was sent out by the Cartel Working Group of the ICN in preparation for the report (*idem* 21).

Epilogue: Perspectives for Network Convergence and Ius Commune

T
HE ECN IS just one of many pan-European networks that have emerged in the last decade relating to judicial matters (both criminal and civil law) or consumer protection, as well as sector-specific networks. But how do these networks interact? A further issue for consideration is the deliberate choice of the Commission to abstain from any harmonisation measures regarding the national procedural rules and investigative powers of NCAs in competition matters, while, at the same time, advocating the need for more uniformity with respect to (certain aspects of) national tort law and the rules of civil procedure to the extent that they are relevant to the private enforcement of competition law.

I. THE NETWORK PHENOMENON

A. Introduction

The issues discussed in the previous chapters were raised in a context where almost all cases display certain transborder elements. This is the result of the interstate-trade criterion of Articles 81 and 82 EC. Obviously, legal matters with cross-border elements always represent a particular challenge for a legal system. At the same time, the Community and the EU continue to be characterised by progressive (economic) integration of the Member States. The closer we come to the effective completion of the internal market, the more cross-border transaction between economic operators in all areas and at all levels of commerce—including producers, traders, distributors and final consumers—there will be. This development will naturally lead to an increase in legal matters and disputes involving persons from different Member States or other types of factual settings which transgress the boundaries of a single Member State. This finding is not limited to the field of competition law, but equally holds true for other areas of law, in particular contract law and consumer law, but also criminal law.[1]

However, in many fields, the substantive national rules, not to mention procedures, have not been unified or harmonised.[2] Moreover, unlike the situation in competition matters, there is generally no central enforcement authority at the EU level. This means that even where certain harmonising measures have been adopted by the Community legislator (eg directives in the field of consumer protection), enforcement of the relevant rules is mostly a matter for the Member States. In view of the increasing number of transfrontier legal matters, it is therefore necessary to address questions such as jurisdiction and applicable law, both substantive and procedural. Without mutual information and the exchange of factual data and possibly even evidentiary material—in other words, without co-operation between the competent national bodies—adequate and reasonable solutions can hardly be found and the efficient operation of national enforcement bodies will not be possible. This may be a reason why the creation of networks to facilitate and enhance co-operation between national authorities in different fields of law recently seems to have become an increasingly popular instrument to foster effective and efficient enforcement of internal market rules, thereby enhancing European integration. The question arises as to what extent the ECN can or does have model character in this context. Another question, however, is whether the creation of more and more sector-specific networks is really a desirable evolution.

B. The Consumer Protection Enforcement Network (CPEN)

One of the recently established networks is the Consumer Protection Enforcement Network (CPEN), created by Regulation (EC) No 2006/2004 of the European Parliament and the Council of 27 October 2004 on co-operation between national authorities responsible for the enforcement of consumer protection laws (the Regulation on consumer protection co-operation).[3] The CPEN only became operative at the end of 2006.

1. Background

In 2001 the Commission launched an extensive debate on the future of the Community's consumer protection policy by publishing the Green Paper on European Union Consumer Protection ('Consumer Protection Green

---

[1] It is well known that international (organised) crime 'benefits' from the creation of an internal market and the fact that border controls in the EU have largely been abolished.

[2] A notable exception is consumer law, where the laws of the Member States have largely been aligned due to a large number of consumer protection directives.

[3] [2004] OJ L364/1.

Paper').[4] The purpose was to determine which regulatory or other measures should best be taken to improve consumer protection in the EU, in particular with regard to cross-border transactions. In the Consumer Protection Green Paper, the Commission highlighted that the internal market represents the largest pool of consumer demand worldwide, and could thus make an important contribution to achieving the EU's goals, notably the 'new strategic goal', proclaimed at the Lisbon European Council in March 2000, of becoming the most competitive economy in the world. Indeed, one may assume that informed, 'confident and demanding consumers drive competition between firms and higher standards by seeking out new products and best value'.[5] However, at the time, the Commission had to note that the 'consumer internal market' was not functioning properly.[6] A lack of certainty and clarity about then 15 different sets of rules regulating business-to-consumer ('B to C') commercial practices worked as a deterrent for businesses, in particular small and medium-sized enterprises, but also for consumers to engage in cross-border transactions. It was thus concluded that additional harmonising measures were required.[7]

According to the Commission, any such regulatory measure had to be linked to adequate enforcement mechanisms as consumer confidence requires a consistent application and effective enforcement of the law throughout the Community. In the Commission's view, this necessitated public enforcement by national authorities acting in co-operation. This form of coordinated market surveillance was considered essential to combat rogue traders who act cross-border by targeting non-domestic customers (eg through the internet or television, or by telephone)[8] or

---

[4] COM(2001) 531 final; 2 October 2001.

[5] S Kaye, 'Regulation EC 2006/2004 on Consumer Protection Co-operation' in G Howells and others (eds), *The Yearbook of Consumer Law 2007* (Aldershot, Ashgate, 2007), 417, 422.

[6] In the words of the Commission, the consumer internal market had 'not achieved its potential and nor matched the development of the internal market in business-to-business transactions' (p 9 of the Consumer Protection Green Paper).

[7] See pp 9–10 of the Consumer Protection Green Paper. The Commission then continued by putting two different methods of regulation up for discussion: the so-called 'specific approach' would require a whole series of detailed directives, each covering a specific aspect of commercial practices (eg advertising, marketing, sales promotions); the 'mixed approach' would essentially consist of a comprehensive framework directive the purpose of which would be to harmonise national fairness rules for B–C commercial practices (possibly by way of a general clause or general test) and which would operate as a kind of safety net to cover situations which fall outside the scope of the sector-specific directives (see pp 10–13 of the Consumer Protection Green Paper). Following the consultation, the Commission opted for the mixed approach and proposed a framework directive which ultimately led to the adoption of Directive 2005/29/EC of the European Parliament and of the Council of 11 May 2005 concerning unfair business-to-consumer commercial practices in the internal market ('Unfair Commercial Practices Directive'), [2005] OJ L149/22.

[8] On the greater opportunities for fraudulent, dishonest or unfair traders in the era of e-commerce and, as a result, the increasing number of cross-border consumer exploitation see also Kaye, above n 5, 418.

relocate to another country and thereby often succeed in evading enforcement.[9]

2. Main Features of the CPEN

Regulation 2006/2004 aims at addressing this issue. The overall objective of the Regulation is to guarantee effective protection of consumers in transborder matters with the ultimate goal of ensuring the smooth functioning of the internal market.[10] To this end, Regulation 2006/2004 provides a framework for seamless co-operation between the national bodies responsible for the enforcement of consumer protection laws in each of the current 27 Member States. This framework shall enable the national enforcement authorities to effectively tackle cross-border infringements of EU consumer protection rules, such as rules on misleading advertising, unfair contract terms and distance selling arrangements.[11]

The framework for the CPEN established by Regulation 2006/2004 has four key elements.

1. It obliges each Member State to designate an authority responsible for the enforcement of consumer protection rules and a single liaison office.
2. It removes barriers to the exchange of confidential information between the national enforcement bodies.
3. It establishes mutual assistance rights and obligations.
4. It allows for wider co-operation in general matters (ie beyond the scope of individual cases) such as training of officials, development of communication tools, standards and guidelines or exchange of officials.[12]

The designation of competent authorities is left to the Member States. Those Member States whose laws do not provide for public enforcement of consumer protection laws (eg Germany, the Netherlands) do not necessarily have to create a new authority; instead, they can designate an existing

---

[9] Pp 16–17 of the Consumer Protection Green Paper. The possible elements of such a co-operation instrument were set out on p 19 of the Consumer Protection Green Paper.

[10] See Art 1 of Reg 2006/2004.

[11] See Kaye, above n 5, 421–2. A list of those consumer protection directives which fall within the scope of co-operation in the CPEN is annexed to Reg 2006/2004. Health and (product) safety issues are excluded.

[12] See Art 16 of Reg 2006/2004. Here, the Community is seen as having a supporting role as regards Member States' efforts to deploy information and education activities which are designed to generally promote consumer interests, as such activities can help to foster the protection of consumer rights. However, this fourth element evidently constitutes a supplementary function of the CPEN, whose principal task is to provide a tool for enforcement co-operation. See para 43 of the Explanatory Memorandum to the Commission's proposal for the Reg on consumer protection co-operation (17 July 2003; COM(2003) 443 final; 'CPC Explanatory Memorandum').

body.[13] However, the facts that each Member State must now have a public enforcement authority and that these authorities must be vested with a minimum of common enforcement powers[14] help ensure consistency and equivalent effectiveness of the implementation of consumer protection rules in the EU. Effective implementation of these rules across the EU ultimately also serves the goal of establishing a level playing field since, where gaps in the Network impede effective and consistent enforcement, law-abiding traders are put at a competitive disadvantage.[15] The nomination of a single liaison office, through which requests for information exchange and mutual assistance are to be channelled,[16] allows for proper coordination and thus facilitates co-operation.

Information exchange takes place either at the request of a particular authority (applicant authority) or spontaneously where a competent authority becomes aware of an intra-Community (ie cross-border) infringement.[17] In both cases, there is an obligation to supply the (requested or relevant) information. In the first case, the requested authority even has to undertake the necessary investigations in order to gather the required information.[18] The regulation also lays down that information the disclosure of which would undermine the protection of the privacy of individuals or commercial interests, ie in particular personal data and business secrets, is covered by the professional secrecy obligation and thus remains confidential.[19]

Mutual assistance is based on the general principle that a competent authority can act against any rogue trader in its own country regardless of the location of the affected consumers.[20] Accordingly, where the information communicated confirms the existence of a cross-border infringement, the requested authority is obliged to bring about the

[13] See paras 28–31 and 36 of the CPC Explanatory Memorandum.

[14] Para 29 of the CPC Explanatory Memorandum.

[15] See recital 2 of Reg 2006/2004 and para 11 of the CPC Explanatory Memorandum. Interestingly, in the field of consumer protection law, where traditionally private enforcement prevailed, the Commission, by causing all Member States to provide equally for public enforcement, somehow took the inverse path of that taken in relation to the modernisation of competition law. In the latter context, the Commission vigorously seeks to enhance private enforcement of the Community's competition rules as a complement to public enforcement measures to be adopted by the Commission or NCAs. See inter alia paras 99–100 of the White Paper and, more importantly, the Commission's Green Paper on damages actions for breach of the EC antitrust rules (COM(2005) 672 final), 19 December 2005 ('Green Paper on Damages Actions').

[16] See Art 12(2) of Reg 2006/2004.

[17] See Arts 6 and 7 of Reg 2006/2004. While spontaneous information exchange is essential to effective market surveillance, exchange on request shall ultimately lead to the prohibition and cessation of the illicit practice (see paras 38 and 39 of the CPC Explanatory Memorandum).

[18] Art 6(2) of Reg 2006/2004.

[19] Such information may only be disclosed if this is necessary to bring about the cessation of an infringement provided that the authority which communicated the information consents to its disclosure. See Art 13(3) of Reg 2006/2004.

[20] Para 41 of the CPC Explanatory Memorandum.

cessation or prohibition of the infringement. But it is free to choose the most efficient and effective method of enforcement.[21] Requests for enforcement measures (or information) may be rejected only in certain circumstances, the default principle being that applications for assistance should be accepted.[22] Since cross-border infringements will often not be limited to bilateral situations, but will affect consumers in multiple Member States, Regulation 2006/2004 further allows for the coordination of surveillance actions or enforcement measures which are undertaken by the competent authorities in several Member States.[23]

The CPEN will be backed by an electronic database, to be maintained by the Commission, in which information communicated under Articles 7, 8 and 9 of Regulation 2006/2004 (mere information exchange, mutual assistance and coordination of multiple surveillance or enforcement measures) will be stored and processed. Accordingly, requests for assistance or information exchange shall be made on a standard form and forwarded electronically via this database.[24]

C. Other Fields and Means of Co-operation

The CPEN is not the only network of national authorities that has recently been created at European level. There are many more examples.

With a view to improving, simplifying and expediting effective judicial co-operation in civil and commercial matters, the Council has established a European Judicial Network in civil and commercial matters ('Civil Matters EJN').[25] This network is to be seen in the context of the 1998 action plan of the Council and the Commission on the implementation of the EU Treaty provisions on an area of freedom, security and justice ('Action Plan').[26] Even though the area of freedom, security and justice is essentially linked to policy fields which are more directly related to the free movement of persons, such as visa, asylum and immigration issues (which are now a Community competence) and police and judicial co-operation in criminal

---

[21] See Art 8 of Reg 2006/2004 and para 39 of the CPC Explanatory Memorandum.

[22] Para 42 of the CPC Explanatory Memorandum. The conditions which may justify a refusal to assist are set out in Art 15(2)–(5) of Reg 2006/2004.

[23] See Art 9 of Reg 2006/2004 and para 40 of the CPC Explanatory Memorandum

[24] See Arts 10(1) and 12(3) of Reg 2006/2004. The language to be used shall be agreed by the competent authorities prior to the sending of the request. If no agreement is reached, each authority (ie the applicant and the requested authority) can use their respective official language.

[25] See Council decision of 28 May 2001 (2001/470/EC), [2001] OJ L174/25 ('2001 Council Decision').

[26] See the Action Plan of the Council and the Commission on how best to implement the provisions of the Treaty of Amsterdam on an area of freedom, security and justice—text adopted by the Justice and Home Affairs Council of 3 December 1998 (1999/C 19/01), [1999] OJ C19/1.

matters,[27] it has been acknowledged that judicial co-operation in civil matters

> represents a fundamental stage in the creation of a European judicial area which will bring tangible benefits for every Union citizen.[28]

On this basis, the creation of the Civil Matters EJN could be considered as one of the flanking measures necessary to complete the internal market.

The Civil Matters EJN aims at improving and facilitating co-operation between judicial bodies of different Member States in general and enhancing the effective and practical application of existing Community instruments relating to judicial co-operation, such as Regulation 44/2001 concerning civil and commercial matters or Regulation 2201/2003 concerning matrimonial and parental matters.[29] Accordingly, it consists of one (or more) contact point(s) for each Member State, as well as central bodies provided for in existing instruments, liaison magistrates and other appropriate authorities, including administrative bodies. Periodic meetings of contact points are convened and chaired by the Commission, as are meetings that are open to all members of the Network.[30] In order to guarantee the practical operation of the Civil Matters EJN, contact points are required to have adequate knowledge of an official language of the Community other than their own.[31] The Civil Matters EJN is supported by a secure limited-access electronic information exchange system, the so-called 'Circa' intranet, managed by the Commission.[32] In addition, an internet-based information system for the public with a dedicated website will gradually be established.[33] The third fundamental objective of the Civil Matters EJN is to promote equal access to justice for citizens in the EU engaging in cross-border litigation.[34] More generally, the Civil Matters EJN serves as a permanent discussion forum regarding cross-border issues of civil justice and contributes to increasing mutual trust between courts in the EU.

The provisions establishing the Civil Matters EJN are modelled upon the

---

[27] See Art 29(1) EU Treaty and Part II of the Action Plan, in particular paras 32–8 and 42–51. See also K Lenaerts and P Van Nuffel, *Constitutional Law of the European Union* (London, Sweet & Maxwell, 2nd edn, 2005), 6-006.

[28] Para 16 of the Action Plan.

[29] Council Regulation (EC) No 2201/2003 of 27 November 2003 concerning jurisdiction and the recognition and enforcement of judgments in matrimonial matters and the matters of parental responsibility, repealing Regulation (EC) No 1347/2000, [2003] OJ L338/1.

[30] See Art 2 and Arts 9–12 of the 2001 Council Decision.

[31] Member States are therefore called upon to encourage language training and promote exchanges between the relevant staff of different Member States. See Art 7 of the 2001 Council Decision.

[32] See Art 13(2) of the 2001 Council Decision.

[33] Art 14 of the 2001 Council Decision. The main purpose of the network's website is to outline the various national systems of civil and commercial law (see background information at www.ec.europa.eu/civiljustice/index_en.htm.

[34] Recital 14 of the 2001 Council Decision.

rules of the European Judicial Network in criminal matters[35] that had been set up in 1998 by the Council acting under Article K.3 of the EU Treaty ('Criminal Matters EJN').[36] The purpose of the Criminal Matters EJN is to further judicial co-operation between the Member States primarily with a view to combating forms of serious (organised) crime, such as drug trafficking and terrorism. It is composed of central authorities of the Member States responsible for international judicial co-operation, as well as judicial or other competent authorities with specific responsibilities within the context of international co-operation. The Joint Action equally provides for the designation of one or more contact points for each Member State which act as intermediaries between (local) domestic and foreign authorities and thus shall have adequate knowledge of a foreign (official) language.[37] Periodic meetings of the members of the Criminal Matters EJN are also envisaged.[38] Further, it was considered that information should be disseminated within the Network by means of an electronic system.[39] It should also be noted that, in addition to the Criminal Matters EJN, a Convention on Mutual Assistance in Criminal Matters between the Member States of the European Union has been established in accordance with Article 34 of the EU Treaty.[40]

Apart from these two judicial networks, there are various sector-specific co-operation instruments in which national regulatory authorities (NRAs) or other national surveillance bodies with sector-specific responsibilities are pooled in a network or engaged in some looser form of co-operation. For instance, the Electronic Communications Framework Directive[41] establishes a harmonised framework for the regulation of electronic communications services and associated facilities, and lays down procedures to ensure the harmonised application of this framework throughout the Community. The regulatory tasks set out in the directive must be assigned by the Member States to a competent and independent

---

[35] Cf para 40(d) of the Action Plan, which lists as one of the measures to be taken within two years: 'examine the possibility of extending the concept of the European judicial network in criminal matters to embrace civil proceedings.'

[36] Joint Action of 29 June 1998, adopted by the Council on the basis of Art K3 of the Treaty on European Union, on the creation of a European Judicial Network (98/428/JHA) ('1998 Joint Action'), [1998] OJ L191/4.

[37] See Arts 2 and 4 of the 1998 Joint Action.

[38] Arts 5–7 of the 1998 Joint Action.

[39] In the words of Art 3 lit c of the 1998 Joint Action: 'an appropriate telecommunications network'; see also Art 10 of the 1998 Joint Action.

[40] Council Act of 29 May 2000, [2000] OJ C197/1. The purpose of this convention is to encourage and modernise co-operation between judicial, police and customs authorities. The instrument lays down the conditions under which mutual assistance is granted and prescribes the applicable procedures. It also allows for spontaneous exchange of information.

[41] Directive 2002/21/EC of the European Parliament and of the Council of 7 March 2002 on a common regulatory framework for electronic communications networks and services (Framework Directive), [2002] OJ 108/33.

national body, ie an NRA.[42] A harmonious development of the internal market in this field and a consistent implementation of the prescribed regulatory tasks evidently requires coordination between the 27 NRAs. Accordingly, Article 7 of the Electronic Communications Framework Directive lays down certain mandatory information and consultation procedures which NRAs have to observe when they intend to adopt a measure that would affect trade between Member States.[43]

A more formalised method of sector-specific co-operation can be found in the financial sector. The so-called *Lamfalussy* regulatory approach, which consists of a four-level system to regulate and monitor the securities markets in the EU,[44] also embraces certain institutional arrangements. It provides, inter alia, for the establishment of a Committee of European Securities Regulators (CESR) which consists of 'high-level representatives from the national public authorities competent in the field of securities'.[45] The CESR thus combines the relevant supervisory authorities of all Member States. One of its tasks is to advise the Commission on the possible content of Level 2 implementing measures.[46] However, the CESR also functions as an instrument to improve and strengthen co-operation between the national regulators and ensure consistent implementation of Level 1 and 2 measures.[47] To this end, the CESR can itself issue, at Level 3, recommendations, guidelines and common standards with a view to coordinating Member States' implementation efforts.[48]

[42] See Arts 1 and 3 of the Electronic Communications Framework Directive. NRAs are typically set up in sectors such as telecommunication, energy or railway which used do be dominated by public operators with monopoly rights and have been liberalised only relatively recently.

[43] See Art 7 of the Electronic Communications Framework Directive. Art 7(5) thereof even provides that the NRA concerned 'shall take the utmost account of comments of other national regulatory authorities and the Commission'. See further Art 8(2)(d) of the Electronic Communications Framework Directive, which generally requires NRAs to co-operate with each other and the Commission 'in a transparent manner'.

[44] A concise but very instructive description of the *Lamfalussy* process is given by W Van Gerven, 'Bringing (Private) Laws Closer to Each Other at the European Level', paper, January 2005, available at www.law.kuleuven.be/ccle/pdf/2005-01-18_WvG_.Impact_courts_on_private_law.pdf (accessed January 2009), 1, 23–6. See also Annex 1 to the Commission's preliminary assessment of 15 November 2004, 'The application of the Lamfalussy process to EU securities markets legislation' (SEC(2004)1459) ('Preliminary Assessment'), which provides an overview of the four-level approach in diagram form.

[45] See Art 3 of the Commission Decision of 6 June 2001 establishing the Committee of European Securities Regulators (2001/527/EC), [2001] OJ 191/43. The Commission even regards the creation of the CESR as one of the key innovations of the *Lamfalussy* approach. See para 6 of its Preliminary Assessment.

[46] At Level 1, the Council and the EP can adopt framework directives, which are then implemented, at Level 2, by the Commission through more technical measures.

[47] Van Gerven, above n 44, 37–8.

[48] See Art 2 of the Commission Decision establishing the CESR and paras 27 *et seq* of the Preliminary Assessment.

D. A Brief Evaluation

A brief evaluation of the development described above, ie the prolifer-ation[49] of ever more different networks at the EU level, leads to two main conclusions. True enforcement networks which seek to enable authorities to coordinate actual investigation and enforcement measures and grant each other mutual administrative assistance such as the ECN or the CPEN have a number of common features, but may still be based on diverging principles. Secondly, the development entails a significant sectoral fragmen-tation of co-operation instruments at the supranational level, but seems to lack sufficient coordination mechanisms between the various networks created, which may have overlapping responsibilities.[50]

1. Common and Diverging Features of ECN and CPEN—Is the ECN Really the Blueprint?

It is probably not surprising that ECN and CPEN, both being networks to further co-operation in the actual enforcement of Community law[51] in transborder cases, have a number of common features. These include:

- 'automatic' provision of information at certain instances;[52]

---

[49] The expression has been borrowed from W Devroe, 'Hoofdstuk VI De verhouding tussen mededingingsautoriteiten en sectoriële toezichthouders in België' in J Stuyck, W Devroe and P Wytinck (eds), *De nieuwe Belgische Mededingingswet 2006* (Mechelen, Kluwer, 2007), 141, para 4. Devroe describes the recent proliferation of supervisory bodies ('proliferatie van toezichthouders') which is triggered by the creation of more and more different sectors combined with the increasing decentralisation of supervision. The latter evolution can be observed not only at the EU level, but also at the Member State level, in particular in Member States with a federal structure where supervisory tasks are assigned to different governmental levels and certain matters are thus distributed between a number of local or regional bodies which entails further fragmentation (*idem*, para 3). The above examples of various novel co-operation instruments show that this phenomenon, the proliferation of supervisory bodies, is carried forward to the networking level.

[50] This statement can be made even though, at the same time, a (fairly limited) trend towards consolidation of supervisory functions (within a certain sector) can be observed at the Member State level. For instance, Germany has recently unified its previously segmented supervisory system in the financial sector by merging the three specialist bodies for banking, insurance and securities into a single supervisory authority for financial services (Bundesanstalt für Finanzdienstleistungsaufsicht). On this trend, see R Lastra, 'The Governance Structure for Financial Reg and Supervision in Europe' (2004) 10 *Columbia Journal of European Law* 49, 50–2.

[51] In the case of the ECN: the Treaty provisions on antitrust; in the case of the CPEN: secondary Community legislation, notably the consumer protection directives listed in the Annex to Reg 2006/2004.

[52] Under Art 7(1) of Reg 2006/2004, a competent authority has to inform its counterparts in other Member States and the Commission of any actual or suspected infringement of the consumer protection laws which has cross-border elements. This information duty is comparable to the routine of NCAs to send initial case reports to the ECN, even though, strictly speaking, supplying this kind of information on new cases is mandatory only vis-à-vis the Commission (see Art 11(3) of Reg 1/2003).

- the right of the participating authorities to share confidential information;
- provisions complementing the former element that oblige all officials involved—both national and Community servants—to abide by the principle of professional secrecy, thereby guaranteeing the confidential treatment of exchanged information;
- the possibility of calling on foreign authorities for assistance in investigating suspected cross-border infringements.[53]

These elements can probably be considered to form the minimum basis of rules that any instrument seeking to make possible and enhance effective co-operation between national bodies should contain.

However, there is one essential aspect in which both networks differ from each other: the CPEN is notably based on a strict reciprocity approach, that is, it provides for mutual assistance rights and obligations. This means that the right of any network member to seek and obtain information or administrative assistance from its counterparts in other Member States is coupled with the obligation of the applicant authority to provide, in (re)turn, the same kind of support to other network members if so requested.[54] And, indeed, this idea of reciprocal duties has been implemented in a very consequent fashion. Mutual assistance (in the broad sense of the word) under Regulation 2006/2004 covers not just information gathering and forwarding, but also actual enforcement measures. For example, pursuant to Article 8 of Regulation 2006/2004, the applicant authority can request its counterpart in another Member State to bring about the cessation or prohibition of a detected intra-Community infringement. On this basis, each Member State can be sure that its consumers will effectively be protected in cases of transborder violations of EC consumer protection legislation.[55]

By contrast, Regulation 1/2003 contains no elements of reciprocity. In fact, the absence of formal mutual obligations between NCAs pervades the entire Regulation. Real information duties and mandatory assistance rules only exist with regard to the vertical relation between Commission and NCAs. The horizontal dimension, ie the relation between NCAs, by contrast, is largely underdeveloped. NCAs are under no obligation to provide information on new cases or evidentiary material in their possession to another NCA, although they may do so on a voluntary

---

[53] In competition matters, an NCA can carry out inspections and other fact-finding measures in its own territory on behalf of a foreign NCA (Art 22(1) of Reg 1/2003). In consumer protection matters, an authority can request the competent authority of another Member State to provide it with information which the requested authority, if necessary, must first gather by undertaking the appropriate investigations (Art 6(1) and (2) of Reg 2006/2004). Both provisions essentially concern the collection of evidentiary material on foreign territory.

[54] Kaye, above n 5, 422.

[55] See para 34 (fifth bullet point) of the CPC Explanatory Memorandum.

basis.[56] Likewise, the rules on mutual assistance (investigations on behalf of another NCA) define a mere faculty. It is thus not surprising that the adoption of enforcement measures by one NCA at the request of another NCA has not been envisaged at all in Regulation 1/2003. Providing such assistance in the actual enforcement of the EC competition rules is likely to be less popular where there is no reciprocal duty of the applicant NCA to grant the same sort of assistance should the requested NCA, in turn, require such relief at a later instance. In view of the facultative character of all forms of mutual support between NCAs, the horizontal co-operation mechanisms of Regulation 1/2003 are significantly weaker than those of 2006/2004.

The strict reciprocity approach in Regulation 2006/2004 may be explained by the fact that, in consumer protection matters, there is no central enforcement agency with powers to implement the relevant rules in the entire Community. This is obviously an important aspect, clearly distinguishing consumer protection from competition matters. In the latter case, not only the NCAs, but also the Commission itself can enforce the Community rules. Against this background, strict reciprocity, in particular a duty for NCAs to effectively take enforcement measures if so requested by another NCA, is strictly speaking not necessary since, as a last resort, the Commission can always be called upon to intervene and enforce the EC antitrust provisions. However, while this difference probably explains why a strict reciprocity approach was indeed necessary in the context of Regulation 2006/2004, it does not, in my view, justify that horizontal co-operation under Regulation 1/2003 essentially is a mere option, not an obligation. Thus, the way in which Regulation 1/2003 incites NCAs to provide support to each other lags behind the level of solidarity created by Regulation 2006/2004. It is submitted that, in this regard, the model character of Regulation 1/2003 is at least doubtful.

Another difference relates to the way in which the protection of confidential information is secured. Article 13(3) of Regulation 2006/2004 describes, in a relatively detailed manner, the kind of personal data, commercially sensitive information and other types of information (eg information relating to legal advice) which shall be subject to the obligation of professional secrecy. Moreover, it makes the disclosure of such confidential information[57] explicitly dependent on the consent of the transmitting authority. Here again, Regulation 1/2003 seems to lag behind the standard achieved in the field of the CPEN in that it does not contain any common rules defining or at least circumscribing the kind of information that shall benefit from confidentiality protection. Where the

---

[56] In practice, summary reports on new cases are in any event uploaded in the ECMS and thus made available to all network members.

[57] Disclosure is only permitted where this is necessary to put an end to the infringement.

protection standards of the receiving authority are lower than those of the transmitting authority, a loss of protection is thus likely to occur. By contrast, under Regulation 2006/2004, this risk is largely eliminated by the consent requirement.[58] It is thus submitted that more legal certainty regarding confidential treatment of information exchanged in the ECN could have been achieved by incorporating some minimum common rules in Regulation 1/2003. This seems all the more feasible as a variety of possible criteria are available at the Community level, *inter alia* in the Commission's Notice on Access to File and Regulation 1049/2001 on public access to documents.[59] As concerns guarantees for the protection of confidential information shared in a network, Regulation 1/2003 therefore does not really provide the prototype solution.

Apart from these two major divergencies, it is interesting to note that Regulation 2006/2004 also contains provisions on the language to be used for communication. While Regulation 1/2003 and even the Network Notice contain no rules on the use of languages, Article 12(4) of Regulation 2006/2004 provides that the authorities concerned shall agree on the language to be used. Obviously, the choice or determination of certain languages, possibly to the exclusion of others, is a very sensitive issue. In view of the general principles laid down in Regulation 1/58[60], the Commission clearly could not exclude a priori, by a simple notice, the use of the official languages of certain Member States as working languages of the ECN.[61] On the other hand, it is equally obvious that any form of co-operation will fail where language barriers impede a proper communication and understanding between the co-operating partners. This is all the more so in a Community of 27, with 23 different official languages. Knowledge and use of languages are therefore crucial factors in any network of national authorities and officials. The Commission apparently

---

[58] Cf also Art 3(5) of the Electronic Communications Framework Directive, which provides that the receiving authority shall ensure the same level of confidentiality as the originating (ie transmitting) authority.

[59] Obviously, other solutions, such as a consent requirement of the transmitting authority or a rule determining that the higher protection standard shall always prevail, could also be envisaged.

[60] Council Reg No 1 determining the languages to be used by the European Economic Community [1958] OJ 17, 385–6 (German, French, Dutch and Italian). Art 1 of that regulation reads: 'Les langues officielles et les langues de travail des institutions de la Communauté sont l'allemand, le français, l'italien et le néerlandais.' In the context of accession of new Member States, Reg 1/58 has regularly been 'updated' so as to include the official languages of the acceding states. It thus expresses the rule that, in principle, the official languages of the Member States are also official languages and working languages of the Communities. The EU currently has 23 official languages (including Irish, which, as of 1 January 2007, has acquired full official language status). It is a prerogative of the Council, acting unanimously, to determine the rules governing the languages of the institutions (see Art 290 EC).

[61] However, a provision similar to that contained in Reg 2006/2006 inviting the NCAs involved each time to jointly determine the language to be used in the event of co-operation would have been possible. See also below n 63.

assumed that language rules would not be necessary for the efficient functioning of the ECN since most members had already developed the practice of using English as the working language.[62] This may be linked to the fact that, in competition matters, there exists a longer tradition of co-operation, inter alia through the Advisory Committee, which already existed under Regulation 17. Moreover, the Commission and NCAs already co-operated closely and exchanged views in the preparation of the various Commission notices complementing Regulation 1/2003. This particular experience probably worked as an indicator that important language issues were not likely to arise. However, this can be very different in other fields of law, where it may well be necessary to develop rules and procedures to tackle actual language problems or at least provide incentives to reduce language barriers.[63] Otherwise such problems could become a real impediment to effective co-operation. On this point also, Regulation 1/2003 therefore does not necessarily have model character.

2. Problems Resulting from the Multiplication of Networks

Two of the main problems raised by the parallel existence of a variety of domain- or sector-specific co-operation networks are the overlap between the responsibilities or tasks of different networks and their members, and the corresponding multiple membership of the participating bodies.

a. Overlap of Responsibilities

Sector-specific supervisory or regulatory bodies often also have to ensure effective competition between the operators in the relevant sector. The legal debate focuses mainly on the relation between NCAs and NRAs since the latter are usually not just responsible for the enforcement of sector-specific regulation, but equally have to enhance free and undistorted competition in the industry sector subject to their supervision.[64] For instance, Article 8(2)(b) of the Electronic Communications Framework Directive provides that NRAs shall promote competition in the provision of electronic communications networks and related services and facilities inter alia by 'ensuring that there is no distortion or restriction of competition in the electronic communications sector'.

These lines echo some of the wording of Article 81 almost verbatim. The overlap of enforcement responsibilities between NCAs and NRAs thus

---

[62] See above Chapter 3, n 95 and accompanying text.

[63] Cf the requirements for foreign language knowledge of contact points laid down both in the 1998 Joint Action creating the Criminal Matters EJN (Art 2(3) thereof) and the 2001 Council Decision establishing the Civil Matters EJN (Art 7 thereof; this latter provision contains a second paragraph seeking to promote language training and exchanges of staff).

[64] Devroe, above n 49, para 6.

becomes all too clear. As a consequence, an NRA has to coordinate its activities with those of the domestic NCA,[65] and possibly also with the activities of other supervisory bodies of the same Member State. This is no simple task. In fact, the complexity of the co-operation requirements is illustrated by Article 3(4) of Electronic Communications Framework Directive, which, in order to ensure proper coordination between the potentially concerned enforcement bodies, provides that:

> Member States shall publish the tasks to be undertaken by national regulatory authorities in an easily accessible form, in particular where those tasks are assigned to more than one body. Member States shall ensure, where appropriate, consultation and co-operation between those authorities, and between those authorities and national authorities entrusted with the implementation of competition law and national authorities entrusted with the implementation of consumer law, on matters of common interest . . .

NRAs are thus explicitly required to co-operate, at the national level, with the domestic NCA and even the domestic consumer protection agency. However, there are no equivalent provisions, let alone a formal mechanism or framework, ensuring coordination at the EU level, ie between NRAs and NCAs of different Member States.[66] As regards the financial sector, the situation is even more complex as there is, already within this 'single' sector, a multiplicity of committees at the supranational level.[67] The lack of coordinating instruments may lead to discrepancies in approach and conflicting measures between NCAs and sector-specific authorities across the EU. Moreover, bilateral consultation between NRA and NCA may not be sufficient, as consumer protection issues may also be involved. Coordination thus becomes a complex process.

b. Multiple Membership

The second problem relates to the fact that competition rules are enforced, in some Member States, by administrative or judicial bodies which also

---

[65] This conclusion is not altered by the fact that NCAs and NRAs can be considered to be complementary in nature since they have different characteristics, in particular, in that NCAs predominantly act *ex post*, while NRAs mostly act *ex ante*. See Devroe, above n 49, para 6.

[66] Devroe, above n 49, para 7.

[67] In fact, the *Lamfalussy* approach already provided for two separate committees at each of Level 2 and Level 3 of the regulatory system, notably the European Securities Committee (ESC; composed of high-ranking national officials such as secretaries of state and chaired by the responsible EU Commissioner) at Level 2 and the aforementioned Level 3 CESR. Later, it was suggested that this dual structure, originally established only with regard to regulation and supervision of the securities markets, should be extended to other segments of the financial sector (inter alia banking and insurance). On these developments, see Lastra, above n 50, 58–9. In the meantime, the relevant directive has been adopted and entered into force (Directive 2005/1/EC regarding a new organisational structure for financial services committees, [2005] OJ L79/9). Against this background, the emergence of a confusing tangle of sectoral bodies and networks at the EU level seems to be unavoidable.

have other responsibilities. These may be sector-specific tasks, for instance in the field of consumer protection, or more general functions in the field of civil or criminal law.

In the UK, the OFT, which is responsible for the enforcement of the EC competition rules, is also the competent authority for enforcing consumer protection laws and will play a pivotal role as a single liaison office under Regulation 2006/2004.[68] Likewise, in France, the DGCCRF, as its name indicates, has responsibilities in the fields of both competition law and consumer protection.[69] These two agencies are thus both members of the ECN and of the CPEN. They will therefore need to distinguish carefully between the different tasks and activities, in particular with regard to information exchange, inter alia because of the diverging confidentiality rules[70] and the different restrictions on the use of the shared information enshrined in both relevant regulations.[71]

In Member States where prohibition decisions and/or decisions imposing fines are adopted by a civil court, such as is the case in Austria (through the Vienna Court of Appeals) and Sweden (through the Stockholm District Court), these courts may be designated as NCAs and may thus be members of the ECN. In addition, they may (also) become engaged in co-operation within the framework of the Civil Matters EJN. Similarly, there are Member States such as the UK and Ireland where breaches of the EC competition rules can represent criminal offences and where these rules are consequently (also) enforced by criminal courts. These criminal courts may thus be part of the Criminal Matters EJN, but may also be involved in information sharing in the ECN. Again, the double membership will require precise rules to ensure that co-operation under both mechanisms, the ECN and EJN, is kept separate internally in order to avoid violations of the respective rules on confidentiality, the limitations on use of exchanged information in evidence, and so on. It seems that these issues have hardly been addressed as yet.

E. Conclusion

The proliferation of supervisory and regulatory authorities, which can be observed at both the EU and national levels and which is carried forward to the area of networking, leads to an increasing fragmentation of regulatory surveillance and law enforcement and a growing number of different networks.

---

[68] Kaye, above n 5, 412.
[69] See also para 36 of the CPC Explanatory Memorandum.
[70] See above n 57 and accompanying text.
[71] Art 12(2) and (3) of Reg 1/2003 and Art 13(1) and (2) of Reg 2006/2004.

A comparison between the ECN and the CPEN has shown that, while both networks have some common features, there are two fundamental differences. Strict reciprocity and a minimum of common rules regarding confidentiality are two important elements of the CPEN arrangements which are, however, absent in the ECN framework. The latter co-operation framework also lacks rules on the language to be used for communications. On these points, it is submitted, the ECN does not unreservedly have model character.

Apart from this, the network phenomenon—that is, the parallel existence of various networks with partly overlapping responsibilities—risks making enforcement co-operation a complex and burdensome task, using up much of the resources of the administrative or judicial bodies involved.[72] This is exacerbated as formal instruments allowing for coordination of activities between the different networks at the EU level are missing. Moreover, it is possible that coordination needs cannot be satisfied bilaterally, but that adequate solutions require multilateral consultations. In addition, some enforcement agencies or courts will have to be represented, concurrently, in several different networks. This again renders matters complicated, at least internally. If the proliferation of networks continues without the Commission developing a more global and coherent approach, this may hamper effective and purposeful co-operation. Will public regulators and enforcers, instead of collaborating closely and thereby fostering actual compliance with EC legislation in cross-border situations, ultimately get lost in 'a tangled web of networks'?

II. HARMONISATION V GRADUAL CONVERGENCE

It may be questioned whether the Commission's assumption is correct that harmonisation or alignment of national (procedural) rules in the field of competition law is not a prerequisite to achieving effective and consistent decentralised enforcement of the EC antitrust provisions. At the beginning of the reform process, the question was raised whether the application of Articles 81 and 82 EC by a multitude of national authorities would not require a certain (minimum) degree of harmonisation of the relevant procedural norms of the Member States.[73] Indeed, several authors consider some

---

[72] On the other hand, the creation of networks could also be seen as a possible way to tackle at least some of the problems arising out of the proliferation of supervisory and regulatory authorities. Grouping the relevant bodies together in a network can enhance co-operation among them and stimulate more coordinated approaches. However, the somewhat uncontrolled emergence of too many 'parallel' networks still entails a number of serious risks, as outlined above (section I.D.2).

[73] See, eg the pre-cited articles by I Forrester, 'Diversity and Consistency: Can They Cohabit?' and C Gauer, 'Does the Effectiveness of the EU Network of Competition Authorities Require a Certain Degree of Harmonisation of National Procedures and Sanctions?' in C-D Ehlermann

form of limited approximation of the procedures and/or sanctions desirable.[74] Others submit that a basic harmonisation of the powers and procedures of NCAs, not limited to investigative powers and penalties, is essential.[75] One scholar even goes so far as suggesting that the concept of the common market tends to make a general harmonisation of antitrust laws, including the substantive national rules, necessary since maintaining a separate set of rules for purely national cases would be difficult to reconcile with the principle of equal treatment.[76] On the other hand, it is not unlikely that, at least in the long term, some convergence between the national procedures applied by the NCAs in the context of implementing Articles 81 and 82 EC will occur. This may, in particular, be expected with regard to those rules and principles that hamper or even impede effective and trustful co-operation within the Network. The crucial question therefore is whether direct harmonisation or even unification through legislative measures at the EU level is really desirable or whether we should rather wait for a spontaneous, but gradual, convergence of the competition procedures of the Member States.

A. Gradual Administrative Convergence[77]

It is a well-known phenomenon that the influence of European integration and European law on the legal systems of the Member States is continuously increasing. In fact, 'today there is virtually no branch of the law, which escapes the impact of Community law'.[78] In particular judge-made law by the Community courts often has significant repercussions on the national legal orders of the Member States. The harmonising effect of the ECJ's case law is particularly visible in the field of legal remedies, where the

---

and I Atanasiu (eds), *European Competition Law Annual 2002: Constructing the EU Network of Competition Authorities* (Oxford, Hart Publishing, 2003), 341 and 187.

[74] L Idot, 'A Necessary Step Towards Common Procedural Standards of Implementation for Articles 81 & 82 EC without the Network' in Ehlermann and Atanasiu, above n 73, 221, suggests that certain aspects (inter alia limitation and sanctions) should be harmonised. Gauer, above n 73, 200, seems to favour an alignment of the applicable sanctions, at least in the medium term.

[75] S Kon, 'The Commission's White Paper on Modernisation: The Need for Procedural Harmonisation' in B Hawk (ed), *1999 Proceedings of the Fordham Corporate Law Institute* (New York, Juris Publishing, 2000), 253.

[76] A von Bogdandy, 'Rechtsgleichheit, Rechtssicherheit und Subsidiarität im transnationalen Wirtschaftsrecht' (2001) 12 *Europäische Zeitschrift für Wirtschaftsrecht* 357, 359. See also the approach taken by the legislators in Belgium and the Netherlands in respect of the treatment of purely national cases, most notably as regards the applicability of (EU) block exemptions (above Chapter 1, n 347).

[77] The term 'convergence' is used here to describe a process whereby national laws, through voluntary or spontaneous action on the part of the Member States, gradually grow together so that discrepancies are reduced or diminish. See Van Gerven, above n 44, 31.

[78] W Van Gerven, 'A Common Law for Europe: The Future Meeting the Past?' (2001) 9 *European Review of Private Law* 485, 491.

requirement to guarantee the effective legal protection of the rights of individuals derived from Community law leads to a certain approximation of Member States' laws in terms of available remedies (including interim relief),[79] and in the field of tort law, where the jurisprudence of the ECJ regarding liability for breaches of Community law tends to reduce disparities between the applicable national tort rules, at least in the Community law sphere.[80]

However, the impact of Community law on the legal orders of the Member States is not limited to the area of private law or civil procedure. Even though administrative law traditionally has had a firmly national character and, in the past, has rarely been inspired by a comparative law approach,[81] it is not exempted from European influences. As long as 20 years ago, a comparative study of European and national administrative laws revealed a certain interdependence and reciprocal influence of the administrative laws of the Member States and the Community.[82] Not only have many general principles of Community law been shaped on the basis of concepts and elements stemming from the legal systems of the Member States;[83] the reverse process is also noticeable: Community law, in turn, has had an impact on the administrative laws of the Member States.[84] This influence is not limited to areas where secondary Community law (through directives or regulations) makes an adaptation of national law necessary. In more general terms, the implementation or execution of Community law by the Member States leads to an alignment of national procedures with the requirements of Community law, in particular the general principles developed by the ECJ in order to ensure the effective and uniform application of Community law throughout the EU.[85] Examples are, inter alia, the principle of proportionality, the duty to state reasons and the

---

[79] One of the most instructive examples in this context is Case C–213/89 *The Queen v Secretary of State for Transport, ex parte: Factortame* [1990] ECR I–2433 where the House of Lords, following the ruling of the ECJ, had to grant an interim injunction against the Crown and, to this end, had to suspend an Act of Parliament, 'two remedies' which were unthinkable pursuant to traditional common law principles.

[80] On these developments (with references to the relevant case law), see W Van Gerven, 'The ECJ Case-law as a Means of Unification of Private Law?' in A Hartkamp and others (eds), *Towards a European Civil Code* (Nijmegen, Ars aequi libri, 2nd edn, 1998), 91, 94–8.

[81] J Schwarze, 'The Convergence of the Administrative Laws of the EU Member States' (1998) 4 *European Public Law* 191, 192.

[82] J Schwarze, *Europäisches Verwaltungsrecht* (Baden-Baden, Nomos, 2nd edn, 2005), CXIII, referring to the first edition of his book on European administrative law published in 1988. Ten years later, in 1998, there was, according to Schwarze, a marked tendency towards approximation of the Member States' administrative law systems. Schwarze, above n 81, 193.

[83] In the early years, influences mainly from the French and German administrative law systems can be observed. Later, the legal systems of the UK and the Scandinavian countries also contributed to the development of Community law. Schwarze, above n 82, CXIV–CXVII.

[84] Schwarze, above n 81, 194. Compared to the situation in 1988 or even 1998, this latter development, ie the repercussion of Community law on the administrative laws of the Member States, is now said to have gained momentum. Schwarze, above n 82, CLIII.

[85] Schwarze, above n 82, CXIX.

protection of legitimate expectations, which have all been incorporated into the legal orders of some Member States to which these principles were essentially alien or where they had a very restricted scope only.[86] This inter-action between the domestic legal orders of the Member States and the Community legal order, which has also been described as a 'process of cross-fertilization',[87] may, at least in the long term, lead to the development of common fundamental principles and standards and thus to some form of basic *ius commune Europaeum* in the field of administrative law.[88]

The protection of competition being one of the core objectives of the Community, competition law has played a central role in the development of EC procedural (administrative) law, which, at least in competition matters, is intrinsically related to the protection of fundamental rights as developed under or inspired by inter alia the fair trial guarantee of Article 6 ECHR. These fundamental rights have gained an increasingly important role in competition litigation before the Community courts.[89] Not surpris-ingly, various principles of Community law have thus been developed in the context of competition matters, in particular principles related to the rights of defence, such as the right to be heard,[90] the right to legal representation, the attorney–client privilege,[91] the protection against (direct) self-incrimi-nation[92] and the conditions governing access to and inspection of business premises.[93] A telling example of convergence in the field of civil law prompted by a competition case is the judgment in *Courage v Crehan*, in which the ECJ essentially extended the *Francovich* jurisprudence[94] on state liability for breaches of Community law to private parties.[95]

---

[86] See Schwarze, above n 81, 195–8.

[87] Van Gerven, above n 44, 14–15. Interestingly, though, Van Gerven seems to analyse the process of interaction in the reverse order to Schwarze. He first describes the influence of Community law on national law and then discusses the role which national law plays in (re)shaping even established Community law. In any event, both approaches underline the strong interdependence of national and Community law. On the opportunities for cross-fertilisation, see also H Vedder, 'Spontaneous Harmonisation of National (Competition) Laws in the Wake of the Modernisation of EC Competition Law' (2004) 1 *The Competition Law Review* 5, 17–18.

[88] See Schwarze, above n 82, CLIII *et seq*.

[89] JP Slot, 'A View from the Mountain: 40 Years of Developments in EC Competition Law' (2004) 41 *CMLRev* 443, 448–51.

[90] Judgment of the ECJ in Case 85/76 *Hoffmann-La Roche v Commission* [1979] ECR 461, para 9.

[91] Judgments of the ECJ in Case 155/79 *AM&S Europe Limited v Commission* [1982] ECR 1575 and Joined Cases T–125/03 and T–253/03 *Akzo Nobel and Akcros Chemicals v Commis-sion* [2007] ECR II–3523.

[92] Judgment of the ECJ in Case 374/87 *Orkem v Commission* [1989] ECR 3283, albeit this case law seems to lag behind the standards developed in the relevant jurisprudence of the ECtHR (see above Chapter 4, n 70).

[93] Judgment of the ECJ in Joined Cases 46/87 and 227/88 *Hoechst v Commission* [1989] ECR 2859.

[94] See above Chapter 6, n 329.

[95] See Case C–453/99 *Courage v Crehan* [2001] ECR I–6297. On the possible impact of this case on the private laws of the Member States, see Van Gerven, above n 44, 19–23. The judgment

It may be expected that the national (procedural) provisions governing the enforcement of Community competition law will also gradually converge.[96] In particular, existing disparities between the rules, concepts or principles of the Member States which lead to difficulties with regard to co-operation in the ECN will put pressure on the Member States to align their competition procedures.[97] For instance, where the protection standards in a certain Member State (eg regarding confidentiality) lag behind the standards applied in other Member States or at the Community level, other authorities may be reluctant to forward sensitive information, or will at least consider more carefully and at length any exchange of documents. This may encourage the Member State concerned to upgrade its own system and bring it in line with the higher standards of the other Network members.[98] Other elements of the procedure which may lend themselves to voluntary harmonisation are the leniency rules and

in *Courage v Crehan* has recently been confirmed by the ECJ in Joined Cases C–295–298/04 *Manfredi v Loyd and others* [2006] ECR I–6619, in particular paras 60–1.

[96] Vedder, above n 87, 5 and 7, describes this phenomenon as 'spontaneous harmonisation' as opposed to intended harmonisation, ie a process of 'convergence of rules of the Member States following the example of comparable rules in the European Union without any express harmonising activity of that Union'. A growing degree of procedural convergence is actually noted by K Dekeyser and M Jaspers, 'A New Era of ECN Cooperation' (2007) 30 *World Competition* 3, 12. According to P Lowe, 'Preventing and Sanctioning Anticompetitive Conduct: Effective Use of Administrative and Criminal Sanctions, Leniency Programmes and Private Action in the EU' in B Hawk (ed), *2006 Proceedings of the Fordham Corporate Law Institute* (New York, Juris Publishing, 2006), 87, 92, many Member States have aligned the basic rules for the imposition of fines with the Community law model as set out in Art 23 of Reg 1/2003. See also P-V Bos, 'Towards a Clear Distribution of Competence between EC and National Competition Authorities' (1995) 16 *European Competition Law Review* 410, 415–16 and the document 'Results of the Questionnaire on the Reform of Member States (MS) National Competition Laws after EC Regulation No 1/2003' published on the website of the ECN, http://ec.europa.eu/competition/ecn/ecn_convergencequest_April2008.pdf.

[97] W Weiß, 'Grundrechtsschutz im EG-Kartellrecht nach der Verfahrensnovelle' (2006) *Europäische Zeitschrift für Wirtschaftsrecht* 263, 268. As concerns the substantive competition provisions of the Member States, these are already harmonised, on a de facto basis, to a large extent by spontaneous national legislation. This trend towards harmonisation of domestic competition laws could already be observed at the beginning of the nineties. B Rodger and A MacCulloch, 'Community Competition Law Enforcement. Deregulation and Re-regulation: the Commission, National Authorities and Private Enforcement' (1998) 4 *Columbia Journal of European Law* 579, 589. See also above Chapter 6, n 129.

[98] See A Burnside and H Crossley, 'Co-operative Mechanisms within the EU: A Blueprint for Future Co-operation at the International Level' (2004) 10 *International Trade Law & Regulation* 25, 33. Cf also R Smits, 'The European Competition Network: Selected Aspects' (2005) 32 *Legal Issues of Economic Integration* 175, 191, who reckons that 'there is bound to be mutual learning and copying'. It is even conceivable that the Member State concerned, in order to maintain the homogeneity of its legal system, will apply the higher standard also in procedures not relating to Community (competition) law. On this basis, gradual convergence of EC law related standards combined with a quest for homogeneity of national systems may even lead to an overall improvement of the quality of legal protection in competition procedures. See W Van Gerven, 'Bridging the Unbridgeable: Community and National Tort Laws After Francovich and Brasserie' (1996) 45 *ICLQ* 507, 539 and J Schwarze, above n 81, 194.

sanctioning powers of the NCAs.[99] The ECN may provide a valuable platform for such unsolicited harmonising steps on the part of the Member States. In this way, divergencies would gradually diminish. However, this form of spontaneous convergence may turn out to be a long and tedious process.[100]

B. Desirability of Harmonising Measures

Harmonisation (or even unification) of national procedural rules would seem to be a feasible option, but it has certain disadvantages. It risks having a disruptive effect on the domestic legal orders of the Member States. Such risks also become apparent if one considers the recent attempts of the Commission to promote private enforcement of competition law as a complementary means of encouraging and ensuring compliance with the Community's antitrust rules.

1. General

An alternative option to the long process of gradual convergence is harmonisation or possibly even unification of national competition procedures through legislative measures of the Community. It is submitted that the Council, acting on the basis of Article 83(1) EC, could lay down a common procedure for the implementation of Articles 81 and 82 EC which would have to be followed (also) by the NCAs when enforcing Community competition law.[101] This common framework could take the form of a directly applicable regulation—similar to the Implementing Regulation[102]— or a directive which would then have to be transposed into the national

---

[99] Vedder, above n 87, 18–19, who further submits that, in view of the qualification of Art 81 EC as a public policy rule (judgment of the ECJ in Case C–126/97 *Eco Swiss v Benetton* [1999] ECR I–3055, paras 36–7), and the provisions of Reg 1/2003 on *amicus curiae* submissions, even the civil procedures of the Member States are likely to converge so that common European procedural rules will emerge (*idem*, 20). See also the examples above n 96 and accompanying text.

[100] Cf Forrester, above n 73, 343. On the other hand, the first voluntary steps of the Member States aiming at an alignment of certain national rules have already been taken by the adoption of the Model Leniency Programme, which was launched in September 2006 at the initiative of the ECN.

[101] Art 83(1) EC empowers the Council to adopt '[t]he appropriate regulations or directives to give effect to the principles set out in Articles 81 and 82'. A common procedure for the application of Arts 81 and 82 EC by NCAs can be considered an appropriate measure giving effect to the competition provisions of the EC Treaty.

[102] See A Riley 'More Radicalism, Please: The Notice on Co-operation between National Courts and the Commission in Applying Articles 85 and 86 of the EEC Treaty' (1993) 14 *European Competition Law Review* 91, 94, and J Temple Lang, 'European Community Constitutional Law and the Enforcement of Community Antitrust Law' in B Hawk (ed), *1993 Proceedings of the Fordham Corporate Law Institute* (New York, Juris Publishing, 1994), 525, 594 *et seq.*

legal order. In the first case, NCAs would act on the basis of truly uniform rules. In the second case, the procedural rules, while being harmonised, would be applied in the form in which they have been transposed into national law.[103] There could thus be variations, depending on the leeway which the directive grants Member States with regard to its implementation.

However, in both cases, the (harmonised or unified) procedural rules would, in the first place, only govern national procedures conducted with a view to enforcing Articles 81 and 82 EC. They would not apply to purely national cases—that is, competition matters which are investigated and decided solely on the basis of the domestic (substantive) antitrust rules of the Member States. The reason for this is that the Community legislature has no power to regulate national competition procedures in general, not to mention a global competence to adopt comprehensive legislation regarding all administrative procedures in the Member States.[104] Because of the principle of 'attribution of competences' or 'conferred powers' (*Prinzip der begrenzten Einzelermächtigung*) resulting from Articles 5(1) and 7(1) EC, the Community institutions can only act in those limited areas for which the EC Treaty has specifically conferred competences or powers on the Community.[105] Since the first *Tobacco* judgment of the ECJ,[106] it has become clear that it should not be taken for granted that Article 95 (ex Article 100a) EC always provides a sufficient legal basis for the Community legislator to enact comprehensive uniform laws or harmonising directives.[107] This analysis has been made in view of certain initiatives, at the Community level, to codify or harmonise large parts of private law or, even more specifically, the law of contract.[108] Namely, it results from the first *Tobacco* judgment that the Community has no general power to regulate the internal market and therefore could not codify or harmonise European contract law in general, at least not to the extent that there is no evidence that the existing divergencies have or are likely to have an adverse impact on the exercise of the 'fundamental freedoms' guaranteed by the EC

---

[103] See S Prechal, 'Judge-made Harmonisation of National Procedural Rules: A Bridging Perspective ' in J Wouters and J Stuyck (eds), *Principles of Proper Conduct for Supranational, State and Private Actors in the European Union: Towards a Ius Commune. Essays in Honour of Walter Van Gerven* (Antwerpen, Intersentia, 2001), 39, 57.

[104] Schwarze, above n 81, 205.

[105] This also means that all Community action must have a legal basis in the EC Treaty. See Lenaerts and Van Nuffel, above n 27, 5-009.

[106] Case C–376/98 *Germany v EP and Council (Tobacco I)* [2000] ECR I–8419, in particular paras 83 and 84.

[107] Pursuant to Art 95 EC, the Council may adopt measures for the approximation of national provisions of the Member States which have as their object the establishment and functioning of the internal market.

[108] See W Van Gerven, 'Codifying European Private Law? Yes, If!', (2002) 27 *EL Rev* 156, 164–5.

Treaty.[109] This does not mean, however, that a limited harmonisation or codification of the law of contract relating only to intra-Community cross-border transactions could not be envisaged.[110] A similar analysis can be made with regard to the administrative procedures in competition matters. A general harmonisation of the relevant national rules would not be possible for lack of a legal basis. On the other hand, the procedural rules applied by NCAs when enforcing Community competition law—those matters which have a cross-border element—could arguably be harmonised. This follows directly from Article 83(1) EC, which limits the power of the Council to rule-making giving effect to the principles enshrined in Articles 81 and 82 EC. Article 95 EC, it would seem, cannot transfer a broader competence since purely national situations have no bearing on the internal market.[111]

One disadvantage of harmonisation is that it will often be achieved not on the basis of the highest standard, but rather on the basis of the smallest common denominator. Harmonisation would then be realised at the expense of those Member States that have particularly high protection standards and to the detriment of companies and individuals, who will be deprived of the benefits of such advanced national systems.

Another disadvantage of this approach is that NCAs would have to apply two sets of different procedural rules depending on whether they enforce Community competition law or (only) national competition law. In other words, the national legal orders of the Member States would have to tolerate not only the existence of two sets of substantive rules (Article 81/82 EC and domestic competition law), but also the introduction of a second set of procedural norms applicable only to 'cross-border' competition matters. The emergence, within the same area of national law, of two parallel legal regimes, one that is modified in accordance with Community law measures or requirements and one that continues to govern purely internal situations and is thus unaffected by Community law, is typical for EC law, regardless of whether the law is judge-made[112] or results from

---

[109] The reasoning in *Tobacco I* was confirmed by the ECJ in Case C–380/03 *Germany v EP and Council (Tobacco II)* [2006] ECR I–11573. In *Tobacco II*, the ECJ notably reiterated that a mere finding of disparities between national rules is not sufficient to justify harmonising measures on the basis of Art 95 EC. However, where 'there are obstacles to trade, or it is likely that such obstacles will emerge in the future, because the Member States have taken, or are about to take, divergent measures with respect to a product or a class of products, which . . . prevent the product or products concerned from moving freely within the Community, Article 95 EC authorises the Community legislature to intervene by adopting appropriate measures'. See paras 37–41 of the judgment in *Tobacco II*.

[110] Van Gerven, above n 108, 166.

[111] The need to create a level playing field for economic operators which are subject to EC and national competition rules has already been accommodated by the convergence rule of Art 3(2) of Reg 1/2003.

[112] Illustrated, for instance, by the *Francovich* case law on state liability for breaches of Community law or the *Factortame* (above n 79) jurisprudence on the availability of legal

Community legislation.[113] However, it is precisely this coexistence of two sets of domestic rules which risks distorting the homogeneity of the national legal systems of the Member States.[114] This disruptive impact on the national legal orders has been described as the 'dark side of EC harmonisation'.[115] Moreover, such a kind of two-pillar system may also hamper the de facto integration of Community law into the national legal order.[116]

On the other hand, these concerns may be exaggerated. After all, the Community has been in existence for over 50 years and harmonisation of national rules has always been a central feature of the integration process.[117] The numerous directives adopted in the field of consumer protection are a good example of this phenomenon. It does not seem to have entailed any serious damage to the integrity of the Member States'

---

remedies (interim relief) for individuals to enforce Community law rights. Here, the case law of the ECJ has the effect of harmonisation or rather judicial approximation of national laws (see Van Gerven, above n 44, 12–14 and also his contribution on case-law as a means of unification, above n 80, 94–7 (with references to the relevant judgments)), but at the same time may cause disruption within the national legal order (see below n 114 and accompanying text). In case of the *Francovich* doctrine (Joined Cases C–6 and C–9/90 *Francovich and Bonfifaci v Italy* [1991] ECR I–5357), for instance, the integrity of the national legal order can in fact only be preserved if either the system of state liability for breaches of Community law is integrated into the existing domestic torts regime or the Community doctrine on (state) liability is applied across the board, ie also to purely domestic situations. M-P Granger, 'National applications of Francovich and the construction of a European administrative jus commune' (2007) 32 *EL Rev* 157, 160–1.

113 Van Gerven, above n 78, 491.

114 See Van Gerven, above n 98, 538–9. The application of the *Francovich* doctrine (above n 112) by national courts can again serve as an example. In this area, concerns regarding the coherence of the national legal system are accommodated in many Member States by requiring applicants to bring their state liability claims within the domestic framework of traditional tort claims. However, this makes the reception of the *Francovich* doctrine ultimately dependent on different national legal traditions relating to tort law and public liability. See Granger, above n 112, 160 and 175–6.

115 Van Gerven, above n 78, 489–90. The discussions on the disruptive effect of increasing Community legislation on the Member States' legal systems mostly centre on private law and the rules of civil procedure. However, in view of the seemingly extended competence not the Community in criminal law matters (see Case C–176/03 *Commission v Council* [2005] ECR I–7879 regarding environmental offences), they have recently also reached the criminal law sphere. See S Peers, 'The European Community's Criminal Law Competence: The Plot Thickens' (2008) 33 *EL Rev* 399, 407–8.

116 See Prechal, above n 103, 57–8. The concern again relates to the judicial protection of individual rights based on Community law. Such rights are usually relied upon in an integrated way, ie not treated as a separate Community law claim. Cf also Granger, above n 112, 175–8. However, a similar concern may arise if separate procedures would have to be followed by NCAs, one harmonised procedure for the enforcement of Community competition law and one that is not harmonised for the enforcement of national competition law. The parallel application of both substantive law regimes (as suggested by Art 3(1) of Reg 1/2003), in terms of procedure, would become a 'technically' complicated and highly complex task. This would certainly not be conducive to the effective enforcement of the EC competition rules at the national level.

117 Even though, in the 1980s, the Commission started to advocate a new approach whereby detailed (technical) harmonisation would be replaced as far as possible by mutual recognition of national standards. See Lenaerts and Van Nuffel, above n 27, 5-212.

legal systems. In the present context, it would be a feasible compromise, in my view, to make the application of national and Community competition law mutually exclusive[118] and harmonise the essential aspects of the procedure applicable in Community law matters. The harmonised rules should certainly cover inspection powers, confidentiality, access to file, legal privilege and rights against self-incrimination. For the rest, the existence of two parallel systems, one harmonised and the other non-harmonised, arguably has to be accepted for the sake of European integration. The disruptive effect on the domestic legal orders of the Member States can be avoided by voluntary harmonisation along the lines of Community law.[119]

2. *Example: the Green Paper on Damages Actions*

The disruptive or disintegrating effect that EC harmonisation can have on the legal orders of the Member States is beautifully illustrated by the various proposals to raise the level of private antitrust litigation in the EU which the Commission recently put up for discussion in the Green Paper on Damages Actions.

Since the beginning of the modernisation process, the Commission has been quite firm on the point that, next to public enforcement by the Commission and NCAs, private enforcement of the EC competition rules would have to be furthered. In the White Paper (1999), the Commission outlined that national courts should play an enhanced role in the enforcement of the competition rules, inter alia through the application of Article 81 EC in proceedings regarding contractual and non-contractual liability and injunction proceedings.[120] The primary means to increase the involvement of national courts in the application of Community competition law is the shift from the notification/authorisation system to the legal

---

[118] This would avert the risk that, in terms of procedure, enforcement would 'technically' become too complex. The main argument put forward in favour of the parallel (or, rather, the alternative, in the sense of *hilfsweise*) application of national competition law (see above Chapter 1, n 344 and accompanying text) are in my view not fully convincing. First, in some Member States such parallel application is already ruled out on the basis of national competition law, which only applies to the extent that Community competition law is not applicable (eg Italy; see A Frignani, 'Competition Law in Italy', in F Vogelaar, J Stuyck, B Van Reeken (eds), *Competition Law in the EU, Its Member States and Switzerland, Volume I* (The Hague, Kluwer Law International, 2000), 361, 375). Secondly, over time, NCAs will gain more experience in the application of Community competition law and, more particularly, the effect-on-trade criterion, so that the parallel approach will no longer be necessary.

[119] Spill-over. See below in this chapter, section II.C.

[120] See paras 99 and 100 of the White Paper. In fact, attempts by the Commission to enhance the role of national courts in the enforcement of Community competition law had already been made prior to the publication of the White Paper, notably by setting out possible avenues for co-operation between the Commission and national courts in the 1993 Co-operation Notice. On these (largely vain) efforts, see Riley, above n 102, 93–6.

exception system, which allows national courts to apply Article 81 EC in full, thereby excluding the possibility that the national proceedings are being blocked by so-called dilatory notifications.[121] Other crucial elements are the improved and unprecedented mechanisms for co-operation with the judiciary which allow the Commission to effectively assist national courts, either at their request or on the Commission's own initiative, where issues of Community antitrust law arise in civil litigation cases before these courts.[122] The key principles of this partly novel form of co-operation are now enshrined in a formal legislative act.[123] They are supplemented by more detailed rules laid down in the National Courts' Notice of the Commission.[124]

However, the Commission obviously deems these modifications of the enforcement system, even in combination with a more intensified co-operation between itself and the national courts, to be insufficient to really stimulate private enforcement actions.[125] The ECJ's judgment in *Courage v Crehan* seems to have given fresh impetus to the Commission's endeavours to effectively establish private enforcement through civil litigation as a real complement to enforcement measures taken by public authorities.[126] In that judgment, the ECJ noted that the full effectiveness of Article 81 EC would be put at risk if individuals could not claim damages for loss caused to them by an infringement of this norm. The court continued:

---

[121] The Commission considered such dilatory notifications to form one of the major obstacles to effective private enforcement. See White Paper, para 100. See also E De Smijter, 'Het Groenboek van de Commissie omtrent schadevorderingen wegens schending van de Europese mededingingsregels' (2007) 2 *TBM-RCB* 3, para 1. This view seems to be widely shared. See A Komninos, 'Public and Private Antitrust Enforcement in Europe: Complement? Overlap?' (2006) 3 *The Competition Law Review* 5, 7 (at fn 13; with further references).

[122] See R Nazzini, 'Parallel and Sequential Proceedings in Competition Law: An Essay on the Modes of Interaction between Community and National Law (2005) 16 *European Business Law Review* 245, 247.

[123] See Art 15 of Reg 1/2003. The novel element is the possibility for the Commission to submit *amicus curiae* briefs without prior request or consent of the national court (Art 15(3) of Reg 1/2003).

[124] The new system is far more advanced than the previous system, which was only based on a Commission notice (the 1993 Co-operation Notice). See Nazzini, above n 122, 255.

[125] Also De Smijter, above n 121, para 6, considers it self-evident that the changes introduced by Reg 1/2003, as such, are not sufficient to boost private enforcement. Similarly, W Van Gerven, 'Private Enforcement of EC Competition Rules in the ECJ – Courage v. Crehan and the Way Ahead' in J Basedow (ed), *Private Enforcement of EC Competition Law* (Kluwer Law International, 2007), 19, 24, submits that the mere fact that national courts may now apply Art 81 EC in full will not in itself encourage more private litigants to seek compensation.

[126] Cf recital 7 of Reg 1/2003. To the extent, however, that the Commission views private enforcement as an additional avenue to increase deterrence by escalating the potential 'penalties' for violators, it is questionable whether this approach really is the most efficient way from a purely economic perspective. Indeed, it has been suggested that the same result could be achieved at less cost (ie without the additional expense of private litigation) by simply imposing higher fines at the end of the public enforcement procedure. See I Segal and M Whinston, 'Public vs Private Enforcement of Antitrust Law: A Survey' (2007) 28 *European Competition Law Review* 306, 309 and 313.

Indeed, the existence of such a right strengthens the working of the Community competition rules and discourages agreements or practices, which are frequently covert, which are liable to restrict or distort competition. From that point of view, actions for damages before the national courts *can make a significant contribution to the maintenance of effective competition* in the Community.[127]

However, the remedies and procedures[128] available for the judicial enforcement of EC competition law by individuals are governed by the domestic laws of the Member States. These rules are therefore subject only to the principles of equivalence and (minimum) effectiveness,[129] and vary considerably from Member State to Member State. Against this background, the Commission published the Green Paper on Damages Actions in December 2005 in order to launch a wide debate on possible ways to encourage and facilitate the institution of successful damages actions before national courts.[130] To that end, the Green Paper seeks to identify the main obstacles to antitrust damages claims and sets out various options which, either in isolation or in combination, could improve the conditions for such claims.[131] The entire approach is based on the assumption that the Member States' current systems regarding damages claims for antitrust violations are totally underdeveloped and that the current level of enforcement through

---

[127] Emphasis added. Paras 26 and 27 of the judgment in *Courage v Crehan* (above n 95). Arguably, it was Advocate General W Van Gerven in Case C–128/92 *HJ Banks v British Coal* [1994] ECR I–1209 who paved the way for this progressive approach of the ECJ towards private damages claims based on a breach of Art 81 or 82 EC: 'I conclude . . . that the right to obtain reparation in respect of loss and damage sustained as a result of an undertaking' s infringement of Community competition rules which have direct effect is based on the Community legal order itself. Consequently, as a result of its obligation to ensure that Community law is fully effective and to protect the rights thereby conferred on individuals, the national court is under an obligation to award damages for loss sustained by an undertaking as a result of the breach by another undertaking of a directly effective provision of Community competition law' (para 45 of his opinion). However, the ECJ held that the relevant provisions (Arts 65 and 66 of the ECSC Treaty) did not have any direct effect and therefore did not have to rule on the compensation issue. It should be noted that private enforcement is not intended to become a substitute for, but rather a complement to, public enforcement. Cf De Smijter, above n 121, para 30. A complementary model combining effective public and private action is also commended by S Waller, 'Towards a Constructive Public-Private Partnership to Enforce Competition Law' (2006) 29 *World Competition* 367, 377. *Accord*, in principle, Komninos, above n 121, 15. *Contra* W Wils, 'Should Private Antitrust Enforcement Be Encouraged in Europe?' (2003) 26 *World Competition* 473, 484–6, who does not see any useful (supplementary) role for private antitrust claims in Europe.

[128] On the distinction between (Community law) rights, remedies and procedures see W Van Gerven, 'Of Rights, Remedies and Procedures' (2000) 37 *CML Rev* 501, 502–4.

[129] Para 29 of the judgement in *Courage v Crehan* (above n 95). On the development of these principles see Prechal, above n 103, 40–2.

[130] The Green Paper only deals with damages claims as these are considered to have a double purpose: they offer compensation for those who have suffered loss by anti-competitive conduct and, at the same time, increase the incentive for companies to comply with the competition rules. P 4 of the Green Paper on Damages Actions.

[131] In fact, the Green Paper on Damages Actions contains 36 different proposals, a number of which are, however, alternative options.

private litigation is poor.[132] The validity of these assumptions is, however, doubted by several commentators.[133] The main issues addressed in the Green Paper on Damages Actions are:

- access to evidence (discovery);
- fault requirement;
- definition and quantification of damages;
- collective actions;
- cost risk/recovery of legal costs;
- jurisdiction and applicable law.

This (incomplete) list clearly demonstrates that harmonisation measures, which might eventually be adopted by the Community after publication of the White Paper (which the Commission published with some delay in April 2008)[134] and a further public consultation procedure, could concern a whole spectrum of different elements of private (competition) litigation. It would not merely have an impact on the relevant procedural rules of the Member States, but could also encroach upon some substantive aspects of tort claims, for instance by modifying the required standard of fault or the concept of damages.[135] The Commission has declared that the various options set out in the Green Paper are presented for further reflection and discussion in order to help the Commission decide whether and what measures should be taken.[136] However, in view of the large scope of the envisaged solutions, it is imperative that the potential impact of any measure on the legal orders of the Member States and, specifically, on their homogeneity is carefully considered. By introducing a special Community law regime for damages claims for antitrust violations on the basis of the options put forward in the Green Paper, the Commission would not only touch upon some of the core elements of national civil law and

[132] See p 4 of the Green Paper on Damages Actions.

[133] For example, M Siragusa, 'A Reflection on Some Private Antitrust Enforcement Issues', paper for the 2006 EU Competition Law and Policy Workshop, European University Institute/RSCAS, Florence, available at http://www.eui.eu/RSCAS/Research/Competition/2006 (pdf)/200610-COMPed-Siragusa.pdf (accessed July 2007), 6, submits that the current procedural framework in the Member States has not yet fully been tested. A similar argument is made by C Hodges, 'Competition Enforcement, Regulation and Civil Justice: What is the Case?' (2006) 43 *CML Rev* 1381, 1396–9. He points to the evolving state of the civil justice systems of the Member States, including recent reforms introduced in some Member States of which the Commission does not seem sufficiently aware. Hodges further criticises the absence of sufficient reliable research substantiating the Commission's assertion (*idem*, 1401–2). The latter point is also raised by Waller, above n 127, 375 *et seq*, who submits that more empirical research is needed to strike the right balance between public and private remedies.

[134] The White Paper on damages actions for breach of the EC antitrust rules ('White Paper on Damages Actions') had originally been announced for the end of 2007, was then postponed to early 2008 and finally published on 2 April 2008 (COM(2008) 165 final). See also below n 148.

[135] Hodges, above n 133, 1400, even submits that virtually all proposals would represent a radical departure from existing civil litigation practice in the EU.

[136] See p 5 of the Green Paper on Damages Actions.

procedure;[137] it would also risk disrupting a whole series of different constituents from the 'normal' rules on damages actions.[138] These different elements are probably spread over a variety of laws, such as tort law, civil procedure, regulations on legal fees and possibly consumer protection legislation. The disintegrating effect of the contemplated measures could thus be huge and the delicate balance of the individual civil justice systems could be seriously distorted, at least if all or the majority of the proposals were adopted.[139] The question must therefore be asked whether it is really appropriate to set special rules for damages claims based on an infringement of the Community competition rules.[140]

It may also be doubted that the suggested changes to national tort and litigation rules would have the desired effect of increasing the level of private enforcement of Community competition law through civil damages claims. Presumably, the Commission's proposals were largely inspired by the US system (eg the possibility of awarding punitive or exemplary damages/'double damages', or introducing some form of group action that would allow a large number of smaller (consumer) claims to be consolidated in a single law suit).[141] However, the US have a very different legal history and a 'private litigation culture' that is essentially alien to European citizens, as in Europe law enforcement has traditionally been in the hands

---

[137] T Eilmansberger, 'The Green Paper on Damages Actions for Breach of the EC Antitrust Rules and Beyond: Reflections on the Utility and Feasibility of Stimulating Private Enforcement Through Legislative Action' (2007) 44 *CML Rev* 431, 439, states that the Green Paper 'consists of a collection of legislative proposals on core areas of civil and procedural law' and the competence of the Community to pass legislation in these core areas of national law is controversial. Arguably, however, Art 83 EC provides a sufficiently broad legal basis to encompass also Community measures facilitating and harmonising damages claims in competition matters. Eilmansberger, above n 137, 440–1; P Oliver, 'Le règlement 1/2003 et les principes d'efficacité et d'équivalence' (2005) 41 *Cahiers de Droit Européen* 351, 392–3.

[138] See Hodges, above n 133, 1400: 'They [the proposals] would carve out competition litigation as a sector subject to special rules.' Cf also M Van Dijk, 'Particuliere handhaving; de burger en zijn advocaat als premiejagers voor de kartelautoriteiten' (2006) 12 *Nederlands tijdschrift voor Europees recht* 265, 265: 'door specifieke oplossingen zouden die in hoge mate afwijken van wat gebruikelijk is in civiele procedures'.

[139] See Hodges, above n 133, 1398. In my view, it is thus not surprising that the reactions to many of the suggestions put forward in the Green Paper on Damages Actions are dismissive (eg as regards the proposal to award double damages; see De Smijter, above n 121, paras 21–2).

[140] Indeed, there may be good reasons to introduce similar rules with regard to other types of damages claims which potentially involve mass consumer interests (eg product liability, environmental damages). See F Vogelaar, 'Interface: EC and Dutch Competition Law—In Which Fields or Areas Would the Netherlands Still Have Autonomous Regulating Powers?' in D Obradovic and N Lavranos (eds), *Interface between EU Law and National Law* (Groningen, Europa Law Publishing, 2007), 185, 200. In that sense, competition damages claims are probably not so unique.

[141] See Van Dijk, above n 138, 268. See also D Walsh, 'Carrots and Sticks—Leniency and Fines in EC Cartel Cases' (2009) 30 *European Competition Law Review* 30, 32. It must be admitted, though, that the Commission has not suggested, in the Green Paper on Damages Actions, introducing a form of representative procedure that would be akin to the US model of opt-out class actions. See De Smijter, above n 121, para 28.

of public bodies.[142] As yet, the public perception that cartels are very harmful to the economy and victims of such cartels should justly be compensated for their loss has not really grown in Europe.[143] It is therefore not certain that even consumers of products or services in Europe that have been overpriced due to illegal cartel arrangements would be easily convinced that they should engage in private antitrust litigation in order to obtain redress.[144] Moreover, it has been suggested that existing national rules provide tools that could well be employed to overcome many of the hurdles that currently seem to discourage private plaintiffs (consumers, but also competitors or corporate clients) from filing a lawsuit for damages sustained as a result of a competition law infringement.[145]

Last but not least, the Commission's efforts to enhance private enforcement of the EC competition rules ironically coincide with a development in the US—the country that seems to have served as a model for many of the Commission's proposals in the Green Paper on Damages Actions—that points in exactly the opposite direction.[146] The US have in

---

[143] Van Dijk, above n 138, 269. See also Van Gerven, above n 125, 26, who contends that the success of private enforcement in the US, as compared to Europe, is largely due to 'the litigious and competitive nature of US society'; W Wils, *The Optimal Enforcement of EC Antitrust Law. Essays in Law and Economics* (The Hague, Kluwer Law International, 2001), 150; C-D Ehlermann, 'The Modernization of EC Antitrust Policy: A Legal and Cultural Revolution' (2000) 37 *CML Rev* 537, 553.

[144] A Riley, 'Beyond Leniency: Enhancing Enforcement in EC Antitrust Law' (2005) 28 *World Competition* 377, 400, seems however fairly optimistic that such perception will grow in due time.

[145] Van Dijk, above n 141, 269, who submits that European consumers may have other preoccupations than enforcing competition rules which, moreover, are largely unfamiliar to them. The author eloquently notes: 'Misschien maken consumenten zich meer druk over geluidsoverlast van Schipol, goede gezondheidszorg voor een redelijke prijs, veiligheid op straat et cetera.' Riley, above n 143, 390 and 400, by contrast, anticipates 'the rise of a powerful European antitrust litigation practice' provided that there is a significant upward shift in public enforcement, which, according to Riley, could be brought about by upgrading the armoury of competition agencies with effective leniency programmes and even a US-type of anti-fraud programme (similar to the Civil False Claims Act 1986) which would engage private parties, against financial reward, in the recovery of monies from those who have defrauded the public purse.

[145] See Riley, above n 143, 383–6, who submits that the principle barrier for private antitrust litigation, notably the lack or weakness of national discovery procedures, could be side-stepped by increased public enforcement, ie by uncovering a greater number of cartels and adopting more prohibition decisions on which private plaintiffs could then rely in national courts. Other procedural obstacles ('secondary barriers') could be tackled by the judiciary, if need be by resorting to Community law principles, such as the effectiveness doctrine. See also Van Dijk, above n 138, 266–8, who gives the examples of the power of the judge to alleviate or even shift the burden of proof in the case of a glaring asymmetry of information between the parties so as to adjust the rules to the requirements of consumer claims (who have, for instance, no access to internal company documents) or the freedom of the judge to estimate the amount of the damage where it cannot be quantified precisely. See also above n 133. *Contra* W Van Gerven, 'Crehan and the Way Ahead', (2006) 17 *EBLRev* 269, 273, who submits that legislative intervention is imperative.

[146] See Waller, above n 127, 368. Also Wils, above n 127, 478, notes that the US administration, which has encouraged the EC in many other aspects of competition law enforcement to

fact taken a number of (legislative) measures in order to restrict private action rights in antitrust litigation, in particular with regard to class actions, the utility of which is not uncontroversial in the US.[147] These factors cast some doubt on the expediency of the Commission's approach. In the light of the above, it seems difficult to justify the introduction, in the Member States, of a separate legal regime that would be applicable only to damages actions brought for violations of the EC competition rules.[148]

On the other hand, there are some elements of civil litigation that are typically linked to private enforcement of the competition rules and therefore are suitable for harmonisation or even uniform regulation at the Community level. These include the following issues:[149]

- evidential status of NCA and Commission decisions;
- access of the claimant to the competition authority's file (access to evidence);
- possibility to award EU-wide damages (as opposed to damages occurring only in the domestic territory of the relevant court);
- applicable law;
- jurisdiction (including rules to avoid forum shopping).

The above issues are peculiar to (follow-on) damages actions in antitrust matters. In order to create equal enforcement opportunities, thereby enhancing effective and uniform private enforcement of Community competition law across the EU, these issues should ideally be subject to the same rules and principles in all Member States.[150] In particular, discrimination and forum shopping should be avoided by ensuring that claimants have access to the file of the competition authority which has already dealt with the relevant infringement regardless of where (in the EU) the law suit is actually filed. Furthermore, it should be possible to lodge a claim in all Member States in which the anti-competitive agreement or practice has had an appreciable effect and where consumers, purchasers or other market operators may consequently have sustained losses irrespective of the place of residence/business of the litigants. The latter point, which concerns jurisdictional issues, is probably a matter for Regulation 44/2001 (also known as 'Brussels I'), which regulates inter alia jurisdiction in civil and commercial matters, while the question of the applicable law (amazingly

take over the US models, has not advocated the introduction, in Europe, of a US-type of private litigation practice.

[147] Waller, above n 127, 372–3. Waller even notes that '[e]veryone agrees that if we were starting afresh in the United States no one would design the system we currently have'. *Idem*, 375.

[148] Not surprisingly, in my view, in the White Paper on Damages Actions, the Commission seems to take up a much more cautious stance on the need for formal harmonising measures than in the preceding Green Paper on Damages Actions.

[149] See the list provided by Vogelaar, above n 140, 201.

[150] See Vogelaar, above n 140, 200–1.

enough) is already covered by the recently adopted 'Rome II' Regulation[151] on conflict of laws, which includes a separate chapter on 'unfair competition and acts restricting free competition'.[152]

C. Conclusion

Considering the risks for the rights of undertakings and natural persons associated with an almost unlimited exchange of evidence, the lack of clear and binding allocation principles and the conduct of parallel procedures, one is struck by the apparent reluctance of the Commission to envisage even a limited harmonisation of national procedural rules. In this respect, the Commission's proposals in the White Paper and later in the Draft Regulation seem to take insufficient account of the disparities between the domestic rules of the Member States in competition matters and the human rights dimension of procedural guarantees in a quasi-criminal law setting. With regard to other aspects of competition law enforcement, by contrast, one is struck by the eagerness and determination with which the Commission advocates the need for a harmonised approach. This is notably the case when it comes to private enforcement of the EC competition rules. Here, the Commission seems to be convinced that the national systems do not provide for adequate solutions and that some form of (harmonising) legislative initiative on the part of the Community is required, even though there is apparently no conclusive evidence which would prove that the low level of civil litigation instituted to enforce the EC antitrust rules is a

---

[151] Regulation (EC) No 864/2007 of the European Parliament and of the Council of 11 July 2007 on the law applicable to non-contractual obligations (Rome II), [2007[OJ L199/40 (hereafter 'Rome II Regulation'). The regulation essentially lays down uniform conflict-of-law rules regarding claims arising out of extra-contractual liability. Next to Brussels I (which covers jurisdiction and enforcement of judgments in civil and commercial matters) and the Rome Convention of 1980 (which sets out common rules on the choice of law in contractual matters and, in all likelihood, will be converted into a Community instrument—see the proposal for a 'Rome I' regulation (COM(2005) 650 final) which was adopted by the EP on 29 November 2007), Rome II is considered a 'natural extension of the unification of the rules of private international law relating to contractual and non-contractual obligations in civil or commercial matters in the Community' (see p 3 of the Explanatory Memorandum to the Commission's 2003 proposal for the Rome II Regulation; COM(2003) 427 final).

[152] Art 6(3)(a) of the Rome II Regulation reads: 'The law applicable to a non-contractual obligation arising out of a restriction of competition shall be the law of the country where the market is, or is likely to be, affected.' This provision was not contained in the initial (2003) proposal for the Rome II Convention (see Art 5 of that proposal (COM(2003) 427 final)). It was only included at a very late stage of the legislative procedure. Presumably, the Commission (or at least DG Competition) is not too happy with this amendment to its proposal as it did not want to pre-empt the debate (on the law applicable to damages claims for breaches of the EC competition rules) that was taking place in the context of the public consultation on the Green Paper on Damages Actions. See COM(2006) 566 final, 3. On that provision see P Mankowski, 'Das neue Internationale Kartellrecht des Art. 6 Abs. 3 der Rom II-Verordnung' (2008) 54 *Recht der Internationalen Wirtschaft* 177.

phenomenon which is unique or limited to the field of competition law. The disruptive impact that such harmonising measures may have on the legal orders of the Member States has been outlined above. As concerns private enforcement, the Commission might thus overshoot the mark while, in respect of decentralised public enforcement, the Commission arguably has not gone far enough.

In the final analysis, the central questions will be how much harmonisation we really need and how much fragmentation a (national) legal system can sustain.[153] Because of the disintegrating effect of harmonising Community measures, both issues are interlinked and should therefore be evaluated together. This is the reason why some authors preach cautiousness in the pursuit of uniformity or harmonisation in order to preserve the homogeneous structure and integrative force of the national legal orders.[154] In the field of competition law, however, it is worthwhile considering the following. In a harmonisation scenario, the threat to the internal coherence of the national systems could at least partly be averted if the Member States, on a voluntary basis, were to opt for 'harmonising' their 'pure' domestic procedures with those affected by the Community law measures.[155] Such a spill-over of the potentially harmonised rules on procedures that govern purely internal competition matters—that is, infringements which have no effect on inter-state trade and are thus evaluated solely on the basis of national competition law—is not unlikely, even if the harmonisation were to be brought about by the Community

[153] Cf Van Gerven, above n 108, 163.

[154] See Prechal, above n 103, 57–8, who actually pleads against unification (of procedures and remedies to enforce Community law rights). Cf also S Meiklejohn, 'You Can't Legislate Perfection: The Virtues of Experimentation in the Design of Antitrust Enforcement Regimes' in B Hawk (ed), *2003 Proceedings of the Fordham Corporate Law Institute* (New York, Juris Publishing, 2004), 55, 73–4, who argues, with regard to the question of whether we need a uniform international antitrust code, that one should rather aim at designing (varying) laws that best suit the interests of the individual jurisdictions. By contrast, Van Gerven is much more favourable towards unification or harmonisation efforts in the field of procedural laws (see above n 128, 526–7, where he advocates full uniformity of the constitutive conditions of Community law remedies; as part of a subsequent contribution, he even submitted a 'discussion draft of a regulation on the substantive law aspects of private remedies before national courts'—see Annex 2 to W Van Gerven, 'Substantive Remedies for the Private Enforcement of EC Antitrust Rules before National Courts' in J Stuyck and H Gilliams (eds), *Modernisation of European Competition Law. The Commission's Proposal for a New Regulation Implementing Articles 81 and 82 EC* (Antwerp, Intersentia, 2002), 93, 132–6) and even private law (see above n 108, 164, where he endorses the idea of codifying large parts of contract law), even though he already recognised in 1996 the 'quest for homogeneity' (see above n 98, 537–9).

[155] See the example, quoted by Van Gerven, above n 80, 95, of the conformation of UK law regarding interim relief: following the *Factortame* judgment (above n 79), the House of Lords decided that the more favourable position of plaintiffs who request interim relief in matters of Community law should be extended to purely national matters. In later writings, Van Gerven describes this phenomenon as convergence (in the sense of internal coherence within a Member State) 'by way of spill-over'. See, eg Van Gerven, above n 44, 32.

legislature rather than by case law.[156] Most Member States have already modelled their substantive competition provisions on the EC Treaty rules.[157] Indeed, it makes little sense to operate a kind of two-standard system whereby substantially different national rules apply with regard to *de minimis* cases which do not fulfil the 'effect on trade' criterion.[158] It would thus be a logical step for these Member States to align their national procedures with those to be applied in Community law matters. In this way, the conformity of the domestic (material and procedural) competition rules with the EC antitrust rules would be maintained for the benefit of the overall coherence of the national system. The example of those Member States could then possibly be followed by other Member States.[159]

As concerns the contemplated (partial) harmonisation of national tort laws and other civil law rules in order to enhance private enforcement, it is suggested that more research should first be done into the question of whether the relative absence of private damages claims based on a violation of the EC competition rules really is so 'abnormal'. There may be a variety of grounds why private parties do not to file law suits to obtain compensation when they have been the victim of a breach of competition law. Many of these grounds, such as cultural, historical and societal reasons, may actually be unrelated to the applicable rules of private law and civil litigation. Moreover, the judgment in *Courage v Crehan* was only rendered in 2001[160] and the direct applicability of Article 81(3) EC was introduced less than four years ago. All in all, Regulation 1/2003 and the 'modernisation package' have paved the way for a more balanced system of public and private enforcement.[161] It might therefore be premature to conclude that private enforcement of Community competition law can be stimulated solely by harmonising certain aspects of the tort laws and civil procedures of the Member States, if it can be stimulated by such measures at all.

---

[156] Cf Van Gerven, above n 78, 492, regarding the so-called 'spill-over'effect of legislative enactments where he also refers to the area of antitrust law.

[157] Recently, even Germany, which for decades maintained a differentiation in legal treatment between horizontal and vertical restrictions, has aligned its national cartel rules with Art 81. See further above Chapter 6, n 129.

[158] A Fuchs, 'Kontrollierte Dezentralisierung der europäischen Wettbewerbsaufsicht' (2005) 40 *Europarecht* (Beiheft 2), 77, 79. Such a two-standard system is also difficult to justify. See C Arhold, 'Die Reform der europäischen Wettbewerbsaufsicht aus praktischer Sicht' (2005) 40 *Europarecht* (Beiheft 2), 119, 120 note 9, see also above n 76 and accompanying text.

[159] According to Schwarze, above n 81, 209–10, there is a certain tendency in the Member States to allow European influences on the national legal order. Supposedly, this tendency will grow because, in the long run, it would hardly be possible to maintain, within a national legal order, two different systems of administrative law.

[160] Above n 95.

[161] G Di Federico and P Manzini, 'A Law and Economics Approach to the New European Antitrust Enforcing Rules' (2004) 1 *Erasmus Law and Economics Review* 143, 160. Cf also Walsh, above n 141, 32, who even goes as far as submitting that the Commission's 'proposal on private actions for damages may lead to the ruination of its own policy on cartels', ie that it might ultimately diminish the current success of public enforcement.

Index

341.424
BRA

530064

Ollscoil na hÉireann, Gaillimh

3 1111 40219 6545